**5**

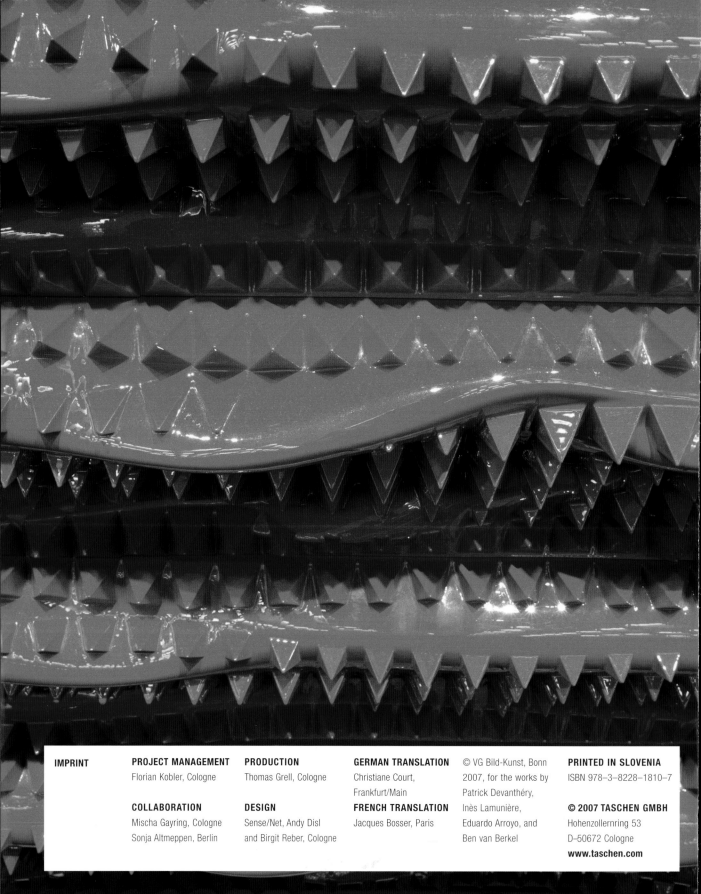

**IMPRINT**

**PROJECT MANAGEMENT**
Florian Kobler, Cologne

**COLLABORATION**
Mischa Gayring, Cologne
Sonja Altmeppen, Berlin

**PRODUCTION**
Thomas Grell, Cologne

**DESIGN**
Sense/Net, Andy Disl
and Birgit Reber, Cologne

**GERMAN TRANSLATION**
Christiane Court,
Frankfurt/Main

**FRENCH TRANSLATION**
Jacques Bosser, Paris

© VG Bild-Kunst, Bonn
2007, for the works by
Patrick Devanthéry,
Inès Lamunière,
Eduardo Arroyo, and
Ben van Berkel

**PRINTED IN SLOVENIA**
ISBN 978–3–8228–1810–7

**© 2007 TASCHEN GMBH**
Hohenzollernring 53
D–50672 Cologne
**www.taschen.com**

# ARCHITECTURE NOW!

*Architektur heute / L'architecture d'aujourd'hui*

*Philip Jodidio*

**TASCHEN**

HONG KONG  KÖLN  LONDON  LOS ANGELES  MADRID  PARIS  TOKYO

# CONTENTS

# CONTENTS

# INTRODUCTION

### THE YOUNG AND THE RESTLESS

In a period that privileges transience, architecture is curiously still prized for its durability. With the thunderous collapse of the World Trade Center towers, it may be, though, that the 21st century will be more a time of superficiality and ruin than of new and lasting monuments to the spirit. Or might there be more hope for the future than this dark picture would suggest? The heavy stones of other eras have already given way to lightness both in form and in concept, often obviating the need to last a lifetime or more—the usually unstated hope of any client, to leave a mark for new generations to admire. This is not to say that architects have broken with the past and the future. I. M. Pei's Mudam in Luxembourg (Musée d'Art Moderne Grand-Duc Jean, Luxembourg, 1999–2006; 1) rises from the walls of fortifications designed by Vauban, and Richard Rogers's National Assembly for Wales (Cardiff, Wales, 1998–2005) was built to stand for at least a 100 years.

There has been a revolution in architecture, however, and its full implications are only beginning to be felt. Where Modernism had built on industrial repetition and assembly-line methods, architects of today are crafting a new architecture, intimately linked to the computer and to the astonishing capacity it offers to create individual parts for any structure. Architects like Renzo Piano have seen this development as a link to the distant past when stone carvers and sculptors made monuments with no two parts exactly alike. The economies of scale that dictated the emergence of today's cities and their geometrically aligned towers have been shattered, freeing the architect to design unique buildings, limited only by the imagination and the willingness of clients to experiment. The culture of instant gratification molds this new freedom almost as much as the diktat of economic "realism"; but there are other signs of great change. Previous volumes of *Architecture Now* have drawn attention to the rise of projects that make explicit the link between architecture and art. Bound by the constraints of practicality, architects are rarely free to indulge their own proclivities for truly artistic expression, but artists step across the unmarked boundary separating disciplines with increasing impunity. What if the spirit of individuality encouraged by such barbaric-sounding tools as CNC machines finally offered architecture the possibility of achieving the kind of unity imagined by figures like John Ruskin (1819–1900).[1] Ruskin made clear his feeling that architecture could claim to be the highest of the arts, allying as it does other forms of spatial expression in a unified whole. Curiously, even the authors of the idea of the *tabula rasa* dreamt of what might be called a "unified field" theory of architecture. In his first Bauhaus manifesto, published in 1919, Walter Gropius wrote: "Together let us desire, conceive and create the new structure of the future, which will embrace architecture and sculpture and painting in one unity, and which will one day rise toward heaven from the hands of a million workers like the crystal symbol of a new faith." Although the almost messianic tone of the pronouncements of Gropius is no longer fashionable, it is a fact that the creation of a new architecture made of individually crafted parts opens a vast horizon where architecture is meeting art but also design.

Works of art that touch on the domain of architecture remain very much a part of this book, as do inevitably the large number of high-quality buildings consecrated to the world of the arts. What might be considered new is the increasingly significant presence of designers who may in many cases have no specific training in architecture. Figures like Evan Douglis in New York are seeking to use the computer to create practical and yet infinitely variable cladding materials that enliven or even completely transform architectural environments. Others, such as the French designer Patrick Jouin, have made absolutely clear their intention to cross the threshold between design and architecture, linking the two in the creation of a work that might ultimately correspond to the call of Gropius. The new faith involved has little to do with religion and much more with an ambition to think about architecture in a different way, encouraged by the ubiquity of computer-assisted design and manufacturing.

Another phenomenon that is surely changing architecture is the rise of practitioners under the age of 40. Given the time required for projects to be carried out, and, above all, for architects to earn the respect of their potential clients, few important figures emerged in the past much before the age of 50. A brief overview of the contents of this volume suggests that that rule may well be changing. Young architects featured here with their respective dates of birth are: Pierre Sartoux and Augustin Rosenstiehl (Atelier SoA, both 1973); Aldo Celoria (1969) and his partner Federica Giovannini (1978); Antón García-Abril Ruiz (1969); Gernot Hertl (1971); the architects of the Swiss firm HHF—Tilo Herlach (1972), Simon Hartmann (1974), and Simon Frommenwiler (1972); Jesse Judd (1975); and Guilherme Machado Vaz (1974). At the opposite end of the scale, it would seem that a successful career in architecture may be a secret to longevity—as witnessed by the very recent work carried out by I. M. Pei (1917), or, still more surprisingly, by Oscar Niemeyer (1907). Even the buildings desigend by Pei and Niemeyer are now put together using the most sophisticated computer methods, though the initial conceptualization of their projects may follow more time-honored paths. Restless young architects and a number of their elders, too, are forging ahead with considerable changes in the way buildings are conceived and erected. One of the pioneers in the dissolution of barriers between disciplines, Frank O. Gehry, recently completed the astonishing Hotel Marqués de Riscal (Elciego, Alava, Spain, 2003–06; 27), where sculptural form, allied with his trusted CATIA software, makes it seem that a new world has opened up for architecture in general. The spiritual sons and daughters of Gehry have no doubts on the subject.

## FUNCTION AND FORM FOLLOW DESIGN

Some architects naturally design a building from the inside out, evolving toward an exterior appearance that is intimately related to interior function and form. The reverse is often true as well—a seductive skin is made to cover whatever space the client requires. Industrial design has many points in common with architecture because it, too, must seek an intimate relationship between form and function, alternatively privileging one or the other. Design has often been seen as the creation of objects that merely inhabit an architectural space, though many pioneers such as Charles (1907–78) and Ray Eames (1912–88) challenged that idea, in this case with their famous Case Study House #8 (Pacific Palisades, California, 1949). An entire generation of designers is now approaching its work in a way that may well be redefining the very nature of architecture. The inventive French brothers Ronan and Erwan Bouroullec, for example, have created more than one system that allows the selective and ephemeral division of space within an existing building. Their Roc system (5) is related to other, even more recent projects that exploit the idea of creating intimate space within relatively cold modern structures. For the Mudam in Luxembourg (designed by I. M. Pei), they created an interior restaurant with textile tiles and a robust Douglas fir structure. As they describe their design, "The tiles covering the wooden structures are elements of a new system of modular textile walls developed in 2006 together with Kvadrat, a textile

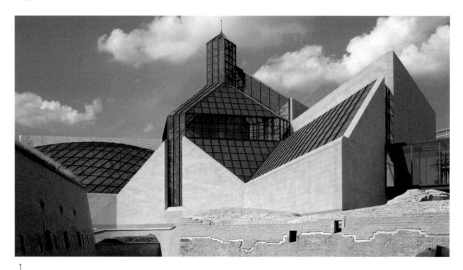

1

manufacturer. After the Algues and Twigs edited by Vitra, this project is a concrete expression of some long-incubated ideas about building spaces with textile material, as they would be warm and soundproof, like Mongol yurts. Thought up as sorts of scales, the tiles can be assembled together by an ingenious folding system that doesn't require any external mechanical element. Four lateral slats are inserted in the slots of the adjacent tiles, giving rhythm and an even volume to the resulting wall. The fine contours of these 50 x 25-centimeter elements have been determined by the functional logics of their assembly. The high modularity of this system makes it possible to consider multiple applications to build autonomous and soundproof spaces, with infinite forms, be they organic or geometrical. The industrialization process of the tiles is surprisingly easy and quick: 20 seconds only are needed to mold the hard foam core between two pieces of textile."

Though design usually implies work with palpable materials, often the same as those employed in architecture, some architects like Lars Spuybroek (NOX, Rotterdam) have experimented with the use of sound or music in order to add a new dimension to their work (Son-O-House, Son en Breugel, The Netherlands, 2000–03). The Brazilian designer Muti Randolph has taken a related concept even further in work such as his D-Edge nightclub (São Paulo, SP, Brazil, 2003; 6), where custom-design software is used to model interior space using both light and sound. In this type of environment, architecture might well be nothing more than an anonymous shell, housing the effects and spaces that are carefully crafted by a designer.

In France, a generation of designers, formed in one way or another by the earlier example of Philippe Starck, has come to international attention, often with a specific interest in crossing the barrier between furniture, interior design and architecture itself. This is certainly the case of both Matali Crasset, who worked with Starck and Thomson Multimédia before creating her own office in 1998, and Patrick Jouin, who was a designer in Starck's studio from 1995 to 1998. Crasset recently completed the remake of the SM's – Stedeljik Museum 's-Hertogen-bosch (The Netherlands, 2004–05), and she has brought her signature bright colors and a sense of design that redefines space and function to the project. Working with industrial sheds built in the Dutch city by Jacob Berend Bakema (1914–81), she demonstrated here that function must not necessarily follow form. Rather, design generates form and even function.

Patrick Jouin, who has established a solid reputation as the architect-designer of the numerous Ducasse (or Spoon) restaurants around the world, has gone on to create an astonishing house in Kuala Lumpur (Malaysia, 2004–07). Handling both the actual architecture and the interior design in an integrated program, Jouin may here be accomplishing the dream of the German Bauhaus—that of the complete work of art (*gesamtkunstwerk*), where all aspects of the creation are born of a determined spirit. Jouin's originality and his use of cutting-edge technology, such as stereo-lithography in his furniture design, mark him as one of the rising stars of international design. Clearly he will not stop with chairs however.

### EAT, SLEEP, THEN SHOP TILL YOU DROP

One of the most obvious areas in which architecture and design come together is in hotels, restaurants and stores. Two recent and spectacular projects in New York surely confirm this idea. The Morimoto NYC restaurant (2005–06; 7) is one of Tadao Ando's first ventures into the field. Working with Stephanie Goto, a young New York architect, Ando transformed an otherwise nondescript industrial space in Man-

*1*
*I.M. Pei, Mudam Luxembourg,*
*Musée d'Art Moderne Grand-Duc*
*Jean, Luxembourg, 1999–2006*

hattan's newly fashionable Meat Packing District into a memorable dining experience. His trademark concrete is present in the form of columns that follow a central stairway leading to the lower-level bar, but here his solidity meets with the plasticity of ceilings and walls draped with undulating canvas shaped with fiberglass reinforcement. A wall of water bottles designed by Ross Lovegrove runs parallel to the steps and further enlivens the space. Furniture by Lovegrove, but also a bar with a Plexiglas top by Ando, confirm that architecture and design have found a meeting place at the highest level in New York.

Another, even more visible blending of various forms of architecture and design occurs in the new Apple Store on Fifth Avenue in New York (2003–06). The work of Bohlin Cywinski Jackson, in collaboration with Apple Chairman Steve Jobs, the featherlight glass cube that sits above the underground store succeeds in giving architectural form to the computer-maker's legendary design quality. It is true, however, that the spiral staircase with a central circular elevator leading to the shop floor most decidedly brings to mind I. M. Pei's design for the Louvre Pyramid. Open every day and all night, the Apple Store on Fifth Avenue might be considered one of the most successful examples of the new integration of design and architecture that is one of the most powerful trends of the moment in retailing, hotels and restaurants.

Another high point of the meeting between architecture and design is the newly refurbished Hotel Duomo in Rimini (Italy, 2003–06; 8). Ron Arad, who has indeed turned his attention more and more to architecture, rendered the link between exterior and interior explicit in Rimini by wrapping the existing façade in a bronze skin that penetrates the building and runs into the back wall of the bar, where it ends as the profile of a bench seat. The enormous ringlike desk in the lobby of the hotel lends a drama to the space that few architects could match. While the architecture of the hotel becomes part of a bench in the bar, the desk in the lobby becomes a defining gesture of architecture. Ron Arad stands apart even in the world of "celebrity" designers, but much of his work is marked by his sense of space. His transition to architecture is all the more natural.

Design and architecture can certainly go hand in hand when there is a meeting of minds between the parties concerned, and surely the client is essential in that mixture. Taking a building a step further, to the point where it can justifiably be considered a work of art, is another matter. Frank O. Gehry's interest in contemporary art is well documented in his own buildings, from the early work in Venice or Santa Monica to the universally acclaimed Guggenheim Bilbao. His approach has consistently urged for a new definition of what constitutes the art of architecture. One of his most recent buildings, the Hotel Marqués de Riscal in Spain, uses a vocabulary of undulating metal sheets for which the California architect is well known, but its exuberance sets it apart in his oeuvre. With its 10-meter-high cantilevers and convoluted shapes, the hotel could most readily be placed in the category of sculpture on a monumental scale. Gehry's audacity has brought him commissions, but his work also encourages visitors in numbers that please his clients. This is not a criticism of the architect; it is merely a statement of the economics at work in such instances. Although his staff makes ample use of computers and such complex forms could hardly be fashioned without CNC milling, Gehry's approach is not that of the young computer fanatics whose star is rising in the architectural profession. Like Frank Stella, an artist of his generation, Gehry set out to liberate form, to redefine the space between architecture and art. With the Hotel Marqués de Riscal, he fashioned a work of art.

2
*Evan Douglis,
REptile–Haku Japanese Restaurant,
New York, NY, USA, 2005*

## COLORS OF SHADOW

The rapport between art and architecture is a rich and varied one, with almost as many forms of expression as there are creators involved. Artists have discovered a fertile area in the interpretation of architectural form, or rather its redefinition. The sculptor Anish Kapoor has long been fascinated by the scale of buildings, but also by their reflection, and their relationship to the space they define. His stunning work *Marsyas* (Turbine Hall, Tate Modern, London, October 9, 2002–April 6, 2003) brought a 155-meter-long, 35-meter-high span of dark-red stretched PVC membrane into the former Bankside Power Station—a work of art on an architectural scale, realized with the assistance of the engineer Cecil Balmond. His *Cloud Gate*, a highly polished stainless-steel sculpture, installed on the promenade of Chicago's Millennium Park, reflects the city's skyline and deforms it in its billowing 10-meter height, 20-meter length and volume. A Chicago newspaper wrote after its July 2004 inauguration that some compared it to "a rift in the very fabric of space and time." More recently, Kapoor installed his *Sky Mirror* (2006; **10**), a 10.7-meter polished stainless-steel mirror, on the axis of the Rockefeller Center near Fifth Avenue in New York. Convex on one side, concave on the other, the mirror gave passersby more than a pause as they contemplated their own distorted images together with those of the familiar Manhattan skyline. In this way, art redefines architecture and even those who use it. It brings buildings to life anew, where in a place like the Rockefeller Center they are merely taken for granted by most.

The artists Michael Elmgreen, born in 1961 in Copenhagen, Denmark, and Ingar Dragset, born in 1969 in Trondheim, Norway, have worked in various ways on the symbolism of architecture and its uses. One of their most surprising pieces, *Prada Marfa* (Valentine, Texas, 2005; **9**), resembles a tiny fashion boutique stranded on the edge of a desert highway. It calls to mind the visual imagery of fashion labels and their utter uselessness in such an environment. Elmgreen and Dragset also play on Prada's signature minimalism to point out links to the work of Donald Judd, who lived and worked in nearby Marfa, Texas. Though it should best be qualified as installation art, *Prada Marfa* is surely as accurate and disturbing a commentary on fashion, design, and architecture as any formulated in recent years. Architecture is deformed here as surely as in Kapoor's *Sky Mirror*, but the artists suggest that beauty (or hatred) is in the eye of the beholder.

Where architects do usually try to make buildings that will last, a number of them have been tempted by more ephemeral works, such as stage sets or designs. The French architect Dominique Perrault, author of the French National Library in Paris, created a staging of *La Cité Radieuse* for the Ballet National de Marseille in 2005 (**11**). Using his trademark metal mesh as the main device, Perrault thus participated in the staging of a ballet concerning Le Corbusier, a rather elegant homage to the Swiss master, and above all a successful transition from architecture to the less permanent art of dance. The choreographer Frédéric Flamand, Director of the Ballet National de Marseille, has called on Zaha Hadid, Thom Mayne, Jean Nouvel, and Diller + Scofidio for past productions, so he is apparently convinced of the virtues of bringing architects into stage work. Perrault's interest in light and in questions of opacity and transparency made him a natural choice for such work. It appears that he, like the other architects who have worked with Flamand, found no difficulty in moving from the construction site to the stage.

Moving in the opposite direction, the noted photographer Hiroshi Sugimoto has frequently explored well-known modern buildings in images, notably in his *Architecture* series (since 1997). He has also tried his hand at actually building, albeit in a traditional Japanese mode (Go'o Shrine, Naoshima, Japan). He recently began a series of images called *Colors of Shadow* (2004–06) in which he explores extremely

2

subtle variations in the light on walls in the apartment he designed in Tokyo. These pictures might be considered more akin to abstract art than to architectural photography, but many contemporary architects, ranging from Steven Holl to Tadao Ando, actively explore the effects of changing light on their spaces. The acuity of Sugimoto's eye is such that he sees the art in a ray of light moving across a wall. Just as he took many nearly abstract images of light on the sea, often with time-lapse photography, Sugimoto, like the architects in a slightly different vein, aims to capture the light and to observe its beauty.

It may be debatable where art ends and illustration begins, but it is certain that architecture of a very different sort than that built of steel and concrete exists on the Internet, in various computer games, or in the world of movies. Whether based on archeology or literature (*Lord of the Rings* and so on), this domain is a rich and flourishing one that cannot help but have an influence on the architecture of tomorrow. For this volume of *Architecture Now*, the work of one such "virtual" architect has been selected. Doug Chiang was born in Taipei in 1962 and studied film at UCLA. He worked as Design Director for Lucasfilm Ltd. on *Star Wars Episode I*, *The Phantom Menace* and *Episode II, Attack of the Clones*, and as a Concept Designer for Steven Spielberg's *War of the Worlds*. His own more personal work, reproduced in this book, is akin to "uchronian" fantasies that purport to depict our world a hypothetical time, either far in the future, or far in the past. Any similarity to the Temple of Ta Phrom (Angkor, Cambodia) in some of his work is purely intentional. The ubiquitous nature of computer games or web sites such as "Second Life" (www.secondlife.com) means that in some ways virtual architecture has a new and developing existence. In "Second Life," players may inhabit or even sell buildings that are designed to exist only on the Internet. Work like Giovanni Battista Piranesi's *Imaginary Prisons* (1749–50/1761*)* engravings of course inform and inhabit these new images, but it would not be a hazardous guess to predict that the virtual world of artists like Doug Chiang will soon spill over even more into the built environment.

## THE WHITE PURITY OF THE COMPLEX

Perhaps if an architect is not the sort to create an artistic statement like Frank Gehry, the next best thing is to design cultural institutions. If the number of new museums and institutes is any indication, this remains one of the most fertile areas in contemporary architecture. Though established names are often preferred over young talents when museum boards and juries vote, cultural buildings are more frequently the object of aesthetic effort than most other types of architecture. According to regional sensibilities, or architects' own aesthetic sense, the new cultural institutions take on an astonishing number of forms, sometimes affirming their presence in an almost programmatic way, and in other circumstances willfully blending into their settings. Art and cultural institutions usually carry with them a positive connotation, but what about a museum dedicated to horror? There is surely no one way to imagine the architectural image of culture, and indeed the variety of solutions represented here might be taken as proof that there is today no one dominant style in architecture itself. Quite the contrary.

Boston is by and large a conservative city when it comes to contemporary architecture, even if Harry Cobb's elegant John Hancock Tower still stands out on the skyline. It might be considered all the more surprising that the Institute of Contemporary Art should select the innovative New York firm Diller Scofidio + Renfro for their new harborside facility (2004–06; **12**). Lost for the moment in a sea of car parks, and next to another, still better-known Boston monument (Anthony's Pier 4 Restaurant), the ICA is an audacious wraparound building with a

3

3
*Patrick Jouin, Gilt Restaurant and Bar, New York, NY, USA, 2005*

dramatic cantilever hanging above an outdoor public space. The gallery space is essentially concentrated on the top floor with various natural and artificial lighting combinations, and an easy subdivision of the space for temporary exhibitions. A spectacular multimedia area with a dramatic view of the water and the building as a whole give a dynamic impression. Though the budget was not as high as it might have been, the building is a resounding success that pleads in favor of improving the architectural quality of buildings in downtown Boston.

An ocean away, the Swiss architects Herzog & de Meuron have been called upon to design an extension of the Tate Modern (2004–12; **13**), the former Bankside Power Plant, whose space they refurbished in 2000. Their irregular piled structure, that gives "the impression of a roughcast, fragmented form in progress," represents an interesting departure from more orderly or apparently coherent buildings. With its engineering and construction assisted by recently developed computer methods, the design may well herald a new generation of buildings whose appearance is more chaotic than aesthetically pleasing. The dynamism of the contemporary art shown here is thus reflected in the architectural scheme. Where Diller Scofidio + Renfro had found it sufficient to form a continuous wrapped construction jutting out toward the water, Herzog & de Meuron appear to wish to look in several directions at once.

Paris, too, has had its share of new institutions dedicated to art, and the most spectacular and visible of these is the new Quai Branly Museum (**14**) designed by Jean Nouvel, working closely with the landscape architect Gilles Clément for the gardens (2001–06). Situated on the Seine River, close to the Eiffel Tower, this museum of primitive art will surely draw crowds for many years to come. And yet its complexity, or even darkness around the displays, makes it an unlikely location for mass tourism. It boasts many splendid works of African, Oceanic or North and South American Indian art, but there is no *Mona Lisa* to draw in the admiring crowds. Rather, the architect and the curators have invited visitors to something of a voyage of discovery. Nouvel speaks of the snaking white ramp that leads from the ground floor to the upper-level exhibition areas in terms of "going up the river." To the heart of darkness then? Elevated off the ground that is potentially exposed to flooding near the river, the museum sits above an extensive garden of grasses and trees selected by Clément. A glass screen limits the site on the quayside, but visitors in general are allowed to stroll through the gardens even if they do not enter the museum. In such a visible location, aligned with various government buildings or Haussmann-style apartment buildings, the Quai Branly Museum stands out and will continue to do so even after its screen of trees makes the building all but invisible from the river. Also responsible for the interior museum design, Jean Nouvel has certainly completed one of his most ambitious and surprising projects in Paris, one that will continue to stir controversy, much as the Pompidou Center did in its time. Not yet a Pritzker Prize winner, like his colleague Christian de Portzamparc, Nouvel nevertheless stands out as the most interesting and inventive living French architect.

I. M. Pei was born in Canton (now Guangzhou), China, in 1917. He went to the United States to study in 1935 and remained in New York. It was only with the Fragrant Hill Hotel (near Beijing, 1979–82) and the later Bank of China Headquarters (Beijing, 1999–2001) that Pei returned to his country of origin. In the case of the Fragrant Hill Hotel, he spoke at the time of attempting to find a "new vernacular" for China, beset with poor-quality modern architecture that has become almost ubiquitous since that time. Pei's family long lived in Suzhou: a city of gardens and canals located about 60 kilometers from Shanghai. His most recent project—the Suzhou Museum—brings him back to his roots, near his former family garden in Suzhou. Here, I. M. Pei has taken on the daunting task of reconciling Chinese tradition with modernity. His

4

gray and white geometric composition embraces a central pond with a tea pavilion, a reminiscence of sorts of the city's remarkable gardens. The new museum, containing a mixture of ancient and contemporary art, is located on the same street as one entry of Suzhou's most famous tourist attraction, the Garden of the Humble Administrator. With clarity and the will to overcome any obstacle, I. M. Pei has in a sense come home again, giving Suzhou and contemporary China ideas for a way forward. A student of Gropius when he was at Harvard, Pei has always espoused a geometric vocabulary, but he quickly moved away from the dour rigor of early Modernism to suffuse his buildings with light and drama. The Suzhou Museum (2003–06; **15**) is less dramatic than the East Building of the National Gallery in Washington, D.C., for example, but it is intimately connected to the architecture and gardens of China—a succession of courts and open spaces. It is a symbolic return to Pei's roots, but also a gift from one of the most celebrated architects in the world to his own country precisely when prosperity risks getting the better of China's ancient traditions.

A Brazilian architect in his 50s jokes that three full generations in his profession have been sacrificed on the altar of Oscar Niemeyer's reputation. He means that Niemeyer long since became the "official" architect of the government and its institutions, and that few others have been granted the major commissions that inevitably go to the man from Rio. At 100 years of age in December of 2007, "ON," as he signs his name, is still creating remarkable, lyrical works. His new Cultural Center in Goiânia (Goiás, Brazil, 2003–07; **17**) is a composition in the grand style of his Ibirapuera Park, inaugurated in 1954, or perhaps of the Memorial for Latin America in São Paulo, designed in 1987, and the so-called Caminho Niemeyer, another current project, located in Niterói, on the opposite side of Guanabara Bay from Rio. Niemeyer remains in a far more geometric gamut of forms than Frank O. Gehry, for example, but his idea of architecture as sculpture predates that of the Californian by 30 years at least. Where another of his recently completed projects, the Ibirapuera Auditorium (São Paulo, 2004–05; **16**), is concerned, the architect wrote of the "necessity to add a triangular building to guarantee the white purity of the complex." His theater is nothing more than an enormous white wedge, just as the "final element" in Goiânia "is the Human Rights Monument, a great red concrete triangle that confers the desired importance to the whole."

Much younger than Niemeyer, Paulo Mendes da Rocha was born in 1928. Winner of the 2006 Pritzker Prize, Mendes da Rocha is a powerful and original architect, surely underestimated in European and American circles because so much of his production is in Brazil. His Leme Gallery (São Paulo, 2004; **18**) is a rough space made of unpolished concrete. The wish of gallery owner Eduardo Leme to present "aesthetics of substance" here takes on a new meaning by bringing together architecture and art at a high level. The rather belated acknowledgment accorded to Mendes da Rocha by the Pritzker jury hardly makes up for the way Oscar Niemeyer was commended in 1988, as a co-winner with Gordon Bunshaft. Niemeyer is undeniably, together with men like Ludwig Mies van der Rohe, Le Corbusier or Frank Lloyd Wright, one of the great figures of modern architecture. Mendes da Rocha has continued and developed Brazil's rich tradition of architecture. Both men have worked at the frontier of art and architecture in ways that will continue to deeply influence contemporary creativity despite any North American or European prejudice against them.

Where Mendes da Rocha has often experimented with very heavy elements, as in his Brazilian Museum of Sculpture (São Paulo, SP, Brazil, 1987–92), a cultural institution in the United States has done its best almost to dissolve into its natural setting. The Glass Pavilion by

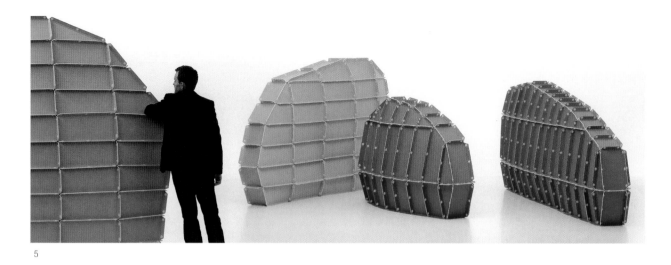

5

the Japanese architects S A N A A (Toledo Museum of Art, Toledo, Ohio, 2003–06; **19**) is an exercise in creating the lightest, most transparent possible building, using some 3000 square meters of glazing and 1.9-centimeter-thick plate steel walls. Kazuyo Sejima and Ryue Nishizawa designed a similarly evanescent structure for the Kanazawa 21st Century Museum of Contemporary Art (Ishikawa, Japan, 2002–04), a circular band of glass with a carefully orchestrated series of internal galleries and courtyards. Given that the Toledo building was intended for a collection of glass, the choice of the architects to make the building itself almost disappear, is an intriguing and undoubtedly successful one.

For a very different commission, the German architects Wandel Hoefer Lorch + Hirsch imagined the Hinzert Documentation Center (Hinzert, Germany, 2003–05) as a sculptural Cor-ten steel hut in a natural setting near the former Hinzert Special SS Concentration Camp. Although the architects have experience with other war memorials in Germany, this particular task required a great deal of subtlety and inventiveness on their part. The resulting structure is very much in the spirit of work that has been done elsewhere using computer design and machining, but the architects do succeed in conveying something of the portentous nature of the place in their building.

## FROM ARCADIA TO LAND'S END

Private houses are often the most interesting work of architects, since they are sometimes freed of tight financial constraints, and when the right client is part of the mix, inventiveness is the name of the game much more than in any large public building, for example. The designer and architect Emilio Ambasz, born in Argentina and based in New York, managed to create his own dream house in Seville 30 years after conceiving it (House of Spiritual Retreat, Seville, Spain, 1975/ 2003–05; **20**). He imagined the surprising façade of the house as "a masklike surrogate for architecture." In fact, from some angles, the residence appears to consist of only two white façades. Seeking "to re-examine architecture as a culturally conditioned process and return to the primeval notion of the abode," Ambasz appears to indulge in a great deal more sophistication than his theoretical goal would allow. The House of Spiritual Retreat may be more than anything a search for an Arcadian solitude where art, architecture and nature come together in a unique whole.

The Iberian Peninsula has been exceedingly inventive in the area of contemporary architecture, to which several projects in this volume testify. Another very surprising residence is the Tóló House (Lugar das Carvalhinhas – Alvite, Freguesia de Cerva, Portugal, 2000–05) designed by the son of Álvaro Siza, Álvaro Leite Siza Vieira. Inserted into a steeply inclined site, the three-bedroom holiday house runs down the hillside like a path leading from top to bottom. Both the architect's father and his colleague Eduardo Souto de Moura, for whom the young architect has also worked, have engaged in active dialogues with their sites, particularly in the case of notable private houses. Here Álvaro Leite Siza Vieira takes the relationship to landscape a step further, making the architecture itself integrate into its site without sacrificing the natural inclination of the land.

The architects of Atelier Tekuto faced a very different kind of site problem with their Lucky Drops House in Tokyo (2004–05; **21**). As is often the case in the Japanese capital, they had to work with very little land (just 59 m²). Combining his talents with those of the noted engineer Masahiro Ikeda, architect Yasuhiro Yamashita produced a very original dwelling with a footprint occupying less than half of the site. The narrowness of the architecture was at a premium given the size constraints, and it was decided to coat the building with fiber-reinforced

*5*
*Ronan and Erwan Bouroullec,*
*Roc, designed for Vitra, 2006*

plastic, allowing daylight in and also achieving a physical lightness that is one time-honored Japanese way to counter the potential effects of earthquakes. The Lucky Drops House might be considered extreme in many respects in another environment, both because of its miniscule presence and because of its unexpected shape and design. Despite their attachment to various forms of tradition, however, the Japanese may be considered more open to inventive architecture than most of their European counterparts.

Though not faced with such a small site, the Swiss architect Aldo Celoria also found a solution for his Trapanese House (Castel San Pietro, Ticino, Switzerland, 2004–05) that makes use of plastic walls (polycarbonate slabs in this instance) to bring ample light into the residence. Set on the same vineyard-covered hillside as his earlier Travella House (2002–04), the new house makes inventive use of interior space, which winds around a central stairway. The entire structure is supported not by any element associated with the façade, but by an internal concrete wall, a device the architect had used albeit in a different form in the Travella House. A graduate of Mario Botta's Mendrisio School of Architecture, Celoria is still under 40, but has shown such a promising start that he appears to be one of the rising stars of architecture in Switzerland. Working on land that originally belonged to his family, Aldo Celoria, like other young architects, has found that the design of private houses is one of the most obvious ways to emerge from the ranks of less inventive colleagues.

Half a world away, another young team—Pezo von Ellrichshausen Arquitectos—has created a surprising block of a house on the edge of a cliff 550 kilometers south of Santiago (Poli House, Coliumo Peninsula, Chile, 2003–05; **22**). The 180-square-meter structure was built with a budget of just 66 600 dollars. Adapting to the sloping site in a "zigzagging way" the architecture assumes a kind of mysterious roughness that fits well into the harsh landscape. A wall so thick it houses the kitchen, bathrooms, closets, and vertical circulation, as well as storage space, makes this one of the more unexpected works of architecture built anywhere in the world in the past few years. With a tiny budget and a sense of space, Mauricio Pezo and Sofía von Ellrichshausen have already left their mark on this southern version of Land's End.

## FLYING OVER THE BONES OF A GHOST VILLAGE

Making a virtue of economic constraints has always been a part of the practice of architecture, and yet, somehow, today's designers, calling on a gamut of industrial materials for example, succeed in creating original spaces with limited budgets or surprising approaches. As it is described by the architect Brian MacKay-Lyons, "Ghost Research Lab is an educational initiative designed to promote the transfer of architectural knowledge through direct experience, project based learning taught in the master builder tradition, with an emphasis on issues of landscape, material culture and community." A two-week summer internship for architects, professors and students, "Ghost Lab" (**23**) is organized "each summer on the coast of Nova Scotia, atop the stone ruins of a nearly 400-year-old village on the MacKay-Lyons farm." MacKay-Lyons may not have the international reputation he deserves, given the location of his practice, but "Ghost Lab" deserves more than a passing interest. Making a virtue of the ephemeral, yet building structures that respect this harsh climate, MacKay-Lyons and his students seem to have created wooden forms that spring from the earth of Nova Scotia with their own logic. "Imagine flying over the bones of a ghost village on the edge of the world," says MacKay-Lyons. The architect is currently completing the Canadian High Commission (Dhaka, Bangladesh, 2007), perhaps an occasion for others to encounter one of the more intriguing and innovative figures in contemporary architecture.

6

6
*Muti Randolph, D-Edge, São Paulo,*
*SP, Brazil, 2003*

The young members of the Office for Subversive Architecture (OSA) have an unusual working arrangement since they are based in London, Rotterdam, Graz, Vienna, Darmstadt, Frankfurt, and Munich, and they come together for specific projects only as circumstances require. Two members of the group, Karsten Huneck and Bernd Trümpler, and their London firm Studio+44, were involved in an intriguing temporary installation on the Blade Factory at Greenland Street in Liverpool (2006; **24**). Using white translucent and red PVC factory curtains and hedges, they created an events space on the roof of the former industrial building. Glowing from within at night, the Blade Factory became a kind of beacon of contemporary art in Liverpool, and showed that engaging architectural form is not only the product of sophisticated computer-driven machine tools and multi-million-dollar budgets. There is a place and, indeed, a growing one for less expensive, but innovative, ideas, which can be avowedly ephemeral without diminishing their architectural interest.

The interest in industrial materials is not only due to the fact that they are cheap and readily available, but also to a certain aesthetic sense that may have been fueled by such figures as the photographers Bernd and Hilla Becher, who began to photograph gas tanks, silos and water towers in the early 1960s. They have long taught photography at the Staatliche Kunstakademie in Düsseldorf and have had a direct influence on such photographers as Thomas Struth, Candida Höfer, and Thomas Ruff. Simply put, these artists have played a role in making industrial buildings "fashionable." Used shipping containers have been employed by a number of contemporary architects, such as Shigeru Ban (Bianimale Foundation/Nomadic Museum, Pier 54, New York, 2005). The new Freitag Flagship Store in Zurich (2006) is a 26-meter-high tower made with 17 shipping containers. Containing 100 square meters of space, the facility was the idea of owners and graphic designers Daniel and Markus Freitag, and was carried out by the Zurich firm spillmann echsle architekten. The Freitag brothers produce and market "bags and accessories made from used materials and found on the road: old truck tarpaulins tanned by exhaust fumes, cycle inner tubes, and used seat belts, as well as the new resource of used airbags." The fact that used, rusted shipping containers blend well with this sales practice is obviously a factor in the design of the new store, but part of its originality comes from the vertical stacking—making a tower out of metal boxes used for transport. It is quite reasonable to predict that such methods will be employed more and more frequently in the future, for reasons of cost and also with reference to a certain vision of aesthetics.

### HEART OF CONCRETE, WINDMILL IN THE SKY

Ben van Berkel and Caroline Bos of UNStudio have shown continuous creativity in their work, starting with the emblematic Erasmus Bridge (1996) that links central Rotterdam to the new Kop van Zuid area of the city. Their new Mercedes-Benz Museum in Stuttgart (2003–06; **25**) is big (35 000 m$^2$), but it is physically and intellectually a highly innovative structure. As Ben van Berkel explains, "The structure is a continuous loop, or a spiral that generates the idea of a time machine. 170 cars are displayed in the 16 500 square meters of exhibition space. A section of the design shows that it is a continuous flower-like structure, a ring that holds itself up without any support in the middle." Heavily involved in computer-assisted design and parametric modeling, UNStudio aims to do things that "have not yet been done in architecture, and to make them work." Indeed, Van Berkel compares the firm's method to that of automobile manufacturers. "In the early work we were interested in geometry and then that turned into play with mathematical diagrams. And now the diagrams have turned into what we call

7
*Tadao Ando, morimoto nyc, New York,*
*NY, USA, 2005–06*

7

'design models.' One strategy for design can turn into a variant, like a prototype for a car, which can generate five or six cars." In their Möbius House (Naarden, The Netherlands, 1993–98), they already experimented with the idea of a continuous loop, applied in Stuttgart on a much larger scale, and to different effect. Van Berkel admits that the parametric modeling of the Mercedes-Benz Museum reaches a degree of complexity that only computer specialists can fully grasp, but the upshot of this system is that unique parts can be fit into the whole design without engaging in the kind of cost overruns that were typical in the past of such innovative buildings. No less than 38 000 working drawings were required for the construction, and entirely new software was conceived during construction to deal with the intricacy of the task.

Aside from its structural and architectural innovations, the Mercedes-Benz Museum is an example of successful collaboration between architects, engineers and designers. Working with the celebrated Stuttgart engineer Werner Sobek, or the exhibition designer H. G. Merz, UNStudio has maintained a high degree of control over the entire project, including the associated outside spaces. Rob Wagemans (Concrete Architectural Associates, Amsterdam) created all of the shop and restaurant spaces in the building, while the well-known Dutch designer Petra Blaisse participated in the project with "sun filtering, darkening, and acoustic curtains, as well as an acoustical wall." In the building's lower-level Espresso Bar, "a concave brush wall is the backdrop to a 'Concrete' interior. The white brush-hairs, inserted into panels covered with gold-colored metal-foil, add a three-dimensional 'veil' to the space and scatter sound waves for an improved acoustic atmosphere." Blaisse goes on to explain her intervention seven floors higher: "A lime-green finned curtain with a black 'Sauerkraut' backing (46 m long x 4 m high) lines an open balcony and envelops the restaurant and the lounge. The curtain's design reacts to the folded white ceiling and its opacity secures the dimmed light conditions of the exhibition space below. The public can peep through the curtain's half-open surface."

Manipulating 120 000 tons of concrete as though it were in a state of continual fluidity, Van Berkel has used 3D computer modeling to create the first truly 21st-century building, where technology is at the service of an idea, profoundly related to nature, but also to the flow of visitors and time itself. Cars stream around the Mercedes-Benz Museum at all hours just as 600 000 visitors a year or more will participate in this unique voyage through time and space. Van Berkel refers to the double helix of DNA as a source of inspiration, but this building can also be compared to a human heart, whose lifeblood is the visitor.

A second building by Dutch architects offers another approach to the questions posed by large structures. The Netherlands Institute for Sound and Vision in Hilversum (2003–06; **26**), by Neutelings Riedijk, is intended to archive all of the audiovisual material ever produced in the country. Roughly half of the 30 000-square-meter building is below ground in order to protect the actual documents, but the above-grade part of the architecture plays on voids and light in an original way. As the architects describe their work: "The central well delivers daylight down to the lowest levels of the vault. In the first instance overhead light streams in through the skylights; in the second, colored and tempered light enters through the glazed frontage of the superstructure. The large well in the superstructure opens to the south so that the afternoon sun penetrates to the core of the building and reflected light can skim over the inner façade wall of the offices. At the entrance the void presences as a deep canyon that dramatically brings home to visitors the scale and the sheer size of the archives/storage vault. One of the canyon's sides is a flush wall, the other rises in a series of inverted terraces. These contain the rooms for receiving clients plus annexes serving the archives and stores; the archives and stores themselves are concealed behind the flush canyon wall. The central well culminates

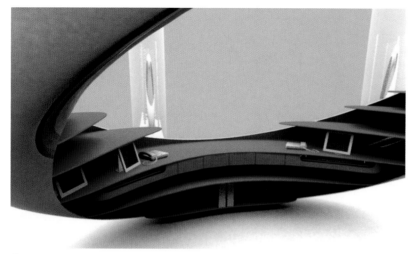

8

in an enormous void where both museum and offices show their best face. The upside down cascade of museum levels registers as a wall sculpture that shapes and scales the internal space of the building." The geological or artistic means used by Neutelings Riedijk to render their ideas explicit in writing reveal their intentions, but one of the most striking features of the architecture is its façade. In the preliminary phase, the architects collaborated with Jaap Drupsteen, who is known for his work on television graphics, but also as the designer of the last of the Dutch guilders. Using Institute archives as their image source, and a new computer-driven process, it was possible to create 748 different glass panes with a great variety of color and relief patterns. It is this colored façade that animates the building both from the outside and from within as the sun shines through.

Designing big buildings in Paris is somewhat of a perilous business. Jean Nouvel's "Tour sans Fins" (1989) was to have been a round spire 100 stories (420 meters) tall located near the Grande Arche and the CNIT building in the Défense business area of the French capital. Despite its apparently "evanescent" appearance, the design was judged too audacious and was never built. Though not quite as high, at 300 meters, the new Phare Tower proposed by Los Angeles architects Morphosis for a similar site seems more likely to be built by 2012. The "fluidity, sensuousness, and softness" of the tower, as described by firm Design Director Thom Mayne, may serve to mollify some opposition, but it remains that no building on this scale has gone up in Paris since the Eiffel Tower (324 meters, 1889). Topped by "futuristic wind mills" that should provide power for the structure's natural ventilation system, the building is just off the celebrated Champs-Elysées axis and would be visible from the city center. Though Thom Mayne and Morphosis, winners of the 2005 Pritzker Prize, are not best known for their skyscrapers, they are familiar with the issues posed by large buildings. If the local authority (EPAD) and the client Unibail were going to take a risk on changing the Paris skyline, they could hardly have found more competent and interesting architects. It does remain to be seen if the shifting political winds in France will allow this project to go forward, but it would represent a symbolic entry into the 21st century for a city that has by and large relied on its historic image.

### YOU SAY YOU WANT A REVOLUTION?

There was a time, not so long ago, when computer-assisted design seemed to be a plaything for the irresponsible. The oddest of blobs appeared on the horizon, accompanied by the inevitable theory about "revolutionary" change. The few examples cited here and the more numerous ones listed in this volume show that the computer has already changed the face (and heart) of contemporary architecture. The key to this transition may be less in the design phase than in the increasing use of computer-driven machines that can produce thousands of individually fashioned parts where repetitive, identical elements were the rule of the past. The importance of this change cannot be underestimated, because it frees the architect from the economic constraints imposed by the assembly-line methods in the past. For those with some ambition, the newfound freedom is being used to redefine architectural space (as in the Mercedes-Benz Museum), or to allow real collaboration with artists or designers to flourish.

An interesting aftereffect of these powerful changes is likely to be what might flippantly be called "the death of style." Architects, no doubt inspired by Michelangelo or other great figures of the past, have long imagined that they should be in the company of artists. And yet,

*8*
*Ron Arad, Duomo Hotel,*
*Rimini, Italy, 2003–06*

8

the mind-numbing mechanics of Modernist production made it very difficult, especially in larger buildings, to do anything other than embroider on standard geometry. The best, like Richard Meier, made a virtue of the grid, while others found that monotonous repetition was their lot in life. A critic or two and a number of architects marched into the 1970s under the banner of "Postmodernism," a theoretical call to revive the Mannerist past, condemned to be no more than an accumulation of sugary façades glued on to otherwise rectangular buildings. But now the very rules have changed and, with the click of a mouse, architecture finally has the potential to become the original and fecund art that John Ruskin imagined—the greatest of the arts perhaps. With the spirit of individuality reborn, it may well be that the kind of collaboration seen in the Mercedes-Benz Museum will become much more common. As art struggles to break free of the Modernist white-cube gallery, might it not find its true place in architecture likewise freed of the constraints of standardization? Frank O. Gehry may well be seen in the future as the pioneer of a historic movement of architecture toward art and the reverse. Despite his personal preference for wiry sketches, Gehry is also the forerunner of computer-driven construction, having used the Dassault CATIA program for the Guggenheim Bilbao and later buildings. But on the path opened by the very personal, sculptural approach of Gehry, others are finding that fundamentally no two buildings ever have to look alike again. The approach of Herzog & de Meuron to the new Tate Modern building, which they describe as "a roughcast, fragmented form in progress," allows for the kind of shifts in curatorial decisions that are typical of the museum process. Might this form without form herald a new generation of architecture without style? Paulo Mendes da Rocha's Leme Gallery in São Paulo might also be described as "a roughcast, fragmented form in progress," and it, too, was made to seek out a kind of symbiosis with contemporary art. The promise of computer-driven design and construction means that not only a small cutting-edge gallery can profit from the intelligence of an individual design. So, too, today, can a museum that receives millions of visitors a year. Style in architecture need no longer be determined by the constraints of assembly-line methods; rather, it is already becoming a more personal affair, defined by architects empowered with new freedom.

*Philip Jodidio, Grimentz 2007*

[1] Computer Numerical Control (CNC) refers to a computer "controller" that drives machine tools, or powered mechanical devices typically used to fabricate metal components by the selective removal of metal. Used in architecture, this system allows the manufacture of individually designed elements at a cost similar to that of traditional standardized manufacturing.

# EINLEITUNG

**THE YOUNG AND THE RESTLESS**[1]

In einer Zeit, die Vergänglichkeit bevorzugt, wird die Architektur seltsamerweise immer noch für ihre Dauerhaftigkeit gepriesen. Angesichts des donnernden Einsturzes der Türme des World Trade Centers könnte es allerdings sein, dass sich das 21. Jahrhundert eher als von Oberflächlichkeit und Verfall gekennzeichnet erweist, denn als eine Zeit der neuen, beständigen Monumente der Hochstimmung. Oder ist die Zukunft vielleicht hoffnungsvoller, als es dieses düstere Bild vermuten lässt? Die schweren Steine anderer Zeitalter sind bereits der Leichtigkeit in Form und Auffassung gewichen, wobei häufig die Verpflichtung außer Acht gelassen wird, lebenslang oder länger zu bestehen – die gewöhnlich unausgesprochene Hoffnung eines jeden Bauherrn, ein Zeichen zu setzen, das kommende Generationen bewundern mögen. Das bedeutet nicht, dass Architekten sämtliche Verbindungen zu Vergangenheit und Zukunft aufgekündigt haben. I. M. Peis Mudam in Luxemburg (Musée d'Art Moderne Grand-Duc Jean, 1999–2006; 1) erhebt sich über den Mauern einer von Vauban konzipierten Befestigung und Richard Rogers National Assembly of Wales (Cardiff, Wales, 1998–2005) wurde mit der Vorgabe errichtet, wenigstens 100 Jahre zu überdauern.

In der Architektur hat sich gleichwohl eine Revolution ereignet, deren Auswirkungen sich gerade erst bemerkbar machen. Wo der Modernismus auf industrielle Reihung und Fließbandfertigung setzte, entsteht gegenwärtig eine neue Architektur, die aufs Innigste mit dem Computer und dessen erstaunlicher Kapazität, individuelle Teile für jegliches Bauwerk herzustellen, verbunden ist. Architekten wie Renzo Piano verstehen diese Entwicklung als Bezug zu einer fernen Vergangenheit, in der Steinmetze und Bildhauer Monumente schufen, bei denen kein Teil einem anderen glich. Die Wirtschaftlichkeitsberechnungen, die in der Massenproduktion einen Vorteil sahen und damit das Erscheinungsbild der heutigen Städte mit ihren geometrisch ausgerichteten Hochhäusern prägten, gelten heute nicht mehr. Das verschaffte den Architekten die Freiheit, beispiellose Bauten zu konzipieren, deren einzige Grenzen die Vorstellungskraft und die Bereitschaft des Auftraggebers zum Experiment darstellen. Diese neue Freiheit wird von einer Kultur der sofortigen Bedürfnisbefriedigung nahezu so stark geprägt wie vom Diktat des ökonomischen »Realismus«, aber es gibt andere Anzeichen eines tief greifenden, derzeitigen Wandels. In früheren Ausgaben von *Architecture Now* war vom Aufkommen von Projekten die Rede, die die Verbindung zwischen Architektur und Kunst thematisierten. Eingeengt von den Beschränkungen der Nützlichkeit können Architekten selten ihren eigenen Neigungen zu wahrhaft künstlerischem Ausdruck frönen, wohingegen Künstler immer häufiger ungestraft die nicht markierten Grenzen zwischen den Disziplinen überschreiten. Was wäre, wenn der von solch barbarisch klingenden Gerätschaften wie CNC-Maschinen beförderte Geist der Individualität der Architektur endlich die Möglichkeit böte, die Art von Einheit zu erreichen, wie sie sich Menschen wie John Ruskin (1819–1900) vorstellten?[2] Er vertrat klar die Meinung, die Architektur könne Anspruch darauf erheben, die höchste aller Künste zu sein, da sie andere Formen räumlichen Ausdrucks zu einem einheitlichen Ganzen vereine. Merkwürdigerweise träumten selbst die Urheber der Vorstellung der Tabula rasa von einer »einheitlichen Feldtheorie« der Architektur. In seinem 1919 veröffentlichten Gründungsmanifest des Bauhauses schrieb Walter Gropius: »Wollen, erdenken, erschaffen wir gemeinsam den neuen Bau der Zukunft, der alles in einer Gestalt sein wird: Architektur und Plastik und Malerei, der aus Millionen Händen der Handwerker einst gen Himmel steigen wird als kristallenes Sinnbild eines neuen kommenden Glaubens.«[3] Wenngleich der beinahe messianische Ton der Gropius'schen Erklärung aus der Mode gekommen ist, bleibt die Tatsache bestehen, dass die Schaffung einer neuen Architektur aus individuell angefertigten Teilen eine weite Sphäre eröffnet, in der Architektur auf Kunst und ebenso auf Design trifft.

9
*Michael Elmgreen & Ingar Dragset,*
Prada Marfa, *Valentine, TX, USA,*
2005

Kunstwerke, die den Bereich der Architektur berühren, machen nach wie vor einen großen Teil dieses Buchs aus, ebenso wie zwangsläufig die große Zahl qualitätvoller, der Welt der Künste gewidmeter Bauwerke. Neuartiger ist die zunehmende Präsenz von Designern, die in vielen Fällen über keine spezifische Architektenausbildung verfügen. Leute wie Evan Douglis in New York wollen den Computer zur Schaffung brauchbarer und doch unendlich variabler Verkleidungsmaterialien nutzen, die Architekturensembles beleben oder sogar vollständig umgestalten können. Andere, wie der französische Designer Patrick Jouin verkünden klar und deutlich ihre Absicht, die Schwelle zwischen Design und Architektur zu überschreiten und beide in der Konzeption eines Werks zu verbinden, das letztlich der Forderung von Gropius entsprechen könnte. Befördert vom allgegenwärtigen computergestützten Entwerfen und Herstellen, hat der damit verbundene neue Glaube wenig mit Religion zu tun, sondern mehr mit dem Ehrgeiz, anders über Architektur zu denken.

Ein weiteres Phänomen, das gewiss zur Veränderung der Architektur beiträgt, ist die zunehmende Zahl noch nicht 40 Jahre alter Architekten. Angesichts der Zeit, die zur Realisierung von Projekten und vor allem zur Vertrauensbildung bei den infrage kommenden Auftraggebern nötig ist, taten sich in der Vergangenheit kaum potenziell bedeutende Persönlichkeiten hervor, die noch keine 50 Jahre alt waren. Ein kurzer Überblick über den Inhalt dieses Bands lässt darauf schließen, dass diese Regel anscheinend dabei ist, ihre Gültigkeit zu verlieren. Hier einige der vorgestellten Architekten mit ihren jeweiligen Geburtsjahren: Pierre Sartoux und Augustin Rosenstiehl (Atelier SoA, beide 1973), Aldo Celoria (1969) und seine Partnerin Federica Giovannini (1978), Antón García-Abril Ruiz (1969), Gernot Hertl (1971), die Architekten des Schweizer Büros HHF – Tilo Herlach (1972), Simon Hartmann (1974) und Simon Frommenwiler (1972), Jesse Judd (1975) und Guilherme Machado Vaz (1974). Auf der anderen Seite scheint eine erfolgreiche Laufbahn in der Architektur ein Garant für ein langes Leben zu sein, wie die jüngsten von I. M. Pei (geboren 1917) realisierten Projekte oder, noch erstaunlicher, Bauten von Oscar Niemeyer (geboren 1907) beweisen. Selbst die Werke von Pei und Niemeyer entstehen heutzutage mithilfe hoch entwickelter Computerverfahren, wenngleich die anfänglichen Entwürfe ihrer Projekte möglicherweise noch auf traditionelle Weise entstanden. Rastlose junge Architekten und auch eine Reihe ihrer Vorläufer bahnen sich den Weg mit tief greifenden Veränderungen der Art und Weise, in der Bauten konzipiert und realisiert werden. Einer der Pioniere bei der Aufhebung der Schranken zwischen den Disziplinen, Frank O. Gehry, stellte unlängst das bemerkenswerte Hotel Marqués de Riscal (Elciego, Alava, Spanien, 2003–06; **27**) fertig, bei dem plastische Formen zusammen mit seiner bewährten Software CATIA der Architektur insgesamt anscheinend eine neue Welt eröffnen. Gehrys Söhne und Töchter im Geiste hegen diesbezüglich keine Zweifel.

### FUNKTION UND FORM FOLGEN DEM DESIGN

Einige Architekten neigen von Natur aus dazu, Bauten von innen nach außen zu planen und gelangen so zu einem Außenbau, der aufs Engste mit Funktion und Form des Interieurs verbunden ist. Oft wird auch genau umgekehrt verfahren – eine attraktive Außenhaut entsteht, um die vom Auftraggeber gewünschten Räumlichkeiten zu umfassen. Industriedesign hat mit Architektur vieles gemein, denn auch hier geht es darum, eine enge Beziehung zwischen Form und Funktion anzustreben und dabei abwechselnd der einen oder der anderen ein Vorrecht einzuräumen. Man hat Design häufig als die Schaffung von Objekten betrachtet, die im architektonischen Raum lediglich präsent sind; einige Pioniere, wie Charles (1907–78) und Ray Eames (1912–88) mit ihrem berühmten Case Study House Nr. 8 (Pacific Palisades, 1949), stellten

10

10
*Anish Kapoor*, Sky Mirror, *New York, NY, USA, 2006*

diese Auffassung allerdings infrage. Eine ganze Generation von Designern geht heute in einer Weise an ihre Arbeit heran, die das eigentliche Wesen von Architektur sehr wohl umdeuten könnte. So schufen beispielsweise die innovativen französischen Brüder Ronan und Erwan Bouroullec mehr als nur ein System, das es gestattet, innerhalb eines bestehenden Gebäudes den Raum nach Wunsch und auch nur zeitweise zu unterteilen. Ihr System Roc (5) steht mit anderen, noch neueren Projekten in Verbindung, die den Gedanken verfolgen, im Inneren eher kühler, moderner Bauten intime Räume zu schaffen. Für das Mudam in Luxemburg (Entwurf von I. M. Pei) konzipierten sie ein Restaurant mit Textilfliesen und einer stabilen Konstruktion aus Douglasfichte. Sie beschreiben ihre Gestaltung mit folgenden Worten: »Die Fliesen, die die Holzkonstruktion verkleiden, sind Elemente eines neuen Systems modularer Textilwände, die 2006 zusammen mit dem Textilhersteller Kvadrat entwickelt wurden. Nach den von Vitra in Auftrag gegebenen Systemen Algues und Twigs handelt es sich bei diesem Projekt um die Realisierung einiger lang gehegter Ideen zum Gestalten von Räumen mit Textilien, um sie warm und schalldicht wie mongolische Jurten zu machen. Die schuppenartigen Fliesen lassen sich dank eines genialen Faltsystems zusammensetzen, das keine externen mechanischen Elemente benötigt. Seitlich werden vier Leisten in die Schlitze benachbarter Fliesen gesteckt, die der Wand Rhythmus und sogar etwas Volumen verleihen. Die eleganten Konturen dieser 50 x 25 cm messenden Elemente werden von den funktionalen Notwendigkeiten ihrer Montage bestimmt. Die hochgradige Anpassungsfähigkeit dieses Systems ermöglicht es, seine Anwendung beim Bau autonomer, schalldichter Räume in großer formaler Vielfalt, ob organisch oder geometrisch, in Betracht zu ziehen. Die industrielle Fertigung dieser Fliesen geht erstaunlich leicht und schnell vonstatten: Um den harten Schaumkern zwischen zwei textilen Lagen zu formen, benötigt man ganze 20 Sekunden.«

Obgleich man beim Design in der Regel von realen Materialien ausgeht, häufig den gleichen, die in der Architektur zur Anwendung kommen, experimentieren einige Architekten wie Lars Spuybroek (NOX, Rotterdam) mit dem Einsatz von Klang oder Musik, um ihre Arbeit durch eine neue Dimension zu erweitern (Son-O-House, Son en Breugel, Niederlande, 2000–03). Der brasilianische Designer Muti Randolph führte in Arbeiten wie seinem Nachtclub D-Edge (São Paulo, Brasilien, 2003; 6) eine ähnliche Idee noch weiter aus, indem er benutzerdefinierte Design-Software dazu verwandte, Innenräume mithilfe von Licht und Klang zu gestalten. In einer solchen Art von Environment wird Architektur auf eine anonyme Hülle reduziert, die von Designern überlegt angefertigte Effekte und Räume enthält.

In Frankreich gelangte eine auf die eine oder andere Weise von ihrem Vorgänger Philippe Starck geprägte Generation von Designern zu internationalem Ansehen, von denen viele speziell daran interessiert sind, die Schranke zwischen Mobiliar, Innenraumgestaltung und Architektur zu überschreiten. Zu nennen wären hier Matali Crasset, die vor Gründung ihres eigenen Büros im Jahr 1998 mit Starck und Thomson Multimédia arbeitete, und Patrick Jouin, der von 1995 bis 1998 in Starcks Büro als Designer tätig war. Crasset beendete unlängst die Erneuerung des Stedelijk Museums in 's-Hertogenbosch (Niederlande, 2004–05) und brachte die für sie typischen leuchtenden Farben sowie ein Gespür für Design, das Raum und Funktion neu bestimmt, in das Projekt ein. Bei ihrer Arbeit mit den Industriehallen, die Jacob Berend Bakema (1914–81) errichtet hatte, zeigte sie, dass Funktion nicht zwangsläufig Form folgen muss. Stattdessen erzeugt Design Form und sogar Funktion.

Patrick Jouin, der sich als Architekt und Gestalter der zahlreichen Restaurants von Ducasse (oder Spoon) auf der ganzen Welt einen Namen gemacht hat, errichtete in der Folgezeit ein erstaunliches Haus in Kuala Lumpur (Malaysia, 2004–07). Weil er hier in einem integrierten Programm sowohl für die eigentliche Architektur als auch für die Gestaltung der Innenräume zuständig ist, könnte Jouin einen Traum des

Bauhauses verwirklichen, und zwar den des Gesamtkunstwerks, bei dem sämtliche Aspekte eines Werks dem entschlossenen Geist eines Einzelnen zu verdanken sind. Jouins Kreativität und sein Gebrauch neuester Technik, wie die Stereo-Lithografie bei seinen Möbelentwürfen, heben ihn als einen der aufgehenden Stars des internationalen Designs hervor. Und ganz gewiss wird er nicht bei Stühlen haltmachen.

### ESSEN, SCHLAFEN, DANN EINKAUFEN BIS ZUM UMFALLEN

Bei Hotels, Restaurants und Läden ist der gemeinsame Auftritt von Architektur und Design nicht zu übersehen. Zwei unlängst in New York entstandene, bemerkenswerte Projekte bestätigen dies besonders eindrucksvoll. Das Restaurant morimoto nyc (2005–06; 7) ist eines von Tadao Andos ersten Projekten auf diesem Gebiet. In Zusammenarbeit mit der jungen New Yorker Architektin Stephanie Goto verwandelte Ando einen ansonsten gesichtslosen Gewerberaum im neuerdings angesagten Meat Packing District in ein einprägsames Speiselokal. Der für ihn typische Beton ist in Form von Pfeilern präsent, die einer zentralen Treppenanlage folgend zu einer Bar im Untergeschoss führen. Hier trifft die Festigkeit des Betons allerdings auf die Plastizität der Decken und Wände, die mit wellenförmigen Segeltuchbahnen verkleidet sind, die ihre Form Versteifungen aus Fiberglas verdanken. Eine von Ross Lovegrove entworfene Wand aus Wasserflaschen verläuft parallel zur Treppe und trägt zur weiteren Belebung des Raums bei. Das Mobiliar von Lovegrove und die Bar mit einem Plexiglastresen von Ando bestätigen, dass Architektur und Design sich in New York auf höchstem Niveau begegnen.

Eine weitere, noch auffälligere Synthese verschiedener Formen von Architektur und Design ist in dem neuen Apple Store an New Yorks Fifth Avenue (2003–06) zu sehen. Dem federleichten Glaskubus, der über dem Ladengeschäft im Erdgeschoss thront, einem Werk von Bohlin Cywinski Jackson in Zusammenarbeit mit Steve Jobs, dem Präsidenten von Apple, gelingt es, der legendären Designqualität des Computerherstellers architektonische Form zu geben. Es lässt sich jedoch nicht leugnen, dass die Wendeltreppe mit dem in ihrem Inneren verlaufenden runden Aufzug, der zur Ladenebene führt, ganz entschieden an I. M. Peis Entwurf der Pyramide im Louvre erinnert. Der rund um die Uhr geöffnete Apple Store kann als eines der gelungensten Beispiele für die neue Integration von Design und Architektur gelten, einem der zurzeit erfolgreichsten Trends bei der Gestaltung von Läden, Hotels und Restaurants.

Ein weiterer Höhepunkt im Zusammenwirken von Architektur und Design ist das renovierte Hotel Duomo in Rimini (Italien, 2003–06; 8). Ron Arad, der sich immer stärker auf Architektur konzentriert, gelingt in Rimini die eindeutige Verbindung zwischen draußen und drinnen, indem er die vorhandene Fassade mit einer Bronzehaut überzieht, die in das Gebäude eindringt und sich bis zur Rückwand der Bar fortsetzt, wo sie als Profil einer Sitzbank endet. Die gewaltige ringförmige Rezeption in der Lobby des Hotels verleiht dem Raum eine Theatralik, mit der es nur sehr wenige Architekten aufnehmen können. Während die Architektur des Hotels zum Teil einer Sitzbank in der Bar wird, wird die Rezeption in der Lobby zum prägenden Detail der Architektur. Selbst in der Gesellschaft berühmter Designer nimmt Ron Arad, dessen Schaffen größtenteils von seinem Gespür für Raum geprägt ist, eine Sonderstellung ein. Seine Hinwendung zur Architektur ist umso naheliegender.

Design und Architektur können mit Gewissheit dann Hand in Hand gehen, wenn die Beteiligten eines Geistes sind, und auch der Bauherr ist in dieser Konstellation von Bedeutung. Beim Bauen allerdings einen Schritt weiter zu gehen, bis zu dem Punkt, an dem ein Gebäude mit Recht als Kunstwerk gelten kann, ist wieder eine andere Sache. Für Frank O. Gehrys Interesse an zeitgenössischer Kunst finden sich in seinen

11
*Dominique Perrault*, La Cité Radieuse,
Ballet National de Marseille, France,
2005

12
*Diller Scofidio + Renfro*,
Institute of Contemporary Art,
Boston, MA, USA, 2004–06

Bauten zahlreiche Hinweise, angefangen bei seinen frühen Häusern in Venice oder Santa Monica bis zum weltweit gefeierten Guggenheim Museum in Bilbao. Seine Arbeitsweise drängt beständig nach einer neuen Bestimmung dessen, was in der Architektur als Kunst gilt. Bei einem seiner jüngsten Bauten, dem Hotel Marqués de Riscal in Spanien, verwendet er die für ihn typische Formensprache gewellter Bleche, aber der hier herrschende Überschwang hebt den Bau aus seinem Œuvre heraus. Mit seinen 10 m tiefen Überhängen und den gewundenen Formen ließe sich das Hotel am ehesten in die Kategorie monumentaler Skulpturen einordnen. Gehrys Wagemut brachte ihm Aufträge ein, aber seine Bauten locken zur Freude seiner Bauherren auch zahllose Besucher an. Dies bedeutet keine Kritik am Architekten, sondern ist lediglich eine Darstellung der in solchen Fällen wirksam werdenden ökonomischen Gesetze. Obwohl sein Büro weidlich Gebrauch von Computern macht und derart komplexe Formen ohne den routinemäßigen Gebrauch von CNC kaum denkbar sind, gleicht Gehrys Vorgehen nicht dem jener jungen Computerfanatiker, deren Stern in der Architektenschaft gerade aufgeht. Wie der seiner Generation angehörende Künstler Frank Stella hat sich Gehry vorgenommen, die Formen zu befreien, den Raum zwischen Architektur und Kunst neu zu bestimmen. Mit dem Hotel Marqués de Riscal ist ihm ein Kunstwerk gelungen.

## FARBEN DES SCHATTENS

Das zwischen Architektur und Kunst herrschende Verständnis ist fruchtbar und vielgestaltig, mit nahezu so vielen Ausdrucksformen wie beteiligten Künstlern. Künstler entdeckten ein dankbares Betätigungsfeld in der Deutung architektonischer Form bzw. in ihrer Neubestimmung. Der Bildhauer Anish Kapoor ist seit Langem fasziniert von der Größe von Bauten, aber auch von ihrer Spiegelung und ihrer Beziehung zum von ihnen definierten Raum. Mit seinem fantastischen »Marsyas« (Turbinenhalle, Tate Modern, London, 9.10.2002–6.4.2003) hielt ein 155 m langer, 35 m hoher Schlauch aus einer dunkelroten, gedehnten PVC-Membran, ein mithilfe des Ingenieurs Cecil Balmond realisiertes Kunstwerk mit der Maßstäblichkeit von Architektur, Einzug im ehemaligen Kraftwerk Bankside. Sein »Cloud Gate«, eine Skulptur aus hochglänzendem Edelstahl, aufgestellt an der Promenade des Millennium Park in Chicago, reflektiert die Skyline der Stadt und verformt sie auf ihrem 10 m hohen und 20 m langen Körper. In einer Chicagoer Zeitung hieß es nach ihrer Einweihung im Juli 2004, einige verglichen sie mit »einem Spalt in der eigentlichen Textur von Raum und Zeit«. In noch jüngerer Zeit installierte Kapoor in der Achse des Rockefeller Center nahe der Fifth Avenue in New York seinen »Sky Mirror« (2006; **10**), einen Spiegel aus poliertem Edelstahl mit einem Durchmesser von 10,7 m. Der auf einer Seite konvexe, auf der anderen konkave Spiegel verschaffte Passanten unterhaltsame Pausen, während sie ihre eigenen verformten Abbilder neben denen der vertrauten Skyline von Manhattan betrachteten. Auf diese Weise nimmt Kunst auf den Charakter von Architektur, ja selbst auf den ihrer Nutzer Einfluss. Sie erweckt Gebäude zu neuem Leben, wo sie an einem Ort wie dem Rockefeller Center meistens gar nicht mehr wahrgenommen werden.

Die Künstler Michael Elmgreen und Ingar Dragset, 1961 in Kopenhagen bzw. 1969 in Trondheim, Norwegen, geboren, arbeiten auf verschiedene Weise am Symbolismus der Architektur und seiner Verwendung. »Prada Marfa« (Valentine, Texas, 2005; **9**), eine ihrer erstaunlichsten Arbeiten, sieht für alle Welt wie eine winzige Modeboutique aus, die es an den Rand eines Highways durch die Wüste verschlagen hat. Sie lässt einen an die Bildsprache von Modemarken und deren völlige Nutzlosigkeit in einer Umgebung wie dieser denken. Elmgreen und Dragset

11

12

heben darüber hinaus auf den für Prada typischen Minimalismus ab, wenn sie auf Verbindungen zum Werk von Donald Judd verweisen, der im nahe gelegenen Marfa, Texas, lebte und arbeitete. Obgleich man »Prada Marfa« am besten als Installation bezeichnen würde, ist das Werk ein so treffender, erschreckender Kommentar zu Mode, Design und Architektur wie kaum ein anderer aus jüngerer Zeit. Die Architektur ist hier ebenso sicher deformiert wie in Kapoors »Sky Mirror«, wenngleich die Künstler zu verstehen geben, dass Schönheit (oder Hass) im Auge des Betrachters liegt.

Während Architekten üblicherweise bestrebt sind, dauerhafte Bauwerke zu errichten, findet eine Reihe von ihnen flüchtigere Arbeiten wie Bühnenbilder verlockend. Der französische Architekt Dominique Perrault, Erbauer der französischen Nationalbibliothek in Paris, schuf 2005 das Bühnenbild für »La Cité Radieuse« für das Ballet National de Marseille (**11**). Dabei verwandte er als Hauptbestandteil sein charakteristisches Metallgewebe und war damit an der Aufführung eines Balletts zum Thema Le Corbusier beteiligt, eine recht elegante Reverenz an den Schweizer Meister und vor allem ein gelungener Übergang von der Architektur zur weniger beständigen Kunst des Tanzes. Der Choreograf Frédéric Flamand, Direktor des Ballet National de Marseille, wandte sich bei früheren Produktionen an Zaha Hadid, Thom Mayne, Jean Nouvel und Diller + Scofidio – er scheint also von den Vorzügen der Beteiligung von Architekten an Bühnenwerken überzeugt zu sein. Perraults Interesse an Licht und an Fragen von Opazität und Lichtdurchlässigkeit machen ihn zum geborenen Kandidaten für eine solche Aufgabe. Es scheint, als sei ihm der Wechsel vom Bauplatz auf die Bühne ebenso leicht gefallen wie den anderen Architekten, die mit Flamand arbeiteten.

Die umgekehrte Richtung schlägt der bekannte Fotograf Hiroshi Sugimoto ein, der häufig mit Bildern bekannter moderner Bauwerke arbeitet, vor allem seit 1997 in seiner Fotoserie »Architecture«. Darüber hinaus versucht er sich selbst als Architekt, wenn auch in traditionell japanischer Weise (Go'o Schrein, Naoshima, Japan). Unlängst begann er mit einer Bilderserie mit dem Titel »Colors of Shadow« (2004–06), in der er die äußerst subtilen Variationen des Lichts auf den Wänden des von ihm entworfenen Apartments in Tokio auslotet. Man mag diese Bilder eher für abstrakte Kunst als für Architekturfotografie halten, aber viele zeitgenössische Architekten, von Steven Holl bis Tadao Ando, experimentieren selbst mit der Wirkung des sich verändernden Lichteinfalls in ihre Räume. Sugimoto verfügt über ein so scharfes Auge, dass er Kunst in einem Lichtstrahl erkennt, der sich über eine Wand bewegt. Ebenso wie er viele, beinahe abstrakte Bilder vom Licht auf dem Meer, etliche davon mit Zeitraffer, aufnahm, versucht Sugimoto in etwas anderer Manier als die Architekten, Licht einzufangen und seine Schönheit zu beobachten.

Man kann sicher darüber streiten, wo Kunst endet und Illustration beginnt, aber es steht fest, dass im Internet, in verschiedenen Computerspielen oder auf der Kinoleinwand Architektur ganz anderer Art als solche aus Stahl und Beton existiert. Dieser Bereich, ob er nun auf Archäologie oder Literatur (*Herr der Ringe* usw.) basiert, ist vielfältig und erfolgreich, so dass er fast zwangsläufig Auswirkungen auf die Architektur von morgen haben muss. Für diesen Band von *Architecture Now* wurde das Schaffen eines solchen »virtuellen« Architekten ausgewählt. Doug Chiang wurde 1962 in Taipeh geboren und studierte Filmwissenschaft an der UCLA. Er war bei Lucasfilm Ltd. als Design Director für »Krieg der Sterne: Episode I – Die dunkle Bedrohung« und »Episode II – Angriff der Klonkrieger« sowie als Concept Designer für Steven Spielbergs »Krieg der Welten« zuständig. Sein in diesem Buch abgebildetes, eigenes Schaffen ähnelt Fantasien einer »anderen Geschichte«, die vorgeben, einen entweder in ferner Zukunft oder Vergangenheit gelegenen Zeitabschnitt unserer Welt darzustellen. Jede in einem Teil seines

Werks vorhandene Ähnlichkeit mit dem Tempel von Ta Phrom (Angkor, Kambodscha) ist absichtlich. Der allgegenwärtige Charakter von Computerspielen oder Websites wie »Second Life« (www.secondlife.com) bedeutet, dass der virtuellen Architektur eine neue, sich weiterentwickelnde Existenz beschieden ist. In »Second Life« können Mitspieler Gebäude bewohnen oder sogar verkaufen, die nur im Internet existieren. Natürlich sind diese neuen Bilder von Werken wie Giovanni Battista Piranesis Radierungsfolge »Carceri« (1749–50/1761) beseelt und durchdrungen, aber man geht mit der Voraussage, dass die virtuelle Welt von Künstlern wie Doug Chiang schon bald auf die gebaute Umwelt übergreifen wird, gewiss kein Risiko ein.

### DIE WEISSE REINHEIT DER ANLAGE

Wenn ein Architekt nicht zu denen gehört, die wie Frank Gehry künstlerische Aussagen hervorbringen, hat er immer noch die Möglichkeit, eine Kultureinrichtung zu bauen. Die Anzahl neuer Museen und Institute lässt darauf schließen, dass es sich hierbei um eines der fruchtbarsten Betätigungsfelder zeitgenössischer Architekten handelt. Obgleich beim Votum von Museumskommissionen und Juroren oft etablierten Namen vor jungen Talenten der Vorzug gegeben wird, sind Kulturbauten häufiger Gegenstand ästhetischer Bemühungen als die meisten anderen Bauaufgaben. Abhängig von regionaler Sensibilität oder dem ästhetischen Empfinden der Architekten selbst, nehmen die neuen Kultureinrichtungen eine erstaunliche Formenvielfalt an, wobei sie bisweilen ihre Präsenz in nahezu programmatischer Weise bekräftigen oder sich unter anderen Voraussetzungen mit voller Absicht in ihre Umgebung einfügen. Kunst und kulturelle Einrichtungen lösen in der Regel positive Konnotationen aus, was aber, wenn ein Museum dem Horror gewidmet ist? Gewiss gibt es nicht die *eine* Vorstellung der kulturgemäßen Architektur und man könnte die Vielfalt der hier vorgestellten Lösungen als Beweis dafür ansehen, dass es heutzutage nicht den einen beherrschenden Architekturstil gibt – ganz im Gegenteil.

Wenn es um zeitgenössische Architektur geht, ist Boston im Großen und Ganzen eine konservative Stadt, selbst wenn der elegante John Hancock Tower von Harry Cobbs immer noch aus der Skyline hervortritt. Umso überraschender also, dass die Wahl des Institute of Contemporary Art (ICA) für sein neues Museum an der Harborside (2004–06; 12) auf das New Yorker Büro Diller Scofidio + Renfro fiel. Gegenwärtig steht es noch etwas verloren in einem Meer von Parkplätzen und neben einem derzeit noch bekannteren Bostoner Denkmal (Anthony's Pier 4 Restaurant). Beim ICA handelt es sich um ein kühn konzipiertes Bauwerk mit einer spektakulären Auskragung über öffentlichem Außenraum. Die Galerieräume befinden sich im Wesentlichen im Obergeschoss, wo verschiedene Tages- und Kunstlichtkombinationen sowie ein leicht unterteilbarer Bereich für Sonderausstellungen vorhanden sind. Von dem tiefer liegenden phänomenalen Multimediaraum bietet sich ein fulminanter Blick aufs Wasser, und das Gebäude hinterlässt insgesamt einen dynamischen, zukunftsorientierten Eindruck. Obgleich sich das Budget in Grenzen hielt, erweist sich der Bau als durchschlagender Erfolg, der dafür spricht, die Qualität der Architektur im Zentrum von Boston zu verbessern.

Auf der anderen Seite des Atlantiks erhielten die Schweizer Architekten Herzog & de Meuron den Auftrag, eine Erweiterung für die Tate Modern zu entwerfen (2004–12; 13), jenes von ihnen im Jahr 2000 zum Museum umgebaute Kraftwerk an der Bankside. Ihr unregelmäßig geschichteter Entwurf, der den »Eindruck einer unfertigen, fragmentierten Form« erweckt, stellt eine interessante Alternative zu methodi-

*13*
*Herzog & de Meuron, Transforming*
*Tate Modern, Bankside, Southwark,*
*London, UK, 2004–12*

13

scheren, offenkundig kohärenten Bauwerken dar. Das Projekt, bei dessen Bautechnik und Konstruktion zweifellos jüngst entwickelte Computerverfahren beteiligt waren, könnte der Vorbote einer neuen Generation von Gebäuden sein, deren Erscheinungsbild eher chaotisch als ästhetisch ansprechend sein wird. Die angebliche Dynamik der hier gezeigten zeitgenössischen Kunst spiegelt sich somit in der architektonischen Programmatik. Wo es Diller Scofidio + Renfro genügte, eine über das Wasser auskragende, durchgehend geschlossene Konstruktion zu erdenken, ist Herzog & de Meuron offenbar daran gelegen, in mehrere Richtungen gleichzeitig zu schauen.

Auch Paris hat seinen Anteil an neuen Institutionen, die der Kunst gewidmet sind; die ungewöhnlichste, auffälligste ist das neue Museum am Quai Branly von Jean Nouvel (2001–06; **14**), der bei den zugehörigen Gärten eng mit dem Landschaftsarchitekten Gilles Clément zusammenarbeitete. In unmittelbarer Nähe des Eiffelturms am Ufer der Seine gelegen, wird dieses Museum für außereuropäische Kunst in den kommenden Jahren ein Anziehungspunkt für zahlreiche Besucher sein. Wegen seiner Komplexität und der dunklen Ausstellungsräume wird es aber vermutlich kein Ziel des Massentourismus werden. Es zeigt zahlreiche exzellente Werke afrikanischer und ozeanischer Künstler sowie Kunst der Indianer Nord- und Südamerikas, aber es gibt keine »Mona Lisa«, um die ehrfürchtigen Massen anzulocken. Stattdessen werden die Besucher vom Architekten und den Kuratoren zu einer Entdeckungsreise eingeladen. Nouvel vergleicht die sich schlängelnde, weiße Rampe, die vom Erdgeschoss zu den oberen Ausstellungsflächen führt, mit einem »Stromaufwärtsgehen«. Und dann ins Herz der Dunkelheit? Wegen des potenziell vom Hochwasser der Seine bedrohten Baugrunds ist das Museum über einer großflächigen Gartenanlage aufgeständert, die mit von Clément ausgewählten Gräsern und Bäumen bepflanzt ist. Zur Kaianlage hin begrenzt eine Glaswand das Gelände, aber allen Besuchern ist es gestattet, durch den Garten zu flanieren, selbst wenn sie das Museum nicht betreten. An einem derart repräsentativen Ort, in der Flucht mit verschiedenen Regierungsgebäuden und Apartmenthäusern im Stil Haussmanns, hebt sich das Museum am Quai Branly ab und wird das auch weiterhin tun, selbst wenn die vorgesehenen Bäume das Gebäude vom Fluss nahezu vollständig abschirmen werden. Jean Nouvel, der auch für die Innenarchitektur des Museums verantwortlich zeichnet, hat hier gewiss eines seiner ehrgeizigsten, ausgefallensten Projekte in Paris vollendet, eines, das auch weiterhin umstritten sein wird, so wie es seinerzeit das Centre Pompidou war. Wie sein Kollege Christian de Portzamparc, der mit dem Pritzker-Preis ausgezeichnet wurde, erweist Nouvel sich als einer der derzeit interessantesten und innovativsten französischen Architekten.

I. M. Pei wurde 1917 in Kanton (heute Guangzhou), China, geboren. 1935 kam er zum Studium in die Vereinigten Staaten und blieb danach in New York. Erst mit dem Bau des Fragrant Hill Hotel (bei Peking, 1979–82) und der späteren Zentrale der Bank of China (Peking, 1999–2001) kehrte Pei in sein Herkunftsland zurück. Beim Fragrant Hill Hotel sprach er damals davon, er wolle versuchen, einen neuen, landschaftsspezifischen Stil für China zu finden, das schon damals von der inzwischen allgegenwärtigen, mittelmäßigen modernen Architektur befallen war. Peis Familie lebte lange Zeit in Suzhou, einer Stadt der Gärten und Kanäle, etwa 60 km von Shanghai entfernt. Sein jüngstes Projekt, das Museum von Suzhou, führte ihn zurück zu seinen wirklichen Wurzeln, in die Nähe des früheren Gartens seiner Familie. Hier übernahm Pei die heikle Aufgabe, chinesische Tradition mit der Moderne zu vereinbaren. Sein grau-weißes, geometrisches Ensemble umgibt einen zentralen Teich mit einem Teepavillon, eine Art Erinnerung an die sehenswerten Gärten der Stadt. Das neue Museum, in dem eine Mischung aus alter und zeitgenössischer Kunst zu sehen ist, liegt an derselben Straße wie einer der Eingänge zu Suzhous größter Touristenattraktion, dem

14

»Garten des bescheidenen Beamten«. Mit klaren Vorstellungen und dem Willen, jegliches Hindernis zu überwinden, ist Pei in gewisser Weise wieder zu Hause angekommen, um Suzhou und dem heutigen China Ideen für einen Weg in die Zukunft zu geben. Pei, der in Harvard bei Gropius studierte, trat stets für eine geometrische Formensprache ein, entfernte sich jedoch schnell von der übermäßigen Strenge des frühen Modernismus, um seine Bauwerke mit Licht und Dramatik zu durchfluten. Das Museum in Suzhou (2003–06; **15**) ist weniger theatralisch als beispielsweise der Ostflügel der National Gallery in Washington, aber es ist dank der Abfolge von Innenhöfen und offenen Räumen mit der Architektur und den Gärten Chinas eng verbunden. Es versinnbildlicht Peis Rückkehr zu seinen Wurzeln, aber es ist auch das Geschenk eines der weltweit berühmtesten Architekten an sein Heimatland, genau zu einem Zeitpunkt, an dem neuer Reichtum Chinas uralte Traditionen zu überrollen droht.

Ein brasilianischer Architekt um die 50 scherzte einmal, drei komplette Generationen seines Berufsstands seien auf dem Altar von Oscar Niemeyers Reputation geopfert worden. Das heißt, dass Niemeyer seit Langem der »offizielle« Architekt der Regierung und ihrer Institutionen ist und dass es nur wenigen anderen vergönnt war, bedeutende Aufträge zu übernehmen, die ansonsten zwangsläufig an den Mann in Rio vergeben werden. Im Alter von fast 100 Jahren gelingen »ON« – so sein als Unterschrift dienendes Kürzel – noch immer bemerkenswert sensible Bauten. Bei seinem neuen Kulturzentrum in Goiânia (Staat Goiás, Brasilien, 2003–07; **17**) handelt es sich um eine Anlage im imposanten Stil seines 1954 eingeweihten Ibirapuera Parks oder vielleicht des 1987 entworfenen Monuments für Südamerika in São Paulo und dem so genannten Caminho Niemeyer, einem weiteren aktuellen Projekt in Niterói auf der Rio gegenüberliegenden Seite der Guanabarabucht. Niemeyer bedient sich eines weit stärker geometrischen Formenkanons als beispielsweise Frank O. Gehry, aber mit seiner Vorstellung von Architektur als Skulptur ist er dem Kalifornier mindestens 30 Jahre zuvorgekommen. Bei einem anderen, vor Kurzem fertiggestellten Projekt, dem Ibirapuera Auditorium (São Paulo, 2004–05; **16**), schrieb der Architekt von der »Notwendigkeit, ein dreieckiges Gebäude hinzuzufügen, um die weiße Reinheit der Anlage zu gewährleisten«. Sein Theater ist nichts weiter als ein gewaltiger weißer Keil, ebenso wie das »entscheidende Element« in Goiânia, »das Denkmal für die Menschenrechte, ein mächtiges, rotes Betondreieck ist, das dem Ganzen die gewünschte Bedeutung verleiht«.

Obwohl Paulo Mendes da Rocha immerhin 1928 geboren wurde, ist er weit jünger als Niemeyer. 2006 mit dem Pritzker-Preis ausgezeichnet, ist Mendes da Rocha ein einflussreicher, schöpferischer Architekt, der in Europa und Nordamerika sicher unterschätzt wird, weil sich ein so großer Teil seiner Bauten in Brasilien befindet. Seine Galerie Leme (São Paulo, 2004; **18**) stellt sich als roh belassener Raum aus unpoliertem Beton dar. Der Wunsch des Galeristen Eduardo Leme »substanzielle Ästhetik« zu präsentieren, erhält hier eine neue Bedeutung, indem Architektur und Kunst auf hohem Niveau zusammentreffen. Dass die Pritzker-Jury – wenn auch spät – Mendes da Rochas Leistung anerkannt hat, kann nicht darüber hinwegtrösten, wie sie Oscar Niemeyer 1988 gemeinsam mit Gordon Bunshaft auszeichnete. Niemeyer gehört zusammen mit Mies van der Rohe, Le Corbusier und Frank Lloyd Wright zweifellos zu den Großen der modernen Architektur. Mendes da Rocha hat die reiche brasilianische Architekturtradition fortgeführt und weiterentwickelt. Beide Architekten waren bisher in einer Weise führend in Kunst und Architektur tätig, die ungeachtet nordamerikanischer und europäischer Vorbehalte, auch weiterhin das heutige künstlerische Schaffen entscheidend mitbestimmen wird.

*14*
*Jean Nouvel, Quai Branly Museum,*
*Paris, France, 2001–06*

Während Mendes da Rocha wie bei seinem Brasilianischen Museum für Skulptur (São Paulo, 1987–92) mit äußerst gewichtigen Elementen experimentierte, setzte eine Kulturinstitution in den Vereinigten Staaten alles daran, mit der umgebenden Landschaft nahezu zu verschmelzen. Der Glaspavillon des japanischen Architekturbüros S A N A A (Toledo Museum of Art, Toledo, Ohio, 2003–06; **19**) ist der Versuch, unter Verwendung von 3000 m$^2$ Glasscheiben und 1,9 cm starken Wänden aus Stahlblech, das denkbar leichteste, transparenteste Bauwerk zu gestalten. Kazuyo Sejima und Ryue Nishizawa entwarfen einen ähnlich vergänglich wirkenden Baukörper für das Kanazawa Museum für zeitgenössische Kunst des 21. Jahrhunderts (Ishikawa, Japan, 2002–04), das in einem flachen, kreisrunden Bauwerk aus Glas mit sorgsam angeordneten Abfolgen von Galerieräumen und Innenhöfen Platz findet. Da der Pavillon in Toledo eine Glassammlung aufnehmen soll, scheint die Entscheidung der Architekten, das Gebäude selbst nahezu verschwinden zu lassen, faszinierend und offenkundig gelungen.

Für einen ganz anderen Auftrag konzipierten die deutschen Architekten Wandel Hoefer Lorch + Hirsch das Dokumentationszentrum in der Nähe des früheren SS-Sonderlagers Hinzert im Hunsrück (2003–05) als in der freien Landschaft stehende, skulpturale Hütte aus Cor-Ten-Stahl. Obgleich die Architekten über Erfahrung mit anderen Kriegsgedenkstätten in Deutschland verfügen, forderte diese besondere Aufgabe von ihnen sehr viel Raffinesse und Einfallsreichtum. Das Zentrum ähnelt Projekten, die andernorts mithilfe von Computerdesign und maschineller Bearbeitung entstanden sind, aber es ist den Architekten gelungen, etwas vom unheilvollen Charakter des Ortes auf ihr Bauwerk zu übertragen.

## VON ARKADIEN BIS LAND'S END

Privathäuser sind häufig die interessantesten Arbeiten von Architekten, da sie bisweilen keinem strikten Budget unterliegen, und wenn der richtige Auftraggeber mit von der Partie ist, kommt schöpferisches Gestalten stärker zum Zuge, als bei jedem großen öffentlichen Gebäude. Dem in Argentinien geborenen, heute in New York ansässigen Architekten und Designer Emilio Ambasz gelang es, in Sevilla sein 30 Jahre zuvor konzipiertes Traumhaus zu realisieren (Casa de retiro espiritual, Sevilla, 1975/2003–05; **20**). Er stellte sich die verblüffende Fassade des Hauses als »maskengleiches Surrogat für Architektur« vor. Tatsächlich scheint das Haus von einigen Blickwinkeln aus gesehen nur aus zwei weißen Wänden zu bestehen. Ambasz, der bestrebt ist, »Architektur als kulturell konditionierten Prozess und Rückkehr zur urzeitlichen Vorstellung der Behausung neu zu überdenken«, scheint sich weit mehr Raffinement zu gönnen, als sein theoretisches Ziel gestatten dürfte. Die Casa de retiro espiritual verkörpert wohl vor allem die Suche nach arkadischer Einsamkeit, in der sich Kunst, Architektur und Natur zu einem einzigen Ganzen vereinen.

Die Iberische Halbinsel tut sich auf dem Gebiet der zeitgenössischen Architektur durch außerordentlichen Erfindungsreichtum hervor, wie mehrere Projekte in diesem Band belegen. Ein weiteres, höchst ausgefallenes Anwesen ist die Casa Tóló (Lugar das Carvalhinhas – Alvite, Freguesia de Cerva, Portugal, 2000–05), ein Entwurf des Sohns von Álvaro Siza, Álvaro Leite Siza Vieira. Das in ein sehr steil abfallendes Grundstück eingefügte Ferienhaus mit drei Schlafzimmern verläuft über den Abhang wie ein zur Talsohle führender Pfad. Sowohl der Vater des Architekten wie auch sein Kollege Eduardo Souto de Moura, für den der junge Architekt auch schon tätig war, setzen sich, besonders bei bedeutenden Privathäusern, äußerst intensiv mit dem jeweiligen Baugelände auseinander. Hier führt Álvaro Leite Siza Vieira

15
*I.M. Pei, Suzhou Museum, Suzhou, China, 2003–06*

die Beziehung zur Landschaft einen Schritt weiter, indem er die Architektur in den Baugrund einbindet, ohne das natürliche Gefälle zu opfern.

Die Architekten des Atelier Tekuto sahen sich bei ihrem Lucky Drops House in Tokio (2004–05; 21) mit einem ganz anderen Geländeproblem konfrontiert. Wie so oft in der japanischen Hauptstadt mussten sie mit sehr wenig Fläche, nämlich ganzen 59 m² auskommen. In enger Zusammenarbeit mit dem bekannten Bauingenieur Masahiro Ikeda gelang dem Architekten Yasuhiro Yamashita eine höchst originelle Behausung mit einer Grundfläche, die weniger als die Hälfte des Geländes einnimmt. Die Dünnwandigkeit des Hauses war angesichts des beschränkten Platzes von größter Bedeutung und man beschloss, das Gebäude mit faserverstärktem Kunststoff zu überziehen, der Tageslicht durchlässt und mit seinem geringen Gewicht einer der uralten japanischen Vorkehrungen gegen die potenziellen Auswirkungen von Erdbeben entspricht. In einer anderen Umgebung könnte das Lucky Drops House in vieler Hinsicht übertrieben wirken, sowohl wegen seiner winzigen Abmessungen als auch wegen seiner ungewöhnlichen Form und Gestalt. Trotz ihrer Bindung an traditionelle Formen erweisen sich Japaner innovativer Architektur gegenüber häufig aufgeschlossener als ihre europäischen Zeitgenossen.

Obgleich der Schweizer Architekt Aldo Celoria es nicht mit einem derart kleinen Bauplatz zu tun hatte, verwendete auch er für seine Casa Trapanese (Castel San Pietro, Tessin, Schweiz, 2004–05) Kunststoffwände, in diesem Fall Platten aus Polycarbonat, um reichlich Licht in das Wohnhaus einfallen zu lassen. Auf dem gleichen, von Weinstöcken bewachsenen Hang gelegen wie seine frühere Casa Travella (2002–04), macht das neue Haus innovativen Gebrauch von dem um eine zentrale Treppe mäandernden Innenraum. Der gesamte Bau wird von keinem mit der Fassade assoziierten Element abgestützt, sondern von einer Innenwand aus Beton, ein Einfall, den der Architekt, wenn auch in anderer Form, schon im Haus Travella verwendet hatte. Celoria, ein Absolvent von Mario Bottas Accademia di Architettura in Mendrisio, ist noch keine 40, gilt aber dank seines vielversprechenden Anfangs als kommender Star der Schweizer Architekturszene. Er bebaut Gelände, das sich früher im Besitz seiner Familie befand, und stellte dabei wie andere junge Architekten fest, dass das Entwerfen von Privathäusern eine der besten Möglichkeiten bietet, sich aus dem Kreis der weniger innovativen Kollegen herauszuheben.

In einer weit entfernten Weltgegend schuf ein anderes junges Team – Pezo von Ellrichshausen Arquitectos – einen ungewöhnlichen Klotz von einem Haus am Rand einer Klippe 550 km südlich von Santiago (Casa Poli, Península de Coliumo, Chile, 2003–05; 22). Das 180 m² große Haus entstand mit einem Budget von nur 66 600 Dollar. Es passt sich mit seiner Zickzackform dem abschüssigen Gelände an und zeichnet sich durch eine eigenartige Rauheit aus, die sich offensichtlich gut in die schroffe Landschaft einfügt. Eine Wand, deren Stärke so gewaltig ist, dass darin Küche, Badezimmer, Schränke, Treppen sowie Stauraum Platz finden, macht dieses Haus zu einem der ungewöhnlichsten Bauwerke, die in den letzten Jahren weltweit realisiert wurden. Mit einem winzigen Etat und einem Gespür für Raum drückten Mauricio Pezo und Sofía von Ellrichshausen dieser Region, die einer südlichen Entsprechung von Land's End ähnelt, bereits ihren Stempel auf.

## ÜBER DIE RUINEN EINES GEISTERDORFS FLIEGEN

Aus ökonomischen Restriktionen eine Tugend zu machen, war immer Bestandteil der Arbeit von Architekten, und es gelingt auch den heutigen Designern, die u. a. auf eine Vielzahl industrieller Materialien zurückgreifen können, mit beschränkten Budgets originelle Räume oder

15

neuartige Ansätze zu erdenken. Der Beschreibung des Architekten Brian MacKay-Lyons zufolge »ist das Ghost Research Lab eine Ausbildungsinitiative, die entstand, um den Transfer architektonischen Wissens durch direkte Erfahrung, projektbezogenes Lernen, das in Baumeistertradition vermittelt wird, mit dem Schwerpunkt auf Fragen der Landschaft, Materialkultur und Gemeinschaft zu fördern«. Das zweiwöchige Praktikum »Ghost Lab« (23) für Architekten, Professoren und Studenten findet »jeden Sommer an der Küste von Nova Scotia auf den steinernen Ruinen eines fast 400 Jahre alten Dorfes auf dem Farmgelände von MacKay-Lyons statt«. In Anbetracht des entlegenen Standorts seines Büros genießt MacKay-Lyons vielleicht nicht das ihm zukommende, internationale Ansehen, für »Ghost Lab« sollte man sich allerdings interessieren. MacKay-Lyons und seine Studenten, die eine Tugend aus den temporären, gleichwohl stabilen Bauten machen, die diesem rauen Klima gewachsen sind, haben hölzerne Formen geschaffen, die mit ihrer eigenen Folgerichtigkeit aus der Erde von Nova Scotia hervorkommen. »Stellen Sie sich vor, Sie flögen über die Ruinen eines Geisterdorfs am Rand der Welt«, sagt MacKay-Lyons. Zurzeit ist der Architekt damit befasst, die kanadische Gesandtschaft in Dhaka (Bangladesh, 2007) fertigzustellen, vielleicht eine Gelegenheit für andere, eine der faszinierendsten und innovativsten Figuren der zeitgenössischen Architektur kennenzulernen.

Die jungen Architekten des Office for Subversive Architecture (OSA) haben ein ungewöhnliches Arbeitsabkommen, da sie in London, Rotterdam, Graz, Wien, Darmstadt, Frankfurt am Main und München ansässig sind und sich nur bei Bedarf für bestimmte Projekte treffen. Zwei Mitglieder der Gruppe, Karsten Huneck und Bernd Trümpler und ihr Londoner Büro Studio+44, waren an einer ungewöhnlichen Installation auf der Blade Factory in Liverpools Greenland Street (2006; 24) beteiligt. Sie verwendeten durchscheinende weiße und rote Fabrikvorhänge und Absperrungen aus PVC und gestalteten damit Eventräume auf dem Dach des aufgelassenen Industriegebäudes. Die bei Nacht von innen leuchtende Blade Factory wurde in Liverpool zu einer Art Leuchtfeuer für zeitgenössische Kunst und demonstrierte, dass interessante Architektur nicht nur durch Einsatz computergesteuerter Werkzeuge und millionenschwerer Budgets möglich ist. Es gibt in der Tat wachsenden Raum für weniger kostenträchtige, aber dafür innovative Ideen, die offenkundig kurzlebig sein können, ohne dass dies ihre architektonische Gültigkeit mindern würde.

Das Interesse an Industriematerialien besteht nicht nur aufgrund der Tatsache, dass sie billig und ohne Weiteres verfügbar sind, sondern hat auch mit einer gewissen ästhetischen Auffassung zu tun, die von Persönlichkeiten wie Bernd und Hilla Becher geschürt wurde, die Anfang der 1960er-Jahre begannen, Gasbehälter, Silos oder Wassertürme zu fotografieren. Sie lehrten lange Zeit Fotografie an der Staatlichen Kunstakademie Düsseldorf und übten direkten Einfluss auf Fotografen wie Thomas Struth, Candida Höfer und Thomas Ruff aus. Einfach ausgedrückt waren diese Künstler an der Renaissance von Industriearchitektur beteiligt. Eine Reihe zeitgenössischer Architekten wie Shigeru Ban (Bianimale Foundation/Nomadic Museum, Pier 54, New York, 2005) verwenden ausgediente Schiffscontainer. Der neue Freitag Flagship Store in Zürich (2006) ist ein aus 17 Schiffscontainern aufgestapelter, 26 m hoher Turm. Die 100 m² umfassende Räumlichkeit war eine Idee der als Gebrauchsgrafiker tätigen Besitzer Daniel und Markus Freitag und wurde von der Zürcher Firma spillmann echsle architekten ausgeführt. Die Gebrüder Freitag produzieren und vertreiben »Taschen und Accessoires aus gebrauchten und auf der Straße gefundenen Materialien: alte, von Abgasen verfärbte Lastwagenplanen, Radschläuche und gebrauchte Sicherheitsgurte sowie als neue Ressource gebrauchte Airbags«. Der Umstand, dass alte, rostige Schiffscontainer sich gut mit dieser Handelsware vertragen, spielte bei der Gestaltung des neuen Ladens natürlich

16

eine Rolle, aber ein Teil seiner Originalität beruht auf der vertikalen Schichtung; es entstand ein Turm aus Transportbehältern aus Metall. Es ist durchaus naheliegend zu prophezeien, dass derartige Methoden aus Kostengründen und darüber hinaus mit Blick auf eine bestimmte ästhetische Richtung künftig immer öfter zum Einsatz kommen werden.

### HERZ AUS BETON, WINDMÜHLEN IM HIMMEL

Beginnend mit der symbolträchtigen Erasmusbrücke (1996), die das Zentrum von Rotterdam mit dem neuen Viertel Kop van Zuid verbindet, haben Ben van Berkel und Caroline Bos von UNStudio in ihren Bauten beständige Kreativität bewiesen. Ihr neues Mercedes-Benz-Museum in Stuttgart (2003–06; 25) erweist sich trotz seiner enormen Größe von 35 000 m² in konkreter wie gedanklicher Hinsicht als äußerst innovatives Bauwerk. Ben van Berkel erläutert: »Der Bau ist eine kontinuierliche Schleife oder Spirale, die die Vorstellung einer Zeitmaschine erzeugt. Auf den 16 500 m² Ausstellungsfläche werden 170 Autos gezeigt. Ein Schnitt durch den Entwurf macht deutlich, dass es sich um eine fortlaufende, blumenartige Konstruktion handelt, um einen Ring, der sich ohne jegliche mittlere Stütze oben hält.« Das intensiv mit computergestütztem Entwerfen und parametrischer Formgebung befasste Büro will Dinge tun, »die in der Architektur bislang nicht getan wurden und sie dann zum Funktionieren bringen«. Van Berkel vergleicht die Vorgehensweise des Büros mit der eines Automobilherstellers: »Bei unseren frühen Bauten interessierte uns Geometrie und daraus wurde dann ein Spiel mit mathematischen Diagrammen. Und das, was inzwischen aus den Diagrammen wurde, bezeichnen wir als ›Entwurfsmodelle‹. Wie beim Prototyp eines Autos, aus dem fünf oder sechs Modelle entstehen können, kann aus einer Entwurfsstrategie eine Variante werden.« Schon bei ihrem Möbius-Haus (Naarden, Niederlande, 1993–98) experimentierten sie mit der Endlosschleife, die sie dann in Stuttgart in weit größerem Maßstab und mit anderer Wirkung verwendeten. Ben van Berkel räumt ein, dass mit der parametrischen Formgebung des Mercedes-Benz-Museums ein Grad von Komplexität erreicht ist, der sich nur Computerspezialisten vollständig erschließt. Andererseits erlaubt dieses System, dass Einzelteile in den Gesamtentwurf eingepasst werden können, ohne die in der Vergangenheit für solch innovative Bauten typischen, weit überzogenen Kosten. Für die Errichtung waren nicht weniger als 38 000 Arbeitszeichnungen nötig und noch während der Bauzeit musste völlig neue Software erstellt werden, um mit den Schwierigkeiten des Auftrags fertig zu werden.

Abgesehen von seinen konstruktiven und architektonischen Neuerungen ist das Mercedes-Benz-Museum ein gutes Beispiel für die erfolgreiche Zusammenarbeit von Architekten, Ingenieuren und Designern. In Kooperation mit dem renommierten Stuttgarter Ingenieur Werner Sobek und dem Ausstellungsdesigner H. G. Merz behielt UNStudio weitgehend die Kontrolle über das gesamte Projekt, einschließlich der zugehörigen Freiflächen. Rob Wagemans (Concrete Architectural Associates, Amsterdam) gestaltete sämtliche Läden und Restaurants im Museum, während die bekannte niederländische Designerin Petra Blaisse mit »Sonnenschutz, Verdunkelung und schallschluckenden Vorhängen sowie mit einer schallabsorbierenden Wand« an dem Projekt beteiligt war. In der Espressobar im Tiefgeschoss bildet »eine konkave Bürstenwand den Hintergrund eines Betoninterieurs. Die in mit Goldblech überzogenen Paneele eingesetzten weißen Borsten bereichern den Raum um einen dreidimensionalen ›Schleier‹ und streuen die Klangwellen zur Verbesserung der Akustik.« Im Folgenden erläutert Blaisse ihre Maßnahmen sieben Geschosse höher: »Ein limonengrüner, gerippter Vorhang mit einem schwarzen ›Sauerkraut‹-Futter (46 m lang und 4 m hoch) säumt

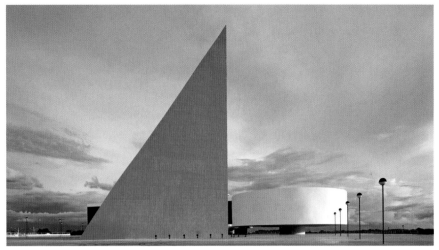

*17*
*Oscar Niemeyer, Cultural Center, Goiâ-*
*nia, Goiás, Brazil, 2003–07*

eine offene Empore und hüllt Restaurant und Lounge ein. Die Gestaltung des Vorhangs antwortet auf die gefaltete weiße Decke und seine Lichtundurchlässigkeit gewährleistet die abgedunkelten Lichtverhältnisse des darunterliegenden Ausstellungsraums. Besucher können durch den halboffenen Vorhang schauen.«

Um 120 000 t Beton so zu handhaben, als befände er sich in permanent flüssigem Zustand, verwendete van Berkel 3D-Computermodeling, um das erste, wahrhaft dem 21. Jahrhundert zugehörige Gebäude zu schaffen, bei dem die Technik einer Vorstellung dient, die eng mit der Natur verbunden ist, aber auch mit dem Fließen des Besucherstroms und der Zeit selbst. Rund um die Uhr wird das Mercedes-Benz-Museum von Autos umfahren, so wie sich pro Jahr etwa 600 000 Besucher auf die einzigartige Reise durch Zeit und Raum begeben werden. Van Berkel beruft sich auf die DNS-Doppelhelix als Inspirationsquelle, aber auch der Vergleich mit dem menschlichen Herzen bietet sich an, als dessen Lebensnerv die Besucher fungieren.

Ein zweites, von niederländischen Architekten konzipiertes Gebäude bietet eine Antwort auf die von großen Bauten aufgeworfenen Fragen. Das Niederländische Institut für Bild und Ton in Hilversum (2003–06; **26**) von Neutelings Riedijk soll als Archiv alle je im Land produzierten audiovisuellen Materialien aufnehmen. Etwa die Hälfte der 30 000 m² Nutzfläche befindet sich zum besseren Schutz der eigentlichen Dokumente unter der Erde, während der oberirdische Teil auf originelle Weise mit Lücken und Licht spielt. Die Architekten beschreiben ihr Werk wie folgt: »Der zentrale Lichtschacht lässt Tageslicht bis in die untersten Ebenen des Kellers einfallen; zum einen dringt Tageslicht durch die Oberlichter ein, zum anderen fällt farbiges, abgeschwächtes Licht durch die verglaste Vorderfront des Baus. Der große Schacht öffnet sich nach Süden, so dass die nachmittägliche Sonne bis in das Gebäudeinnere vordringen und reflektiertes Licht über die innere Fassadenwand der Büros streifen kann. Am Eingang stellt sich der Hohlraum als tiefe Schlucht dar, die den Besuchern Maßstab und schiere Größe des Archivgewölbes drastisch zu Bewusstsein bringt. Die eine Seite der Schlucht ist eine glatte Wand, die andere steigt in einer Folge verkehrter Terrassen an. Diese enthalten Empfangsräume für Kunden sowie Nebenräume der Archive und Läden; Archive und Läden selbst verbergen sich hinter der glatten Wand der Schlucht. Der zentrale Schacht mündet in einen riesigen Hohlraum, wo Museum und Büros ihre Schauseite präsentieren. Die umgekehrte Kaskade der Museumsebenen prägt sich als Wandskulptur ein, von der die Innenräume des Gebäudes Form und Maßstab erhalten.« Die geologischen und künstlerischen Begriffe, die Neutelings Riedijk verwenden, um ihre Vorstellungen in schriftlicher Form festzuhalten, verdeutlichen ihre Absichten; einer der auffallendsten Aspekte der Architektur ist allerdings die Fassade. Bei der Vorbereitung arbeiteten die Architekten mit Jaap Drupsteen zusammen, der für seine Arbeit mit Fernsehgrafik, aber auch als Gestalter der letzten niederländischen Guldenserie bekannt ist. Mit den Institutsarchiven als Bildquelle und einem neuen computergestützten Verfahren war es möglich, 748 verschiedene Glasscheiben mit einer großen Vielfalt an Farben und Reliefmustern zu erzeugen. Diese farbige Fassade belebt das Gebäude von außen und bei einfallendem Sonnenlicht auch von innen.

In Paris große Bauten zu gestalten, ist ein einigermaßen riskantes Unterfangen. Jean Nouvels »Tour sans Fins« (1989) sollte ein 100-geschossiger, runder Turm mit einer Höhe von 420 m werden, der in der Nähe der Grande Arche und des CNIT-Gebäudes im La-Défense-Viertel von Paris entstehen sollte. Trotz seines offenbar »endlichen« Äußeren wurde der Entwurf für zu gewagt befunden und nie realisiert. Der mit 300 m deutlich niedrigere neue Phare Tower, den das in Los Angeles ansässige Büro Morphosis für einen ähnlichen Standort plant, hat besse-

18
Paulo Mendes da Rocha,
Leme Gallery, São Paulo, SP,
Brazil, 2004

18

re Chancen, bis 2012 erbaut zu werden. Thom Mayne, leitender Designer des Büros, beschreibt den Turm als »fließend, sinnlich und abgerundet« und könnte damit einige Kritiker besänftigen, wenngleich in Paris seit dem Eiffelturm (1889, 324 m hoch) kein Bauwerk dieser Höhe entstanden ist. Bekrönt von »futuristischen Windrädern«, die das Belüftungssystem des Gebäudes mit Strom versorgen sollen, käme der Turm unweit der berühmten Achse der Champs-Elysées zu stehen und wäre vom Stadtzentrum aus sichtbar. Obschon Thom Mayne und Morphosis, die 2005 mit dem Pritzker-Preis ausgezeichnet wurden, nicht unbedingt für ihre Hochhäuser bekannt sind, sind ihnen die mit großen Bauvorhaben zusammenhängenden Probleme vertraut. Falls die örtliche Behörde (EPAD) und der Bauherr Unibail das Risiko eingehen sollten, die Skyline von Paris zu verändern, hätten sie dafür kaum fähigere, interessantere Architekten finden können. Es bleibt abzuwarten, ob die veränderlichen politischen Verhältnisse in Frankreich das Projekt positiv beeinflussen werden; in jedem Fall wäre es der symbolische Einzug ins 21. Jahrhundert für eine Stadt, die sich bisher im Großen und Ganzen mit ihrem historischen Erscheinungsbild rühmt.

### YOU SAY YOU WANT A REVOLUTION?

Es ist noch nicht allzu lange her, dass computergestütztes Entwerfen als eine Spielerei von Verantwortungslosen galt. Die seltsamsten Formen tauchten auf, begleitet von den unvermeidlichen Theorien zum »revolutionären« Wandel. Die wenigen, hier angeführten und die zahlreichen in diesem Band genannten Beispiele belegen, dass der Computer Angesicht (und Herz) der zeitgenössischen Architektur bereits verändert hat. Der Auslöser für diesen Wandel mag weniger im Entwurfsstadium zu suchen sein als im zunehmenden Gebrauch computergesteuerter Maschinen, die Tausende von eigens angefertigten Teilen produzieren können, während in der Vergangenheit sich wiederholende, identische Elemente die Regel waren. Die Bedeutung dieses Wandels kann nicht hoch genug eingeschätzt werden, weil er den Architekten von den durch die Fließbandfertigung verursachten, ökonomischen Restriktionen befreit. Die Ehrgeizigeren nutzen diese Freiheit, um den architektonischen Raum neu zu definieren (wie im Fall des Mercedes-Benz-Museums) oder um ein echtes Zusammenwirken mit Künstlern oder Designern zu ermöglichen.

Eine interessante Folge dieser tief greifenden Veränderungen könnte – etwas oberflächlich ausgedrückt – der »Tod des Stils« sein. Von Michelangelo oder anderen großen historischen Figuren inspirierte Architekten sahen sich seit Langem am ehesten in der Gesellschaft von Künstlern. Und doch erschwerten die geisttötenden Mechanismen moderner Fertigung es besonders bei Großbauten sehr, über das Variieren herkömmlicher Formen hinauszukommen. Die Besten, wie Richard Meier, machten eine Tugend aus dem Raster, während andere in monotoner Wiederholung ihre Lebensaufgabe fanden. Ein oder zwei Kritiker und einige Architekten marschierten unter dem Banner der »Postmoderne« in die 1970er, ein theoretischer Aufruf zur Wiederbelebung der manieristischen Vergangenheit, dazu verdammt sich darauf zu beschränken, eine Anhäufung abgeschmackter Fassaden auf ansonsten rechteckige Gebäude zu kleben. Inzwischen haben sich allerdings die Regeln selbst verändert und der Architektur bietet sich mittels einiger Mausklicks endlich die Gelegenheit, zu jener unabhängigen, schöpferischen Kunst zu werden, wie sie sich John Ruskin vorstellte – vielleicht zur größten aller Künste. Nach der Wiedergeburt des Geistes der Individualität ist es gut möglich, dass die beim Mercedes-Benz-Museum stattgefundene Zusammenarbeit immer alltäglicher werden wird. Könnte die Kunst, die dabei ist, sich aus den weiß verputzten Ausstellungsräumen zu befreien, nicht ihre wahre Heimat in gleichermaßen von den Zwängen der

Standardisierung befreiter Architektur finden? Es ist gut möglich, dass man Frank Gehry künftig als Pionier einer historischen Bewegung der Architektur hin zur Kunst und umgekehrt betrachten wird. Da er für das Guggenheim in Bilbao und spätere Bauten das CATIA-Programm von Dassault verwendete, kann er, ungeachtet seiner persönlichen Vorliebe für gekritzelte Skizzen, ebenso als Vorreiter des computergestützten Bauens gelten. Auf dem von Gehry mit seinem sehr persönlichen, plastischen Ansatz geebneten Weg stellen indessen auch andere fest, dass sich zwei Bauten nie genau gleichen müssen. Die Einstellung von Herzog & de Meuron zum Gebäude der Tate Modern, das sie als »eine unfertige, fragmentierte Form im Werden« beschreiben, gestattet die für Museumsarbeit typischen Veränderungen von kuratorischen Entscheidungen. Könnte diese formlose Form Vorbote einer neuen, »stillosen« Architektur sein? Auch Paulo Mendes da Rochas Galerie Leme in São Paulo könnte man als »eine unfertige, fragmentierte Form im Werden« beschreiben und auch sie entstand auf der Suche nach einer Art von Symbiose mit zeitgenössischer Kunst. Die Zukunft computergesteuerten Entwerfens und Bauens bedeutet, dass nicht nur eine kleine Avantgardegalerie von der Intelligenz eines einzelnen Entwurfs profitieren kann, dasselbe gilt auch für Museen, die pro Jahr Millionen von Besuchern erwarten. Architektonischer Stil ist nicht länger den Beschränkungen der Fließbandverfahren unterworfen; er ist bereits zu einer persönlicheren Angelegenheit geworden, die im Ermessen der mit neuer Freiheit ausgestatteten Architekten liegt.

*Philip Jodidio, Grimentz 2007*

[1] Titel der seit 1973 ausgestrahlten, ältesten Soap im US-Fernsehen (etwa: Die Jungen und die Ruhelosen)

[2] CNC (Computer Numerical Control/computerisierte, numerische Steuerung) bezieht sich auf computerisierte Geräte zur Steuerung von Werkzeugmaschinen, die zur Herstellung von Metallteilen verwendet werden. In der Architektur erlaubt dieses System die Fertigung individuell gestalteter Elemente zu einem mit traditioneller Serienfertigung vergleichbaren Preis.

[3] Zitiert nach: Conrads, Ulrich (Hrsg.), *Programme und Manifeste zur Architektur des 20. Jahrhunderts*, Braunschweig 1986, S. 47.

# INTRODUCTION

**JEUNES ET TURBULENTS**

Dans une époque qui privilégie de plus en plus la nature passagère des choses, l'architecture reste curieusement appréciée pour sa durabilité. Cependant, après avoir débuté dans le tonnerre de l'effondrement des tours du World Trade Center, le XXIe siècle sera peut-être davantage marqué par le superficiel et les ruines que par de grands monuments nouveaux et pérennes. Le futur nous réserve-t-il un espoir que masquerait cette sombre prévision ? Les lourdes constructions en pierre des siècles précédents ont déjà cédé la place à la légèreté, aussi bien dans la forme que dans la conception, écartant souvent le besoin de pérennité, généralement inexprimé mais bien réel chez tout client qui souhaite laisser un témoignage de son action aux générations suivantes. Ceci ne veut pas dire que les architectes ont renoncé à tout lien avec le passé et le futur. Par exemple, le Mudam d'I. M. Pei à Luxembourg (Musée d'Art Moderne Grand-Duc Jean, Luxembourg, 1999–2006 ; 1) se dresse sur des fortifications conçues par Vauban, et l'Assemblée nationale du Pays de Galles signée Richard Rogers (Cardiff, Pays de Galles, 1998–2005) a été édifiée pour durer au moins une centaine d'années.

L'architecture connaît ce faisant une révolution dont les implications pleines et entières commencent seulement à se faire sentir. Alors que le modernisme s'appuyait sur la répétitivité industrielle et les méthodes de la chaîne de montage, l'époque actuelle élabore une architecture intimement liée à l'ordinateur et à son étonnant pouvoir de permettre de créer des pièces uniques pour n'importe quel type de construction. Des architectes comme Renzo Piano ont pu voir dans ces développements un lien avec un passé lointain, lorsque tailleurs et sculpteurs de pierre élevaient des monuments sans que deux pierres ne soient exactement semblables. Le principe des économies d'échelle, qui ont favorisé l'émergence des villes actuelles prises dans les alignements de leurs tours, est bousculé, offrant ainsi à l'architecte la liberté de créer des bâtiments uniques dont les seules limites sont l'imagination, mais aussi la capacité des clients à accepter ces expériences. La culture de la récompense instantanée alimente cette nouvelle liberté presque autant que le diktat du « réalisme » économique, mais on observe par ailleurs d'autres signes d'un changement profond. Les précédents volumes d'*Architecture Now* avaient attiré l'attention des lecteurs sur la montée en force de projets qui mettaient en avant les liens entre l'art et l'architecture. Tenus par les contraintes pratiques, les architectes sont rarement libres de s'abandonner à leurs penchants pour une expression vraiment artistique, mais les artistes ont franchi les barrières invisibles qui séparent les disciplines et bénéficient d'une impunité croissante. L'esprit d'individualisme encouragé par des outils aux noms barbares comme les machines à commande numérique ouvrirait-il finalement à l'architecture l'accès à cette unité qu'imaginaient des auteurs comme John Ruskin (1819–1900) ?[1] Ruskin avait brillamment expliqué que l'architecture pouvait prétendre être le plus grand de tous les arts puisqu'elle alliait plusieurs formes d'expression spatiale en un tout unifié. Curieusement d'ailleurs, même les pères de l'idée de la *tabula rasa* rêvaient de ce que l'on pourrait appeler la théorie d'un « champ unifié » de l'architecture. Dans le premier manifeste du Bauhaus publié en 1919, Walter Gropius écrivait ainsi : « Voulons, imaginons, créons ensemble le nouveau bâti de l'avenir, qui intégrera tout en une forme unique : architecture et sculpture et peinture, et qui, issu de millions de mains de travailleurs, montera un jour jusqu'au ciel, symbole cristallin d'une nouvelle foi qui s'annonce. » Bien que le ton quasi messianique de cette proclamation ne soit plus à la mode, il faut être conscient que la création d'une architecture nouvelle composée de parties réalisées une à une ouvre d'immenses horizons qui verront cette discipline se porter à la rencontre de l'art mais aussi du design.

19
Kazuyo Sejima + Ryue
Nishizawa / S A N A A, Glass Pavilion,
Toledo Museum of Art, Toledo, OH,
USA, 2003–06

Les œuvres d'art qui touchent au domaine de l'architecture occupent une place importante dans ce livre, de même, bien sûr, que le grand nombre de réalisations de qualité consacrées au monde de la culture. Un phénomène nouveau est la présence de plus en plus significative de designers qui, dans de nombreux cas, ne possèdent pas de formation architecturale spécifique. Des individualités comme le New-Yorkais Evan Douglis cherchent à travers l'ordinateur à créer des matériaux d'habillage pratiques et cependant infiniment diversifiables qui animent ou transforment complètement les environnements architecturaux. D'autres comme le designer français Patrick Jouin ont clairement exprimé leur intention de franchir le seuil entre design et architecture en les fusionnant dans une œuvre qui pourrait finalement répondre à l'appel de Gropius. La « nouvelle foi » évoquée par celui-ci n'a pas grand-chose à voir avec la religion mais beaucoup plus avec une ambition de penser l'architecture de façon différente, encouragée par l'omniprésence grandissante de la conception et de la fabrication assistées par ordinateur.

Autre phénomène qui modifie certainement l'architecture : la montée en puissance de praticiens de moins de 40 ans. Dans le passé, le temps de la mise en œuvre des projets et celui nécessaire pour s'établir une réputation auprès de clients potentiels expliquent qu'il était difficile de se faire un nom avant 50 ans. Un survol rapide du contenu de ce volume suggère que cette règle est sans doute en train de changer. Parmi les architectes présentés ici (la date de naissance est indiquée entre parenthèses) figurent ainsi Pierre Sartoux et Augustin Rosenstiehl, Atelier SoA (tous deux 1973), Aldo Celoria (1969) et son associée Federica Giovannini (1978), Antón García-Abril Ruiz (1969), Gernot Hertl (1971), les architectes de l'agence suisse HHF, Tilo Herlach (1972), Simon Hartmann (1974) et Simon Frommenwiler (1972), Jesse Judd (1975) et Guilherme Machado Vaz (1974). À l'autre bout de l'échelle, il semble qu'une brillante carrière en architecture soit un secret de longévité comme le montrent les œuvres très récentes de I. M. Pei (1917) ou, plus étonnant encore, d'Oscar Niemeyer (1907). Mais même leurs travaux font aujourd'hui appel aux méthodes informatiques les plus sophistiquées, bien que la phase initiale de conception de leurs projets suive encore des chemins plus classiques. De jeunes architectes impatients et un certain nombre de leurs aînés nous annoncent de profonds changements dans la façon dont le bâti sera conçu et réalisé. L'un des pionniers de cette dissolution des barrières interdisciplinaires, Frank O. Gehry a récemment achevé l'étonnant Hôtel Marqués de Riscal (Elciego, Alava, Espagne, 2003–06; 27) dont la forme sculpturale, qui doit beaucoup à son fidèle logiciel CATIA, donne l'impression qu'un monde nouveau s'ouvre à l'architecture. Les fils et filles spirituels de Gehry n'ont aucun doute à ce sujet.

### QUAND LA FONCTION ET LA FORME SUIVENT LE DESIGN

Certains architectes conçoivent tout naturellement un bâtiment de l'intérieur vers l'extérieur, son apparence finale étant intimement liée aux fonctions et à la forme de l'intérieur. L'inverse est souvent tout aussi vrai, une « peau » séduisante pouvant recouvrir le volume dont a besoin le client. Le design industriel présente de nombreux points communs avec l'architecture car lui aussi recherche une relation intime entre la forme et la fonction, privilégiant alternativement l'une ou l'autre. Il a souvent été considéré comme la création d'objets qui tout au plus occupent un espace architectural, bien que de nombreux pionniers aient remis cette idée en perspective, comme Charles (1907–78) et Ray Eames (1912–88) dans leur fameuse Case Study House n° 8 (Pacific Palisades, Californie, 1949). Toute une génération de designers

20
*Emilio Ambasz,
House of Spiritual Retreat, Seville,
Spain, 1975/2003–05*

approche maintenant son travail d'une manière qui pourrait bien à terme redéfinir la nature même de l'architecture. Les très inventifs frères français Ronan et Erwan Bouroullec, par exemple, ont créé plusieurs dispositifs qui permettent la partition sélective éphémère de l'espace dans un bâti existant. Leur système Roc (5) est voisin d'autres projets même plus récents encore qui exploitent l'idée de créer un espace intime dans des constructions modernes relativement neutres. Pour le Mudam à Luxembourg (conçu par I. M. Pei), ils ont créé un restaurant à partir d'une robuste structure en pin de Douglas et de tuiles textiles. Ils expliquent ainsi que «ces tuiles qui recouvrent les structures en bois sont les éléments d'un nouveau système de mur textile modulaire mis au point en 2006 en collaboration avec le fabricant de tissus Kvadrat. Après les projets Algues et Twigs édités par Vitra, ce projet est l'expression concrète d'idées auxquelles nous travaillons depuis longtemps sur des espaces construits et des matériaux textiles qui seraient à la fois chaleureux et isolés phoniquement comme des yourtes mongoles. Sorte d'écailles, ces tuiles peuvent s'assembler grâce à un ingénieux système de pliage qui ne demande aucune intervention mécanique extérieure. Quatre volets latéraux s'insèrent dans les fentes des tuiles adjacentes, ce qui crée un rythme et même un volume sur l'ensemble du mur. Les contours de ces éléments de 50 x 25 cm ont été déterminés par la logique fonctionnelle de leur assemblage. La très grande modularité de ce système lui permet de s'adapter à de multiples applications pour construire des espaces autonomes et insonorisé dans une infinie variété de formes, qu'elles soient organiques ou géométriques. Le processus d'industrialisation de ces tuiles est étonnamment simple et rapide : il ne faut que vingt secondes pour mouler le noyau en mousse dense entre deux pièces de textile. »

Bien que le design implique généralement un travail sur des matériaux bien réels, souvent les mêmes que ceux employés en architecture, certains architectes comme Lars Spuybroek (NOX, Rotterdam) se sont orientés vers le son ou la musique pour enrichir leur œuvre d'une nouvelle dimension (Son-O-House, Son en Breugel, Pays-Bas, 2000–03). Le designer brésilien Muti Randolph a poussé un concept voisin encore plus loin pour son night-club D-Edge (São Paulo, SP, Brésil, 2003 ; 6) dans lequel un logiciel spécifique sert à modeler l'espace à partir de la lumière et de sons. Dans ce type d'environnement, l'architecture pourrait bien ne plus être qu'une coquille anonyme abritant des effets et des espaces imaginés et mis en œuvre par un designer.

En France, une génération de designers, formés d'une façon ou d'une autre par Philippe Starck, accède à la notoriété internationale, et montre souvent son envie de sauter les barrières entre mobilier, architecture intérieure et architecture. C'est certainement le cas de Matali Crasset, qui a travaillé pour Starck chez Thomson Multimédia avant de créer sa propre agence en 1998, ou celui de Patrick Jouin, designer chez Starck de 1995 à 1998. M. Crasset a récemment achevé le remodelage du SM's – Stedelijk Museum 's-Hertogenbosch (Pays-Bas, 2004–05) où elle a mis en scène sa déjà célèbre gamme chromatique et son approche d'un design qui redéfinit l'espace et la fonction du projet. Travaillant sur des *sheds* industriels construits par Jacob Berend Bakema (1914–81), elle montre ici que la fonction ne suit pas forcément la forme mais plutôt que le design génère la forme et même la fonction.

Patrick Jouin, qui s'est fait une solide réputation d'architecte-designer à l'occasion des nombreux chantiers des restaurants Ducasse (ou Spoon) dont il a été chargé dans le monde, vient de réaliser une très étonnante maison à Kuala Lumpur (Malaisie, 2004–07). Maîtrisant à la fois l'architecture et l'aménagement intérieur dans un programme intégré, il a peut-être réalisé ici le rêve du Bauhaus allemand, celui de l'œuvre d'art globale, de la *Gesamtkunstwerk*, dans laquelle tous les aspects de la création sont issus d'un même esprit déterminé. Son origi-

20

nalité et son recours à des technologies d'avant-garde, comme la stéréo-lithographie sur ses meubles, font de lui l'une des étoiles montantes du design international. À l'évidence, il n'a pas envie de se cantonner aux sièges.

### MANGER, DORMIR, ET ACHETER JUSQU'À PLUS SOIF

L'un des secteurs dans lesquels l'architecture et le design se trouvent mariés avec la plus grande évidence est celui des hôtels, des restaurants et des magasins. Deux spectaculaires projets new-yorkais récents le confirment. Le restaurant morimoto nyc (2005–06; 7) est l'une des premières interventions de Tadao Ando dans ce domaine. En collaboration avec une jeune architecte locale, Stephanie Goto, il a transformé un volume industriel par ailleurs sans intérêt dans le nouveau quartier à la mode du Meat Packing District à Manhattan en un lieu de dîners mémorables. Le béton qui est sa marque est, bien entendu, présent sous forme de colonnes qui accompagnent l'escalier central conduisant au bar au sous-sol, mais cette solidité affichée se mélange ici avec la plasticité des plafonds et des murs drapés d'une toile sinueuse renforcée de fibre de verre. Un mur de bouteilles d'eau dessiné par Ross Lovegrove court parallèlement aux marches et anime encore davantage cet espace. Le mobilier de Lovegrove mais aussi le bar en Plexiglas d'Ando confirment que l'architecte et le designer se rencontrent ici au plus haut niveau.

Cette fusion architecture-design est encore plus nette dans le nouvel Apple Store sur Cinquième Avenue, toujours à New York (2003–06). Œuvre de Bohlin Cywinski Jackson en collaboration avec le président d'Apple, Steve Jobs, il s'agit d'un cube de verre à la légèreté d'une plume, posé au-dessus de la boutique souterraine, qui réussit à donner une forme architecturale à la légendaire qualité de design du fabricant d'ordinateurs. Il est vrai cependant que l'escalier en spirale à ascenseur circulaire central qui conduit au magasin rappelle très fortement celui de I. M. Pei sous la pyramide du Louvre. Ouvert jour et nuit, l'Apple Store peut être considéré comme l'un des exemples les plus réussis de la nouvelle intégration du design et de l'architecture, l'une des plus fortes tendances du moment dans les secteurs de la distribution, de l'hôtellerie et de la restauration.

Autre sommet de cette rencontre, l'Hôtel Duomo à Rimini (Italie, 2003–06; 8) qui vient d'être rénové. Ron Arad, qui se tourne de plus en plus vers l'architecture, a explicité le lien entre extérieur et intérieur en enveloppant la façade existante d'une peau de bronze qui pénètre dans l'immeuble et court le long du mur du fond du bar avant de se terminer en une banquette. Dans le hall, l'énorme banque d'accueil en anneau confère à cet espace un caractère spectaculaire pratiquement sans équivalent aujourd'hui. Si l'architecture se transforme en banc dans le bar, cette banque devient en soi un geste architectural. Arad est une personnalité à part, même dans le monde des « stars » du design, et une grande partie de son œuvre est marquée par ce sens de l'espace. Sa transition vers l'architecture en est d'autant plus naturelle.

Le design et l'architecture peuvent sûrement cheminer main dans la main lorsque se produit une rencontre entre les parties impliquées, concert dans lequel le rôle du client est essentiel. Faire avancer un projet au point où il peut être valablement considéré comme une œuvre d'art est une autre affaire. L'intérêt de Frank O. Gehry pour l'art contemporain est largement présent dans ses réalisations, de ses premiers projets à Venice ou Santa Monica jusqu'au musée Guggenheim de Bilbao universellement applaudi. Son approche nous oriente depuis longtemps vers une nouvelle définition de ce que pourrait être l'art en architecture. L'une de ses œuvres les plus récentes, l'Hôtel Marqués de

21

21
Atelier Tekuto, Lucky Drops House,
Setagaya-ku, Tokyo, Japan, 2004–05

Riscal en Espagne fait appel au vocabulaire d'ondulations métalliques qui l'ont rendu célèbre, mais l'exubérance dont elle témoigne ici est hors du commun. Avec ses porte-à-faux de 10 mètres et ses formes contournées, l'hôtel pourrait facilement entrer dans la catégorie des sculptures monumentales. L'audace de Gehry lui attire des commandes, mais son travail déplace également des foules de visiteurs, ce qui est fort agréable pour ses clients. Ce n'est pas une critique de l'architecte mais plutôt une constatation des réalités économiques en jeu. Bien que son équipe se serve abondamment de l'ordinateur et que des formes aussi complexes ne pourraient guère être produites sans l'aide des procédés de fabrication par CNO, l'approche de Gehry n'est pas celle d'un jeune fanatique de l'informatique dont l'étoile monterait. Comme Frank Stella, artiste de la même génération, il travaille à la libération de la forme et à la redéfinition de l'espace entre l'architecture et l'art. À l'Hôtel Marqués de Riscal, il a modelé une œuvre d'art.

### LES COULEURS DE L'OMBRE

Les rapports entre l'art et l'architecture sont riches et variés et l'on peut découvrir à travers eux autant de formes d'expression que de créateurs. Dans l'interprétation, ou plutôt la redéfinition, de la forme architecturale, les artistes trouvent un champ particulièrement fertile. Le sculpteur Anish Kapoor a longtemps été fasciné par l'échelle des bâtiments, mais aussi par leurs reflets et les relations qu'ils entretiennent avec l'espace qu'ils définissent. Œuvre d'art d'échelle résolument architecturale, son étonnante *Marsyas* (Turbine Hall, Tate Modern, Londres, 9 octobre 2002 – 6 avril 2003) réalisée avec l'aide de l'ingénieur Cecil Balmond mettait en scène une membrane en PVC rouge foncé étirée sur 155 mètres de long et 35 mètres de haut, qui occupait le volume de l'immense hall de la centrale électrique de Bankside. La *Cloud Gate*, toujours de Kapoor, est une sculpture en acier inoxydable hyperpoli, installée sur la promenade du Millennium Park à Chicago. Elle reflète le panorama urbain et le déforme en volume. Après son inauguration en juillet 2004, un journal local a parlé de « faille dans le tissu même du temps et de l'espace ». Plus récemment, l'artiste a installé son *Sky Mirror* (2006; **10**), un miroir en acier poli de 10,7 mètres de diamètre, sur l'axe du Rockefeller Center près de la Cinquième Avenue à New York. Convexe d'un côté, concave de l'autre, ce « miroir » interpelle les passants qui contemplent leur image déformée sur le fond du panorama familier de Manhattan. De cette façon, l'art redéfinit l'architecture et même ses usagers. Il redonne une nouvelle vie au bâti, dans un lieu comme le Rockefeller Center où il est plutôt considéré comme une donnée fixe.

Les artistes Michael Elmgreen, né à Copenhague au Danemark en 1961, et Ingar Dragset, née à Trondheim en Norvège en 1969, ont travaillé de différentes façons sur le symbolisme de l'architecture et ses usages. L'une de leurs œuvres les plus surprenantes, *Prada Marfa* (Valentine, Texas, 2005; **9**) n'évoque rien d'autre qu'une minuscule boutique de mode perdue en bordure d'une autoroute dans le désert. Elle rappelle l'imagerie des marques de mode et leur inutilité finale dans un tel environnement. Elmgreen et Dragset jouent également sur le minimalisme attribué à Prada pour pointer des liens avec l'œuvre de Donald Judd, qui a vécu et travaillé à Marfa, non loin de là. Bien que ce soit surtout une installation, *Prada Marfa* est certainement un commentaire tout aussi précis et dérangeant sur la mode, le design et l'architecture que bien d'autres apparus au cours de ces dernières années. L'architecture est ici déformée aussi certainement que dans le *Sky Mirror* de Kapoor, mais les artistes suggèrent que la beauté (ou la haine) réside d'abord dans le regard du spectateur.

Si les architectes s'efforcent généralement de réaliser des constructions qui durent, un certain nombre d'entre eux ont été tentés par des travaux plus éphémères comme la scénographie ou les décors de scène. L'architecte français Dominique Perrault, auteur de la Bibliothèque nationale de France à Paris, a ainsi créé le décor de *La Cité radieuse* pour le Ballet national de Marseille en 2005 (**11**). À l'aide des maillages métalliques qui sont sa marque, il a ainsi participé à la mise en scène de ce ballet sur Le Corbusier, hommage assez élégant au grand maître suisse et surtout à une transition réussie entre l'architecture et cet art beaucoup moins permanent qu'est la danse. Dans le passé, le chorégraphe Frédéric Flamand, directeur du Ballet national de Marseille et apparemment convaincu des vertus du travail des architectes sur les dispositifs scéniques, a fait appel à Zaha Hadid, Thom Mayne, Jean Nouvel et Diller + Scofidio pour d'autres productions. L'intérêt de Perrault pour la lumière, l'opacité et la transparence faisaient de lui un choix naturel pour un travail de ce type. Comme d'autres architectes qui ont travaillé avec Flamand, il semble n'avoir rencontré aucune difficulté particulière à passer du chantier à la scène.

Dans une direction opposée, le célèbre photographe Hiroshi Sugimoto a fréquemment exploré en image depuis 1997 des constructions modernes connues, en particulier dans sa série *Architecture*. Il s'est également essayé à construire, bien que sur un mode japonais traditionnel (Go'o Shrine, Naoshima, Japon). Il a récemment entamé une série photographique intitulée *Colors of Shadow* (2004–06) dans laquelle il s'intéresse aux variations extrêmement subtiles de la lumière sur les murs d'un appartement qu'il a conçu à Tokyo. Ces photos peuvent être jugées plus proches de l'art abstrait que de la photographie architecturale, mais beaucoup d'architectes contemporains, de Steven Holl à Tadao Ando, travaillent concrètement sur les effets des modifications de lumière dans les espaces qu'ils conçoivent. L'acuité de son regard est telle qu'il voit de l'art jusque dans le déplacement d'un rai de lumière sur un mur. De même qu'il a longtemps pris des images abstraites de la lumière sur la mer, souvent en pause longue, Sugimoto, comme les architectes mais dans une veine légèrement différente, se propose de la capter et d'observer sa beauté.

Si l'on peut débattre du moment où l'art fini et l'illustration commence, il est néanmoins certain qu'une architecture d'une espèce très différente de celle du béton et de l'acier est apparue sur Internet dans divers jeux électroniques ou dans l'univers cinématographique. Qu'il s'appuie sur l'archéologie ou la littérature (*Le Seigneur des anneaux*, etc.), ce domaine riche et florissant ne peut manquer d'exercer une influence sur l'architecture de demain. Des travaux d'un de ces architectes « virtuels » ont été sélectionnés pour ce volume (voir page 000). Ainsi Doug Chiang, né à Taipeh en 1962, a étudié le cinéma à UCLA puis a été directeur de conception pour Lucasfilm Ltd. sur *Star Wars Episode I, La Menace fantôme* et *Episode II, L'Attaque des clones* et designer de concept pour la *Guerre des mondes* de Steven Spielberg. Son travail plus personnel, reproduit ici, fait penser à ces fantaisies « uchronienne » qui décrivent un futur ou un passé lointains hypothétiques. Toute similarité entre certaines de ses interventions et le temple de Ta Phrom (Angkor, Cambodge) est purement intentionnelle. L'ubiquité naturelle aux jeux vidéos ou aux sites Internet comme « Second Life » (www.secondlife.com) signifie que, vue d'une certaine façon, l'architecture virtuelle possède une existence nouvelle et en plein développement. Dans « Second Life », les joueurs peuvent habiter ou même vendre des immeubles qui n'existent que sur Internet. Des œuvres comme les gravures des *Prisons imaginaires* de Giovanni Battista Piranesi (1749–50/1761) ont, bien entendu, influé sur ces images, et ce ne serait guère prendre de risques que de penser que les mondes virtuels d'artistes comme Doug Chiang se répandront bientôt sur notre environnement construit.

22

## LA PURETÉ IMMACULÉE DU COMPLEXE

Pour un architecte qui ne possède pas le goût artistique affirmé d'un Frank Gehry, la conception d'institutions culturelles est peut-être ce qui s'en rapproche le plus. Si le nombre des musées et nouveaux instituts divers est une indication, il est certain qu'il s'agit là du domaine le plus fertile et le plus ouvert pour l'architecture contemporaine. Même si les noms bien établis sont souvent préférés à ceux de talents plus jeunes dès que des conseils d'administration ou des jurys doivent voter, les bâtiments culturels font plus fréquemment l'objet de réels efforts esthétiques que la plupart des autres types architecturaux. En fonction des sensibilités locales, ou du sens esthétique propre à chaque praticien, ces nouvelles institutions peuvent revêtir une étonnante multiplicité de formes, affirmant parfois leur présence de manière quasi programmatique ou, dans d'autres circonstances, se fondant volontairement dans leur environnement. Les institutions culturelles et artistiques bénéficient généralement de connotations positives, mais que se passerait-il à propos d'un musée consacré à l'horreur ? Il existe très certainement plus d'une façon de concevoir l'image architecturale de la culture, et la diversité des solutions présentées dans ces pages est sans doute la preuve qu'il n'existe plus de style dominant dans l'architecture d'aujourd'hui. La situation est même à l'opposé.

Tout bien considéré, Boston est une ville conservatrice en matière d'architecture contemporaine, même si l'élégante Tour John Hancock de Harry Cobb se détache toujours de son panorama. On peut donc être surpris que l'Institute of Contemporary Art ait sélectionné la très novatrice agence new-yorkaise Diller Scofidio + Renfro pour leurs nouvelles installations sur le port (2004–06 ; **12**). Perdu pour le moment dans une mer de parkings, et non loin d'une autre institution locale, pour l'instant la plus célèbre, l'Anthony's Pier 4 Restaurant, l'ICA est un audacieux bâtiment à enveloppe doté d'un spectaculaire porte-à-faux dominant un espace public extérieur. Les galeries, essentiellement concentrées au niveau supérieur, bénéficient de diverses combinaisons d'éclairages naturel et artificiel et d'un système de division aisée du volume pour les expositions temporaires. Un espace multimédia spectaculaire descend en gradins vers une étonnante vue sur l'eau, et l'ensemble donne une impression de dynamisme. Bien que le budget n'ait pas été aussi élevé qu'il aurait dû, ce centre culturel est un brillant succès qui plaide en faveur de l'amélioration de la qualité architecturale du centre de Boston.

De l'autre côté de l'océan, les architectes suisses Herzog & de Meuron ont été rappelés pour concevoir l'extension de la Tate Modern (2004–12 ; **13**), l'ancienne centrale électrique de Bankside, dont ils avaient réaménagé les volumes en 2000. Ici la structure, irrégulièrement empilée, qui donne « l'impression d'une forme fragmentée échafaudée en cours de construction », représente une intéressante évolution par rapport à leur production généralement plus ordonnée ou apparemment cohérente. Ce projet, dont la conception et l'ingénierie font sans aucun doute appel à de nouveaux logiciels informatiques, pourrait bien annoncer une nouvelle génération de bâtiments dont l'aspect serait plus chaotique que séduisamment esthétique. Le dynamisme supposé de l'art contemporain qui y sera exposé se refléterait ainsi dans les plans suisses. Alors que Diller Scofidio + Renfro se contentent d'une forme enveloppée projetée vers l'eau, Herzog & de Meuron semblent avoir voulu regarder dans plusieurs directions à la fois.

Paris possède également sa part d'institutions nouvelles consacrées à l'art, la plus récente et la plus visible étant le nouveau musée du quai Branly (**14**) conçu par Jean Nouvel, en étroite collaboration avec l'architecte-paysagiste Gilles Clément pour les jardins (2001–06). Situé au bord de la Seine, près de la tour Eiffel, ce musée de l'art primitif va sûrement attirer les foules dans les années qui viennent. Pourtant sa

23
MacKay-Lyons Sweetapple,
"Ghost Lab," Nova Scotia, Canada,
1994–1997, 2002–

23

complexité, et même l'obscurité entretenue autour des pièces exposées, ne le prédisposent pas vraiment au tourisme de masse. Il se félicite de posséder de multiples œuvres splendides d'Afrique, d'Océanie ou d'Amérique du Nord et du Sud, mais pas de *Mona Lisa* qui puisse mobiliser les foules. L'architecte et les conservateurs ont préféré convier les visiteurs à une sorte de voyage de découverte. Nouvel parle ainsi d'une rampe d'accès qui « serpente » du rez-de-chaussée jusqu'au niveau des expositions pour « remonter le courant d'une rivière ». Au cœur de la jungle ? Surélevé sur pilotis par rapport au terrain exposé aux inondations par sa proximité du fleuve, le musée domine un grand jardin de végétaux et d'arbres choisis par Clément. Un écran de verre limite le site côté Seine, mais on peut se promener dans les jardins, même si l'on ne visite pas le musée. Dans un lieu aussi visible, aligné sur divers bâtiments publics et immeubles haussmanniens, le musée se fait remarquer et continuera à l'être même lorsque son écran d'arbres l'aura masqué par rapport au quai. Également responsable de la muséographie, Jean Nouvel a certainement réalisé là l'un de ses projets parisiens le plus ambitieux et le plus surprenant. Il suscitera longtemps la controverse comme l'a fait en son temps le Centre Pompidou. Comme son confrère Christian de Portzamparc, distingué par le Pritzker Prize, Jean Nouvel se distingue comme l'un des plus intéressant et inventif architecte français vivant.

I. M. Pei, né à Canton en Chine en 1917, est arrivé aux États-Unis pour ses études en 1935, pour finalement décider de s'installer à New York. Ce n'est qu'à l'occasion de son Fragrant Hill Hotel (près de Pékin, 1979–82), puis du siège de la Banque de Chine (Pékin, 1999–2001), qu'il est revenu dans son pays natal. Pour l'hôtel, il parla à l'époque d'une tentative de trouver « un nouveau style vernaculaire » pour la Chine, accablée par la qualité médiocre d'une architecture omniprésente dite moderne. La famille de Pei avait longtemps vécu à Suzhou, ville de jardins et de canaux à 60 km environ de Shanghai. Le plus récent projet de l'architecte, le Musée de Suzhou, traduit donc un retour à ses racines, non loin de l'ancien jardin de la propriété familiale. Il s'y est livré à une tâche audacieuse : réconcilier les traditions chinoises avec la modernité. Sa composition géométrique de couleur grise et blanche entoure un étang central bordé d'un pavillon de thé qui rappelle les remarquables jardins de la cité historique. Le nouveau musée, dont les collections contiennent des œuvres anciennes et contemporaines, est situé dans la même rue que l'une de plus célèbres attractions touristique locales : le Jardin de l'humble administrateur. Très clairement, avec aussi la volonté de surmonter tous les obstacles, I. M. Pei est d'une certaine manière revenu chez lui, en offrant à sa ville et à la Chine contemporaine de nouvelles idées qui devraient leur permettre d'avancer. Élève de Gropius à Harvard, il est resté fidèle à un vocabulaire géométrique, mais s'est rapidement éloigné de la rigueur austère du premier modernisme pour faire pénétrer dans ses projets la lumière et le spectaculaire. Le Musée de Suzhou (2003–06; **15**) l'est moins que l'aile Est de la National Gallery de Washington par exemple, mais est intimement lié à l'architecture et aux jardins chinois dans sa succession de cours et de volumes. Il constitue le présent d'un des architectes les plus célèbres du monde à son pays natal, au moment où la prospérité de celui-ci risque de venir à bout du meilleur des anciennes traditions chinoises.

Un architecte brésilien âgé d'une cinquantaine d'années aime à dire que trois générations entières de sa profession ont été sacrifiées sur l'autel de la réputation d'Oscar Niemeyer. Il veut signifier par là que Niemeyer est depuis longtemps l'architecte « officiel » du gouvernement et de ses institutions et que peu d'autres représentants de cette discipline ont pu accéder aux grandes commandes qui vont systématiquement à l'homme de Rio. Âgé de 100 ans en décembre 2007, « ON » comme il signe, continue à créer de remarquables œuvres lyriques. Son nouveau Centre culturel à Goiânia (Goiás, Brésil, 2003–07; **17**) est une composition dans le superbe style qu'il avait appliqué au parc Ibi-

24

rapuera inauguré en 1954 et peut-être du Mémorial pour l'Amérique latine (São Paulo, 1987) et du fameux Caminho Niemeyer, autre projet en développement à Niterói, au bord de la baie de Guanabara, face à Rio. Il reste dans une gamme de formes beaucoup plus géométriques que Frank O. Gehry, par exemple, mais sa vision de l'architecture considérée comme une sculpture précède celle du Californien de trente années au moins. Au sujet de l'un de ces récents projets, l'auditorium d'Ibirapuera (São Paulo, 2004–05; **16**), il parle de « la nécessité d'ajouter au programme un bâtiment triangulaire pour renforcer la pureté immaculée du complexe ». Son théâtre n'est rien de plus qu'un énorme coin blanc, de même que « l'élément final » à Goiânia est « le Monument aux droits de l'homme, un grand triangle de béton rouge qui confère à l'ensemble l'importance voulue ».

Moins âgé que Niemeyer, Paulo Mendes da Rocha est né en 1928. Titulaire du Pritzker Prize 2006, c'est un architecte puissant et original, certainement sous-estimé dans les cercles européens ou américains parce que l'essentiel de sa production se trouve au Brésil. Sa galerie Leme (São Paulo, 2004; **18**) est un volume de béton brut. Son propriétaire, Eduardo Leme, souhaitait mettre en scène une « esthétique de la substance » qui prend ici un sens nouveau par la réunion de l'art et de l'architecture au plus haut niveau. La reconnaissance relativement tardive accordée à Mendes da Rocha par le jury du Pritzker compense mal la façon dont Niemeyer a été récompensé en 1988 : *ex aequo* avec Gordon Bunshaft… Comme Mies van der Rohe, Le Corbusier ou Frank Lloyd Wright, Niemeyer est indiscutablement l'une des plus grandes personnalités de l'architecture moderne. Mendes da Rocha poursuit et développe la riche tradition de l'architecture brésilienne. Les deux hommes ont travaillé à la frontière de l'art et de l'architecture d'une manière qui continuera à influencer en profondeur la créativité contemporaine, quels que soient les préjugés nord-américains et européens dont ils peuvent souffrir.

Alors que Mendes da Rocha s'est souvent lancé dans des expérimentations à partir d'éléments massifs comme dans son Musée brésilien de la sculpture (São Paulo, 1987–92), une institution culturelle américaine fait de son mieux pour se dissoudre dans son cadre naturel. Le Pavillon de verre des architectes japonais S A N A A (Toledo Museum of Art, Toledo, Ohio, 2003–06; **19**) est une recherche sur la plus grande légèreté et la plus grande transparence possibles. Il utilise 3 000 m² de verre et des murs en tôle d'acier de 1,9 cm d'épaisseur. Kazuyo Sejima et Ryue Nishizawa ont conçu une autre structure tout aussi évanescente pour le Musée d'art contemporain du XXIe siècle de Kanazawa (Ishikawa, Japon, 2002–04), bandeau circulaire de verre dont l'intérieur comporte une succession soigneusement orchestrée de cours et de galeries. Le projet de Toledo étant destiné à une collection de verreries, le choix de ces architectes de faire quasiment disparaître les murs ne manque pas de pertinence.

Pour une demande de nature très différente, les architectes allemands Wandel Hoefer Lorch + Hirsch ont imaginé pour le Centre de documentation d'Hinzert (Hinzert, Allemagne, 2003–05) une sorte de hutte sculpturale en acier Cor-Ten, implantée dans un environnement naturel non loin de l'ancien camp de concentration spécial des SS. Bien que les architectes possèdent déjà l'expérience de ces monuments de mémoire en Allemagne, ce projet très particulier a demandé beaucoup de subtilité et d'invention. Si dans l'esprit, le résultat est proche d'œuvres réalisées à l'aide d'ordinateurs et de machines pilotées par informatique, les architectes ont néanmoins réussi à traduire quelque chose de la nature funeste du lieu.

*24*
*OSA – Office for Subversive Architecture,* Kunsthülle LPL, *Blade Factory, Greenland Street, Liverpool, UK, 2006*

## DE L'ARCADIE AU BOUT DU MONDE

Les résidences privées figurent souvent parmi les projets les plus intéressants d'un architecte car ces chantiers sont plus facilement libérés de contraintes financières. Lorsque le client joue le jeu, l'inventivité peut se déployer avec plus de générosité que dans les grands bâtiments publics, par exemple. Le designer et architecte Emilio Ambasz, né en Argentine et basé à New York, a réussi à construire pour lui-même la maison dont il rêvait à Séville près de trente ans après l'avoir conçue (Maison de retraite spirituelle, Séville, 1975/2003–05; **20**). Il a imaginé la surprenante façade de cette maison en « substitut d'architecture en forme de masque ». En fait, sous certains angles, cette résidence donne l'illusion de ne se composer que de deux façades. Cherchant à « réexaminer l'architecture qui est un processus conditionné par la culture et par le retour à la notion primitive de demeure-abri », Ambasz semble s'autoriser beaucoup plus de sophistication que son objectif théorique ne pourrait le laisser entendre. Cette maison correspond peut-être avant tout à la quête d'une solitude arcadienne dans laquelle l'art, l'architecture et la nature fusionnent en un tout unique.

La Péninsule ibérique se montre parfois incroyablement inventive dans le domaine de l'architecture contemporaine comme en témoignent plusieurs projets présentés dans ces pages. Ainsi, cette très surprenante résidence, la maison Tóló (Lugar das Carvalhinhas – Alvite, Freguesia de Cerva, Portugal, 2000–05) conçue par le fils d'Álvaro Siza, Álvaro Leite Siza Vieira. Insérée dans un site en forte déclivité, cette maison de vacances de quatre pièces suit un flanc de colline selon un cheminement de haut en bas. Le père de l'architecte et son confrère Eduardo Souto de Moura pour lesquels le jeune praticien a également travaillé apprécient également le dialogue actif avec le site, en particulier dans leurs réalisations de résidences privées. Ici, Álvaro Leite Siza Vieira pousse encore plus loin la relation avec le paysage, en faisant en sorte que l'architecture s'intègre en respectant l'inclinaison naturelle du sol.

Les architectes de l'Atelier Tekuto étaient confrontés à un problème très différent pour leur « Lucky Drops House » à Tokyo (2004–05; **21**). Comme c'est souvent le cas dans la capitale japonaise, ils ne disposaient que d'un minuscule terrain d'à peine 59 m². En associant son talent à celui de l'ingénieur Masahiro Ikeda, Yasuhiro Yamashita a réalisé une très originale petite habitation dont l'empreinte au sol occupe moins de la moitié du terrain. La « finesse » de cette architecture était quasi obligatoire étant donné la contrainte de dimensions. Elle a été habillée de plastique fibré pour permettre la pénétration de la lumière naturelle et assurer une légèreté physique qui est aussi une manière de se prémunir contre les effets des tremblements de terre fréquents au Japon. Dans un autre environnement, la présence réduite, la forme et la conception de cette maison seraient, à de nombreux égards, jugées extrémistes. Malgré leur attachement à diverses formes de traditions, les Japonais sont fréquemment bien plus ouverts à l'inventivité architecturale que la plupart des Européens.

Bien qu'il n'ait pas été confronté à un terrain aussi limité, l'architecte suisse Aldo Celoria a trouvé pour sa maison Trapanese (Castel San Pietro, Tessin, Suisse, 2004–05) une solution à base de murs en plastique (dalles de polycarbonate) qui permet d'éclairer généreusement les volumes intérieurs. Implantée sur le même flanc de colline aux vignobles que sa précédente maison Travella (2002–04), cette nouvelle réalisation utilise de manière inventive l'espace interne qui s'enroule autour d'un escalier en spirale. La structure est dans sa totalité soutenue par un mur de béton intérieur et non par la façade, technique que l'architecte avait déjà utilisée sous une forme différente dans la maison Travella. Diplômé de l'École d'architecture de Mendrisio animée par Mario Botta, Celoria est âgé de moins de 40 ans mais ses débuts sont si prometteurs qu'il est déjà considéré comme l'une des stars montantes de l'architecture suisse. Travaillant sur un terrain qui appartenait à l'origine à sa famille, il découvre, comme d'autres jeunes architectes, que la conception de résidences privées est l'une des voies les plus évidente pour se distinguer de confrères moins inventifs.

De l'autre côté du monde, une autre jeune équipe – Pezo von Ellrichshausen Arquitectos – vient de créer une sorte de maison-cube au bord d'une falaise située à 550 km au sud de Santiago du Chili (Maison Poli, Péninsule de Coliumo, Chili, 2003–05; **22**). Cette construction de 180 m$^2$ a été réalisée pour un budget de tout juste 66 600 dollars. S'adaptant à la façon d'un zigzag à la pente du terrain, l'architecture affiche une sorte de brutalité mystérieuse qui semble se marier à la rudesse du paysage. Son mur, si épais qu'il abrite la cuisine, les salles de bains, les toilettes, la circulation verticale et un espace de rangement, en fait l'une des œuvres architecturales les plus inattendues construites au cours de ces dernières années dans le monde. Pour un maigre budget mais un grand sens de l'espace, Mauricio Pezo et Sofía von Ellrichshausen ont déjà laissé leur marque sur ce lointain « bout du monde ».

### VOL AU-DESSUS D'UN VILLAGE FANTÔME

Faire d'une contrainte économique une vertu a toujours été une qualité d'architecte et, par exemple, les concepteurs actuels qui font appel à la panoplie des matériaux industriels réussissent souvent à créer des volumes originaux dans le cadre de budgets limités ou d'approches étonnantes. Comme le décrit l'architecte Brian MacKay-Lyons : « Le Ghost Research Lab (Laboratoire fantôme de recherche) est une initiative éducative destinée à promouvoir le transfert des connaissances architecturales *via* l'expérience directe et un enseignement sur le projet dispensé dans la tradition du maître constructeur, en mettant l'accent sur les enjeux de paysage de culture matérielle et de communauté. » Stage d'été de deux semaines réservé aux architectes, professeurs et étudiants, ce « Ghost Lab » (**23**) est organisé « chaque été sur la côte de la Nouvelle-Écosse, au-dessus des ruines d'un village vieux de près de quatre cents ans dans la ferme MacKay-Lyons ». La localisation de son agence n'aide pas l'architecte à accéder à la réputation internationale qu'il mérite, mais son « Ghost Lab » est plus qu'une simple curiosité. Dans un esprit éphémère mais aussi à travers un mode de construction adapté à la rudesse du climat, le professeur et ses étudiants créent des formes en bois qui semblent surgir du sol de la Nouvelle-Écosse par leur propre logique. « Imaginez survoler les vestiges d'un village fantôme dans un pays perdu », explique-t-il. Il achève actuellement le bâtiment de la Haute Commission canadienne à Dhaka (Bangladesh, 2007), occasion pour ses confrères de faire la connaissance de l'une des figures les plus intrigantes et innovantes de l'architecture contemporaine.

Les jeunes membres de l'Office for Subversive Architecture (OSA) se sont organisés selon une configuration inhabituelle puisqu'ils sont basés à la fois à Londres, Rotterdam, Graz, Vienne, Darmstadt, Francfort et Munich et se réunissent pour des projets spécifiques en fonction des circonstances. Deux membres du groupe, Karsten Huneck, Bernd Truempler et leur agence londonienne Studio+44, ont réalisé une étonnante installation temporaire dans la Blade Factory, Greenland Street, à Liverpool (2006; **24**). À partir de rideaux et de claustras de type industriel en PVC rouge et blanc translucide, ils ont créé un espace pour événements sur le toit d'un ancien bâtiment d'usine. Irradiant de lumière la nuit, la Blade Factory est devenue une sorte de lieu-phare de l'art contemporain à Liverpool et montre qu'une forme architecturale

*25*
*UNStudio, Mercedes-Benz Museum,*
*Stuttgart, Germany, 2003–06*

25

séduisante n'est pas forcément le produit d'outils pilotés par ordinateur ni de budgets de millions de dollars. Il existe une place, et même une place grandissante, pour des idées moins coûteuses et plus innovantes capables de viser ouvertement à l'éphémère sans que cela ne diminue en rien leur intérêt architectural.

Cet intérêt pour les matériaux industriels est non seulement lié à leur disponibilité et à leur faible coût mais aussi à une certaine esthétique qui a nourri des créateurs comme les photographes Bernd et Hilla Becher. Ces enseignants de la Staatliche Kunstakademie de Düsseldorf qui ont commencé à photographier des réservoirs de gaz, des silos ou des châteaux d'eau au début des années 1960 ont exercé une influence directe sur des photographes comme Thomas Struth, Candida Höfer et Thomas Ruff. Sous un autre angle, ces artistes ont également joué un rôle dans la « mode » des bâtiments industriels. De vieux conteneurs de transport ont ainsi été utilisés par un certain nombre d'architectes contemporains tels Shigeru Ban (Fondation Bianimale/Nomadic Museum, Pier 54, New York 2005). Le nouveau magasin Freitag à Zurich (2006) est une tour de 26 mètres de haut composée de dix-sept conteneurs. De 100 m² de surface, cette installation est une idée des propriétaires et graphistes Daniel et Markus Freitag, réalisée par l'agence zurichoise spillmann echsle architekten. Les frères Freitag fabriquent et vendent des « sacs et accessoires réalisés à partir de matériaux de récupération, ou trouvés au bord des routes : vieux camions, toiles à bâche tannées par les gaz d'échappement, cadres de vélos, vieilles ceintures de sécurité ainsi qu'une nouvelle trouvaille, les airbags ». Que ces vieux conteneurs rouillés correspondent à ce programme commercial a évidemment constitué un facteur clé dans la conception de ce nouveau magasin, mais une part de son originalité vient de leur empilement vertical. On peut raisonnablement prévoir que des méthodes de ce type seront utilisées de plus en plus fréquemment pour des raisons de coût mais aussi pour une certaine vision esthétique.

### UN CŒUR DE BÉTON, DES MOULINS DANS LE CIEL

Ben van Berkel et Caroline Bos de UNStudio peuvent se targuer de leur continuité créative, remarquée dès leur emblématique pont Érasme (1996) reliant le centre de Rotterdam au nouveau quartier de Kop van Zuid. Leur vaste nouveau Musée Mercedes-Benz à Stuttgart (2003–06; **25**), construit sur 35 000 m², est, tant structurellement qu'intellectuellement, novateur. Comme l'explique Ben van Berkel : « La structure forme une boucle en continu, ou spirale, qui illustre une idée de machine à remonter le temps. Cent-soixante-dix voitures sont exposées dans les 16 500 m² de l'espace d'exposition. Une coupe montre qu'il s'agit d'une structure en forme de fleur continue, un anneau qui se maintient de lui-même, sans support central. » Plongé dans la conception assistée par ordinateur et la modélisation paramétrique, UNStudio veut « créer des choses qui n'ont pas encore été réalisées en architecture et faire en sorte qu'elles fonctionnent. » Van Berkel compare d'ailleurs la méthode de son agence à celle d'un fabricant d'automobiles. « Dans les premières étapes du projet, nous nous intéressons à la géométrie, ce qui nous conduit à faire intervenir des diagrammes mathématiques. Puis ceux-ci deviennent ce que nous appelons des « modèles de conception ». Une stratégie de conception peut se transformer en variante, comme dans le cas d'un prototype de voiture, qui peut générer cinq ou six véhicules différents. » Leur maison Möbius (Naarden, Pays-Bas, 1993–98) expérimentait déjà l'idée d'anneau continu reprise à Stuttgart à beaucoup plus grande échelle pour un effet différent. Ben van Berkel admet que la modélisation paramétrique de ce musée a atteint un niveau de complexité tel que seuls des informaticiens peuvent l'appréhender entièrement, mais le résultat est unique en ce

26

26
Neutelings Riedijk,
Netherlands Institute for Sound
and Vision, Hilversum,
The Netherlands, 2003–06

que des pièces peuvent s'intégrer dans l'ensemble sans entraîner, comme par le passé, les dépassements de coûts typiques à ces constructions-prototypes. Pas moins de 38 000 dessins techniques ont été réalisés et un logiciel entièrement nouveau a été conçu pendant le chantier pour gérer la complexité des tâches.

En dehors de ses innovations structurelles et architecturales, le Musée Mercedes-Benz est un exemple de collaboration fructueuse entre des architectes, des ingénieurs et des designers. Collaborant avec le célèbre ingénieur de Stuttgart, Werner Sobek, ou le concepteur d'expositions, H. G. Merz, UNStudio a néanmoins conservé un degré de contrôle élevé sur le projet tout entier, y compris les espaces extérieurs. Rob Wagemans (Concrete Architectural Associates, Amsterdam) a créé l'ensemble des boutiques et restaurants tandis que la célèbre designer néerlandaise, Petra Blaisse, a participé au projet par des «rideaux acoustiques assombrissants et filtrant le soleil et un mur acoustique». Dans l'Espresso-Bar du niveau inférieur, «un mur-brosse concave sert de fond à un intérieur «béton». Les poils de brosse blancs insérés dans des panneaux recouverts d'un film de métal doré créent un «voile» tridimensionnel dans cet espace et éparpillent les ondes sonores pour améliorer le confort acoustique». Blaisse explique également son intervention sept niveaux plus haut: «Un rideau d'ailettes vert tilleul à support noir «choucroute» (46 mètres de long x 4 mètres de haut) recouvre un balcon ouvert et enveloppe le restaurant et le salon. Le dessin de ce rideau réagit au plafond blanc à plis et son opacité filtre la lumière pour l'espace d'exposition en dessous. Le public peut regarder à travers le plan semi-ouvert du rideau.»

Pour édifier cette construction qui est véritablement du XXIe siècle, il aura fallu traiter ces 120 000 tonnes de béton en flux continu grâce à une modélisation en 3D. La technologie était ici au service d'un concept étroitement lié à la nature mais également au flux des visiteurs et du temps. Les voitures affluent autour du musée à toute heure, et l'on pense que 600 000 visiteurs par an au moins vont participer à ce voyage exceptionnel à travers le temps et l'espace. Si l'architecte se réfère à la structure en double hélice de l'ADN, ce musée peut aussi se comparer à un cœur humain dont le flux sanguin serait en fait les visiteurs.

Une autre réalisation d'architectes néerlandais apporte une réponse différente aux questions soulevées par les constructions à grande échelle. Il s'agit de l'Institut néerlandais pour le son et la vision d'Hilversum (2003–06; **26**) par Neutelings Riedijk, destiné à l'archivage de tous les matériaux audiovisuels produits dans ce pays. Environ 30 000 m$^2$ de l'immeuble sont en sous-sol pour assurer une meilleure protection des documents, et la partie émergeante joue sur les pleins, les vides et la lumière de façon originale. Selon le descriptif de l'agence: «Le puits central laisse pénétrer la lumière naturelle jusqu'au fond des réserves. Tout d'abord, la lumière zénithale franchit les verrières, puis une lumière colorée et adoucie pénètre à travers la façade vitrée de l'immeuble. Le vaste puits creusé dans la superstructure s'ouvre au sud pour que le soleil de l'après-midi pénètre jusqu'au cœur du bâtiment, tandis que la lumière réfléchie balaie le mur de façade intérieur des bureaux. À l'entrée, le vide forme un profond canyon qui fait percevoir aux visiteurs l'échelle spectaculaire et les dimensions impressionnantes des archivages. L'un des côtés de ce canyon est un mur arasé, les autres s'élèvent en une série de terrasses inversées qui contiennent des salles pour la réception de la clientèle et des annexes pour les archives et les magasins de stockage. Ces derniers sont dissimulés derrière le mur lisse du canyon. Le puits central culmine en un énorme vide où le musée et les bureaux se montrent sous leur meilleur angle. La cascade inversée des niveaux du musée crée une sorte de sculpture murale qui donne forme et échelle aux volumes intérieurs de l'ensemble.» Les qualificatifs géologiques ou artistiques utilisés par Neutelings Riedijk pour expliciter leur pensée révèlent leurs intentions, mais l'un des éléments les plus frappants de cette réalisation reste sa façade. Dans la phase préliminaire, les architectes ont collaboré avec Jaap Drupsteen, connu pour son travail d'habillages graphiques pour la télévision et le dessin du dernier florin. Utilisant les archives de l'Institut comme source iconographique et un nouveau processus de fabrication piloté par ordinateur comme outil de créations, 748 panneaux de verre différents ont été réalisés dans une grande variété de couleurs et de textures. C'est cette façade colorée qui anime ce bâtiment aussi bien de l'extérieur que de l'intérieur lorsque les rayons du soleil la traversent.

Construire des immeubles de grande hauteur à Paris est une entreprise périlleuse. La « Tour sans Fins » de Jean Nouvel (1989) aurait due être une flèche cylindrique de 100 étages et 420 mètres de haut dressée près de la Grande Arche de La Défense et du bâtiment du CNIT. Malgré son aspect « évanescent », le projet fut jugé trop audacieux et rejeté. Bien que moins haute – 300 mètres – la nouvelle « Tour Phare » proposée par l'agence de Los Angeles, Morphosis, pour pratiquement le même site semble avoir plus de chance d'être réalisée d'ici 2012. La « fluidité, la sensualité et la douceur » de cette dernière telle qu'elle est décrite par l'agence du responsable de la conception, Thom Mayne, réussiront sans doute à réduire quelques oppositions, mais il reste qu'aucun bâtiment de cette taille n'a été édifié dans la capitale française depuis la tour Eiffel (1889, 324 mètres). Surmonté de « moulins à vent futuristes » qui devraient fournir l'énergie nécessaire pour le système de ventilation naturelle de la tour, l'immeuble légèrement décalé par rapport à l'axe des Champs-Élysées sera visible du centre de la capitale. Bien que Thom Mayne et Morphosis, Pritzker Prize 2005, ne soient pas spécialement réputés pour leurs gratte-ciel, ils sont familiers des enjeux posés par les immeubles de grandes dimensions. Si l'autorité administrative de La Défense (EPAD) et le client, Unibail, veulent prendre le risque de modifier le panorama parisien, ils auraient difficilement pu trouver une équipe plus compétente et passionnante. Il reste à voir si les changements politiques en France permettront de donner le feu vert à ce projet, mais il offrirait une entrée symbolique dans le XXIᵉ siècle à une ville qui s'est beaucoup reposée sur son image historique.

## VOUS VOULIEZ UNE RÉVOLUTION?

Il y eut un temps, qui n'est pas si éloigné d'ailleurs, où la conception assistée par ordinateur semblait un jouet pour irresponsables. Les *blobs* les plus bizarres apparaissaient à l'horizon accompagnés d'une inévitable « théorie » du changement. Les quelques exemples cités dans cette introduction et ceux encore plus nombreux présents dans ce volume montrent que l'ordinateur a déjà modifié le visage et le cœur de l'architecture contemporaine. La clé de cette transition se cache peut-être moins dans la phase de conception que dans l'utilisation de plus en plus répandue de machines-outils pilotées par ordinateur qui peuvent produire des milliers de pièces sur mesure, alors que la règle était naguère à la répétitivité d'éléments identiques. L'importance de ce changement ne doit pas être sous-estimée car elle libère les architectes de contraintes économiques imposées par les anciennes méthodes de chaîne de montage. Pour le plus ambitieux, cette nouvelle liberté est un outil de redéfinition de l'espace architectural – comme dans le Musée Mercedes-Benz par exemple –, ou de développement de collaborations réelles avec des artistes ou des designers.

Une conséquence intéressante de ces grands changements est probablement ce que l'on pourrait appeler irrévérencieusement la

27

27

« mort du style ». Les architectes, sans aucun doute inspirés par Michel-Ange ou d'autres grandes figures du passé, se sont longtemps imaginé qu'ils devaient être rangés en compagnie des artistes. Cependant la mécanique engourdissante de la production moderniste rend très difficile, en particulier dans les immeubles de grandes dimensions, de faire autre chose que de broder sur une base géométrique standard. Les meilleurs, comme Richard Meier, font de la trame une vertu, tandis que d'autres découvrent que la monotonie de la répétition est devenue leur lot. Quelques critiques et un certain nombre d'architectes ont défilé dans les années 1970 sous la bannière du postmodernisme, appel théorique à revivifier un passé maniériste, condamné dans les faits à ne guère aller plus loin qu'une accumulation de façades façon gâteau d'anniversaire, collées sur des immeubles par ailleurs parfaitement rectilignes. Mais aujourd'hui, les règles ont changé et, d'un clic de souris, l'architecture s'est enrichie de la possibilité de devenir cet art original et fécond dans lequel John Ruskin voyait peut-être le plus grand de tous les arts. L'esprit d'individualisme revivifié, il est bien possible que le type de collaboration aperçu dans le projet Mercedes-Benz se répande de plus en plus. De même que l'art se bat pour rompre avec le cube blanc moderniste de la galerie, ne pourrait-il trouver sa vraie place dans l'architecture qui s'est, elle aussi, libérée de la standardisation ? Frank O. Gehry sera peut-être considéré dans le futur comme le pionnier d'un mouvement historique de l'évolution de l'architecture vers l'art et l'inverse. Malgré ses préférences personnelles pour les croquis nerveux, Gehry est également le pionnier de la construction assistée par ordinateur, ayant utilisé le logiciel Dassault CATIA pour le Musée Guggenheim de Bilbao et d'autres réalisations ultérieures. Sur le chemin ouvert par cette approche sculpturale très personnelle, d'autres découvrent que, fondamentalement, il n'est plus nécessaire que deux constructions se ressemblent. L'approche d'Herzog & de Meuron pour le nouveau bâtiment de la Tate Modern qu'ils décrivent comme « une forme fragmentée en devenir » permet les changements de cap des conservateurs devenus typiques dans le travail des musées. Cette forme sans forme annonce-t-elle une nouvelle génération d'architecture sans style ? La galerie Leme de Paulo Mendes da Rocha à São Paulo pourrait aussi être décrite de la même façon puisqu'elle aussi recherche une symbiose avec l'art contemporain. Les promesses de la conception et de la construction assistées par ordinateur signifient que ce ne sont pas seulement des musées d'avant-garde qui peuvent bénéficier d'une conception spécifique intelligente, mais aussi des musées qui vont recevoir des millions de visiteurs chaque année. Le style en architecture n'a plus à être déterminé par des contraintes de méthodes de construction en séries, mais devient plutôt quelque chose de plus personnel défini par des architectes qui ont su conquérir une nouvelle liberté.

*Philip Jodidio, Grimentz 2007*

[1] La commande numérique par ordinateur (CNO) se réfère à un ordinateur « contrôleur » qui pilote des machines-outils (MOCN), ou des mécanismes utilisés par exemple pour fabriquer des pièces métalliques par suppression sélective de métal. Utilisé en architecture, ce système permet la fabrication d'éléments individualisés à un coût similaire à celui d'une fabrication standardisée traditionnelle.

# MARCOS ACAYABA

*Marcos Acayaba Arquitetos Ltda*
*Rua das Magnólias 70*
*05674–000, São Paulo, SP*
*Brazil*

*Tel/Fax: +55 11 3815 5465*
*E-mail: macayaba@uol.com.br*
*Web: www.marcosacayaba.arq.br*

**MARCOS ACAYABA** was born in São Paulo, Brazil, in 1944. From 1964 to 1969, he studied at the Architecture and Urban Planning School of the University of São Paulo (FAUUSP), from which he obtained his doctorate in 2005. He has served as a Project Professor at the FAUUSP from 1972 to 1976, and since 1994. He won the Grand Prize at the São Paulo International Architecture Biennale (1997, ex-aequo). His most significant works include the Cidade Jardim House (São Paulo, SP, 1972–75); Alphaville House (Barueri, SP, 1981–82); Pindorama Pavilion (Cabreúva, SP, 1984–85); Morumbi Residence (São Paulo, SP, 1986–87); Jardim Vitória Régia House (São Paulo, SP, 1987–90); Iporanga House (Guarujá, SP, 1990–91); Acayaba House (Guarujá, SP, 1996–97, renovated in 2005, published here); Vila Butantã Housing (São Paulo, SP, 1998–2004); and most recently, the FDE State School, Jardim Bela Vista II (Mogi das Cruzes, SP, 2004–05), all in Brazil. Explaining his philosophy, Marcos Acayaba writes, "I try not to use any material that is not absolutely indispensable for construction. All the material should be employed in the fullness of its characteristics. I also try to consider the use of the building, the work that time will do and how it will be maintained. From the initial conception of the project on, I try to prevent or minimize maintenance problems."

**MARCOS ACAYABA** wurde 1944 in São Paulo geboren. Von 1964 bis 1969 studierte er am Fachbereich Architektur und Stadtplanung der Universität von São Paulo (FAUUSP), an der er 2005 promoviert wurde. Er lehrte von 1972 bis 1976 und dann wieder seit 1994 an der FAUUSP. Bei der Internationalen Architekturbiennale von São Paulo wurde er 1997 mit dem Großen Preis ausgezeichnet. Zu seinen wichtigsten Bauten zählen: das Haus Cidade Jardim (São Paulo, 1972–75), Haus Alphaville (Barueri, 1981–82), Pindorama Pavillon (Cabreúva, 1984–85), Residenz Morumbi (São Paulo, 1986–87), Haus Jardim Vitória Régia (São Paulo, 1987–90), Haus Iporanga (Guarujá, 1990–91), Haus Acayaba (Guarujá, 1996–97, 2005 renoviert, hier publiziert), die Bebauung Vila Butantã (São Paulo, 1998–2004) und als neuester Bau die Staatliche Schule der FDE, Jardim Bela Vista II (Mogi das Cruzes, 2004–05), sämtliche in Brasilien. Zur Erläuterung seiner Philosophie schreibt Acayaba: »Ich versuche, nur Materialien zu verwenden, die für den Bau absolut unverzichtbar sind. Die Materialien sollen so verwendet werden, dass all ihre typischen Merkmale zur Wirkung kommen. Ich versuche darüber hinaus, die Nutzung des Gebäudes, seine Instandhaltung und Alterung zu berücksichtigen. Schon vom ersten Entwurf eines Projekts an versuche ich, Probleme der Instandhaltung zu verhindern oder zumindest zu minimieren.«

**MARCOS ACAYABA**, né à Sao Paulo au Brésil en 1944, étudie à l'École d'architecture et d'urbanisme de l'Université de Sao Paulo (FAUUSP) de 1964 à 1969 où il passe son doctorat en 2005. Il est professeur de projet à la FAUUSP de 1972 à 1976, puis de nouveau depuis 1994. Il remporte, *ex aequo*, le Grand Prix de la Biennale internationale d'architecture de Sao Paulo en 1997. Toutes situées au Brésil, ses réalisations les plus notables comprennent la Maison Cidade Jardim à Sao Paulo (1972–75) ; la Maison Alphaville, Barueri (1981–82) ; le Pavillon Pindorama, Cabreúva (1984–85) ; la résidence Morumbi, Sao Paulo (1986–87) ; la Maison Jardim Vitória Régia, Sao Paulo (1987–90) ; la Maison Iporanga, Guaruja (1990–91) ; la Maison Acayaba, Gauruja (1996–97), rénovée en 2005 et publiée ici ; l'immeuble de logements Vila Butanta à Sao Paulo (1998–2004) et, plus récemment, l'École nationale FDE, Jardim Bela Vista II, Mogi das Cruzes (2004–05). Sur sa philosophie, il précise : « J'essaie de ne pas utiliser de matériau qui ne soit pas absolument indispensable dans la construction. Chaque matériau doit être utilisé dans la plénitude de ses caractéristiques. J'essaie aussi de prendre en compte l'utilisation du bâtiment, l'effet prévisible du temps et la façon dont il sera entretenu. Dès la conception initiale, je tente de prévoir ou de minimiser les problèmes de maintenance. »

# ACAYABA HOUSE

*Tijucopava, Guarujá, SP, Brazil, 1996–97, renovated in 2005*

*Site area: 1993 m². Floor area: 252 m². Client: Marcos Acayaba.*
*Cost: $150 000*

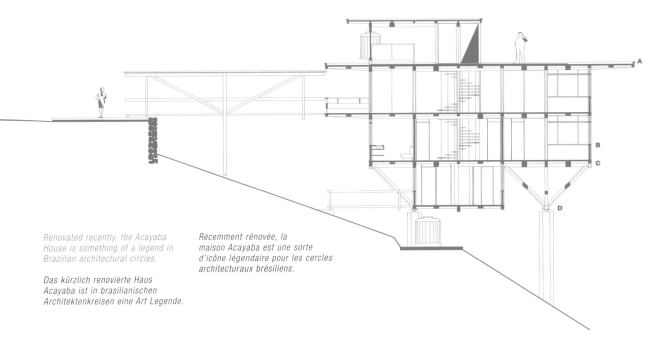

*Renovated recently, the Acayaba
House is something of a legend in
Brazilian architectural circles.*

*Récemment rénovée, la
maison Acayaba est une sorte
d'icône légendaire pour les cercles
architecturaux brésiliens.*

*Das kürzlich renovierte Haus
Acayaba ist in brasilianischen
Architektenkreisen eine Art Legende.*

Considered something of a classic in recent Brazilian architecture, the house of Marcos Acayaba was renovated in 2005, when he redesigned the access bridge with a new truss system more specifically thought out for the frequent tropical rains on the site. Built on a wooded hillside 150 meters from the ocean, the house sits about 70 meters above the beach. In an effort to preserve the native Mata Atlântica forest, only three pillars were used to support the house and they were erected between the main existing trees. As Acayaba explains, "The triangular structure that expands up like a tree was assembled with industrialized elements: wooden pillars and beams, steel cables and connections." Lightweight triangular precast concrete panels were used for the roof and floors, while the walls and parapets were made with industrially produced plywood panels. The architect's focus on small, light construction elements allowed just four workers to build the house in four months. One spectacular feature of the house is its roof terrace that functions like "an open-air living room, looking down on the tops of the trees and the ocean beyond." A 2-meter cantilevered edge on the terrace was designed to protect the space from tropical rains. The main level, including the kitchen and living room, is accessed through a covered bridge, while the service area, connected to the ground by its own bridge, is hung between three sets of diagonal trusses below the living area.

Das in der jüngeren Architektur Brasiliens als eine Art Klassiker geltende Haus von Marcos Acayaba wurde 2005 renoviert, als er die Zugangsbrücke mittels einer neu konzipierten Fachwerkkonstruktion umgestaltete, die den hier häufig niedergehenden tropischen Regenfällen besser gewachsen ist. Das 150 m vom Meer entfernt auf einem bewaldeten Hügel erbaute Haus steht etwa 70 m hoch über dem Strand. Um den hier heimischen Mata-Atlântica-Regenwald zu schützen, wurde das Haus mit nur drei Stützpfeilern erbaut, die zwischen die vorhandenen Bäume gestellt wurden. Acayaba erläutert: »Der dreieckige Bau, der sich wie ein Baum nach oben entfaltet, wurde aus industriell gefertigten Teilen montiert: Holzpfosten, Stahlseile und Verbindungen.« Für Dach und Böden wurden dreieckige, vorgefertigte Leichtbetonplatten verwendet, während Wände und Brüstungen aus industriell produzierten Sperrholztafeln gefertigt wurden. Da der Architekt kleine, leichtgewichtige Bauteile bevorzugte, konnten nur vier Arbeiter das Haus in vier Monaten errichten. Ein Element des Hauses ist seine Dachterrasse, die »als Freiluftwohnzimmer dient, von dem aus man auf die Wipfel der Bäume und das dahinter liegende Meer schauen kann«. Das 2 m vorkragende Dach soll das Haus vor dem Tropenregen schützen. Man erreicht die Hauptebene mit Küche und Wohnraum über eine überdachte Brücke, während die Funktionsebene, die mittels einer eigenen Brücke mit dem Boden verbunden ist, unterhalb des Wohnbereichs zwischen drei Bündeln diagonaler Fachwerkstreben hängt.

Considérée comme une quasi icône de l'architecture brésilienne récente, la maison de Marcos Acayaba a été rénovée en 2005. À cette occasion, elle a été dotée d'une nouvelle passerelle d'accès en poutres de bois, plus spécifiquement adaptée aux fréquentes pluies tropicales. Édifiée sur un flanc de colline boisée à 150 m de l'océan, la maison surplombe la plage de 70 m. Pour préserver la forêt naturelle de la Mata Atlântica, seuls trois piliers dressés entre des arbres existants soutiennent l'ensemble. Comme l'explique l'architecte : « La structure triangulaire qui se développe vers le haut à la manière d'un arbre a été assemblée à partir d'éléments industriels : piliers et poutres de bois, câbles et connexions en acier. » Des panneaux triangulaires préfabriqués en béton léger constituent les sols et la couverture, les murs et panneaux de remplissage étant en panneaux de contreplaqué industriel. Le choix d'éléments constructifs légers et de faibles dimensions a permis le montage de la maison par quatre ouvriers en quatre mois. Un de ses éléments les plus spectaculaires est le toit-terrasse qui sert de « séjour à l'air libre, dominant la cime des arbres et l'océan ». Un auvent en porte-à-faux de 2 m de profondeur le protège des pluies tropicales. Le niveau principal, qui comprend la cuisine et le séjour, est accessible par une passerelle couverte tandis que la zone de services est reliée au sol par sa propre passerelle suspendue sous le séjour entre trois jeux de poutres en diagonale.

*Set on a steep hillside, the Acayaba House makes use of the topographic situation of the site to project into the forest, and sits above it.*

*Das an einem Steilhang stehende Haus Acayaba nutzt die topografische Situation, um in den Wald hinein vorzukragen und sich gleichzeitig über ihn zu erheben.*

*Implantée au flanc d'une colline escarpée, la maison met à profit la topographie pour se projeter dans et au-dessus de la forêt.*

At nightfall, the house glows from within—like an occupied tree house in the Brazilian jungle.

*Bei Nacht leuchtet das Haus von innen gleich einem bewohnten Baumhaus im brasilianischen Dschungel.*

*À la tombée de la nuit, la résidence irradie de l'intérieur comme une maison dans les arbres, perdue dans la jungle brésilienne.*

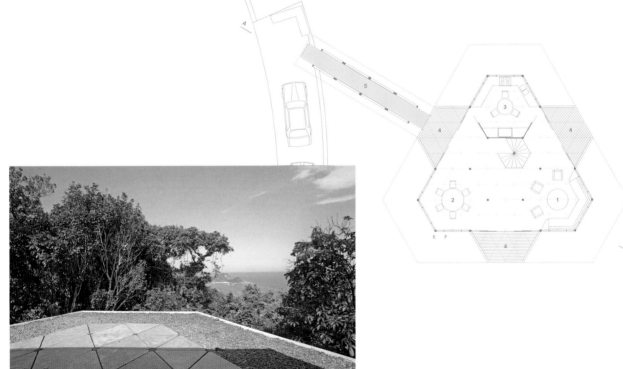

With its plan consisting of two super-
imposed truncated triangles, the
house is reached by a bridge, which
was the object of recent renovations.

*Das Haus, dessen Grundriss aus zwei
abgestumpften Dreiecken besteht,
erreicht man über eine Brücke, die
kürzlich umgestaltet worden ist.*

*Le plan se compose de deux triangles
tronqués superposés. La maison est
accessible par une passerelle qui a
récemment été rénovée.*

# EMILIO AMBASZ

*Emilio Ambasz & Associates, Inc.*
*8 East 62nd Street / New York, NY 10021 / USA*

*Tel: +1 212 751 3517*
*Fax: +1 212 751 0294*
*E-mail: info@ambasz.com*
*Web: www.ambasz.com*

**EMILIO AMBASZ** was born in 1943 in Argentina, and studied at Princeton University where he received an M.Arch degree. He taught at Princeton University's School of Architecture, was a Visiting Professor at the Hochschule für Gestaltung in Ulm, Germany, and has lectured at several American universities. He served as Curator of Design at the Museum of Modern Art in New York (1970–76), where he directed and installed numerous exhibitions on architecture and industrial design. Ambasz was a two-term President of the Architectural League (1981–85). His projects include the Nichii Obihiro Department Store (Hokkaido, Japan, 1987, unbuilt); Lucille Halsell Conservatory at the San Antonio Botanical Center (San Antonio, Texas, 1988); Mycal Sanda Cultural and Athletic Center (Hyogo Prefecture, Japan, 1990–94); Fukuoka Prefectural International Hall (Fukuoka, Japan, 1995, winner of the 2001 DuPont Benedictus Award); and House of Spiritual Retreat (Seville, Spain, 1975/2003–05, published here). Founded in 1976, Emilio Ambasz & Associates, Inc. offers a full range of design services. Ambasz states: "It is my deep belief that design is an act of invention. I believe that its real task begins once functional and behavioral needs have been satisfied. It is not hunger, but love and fear, and sometimes wonder, which make us create. Our milieu may change from generation to generation, but the task, I believe, remains the same: give poetic form to the pragmatic." More recently, he has been engaged on the construction of a 600-bed hospital and an Advanced Ophthalmologic Research Laboratory (Venice-Mestre) as well as residential and hotel projects in Puglia, Rimini-Bellaria and Frossinone, all in Italy.

**EMILIO AMBASZ** wurde 1943 in Argentinien geboren und studierte in Princeton, wo er den Grad eines M.Arch erhielt. Er lehrte an der Architekturfakultät in Princeton, war Gastprofessor an der Hochschule für Gestaltung in Ulm und hielt an verschiedenen amerikanischen Universitäten Vorträge. Von 1970 bis 1976 war er als Kurator für den Bereich Design am Museum of Modern Art in New York tätig. Zwischen 1981 und 1985 war er zwei Amtszeiten lang Präsident der Architectural League. Zu seinen Arbeiten zählen: das Kaufhaus Nichii Obihiro (Hokkaido, Japan, 1987, unrealisiert), das Lucille Halsell Conservatory am San Antonio Botanical Center (San Antonio, Texas, 1988), das Mycal Sanda Cultural and Athletic Center (Präfektur Hyogo, Japan, 1990–94), Fukuoka Prefectural International Hall (Fukuoka, Japan, 1995, Gewinner des DuPont Benedictus Award 2001) sowie die hier vorgestellte Casa de retiro espiritual (Sevilla, 1975/2003–05). Das 1976 gegründete Büro Emilio Ambasz & Associates, Inc. bietet die komplette Bandbreite von Entwurfsarbeiten. Ambasz erklärt: »Ich bin zutiefst davon überzeugt, dass es bei Design um einen genuinen Akt der Erfindung geht. Ich glaube, dass die eigentliche Aufgabe anfängt, sobald die Anforderungen an Funktion und Handhabung erfüllt sind. Wir werden nicht aus Hunger, sondern aus Liebe und Furcht und bisweilen vor Staunen kreativ. Unser Milieu mag sich von Generation zu Generation verändern, aber die Aufgabe bleibt nach meiner Überzeugung dieselbe: dem Pragmatischen zu poetischer Form zu verhelfen.« Unlängst war er mit dem Bau eines Krankenhauses mit 600 Betten und eines hochmodernen ophthalmologischen Forschungslabors in Venedig-Mestre sowie Wohn- und Hotelprojekten in Puglia, Rimini-Bellaria und Frossinone, alle in Italien, beschäftigt.

Né en 1943 en Argentine, **EMILIO AMBASZ** a étudié, puis enseigné à Princeton. Il a aussi été Professeur invité à la Hochschule für Gestaltung à Ulm en Allemagne et dans plusieurs universités américaines. Conservateur pour le design au Museum of Modern Art de New York (1970–76), il y a fait entrer de nombreuses pièces d'architecture et de design industriel. Il a été président de l'Architectural League pendant deux mandats (1981–85). Parmi ses projets : le grand magasin Nichii Obihiro à Hokkaido au Japon (1987, non construit) ; le Lucille Halsell Conservatory au San Antonio Botanical Center à San Antonio, Texas (1988) ; le Mycal Cultural and Athletic Center à Shin-Sanda, préfecture de Hyogo, Japon (1990–94) ; le Hall international de la préfecture de Fukuoka, Fukuoka, Japon (1995) qui a remporté le DuPont Benedictus Award 2001, et sa « maison de retraite spirituelle » à Séville, Espagne (1975–2003/05), publiée ici. Fondée en 1976, l'agence Emilio Ambasz & Associates, Inc. offre une gamme complète de services. Ambasz a déclaré : « Je crois profondément que le design est un acte d'invention. Je pense que son objet réel débute une fois que les besoins fonctionnels et comportementaux ont été satisfaits. Ce n'est pas la faim, mais l'amour et la peur, et parfois l'émerveillement, qui nous rendent créatifs. Le milieu dans lequel nous vivions peut changer de génération en génération mais la tâche, je crois, reste la même : donner une forme poétique au pragmatique. » Plus récemment, il a commencé à travailler à plusieurs projets en Italie : un hôpital de 600 lits et un laboratoire de recherche ophtalmologique à Venise-Mestre ainsi que des complexes résidentiels et d'hôtellerie dans les Pouilles, à Rimini-Bellaria et Frossinone.

# HOUSE OF SPIRITUAL RETREAT

*Seville, Spain, 1975/2003–05*

*Floor area: 280 m². Client: RODA S. L. Cost: not disclosed.*
*Architect of Record (Associate Architect): Felipe Palomino Gonzalez*

Originally designed in 1975, this house received a number of awards (Progressive Architecture Project First Prize Award, 1975) long before it was actually built, in 2005. This work even became something of a myth, in part because of the ambitious theoretical background of its conception. Emilio Ambasz stated, "The only thing to stand was the façade, which would be like a mask—a surrogate for architecture. You might say that by this device I rhetorically sought to re-examine architecture as a culturally conditioned process and return to the primeval notion of the abode. It is an architecture that is both here and not here. With it I hope to place the user in a new state of existence, a celebration of human majesty, thought, and sensation. Though apparently quite new, there are devices—both primitive and ancient—permeating this design." Set above a man-made lake in a 600-hectare estate located about 40 kilometers north of Seville, the house was the object of an exhibition at the Museum of Modern Art in New York ("In-Depth: The House of Spiritual Retreat by Emilio Ambasz," November 23, 2005–March 6, 2006). The house appears to be constituted almost of nothing other than two tall, rough stucco walls that meet at a right angle, sheltering the residence from northern winds. In a fashion typical of the interest of Ambasz in integrating nature into his work, the living area is insulated by earth placed on the roof. In a reference to traditional Andalusian houses, the house opens onto a patio. As the architect explains, "The house consists, simply, of a large continuous space, contained by sinuous walls, with different areas defined by smooth cavities excavated into the floor and echoed by the ceiling above."

Das 1975 entworfene Haus wurde lange vor seiner Fertigstellung im Jahr 2005 mit einer Reihe von Preisen (Progressive Architecture Project First Prize Award, 1975) ausgezeichnet. Wegen des anspruchsvollen theoretischen Hintergrunds der Konzeption wurde das Haus sogar zu einer Art Mythos. Emilio Ambasz führt aus: »Das einzige stehende Element war die Fassade, die wie eine Maske wirkt, wie ein Architekturersatz. Man könnte sagen, dass ich mit diesem Einfall versuchte, Architektur als kulturell konditionierten Prozess und Rückkehr zur urzeitlichen Vorstellung der Behausung neu zu überdenken. Diese Architektur ist gleichzeitig existent und nicht-existent. Ich hoffe, den Bewohner damit in einen neuen Daseinszustand zu versetzen, zur Feier der Erhabenheit des Menschen, seines Denkens und Fühlens. Obwohl der Entwurf offenkundig recht neu ist, durchdringen ihn urzeitliche wie altertümliche Elemente.« Das auf einem 600 ha großen Grundstück, 40 km nördlich von Sevilla, oberhalb eines künstlichen Sees liegende Haus war Gegenstand einer Ausstellung im Museum of Modern Art in New York »In-Depth: The House of Spiritual Retreat by Emilio Ambasz«, 23.11.2005–6.3.2006). Das Haus scheint tatsächlich aus wenig mehr als zwei hoch aufragenden, verputzten Mauern zu bestehen, die im rechten Winkel aufeinandertreffen und so das Wohnhaus vor dem Nordwind schützen. Stets bestrebt, die Natur in sein Werk einzubeziehen, bedeckt Ambasz hier in typischer Manier den Wohnbereich zur Wärmedämmung mit Erde. In Anspielung auf traditionelle andalusische Häuser öffnet sich das Haus zu einem Patio. Der Architekt führt aus: »Das Haus besteht einfach aus einem großen, durchgehenden Raum, der von sich windenden Wänden umfasst ist, mit verschiedenen Bereichen, die durch in den Boden gegrabene Höhlungen bestimmt sind und vom Himmel wiederholt werden.«

Conçue dès 1975, cette maison a reçu un certain nombre de distinctions (prix du premier projet de Progressive Architecture, 1975) longtemps avant d'être construite en 2005. Elle fut même un temps une sorte de mythe, en partie pour son ambitieuse base théorique. «La seule chose dressée serait la façade, qui serait comme un masque – un subrogé d'architecture. Vous pourriez dire que par ce procédé je cherchais à réexaminer sur le plan rhétorique l'architecture en tant que processus conditionné par la culture, et à revenir à la notion primitive d'abri. C'est une architecture qui est à la fois ici et pas ici. J'espère, à travers elle, placer l'utilisateur dans un nouvel état d'existence, une célébration de la majesté de la pensée et de la sensibilité humaines. Bien qu'apparemment assez nouveaux, des procédés à la fois primitifs et anciens imprègnent cette construction.» Érigée au-dessus d'un lac artificiel dans un domaine de 600 hectares à 40 km environ au nord de Séville, cette maison a été l'objet d'une exposition au Museum of Modern Art à New York («In-Depth: The House of Spiritual Spiritual Retreat by Emilio Ambasz», 23 novembre 2005–6 mars 2006). Elle ne semble constituée que de deux hauts murs de stuc brut disposés à angle droit. Ils la protègent des vents du nord. Dans un geste caractéristique de l'intérêt que porte Ambasz à l'intégration de la nature dans son œuvre, le séjour est isolé par une couverture de terre. Dans une référence à l'architecture traditionnelle des maisons andalouses, celle-ci s'ouvre aussi sur un patio. Comme l'explique l'architecte: «La maison se compose d'un vaste espace continu pris entre deux murs sinueux, différentes zones étant définies par des cavités aux formes douces creusées dans le sol qui se retrouvent en écho dans les plafonds.»

The house of Emilio Ambasz is more of a singularity than it is in any sense related to existing building types. Its external appearance is like that of a belvedere with a balcony or window set at the angle of the white walls.

Emilio Ambasz' Haus ist eher singulär als in irgendeiner Weise mit einem vorhandenen Bautypus verwandt. Von außen wirkt es wie ein Belvedere mit einem Balkon oder Fenster, das auf den Winkel der weißen Wände gesetzt ist.

La maison d'Emilio Ambasz est une singularité, sans aucun lien avec d'autres types de construction existants. Son aspect extérieur fait penser à un belvédère doté d'un balcon ou d'une fenêtre au point de jonction de ses murs blancs.

Despite its curious appearance, the visible plan of the house, seen in the computer view below, is made up of a square and a V-shaped protective wall. The interest of Ambasz in landscape design is made clear by the immediate environment of the residence.

Ungeachtet seines ungewöhnlichen Erscheinungsbilds besteht der unten in einer Computeransicht zu sehende Grundriss des Hauses aus einem Quadrat und einer V-förmigen Schutzwand. Ambasz' Interesse an Landschaftsgestaltung wird durch die unmittelbare Umgebung des Wohnhauses deutlich.

Malgré cette curieuse apparence, le plan de la maison, visible dans l'image de synthèse ci-dessous, est fait d'un carré et d'un mur protecteur en forme de « V ». L'intérêt de Ambasz pour le design paysager est confirmé par l'environnement de la maison.

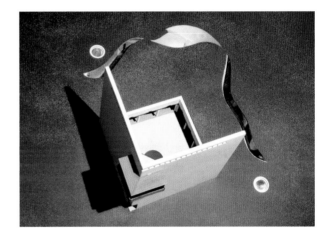

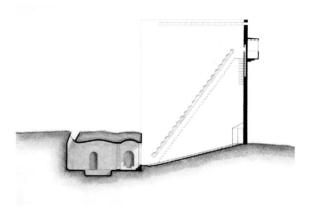

With its curious external steps
leading up the sheer face of one
wall, the house is full of surprises,
including areas below grade that
are not immediately visible when
approaching the house.

Das Haus ist voller Überraschungen
wie die merkwürdigen Außentreppen,
die an den glatten Wandflächen
hochführen, sowie die den Blicken
weitgehend entzogenen, unterirdischen Bereiche.

Avec ce curieux escalier extérieur
qui monte en haut de l'un des murs,
la maison réserve de nombreuses
surprises, dont ses parties en sous-
sol imperceptibles de l'extérieur.

The colonnaded underground space
is shown in the photograph above,
and in the section drawing below.

Der unterirdische Raum mit dem um
eine Ecke verlaufenden Säulengang
ist auf der Abbildung oben sowie auf
der Schnittzeichnung unten zu sehen.

Vu de l'intérieur, l'espace souterrain
à colonnade, ci-dessus, et en coupe
dans le dessin ci-dessous.

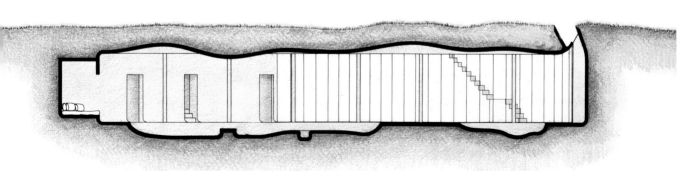

# TADAO ANDO

*Tadao Ando Architect & Associates*
*Osaka 531*
*Japan*

Born in Osaka in 1941, **TADAO ANDO** was self-educated as an architect, largely through his travels in the United States, Europe and Africa (1962–69). He founded Tadao Ando Architect & Associates in Osaka in 1969. He has received the Alvar Aalto Medal, Finnish Association of Architects (1985); Medaille d'Or, French Academy of Architecture (1989); 1992 Carlsberg Prize, and the 1995 Pritzker Prize. He has taught at Yale (1987), Columbia (1988) and Harvard (1990). Notable buildings include: Rokko Housing (Kobe, Japan, 1983–93); Church on the Water (Hokkaido, Japan, 1988); Japan Pavilion Expo '92 (Seville, Spain, 1992); Forest of Tombs Museum (Kumamoto, Japan, 1992); and Suntory Museum (Osaka, Japan, 1994). Recent work includes the Awaji Yumebutai (Awajishima, Hyogo, Japan, 1997–2000); the Pulitzer Foundation for the Arts (Saint Louis, Missouri, 1997–2000); the Modern Art Museum of Fort Worth (Texas, 1999–2002); and the restaurant morimoto nyc (New York, 2005–06, published here). He completed the Chichu Art Museum on the Island of Naoshima in the Inland Sea in 2003, part of the continuing project that led him to create the Benesse House Museum and Hotel there beginning in the early 1990s. He won the competition to design the Pinault Foundation on the Île Seguin in Paris, but the project was canceled in 2005 and he subsequently remodeled Palazzo Grassi in Venice, Italy, for the French arts patron.

Der 1941 in Osaka geborene **TADAO ANDO** ist als Architekt Autodidakt und bildete sich hauptsächlich durch seine Reisen in den Vereinigten Staaten, Europa und Afrika (1962–69). 1969 gründete er Tadao Ando Architect & Associates in Osaka. 1985 erhielt er von der Finnish Association of Architects die Alvar-Aalto-Medaille, 1989 von der französischen Academie d'Architecture die Medaille d'Or, 1992 den Carlsberg-Preis und 1995 den Pritzker-Preis. Er lehrte an den Universitäten Yale (1987), Columbia (1988) und Harvard (1990). Zu seinen beachtenswerten Bauten zählen: Rokko-Wohnanlagen (Kobe, 1983–93), die Kirche auf dem Wasser (Hokkaido, 1988), der Japanische Pavillon auf der Expo '92 (Sevilla, 1992), das Gräberwald-Museum (Kumamoto, 1992) und das Suntory Museum (Osaka, 1994). Neueren Datums sind das Awaji Yumebutai (Awajishima, Hyogo, 1997–2000), die Pulitzer Foundation for the Arts (Saint Louis, Misouri, 1997–2000), das Modern Art Museum in Fort Worth (Texas, 1999–2002) sowie das Restaurant morimoto nyc (New York, 2005–06, hier publiziert). 2003 stellte er das Kunstmuseum Chichu auf der Insel Naoshima im Binnenmeer fertig, Teil eines weitergehenden Projekts, zu dem er Anfang der 1990er-Jahre das Benesse-Haus (Museum und Hotel) geschaffen hatte. Er konnte den Wettbewerb für den Entwurf der Fondation Pinault auf der Île Seguin in Paris für sich entscheiden, aber das Projekt wurde 2005 eingestellt. In der Folgezeit baute er für den französischen Kunstmäzen Pinault den Palazzo Grassi in Venedig um.

Né à Osaka en 1941, **TADAO ANDO** est un architecte autodidacte formé en grande partie lors de voyages aux États-Unis, en Europe et en Afrique (1962–69). Il fonde Tadao Ando Architect & Associates à Osaka en 1969. Parmi ses prix et distinctions : l'Alvar Aalto Medal de l'Association finlandaise des architectes (1985), la médaille d'or de l'Académie d'architecture (Paris, 1989), le Carlsberg Prize (1992) et le Pritzker Prize (1995). Il a enseigné à Yale (1987), Columbia (1988) et Harvard (1990). Il a notamment réalisé les immeubles d'appartements Rokko, Kobé, Japon (1983–93) ; l'église sur l'eau, Hokkaido, Japon (1988) ; le pavillon japonais d'Expo '92, Séville, Espagne (1992) ; le Musée de la forêt des tombes, Kumamoto, Japon (1992) et le Musée Suntory, Osaka, Japon (1994). Plus récemment, il a conçu le Awaji Yumebutai, Awajishima, Hyogo, Japon (1997–2000) ; la Pulitzer Foundation for the Arts, Saint Louis, Missouri (1997–2000) ; le Modern Art Museum de Fort Worth, Texas (1999–2002) ; et le restaurant morimoto nyc, New York (2005–06), publié ici. Il a achevé le Musée d'art Chichu sur l'île de Naoshima dans la Mer intérieure du Japon en 2003, dans le cadre d'un projet à long terme pour lequel il avait déjà conçu le musée et hôtel de la maison Benesse au début des années 1990. Il a remporté le concours pour la Fondation Pinault sur l'île Seguin à Paris, et à la suite de l'abandon de ce projet en 2005, a remodelé le Palazzo Grassi à Venise pour le mécène français.

# MORIMOTO NYC

*New York, New York, USA, 2005–06*

*Floor area: 1230 m². Client: Starr Restaurant Organization (Stephen Starr).*
*Cost: not disclosed. Architects: Tadao Ando Architect & Associates (Tadao Ando, Masataka Yano).*
*New York Project Architect: Stephanie Goto Design Group (Stephanie Goto).*
*Architect of Record and Construction Supervision: Guggenheimer Architects (Amy Beckman, Margaret Kim).*
*Project Manager: Gardiner & Theobald, Inc. (Andrew Demming, Christopher Burke).*
*Structural Engineer: Leslie Robertson Associates Consulting Structural Engineers.*
*Furniture Design: Lovegrove (Ross Lovegrove)*

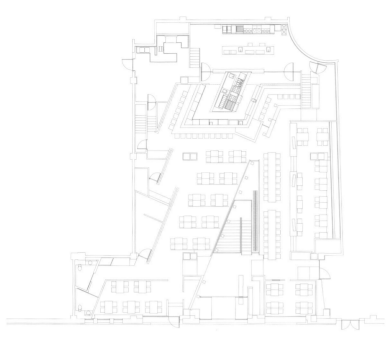

A traditional noren curtain marks the entrance while interior views show the unusual fiberglass-reinforced canvas ceiling, or the wall made of water bottles designed by Ross Lovegrove (left).

Ein traditioneller Noren-Vorhang markiert den Eingang; auf den Innenansichten sind die Decken aus mit Fiberglas verstärkten Segeltuchbahnen und die von Ross Lovegrove gestaltete Wand aus Wasserflaschen (links) zu sehen.

Un rideau Noren traditionnel signale l'entrée. Les vues intérieures montrent le curieux plafond de toile renforcée de fibre de verre ou le mur de bouteilles d'eau, créé par Ross Lovegrove (à gauche).

Located at 88 10th Avenue in New York's newly fashionable Meat Packing District, this restaurant was created by Tadao Ando in a former loading dock of the Chelsea Market, within a century-old masonry building located near the former High Line elevated rail tracks, themselves due for a spectacular renovation by the architects Diller Scofidio + Renfro. A constant, subtle Japanese theme is maintained throughout the project, beginning with the black galvanized steel-panel exterior marked by a traditional orange *noren* curtain used to indicate the presence of a Japanese restaurant. The main restaurant, seating 164, is located on the ground floor, while a 26-seat bar is downstairs. The undeniably theatrical main kitchen, where Masaharu Morimoto, its famous Japanese Iron Chef, and his assistants preside, is fully visible at the rear of the ground-floor space. Powerful columns immediately bring Ando's signature concrete to the fore, while an unusual wall of filled plastic water bottles designed by Ross Lovegrove and backlit with LEDs runs near the stairway. Ceilings and walls are marked with undulating canvas shaped with fiberglass reinforcement. Interior floors are clad in oak panel or concrete. The whole shows that talented architects and designers like Ando and Lovegrove can successfully collaborate on a quintessentially ephemeral environment—that of the fashionable New York restaurant.

Dieses Restaurant an der 10th Avenue 88 im aufstrebenden Meat Packing District New Yorks wurde von Tadao Ando auf einer früheren Ladeplattform des Chelsea Market geschaffen, und zwar innerhalb eines 100-jährigen Gebäudes in der Nähe der ehemaligen Hochbahngleise, die selbst für eine spektakuläre bauliche Neugestaltung durch das Architekturbüro Diller Scofidio + Renfro vorgesehen sind. Das gesamte Projekt hat eine subtile japanische Anmutung, angefangen bei dem mit schwarzen, verzinkten Stahlplatten verkleideten Äußeren, das ein traditioneller, orangefarbener Türvorhang (Noren) als japanisches Restaurant kennzeichnet. Der Hauptraum mit 164 Plätzen befindet sich im Erdgeschoss, darunter gibt es eine Bar mit Platz für 26 Gäste. Die fraglos theatralische Hauptküche, Reich des berühmten japanischen »Iron Chef« Masaharu Morimoto und seiner Assistenten, ist am hinteren Ende des Restaurantraums in voller Breite einzusehen. In Form einer Reihe mächtiger Pfeiler ist Andos bevorzugtes Material Beton sofort sichtbar, während seitlich der Treppe eine von Ross Lovegrove gestaltete, ungewöhnliche Wand aus gefüllten Plastikflaschen verläuft, die von hinten mit Lichtdioden illuminiert wird. Decken und Wände sind mit gebauschten, durch Fiberglas verstärkten Segeltuchbahnen verkleidet, die Böden im Inneren mit Eichenparkett oder Beton belegt. Das Ganze zeigt, dass begabte Architekten und Designer wie Ando und Lovegrove gemeinsam die im Grunde kurzlebige Umgebung eines angesagten New Yorker Restaurants erfolgreich gestalten können.

Situé au 88 de la 10th Avenue dans le quartier depuis peu à la mode du Meat Packing District à New York, ce restaurant a été créé par Ando sur un ancien quai de chargement du Chelsea Market dans un bâtiment centenaire en maçonnerie non loin des anciennes voies ferrées surélevées de la High Line, elles-mêmes vouées à une rénovation spectaculaire par les architectes Diller Scofidio + Renfro. Une subtile et omniprésente thématique japonaise imprègne ce projet, à commencer par l'habillage en panneaux d'acier galvanisé noir interrompu par un rideau Noren traditionnel orange qui signale la présence d'un restaurant japonais. La salle principale de 194 couverts est implantée au rez-de-chaussée, tandis que le bar de 26 places occupe le sous-sol. À l'arrière de la salle du rez-de-chaussée, la cuisine principale, de caractère très théâtral, où préside le fameux chef japonais Masaharu Morimoto entouré de ses assistants, est entièrement visible. Des colonnes très présentes rappellent le béton qui est la signature d'Ando, tandis qu'un curieux mur de bouteilles en plastique pleines d'eau conçu par Ross Lovegrove et rétro-éclairé par des LEDs longe l'escalier. Les plafonds et les murs sont doublés de toile souple renforcée de fibre de verre. Les sols sont en panneaux de chêne ou en béton. Cette réalisation montre que des architectes et des designers de talent comme Ando et Lovegrove peuvent collaborer avec succès sur cet environnement par nature éphémère qu'est un élégant restaurant new-yorkais.

A sketch by Tadao Ando (below) gives the impression of sweeping volumes inserted into this former loading dock. Above, a view taken from the entrance area showing the steps leading down to the bar and concrete columns designed by Ando that end before reaching the ceiling.

Eine Skizze von Tadao Ando (unten) vermittelt einen Eindruck von den in diese ehemalige Laderampe eingefügten ausgedehnten Räumlichkeiten. Oben ein Blick auf den Eingangsbereich mit der nach unten zur Bar führenden Treppe und den von Ando entworfenen Betonpfeilern, die nicht ganz bis zur Decke reichen.

Un croquis de Tadao Ando (ci-dessous) donne l'impression de volumes incurvés qui auraient été insérés dans cet ancien entrepôt. Au-dessus, vue prise de l'entrée montrant l'escalier qui descend vers le bar, et des colonnes de béton dessinées par Ando, qui ne touchent pas le plafond.

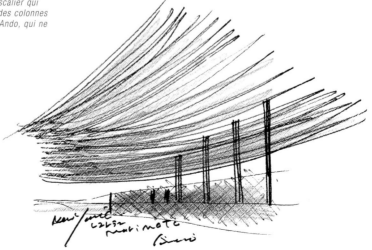

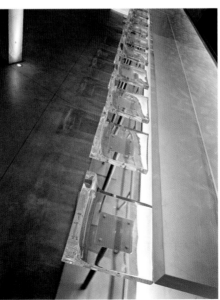

The lower-level bar seen here is made with a Plexiglas countertop designed by Ando.

*Für die Bar im Untergeschoss entwarf Ando eine Theke aus Plexiglas.*

*Le bar du niveau inférieur a été dessiné par Ando.*

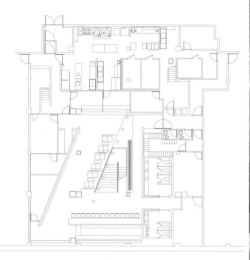

Screens and varied lighting effects give a certain ambiguity to the space, where design, architecture and haute-cuisine *come together.*

*Transluzente Raumteiler und variable Lichteffekte verleihen dem Raum eine gewisse Mehrdeutigkeit, in der Design, Architektur und Haute Cuisine sich treffen.*

*Des écrans et divers effets d'éclairage entretiennent une certaine ambiguïté dans cet espace où fusionnent design, architecture et « haute-cuisine ».*

# RON ARAD

*Ron Arad Associates*
*62 Chalk Farm Road*
*London NW1 8AN*
*UK*

*Tel: +44 20 7284 4963*
*Fax: +44 20 7379 0499*
*E-mail: info@ronarad.com*
*Web: www.ronarad.com*

**RON ARAD** was born in Tel Aviv, Israel, in 1951. An industrial designer, artist and architect, he attended the Jerusalem Academy of Art (1971–73) and the Architectural Association (AA) in London (1974–79), where he worked under Peter Cook and Bernard Tschumi. In 1981, he created One Off Ltd., design studio workshops and showroom in Covent Garden, London, with Caroline Thorman. In 1989, the pair founded Ron Arad Associates. He was a Professor of Design at the Hochschule für Angewandte Kunst in Vienna from 1994 to 1997. He has produced furniture and lighting design for several companies, including Alessi, Vitra, Flos, Artemide, and Kartell, notably the Tom Vac stackable chair, Well Tempered Chair for Vitra (1986), and the Book Worm for Kartell (1996). His architectural work includes: Tel Aviv Opera Foyer in Israel (with Alison Brooks, 1994); Belgo Noord and Belgo Centraal restaurants in London (1994 and 1995); Selfridges Technology Hall in London (2001); Headquarters for Maserati (Modena, Italy, 2003); Y's Store for Yohji Yamamoto (Tokyo, 2003); and Hotel Duomo (Rimini, Italy, 2003–06, published here). Gallery and exhibition designs include "Winning: The Design of Sports" for the Glasgow 1999 UK City of Architecture and Design. He is the Head of Design Products Department at the Royal College of Art in London. Current work includes Upperworld, a plan for a luxury hotel on the roof of Battersea Power Station in London; a new design museum for Holon, Israel; and the headquarters for the domestic products manufacturer Magis in Treviso, Italy.

**RON ARAD** wurde 1951 in Tel Aviv, Israel, geboren. Der Industriedesigner, Künstler und Architekt besuchte die Kunstakademie in Jerusalem (1971–73) und die Architectural Association in London (1974–79), wo er mit Peter Cook und Bernard Tschumi arbeitete. 1981 gründete er mit Caroline Thorman One Off Ltd., Design-Studio, Werkstätten und Ausstellungsraum. 1989 gründeten die beiden Ron Arad Associates. Von 1994 bis 1997 war er als Professor für Design an der Hochschule für Angewandte Kunst in Wien tätig. Er entwarf Möbel und Leuchten für mehrere Firmen, darunter Alessi, Vitra (Well Tempered Chair, 1986, Stapelstuhl Tom Vac), Flos, Artemide und Kartell (Book Worm, 1996). Zu seinen architektonischen Werken zählen das Opernfoyer von Tel Aviv (mit Alison Brooks, 1994), die Restaurants Belgo Noord und Belgo Centraal in London (1994 und 1995), Selfridges Technology Hall in London (2001), die Zentrale von Maserati (Modena, 2003), Y's Store für Yohji Yamamoto (Tokio, 2003) sowie das hier vorgestellte Hotel Duomo in Rimini (2003–06). Zu seinen Galerie- und Ausstellungsgestaltungen zählt »Winning: The Design of Sports« für Glasgow, City of Architecture and Design 1999. Er leitet die Abteilung für Produktdesign am Royal College of Art in London. An neueren Arbeiten sind Upperworld, Planung für ein Luxushotel auf dem Dach des Kraftwerks Battersea in London, zu nennen, außerdem ein neues Designmuseum für Holon, Israel, sowie die Zentrale von Magis, einem Hersteller von Haushaltswaren in Treviso, Italien.

**RON ARAD** naît à Tel-Aviv, Israël, en 1951. Designer, artiste et architecte, il étudie à l'Académie d'art de Jérusalem (1971–73) et à l'Architectural Association à Londres (1974–79), sous la direction de Peter Cook et Bernard Tschumi. En 1981, il crée One Off Ltd. atelier, showroom et agence de design à Covent Garden à Londres en association avec Caroline Thorman. En 1989, ils fondent ensemble Ron Arad Associates. Il exerce en qualité de professeur de design à la Hochschule für Angewandte Kunst à Vienne de 1994 à 1997 et crée des meubles et des luminaires pour plusieurs marques dont Alessi, Vitra, Flos, Artemide et Kartell, en particulier la chaise empilable « Tom Vac », et la « Well Tempered Chair » (1986) pour Vitra ainsi que la bibliothèque « Book Worm » (1996) pour Kartell. Parmi ses interventions architecturales, on trouve le foyer de l'opéra de Tel-Aviv (avec Alison Brooks, 1994) ; les restaurants Belgo Noord et Belgo Centraal à Londres (1994 et 1995) ; le Hall de la technologie de Selfridges à Londres (2001) ; le siège de Maserati à Modène, Italie (2003) ; le Y's Store pour Yohji Yamamoto à Tokyo (2003) et l'hôtel Duomo à Rimini, Italie (2003–06) publié ici. Dans le domaine des expositions, il a conçu, entre autres « Winning : The Design of Sports » pour Glasgow, ville désignée en 1999 « UK City of Architecture and Design ». Il dirige le département du design qu'abrite le Royal College of Art à Londres. Actuellement, il travaille au projet d'Upperworld, un hôtel de luxe sur le toit de la Battersea Power Station à Londres, à celui d'un nouveau musée du design à Holon, Israël, et du siège de Magis, fabricant de meubles à Trévise, Italie.

# HOTEL DUOMO

*Rimini, Italy, 2003–06*

*Floor area: 2650 m². Client: Pierpaolo Bernardi. Cost: €5.5 million (including furnishings, excluding cost of original building).*
*Architects: Ron Arad Associates, Ron Arad, Julian Gilhespie, Geoff Crowther, James Foster, Asa. Bruno, Taishi Kanemura.*
*Executive Architects: Pierandrei Associati (Milan).*

Ron Arad was asked in 2003 to redesign an existing hotel set in a narrow street in the historic center of Rimini. The owners wished to keep pace with a younger clientele. Arad first decided to wrap the existing façade in a bronze skin that penetrates the building and runs into the back wall of the bar, where it ends as the profile of a bench seat. Other interventions in the hotel are nothing short of spectacular. As the architects explain, "The entrance to the hotel is through giant pin-ball-flipper-like doors framing the view to the reception desk, which becomes the focal point of the hotel. The desk takes the form of a tapering stainless-steel ring dramatically leaning at an angle against a polished steel column. Shelves are imbedded into the ring expressing the horizontal topography of the desk. The wall behind is formed using a series of aluminum fins allowing natural daylight to flood the space and enabling a filtered view into the office behind." A focal point of activity of the hotel, the bar was imagined as "a large island with fjord-like scoops routed out of it for the patrons to eat and drink at." The rolling glass shutters of the bar open the space to the street. A number of Arad's pieces of furniture as well as custom-designed bathroom pods feature in the rooms.

Ron Arad erhielt 2003 den Auftrag, ein bestehendes Hotel in einer engen Straße im historischen Zentrum Riminis umzugestalten. Den Betreibern des Hotels ging es darum, mit einer jüngeren Klientel Schritt zu halten. Als Erstes beschloss Arad, die bestehende Fassade mit einer bronzenen Schicht zu überziehen, die in das Gebäude eindringt und sich bis zur Rückwand der Bar zieht, wo sie als Profil einer Sitzbank endet. Andere Eingriffe in das Hotel sind nicht weniger spektakulär. Der Architekt erläutert: »Der Eingang zum Hotel führt durch riesige, wie Flipperautomaten gestaltete Türen, die den Blick auf den Empfang rahmen, der zum Dreh- und Angelpunkt des Hotels wird. Der Empfangstresen hat die Form eines sich verjüngenden Edelstahlrings, der sich an einer Ecke eindrucksvoll auf eine hochglänzende Stahlsäule stützt. In den Ring eingefügte Ablageböden betonen das Horizontale des Empfangstresens. Die dahinter liegende Wand besteht aus gestaffelten Fensterstreben aus Aluminium, die Tageslicht in den Raum einfallen lassen und einen gefilterten Blick in das dahinter liegende Büro gestatten.« Die Bar, Zentrum des Geschehens im Hotel, ist als »große Insel mit ausgefrästen, fjordartigen Mulden konzipiert, an denen die Gäste essen und trinken.« In der wärmeren Jahreszeit öffnen die gläsernen Rollläden der Bar den Raum zur Straße hin. Auch der Gestaltung der Gästezimmer schenkte Ron Arad volle Aufmerksamkeit. Neben speziell angefertigten Sanitärzellen verwendete er eine Reihe selbst entworfener Möbelstücke.

C'est en 2003 que Ron Arad s'est vu demander le réaménagement d'un hôtel existant, situé dans une rue étroite du centre historique de Rimini. L'hôtel souhaitait s'adresser à une clientèle plus jeune. Arad a d'abord décidé d'envelopper la façade existante d'une peau de bronze qui pénètre à l'intérieur du bâtiment et court jusqu'au mur du fond du bar où elle se transforme en banquette. Plusieurs autres interventions sont tout aussi spectaculaires. Comme Arad l'explique : « L'entrée de l'hôtel se fait par de grandes portes qui, comme dans un flipper, cadrent le comptoir de réception, point focal d'attraction. Il se présente sous forme d'un anneau en acier inoxydable incliné de manière spectaculaire et posé contre une colonne d'acier poli. Des étagères y sont intégrées qui expriment la topographie horizontale nécessaire du plan de travail. Le mur à l'arrière est constitué d'une séquence d'ailettes d'aluminium qui laissent pénétrer un généreux éclairage naturel et filtre la vue sur le bureau au second plan. » Le bar, autre lieu d'attractions de l'hôtel, a été imaginé comme « un vaste îlot équipé de tables en forme de fjord autour desquelles les clients peuvent s'installer pour boire et manger ». Pendant les mois les plus chauds, les volets roulants en verre du bar s'ouvrent sur la rue. Ron Arad a également prêté beaucoup d'attention à la conception des chambres avec certains de ses propres meubles et dotées d'enclaves-salles de bains dessinées sur mesure.

*The ring-shaped desk in the lobby of the hotel is one of the most distinctive elements in the design of the hotel, where smooth surfaces and carefully controlled lighting contribute to the atmosphere of cutting-edge design.*

*Der ringförmige Empfangstresen in der Hotellobby ist eines der prägendsten Elemente des Hoteldesigns – glatte Oberflächen und präzise ausgerichtete Beleuchtung tragen zur Atmosphäre avantgardistischer Gestaltung bei.*

*Le comptoir d'accueil à la forme d'anneau dans le hall est l'un des éléments les plus caractéristiques de ce projet d'hôtel où surfaces lisses et éclairages soigneusement contrôlés contribuent à cette atmosphère avant-gardiste.*

*Interior design and color patterns are part of the intervention of Ron Arad, seen to the left, for example, in one of his Tom Vac chairs and a custom-designed table integrated into a wall of a room.*

*Innengestaltung und Farbmuster sind Teil von Ron Arads Planung, links ist z. B. einer seiner Tom-Vac-Stühle zu sehen und ein in die Wand eines Zimmers integrierter, speziell entworfener Tisch.*

*L'architecture intérieure et la gamme chromatique relèvent de Ron Arad, comme, à gauche, ses fauteuils Tom Vac et cette console spécialement dessinée, intégrée au mur d'une chambre.*

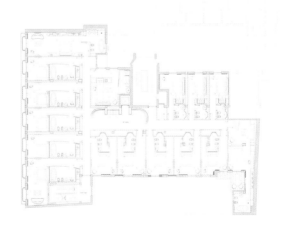

Furniture and fixtures designed by
Ron Arad continue the atmosphere
developed in the lobby and entrance
areas into the rest of the hotel.

Von Ron Arad entworfene Möbel und
Installationsobjekte setzen die in
Lobby und Eingangsbereich geschaffene Atmosphäre im übrigen Hotel
fort.

Le mobilier et les accessoires conçus
par Ron Arad développent dans tout
l'hôtel l'atmosphère créée dès l'entrée
et le hall de réception.

Restaurant and bar plans, drawn up
by the designer-architect, emphasize
an impression of continuity, in both
the aesthetic and the physical senses
of the term.

Die vom Designer und Architekten
entworfenen Grundrisse von Restaurant und Bar unterstreichen den
Eindruck von Kontinuität sowohl im
ästhetischen wie wörtlichen Sinn
des Begriffs.

Les plans du restaurant et du bar
dessinés par le designer-architecte
soulignent l'impression de continuité
dans un sens à la fois esthétique
et physique.

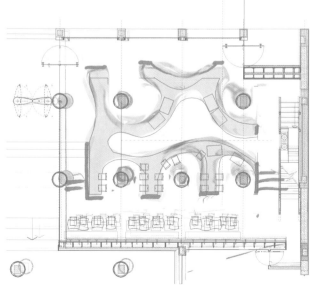

Mirrors or shiny surfaces alternate
with more matte or opaque materials
in the constantly surprising environment developed by Ron Arad for the
hotel.

Bei der von Ron Arad für das Hotel
geschaffenen, immer wieder überraschenden Ausstattung wechseln
sich Spiegel oder glänzende Oberflächen mit eher matten oder opaken
Materialien ab.

Des miroirs ou des surfaces brillantes
alternent avec des matières plus
mates ou opaques dans cet environnement, toujours étonnant, mis au
point par Ron Arad.

# ASYMPTOTE

*Asymptote Architecture Group*
*160 Varick Street, Floor 10 / New York, NY 10013 / USA*
*Tel: +1 212 343 7333 / Fax: +1 212 343 7099*
*E-mail: info@asymptote.net / Web: www.asymptote.net*

Hani Rashid received his M.Arch degree from the Cranbrook Academy of Art, Bloomfield Hills, Michigan. He is presently a Professor of Architecture at Columbia University in New York and at the Graduate School of Design at Harvard. He is also a member of the Steering Committee of the Aga Khan Award for Architecture. Lise Anne Couture received her B.Arch degree from Carlton University, Canada, and her M.Arch degree from Yale. Couture currently holds the Davenport Chair at Yale University School of Architecture. They created **ASYMPTOTE** in 1987. In 2004, they were awarded the Kiesler Prize for Art and Architecture. Projects include their Los Angeles West Coast Gateway (1989); a housing project for Brig, Switzerland; and their participation in the 1993 competition for an Art Center in Tours, France. More recent work includes a theater festival structure built in Denmark in 1997; a virtual trading floor for the New York Stock Exchange (1999); and the Guggenheim Virtual Museum (2000). In 2001, Asymptote participated in competitions for the Daimler-Chrysler and Mercedes-Benz Museums in Stuttgart, an expansion of the Queen's Museum, and the Eyebeam Center in New York. Most recently Asymptote completed the construction of Hydra-Pier in Haarlemmermeer, The Netherlands, and finished the Carlos Miele Flagship Store on West 14th Street in Manhattan in 2003. Asymptote was involved in the design of the 2004 Venice Biennale of Architecture, "Metamorph." They designed the Beukenhof Crematorium and Memorial Chapel in Rotterdam, recently completed the Alessi Flagship Store in the SoHo area of Manhattan, and are currently working on the Penang Towers in Malaysia (published here); two commercial office towers in Budapest, Hungary; a luxury mid-rise residential tower in New York's West Village; a 50-story luxury residential tower in Abu Dhabi; and a 560 m tall tower in Busan, Korea.

Hani Rashid machte seinen Abschluss als Master of Architecture an der Cranbrook Academy of Art in Bloomfield Hills, Michigan. Gegenwärtig lehrt er als Architekturprofessor an der Columbia University in New York und an der Graduate School of Design in Harvard. Er ist Mitglied des Steering Committee für den Aga Khan Award for Architecture. Lise Anne Couture legte die Prüfung zum Bachelor of Architecture an der Carlton University in Kanada, die zum Master in Yale ab. Zurzeit hat sie die Davenport-Professur am Fachbereich Architektur der Universität Yale inne. 1987 gründete sie mit Rashid das Büro **ASYMPTOTE**. 2004 erhielten sie den Kiesler Prize for Art and Architecture. Zu ihren Projekten zählen der Los Angeles West Coast Gateway (1989), ein Wohnungsbauprojekt in Brig in der Schweiz sowie die Teilnahme am Wettbewerb für ein Kunstzentrum in Tours (1993). Zu den neueren Arbeiten gehören ein 1997 in Dänemark errichteter Bau für ein Theaterfestival, ein virtueller Saal für die New Yorker Börse (1999) und das Virtuelle Guggenheim Museum (2000). 2001 beteiligte sich Asymptote an dem Wettbewerb für das Daimler-Chrysler- und das Mercedes-Benz-Museum in Stuttgart, für eine Erweiterung des Museums in Queens und für das Eyebeam Center in New York. In jüngster Zeit beendete Asymptote den Bau des Hydra-Pier in Haarlemmermeer, Niederlande. Außerdem stellten sie 2003 den Carlos Miele Flagship Store an der West 14th Street in Manhattan fertig. Asymptote war an der Gestaltung der Architekturbiennale »Metamorph« 2004 in Venedig beteiligt, entwarf das Krematorium Beukenhof mit Gedenkkapelle in Rotterdam, stellte unlängst den Alessi Flagship Store in SoHo in Manhattan fertig und arbeitet gegenwärtig an den hier publizierten Penang-Towers in Malaysia, zwei Bürohochhäusern in Budapest, einem Luxusapartmenthaus in New Yorks West Village, einem weiteren mit 50 Stockwerken in Abu Dhabi und einem 560 m hohen Turm in Busan, Korea.

Hani Rashid a obtenu son master d'architecture à la Cranbrook Academy of Art, Bloomfield Hills, Michigan. Il est actuellement professeur d'architecture à Columbia University à New York et à la Graduate School of Design d'Harvard ; il est également membre du comité de direction du Prix Aga Khan d'architecture. Lise Anne Couture a fait ses études à la Carlton University, Canada, et a obtenu son master d'architecure à Yale. Elle est actuellement titulaire de la chaire Davenport de la Yale University School of Architecture. Ils ont fondé **ASYMPTOTE** en 1987. En 2004, ils ont reçu le Kiesler Prize pour l'art et l'architecture. Leurs projets comprennent  la Los Angeles West Coast Gateway (1989) ; des logements à Brig, Suisse, et leur participation au concours pour un Centre d'art à Tours (1993). Plus récemment, ils ont réalisé au Danemark une structure pour un festival de théâtre (1997) ; une salle des marchés virtuelle pour le New York Stock Exchange (1999) et le Musée virtuel Guggenheim (2000). En 2001, Asymptote a participé aux concours pour les musées Daimler-Chrysler et Mercedes-Benz à Stuttgart, pour une extension du Queen's Museum et pour le Eyebeam Center à New York. Ils ont récemment achevé la construction de Hydra-Pier à Haarlemmermeer aux Pays-Bas, et, en 2003, le Carlos Miele Flagship Store, West 14th Street à Manhattan. Asymptote a participé à la Biennale d'architecture de Venise à travers le concept « Metamorph ». Ils ont conçu le crématorium et la chapelle du souvenir du Beukenhof à Rotterdam, récemment terminé le magasin Alessi dans le quartier de SoHo à Manhattan et travaillent actuellement sur le projet des Penang Towers en Malaisie, publié ici ; deux tours de bureaux à Budapest, Hongrie ; une tour moyennne d'appartements de luxe dans le West Village à New York ; une tour résidentielle de 50 étages à Abu Dhabi ; une tour de 560 mètres de haut à Busan, Corée.

# PENANG TOWERS

*Penang, Malaysia, 2006–10*

Floor area: 385 000 m².
Client: Equine Capital. Cost: $2.2 billion

Penang is an island in the Straits of Malacca, and also one of the states of Malaysia, located on the northwest coast of peninsular Malaysia. It is nicknamed "Pulau Mutiara," or Pearl of the Orient. The complex designed by Asymptote there is intended to become "a new 21st-century symbol for Penang on both a local and global scale through the simultaneous embrace of both natural landscape and contemporary urbanism." To be built at the base of the Penang Hill nature reserve, the complex overlooks the city and the sea beyond, with two towers willfully marking its presence. The complex is to include a convention center, a hotel, as well as commercial and office space. Outdoor public spaces are designed to accommodate public gatherings, festivals, outdoor performances, and exhibitions, as well as "shopping and socializing." The rather futuristic design of Asymptote seeks nothing less than to redefine the urban presence of this part of Malaysia, a country that has proven itself to be forward-looking in many areas, assuming its role as a regional meeting point and an emerging industrial and financial center. The project looks beyond questions of Muslim or Asian identity to signal the intention of Malaysia to forge bold initiatives that will make it very much part of the vanguard of international development. Asymptote is well chosen to convey this message.

Penang ist eine Insel in der Straße von Malakka und einer der Bundesstaaten Malaysias an der Nordwestküste der Halbinsel Malaysia, der auch als »Pulau Mutiara« oder Perle des Orients bekannt ist. Der von Asymptote entworfene Komplex soll zum »neuen Symbol des 21. Jahrhunderts für Penang werden und zwar auf lokaler wie globaler Ebene, indem natürliche Landschaft und zeitgenössische Stadtplanung einbezogen werden.« Der am Fuß des Naturreservats Penang Hill geplante Komplex überschaut Stadt und Meer und macht durch zwei eigenwillig gestaltete Türme auf sich aufmerksam. Die Anlage soll ein Tagungszentrum, ein Hotel sowie Ladengeschäfte und Büroflächen umfassen. Öffentliche Freiflächen sind für Versammlungen, Festivals, Aufführungen und Ausstellungen sowie zum Einkaufen und Flanieren vorgesehen. Der recht futuristische Entwurf von Asymptote soll die Urbanität dieses Teils von Malaysia neu definieren, einem Land, das sich auf vielen Gebieten als zukunftsorientiert erwiesen und eine Rolle als regionaler Treffpunkt und aufstrebendes Industrie- und Finanzzentrum übernommen hat. Das Projekt weist über Fragen muslimischer oder asiatischer Identität hinaus, um die Absicht Malaysias zu signalisieren, mithilfe kühner Initiativen zu einem Teil der internationalen Avantgarde zu werden. Die Wahl von Asymptote ist bestens geeignet, diese Botschaft zu vermitteln.

Penang est une île du détroit de Malacca sur la côte nord-ouest de la péninsule malaise et l'un des États constituant la Malaisie. Elle est surnommée « Pulau Mutiara » ou Perle de l'Orient. Le complexe conçu par Asymptote devrait être « un symbole du XXIᵉ siècle pour Penang, aussi bien à l'échelle locale que globale, par l'intégration simultanée du paysage naturel et de l'urbanisme contemporain ». Prévu au pied de la réserve naturelle de Penang Hill, il domine la ville et la mer dans le lointain de ses deux tours qui signalent avec force sa présence. Il devrait contenir un centre de congrès, un hôtel, des bureaux et des commerces. Les espaces publics extérieurs sont prévus pour accueillir des rassemblements, des festivals, des spectacles de plein air et des expositions, mais aussi pour se prêter « au shopping et à la socialisation ». La conception assez futuriste d'Asymptote cherche avant tout à redéfinir la présence urbaine dans cette région de la Malaisie, nation qui témoigne de son esprit de progrès dans de nombreux domaines, et veut assumer son rôle de point de rencontre régional et de centre industriel et financier en plein essor. Le projet dépasse l'identité musulmane ou asiatique pour afficher la volonté du pays à prendre des initiatives audacieuses qui la propulseront à l'avant-garde du développement international dans cette partie du monde. Asymptote est sans doute un bon choix pour accomplir cette tâche.

*The architects have developed a new and surprising architectural vocabulary for the complex that is employed in the pedestrian areas and in the overall scheme.*

*Die Architekten entwickelten für den Komplex eine neue, überraschende Architektursprache, die ihre Entsprechung bei den Fußgängerbereichen und in der gesamten Anlage findet.*

*Les architectes ont défini un vocabulaire architectural nouveau et surprenant pour ce complexe, constaté aussi bien au niveau des zones piétonnières que dans le projet d'ensemble.*

# ATELIER SOA

*Atelier SoA architectes*
*101 rue Damrémont*
*75018 Paris*
*France*

*Tel: +33 1 42 62 18 11*
*Fax: +33 1 42 62 18 98*
*E-mail: info.soa@wanadoo.fr*
*Web: www.ateliersoa.fr*

*La Tour Vivante*

Pierre Sartoux was born in 1973 and became a registered architect in 2003. He studied industrial design at the École des Beaux-Arts in Orléans, and interior design at the École des Beaux-Arts in Tours. In 2001, he worked with the firm Lipsky & Rollet in Paris and became a Project Director and co-manager of **ATELIER SOA**. Augustin Rosenstiehl is an architect and ethnologist. Born in 1973, he obtained a Master's degree in Ethnology at Nanterre University near Paris (1997). He worked with Atelier Dhan and Lipsky & Rollet in Paris, before becoming a Project Director and co-manager of Atelier SoA in 2001. Born in 1970, Aline Aviron studied design in Orléans and interior architecture at the École des Beaux-Arts in Tours. A partner of Atelier SoA, she is specialized in interior design. The three partners focus on the theoretical background of their work, and seek to blend the influences that they are familiar with—art, ethnology, design, and architecture. They completed the Ogilvy One Advertising Agency office on the Champs-Elysées in Paris in 2002, and the extension and restructuring of a 1930s house in Clamart, France, in 2004. They are presently working on the transformation of a farm into two houses with an indoor swimming pool, in Mansat-la-Courrière, France, and the Tour Vivante in Rennes, France (published here).

Pierre Sartoux wurde 1973 geboren und erhielt 2003 die Zulassung als Architekt. Er studierte Industriedesign an der École des Beaux-Arts in Orléans und Innenarchitektur an der École des Beaux-Arts in Tours. 2001 arbeitete er mit dem Büro Lipsky & Rollet in Paris und wurde Projektleiter und Co-Manager von **ATELIER SOA**. Der 1973 geborene Augustin Rosenstiehl ist Architekt und Ethnologe. Er machte 1997 an der Universität Nanterre bei Paris seinen Magister in Ethnologie. Er arbeitete mit dem Atelier Dhan und Lipsky & Rollet in Paris, ehe er 2001 Projektleiter und Co-Manager beim Atelier SoA wurde. Die 1970 geborene Aline Aviron studierte Design in Orléans und Innenarchitektur an der École des Beaux-Arts in Tours. Als Partnerin beim Atelier SoA ist sie auf Innenarchitektur spezialisiert. Die drei Partner konzentrieren sich auf den theoretischen Hintergrund ihrer Arbeit und sind bestrebt, die ihnen vertrauten Einflüsse – Kunst, Ethnologie, Design und Architektur – miteinander zu verschmelzen. 2002 stellten sie das Büro der Werbeagentur Ogilvy One an den Champs-Elysées in Paris fertig und 2004 den An- und Umbau eines Hauses aus den 1930er-Jahren in Clamart, Frankreich. Zurzeit arbeiten sie in Mansat-la-Courrière, Frankreich, an der Umgestaltung einer Farm in zwei Häuser mit Innenschwimmbad und der hier vorgestellten Tour Vivante in Rennes.

Pierre Sartoux, né en 1973, est architecte diplômé depuis 2003. Il a étudié le design industriel à l'École des Beaux-arts d'Orléans et l'architecture intérieure à l'École des Beaux-arts de Tours. En 2001, il travaille pour l'agence Lipsky & Rollet à Paris et devient directeur de projets et cogérant de l'**ATELIER SOA**. Augustin Rosenstiehl est architecte et ethnologue. Né en 1973, il obtient son mastère d'ethnologie à l'Université de Nanterre en 1997. Il travaille pour l'Atelier Dhan puis Lipsky & Rollet à Paris, avant de devenir directeur de projet et cogérant de l'Atelier SoA en 2001. Née en 1970, Aline Aviron a étudié le design à Orléans et l'architecture intérieure à l'École des Beaux-arts de Tours. Partenaire dans l'Atelier SoA, elle est spécialisée en architecture intérieure. Les trois associés attachent beaucoup d'intérêt au contenu théorique de leur travail et cherchent à fusionner les influences qui leur sont familières : l'art, l'ethnologie, le design et l'architecture. Ils ont achevé les bureaux de l'agence de publicité Ogilvy One, avenue des Champs-Élysées à Paris, en 2002 et l'extension et la restructuration d'une maison des années 1930 à Clamart, France, en 2004. Ils travaillent actuellement à la transformation d'une ferme en deux maisons avec piscine intérieure à Mansat-la-Courrière, France, et au projet de la Tour Vivante à Rennes, France, publié ici.

# LA TOUR VIVANTE

*Rennes, France, 2005–*

*Floor area: 50 471 m².*
*Clients: City of Rennes and Cimbéton. Cost: not disclosed*

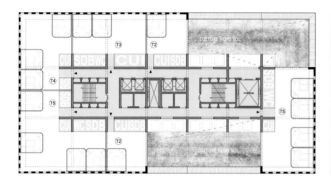 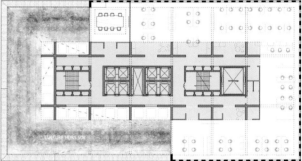

This planned building consists of 127 apartments, 8400 square meters of office space, 6748 square meters of shopping areas, 6957 square meters of greenhouse space, and a neighborhood library. The architects have attempted to reformulate the question of how such diverse functions can coexist in a single structure. They explain that their Tour Vivante (Living Tower) "was conceived as an autonomous ecological machine." They intend for the working greenhouses to provide an unexpected link between the other functions. Located between the city center and the periphery, the tower was designed to offer views of Rennes, and to fit into the local urban pattern. Set near a prison and railway tracks, the Tour Vivante is in a quintessentially urban location, a fact that the architects seek to emphasize rather than hiding inconvenient reality. The automated greenhouses are to produce a large quantity of fruits and vegetables, with an active program of waste and rainwater recycling employed in the agricultural process. Using heavy concrete elements to manage solar gain and thermal stability, the 30-story tower relies on a "chimney effect" created by the stacked greenhouses. Two windmills at the top of the tower provide part of the building's electricity requirements (300 kW), and assist in the recycling of rainwater, waste water and drinking water stored in reservoirs. Photovoltaic panels are integrated into the southern façade as a supplementary power source. University studies and guided tours for the public will explain the functioning of the greenhouses.

Der geplante Bau umfasst 127 Apartments, 8400 m² Bürofläche, 6748 m² Einkaufszonen, 6957 m² Gewächshausfläche sowie eine Stadtteilbibliothek. Die Architekten versuchten, die Frage, wie solch unterschiedliche Funktionen in einem einzigen Bau nebeneinander bestehen können, neu zu beantworten. Sie erläutern, dass ihre Tour Vivante (Lebender Turm) »als autonome, ökologische Maschine konzipiert sei«. Sie möchten mit den betriebsfähigen Gewächshäusern ein überraschendes Bindeglied zwischen den übrigen Funktionen anbieten. Der zwischen Stadtzentrum und Peripherie stehende Turm soll Ausblicke auf Rennes ermöglichen und sich in das lokale urbane Gefüge einpassen. Unweit eines Gefängnisses und von Bahngleisen gelegen, befindet sich die Tour Vivante an einem typisch urbanen Ort, eine Tatsache, die die Architekten eher betonen als die unbequeme Realität zu kaschieren. Die vollautomatisierten Gewächshäuser sollen große Mengen Obst und Gemüse erzeugen und dabei mit Abfall- und Regenwasserwiederaufbereitung arbeiten. Damit die Räume sich unter der Sonneneinstrahlung nicht zu sehr aufheizen und die Temperaturen konstant gehalten werden können, wurden beim Bau des 30-geschossigen Turms schwere Betonelemente verwendet; die übereinander gestapelten Gewächshäuser sorgen überdies für die gewünschte »Kaminwirkung«. Zwei Windräder auf dem Dach des Turms erzeugen einen Teil der nötigen Elektrizität (300 kW) und helfen bei der Wiederaufbereitung von in Speicherbecken gesammeltem Regen-, Trink- und Abwasser. In die Südfassade sind zur zusätzlichen Energiegewinnung Solarzellen integriert. In Universitätskursen und bei öffentlichen Führungen wird die Wirkungsweise der Gewächshäuser erläutert.

Cet immeuble dont la construction est planifiée contiendra 127 appartements, 8 400 m² de bureaux, 6 748 m² de commerces, 6 957 m² de serres et une bibliothèque de quartier. Les architectes ont tenté de reformuler ici le problème de la coexistence de fonctions aussi diversifiées dans le cadre d'une structure unique. Ils expliquent que leur Tour Vivante « a été conçue comme une machine écologique autonome ». Les serres – réelles – créent un lien inattendu entre les autres fonctions. Implantée entre le centre-ville et la périphérie, elle offre des vues sur Rennes et s'intègre dans le tissu urbain. Proche d'une prison et de voies ferrées, elle se trouve néanmoins dans un site par essence urbain, ce que les architectes ont cherché à mettre en valeur plutôt que de masquer une réalité incommode. Les serres automatisées devraient produire de grandes quantités de fruits et de légumes et bénéficieront d'un programme de recyclage des déchets et de l'eau de pluie pour en alimenter les cultures. Construite en éléments lourds en béton pour mieux gérer le gain solaire et la stabilité thermique, cette tour de 30 niveaux met à profit l'effet de cheminée créé par l'empilement des serres. À son sommet, deux éoliennes fourniront une partie de l'énergie consommée par la tour (300 kW) et participeront au recyclage de l'eau de pluie, des eaux usées et de l'eau potable stockée dans des réservoirs. Des panneaux photovoltaïques intégrés à la façade sud apporteront un complément d'énergie. Le fonctionnement des serres sera l'objet d'études universitaires et de visites guidées ouvertes au public.

# la Tour Vivante

The integration of planted areas into the complex at every level, with a kind of green-band continuity, gives an unexpected appearance and an ecologically conscious presence to the tower.

*Die Einbeziehung von Grünbereichen auf jeder Ebene des Komplexes und eine Art kontinuierliches grünes Band geben dem Turm ein ungewöhnliches Aussehen und zeugen von ökologischer Verantwortung.*

*L'intégration de zones végétalisées tout au long d'une sorte de bandeau vert continu donne un aspect inattendu, et marque la personnalité écologique de la tour.*

The air and energy circulation within the building is carefully thought out, making use of the internal greenhouses.

*Der Verlauf der Luft- und Energiezirkulation innerhalb des Gebäudes ist gut durchdacht und nutzt die internen Gewächshäuser.*

*Les circuits de circulation d'air ou d'énergie à l'intérieur du bâtiment ont été soigneusement pensés et profitent des effets provoqués par les serres intérieures.*

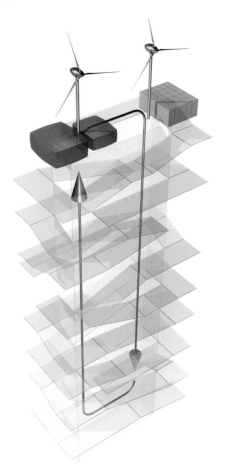

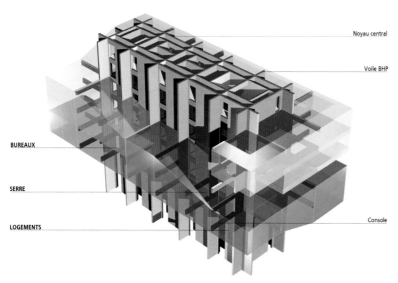

Noyau central

Voile BHP

BUREAUX

SERRE

LOGEMENTS

Console

A computer perspective from within the lower commercial center looking up toward the tower with its rooftop windmills emphasizes the intention to create a new image of architecture.

*Eine Computerperspektive aus dem Inneren der unteren Ladenpassage mit Blick auf den Turm mit den ihn bekrönenden Windrädern unterstreicht die Absicht, ein neues Bild von Architektur zu schaffen.*

*Une perspective en image de synthèse, vue de l'intérieur du centre commercial en regardant vers la tour et ses éoliennes de toiture, souligne la volonté de créer une nouvelle image architecturale.*

# ATELIER TEKUTO

*Atelier Tekuto Co. Ltd.*
*6-15-16-301 Honkomagome*
*Bunkyo-ku*
*Tokyo 113–0021*
*Japan*

*Tel: +81 3 5940 2770*
*Fax: +81 3 5940 2780*
*E-mail: info@tekuto.com*
*Web: www.tekuto.com*

*Lucky Drops House*

Yasuhiro Yamashita was born in Kagoshima, Japan, in 1960. He graduated from the Shibaura Institute of Technology (B.Arch.) and received his M.Arch degree from the same school in 1986. He worked with Yutaka Saito Architect & Associates, PANOM and Shunji Kondo Architects, before founding his own firm, Yamashita Kai Architectural Office, in 1991 in Tokyo. The firm was renamed **ATELIER TEKUTO** in 1995. The office has 10 employees. Yamashita has been a lecturer at the Shibaura Institute of Technology since 1999. His main projects are houses located in or near Tokyo: Penguin House (2002); Wafers (2004); Crystal Brick (2004); Cell Brick (2004); the aLuminum-House (2005); Lucky Drops House (2005, published here); and Wakka (2005). His recent work includes Reflection of Mineral (Nakano, Tokyo, 2006), Glucks Garten (Hiiyoshi, Kanagawa, 2007), and their 1st-prize-winning Busan Eco Center, a natural resource museum that opened in June 2007 in Korea.

Yasuhiro Yamashita wurde 1960 in Kagoshima, Japan, geboren. Er legte am Shibaura Institute of Technology die Prüfung zum B.Arch. ab, 1986 gefolgt vom M.Arch. Ehe er 1991 in Tokio sein eigenes Büro Yamashita Kai Architectural Office gründete, arbeitete er bei Yutaka Saito Architect & Associates, PANOM und Shunji Kondo Architects. 1995 wurde das Büro in **ATELIER TEKUTO** umbenannt. Es hat zurzeit 10 Angestellte. Yamashita ist seit 1999 als Lehrkraft am Shibaura Institute of Technology tätig. Bei seinen Projekten handelt es sich in der Hauptsache um Häuser in oder bei Tokio: Penguin House (2002), Wafers (2004), Crystal Brick (2004), Cell Brick (2004), aLuminum-House (2005), Lucky Drops House (2005, hier publiziert) und Wakka (2005). Zu seinen jüngere Bauten gehören Reflection of Mineral (Nakano, Tokio, 2006), Glucks Garten (Hiiyoshi, Kanagawa, 2007) und sein preisgekröntes Busan Eco Center, ein Museum für natürliche Ressourcen, das im Juni 2007 in Korea eröffnet wurde.

Yasuhiro Yamashita est né à Kagoshima, au Japon, en 1960. Il est diplômé et M. Arch. (1986) de l'Institut de technologie Shibaura. Il travaille avec Yukata Saito Architects & Associates, PANOM et Shunji Kondo Architects avant de créer en 1991 sa propre agence, l'**ATELIER TEKUTO**, qui emploie 10 collaborateurs. Il enseigne à l'Institut Shibaura depuis 1999. Ses principaux projets consistent en des résidences privées situées dans ou près de Tokyo : Maison Penguin (2002), Wafers (2004), Crystal Brick (2004), Maison aLuminum (2005), Maison Lucky Drops (2005) publiée ici et Wakka (2005). Parmi ses réalisations récentes : Reflection of Mineral à Nakano, Tokyo (2006), Glucks Garten, à Hiiyoshi, Kanagawa (2007), et le Busan Eco Center, musée des ressources naturelles inauguré en juin 2007 en Corée, et primé.

# LUCKY DROPS HOUSE

*Setagaya-ku, Tokyo, Japan, 2004–05*

*Floor area: 61 m². Client: not disclosed. Cost: not disclosed.*
*Design: Yasuhiro Yamashita (Atelier Tekuto)*
*with Masahiro Ikeda (Masahiro Ikeda Co. Ltd.)*

Located in the Setagaya district of Tokyo, this house was built for a "married couple with a cat." 6.8 meters high, the building is made of steel with an "FRP (3-mm Fiber Reinforced Plastic) and +EB film (Electron Beam Film)" skin. As is often the case in Japan, the house was built on an extremely small lot (59 square meters) with a building footprint of only 22 square meters. Local zoning rules required a 50-centimeter setback of the external walls of the house from adjacent buildings. This rule did not apply to underground spaces, so the main living spaces are below grade. As the architect explains, "It was agreed from the outset to take advantage of the site's characteristics by ensuring a maximum length for the building; providing a space for fun and structural reinforcement to the building by introducing a slope inside; making the best use of underground space; and turning the entire building into a skin. The above-ground section features skinlike external walls with added transparency letting sunlight permeate the entire building. The floor material is expanded metal letting sunlight penetrate underground, in an attempt to deviate from the usual function of the floor."

Dieses im Setagaya-Distrikt von Tokio gelegene Haus wurde für ein »Ehepaar mit einer Katze« erbaut. Das 6,8 m hohe Bauwerk besteht aus Stahl mit einem Überzug aus »FRP (3-mm-faserverstärktem Kunststoff) und +EB Film (Elektronenstrahlfilm)«. Wie so häufig in Japan wurde das Haus mit einer Grundfläche von nur 22 m² auf einem extrem kleinen Grundstück errichtet (59 m²). Örtliche Bauvorschriften forderten, dass die Außenmauern einen Abstand von 50 cm zur benachbarten Bebauung einhielten. Diese Regel erstreckt sich nicht auf unterirdische Räume, so dass sich die Hauptwohnräume unter der Erde befinden. Der Architekt erklärt »Von Anfang an stand fest, dass wir die Charakteristika des Grundstücks nutzen wollten, indem wir dem Haus die maximale Länge sicherten; indem wir im Innenraum ein Gefälle einplanten, das einen Raum für Freizeitaktivitäten und gleichzeitig die konstruktive Versteifung des Gebäudes ermöglichte, indem wir die Souterrainräume optimal nutzten und indem wir schließlich das ganze Haus in eine Haut verwandelten. Den oberirdischen Bereich kennzeichnen hautähnliche Außenwände, die dank zusätzlicher Transparenz Sonnenlicht in den gesamten Bau eindringen lassen. In dem Versuch, die übliche Funktion von Boden abzuwandeln, bestehen die Fußböden aus Streckmetall, das Tageslicht ins Souterrain einfallen lässt.«

Située dans le quartier de Setagaya à Tokyo, cette maison a été construite pour « un couple marié avec chat ». Haute de 6,8 mètres, sa structure est en acier recouverte d'une peau en FRP (plastique renforcé de fibres) de 3 mm d'épaisseur et d'un film +EB (film traité sous faisceau électronique). Comme souvent au Japon, elle a été édifiée sur une parcelle minuscule (59 m²) et son emprise au sol n'est que de 22 m². La réglementation locale de *zoning* exigeait un retrait de 50 cm des murs extérieurs par rapport aux constructions adjacentes. Cette règle ne s'appliquant pas aux volumes en sous-sol, les principaux espaces à vivre y ont été implantés. Comme l'explique l'architecte : « Dès le départ, nous avons décidé de mettre à profit les caractéristiques du terrain en allongeant au maximum la maison, en créant un espace de loisirs et en renforçant structurellement la construction par l'introduction d'une pente intérieure, ainsi que de profiter au maximum du volume en sous-sol et de transformer la construction toute entière en une « peau ». La partie au-dessus du niveau du sol se définit par des murs extérieurs réalisés en une peau dont la transparence permet d'éclairer naturellement toute la maison. Le matériau de sol est un métal déployé qui laisse lui aussi pénétrer la lumière jusqu'au sous-sol dans un essai de détournement de la fonction habituelle d'un plancher. »

*The tiny Lucky Drops House makes use of its narrow lot in an innovative fashion. The density of Japan's urban areas demands new solutions.*

*Das kleine Haus nutzt das schmale Grundstück auf innovative Weise. Die dichte Bebauung japanischer Städte erfordert neue Lösungen.*

*La minuscule maison utilise son étroite parcelle de façon originale. Au Japon, la densité urbaine impose la recherche de solutions nouvelles.*

*Standing out from an otherwise traditional architectural environment, the house imposes its pointed lozenge form on the street, slanting up to a maximum height near the entrance.*

*Das Haus zwängt seine zugespitzte Parabelform in die ansonsten traditionell bebaute Umgebung und erhebt sich an der Eingangsseite zu maximaler Höhe.*

*Détachée de son environnement architectural traditionnel, la maison affiche sa forme de losange effilé. Sa hauteur maximale se trouve au-dessus de l'entrée.*

The section drawing below shows how the house slants upward near the entrance, making space for the living room below and the bedroom above.

*Die unten abgebildete Schnittzeich-nung zeigt, wie das Haus nahe dem Eingang aufragt und damit Raum schafft für das Wohnzimmer unten und den darüberliegenden Schlafraum.*

*Le dessin de coupe ci-dessous montre l'élévation de la maison près de l'entrée. Le séjour est en bas et une chambre occupe l'étage.*

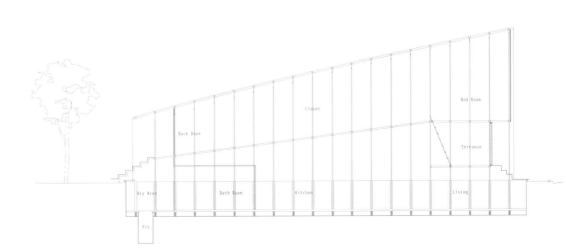

The essentially triangular plan of the house is visible below—interior spaces seem long and curiously generous given the very limited floor space available.

*Der im Grunde dreieckige Grundriss des Hauses ist unten zu sehen – die Innenräume erscheinen angesichts des äußerst begrenzten verfügbaren Raums lang gestreckt und erstaunlich großzügig.*

*Ci-dessous, le plan triangulaire de la maison. Les volumes intérieurs allongés semblent étrangement généreux par rapport à la surface au sol très limitée.*

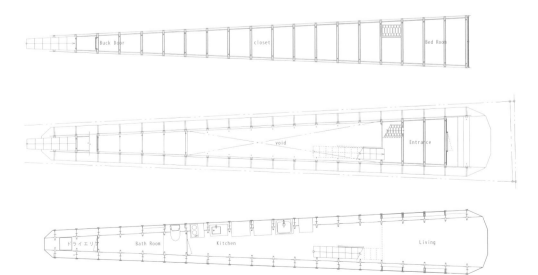

*Coimbra Footbridge*

# CECIL BALMOND

*Arup / 13 Fitzroy Street / London W1T 4BQ / UK*
*Tel: +44 20 7755 4248 / Fax: +44 20 7755 2994*
*E-mail: webmail@arup.com / Web: www.arup.com*

Born in Sri Lanka, **CECIL BALMOND** went to London for postgraduate studies and joined Arup in 1968. He is an internationally recognized designer, structural engineer and author and has been Deputy Chairman of the multidisciplinary engineering firm Arup since 2004. He founded the Advanced Geometry Unit (AGU) at Arup. His interest lies in the genesis of form using numbers, music, and mathematics as vital sources which has led to successful collaborations with major international architects. Aside from the Serpentine Pavilion in London designed with Rem Koolhaas (published here), he worked with the Dutch architect on the Kunsthal (Rotterdam, The Netherlands, 1994); Grand Palais (Lille, France, 1994); Seattle Central Library (Seattle, Washington, 2004); Casa da Musica (Porto, Portugal, 2005); and CCTV Headquarters, Beijing, China. He worked with Álvaro Siza on the Portuguese National Pavilion for Expo '98 in Lisbon, Daniel Libeskind on the latter's ill-fated World Trade Center projects and the artist Anish Kapoor on the sculpture *Marsyas*, presented in the Turbine Hall of the Tate Modern in 2002. Other projects include the redevelopment of the Battersea Power Station (London, 1999–); the design of the new Metz Pompidou Center (with Shigeru Ban); and the Coimbra Footbridge (Portugal, published here). He is an external examiner at the Architectural Association (AA) in London, and Senior Design Fellow at the London School of Economics. His notable books include *Number 9: The Search for the Sigma Code* (Prestel, 1998), and *Informal* (Prestel, 2002). Other projects outside Europe include the Net Bridge in Beirut, Lebanon, with architect and sculptor Nadim Karam, and a collaboration with Heneghan Peng on the Grand Museum of Egypt in Cairo. In 2004, he was appointed the Paul Philippe Cret Professor of Architecture at the University of Pennsylvania, where he is also Director of the NISO (Non-Linear Systems Organization).

Der in Sri Lanka geborene **CECIL BALMOND** kam zu weiterführenden Studien nach London und schloss sich 1968 dem Büro Arup an. Balmond ist ein international bekannter Designer, Bauingenieur, Autor und seit 2004 stellvertretender Vorsitzender des multidisziplinären Ingenieurbüros Arup, wo er die Advanced Geometry Unit (AGU) gründete. Er interessiert sich für die Genese von Formen durch Zahlen, Musik und Mathematik als wesentliche Quellen. Sein Interesse an Architektur und Design führte zur erfolgreichen Zusammenarbeit mit international bedeutenden Architekten. Neben dem hier vorgestellten Serpentine Pavilion, den er mit Rem Koolhaas gestaltete, arbeitete er mit dem niederländischen Architekten an der Kunsthal Rotterdam (1994), dem Grand Palais (Lille, 1994), der Seattle Central Library (Seattle, 1994), der Casa da Musica (Porto, 2005) und an der zurzeit in Bau befindlichen Zentrale von CCTV in Peking. Mit Álvaro Siza arbeitete er am Portugiesischen Pavillon für die Expo `98 in Lissabon und mit Daniel Libeskind an dessen vom Unglück verfolgten Projekt für das World Trade Center (Ground Zero). Überdies kooperierte er mit dem Künstler Anish Kapoor bei dessen Skulptur »Marsyas«, die 2002 in der Turbinenhalle der Tate Modern in London vorgestellt wurde. Weitere Projekte, an denen er beteiligt war, sind das Kraftwerk Battersea (London, 1999–), der Entwurf des Centre Pompidou in Metz (mit Shigeru Ban) sowie die hier gezeigte Fußgängerbrücke in Coimbra, Portugal. Er fungiert als externer Prüfer bei der Architectural Association in London und als Senior Design Fellow an der London School of Economics. Zu seinen wichtigen Büchern gehören *Number 9: The Search for the Sigma Code* (Prestel, 1998) und *Informal* (Prestel, 2002). Seine außereuropäischen Projekte umfassen die Net Bridge in Beirut mit dem Architekten und Bildhauer Nadim Kara sowie eine gemeinschaftliche Arbeit mit Heneghan Peng am Ägyptischen Museum in Kairo. 2004 wurde er als Paul Philippe Cret Professor of Architecture an die Universität von Pennsylvania berufen, wo er außerdem als Leiter der NISO (Non-Linear Systems Organization) fungiert.

Né au Sri Lanka, **CECIL BALMOND** est venu à Londres pour y poursuivre des études supérieures et a rejoint Arup en 1968. Concepteur et ingénieur structurel, auteur, il est vice-président de l'agence d'ingénierie multidisciplinaire Arup depuis 2004. Il s'intéresse particulièrement à la genèse de formes issues des nombres, des mathématiques et de la musique. Son goût pour l'architecture et la conception l'a conduit à des collaborations applaudies avec quelques-uns des plus grands architectes mondiaux. En dehors du Serpentine Pavilion à Londres, conçu avec Rem Koolhaas, publié ici, il a travaillé avec l'architecte néerlandais sur le Kunsthal de Rotterdam (1994), le Grand Palais de Lille (1994), la bibliothèque centrale de Seattle, Washington (2004), la Casa da Musica à Porto (2005) et le siège de CCTV en cours de construction à Pékin. Il a collaboré avec Álvaro Siza sur le Pavillon national portugais pour Expo '98 à Lisbonne, et avec Daniel Libeskind sur ses projets au destin malheureux pour le World Trade Center. Il a également apporté son aide à l'artiste Anish Kapoor pour la sculpture *Marsyas* installée dans le Turbine Hall de la Tate Modern à Londres (2002). Parmi ses autres projets, on compte la restructuration de la Battersea Power Station, Londres (depuis 1999) ; la conception du Centre Pompidou de Metz (avec Shigeru Ban) et la passerelle de Coimbra publiée ici. Il est examinateur invité à l'Architectural Association de Londres et Senior Design Fellow de la London School of Economics. Parmi ses écrits notables : *Number 9: The Search for the Sigma Code* (Prestel, 1998) et *Informal* (Prestel, 2002). Parmi ses autres projets hors d'Europe, le Net Bridge à Beyrouth, avec l'architecte et sculpteur Nadim Karam, et une collaboration avec Heneghan Peng sur le Grand musée d'Égypte au Caire. En 2004, il a été nommé Paul Philippe Cret Professor of Architecture à l'Université de Pennsylvanie où il dirige également le NISO (Organisation de systèmes non linéaires).

# COIMBRA FOOTBRIDGE

*Mondego River, Coimbra, Portugal, 2005–06*

*Client: Coimbra Polis/AFA Consulting SA. Length: 274.5 m. Width: 4 m. Cost: €3.5 million.*
*Design: Cecil Balmond, AGU, with António Fonseca, AFA Consulting SA. AGU Team: Cecil Balmond, Daniel Bosia, Charles Walker, Lip Chiong*

Built with concrete, laminated steel and a 1150-square-meter Guayacan timber pavement, the Coimbra Footbridge is a much more unexpected structure than it might at first appear. Cecil Balmond writes, "I wanted to walk over that stretch of water and linger, stop and start. The idea came to have two halves for the bridge, with neither meeting in their journey across water: two curves that would slip past each other. The middle then would become a crossover zone, not just for pedestrians but also for structure [...] and so, one half in full elevation, the other in shadow due to sun angle and offset. With no support in the middle this leads to an optical illusion, a vision of a bridge that never meets." The project engineer, António Fonseca, explains that the Mondego River is the largest to run exclusively through Portuguese territory, and that this crossing at Coimbra provides "the city [with] a landmark for the 21st century: a point of reference in innovative structural solutions." Cecil Balmond and António Fonseca imagined a very flat arched bridge, "In fact an arch bridge defining two large-size triangular structures." The two halves of the bridge hold each other up, giving an impression that the whole could topple into the river. Faceted panels of glass were designed by Balmond and AGU for the bridge giving the structure an equally unexpected note of bright color. The Mayor of Coimbra linked this unusual footbridge to an old story of love, deceit and murder between Pedro, an heir to the Portuguese throne, and the Galician noblewoman Inês de Castro. Murdered in Coimbra's Quinta das Lágrimas Palace in 1355 on the orders of Pedro's father, Inês de Castro was exhumed when Pedro became king and posthumously declared queen of Portugal. The Pedro and Inês Bridge was inaugurated by the President of Portugal on November 26, 2006.

Die aus Beton, Mehrschichtstahl und einem 1150 m² großen Belag aus Guayacanholz erbaute Fußgängerbrücke in Coimbra ist ein weit ungewöhnlicheres Bauwerk, als es zunächst den Anschein hat. Cecil Balmond schreibt: »Ich wollte über diesen Wasserlauf gehen, verweilen, stehenbleiben und wieder loslaufen. Es entstand die Idee, eine Brücke aus zwei Hälften zu bauen, die sich bei ihrem Weg über das Wasser nicht treffen sollten: zwei aneinander vorbei gleitende Kurven. Die Mitte würde so zu einer Kreuzungszone werden, nicht nur für Passanten, sondern auch für das Bauwerk [...] die eine Hälfte in voller Ansicht, die andere wegen Sonnenstand und Versatz im Schatten liegend. Ohne Stütze in der Mitte führt das zu einer optischen Täuschung, das Bild einer Brücke, die nie aufeinander trifft.« Der Entwurfsingenieur António Fonseca erläutert, dass es sich beim Mondego um den längsten, ausschließlich auf portugiesischem Gebiet verlaufenden Fluss handelt, und dass diese Überquerung in Coimbra »der Stadt ein markantes Bauwerk für das 21. Jahrhundert verschafft: einen Bezugspunkt für innovative, konstruktive Lösungen«. Cecil Balmond und António Fonseca stellten sich eine Brücke mit sehr flachen Bögen vor, »eine Bogenbrücke, die aus zwei großen, dreieckigen Bauteilen besteht«. Die beiden Brückenhälften stützen sich gegenseitig und es entsteht der Eindruck, das Ganze könnte in den Fluss kippen. Balmond und AGU entwarfen facettierte Glasscheiben für die Brücke, die dem Bauwerk eine überraschende leuchtende Farbigkeit schenken. Der Bürgermeister von Coimbra verbindet diese ungewöhnliche Fußgängerbrücke mit einer alten Geschichte von Liebe, Betrug und Mord zwischen Pedro, Anwärter auf den portugiesischen Thron, und der galicischen Adligen Inês de Castro. Letztere, die man 1355 auf Befehl von Pedros Vater im Palast Quinta das Lágrimas in Coimbra ermordete, wurde nach Pedros Krönung exhumiert und posthum zur Königin von Portugal erklärt. Die Pedro-und-Inês-Brücke wurde am 26. November 2006 vom portugiesischen Präsidenten eingeweiht.

En béton et acier feuilleté, son tablier revêtu de 1 150 m² de bois de Guayacan, cette passerelle est encore plus étonnante qu'elle ne peut sembler à première vue. Cecil Balmond a écrit à son sujet : « Je voulais pouvoir marcher au-dessus de cette eau, flâner, m'arrêter et repartir. L'idée m'est venu de dessiner ce pont en deux moitiés qui ne se rejoignent pas dans leur avancée au-dessus des flots, comme deux courbes glissant l'une contre l'autre en se frôlant. La partie centrale deviendrait alors le franchissement, pas seulement pour les piétons mais aussi de la structure elle-même, [...] dont une moitié est en pleine élévation, l'autre dans l'ombre provoquée par la position du soleil, comme effacée. L'absence de support central provoque une illusion d'optique, la vision d'un pont qui ne rejoint jamais la rive. » L'ingénieur de projet António Fonseca explique par ailleurs que le Mondego est le plus grand fleuve à couler exclusivement en territoire portugais et que son franchissement à Coimbra offre « à la ville un monument pour le XXIe siècle, un point de référence dans le domaine des solutions structurelles novatrices ». Balmond et Fonseca ont dessiné un ouvrage à arche surbaissée, « en fait, un pont en arches défini par deux structures triangulaires de grandes dimensions ». Les deux moitiés se tiennent par le haut, donnant l'impression que l'ensemble pourrait presque basculer dans l'eau. Des panneaux de verre facetté spécialement conçus par Balmond et AGU confèrent aux parapets une touche de couleur vive inattendue. Le maire de Coimbra a fait un lien entre cette surprenante passerelle et une très ancienne histoire de passion, de mensonge et de meurtre entre Pedro, prince héritier du trône du Portugal, et une jeune noble galicienne Inês de Castro. Assassinée au palais Quinta das Lagrimas à Coimbra en 1355 sur l'ordre du père de Pedro, la jeune fille fut exhumée lorsque ce dernier devint roi et déclarée reine du Portugal à titre posthume. Le pont « Pedro et Inês » a été inauguré par Aníbal Cavaco Silva, le président portugais, le 26 novembre 2006.

The footbridge has a light presence on the river, almost appearing to hover over the water, or rather to skip over it.

Die Fußgängerbrücke zeichnet sich durch ihre optische Leichtigkeit aus und scheint fast über dem Fluss zu schweben oder besser, ihn zu überspringen.

D'une présence pleine de légèreté, l'ouvrage semble presque en suspension au-dessus de l'eau, ou la franchir d'un bond.

Colored-glass, an irregularly formed handrail, and an unusual form give the bridge a movement and sense of gaiety that it would otherwise have lacked.

Farbiges Glas, ein unregelmäßig geformtes Geländer und eine ungewöhnliche Form verleihen der Brücke Bewegung und eine sonst vielleicht fehlende Fröhlichkeit.

Un garde-corps de forme irrégulière en panneaux de verre de couleur crée un sentiment inattendu de mouvement ludique.

# SERPENTINE GALLERY PAVILION

*Kensington Gardens, London, UK, 2006*

*Surface of Egg: 1800 m². Diameter/Height of Egg: 30 m/21 m. Client: Serpentine Gallery Trust.*
*Cost: not disclosed. Design: Rem Koolhaas and Cecil Balmond with Arup.*
*Arup Team: Cecil Balmond, Carolina Bartram, Tristan Simmonds, Chris Carroll, Andrew Grant,*
*Willliam Whitby, Steve Walker, Phil Greenup*

This project was the product of a collaboration between Rem Koolhaas and Cecil Balmond. Conceived by Julia Peyton-Jones, Director of the Serpentine Gallery, the summer pavilions erected near the Gallery in Kensington Gardens have been the work of Zaha Hadid (2000), Daniel Libeskind with Arup (2001), Toyo Ito with Arup (2002), Oscar Niemeyer (2003), MvRdV (2004, unrealized) and Álvaro Siza and Eduardo Souto de Moura with Cecil Balmond – Arup (2005). Cecil Balmond explains: "These Pavilions have evolved with various structural typologies and materials, provoking a debate on architecture; this year the exploration continues not only with typology and material, but with the very definition of Pavilion." As Arup describes the project, open to the public between July 13 and October 15, 2006, "The *Cosmic Egg* perches 5 meters above the ground on top of the 21-meter-diameter translucent polycarbonate hub that hosted this year's expanded itinerary of art events." The main hull of the Egg, which was intended to be inflated with 6000 cubic meters of helium and a further 2000 cubic meters of pressurized air, and made to float 10 meters above the ground, consisted of almost 2000 square meters (over 1 ton) of a PVC coated polyester cloth, specially made for the project for its combined transparency and strength. The architects state that "the aim of translucency and physical lightness inspired the use of new materials in innovative ways." The construction and use of the Pavilion coincided with an exhibition of the German artist Thomas Demand (6 June–20 August, 2006). Some of the artwork was used inside the Pavilion as decoration.

Dieses Projekt ist das Ergebnis einer Zusammenarbeit von Rem Koolhaas und Cecil Balmond. Die bisher von Julia Peyton-Jones, der Direktorin der Serpentine Gallery initiierten Sommerpavillons, die jeweils unweit der Galerie in Kensington Gardens entstanden, waren Werke von Zaha Hadid (2000), Daniel Libeskind mit Arup (2001), Toyo Ito mit Arup (2002), Oscar Niemeyer (2003), MvRdV (2004, unrealisiert) und Álvaro Siza und Eduardo Souto de Moura mit Cecil Balmond (Arup, 2005). Letzterer führt aus: »Diese Pavillons entwickelten unterschiedliche konstruktive Typologien und Materialien und stießen eine Debatte über Architektur an; in diesem Jahr geht es nicht nur um Typologie und Material, sondern um die eigentliche Definition des Pavillons.« Arup beschreibt das für die Öffentlichkeit vom 13. Juli bis 15. Oktober 2006 zugängliche Projekt wie folgt: »Das ›Kosmische Ei‹ sitzt 5 m über dem Boden auf einem Unterbau aus lichtdurchlässigem Polycarbonat. In diesem Sockel mit einem Durchmesser von 21 m fanden die diesjährigen erweiterten Art Events statt.« Die Haupthülle des Eis, die mit 6000 m³ Helium und weiteren 2000 m³ Druckluft befüllt wurde und 10 m über dem Boden schwebte, bestand aus fast 2000 m² eines mit PVC beschichteten Polyestergewebes (mehr als 1 t schwer), das wegen seiner gleichzeitigen Transparenz und Haltbarkeit eigens für dieses Projekt hergestellt wurde. Den Architekten zufolge »regte der Wunsch nach Transluzenz und physischer Leichtigkeit den Gebrauch neuer Materialien in innovativer Weise an«. Errichtung und Nutzung des Pavillons fielen zeitlich mit einer Ausstellung des deutschen Künstlers Thomas Demand zusammen (6.6.–20.8.2006). Ein Teil der Arbeit wurde im Pavillon ausgestellt.

Ce projet est le fruit d'une collaboration entre Rem Koolhaas et Cecil Balmond. Dans le cadre d'un projet conçu par Julia Peyton-Jones, directrice de la Serpentine Gallery, la construction annuelle d'un pavillon temporaire, non loin de la galerie des jardins de Kensington, a été confiée à Zaha Hadid (2000), Daniel Libeskind en collaboration avec Arup (2001), Toyo Ito également avec Arup (2002), Oscar Niemeyer (2003), MvRdV (2004, non réalisé) et Álvaro Siza et Edouardo Souto de Moura avec Cecil Balmond pour Arup (2005). Cecil Balmond explique : « Ces pavillons ont évolué selon diverses typologies et types de matériaux structurels et ont provoqué un débat sur l'architecture. Cette année, l'exploration se poursuit non seulement sur la typologie et les matériaux, mais sur la définition même du pavillon. » Arup décrit ainsi ce projet, ouvert au public du 13 juillet au 15 octobre 2006 : « Le Cosmic Egg (œuf cosmique) perché à cinq mètres au-dessus du sol présente la forme d'un ballon de 21 mètres de diamètre en polycarbonate translucide et a été conçu pour accueillir un ensemble de manifestations artistiques très diverses. Le ballon, gonflé de 6 000 m³ d'hélium et de 2 000 m³ d'air pressurisé pour flotter à 10 mètres au-dessus du sol, est fait d'environ 2 000 m² (plus d'une tonne) de toile enduite de polyester, spécialement fabriquée pour combiner transparence et résistance… L'objectif de transparence et de légèreté concrète nous a conduit à utiliser de nouveaux matériaux de façon novatrice. » La construction et le fonctionnement du pavillon ont coïncidé avec l'exposition de l'artiste allemande Thomas Demand (6 juin – 20 août 2006), dont une partie était exposée dans le pavillon.

*Standing out behind the much more traditional building of the Serpentine Gallery, the Pavilion had a presence akin to an unidentified flying object temporarily anchored in the Park.*

*Der hinter dem wesentlich traditionelleren Gebäude der Serpentine Gallery ins Auge fallende Pavillon verfügt über eine Präsenz, die der eines zeitweilig im Park gelandeten UFOs gleicht.*

*S'élevant derrière le bâtiment beaucoup plus traditionnel de la Serpentine Gallery, le Pavillon faisait penser à un objet volant non identifié venu s'arrimer temporairement dans le parc.*

*The Pavilion was conceived rather like a balloon, ready to hover up from its mooring next to the Serpentine—as seen in the sketches of Cecil Balmond, to the right.*

*Der Pavillon ist wie ein Ballon konzipiert, bereit, von seinem Ankerplatz an der Serpentine loszuschweben, wie es auf den Skizzen von Cecil Balmond rechts zu sehen ist.*

*Le pavillon a été conçu comme une sorte de ballon prêt à se détacher de son ancrage au bord de la Serpentine, comme le montrent les croquis de Cecil Balmond, à droite.*

*A view at nightfall makes the presence of the Pavilion even more ethereal than it was during the day, an idea confirmed by the lightness of the structure at its base.*

*Die nächtliche Ansicht lässt den Pavillon noch ätherischer erscheinen als bei Tag, eine von der Leichtigkeit des Unterbaus verstärkte Anmutung.*

*Cette vue à la tombée de la nuit rend la présence du Pavillon encore plus éthérée que pendant la journée, effet renforcé par la légèreté de la structure de sa base.*

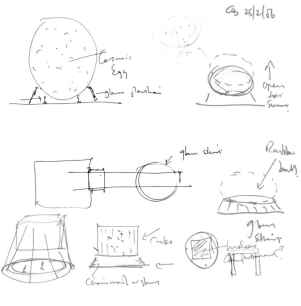

In the views on this page, the upper structure of the Pavilion floats free of its base, with the work of Thomas Demand lining its lower edge.

Auf den Abbildungen dieser Seite scheint der Oberbau des Pavillons, dessen unterer Rand von Werken Thomas Demands gesäumt ist, über dem Sockel zu schweben.

Sur cette page, la partie supérieure du Pavillon flotte, libérée de sa base. Une œuvre de Thomas Demand vient en doublage de sa partie inférieure.

# BÖGE LINDNER ARCHITEKTEN

*Böge Lindner Architekten*
*Brooktorkai 15*
*20457 Hamburg*
*Germany*

*Tel: +49 40 3250 660*
*Fax: +49 40 3250 6666*
*E-mail: info@boegelindner.de*
*Web: www.boegelindner.de*

*Practice Burning House*

Jürgen Böge was born in Bunsoh, Schleswig-Holstein, Germany, in 1950. He received his education in architecture at the Technical Universities of Braunschweig (1971), and Stuttgart (1973–77). He worked in the offices of Wolske + Erler in Hamburg (1978), before creating Büro Böge, Friedrich, Lindner in Hamburg (1981) and then **BÖGE LINDNER ARCHITEKTEN** in the same city in 1986. Ingeborg Lindner-Böge was born in Bremen, Germany, in 1951. She also studied architecture in Braunschweig (1970) and Stuttgart (1973–77), before working in the office of APB in Hamburg (1978) and becoming a founding partner of Böge, Friedrich, Lindner in Hamburg and then Böge Lindner Architekten. Their recent work includes various academic projects for the International University in Bremen amongst others. They completed the Central Fire Station in Gelsenkirchen (2000–05; only the Practice Burning House, a part of this project, is published here); the Ocean's End building in Hamburg (2001–05); and the Esplanade-Spielbank Building in Hamburg (2004–06).

Jürgen Böge wurde 1950 in Bunsoh, Schleswig-Holstein, geboren. Sein Architekturstudium absolvierte er an der Technischen Universität Braunschweig (1971) und der Universität Stuttgart (1973–77). Er war im Büro von Wolske + Erler in Hamburg tätig (1978), ehe er ebenfalls dort 1981 zuerst das Büro Böge, Friedrich, Lindner und dann **BÖGE LINDNER ARCHITEKTEN** gründete (1986). Ingeborg Lindner-Böge wurde 1951 in Bremen geboren. Sie studierte ebenfalls in Braunschweig (1970) und Stuttgart (1973–77) Architektur, ehe sie im Büro APB in Hamburg tätig war und dann Mitgründerin von Böge, Lindner, Friedrich und anschließend Böge Lindner Architekten in Hamburg wurde. Zu ihren neueren Bauten gehören verschiedene Projekte für Hochschulen, u. a. für die Internationale Universität in Bremen. Sie errichteten die zentrale Feuer- und Rettungswache in Gelsenkirchen (2000–05, von der hier nur ein Teil, das Brandübungshaus, publiziert ist), das Gebäude »Ocean's End« in Hamburg (2001–05) sowie das Casino Esplanade in Hamburg (2004–06).

Né à Bunsoh dans le Schleswig-Holstein, Allemagne, en 1950, Jürgen Böge a étudié l'architecture à l'Université Technique de Braunschweig (1971) et à celle de Stuttgart (1973–77). Il a travaillé dans les agences de Wolske + Erler à Hambourg (1978), avant de fonder Böge, Friedrich, Lindner en 1981, puis **BÖGE LINDNER ARCHITEKTEN**, toujours à Hambourg en 1986. Ingeborg Lindner-Böge, née à Brême en 1951, a également étudié l'architecture à Braunschweig (1970) et Stuttgart (1973–77) avant de travailler dans l'agence APB à Hambourg (1978) et de devenir associée fondatrice de Böge, Friedrich, Lindner, puis de Böge Lindner Architekten. Leurs projets récents comprennent diverses interventions dans le domaine universitaire, entre autres pour l'Université internationale de Brême. Ils ont récemment achevé le Centre de secours incendie de Gelsenkirchen (2000–05) dont seule la maison d'exercices d'incendie est publiée ici, et, à Hambourg, les immeubles Ocean's End (2001–05) et Esplanade-Spielbank (2004–06).

# PRACTICE BURNING HOUSE

*Central Fire and Rescue Station, Gelsenkirchen, Germany, 2004–05*

*Floor area: 281 m². Client: City of Gelsenkirchen. Cost: not disclosed.*
*Project Architect: Peter Lehmann*

Although its intentions are the very practical training of firemen, the *Brandübungshaus*, or Practice Burning House, was intended by the architects as a kind of "architectural icon" opposite the new Modernist fire station they designed in Gelsenkirchen. The Practice Burning House had to be able to resist fire for at least 90 minutes and to be water resistant both from the outside and the inside. Insulation was of no use in this instance, so the structure is an almost monolithic block of reinforced concrete colored red with ferrous oxide aggregates. Flush steel blinds on the windows accentuate an impression of curious impenetrability, despite the cosy pitched-roof building type. Because of the rapid cooling brought on by practice fires being put out by water, the concrete had to be protected in certain areas by a layer of Cor-ten steel. Mock-up furniture made of stainless steel is made to burn automatically with liquid petroleum gas during practice sessions that occur no less than 200 days a year. Although the structure is intended to resemble a real house inside, it contains a large technical support room in the center.

Obgleich es der praktischen Ausbildung von Feuerwehrleuten dient, planten die Architekten das Brandübungshaus als eine Art »architektonischer Ikone« gegenüber der ebenfalls von ihnen entworfenen, modernistischen neuen Feuerwache in Gelsenkirchen. Das Brandübungshaus muss wenigstens 90 Minuten lang einem Feuer standhalten können und von außen wie von innen wasserfest sein. Da in diesem Fall eine Isolierung nutzlos ist, ist der Bau ein fast monolithischer Block aus Stahlbeton, der durch Eisenoxidzuschläge seine rote Farbe erhielt. Ungeachtet des gemütlich wirkenden Satteldachs unterstreichen bündig abschließende Stahlblenden an den Fenstern den Eindruck einer eigenartigen Undurchdringlichkeit. Wenn Übungsfeuer mit Wasser gelöscht werden, kommt es zu einer raschen Abkühlung. Der Beton musste deshalb an bestimmten Stellen durch eine Schicht aus Cor-Ten-Stahl geschützt werden. Aus Edelstahl bestehende Möbelattrappen werden bei den Übungen, die an mindestens 200 Tagen im Jahr stattfinden, mittels flüssigen Petroleumgases automatisch zum Brennen gebracht. Obgleich der Bau im Inneren einem wirklichen Haus ähneln soll, enthält er im Zentrum einen großen, technischen Versorgungsraum.

Bien que sa fonction soit la formation pratique des pompiers, cette *Brandübungshaus* ou maison d'exercices d'incendie, a été voulue par les architectes comme une sorte « d'icône architecturale », face au nouveau Centre de secours incendie qu'ils ont conçu pour Gelsenkirchen. Elle doit pouvoir résister au feu (au moins 90 minutes) et à l'eau aussi bien à l'intérieur qu'à l'extérieur. L'isolation n'ayant en l'occurrence pas d'objet, la structure est pratiquement constituée d'un seul bloc monolithique en béton armé coloré en rouge à l'oxyde de fer. Des volets d'acier à fleur de fenêtres accentuent l'impression d'impénétrabilité malgré le type de construction choisi à toiture à double pente. Pour éviter les effets du refroidissement accéléré entraîné par les projections d'eau, le béton a été protégé dans certaines zones par des tôles en acier Cor-Ten. Le faux mobilier en acier inoxydable est mis à feu automatiquement par un gaz de pétrole liquide pendant les sessions d'entraînement qui ne se déroulent pas moins de 200 jours par an. Bien que la structure soit censée ressembler à une vraie maison, elle contient en partie centrale une importante salle technique.

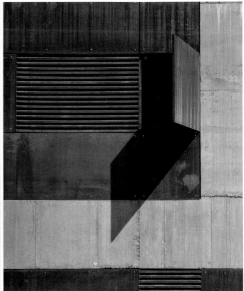

*The Practice Burning House is interesting because of its materials and configuration—based on a typical house, but also on the physical laws that govern fires.*

*Das Brandübungshaus ist wegen seiner Materialien und seiner Bauform interessant, die einerseits einem typischen Haus gleicht und andererseits auf den naturwissenschaftlichen Gesetzen basiert, nach denen Feuer ablaufen.*

*La maison d'exercices d'incendie est intéressante par ses matériaux et sa configuration classiques, mais aussi par son intégration des lois physiques qui ont trait au développement des incendies.*

*Made to resist intense heat, the house is also designed as a typical house might be, except that most of its elements are meant to resist fire.*

*Das Gebäude, das großer Hitze standhalten muss, ähnelt gleichwohl einem typischen Haus, außer dass die meisten Elemente feuerresistent sein müssen.*

*Construite pour résister à une chaleur intense, la maison est conçue comme une construction banale à la différence près que la plupart de ses constituants doivent résister au feu.*

Despite its strictly practical use, the Practice Burning House might be considered to have an "artistic" element—like a work of art that is meant to be burned again and again.

Trotz seines rein praktischen Zwecks kann man dem Brandübungshaus ein künstlerisches Element kaum absprechen – ähnlich einem Kunstwerk, das wieder und wieder verbrennen soll.

Strictement pratique dans sa fonction, ce petit centre de formation n'est pas sans revêtir un élément « artistique », celui d'une œuvre d'art qui serait faite pour être sans cesse brûlée.

# BOHLIN CYWINSKI JACKSON

Bohlin Cywinski Jackson
49 Geary Street, Suite 300
San Francisco, CA 94108
USA

Tel: +1 415 989 2100
Fax: +1 415 989 2101
E-mail: info_request@bcj.com
Web: www.bcj.com

**BOHLIN CYWINSKI JACKSON** was founded in 1965 by Peter Bohlin and Richard Powell in Wilkes-Barre, Pennsylvania. Peter Bohlin received a B.Arch degree from Rensselaer Polytechnic Institute (1959), and an M.Arch degree from Cranbrook Academy of Art (1961). Today the principals are Peter Bohlin, Bernard Cywinski, Jon Jackson, Dan Haden, Frank Grauman, William Loose, Randy Reid, Russell Roberts, Karl Backus, and Gregory Mottola. The firm has additional offices in Pittsburgh, Philadelphia, Seattle, and San Francisco. In 1994, the practice received the Architecture Firm Award from the American Institute of Architects and has received over 300 regional, national and international design awards. Significant work includes: Forest House (Cornwall, Connecticut, 1975); Software Engineering Institute (Pittsburgh, Pennsylvania, 1987); Pacific Rim Estate (Medina, Washington, 1997, joint venture with Cutler Anderson Architects); Headquarters for Pixar Animation Studios (Emeryville, California, 2001); Farrar Residence (Park City, Utah, 2000–05, published here); and Liberty Bell Center Independence National Historical Park (Philadelphia, Pennsylvania, 2003). Current work includes: Williams College Library and Faculty Buildings (Williamstown, Massachusetts); California Institute of Technology Chemistry Building (Pasadena, California); Trinity College Master Plan (Hartford, Connecticut); Peace Arch U.S. Port of Entry (Blaine, Washington); the prototype and a series of high-profile retail stores for Apple Computer (published here, various locations worldwide).

**BOHLIN CYWINSKI JACKSON** wurde 1965 von Peter Bohlin und Richard Powell in Wilkes-Barre, Pennsylvania, gegründet. Peter Bohlin erwarb 1959 einen B.Arch. am Rensselaer Polytechnic Institute und 1961 einen M.Arch. an der Cranbrook Academy of Art. Heute sind die Hauptmitarbeiter Peter Bohlin, Bernard Cywinski, Jon Jackson, Dan Haden, Frank Grauman, William Loose, Randy Reid, Russell Roberts, Karl Backus und Gregory Mottola. Das Büro verfügt über Zweigstellen in Philadelphia, Pittsburgh, Seattle und San Francisco. 1994 wurde das Büro vom American Institute of Architects mit dem Architecture Firm Award und insgesamt mit über 300 regionalen, nationalen und internationalen Designpreisen ausgezeichnet. Wichtige Bauwerke sind: Forest House (Cornwall, Connecticut, 1975), Software Engineering Institute (Pittsburgh, Pennsylvania, 1987), Pacific Rim Estate (Medina, Washington, 1997, Gemeinschaftsarbeit mit Cutler Anderson Architects), der Hauptsitz von Pixar Animation Studios (Emeryville, Kalifornien, 2001), Farrar Residence (Park City, Utah, 2000–05, hier publiziert) und Liberty Bell Center Independence National Historical Park (Philadelphia, Pennsylvania, 2003). Zu den laufenden Projekten gehören: Bibliothek und Fakultätsbauten des Williams College (Williamstown, Massachusetts), das Chemiegebäude des California Institute of Technology (Pasadena, Kalifornien), der Gesamtplan für das Trinity College (Hartford, Connecticut), Peace Arch U.S. Port of Entry (Blaine, Washington) sowie der Prototyp und eine Reihe hochwertiger Läden für Apple Computer (hier vorgestellt, mehrere Standort weltweit).

L'agence **BOHLIN CYWINSKI JACKSON** a été fondée en 1965 par Peter Bohlin et Richard Powell à Wilkes-Barre en Pennsylvanie. Peter Bohlin est diplomé du Rensselaer Polytechnic Institute (1959) et de la Cranbrook Academy of Art (1961). Les associés actuels sont Peter Bohlin, Bernard Cywinski, Jon Jackson, Dan Haden, Frank Grauman, William Loose, Randy Reid, Russell Roberts, Karl Backus et Gregory Mottola. L'agence possède des bureaux à Pittsburgh, Philadelphie, Seattle et San Francisco. En 1994, elle a reçu le prix de l'agence d'architecture de l'American Institute of Architects et, depuis, plus de trois cents distinctions régionales, nationales et internationales. Parmi ses réalisations les plus significatives : Forest House, Cornwall, Connecticut (1975) ; le Software Engineering Institute, Pittsburgh, Pennsylvanie (1987) ; le Pacific Rim Estate, Medina, Washington (1997) en coopération avec Cutler Anderson Architects ; le siège des Pixar Animation Studios, Emeryville, Californie (2001) ; Farrar Residence, Park City, Utah (2000–05) publiée ici et le Liberty Bell Center Independence National Historical Park, Philadelphia, Pennsylvanie (2003). Parmi ses réalisations récentes : la Williams College Library et les bâtiments des enseignants à Williamstown, Massachusetts ; le bâtiment de la chimie du California Institute of Technology à Pasadena, Californie ; le plan directeur de Trinity College à Hartford, Connecticut ; le Peace Arch U.S. Port of Entry à Blaine, Washington ; le prototype d'une série de magasins de ventes de prestige pour Apple Computer, publié ici et destiné au monde entier.

# FARRAR RESIDENCE

*Park City, Utah, USA, 2000–05*

*Floor area: 1115 m². Client: Dennis and Vicki Farrar.*
*Cost: not disclosed. Architects: Peter Bohlin, Gregory Mottola,*
*Karl Backus, George Bradley*

Located on a 5.26-hectare mountain site, this house is near the ski runs of Park City and is surrounded by forest. Visitors immediately discover a view of the Wasatch Valley as they enter the residence. The design consists of two rectangular volumes that intersect in the "public" areas of the house. The north-south box with its poured-in-place concrete base and steel structure contains the entry, kitchen, guest rooms, garage, pool, and a concrete, barrel-vault wine cellar. The indoor, steel-framed pool offers the owners the possibility of taking a swim even as they watch the snow fall outside. The east-west wing is a timber composition containing the living and dining areas. Douglas fir is used for the roof and ceiling, whereas cedar siding clads both exterior and interior surfaces. Large windows permit a close connection to the natural setting, while the use of thick concrete walls or the large, rough stone-clad chimney in the center of the living area recall the mineral strength of the mountain itself. Set on three levels, the house is both luxurious and well adapted to its setting, where winters are harsh. The contrast of materials, from concrete to steel and on to wood or stone, gives this house an agreeable complexity and an undeniable solidity.

Dieses von Wald umgebene Haus unweit der Skipisten von Park City steht auf einem 5,26 ha großen Grundstück in den Bergen. Beim Betreten des Hauses entdecken Besucher sofort die Aussicht auf das Wasatch Valley. Der Entwurf setzt sich aus zwei rechteckigen Baukörpern zusammen, die sich in den »öffentlichen« Bereichen des Hauses durchdringen. Der in Nord-Süd-Richtung stehende Bauteil mit einem vor Ort gegossenen Betonfundament und einer Stahlkonstruktion enthält Eingang, Küche, Gästezimmer, Garage, Pool und einen Weinkeller mit einem Tonnengewölbe aus Beton. Dank des im Hausinneren untergebrachten Pools können die Bewohner schwimmen, während es draußen schneit. In dem in ost-westlicher Richtung liegenden Flügel, einem Holzbau, sind die Wohn- und Essbereiche untergebracht. Für Dach und Decken wurde das Holz der Douglasfichte verwendet, während die Außen- und Innenwände mit Zedernholz verschalt sind. Große Fensteröffnungen ermöglichen eine enge Verbindung zur umgebenden Landschaft, dieweil die Präsenz der dicken Betonwände und des großen, mit Naturstein verkleideten Kamins im Zentrum des Wohnbereichs an die mineralische Qualität des Berges erinnert. Das sich auf drei Ebenen verteilende Haus ist sowohl luxuriös als auch gut an seine Umgebung mit ihren harten Wintern angepasst. Die kontrastierenden Materialien, von Beton über Stahl bis zu Holz und Stein, verleihen dem Haus eine sympathische Vielschichtigkeit und eindeutige Solidität.

Implantée sur un terrain de 5,26 hectares, cette maison en forêt se trouve près des pistes de ski de Park City. Les visiteurs découvrent à leur entrée une vue spectaculaire sur la Wasatch Valley. Le plan consiste en deux volumes rectangulaires à l'intersection desquels se trouve la zone « publique » de la maison. La boîte nord-sud, construite sur une base de béton coulé sur place et à structure en acier, contient l'entrée, la cuisine, les chambres d'amis, le garage, une piscine et une cave à vin à voûte en berceau de béton. La piscine intérieure à structure d'acier offre aux occupants la possibilité de se baigner tout en regardant la neige tomber au-dehors. L'aile est-ouest, en bois, contient le séjour et l'aire des repas. La toiture et les plafonds sont en pin de Douglas et les plans verticaux extérieurs et intérieurs sont doublés de cèdre. De vastes fenêtres assurent un lien étroit avec le cadre naturel, tandis qu'un des murs épais en béton et une cheminée habillée de pierre brute au centre du séjour rappellent la puissante présence minérale de la montagne. Cette maison sur trois niveaux est à la fois luxueuse et bien adaptée à cette région aux hivers rigoureux. Le contraste entre les matériaux – béton, acier, bois et pierre – apporte une agréable complexité et un sentiment indéniable de solidité.

The Farrar Residence sits on a slope and is made to blend into its natural setting, both when seen from the exterior and when its residents look out onto its Utah site.

Implantée à flanc de colline dans l'Utah, la résidence Farrar a été conçue pour se fondre dans son cadre naturel, aussi bien de l'extérieur, que pour ses occupants regardant vers l'extérieur.

Die Farrar Residence steht an einem Hang und soll sich in seine natürliche Umgebung einfügen, und zwar sowohl von außen gesehen als auch von innen, wenn seine Bewohner in die Landschaft von Utah hinausschauen.

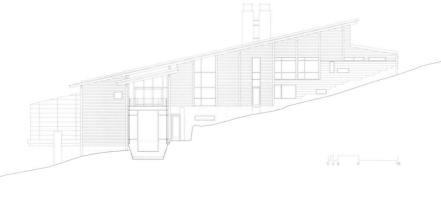

0 2 4      8              16

Even the indoor swimming pool seen above and right is designed so that the end facing the forest opens out to the trees. The dining room, left, is similarly open to the natural environment.

Sogar das oben und rechts abgebildete eingebaute Schwimmbad ist so gestaltet, dass seine dem Wald zugewandte Seite den Blick auf die Bäume ermöglicht. Das Esszimmer links ist ebenfalls zur natürlichen Umgebung geöffnet.

La piscine intérieure (ci-dessus et à droite) est conçue de telle façon que son extrémité donne sur les arbres. De même, la salle à manger, à gauche, s'ouvre sur la nature.

Long and narrow, the pool reflects the trees outside in the view below. Surrounded by glass, it gives the impression that users are outdoors.

In der Ansicht oben spiegeln sich die Bäume in dem langen, schmalen Wasserbecken. Da es ganz von Glas umgeben ist, entsteht der Eindruck, die Nutzer befänden sich im Freien.

La longue et étroite piscine reflète les arbres, ci-dessous. Clôturée de verre, elle donne à ses utilisateurs l'impression d'être déjà dehors.

The use of wood, inside and outside the house, emphasizes its rapport with the forest, and yet it offers a far greater degree of luxury than most mountain houses.

Die Verwendung von Holz im Innen- und Außenbereich unterstreicht die enge Beziehung zum Wald und doch bietet das Haus weit größeren Komfort als die meisten Berghütten.

L'utilisation du bois, à l'intérieur comme à l'extérieur, renforce le lien avec la forêt tout en offrant un degré de luxe supérieur à celui de beaucoup de maisons de montagne.

# APPLE STORE FIFTH AVENUE

*New York, New York, USA, 2003–06*

*Store area: 1858 m². Client: Apple Computer Inc. Size of cube: 9.75 m per side (length, width, height).*
*Cost: not disclosed. Architects: Peter Bohlin, Karl Backus, Jon Jackson.*
*Project Managers: Rosa Sheng, Nick Anderson.*
*Developer's Architect for the General Motors Building: Dan Shannon, Moed de Armas & Shannon*

Located at 767 Fifth Avenue between 58th and 59th Streets on the plaza in front of the former General Motors Building, the new Apple Store is certainly visible, a fact emphasized by its 24-hour-a-day operations. Although the actual retail space is located below grade, the most spectacular element of the design is the the entrance volume. "Entirely free of structural steel," according to the architects, "the glass cube is self-supporting through the integration of a taut glass skin, vertical glass fins and a grid of glass beams. Stainless-steel fittings are used to interlock all glass components into one assembly. Functioning as an entry, this precise glass cube floats on the plaza with the glow of the store emanating from below." The elegant design of this entrance, together with that of the shopping area, blends in a seamless manner with Apple's own careful attention to the design of its products. The "Genius Bar," "iPod Bar" and "Studio Bar" provide "hands-on technical support and creative learning." Gray limestone floors and bead-blasted stainless-steel wall panels are combined with a custom ceiling system comprising narrow bands of perforated stainless-steel plate and tightly stretched white fabric. The idea of a pure geometric form, in this instance a cube, with a spiral staircase encircling a circular elevator leading down to public spaces, may seem familiar to those who have visited I. M. Pei's Louvre Pyramid in Paris. Bohlin Cywinski Jackson worked closely with Dan Shannon of the New York firm Moed de Armas & Shannon on the redesign of the plaza and the integration of the store with its overall design. As Peter Bohlin explains his relationship with the client, "We have worked closely with Steve Jobs since the inception of the high-profile store design program. One of the great things about Steve and the entire team at Apple is their high level of involvement in all aspects of design for every store and their commitment to the highest standards of design. This collaboration has achieved extraordinary results."

Der neue Apple Store, ein optisch überaus präsentes und zudem 24 Stunden am Tag geöffnetes Ladengeschäft, befindet sich an der Fifth Avenue 767, zwischen 58th und 59th Street auf der Plaza vor dem ehemaligen General-Motors-Gebäude. Das spektakulärste Element des Entwurfs ist der Eingangsbereich, während die eigentliche Einkaufsfläche im Souterrain liegt. Der den Architekten zufolge »gänzlich ohne Baustahl« errichtete »gläserne Kubus ist selbsttragend durch eine straff gespannte Glashaut, vertikale Glasrippen und ein Netz gläserner Unterzüge. Um sämtliche Glaskomponenten zu einer Einheit zu verzahnen, wurden Beschläge aus Edelstahl verwendet. Dieser als Eingang dienende präzise Glaskubus scheint über der Plaza zu schweben und wird von unten durch den Laden beleuchtet.« Dieser elegant gestaltete Eingang passt in Einklang mit der hochwertigen Einkaufsgegend nahtlos zu Apples sorgfältigem Produktdesign. »Genius Bar«, »iPod Bar« und »Studio Bar« bieten »praktische technische Unterstützung und kreatives Lernen«. Böden aus grauem Kalkstein und perlengestrahlte Edelstahlwandplatten werden kombiniert mit einem speziell angefertigten Deckensystem aus schmalen Bändern aus perforiertem Edelstahlblech und straff gespanntem weißem Gewebe. Denjenigen, die I. M. Peis Pyramide im Louvre kennen, wird die Idee der reinen geometrischen Form, in diesem Fall eines Kubus, mit einer Wendeltreppe um einen kreisrunden Aufzug, der in unterirdische öffentliche Bereiche führt, bekannt vorkommen. Bohlin Cywinski Jackson arbeiteten bei der Neugestaltung der Plaza und der Integration des Ladens in das Gesamtdesign eng mit Dan Shannon von der New Yorker Firma Moed de Armas & Shannon zusammen. Peter Bohlin erklärt seine Beziehung zum Auftraggeber: »Seit Beginn des viel beachteten Ladengestaltungsprogramms arbeiten wir eng mit Steve Jobs zusammen. Großartig an Steve und dem gesamten Apple-Team ist ihre Beteiligung an sämtlichen Aspekten des Designs für jeden Laden und ihre Verpflichtung auf höchste Designqualität. Diese Zusammenarbeit hat zu großartigen Ergebnissen geführt.«

Situé au 767 de la Cinquième Avenue entre les 58th et 59th Streets sur la *plaza* devant l'ancien immeuble General Motors, le nouveau magasin Apple est hautement visible et de plus ouvert 24 heures sur 24. Bien que l'espace de vente se trouve en réalité au sous-sol, la partie la plus spectaculaire de ce projet est le volume de l'entrée. «Entièrement libéré de tout élément structurel en acier, expliquent les architectes, le cube de verre est autoporteur grâce à une conception intégrant une peau de verre tendue, des ailettes de verre verticales et une trame de poutrelles de verre. Des pièces d'assemblage en acier inoxydable rigidifient l'ensemble de la composition structurelle. Servant d'entrée, ce cube de verre, au dessin très précis, flotte au-dessus de la *plaza,* porté par la lumière qui irradie du magasin en sous-sol. » L'élégant dessin de cette entrée ainsi que celui de l'espace de vente se marie avec aisance avec le design des produits de la marque. Le *Genius Bar*, l'*iPod Bar*, et un *Studio Bar* offrent une assistance technique et une formation créative concrètes. Des sols en calcaire gris et des panneaux muraux en acier inoxydable traité par projection de billes de verre viennent en contrepoint d'un système de plafond original en étroits bandeaux de tôle d'acier inox et de tissu blanc étiré. L'idée de forme géométrique pure, ici un cube, et d'un escalier en spirale encerclant un ascenseur circulaire conduisant vers les espaces de vente pourra sembler familier aux visiteurs de la Pyramide du Louvre d'I. M. Pei à Paris. Bohlin Cywinski Jackson ont travaillé en étroite collaboration avec Dan Shannon de l'agence new-yorkaise Armas & Shannon sur la rénovation de la *plaza* et l'intégration du magasin dans leurs plans. Peter Bohlin présente ainsi sa relation avec son client : «Nous avons travaillé en étroite collaboration avec Steve Jobs depuis le départ de ce projet. L'un des grands avantages de travailler avec Steve et toute l'équipe d'Apple réside dans leur haut niveau d'implication sur tous les aspects de la conception de chaque magasin, et leur souscription au plus hauts critères de création. Ce partenariat a donné des résultats extraordinaires. »

*Located on Fifth Avenue in Manhattan, the Apple Store appears to be an empty glass cube with only the firm's white symbol hanging inside. In fact, the store itself is below grade.*

*Der Apple Store an der Fifth Avenue in Manhattan erscheint als leerer Glaskubus, in dem sich einzig das Firmenlogo befindet. Tatsächlich liegt der Laden selbst unter der Erde.*

*L'Apple Store de Manhattan se présente sous forme d'un cube de verre évidé sur lequel seul se détache le logotype de la marque. Le magasin lui-même est en sous-sol.*

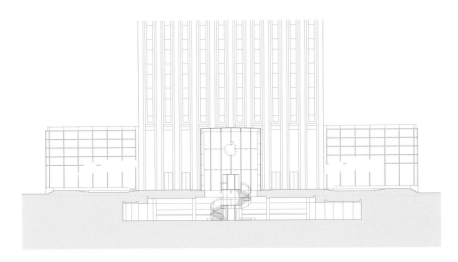

Located on the plaza in front of the former General Motors Building, the Apple store is at once very visible and yet somehow ethereal given its extremely light supporting structure and overall glass conception.

Der auf der Plaza vor dem früheren General Motors Building stehende Apple Store ist zugleich sichtbar und doch irgendwie ätherisch dank seiner extrem leichten Glasbauweise.

Sur une place, devant l'ancien immeuble de General Motors, l'Apple Store est à la fois très visible et éthéré, tant est discrète la structure qui soutient ses parois de verre.

*A spiral staircase and an elevator lead down from the street level to the generous underground spaces of the shop.*

*Von der Straßenebene führen eine Wendeltreppe und ein Lift in die großzügig bemessenen unterirdischen Ladenräume hinunter.*

*Un escalier en spirale et un ascenseur conduisent aux généreux volumes souterrains du magasin.*

Above, the spiral staircase encloses a glass, cylindrical elevator that takes visitors down to the level where the Macintosh computers and accessories are on display.

Die Wendeltreppe umschließt den runden, verglasten Lift, der die Besucher auf die Ebene hinunter bringt, auf der die Macintosh-Computer und ihr Zubehör ausgestellt sind.

L'escalier en spirale entoure un ascenseur cylindrique en verre qui conduit les visiteurs au niveau où sont exposés les ordinateurs et les accessoires Apple.

The very elegant and light spiral staircase as seen from the lower level and from below, looking up to the neighboring skyscrapers (below right).

Ansicht der äußerst eleganten, leichten Wendeltreppe auf der unteren Ebene und der Blick von unten auf die benachbarten Hochhäuser (unten rechts).

Léger et très élégant, l'escalier en spirale, vu du niveau inférieur, en regardant vers les gratte-ciel qui entourent la place (en bas à droite).

 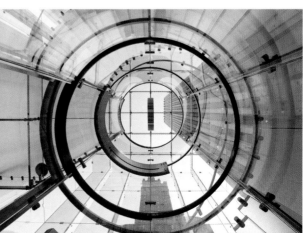

# ALDO CELORIA

*celoria Architects sagl*
*Via delle Fornaci 8c*
*6828 Balerna*
*Switzerland*

*Tel: +41 91 682 4388*
*Fax: +41 91 682 4390*
*E-mail: info@celoria.ch*
*Web: www.celoria.ch*

**ALDO CELORIA** was born in 1969 in Mendrisio, Switzerland. In 1992 he was granted a Diploma in Industrial Design at the Scuola Politecnica di Design in Milan. From 1993 to 1995 he worked in collaboration with several design offices in Ticino, Switzerland. In 1997–98 he lived in Buenos Aires (Argentina), where he worked in the office of Clorindo Testa. In 2002 he graduated in architecture from the Accademia di Architettura di Mendrisio, where he studied under Mario Botta, Peter Zumthor and Kenneth Frampton. In the same year he opened his own office in Balerna, where he undertakes architecture, urban-design and theoretical-research projects. His partner **FEDERICA GIOVANNINI** was born in Como, Italy, in 1978. She graduated in 2002 from the Accademia di Architettura di Mendrisio, where she worked under Aurelio Galfetti. In 2003–05 she participated in the research on the Panos Koulermos archive, which led to an exhibition and a monograph by Kenneth Frampton. In 2004 she received a grant from the FNSNF (Swiss National Science Foundation) for research on "The debate on modern architecture in Italian and Swiss publishing between 1945–60." In 2004 Celoria won two competitions—one for a Balerna school extension, and the second for the urban design of a square in Tenero near Locarno. The same year he completed the Travella House (Castel San Pietro, Ticino, Switzerland) on a site almost adjacent to Trapanese House, published here.

**ALDO CELORIA** kam 1969 in Mendrisio, Schweiz, zur Welt. 1992 erwarb er ein Diplom in Industriedesign an der Scuola Politecnica di Design in Mailand. Von 1993 bis 1995 arbeitete er mit verschiedenen Designbüros im Tessin zusammen. 1997 bis 1998 lebte er in Buenos Aires (Argentinien), wo er im Büro von Clorindo Testa tätig war. 2002 schloss er sein Architekturstudium an der Accademia di Architettura di Mendrisio ab, wo er bei Mario Botta, Peter Zumthor und Kenneth Frampton studiert hatte. Im selben Jahr eröffnete er sein eigenes Büro in Balerna, in dem er sich mit Architektur, Stadtplanung und theoretischer Forschung befasst. Seine Partnerin **FEDERICA GIOVANNINI** wurde 1978 in Como, Italien, geboren. Auch sie schloss ihre Architekturausbildung 2002 an der Accademia di Architettura di Mendrisio ab, wo sie mit Aurelio Galfetti gearbeitet hatte. 2003 bis 2005 war sie an der Forschung zum Panos-Koulermos-Archiv beteiligt, die zu einer Ausstellung und einer Monografie von Kenneth Frampton führte. 2002 erhielt sie ein Stipendium des Schweizerischen Nationalfonds zur Förderung der wissenschaftlichen Forschung (FNSNF) zur Bearbeitung der Thematik »Die Debatte über die moderne Architektur in italienischen und schweizerischen Veröffentlichungen zwischen 1945 und 1960«. 2004 konnte Celoria zwei Wettbewerbe für sich entscheiden – einen für die Erweiterung einer Schule in Balerna, den zweiten für die Gestaltung einer Platzanlage in Tenero bei Locarno. Im gleichen Jahr stellte er die Casa Travella in Castel San Pietro im Tessin auf einem fast an die hier vorgestellte Casa Trapanese angrenzenden Grundstück fertig.

Né en 1969 à Mendrisio, Suisse, **ALDO CELORIA** est diplômé de design industriel de la Scuola Politecnica di Design de Milan en 1992. De 1993 à 1995, il collabore à plusieurs agences de design tessinois (Suisse). En 1997–98, il vit à Buenos Aires (Argentine) où il travaille dans l'agence de Clorindo Testa. En 2002, il est diplômé en architecture de l'Accademia di Architettura di Mendrisio, où il a étudié sous la direction de Mario Botta, Peter Zumthor et Kenneth Frampton. La même année, il ouvre à Balerna son agence d'architecture, d'urbanisme et de recherche théorique. Son associée **FEDERICA GIOVANNINI** est née à Côme (Italie) en 1978. Elle sort diplômée en 2002 de l'Accademia di Architettura di Mendrisio où elle avait étudié sous la direction d'Aurelio Galfetti. En 2003–05, elle participe à une recherche sur les archives de Panos Koulermos qui débouche sur une exposition et une monographie de Kenneth Frampton. En 2004, elle reçoit une bourse de recherche de la FNSNF (Fonds national suisse pour la recherche scientifique) sur « Le débat sur l'architecture moderne dans l'édition suisse et italienne de 1945 à 1960 ». En 2004, Celoria remporte deux concours pour une extension d'école à Balerna et les plans d'une place à Tenero, près de Locarno. La même année, il achève la maison Travella (Castel San Pietro, Suisse) sur un terrain presque adjacent à celui de la maison Trapanese publiée ici.

# TRAPANESE HOUSE

*Castel San Pietro, Ticino, Switzerland, 2004–05*

*Floor area: 318 m². Client: Giovanni and Barbara Trapanese.*
*Cost: €525 128*

Built at the opposite end of the same lot used for his Travella House in Castel San Pietro, the Trapanese House is Aldo Celoria's second completed project. With an overall floor area of 318 square meters (106 m² per floor), it has certain similarities with the earlier residence. The garage is also located on the lower, street level and the floors above have the same height as those of the Travella House. As Celoria explains, "The plan and the section of the house were associated with the idea of a 'chromosome' intended as a double intersection: common spaces with private spaces. The stairs are in the center, creating a hinge of rotation from which all the different areas are organized on the different levels. This double-height void associated with the stairway also connects the earth with the sky." Rather than the glass and copper used in his first project, Celoria opts here for cladding the house entirely with polycarbonate slabs. This surface permits a good deal of diffused natural light to penetrate the interior. As he did in the Travella House, where the snaking interior concrete wall supports the entire structure, Celoria used an unusual structural idea here. He explains, "The structural idea is that the perimeter of the upper floor works as a suspended Vierendeel beam. The forces run down to the ground through the four asymmetrically aligned walls. The beam is also displaced in section according to the different room levels. The windows pursue this structural idea. The voids mirror the structural function of the beam." A Vierendeel frame, invented by the Belgian engineer and writer Arthur Vierendeel (1852–1940), has rigid upper and lower elements connected by vertical beams.

Aldo Celorias zweites fertiggestelltes Projekt befindet sich am gegenüberliegenden Ende des Grundstücks in Castel San Pietro, auf dem seine Casa Travella steht. Mit einer Gesamtfläche von 318 m² (106 m² pro Geschoss) weist es einige Ähnlichkeit mit dem früheren Wohnhaus auf. Auch hier liegt die Garage auf der unteren Ebene auf Straßenhöhe und die darüber liegenden Geschosse haben die gleiche Höhe wie die der Casa Travella. Celoria erläutert: »Grundriss und Schnitt des Hauses standen mit der Vorstellung eines als doppelte Kreuzung gedachten ›Chromosoms‹ in Verbindung: Gemeinschaftsräume mit Privaträumen. Die Treppen befinden sich im Zentrum und bilden ein Drehgelenk, um das sich die verschiedenen Bereiche auf den unterschiedlichen Ebenen gruppieren. Diese im Zusammenhang mit der Treppe entstandene, doppelgeschossige Leerstelle verbindet darüber hinaus die Erde mit dem Himmel.« Anstelle von Glas und Kupfer, die er bei seinem ersten Haus verwendete, entschied sich Celoria hier dafür, das Haus vollständig mit Polycarbonatplatten zu verkleiden. Diese Oberfläche lässt ziemlich viel diffuses Tageslicht ins Innere eindringen. Genauso wie bei der Casa Travella, wo die gewundene Innenwand aus Beton den gesamten Bau trägt, griff Celoria auch hier auf einen ungewöhnlichen konstruktiven Einfall zurück. Er erklärt: »Die konstruktive Idee ist, dass der Umkreis des Obergeschosses als hängender Vierendeelträger fungiert. Die Kräfte werden durch die vier asymmetrisch stehenden Wände auf den Boden abgeleitet. Der Träger wird darüber hinaus den verschiedenen Raumebenen entsprechend abschnittsweise versetzt. Die Fenster führen diesen konstruktiven Gedanken fort. Die Leerstellen spiegeln die konstruktive Funktion des Trägers.« Der von dem belgischen Ingenieur und Autor Arthur Vierendeel (1852–1940) erfundene Vierendeelträger zeichnet sich durch feststehende obere und untere Elemente aus, die durch vertikale Träger verbunden sind.

Construite à Castel San Pietro à l'extrémité opposée de la parcelle sur laquelle se trouve déjà la maison Travella, avec laquelle elle partage certaines similarités, cette maison de 318 m² (106 m² par niveau) est le second projet réalisé par Aldo Celoria. Son garage, implanté au niveau inférieur, celui de la rue, et les autres niveaux sont de la même hauteur. Comme l'explique l'architecte : « Le plan et la coupe viennent d'une image de « chromosome » en double intersection : espaces communs et espaces privés. L'escalier, positionné au centre, crée une charnière de rotation à partir de laquelle les diverses zones s'organisent sur différents niveaux. Ce vide sur double hauteur généré par l'escalier connecte la terre au ciel. » À la place du verre et du cuivre retenus pour le premier projet, Celoria a opté pour un habillage entièrement en plaques de polycarbonate ce qui permet la pénétration d'une abondante lumière naturelle diffuse à l'intérieur. Comme pour la maison Travella, où un mur en béton sinueux constitue la structure, Celoria a trouvé une solution originale : « L'idée structurelle est que le périmètre de l'étage supérieur fonctionne comme une poutre Vierendeel suspendue. Les forces sont dirigées vers le sol par quatre murs alignés asymétriquement. La poutre est également décalée en section en fonction des niveaux différents des pièces. Les fenêtres reprennent la même idée structurelle. Les vides rappellent la fonction de la poutre. » Ce type de poutre inventé par l'ingénieur et auteur belge Arthur Vierendeel (1852–1940) se caractérise par des membres supérieurs et inférieurs rigides réunis par des poutres verticales.

Set in a vineyard-covered hill, the house is due to have two other houses designed by Aldo Celoria built next to it in the near future. Its polycarbonate façades will make it stand out from the neighborhood in any case.

Neben dem auf einem von Weinstöcken bewachsenen Hügel stehenden Haus werden in Kürze zwei weitere von Aldo Celoria entworfene Häuser entstehen. In jedem Fall wird das Haus sich durch seine Polycarbonatfassade von der Umgebung abheben.

Édifiée sur une colline couverte de vigne, la maison devrait bientôt s'accompagner de deux voisines, également conçues par Aldo Celoria. Ses façades en polycarbonate la distinguent de son voisinage.

*The house seems to sit lightly on the ground, although it is in fact built over its own garage. The façade changes with the seasons.*

*Obwohl das Haus über der Garage errichtet wurde, scheint es doch nicht auf dem Boden zu lasten. Die Fassade verändert sich mit den Lichtverhältnissen.*

*La maison semble à peine s'appuyer sur le sol. Sa façade en plastique se modifie au gré des variations de la lumière et des saisons.*

The interior with its kitchen is carefully thought out, with nearly open façades.

Das Innere des Hauses mit der Küche ist passend zu den nahezu offenen Fassaden genau durchdacht.

L'intérieur, dont la cuisine sur l'arrière, a été soigneusement aménagé en fonction des façades ouvertes.

Red concrete floors on the lower level give way to parquet in the bathroom above.

An die Stelle der roten Betonböden der unteren Ebene tritt oben im Badezimmer Parkett.

Les sols en béton rouge du rez-de-chaussée laissent place à l'étage à un parquet comme dans la salle de bains.

Concrete stairs leading from the ground floor up to the roof take on an architectonic presence in the hands of Aldo Celoria.

Die Betontreppen, die vom Erdgeschoss nach oben aufs Dach führen, gewinnen in den Händen Aldo Celorias architektonische Präsenz.

Dessinés par Aldo Celoria, les escaliers en béton qui mènent respectivement du rez-de-chaussée à l'étage et de celui-ci au toit prennent une présence quasi architectonique.

# DOUG CHIANG

*Doug Chiang
P. O. Box 151617
San Rafael, CA 94915
USA*

*E-mail: doug@dchiang.com
Web: www.dchiang.com*

**DOUG CHIANG** was born in 1962 in Taipei, Taiwan. He studied Film at UCLA, and Industrial Design at the Center of Creative Studies, College of Art and Design. Chiang began work as a stop motion animator on the *Pee Wee's Playhouse* television series. He became a commercial director and designer for Rhythm and Hues, Digital Productions, and Robert Abel and Associates. In 1989, he joined Industrial Light and Magic, where he became the Creative Director in 1993. During this time, he worked as Visual Effects Art Director for films including *Ghost*, *The Doors*, *Terminator 2*, *Death Becomes Her*, *Forrest Gump*, *Jumanji*, and *The Mask*. He has earned both an Academy Award and a British Academy Award for *Death Becomes Her*, and another British Academy Award for *Forrest Gump*. Chiang left ILM in 1995 to serve as Design Director for Lucasfilm Ltd. on *Star Wars Episode I, The Phantom Menace*, and *Episode II, Attack of the Clones*. In 2002, he served as Production Designer for Robert Zemeckis's *The Polar Express*. His book *Robota* was published by Chronicle Books in 2003 (see images published here) and he is currently collaborating with Sony Picture Imageworks to develop a video game based on the film. Chiang is currently Production Designer for Zemeckis's *Beowulf*, to be released in 2007. In addition, he also served as Art Director for *Monster House* and Concept Designer for Steven Spielberg's *War of the Worlds*.

**DOUG CHIANG** wurde 1962 in Taipeh, Taiwan, geboren. Er studierte an der UCLA Filmwissenschaft und Industriedesign am Center of Creative Studies, College of Art and Design. Chiang begann seine berufliche Laufbahn als Stop Motion Animator bei der Fernsehserie »Pee Wee's Playhouse«. Für Rhythm and Hues, Digital Productions und Robert Abel and Associates arbeitete er kommerziell als Regisseur und Designer. 1989 fing er bei Industrial Light and Magic (ILM) an, wo er 1993 Creative Director wurde. Während dieser Zeit war er als Art Director für visuelle Effekte bei Filmprojekten, darunter »Ghost«, »The Doors«, »Terminator 2«, »Death Becomes Her«, »Forrest Gump«, »Jumanji« und »The Mask«, tätig. Für »Death Becomes Her« wurde er sowohl mit einem Academy Award (Oscar) als auch einem British Academy Award ausgezeichnet; für »Forrest Gump« erhielt er einen weiteren British Academy Award. 1995 verließ Chiang ILM, um bei Lucasfilm Ltd. als Design Director bei »Star Wars Episode I, The Phantom Menace« und »Episode II, Attack of the Clones« zu arbeiten. 2002 wirkte er bei Robert Zemeckis' »Polar Express« als Production Designer mit. Bei Chronicle Books erschien 2003 sein Buch *Robota* (vgl. die hier publizierten Abbildungen); gegenwärtig arbeitet er mit Sony Picture Imageworks an der Entwicklung eines auf der Verfilmung basierenden Videospiels. Außerdem fungiert er als Production Designer bei Robert Zemeckis' für 2007 angekündigtem Film »Beowulf«. Darüber hinaus war er auch als Art Director für »Monster House« zuständig und als Concept Designer für Steven Spielbergs »War of the Worlds«.

**DOUG CHIANG**, né à Taipeh (Taiwan) en 1962, étudie le cinéma à UCLA et le design industriel au Center of Creative Studies du College of Art and Design. Il commence sa carrière comme dessinateur pour dessins animés dans la série télévisée *Pee Wee's Playhouse*, puis devient directeur commercial et designer pour Rhythm and Hues, Digital Productions et Robert Abel and Associates. En 1989, il rejoint Industrial Light and Magic, dont il devient directeur de la création en 1993. Pendant cette période, il est directeur artistique pour les effets visuels de films comme *Ghost, The Doors, Terminator 2, La Mort vous va si bien, Forrest Grump, Jumanji et Le Masque*. Il a remporté un Academy Award et un British Academy Award pour *La Mort vous va si bien* ainsi qu'un British Academy Award *pour Forrest Grump*. Il quitte ILM en 1995 pour devenir directeur de conception pour Lucasfilm Ltd. sur *Star Wars Episode I, La Menace fantôme, Episode II et L'Attaque des clones*. En 2002, il est designer de production pour *Le Pôle Express* de Robert Zemecki. Son livre *Robota* est publié en 2003 par Chronicle Books (voir les images reproduites ici) et il collabore actuellement avec Sony Picture Imageworks au développement d'un jeu vidéo d'après le film qui en a été tiré. Il est actuellement designer de production pour le *Beowulf* de Zemecki, diffusé en 2007. Par ailleurs, il a été directeur artistique de *Monster House* et designer de concept pour *La Guerre des mondes*, le film de Steven Spielberg.

# ROBOTA

*2002*

Doug Chiang wrote his own commentary for these images, destined to appear in *Architecture Now*, volume 5: "As a film Production Designer, I strive to suspend disbelief and inspire awe and amusement with my designs. Whether it's designing castles for *Beowulf* or an imaginary North Pole for the *Polar Express* or the futuristic City States of *Star Wars*, the designs are often gestures, suggestions of alternative realms that exist only for the camera. Nevertheless, they need to be visually plausible in order to convince the viewer it exists when in fact it doesn't. I'm not a trained architect even though the sets and designs I build for films require some of the same sensibilities, the biggest difference being that I'm not restricted by reality or physics or materials!"

Doug Chiang schrieb für *Architecture Now*, Band 5, einen eigenen Kommentar zu diesen Bildern: »Als Production Designer beim Film bemühe ich mich mit meinen Entwürfen, Zweifel zu unterdrücken und Ehrfurcht und Vergnügen zu erzeugen. Ob es um die Schlösser bei ›Beowulf‹, einen imaginären Nordpol für ›Polar Express‹ oder um futuristische Stadtstaaten in ›Star Wars‹ geht – oft sind die Entwürfe Gesten und Andeutungen von anderen Welten, die nur für die Kamera existieren. Trotzdem müssen sie visuell nachvollziehbar sein, um den Betrachter davon zu überzeugen, dass sie existieren, auch wenn sie es tatsächlich nicht tun. Ich bin kein ausgebildeter Architekt, aber die Entwürfe und Sets, die ich für Filme baue, erfordern dasselbe Empfindungsvermögen. Der größte Unterschied ist, dass ich weder durch die Realität, noch durch die Physik oder Materialien beschränkt bin.«

Doug Chiang a rédigé ses propres commentaires sur les images sélectionnées pour *Architecture Now 5*. « Designer de production pour le cinéma, je m'efforce à travers mes dessins de faire oublier ce qui est incroyable et d'inspirer le respect et l'amusement. Que ce soit dans les châteaux pour *Beowulf*, le pôle Nord imaginaire de *Pôle Express* ou les cité-états futuristes de *Star Wars*, ces dessins sont souvent des gestes, des suggestions de domaines alternatifs qui n'existent que pour la caméra. Néanmoins, ils doivent être visuellement plausibles pour convaincre le spectateur qu'ils existent alors qu'ils n'existent pas en fait. Je ne suis pas architecte de formation, même si les décors et projets que j'élabore pour les films réclament une sensibilité de même nature, la très grande différence étant que je ne suis pas limité par la réalité, la physique ou les matériaux. »

*Chiang's images of "Decay City" above are inspired by the Cambodian temple of Ta Phrom. To the right, his skyscrapers rise up out of the sea. "This is my homage to Hugh Ferris," says Chiang.*

*Chiangs Bilder von »Decay City«, oben, sind vom kambodschanischen Tempel Ta Phrom inspiriert. Seine schlanken Hochhäuser erheben sich direkt aus dem Meer. »Dies ist meine Hommage an Hugh Ferris«, sagt Chiang.*

*Les images de Chiang et sa « Decay City » sont inspirées du temple cambodgien de Ta Phrom. À droite, ses gratte-ciel acérés surgissent tout droit de la mer. « C'est mon hommage à Hugh Ferris », précise Chiang.*

To the left, "Kantuur City." "In the book Robota," says Chiang, "this city is the home of the robots. Built on a natural magnetic rock formation, it floats over the center of large ocean sink holes, and I imagined this city to be a mix of architectural styles, but mostly Moorish influence. I like the eclectic look of Venice and thought this city would be modeled like a futuristic merchant city."

Links: »Kantuur City«. »In dem Buch Robota wohnen in dieser Stadt die Roboter. Auf einer von Natur aus magnetischen Felsformation erbaut, schwebt sie über der Mitte großer Senkgruben im Ozean. Ich stellte mir diese Stadt als Mischung von Architekturstilen vor, aber überwiegend maurisch geprägt. Ich mag das eklektische Aussehen von Venedig und dachte, diese Stadt würde wie eine futuristische Handelsstadt aussehen.«

À gauche, « Kantuur City » : « Dans mon livre « Robota », explique Chiang, cette ville est celle des robots. Édifiée sur une formation rocheuse magnétique, elle flotte au-dessus d'immenses déversoirs dans l'océan. Je l'ai imaginée composée de styles architecturaux divers, mais surtout d'influence islamique. J'aime l'allure éclectique de Venise, et j'ai pensé que cette cité pourrait être une ville marchande du futur. »

Above, "Flying Rock City." "Again using mushrooms as inspiration, I wanted to create an impossible, levitating human structure. The dome-shaped cap building is supported by a highly charged magnetic core that gives it its floating capability. Like a hot-air balloon, this city is transient, floating with the air currents."

Oben: »Flying Rock City«. »Wiederum von Pilzen inspiriert, wollte ich eine unmögliche, frei schwebende, menschliche Struktur gestalten. Das kuppelförmige, aufgesetzte Gebäude wird von einem hoch aufgeladenen magnetischen Kern getragen, der ihn schweben lässt. Gleich einem Heißluftballon ist diese Stadt flüchtig, mit den Luftströmungen schwebend.«

En haut, « Flying Rock City » : « Là encore partant des champignons, je voulais créer une structure en lévitation, inimaginable. Le bâtiment surmonté d'une coupole est soutenu par un noyau à haute charge magnétique qui lui permet de flotter. Comme un ballon gonflé à l'air chaud, la ville se déplace, flotte sur les courants d'air. »

Above, "Rock Dwelling." "Mushrooms were the inspiration for this structure," says Chiang. "I thought it would be interesting to create a human structure that combines the organic shapes of mushrooms with huge rock formations."

Oben: »Rock Dwelling«. »Zu diesen Bauten wurde ich von Pilzen angeregt. Ich dachte, es wäre interessant, eine menschliche Struktur zu schaffen, bei der sich die organischen Formen von Pilzen mit riesigen Felsformationen vereinen.«

Ci-dessus, « Rock Dwelling » : « Les champignons ont inspiré cette structure, explique Chiang. Il m'a semblé intéressant de créer une structure pour les hommes qui combine les formes organiques du champignon à d'énormes formations rocheuses. »

# DAVID CHIPPERFIELD

*David Chipperfield Architects*
*1A Cobham Mews, Agar Grove / London NW1 9SB / UK*
*Joachimstrasse 11 / 10119 Berlin / Germany*

*Tel: +44 20 7267 9422*
*Fax: +44 20 7267 9347*
*E-mail: info@davidchipperfield.com*
*Web: www.davidchipperfield.com*

*Museum of Modern Literature*

Born in London in 1953, **DAVID CHIPPERFIELD** obtained his Diploma in Architecture from the Architectural Association (AA), London, in 1977. He worked at the practices of Richard Rogers and Norman Foster before establishing David Chipperfield Architects in 1984. In 2004, David Chipperfield was appointed Commander of the Order of the British Empire (CBE) for services to architecture. In 2006, he was appointed Royal Designer for Industry (RDI), and in 2007 he was made an Honorary Fellow of the American Institute of Architects (AIA). Built work includes: Gotoh Museum (Chiba, Japan, 1991), River and Rowing Museum (Henley-on-Thames, UK, 1997); private house (Corrubedo, Spain, 2002); Ernsting's Service Center (Coesfeld-Lette, Germany, 2002); Villaverde housing (Madrid, 2005); Figge Art Museum (Davenport, Iowa, USA, 2005); Des Moines Public Library (Des Moines, Iowa, USA, 2006); Museum of Modern Literature (Marbach, Germany, 2006, published here); and America's Cup Building "Veles e Vents" (Valencia, Spain, 2006). Current work includes: San Michele Cemetery (Venice, Italy, 1998–2013); restoration of the Neues Museum (Berlin, Germany, 2000–09); and City of Justice (Barcelona, 2002–08).

Der 1953 in London geborene **DAVID CHIPPERFIELD** erwarb 1977 sein Diplom in Architektur bei der Architectural Association in London. Er arbeitete in den Büros von Richard Rogers und Norman Foster, ehe er 1984 in London David Chipperfield Architects begründete. 2004 wurde er für seine Dienste auf dem Gebiet der Architektur zum Commander of the Order of the British Empire (CBE) ernannt, 2006 zum Royal Designer for Industry (RDI) und 2007 zum Ehrenmitglied des American Institute of Architects (AIA). Zu seinen realisierten Projekten gehören: Gotoh Museum (Chiba, Japan, 1991), River and Rowing Museum (Henley-on-Thames, Grossbritannien, 1997), Privathaus (Corrubedo, Spanien, 2002), Ernsting's Service Center (Coesfeld-Lette, Deutschland, 2002), Wohnanlage Villaverde (Madrid, 2005), Figge Art Museum (Davenport, Iowa, 2005), Öffentliche Bibliothek Des Moines (Des Moines, Iowa, 2006), Literaturmuseum der Moderne (Marbach, Deutschland, 2006, hier vorgestellt) und das America's Cup Building »Veles e Vents« (Valencia, Spanien, 2006). Zur Zeit im Bau befinden sich: Friedhof San Michele (Venedig, Italien, 1998–2013), Umgestaltung des Neuen Museums (Berlin, 2000–09) und die City of Justice (Barcelona, 2002–08).

Né à Londres en 1953, **DAVID CHIPPERFIELD** est diplômé en architecture de l'Architectural Association (Londres, 1977). Il a travaillé dans les agences de Richard Rogers et Norman Foster avant de créer David Chipperfield Architects à Londres en 1984. Il a été fait Commander of the Order of the British Empire (CBE) pour services rendus à l'architecture en 2004, a été nommé Royal Designer for Industry (RDI) en 2006 et Honorary Fellow de l'American Institute of Architects (AIA) en 2007. Parmi ses réalisations : le Gotoh Museum, Chiba, Japon (1991) ; le River and Rowing Museum, Henley-on-Thames, Royaume-Uni (1997) ; une résidence privée à Corrubedo, Espagne (2002) ; le Ernsting's Service Center à Coesfeld-Lette, Allemagne (2002) ; des logements à Villaverde, Madrid (2005) ; le Figge Art Museum à Davenport, Iowa (2005) ; la Bibliothèque publique Des Moines, Iowa (2006) ; le Musée de la littérature moderne de Marbach, Allemagne (2006) publié ici ; le bâtiment de l'America's Cup « Veles e Vents » à Valence en Espagne (2006), la restauration du Neues Museum, Berlin (2000–09) et la Cité de la Justice à Barcelone (2002–08).

# MUSEUM OF MODERN LITERATURE

*Marbach am Neckar, Germany, 2002–06*

*Floor area: 3800 m². Client: Deutsches Literaturarchiv Marbach, Prof. Dr. Ulrich Raulff,*
*Dr. Heike Gfrereis, Dr. Roland Kamzelak. Cost: not disclosed.*
*Architect: David Chipperfield Architects. Project Team: Alexander Schwarz, Harald Müller,*
*Martina Betzold, Barbara Koller, Laura Fogarasi, Hannah Jonas*

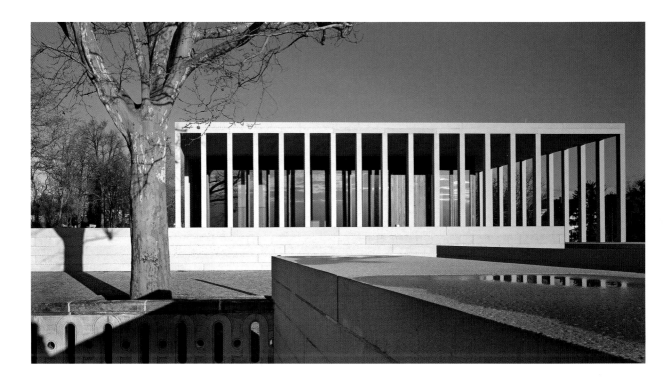

Inaugurated by Germany's Federal President Horst Köhler on June 6, 2006, this new museum is located in Marbach, the birthplace of Friedrich Schiller, and over-looks the Neckar River. Offering panoramic views of the landscape, the structure is "embedded in its topography" and makes full use of the steep slope of the site near the National Schiller Museum. A pavilion-like volume on the uppermost level marks the entrance to the museum, leading down toward dark timber-paneled exhibition galleries. In the galleries, only artificial light is used, given the light-sensitivity of the books and works on paper it houses. "At the same time," the architects explain, "each of these environmentally controlled spaces borders onto a naturally lit gallery, so as to balance views inward to the composed, internalized world of texts and manuscripts with the green and scenic valley on the other side of the glass." As is often the case, Chipperfield uses sober materials such as fair-faced concrete, sand-blasted reconstituted stone with limestone aggregate, limestone, wood, felt and glass to give the solid, modern feeling that he masters so well.

Dieses vom deutschen Bundespräsidenten Horst Köhler am 6. Juni 2006 eingeweihte neue Museum liegt hoch über dem Neckar in Marbach, dem Geburtsort Friedrich Schillers. Der »in seine Topografie eingebettete Bau« bietet Panoramablicke auf die umgebende Landschaft und nutzt seine Lage auf dem Steilhang unweit des Schiller-Nationalmuseums vollkommen aus. Ein pavillonartiger Baukörper auf der obersten Ebene markiert den Museumseingang und führt hinunter zu den mit dunklem Holz verschalten Ausstellungsräumen. Angesichts der Lichtempfindlichkeit von Büchern oder allgemein von Arbeiten auf Papier, wird in den Galerien nur Kunstlicht ver-wendet. »Gleichwohl«, erläutern die Architekten, »grenzt jeder dieser klimakontrollierten Räume an eine Galerie mit Tageslicht, um so einen Ausgleich zwischen den Blicken nach innen auf die Welt der Texte und Manuskripte und auf das auf der anderen Seite der Glaswand gelegene grüne, malerische Tal herzustellen.« Wie so häufig ver-wendet Chipperfield nüchterne Materialien wie Sichtbeton, sandgestrahlten Kunststein mit Kalksteinzuschlag, Kalkstein, Holz, Filz und Glas, um die ihm so geläufige, kom-pakt-moderne Anmutung zu erzeugen.

Inauguré le 6 juin 2006 par le président allemand Horst Köhler, ce nouveau musée situé à Marbach, lieu de naissance de Friedrich Schiller, donne sur le Neckar. Offrant des vues panoramiques sur le paysage, le bâtiment est « incrusté dans la topographie » et met pleinement à profit la pente de son terrain, à proximité du Musée national Schiller. Le volume en pavillon au niveau supérieur marque l'entrée qui conduit en descendant vers les galeries d'exposition lambrissées de bois sombre. Elles ne reçoivent qu'un éclairage artificiel établi en fonction de la forte sensibilité des livres et des œuvres sur papier à la lumière. « En même temps, explique l'architecte, chacun de ces espaces à environnement contrôlé borde une galerie à éclairage naturel de façon à équilibrer les vues vers l'intérieur sur l'univers composé et intériori-sé des textes et des manuscrits et celles de la belle vallée verte de l'autre côté des vitrages. » Comme souvent, Chipperfield utilise des matériaux sobres comme une pierre reconstituée en béton à agrégats de calcaire sablé doux au toucher, de la pierre calcaire, du bois et du verre pour aboutir à cette impression de modernité et de solidité qu'il maîtrise si bien.

Standing like a temple on its stone plinth, the Museum of Modern Literature renews the vocabulary of classic architecture and brings it into the realm of the modern.

Das gleich einem Tempel auf seinem steinernen Sockel stehende Literaturmuseum der Moderne erneuert die Formensprache der antiken Architektur und transponiert sie in die Moderne.

Se dressant comme un temple sur une plinthe de pierre, le musée de la Littérature moderne renouvelle le vocabulaire de l'architecture classique qu'il transfère dans la sphère moderne.

The interior of the museum, like its exterior, is strict and rather austere, with natural light giving variety and life to the spaces where it is admitted.

Die Innenräume des Museums wirken wie das Äußere streng und recht nüchtern, wobei das Tageslicht in den dafür vorgesehenen Räumen für Abwechslung und Belebung sorgt.

Comme pour l'extérieur, l'intérieur du musée est d'aspect strict, presque dur. L'éclairage naturel apporte à l'occasion la variété et la vie dans les volumes.

Chipperfield ist dafür bekannt, seine Architektur auf das Wesentliche zu reduzieren. In diesem Fall dominiert geradlinige Schlichtheit.

Chipperfield is known for paring down his architecture to the essentials. In this instance, rectilinear severity is the rule.

David Chipperfield est réputé pour une architecture qui va à l'essentiel. Ici, règne la ligne droite dans toute sa sévérité.

DER LANDSBERGER POESIEAUTOMAT VON HANS MAGNUS ENZENSBERGER

TROPFENWEISE ERPRESSUNGEN ZUM FRÜHSTÜCK. DIESER GELEHRIGE KAFFEEKLATSCH VOR DEM ERBRECHEN.

UND DIESE KOSTSPIELIGEN MAGENKRÄMPFE: ZUGEGEBEN: ANSONSTEN GELINGT UNS DOCH MANCHES

STATTDESSEN ZUR ABWECHSLUNG ZAHLFLÜSSIGE PROTESTE. PÜNKTLICH KAPITULIEREN!

BETEUERUNGEN. ("IHR SEID AUCH SO GIERIG.") AN DER BASIS PANIKSTIMMUNG.

DAS NACKTE ERBARMEN VERLEIDET UNS NOCH IMPOTENZ. UNTER UNS GESAGT ESSEN WIR IMMERZU.

BERÜHRUNGEN. VALIUM. FOSSILE MUNDMALE. ANSCHEINEND TUT ES NICHT WEH.

*The architect uses horizontal beams much as he has employed columns outside the building, creating a sense of lightness out of the fundamental solidity of the structure.*

*Light penetrates interior spaces in calculated ways, creating variety where the architecture itself is unmoving.*

*Der Architekt verwendet horizontale Balken ebenso wie am Außenbau Pfeiler, die der ausgeprägten Stabilität des Gebäudes zu einer gewissen Leichtigkeit verhelfen.*

*L'architecte utilise les poutres horizontales dans le même esprit que les colonnes extérieures. Il crée une impression de légèreté à partir d'une structure fondamentalement massive.*

*Licht fällt in wohl überlegter Weise in die Innenräume ein und sorgt in einer unbewegten Architektur für Abwechslung.*

*La lumière apporte la diversité dans les volumes intérieurs selon des chemins calculés, tandis que l'architecture en elle-même reste froide.*

# MATALI CRASSET

Matali Crasset
26, rue du Buisson Saint-Louis
75010 Paris
France

Tel: +33 1 4240 9989
Fax: +33 1 4240 9998
E-mail: matali.crasset@wanadoo.fr
Web: www.matalicrasset.com

Born in 1965 in Châlons-en-Champagne, France, **MATALI CRASSET** studied at the École Nationale Supérieure de Création Industrielle in Paris. She received her diploma in 1991 and left for Milan, where she worked as a designer. She returned to Paris to work with Philippe Starck and Thomson Multimedia, before creating her own office in 1998. Matali Crasset has designed furniture and domestic objects, as well as worked on exhibition design and interiors. Her exhibition work includes the "Paris-Milano" and "Bulb" shows for the design magazine *Intramuros*, as well as the "Tendance" fair in Frankfurt (2000), "Archilab" in Orléans (2001), and several projects for Hermès. She has also created installations whose point is to pose questions about architectural space (*Casaderme*, 2002). Her work as an interior architect includes the Red Cell Advertising Agency (Paris, 2001); her own studio-house (Paris, 2001); a private house near Lake Annecy (France, 2001); the Hi Hotel in Nice (2003); the BHV Store in Belle-Epine (France, 2005); Vegetable, an ephemeral restaurant in Paris (2005); the Lieu Commun Store in Paris (2005); the Vert Anis Restaurant (Annecy, 2005); and the SM's – Stedelijk Museum in 's-Hertogenbosch (The Netherlands, 2004–05, published here). Her current work includes a residence in Tarifa (Spain); the Sleg House in Nice (France); and the Dar'Hi Hotel in Nefta (in the south of Tunisia near the desert).

Die 1965 in Châlons-en-Champagne geborene **MATALI CRASSET** studierte an der École Nationale Supérieure de Création Industrielle in Paris. 1991 erhielt sie ihr Diplom und ging nach Mailand, wo sie als Designerin tätig war. Sie kehrte nach Paris zurück und arbeitete mit Philippe Starck und Thomson Multimedia, ehe sie 1998 ihr eigenes Büro gründete. Matali Crasset entwarf Möbel und Hausgeräte und gestaltete Ausstellungen und Innenräume. Zu ihren Ausstellungsprojekten gehören »Paris-Milano« und »Bulb« für die Designzeitschrift *Intramuros* ebenso wie die Messe »Tendance« 2000 in Frankfurt am Main, »Archilab« in Orléans (2001) sowie mehrere Projekte für Hermès. Darüber hinaus schuf sie Installationen, die Fragen zum architektonischen Raum aufwerfen sollen (»Casaderme«, 2002). Als Innenarchitektin zeichnet sie für die Werbeagentur Red Cell (Paris, 2001) verantwortlich sowie für ihr eigenes Atelierhaus (Paris, 2001), ein Privathaus am Lac d'Annecy (Frankreich, 2001), das Hi Hotel in Nizza (2003), die BHV-Filiale in Belle-Epine (Frankreich, 2005), Vegetable, ein Restaurant in Paris (2005), das Geschäft Lieu Commun in Paris (2005), das Restaurant Vert Anis (Annecy, 2005) und das hier vorgestellte SM's, das Städtische Museum in 's-Hertogenbosch (Niederlande, 2004–05). Zurzeit arbeitet sie an einem Wohnhaus in Tarifa, Spanien, dem Sleg House in Nizza und am Dar'Hi-Hotel in Nefta im Süden Tunesiens nahe der Wüste.

Née en 1965 à Châlons-en-Champagne, France, **MATALI CRASSET** a étudié à l'École nationale supérieure de création industrielle à Paris dont elle est sortie diplômée en 1991. Elle a ensuite travaillé comme designer à Milan avant de collaborer avec Philippe Starck pour Thomson Multimédia et de créer sa propre agence en 1998. Elle conçoit des meubles et des objets pour la maison ainsi que des expositions et des aménagements intérieurs. Ses interventions dans le domaine des expositions comprennent les présentations « Paris-Milano » et « Bulb » pour le magazine de design *Intramuros*, ainsi que « Tendance » pour la foire de Francfort (2000), « Archilab » à Orléans (2001) et plusieurs projets pour Hermès. Elle a aussi créé des installations qui remettent en question l'espace architectural comme « Casaderme » (2002). Architecte d'intérieur, elle a conçu les locaux de l'agence de publicité Red Cell à Paris (2001), sa propre maison-atelier à Paris (2001), une résidence privée près du lac d'Annecy, France (2001), le Hi Hôtel à Nice (2003), le magasin BHV de Belle Épine, France (2005), le restaurant Vert-Anis, Annecy (2005) et le Musée d'art contemporain SM's – Stedelijk Museum à Hertogenbosch, Pays-Bas (2004–05) publié ici. Elle travaille actuellement sur un projet de maison à Tarifa, Espagne, sur celui de la maison Sleg à Nice, et le Dar'Hi Hôtel en Tunisie, aux portes du désert.

tentoonstellingen
exhibitions

# SM'S – STEDELIJK MUSEUM

*'s-Hertogenbosch, The Netherlands, 2004–05*

*Floor area: 5000 m². Client: SM's – Stedelijk Museum 's-Hertogenbosch.*
*Cost: € 750 000. Global Concept (interior architecture, furniture design and graphic design): Matali Crasset,*
*Matali Crasset Productions with Marco Salgado and Francis Fichot.*
*Associated Architects: Molenaar en Koeman Architecten: Frank van Dillen, Martijn Poelen*

SM's – Stedelijk Museum 's-Hertogenbosch is a museum of contemporary art and design with an emphasis on ceramics and jewelry. Formerly known as the Museum Het Kruithuis, it was created in 1956. Het Kruithuis was granted the status of Municipal Museum of Contemporary Art in 1985. In 1994, the City Council decided to expand it and selected the Czech designer Borek Sipek. Six years of planning difficulties led to the cancellation of the project. SM's is theoretically awaiting the construction of new premises by the Dutch architects Henket Partners, but Matali Crasset was asked to renovate a temporary site, industrial sheds designed by Jacob Berend Bakema (1914–81). Describing her concept for this project, Crasset wrote, "The museum is a very long empty space; the project's goal is to inject life and as a central vein irrigating zones with different functions: restaurant, shop, bookspace […]. As it is an old factory the project must provide intimacy to each part and a specific organization. The organization is based on a central path and smaller paths, each leading to specific places. This structure injects life and people, like a plant provides food to each leaf." Using her trademark bright, cheerful colors, overseeing the furniture and graphic design as well as the interior architecture, Matali Crasset has shown that her style fits as well in a museum environment as it does in a commercial one. Despite its avowedly temporary nature, the SM's may serve for some time as the city's museum of contemporary art.

Das SM's – Stedelijk Museum 's-Hertogenbosch ist ein Museum für zeitgenössische Kunst und Design mit einem Schwerpunkt auf Keramik und Schmuck. Das 1956 gegründete Haus war vormals unter dem Namen Museum Het Kruithuis bekannt. Het Kruithuis erhielt 1985 den Rang eines Städtischen Museums für zeitgenössische Kunst. 1994 beschloss der Stadtrat die Erweiterung des Museums und wählte dafür den tschechischen Designer Borek Sípek aus. Sechs Jahre planerischer Schwierigkeiten hatten die Stornierung des Projekts zur Folge. Theoretisch wartet SM's auf die Errichtung neuer Räumlichkeiten durch das niederländische Architekturbüro Henket Partners, aber Matali Crasset wurde für die Zwischenzeit mit der Renovierung eines Gebäudes betraut, bei dem es sich um Industriehallen von Jacob Berend Bakema (1914–81) handelt. Matali Crasset beschreibt ihr Konzept für dieses Projekt wie folgt: »Bei dem Museum handelt es sich um einen sehr langen, leeren Raum. Ziel des Projekts ist es, diesen Raum mit Leben zu füllen und durch eine zentrale Achse zu gliedern, die unterschiedliche Funktionszonen wie Restaurant, Bücherei erschließt. […] Da es sich um alte Bausubstanz handelt, muss das Projekt jedem Bereich Intimität und eine spezifische Aufteilung bieten. Die Aufteilung beruht auf einem zentralen Weg und nebengeordneten Pfaden, die jeweils zu bestimmten Orten führen. Dieses Gefüge injiziert Leben und Leute, so wie eine Pflanze jedes Blatt mit Nahrung versorgt.« Matali Crasset, die auch für Möblierung, grafische Gestaltung und Innenarchitektur zuständig war und dabei ihr typisches, leuchtend-fröhliches Farbkonzept verwendete, konnte hier beweisen, dass ihr Stil ebenso gut zu einem Museum wie zu einer kommerziellen Nutzung passt. Ungeachtet seines angeblich temporären Charakters, könnte das SM's lange Zeit als Städtisches Museum für zeitgenössische Kunst dienen.

Le SM's – Stedelijk Museum 's-Hertogenbosch est un musée d'art contemporain et de design qui met l'accent sur la céramique et la joaillerie. Anciennement connu sous le nom de Museum Het Kruithuis, il a été fondé en 1956, puis est devenu musée municipal d'art contemporain en 1985. En 1994, le conseil municipal avait décidé de l'agrandir et choisit pour cela le designer tchèque Borek Sipek. Six années de difficultés aboutirent à l'annulation du projet. Le musée attend la construction de nouvelles installations confiées aux architectes néerlandais Henket & Partners, mais a demandé à Matali Crasset de rénover un site temporaire, sous des *sheds* industriels conçus par Jacob Berend Bakema (1914–81). Dans la présentation de son concept, Matali Crasset écrit : « Le musée est un espace long et vide. L'objectif du projet est d'y injecter la vie et une veine centrale irrigue ainsi les zones des différentes fonctions : restaurant, boutique, espace de bibliothèque… Comme il s'applique à un bâtiment ancien, le projet doit s'efforcer d'apporter l'intimité dans chaque partie et en même temps une organisation spécifique. Celle-ci repose sur une circulation centrale et secondaire conduisant vers des lieux spécifiques. Cette structure injecte la vie et les visiteurs comme une plante apporte la nourriture à chaque feuille. » Utilisant ses couleurs vives et chaleureuses, supervisant le mobilier et la signalétique ainsi que l'architecture intérieure, Crasset montre que son style s'adapte à des environnements aussi bien muséaux que commerciaux. En dépit de sa nature temporaire, le SM's servira peut-être longtemps de musée d'art contemporain municipal.

Matali Crasset's refit of these former industrial sheds might be considered the opposite of David Chipperfield's approach seen in the preceding pages. She brings color and a sense of gaiety to otherwise dull, repetitive architecture.

Man könnte Matali Crassets Umnutzung dieser ehemaligen Industriehallen für das genaue Gegenteil der auf den vorhergehenden Seiten gezeigten Vorgehensweise von David Chipperfield halten. Sie belebt eine ansonsten banal-gleichförmige Architektur mittels Farbe und Fröhlichkeit.

L'aménagement par Matali Crasset de ces anciens entrepôts industriels est à l'opposé du travail de David Chipperfield vu aux pages précédentes. Elle a insufflé de la couleur et de la gaieté dans une architecture répétitive ennuyeuse.

Crasset attempts to rethink the function of the space itself and to give visitors a more enjoyable experience than they might have had if a strictly museum-oriented approach been used.

Crasset versucht, die Funktion des Raums selbst zu überdenken und den Besuchern eine erfreulichere Erfahrung zu bieten, als sie sie in einer an rein musealen Gesichtspunkten orientierten Lösung gehabt hätten.

Crasset s'efforce de repenser la fonction de l'espace et d'offrir aux visiteurs une expérience plus agréable que ce qu'aurait pu proposer un musée de conception plus classique.

An axonometric plan of the installation gives an idea of its complexity. The irregular placement of objects or furniture enlivens the visitor's experience, as can be deduced from the photo above.

Eine Axonometrie macht deutlich, wie komplex die Installation ist. Die unregelmäßige Platzierung von Objekten und Möbeln macht den Museumsbesuch zu einem Erlebnis, wie man sich beim Anblick des Fotos oben vorstellen kann.

La perspective axonométrique donne une idée de la complexité de l'installation. Comme le montre la photographie ci-dessus, les meubles et les objets ont une place inhabituelle ce qui stimule l'expérience des visiteurs.

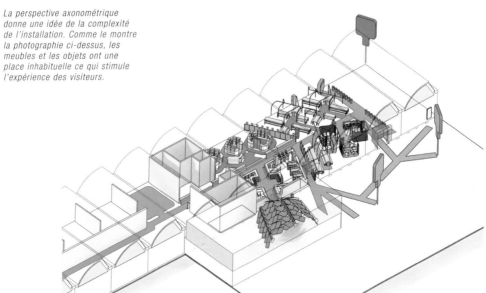

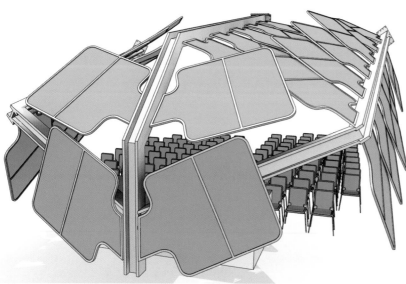

Moveable panels enclose a lecture area, emphasizing the flexibility that Crasset has introduced.

Bewegliche Paneele teilen einen Vortragsraum ab und unterstreichen die von Crasset angestrebte Flexibilität.

Des panneaux mobiles recouvrent une aire de lecture, illustration de la souplesse d'aménagement introduite par Crasset.

Crasset's vibrant use of colors, like this apple green, is certainly unexpected in the museum world, where muted tones are still very much the rule. She takes an overall view at the way both objects and the space they are placed in interact.

Der Gebrauch kraftvoller Farben, wie dieses Apfelgrün, überrascht in einer ansonsten gedämpfte Farbtöne bevorzugenden Museumswelt. Matali Crasset berücksichtigt den Gesamteindruck, den die Objekte und der ihnen zugedachte Raum ergeben.

L'utilisation de couleurs vibrantes comme ce vert pomme est surprenante dans un monde muséal où les couleurs assourdies sont la règle. Crasset possède une vision globale de la manière dont les objets et l'espace peuvent interagir.

# CURIOSITY

Gwenaël Nicolas
Curiosity Inc.
2–13–16 Tomigaya, Shibuya-ku
Tokyo 151–0063
Japan

Tel: +81 3 5452 0095
Fax: +81 3 5454 9691
E-mail: info@curiosity.jp
Web: www.curiosity.jp

*C-1 (Curiosity One) House*

Gwenaël Nicolas was born in France in 1966. He studied Interior Design at the École Supérieure d'Arts Graphiques et d'Architecture d'Interieure (ESAG, 1984–88). He obtained a Master's degree in Industrial Design from the Royal College of Art, London (1991), and moved the same year to Japan. In 1998, he established his firm **CURIOSITY** Inc. in Tokyo. He worked on a number of shops for Issey Miyake, including the Pleats Please Boutique in the SoHo area of New York (with Toshiko Mori, 1998). The firm has also created a showroom for Sony and shops for the watchmaker Tag Heuer. More recent work includes two houses in Tokyo, such as C-1 (Curiosity One) House (2004–05, published here).

Gwenaël Nicolas wurde 1966 in Frankreich geboren. Er studierte Innenarchitektur an der ESAG (École Supérieure d'Arts Graphiques et d'Architecture, 1984–88). Am Royal College of Art in London erwarb er 1991 einen Magisterabschluss in Industriedesign und verlegte im gleichen Jahr seinen Wohnsitz nach Japan, wo er 1998 in Tokio das Büro **CURIOSITY** Inc. gründete. Er arbeitete an einer Reihe von Läden für Issey Miyake, darunter die Pleats Please Boutique im SoHo-Viertel von New York (mit Toshiko Mori, 1998). Außerdem gestaltete das Büro einen Ausstellungsraum für Sony und Läden für den Uhrenhersteller Tag Heuer. Zu seinen jüngeren Arbeiten zählen zwei Häuser in Tokio, wie das hier gezeigte Haus Curiosity One (2004–05).

Né en France en 1966, Gwenaël Nicolas a étudié l'architecture intérieure à l'ESAG (École supérieure d'arts graphiques et d'architecture intérieure, 1984–88). Il obtient un Master en design industriel au Royal College of Art à Londres (1991) et s'installe la même année au Japon. En 1998, il crée son agence, **CURIOSITY** Inc., à Tokyo. Il travaille sur un certain nombre de projets de boutiques pour Issey Miyake, dont celle de Pleats Please à SoHo (New York, avec Toshiko Mori, en 1998). L'agence a également créé un showroom pour Sony et des magasins pour le fabricant de montres Tag Heuer. Plus récemment, il a conçu deux maisons à Tokyo dont la C-1 (Curiosity One) publiée ici (2004–05).

# C-1 (CURIOSITY ONE) HOUSE

*Tokyo, Japan, 2004–05*

*Floor area: 400 m². Client: Curiosity. Cost: $1 million*
*Associated Architect: Tomoyuki Utsumi (Milligram Studio)*

*The ramped, angled design of the house assures that its levels are not as completely distinct from each other as typical floors. Movement in space is emphasized too by the very nature of these photos.*

*Das mit Rampen und Schrägen gestaltete Haus gewährleistet, dass seine Ebenen nicht wie übliche Geschosse vollständig voneinander getrennt sind. Bewegung im Raum wird darüber hinaus durch den Charakter dieser Fotos unterstrichen.*

*La conception de la maison en suivant une rampe inclinée fait que les différents niveaux se distinguent moins les uns des autres que dans une configuration classique. La mobilité de l'espace est mise en valeur par la nature de ces photos.*

This house is essentially a glass box surrounded by a walkway or gallery. The design was created before a site was identified. Gwenaël Nicolas imagined the building like a space in which the user would appear and disappear as though being filmed. The steel slab floors are just 25 millimeters thick (60 mm with the added flooring material). 3D animation was used as a design tool for a structure where the architects sought nothing less than to challenge common perceptions of the use of space. A melamine surface was used for the exterior, in an attempt to do away with all reference to a specific architectural scale. The same is true of the interior where the kitchen was so carefully designed: it does not "seem to exist." Nicolas states of C-1 that "it is designed like a unique, independent product, a seamless space where architecture and interior furnishings become part of a unique, interconnected emotional experience." Gwenaël Nicolas's background in interior or industrial design, as blended here with the architectural thinking of Tomoyuki Utsumi, makes for an unusual "product," in which the very boundary between architecture and design is dissolved.

Dieses Haus ist im Grunde ein von einem Umgang oder einer Galerie umzogener Glaskasten. Der Entwurf entstand bevor ein Grundstück ausgewiesen war. Gwenaël Nicolas stellte sich das Haus wie einen Raum vor, in dem der Bewohner wie in einem Film auf- und abtritt. Die Bodenplatten aus Stahl sind nur 25 mm stark (60 mm mit zusätzlichen Bodenbelägen). Für den Entwurf dieses Hauses, bei dem die Architekten nichts Geringeres anstrebten, als die übliche Vorstellung von Raumnutzung infrage zu stellen, wurde 3D-Computeranimation als Hilfsmittel verwendet. Der Außenbau wurde mit einer Melaminbeschichtung versehen, in dem Bemühen jeglichen Hinweis auf einen spezifischen architektonischen Maßstab zu beseitigen. Dasselbe gilt für das Hausinnere, wo die Küche so wohl überlegt gestaltet wurde, dass sie »scheinbar nicht vorhanden ist«. Gwenaël Nicolas behauptet von C-1, es sei »wie ein einmaliges, selbstständiges Produkt – ein nahtloser Raum, in dem Architektur und Innenausstattung Teil einer einmaligen, vernetzten emotionalen Erfahrung werden«. Durch die Verbindung von Gwenaël Nicolas' Herkunft von Innenarchitektur und Industriedesign mit dem architektonischen Denken Tomoyuki Utsumis entsteht ein ungewöhnliches »Produkt«, bei dem sich die Grenze zwischen Architektur und Design auflöst.

Conçue avant que son terrain n'ait été trouvé, cette maison consiste essentiellement en une boîte de verre entourée d'une coursive ou galerie. Gwenaël Nicolas l'a imaginée sous la forme d'un espace dans lequel l'occupant apparaît et disparaît comme s'il était filmé. Les sols en dalles d'acier ne sont que de 25 mm d'épaisseur (60 mm avec les matériaux de revêtement). L'animation en 3D a permis de dessiner une structure dans laquelle les architectes ne cherchent rien de moins qu'à relever l'enjeu de la perception commune de l'utilisation de l'espace. L'extérieur est habillé de mélamine afin d'effacer tout référence à une échelle architecturale précise. De même, à l'intérieur, la cuisine a été dessinée avec un tel soin qu'« elle ne semble pas exister ». Gwenaël Nicolas écrit que cette maison « est conçue comme un produit unique, indépendant, un espace continu dans lequel l'architecture et le mobilier s'intègrent dans une expérience sensible unique et interconnectée ». Sa formation d'architecte intérieur et de designer, associée ici à la pensée architecturale de Tomoyuki Utsumi, a permis la naissance à un « produit » étonnant dans lequel les frontières entre architecture et design se dissolvent.

*Furniture and spaces are designed to fulfill the same functions, doing away with the frequent dichotomy between design and architecture.*

*Möbel und Räume sollen den gleichen Zwecken dienen und schaffen den oft vorhandenen Gegensatz zwischen Design und Architektur ab.*

*Meubles et volumes sont conçus pour remplir les mêmes fonctions, à l'encontre de la fréquente dichotomie entre design et architecture.*

A Japanese sparseness inhabits the
C-1 House, and spaces are frequently
subject to interpenetration that
allows views through the volumes.

Das Haus C-1 ist von einer typisch
japanischen Kargheit erfüllt und die
Räume durchdringen sich häufig
gegenseitig, so dass Blickachsen
entstehen.

Une économie de moyens à la
japonaise caractérise la maison C-1.
Les espaces sont soumis à des
interpénétrations qui ménagent des
perspectives à travers les volumes.

*Muted light sources and smooth, continuous surfaces seek to break down the normal hierarchy of residential or office spaces.*

*Gedämpfte Lichtquellen und glatte, durchgehende Oberflächen durchbrechen die übliche Hierarchie von Wohn- oder Büroräumen.*

*Des sources de lumière atténuée et la continuité des plans rompent avec la hiérarchie normale des espaces résidentiels ou de bureau.*

The exploded axonometric drawing shows the interior structure of the house, with its diagonal ramps. Furniture here, as elsewhere, takes on a strictly geometric appearance.

Die Axonometrie rechts erklärt die Binnengliederung des Hauses durch die diagonalen Rampen. Das Mobiliar hat überall rein geometrische Formen.

L'axonométrie explique la structure intérieure de la maison et de ses rampes en diagonale. Partout, le mobilier est strictement géométrique.

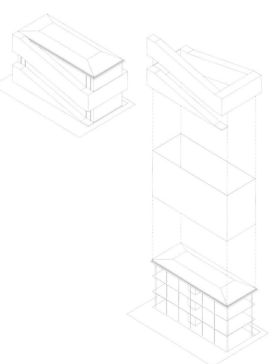

*Alpine Barn and Stable*

# DEVANTHÉRY & LAMUNIÈRE

*Devanthéry & Lamunière*
*7, rue du Tunnel*
*1227 Carouge-Geneva*
*Switzerland*

*Tel: +41 22 307 0130*
*Fax: +41 22 343 0554*
*E-mail: mail@devanthery-lamuniere.ch*
*Web: www.devanthery-lamuniere.ch*

**PATRICK DEVANTHÉRY** and **INÈS LAMUNIÈRE** were born respectively in Sion and in Geneva in 1954. They both completed their studies at the École Polytechnique Fédérale de Lausanne (EPFL) in 1980. In 1983, they created their firm Devanthéry & Lamunière in Geneva and Lausanne, and an urban design affiliate in Geneva in 2001 under the name Devanthéry, Lamunière & Marchand. They have taught at the Harvard Graduate School of Design (1996 and 1999), at the Université de Nancy (1994), and at the ETH in Zurich (1991–93 and 1994). Inès Lamunière is currently a Professor of Architectural Theory and Project at the EPFL in Lausanne. In 2001, she created the Laboratory of Architecture and Urban Mobility at the EPFL. They have both participated on the editorial committee of the magazine *Faces* (1989–2004). Their work includes numerous restoration projects, as well as new buildings such as a psychiatric clinic in Yverdon (1995–2003); the Hôtel Cornavin in Geneva (1996–99 and 2006); an urban housing district in the city of Neuchâtel completed in 2004; a 300-room hotel located on the Guisanplatz in Bern (1999–2004); Philip Morris International Headquarters in Lausanne (2002–07); the alpine barn and stable in the Valais (2003–04, published here); Ber-Scott Villa (Geneva, 2006); and SIP, transformation of an industrial area into lofts and offices (Geneva, 2006), all in Switzerland. Current projects include the Bloch-Pasche Villa (Paudex, 2007); Life Sciences Faculty, EPFL (Lausanne, 2008); TV Tower (Geneva, 2009); the Opera (Lausanne, 2009) and the Prieuré, EMS and residences (La Gradelle, Geneva, 2004–10).

**PATRICK DEVANTHÉRY** und **INÈS LAMUNIÈRE** wurden 1954 in Sion bzw. Genf geboren. Beide beendeten 1980 ihr Studium an der École Polytechnique Fédérale de Lausanne (EPFL). Die Büros Devanthéry & Lamunière eröffneten sie in Genf und Lausanne, außerdem unter dem Namen Devanthéry, Lamunière & Marchand 2001 in Genf eine Dependance für Stadtplanung. In den Jahren 1996 und 1999 unterrichteten sie an der Harvard Graduate School of Design, 1994 an der Université de Nancy und 1991 bis 1993 und 1994 an der ETH Zürich. Inès Lamunière hat zurzeit eine Professur für Architekturtheorie an der EPFL in Lausanne inne. Dort richtete sie 2001 das Laboratoire d'Architecture et Mobilité Urbaine ein. Von 1989 bis 2004 gehörten beide der Redaktion der Zeitschrift *Faces* an. Ihr Arbeitsgebiet umfasst zahlreiche Restaurierungsprojekte ebenso wie Neubauten, so die Psychiatrische Klinik in Yverdon (1995–2003), das Hotel Cornavin in Genf (1996–99 und 2006), ein 2004 fertiggestelltes städtisches Wohnviertel in Neuchâtel, ein Hotel mit 300 Zimmern am Guisanplatz in Bern (1999–2004), den internationalen Hauptsitz von Philip Morris in Lausanne (2002–07), das hier vorgestellte Ensemble aus Scheune und Stall im Wallis (2003–04), die Villa Ber-Scott (Genf, 2006) sowie SIP, die Umwandlung eines Industriegebiets in Lofts und Büros (Genf, 2006), alle in der Schweiz. Aktuelle Projekte sind die Villa Bloch-Pasche (Paudex, 2007), die Fakultät für Biowissenschaften an der EPFL, Lausanne (2008), ein Fernsehturm (Genf, 2009), die Oper in Lausanne (2009) und die Prieuré und Wohnhäuser in La Gradelle (Genf, 2004–10).

**PATRICK DEVANTHÉRY** et **INÈS LAMUNIÈRE** sont nés respectivement à Sion et Genève en 1954. Tous deux ont achevé leurs études à l'École polytechnique fédérale de Lausanne (EPFL) en 1980. En 1983, ils créent leur agence Devanthéry & Lamunière à Genève et Lausanne et ouvrent un bureau d'urbanisme en 2001 à Genève : Devanthéry, Lamunière & Marchand. Ils ont enseigné à l'Harvard Graduate School of Design (1996 et 1999), à l'Université de Nancy (1994) et à l'ETH de Zurich (1991–93 et 1994). Inès Lamunière est actuellement professeur de théorie et projet de l'architecture à l'EPFL de Lausanne. En 2001, elle a créé le Laboratoire d'architecture et de mobilité urbaine de l'EPFL. Ils ont tous deux participé au comité éditorial du magazine *Faces* (1989–2004). Leur œuvre, entièrement réalisée en Suisse, comprend de nombreux projets de restauration ainsi que des constructions neuves dont une clinique de psychiatrie à Yverdon (1995–2003) ; l'Hôtel Cornavin à Genève (1996–99 et 2006) ; un quartier de logements à Neufchâtel achevé en 2004 ; un hôtel de 300 chambres sur la Guisanplatz à Berne (1999–2004) ; le siège international de Philip Morris à Lausanne (2002–07) une grange-écurie dans le Valais (2003–04) publiée ici ; la villa Ber-Scott (Genève, 2006) et SIP, transformation d'une zone industrielle en lofts et bureaux à Genève (2006). Parmi leurs projets actuels : la villa Bloch-Pasche à Paudex (2007) ; la faculté des sciences de la vie, EPFL, Lausanne (2008) ; une tour de télévision à Genève (2009) ; l'opéra de Lausanne (2009) et le Nouveau Prieuré, EMS et résidences de La Gradelle, Genève (2004–10).

# ALPINE BARN AND STABLE

*Evolène, Valais, Switzerland, 2003–04*

*Floor area: 86 m². Client: not disclosed. Cost: not disclosed.*
*Collaborators: Frédéric Dayer, Christian Pesch*

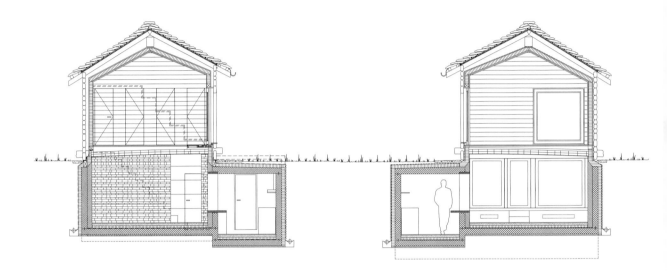

Located in the Val d'Hérens (Valais) region of Switzerland, this former barn and stable were built in a high mountain pasture with a view of the Dent Blanche mountain. Designed in 2002, and completed in 2004, the project of Devanthéry & Lamunière specifically addresses the potential danger of avalanches on this site. The stone stable and timber barn were combined in a precise 4 x 5 x 3 meter configuration. Carefully dismantled, the structures were rebuilt behind a solid protective concrete wall whose presence is affirmed through its blue-green color. A stone roof, typical of local architecture, was added. A kitchen and bathroom were added to living space in the structures that were not originally intended for more than short-term occupation. The architect Inès Lamunière made this project a cornerstone of her book *Habiter la Menace* (Inhabiting Danger; PPUR, 2006). The book and, indeed, this converted barn and stable confront danger, in this case with an appropriate design.

Diese beiden ehemals landwirtschaftlich genutzten Gebäude in der Region Val d'Hérens/Wallis entstanden auf einer Hochalm mit Blick auf den Dent Blanche. Mit diesem 2002 entworfenen und 2004 fertiggestellten Projekt sprechen Devanthéry & Lamunière ganz explizit die potenzielle Lawinengefahr dieser Gegend an. Der gemauerte Stall und die aus Holz errichtete Scheune wurden in einer genau 4 x 5 x 3 m messenden räumlichen Anordnung vereint. Die sorgfältig demontierten Gebäude wurden hinter einer massiven Schutzmauer aus Beton, deren Präsenz dank ihres blau-grünen Anstrichs nicht zu übersehen ist, neu errichtet. Ein für die hiesige Architektur typisches, mit Steinen gedecktes Dach kam hinzu. Der Wohnraum in den ursprünglich nur für kurzzeitige Aufenthalte gedachten Bauten wurde um Küche und Bad ergänzt. Die Architektin Inès Lamunière verwendete dieses Projekt als Anlass für ihr Buch *Habiter la Menace* (Gefahr bewohnen, PPUR 2006). Das Buch und in der Tat auch die umgebaute Scheune und der Stall stellen sich durch eine angemessene Gestaltung wissentlich der Gefahr.

Située dans Val d'Hérens en Valais, Suisse, cette ancienne grange et écurie avait été construite dans des alpages donnant sur la Dent blanche. Conçu en 2002 et achevé en 2004, le projet des architectes répond spécifiquement au danger potentiel d'avalanches. La grange en pierre et l'écurie de bois ont été réunies dans une nouvelle configuration de 4 x 5 x 3 mètres. Les constructions ont été démontées avec soin, puis remontées derrière un solide mur de protection en béton dont la présence s'affirme à travers le choix d'une couleur bleu-vert. Un toit en pierres, de style typiquement local, a été posé. Une cuisine et une salle de bains ont été adjointes au séjour dans cet ensemble prévu à l'origine pour de très courts séjours. Ce projet est l'élément clé de l'ouvrage d'Inès Lamunière, *Habiter la menace* (PPUR, 2006), où comment faire consciemment face à un danger grâce à une conception adaptée.

*Far removed from the urban sophistication of Tokyo seen in the C-1 House on the previous pages, this former barn and stable has been converted into a house, in a fundamentally hostile environment—as the thick avalanche wall to the rear demonstrates.*

*Zwischen dem von Tokios urbaner Perfektion geprägten Haus C-1 auf den vorhergehenden Seiten und diesen in ein Wohnhaus umgewandelten ehemaligen landwirtschaftlichen Nutzbauten liegen Welten. Wie die dicke Lawinenmauer auf der Rückseite zeigt, befinden sie sich in einer unwirtlichen Umgebung.*

*Loin de la sophistication urbaine de la maison C-1 de Tokyo vue précédemment, cette ancienne grange et écurie a été aménagée en maison dans un environnement fondamentalement hostile comme le montre l'épais mur anti-avalanche élevé à l'arrière.*

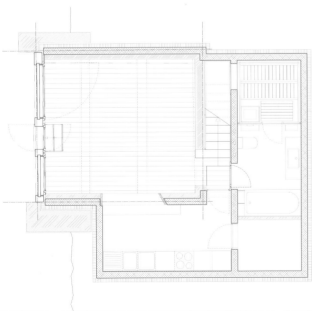

The rough external appearance of
the house gives way to a spartan but
modern comfort inside, with remarkable views of the Alps in the Val
d'Hérens.

Das von außen eher primitiv wirkende Haus verfügt über Innenräume, die
mit einfachem aber modernem Komfort ausgestattet sind. Von dieser
Hochalm im Val d'Hérens bieten sich
großartige Ausblicke auf die Alpen.

L'aspect extérieur brut de la maison
laisse place à l'intérieur à un aménagement moderne mais spartiate. Les
vues sur le Val d'Hérens, dans les
Alpes, sont remarquables.

Stone and wood, the two most typical local building materials, are the visible elements of the interior design—with the heavy concrete of the rear wall here no longer in evidence.

Die typischen heimischen Baumaterialien, Stein und Holz, sind die sichtbaren Elemente der Innenraumgestaltung – da der wuchtige Beton der Lawinenmauer hier nicht zu sehen ist.

La pierre et le bois, deux matériaux de construction typiquement locaux, sont partout présents à l'intérieur. L'épais mur anti-avalanches en béton est maintenant imperceptible.

# DILLER SCOFIDIO + RENFRO

*Diller Scofidio + Renfro*
*601 W26th Street, Suite 1815 / New York, NY 10001 / USA*
*Tel: +1 212 260 7971 / Fax: +1 212 260 7924*
*E-mail: disco@dsrny.com / Web: www.dsrny.com*

**ELIZABETH DILLER** was born in Lodz, Poland, in 1954. She received her B. Arch from the Cooper Union School of Arts in 1979. She is a Professor of Architecture at Princeton University. **RICARDO SCOFIDIO**, born in New York in 1935, graduated from the Cooper Union School of Architecture and Columbia University, where he is currently a Professor of Architecture. They founded Diller+Scofidio in 1979. **CHARLES RENFRO** became a partner in 2004. Renfro was born in Houston, Texas in 1964. He graduated from Rice University and Columbia, where he taught for three years. DS+R works today with a permanent staff of 40. According to their own description, "DS+R is a collaborative, interdisciplinary studio involved in architecture, the visual arts and the performing arts. The team is primarily involved in thematically-driven experimental works that take the form of architectural commissions, temporary installations and permanent site-specific installations, multimedia theater, electronic media, and print." They recently completed the Blur Building (Expo '02, Yverdon-les-Bains, Switzerland, 2000–02); and the Viewing Platforms at Ground Zero in Manhattan (New York). Other works include: The Brasserie (Seagram Building, New York, 1998–99); Slither, a social housing building in Gifu (Japan); Jet Lag, a multimedia work for the stage in collaboration with the Builders Association; two dance collaborations with the Lyon Opera Ballet of France and Charleroi/Danses of Belgium. Current work includes: Lincoln Center projects including the expansion of the Juilliard School of Music and a renovation of Alice Tully Hall; the redevelopment of Tivoli Gardens in Copenhagen (Denmark); the conversion of the High Line, a 2.4 kilometer stretch of elevated railroad into a New York City park. Design of the Institute of Contemporary Art in Boston, published here, began in 2001.

**ELIZABETH DILLER** wurde 1954 im polnischen Lodz geboren. Den Grad des Bachelor of Architecture erwarb sie 1979 an der Cooper Union School of Arts. Sie lehrt als Architekturprofessorin an der Universität Princeton. Der 1935 in New York geborene **RICARDO SCOFIDIO** erhielt seine Ausbildung an der Cooper Union School of Architecture und der Columbia University, wo er gegenwärtig eine Professur im Fach Architektur innehat. 1979 gründeten sie das Büro Diller+Scofidio. 2004 kam der 1964 in Houston geborene **CHARLES RENFRO** als Partner hinzu. Er erwarb Abschlüsse an der Rice und Columbia University, wo er drei Jahre lang unterrichtete. DS+R arbeitet heute mit einer ständigen Belegschaft von 40 Angestellten. Ihrer eigenen Beschreibung zufolge ist "DS+R ein interdisziplinäres gemeinschaftliches Büro, das sich mit Architektur, bildender und darstellender Kunst beschäftigt. Das Team arbeitet in erster Linie an thematisch ausgerichteten experimentellen Projekten in Form von Bauaufträgen, temporären Installationen und dauerhaften, ortsspezifischen Installationen, multimedialem Theater sowie elektronischen und gedruckten Medien." Zu ihren Projekten gehören: das Blur Building (Expo '02, Yverdon-les-Bains, Schweiz, 2000–02), die Aussichtsplattformen am Ground Zero in Manhattan, The Brasserie (Seagram Building, New York, 1998–99), Slither, ein Komplex mit Sozialwohnungen in Gifu (Japan), Jet Lag, eine Multimediaarbeit für die Bühne in Zusammenarbeit mit der Builders Association, zwei gemeinsam mit dem französischen Ballet de l'Opera in Lyon und dem Charleroi/Danses Belgien erarbeitete Tanzprojekte. Neuere Arbeiten umfassen: Neugestaltung des Lincoln Center mit Erweiterung der Juilliard School of Music und Renovierung der Alice Tully Hall, Umgestaltung des Tivoli in Kopenhagen, die Umwandlung der High Line, eine 2,4 km lange Hochbahnstrecke, in einen städtischen Park in New York City. Die Entwurfsarbeit an dem hier vorgestellten Institute of Contemporary Art in Boston begann 2001.

**ELIZABETH DILLER**, née à Lodz, Pologne, en 1954 est B. Arch. de la Cooper Union School of Arts (1979). Elle est professeur d'architecture à Princeton University. **RICARDO SCOFIDIO**, né à New York en 1935, est diplômé de la Cooper Union School of Architecture et de Columbia University, New York, où il enseigne actuellement l'architecture. Ils fondent Diller+Scofidio en 1979, agence à laquelle s'associe **CHARLES RENFRO** en 2004. Renfro, né à Houston en 1964 est diplômé de la Rice University et de Columbia, où il a enseigné trois ans. DS+R emploient actuellement 40 collaborateurs permanents. Ils se présentent comme « une agence interdisciplinaire coopérative se consacrant à l'architecture, aux arts plastiques et arts de la scène. L'équipe travaille essentiellement sur des recherches thématiques expérimentales qui peuvent prendre la forme de commandes architecturales, d'installations temporaires, d'installations permanentes adaptées au site, de théâtres multimédia, de médias électroniques et d'édition. » Parmi leurs réalisations : le Blur Building, Expo '02, Yverdon-les-Bains, Suisse (2000–02) ; la plate-forme d'observation de Ground Zero à Manhattan (New York); The Brasserie, Seagram Building, New York (1998–99) ; Slither, un immeuble de logements sociaux à Gifu, Japon ; Jet Lag, un travail multimédias pour la scène en collaboration avec la Builders Association ; deux collaborations avec le Ballet de l'opéra de Lyon, France et Charleroi/Danses en Belgique. Plus récemment, ils ont travaillé sur le Lincoln Center dont l'agrandissement de la Juilliard School of Music et la rénovation de l'Alice Tully Hall ; la rénovation des Jardins de Tivoli à Copenhague, Danemark; la conversion de la High Line, une section de voie de chemin de fer surélevée de 2,4 km de long dans un parc de New York. Le design pour l'Institute of Contemporary Art à Boston, publié ici, a débuté en 2001.

# INSTITUTE OF CONTEMPORARY ART

*Boston, Massachusetts, USA, 2004–06*

*Floor area: 5760 m². Client: The Institute of Contemporary Art. Cost: $41 million.*
*Project Leader: Flavio Stigliano.*
*Associate Architects: Perry Dean Rogers and Partners*

The extreme cantilever of the institute is visible in the elevation below. Photos show this overhang, which can be used as an outdoor theater facing Boston Harbor.

Die sehr stark vorkragenden Obergeschosse des Museums sind im Aufriss unten zu erkennen. Die Abbildungen zeigen, dass dieser Überhang sich als Freilufttheater mit Blick auf den Hafen von Boston nutzen lässt.

Dans la coupe ci-dessous, l'énorme porte-à-faux de l'Institut. Les photographies montrent qu'il peut servir d'abri à un théâtre de plein air aménagé face au port de Boston.

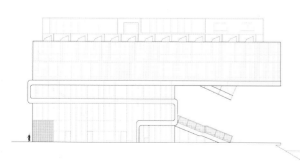

The unusual structure designed for the Institute of Contemporary Art in Boston by the architects Diller Scofidio + Renfro is located at the water's edge, on Fan Pier. With its 1672 square meters of gallery space, a performing arts theater, restaurant, bookstore, education/workshop facilities, and administrative offices, the facility will considerably upgrade the cultural profile of south Boston. The Institute is presently surrounded by parking lots, but the area, near South Station and Government Center, is promised a rapid development, which is slated to include an upgraded Harborwalk, one of the metaphorical starting points for the design. A kind of "grandstand" is sheltered by the cantilevered upper levels of the Institute, looking across the harbor toward Logan Airport. The wooden surface that wraps around this exterior space penetrates into the building, lending the continuity to the public space. The gallery spaces, which can receive natural overhead lighting, are located almost entirely on the upper level of the curving, wrapping building. Though it is easy to subdivide the gallery space, its entire volume, with ceilings almost 5 meters high, is column-free. Inaugurated in December 2006, the new ICA was labeled "audacious and venturesome" by the Boston *Globe*, and indeed the New York architects seem to have brought a new level of architectural quality and drama to the Boston waterfront.

Dieser von der Architektengemeinschaft Diller Scofidio + Renfro für das Institute of Contemporary Art in Boston entworfene, ungewöhnliche Bau steht auf dem Fan Pier am Ufer des alten Hafengeländes. Die Einrichtung mit 1672 m² Ausstellungsfläche, Theatersaal, Restaurant, Buchladen, Lehr- und Werkstatträumlichkeiten sowie Verwaltungsbüros wird das kulturelle Profil von Südboston erheblich aufwerten. Gegenwärtig ist der Bau von Parkplätzen umgeben, aber der Gegend unweit von South Station und Government Center sagt man eine rasche Entwicklung voraus, zu der auch ein ausgebauter »Harborwalk« gehören soll, einer der metaphorischen Ausgangspunkte für das Projekt. Eine Art Tribüne wird von den vorkragenden Obergeschossen des Institutes mit Blick auf Logan Airport überfangen. Die Holzoberflächen, die diesen Außenraum bedecken, setzen sich im Innenraum fort und implizieren damit die Kontinuität des öffentlichen Raums. Die Galerieflächen, die Tageslicht erhalten können, befinden sich fast zur Gänze auf der oberen Ebene des Museums. Obwohl sich die Ausstellungsfläche leicht unterteilen lässt, ist der gesamte, nahezu 5 m hohe Raum stützenfrei. Der *Boston Globe* nannte das im Dezember 2006 eingeweihte neue ICA »kühn und gewagt« und tatsächlich haben die New Yorker Architekten anscheinend einen neuen Grad architektonischer Qualität und Dramatik an das Gestade von Boston gebracht.

Ce curieux bâtiment conçu pour l'Institute of Contemporary Art est situé en bordure de l'eau, sur Fan Pier. Comprenant 1 672 m² de galeries d'exposition, un théâtre, un restaurant, une librairie, des ateliers éducatifs et des bureaux, cet équipement public devrait considérablement améliorer le niveau d'équipement culturel du sud de Boston. L'institut est actuellement entouré de parkings, mais ce quartier, non loin de la gare du Sud et du Government Center, est promis à un développement rapide comprenant une promenade le long du port, qui est d'ailleurs l'un des points de départs métaphoriques du projet. Une sorte de « tribune » s'élève à l'abri des niveaux en porte-à-faux qui donnent sur le port d'où la vue porte jusqu'à aéroport Logan. L'habillage de bois qui enveloppe le bâtiment pénètre dans celui-ci pour signifier la continuité de l'espace public. Les galeries, qui peuvent être éclairées zénitalement, sont presque entièrement groupées au niveau supérieur. Leur volume tout entier à plafonds de 5 mètres de haut est libre de toute colonne et donc facilement subdivisable. Inauguré en décembre 2006, le nouvel ICA a été qualifié « audacieux et aventureux » par le *Boston Globe*. Il semble bien que les architectes new-yorkais aient réussi à faire entendre sur les quais de Boston une approche nouvelle et spectaculaire de la qualité architecturale.

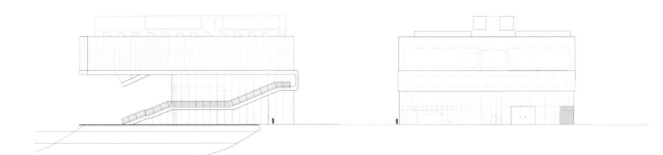

Sitting almost on the water, the
structure provides a striking contrast
to the high-rise office buildings of
downtown Boston. Its spatial divisions
are intentionally rather ambiguous.

Das unmittelbar am Wasser stehende
Gebäude stellt einen Kontrast zu den
Bürohochhäusern in Bostons Innenstadt
dar. Sein mehrdeutig gegliederter Baukörper ragt weithin sichtbar auf.

Quasi posé sur l'eau, le bâtiment
contraste avec les grands immeubles
de bureaux du centre de Boston. La
division des espaces est volontairement ambiguë.

The auditorium space above can be opened to the harbor, while the multimedia room (left) is skewed down to the water, allowing views only of the waves. Structurally innovative, the building proclaims its allegiance to the contemporary in all forms.

Das Auditorium (oben) lässt sich zum Hafen hin öffnen, während der Multimediaraum (links) zum Wasser hin abgeschrägt ist, sodass einzig die Wellen zu sehen sind. Das in seiner Konstruktion innovative Gebäude kündet mit jedem Detail von seiner Bindung an die Gegenwart.

L'auditorium s'ouvre sur le port, tandis que la salle multimédia (à gauche) s'incline vers l'eau pour offrir une vue sur les vagues. De structure novatrice, cet équipement culturel proclame une allégeance à la modernité contemporaine sous toutes ses formes.

# EVAN DOUGLIS

Evan Douglis Studio
1205 Manhattan Avenue, 1-2-14 / Brooklyn, NY 11222 / USA
Tel: +1 718 302 2033
E-mail: info@evandouglis.com / Web: www.evandouglis.com

**EVAN DOUGLIS** participated in the Exchange Program of the Architectural Association (AA) in London (1980), before obtaining his B. A. degree from Cooper Union (1983) and his M.Arch. from the Harvard Graduate School of Design (1991). He worked from 1982 to 1985 in the office of Tod Williams and Billie Tsien in New York, from 1985 to 1987 with Emilio Ambasz and from 1991 to 1992 with Agrest and Gandelsonas. Since its creation in 1992, the Evan Douglis Studio has been an architecture and interdisciplinary design firm "committed to the research and application of new self-generative systems, membrane technology, and contemporary fabrication techniques as applied to a range of projects." Evan Douglis is currently the Chair of the Undergraduate School of Architecture at Pratt Institute. Prior to this appointment he was an Associate Assistant Professor at Columbia University, the Director of Columbia University's Architecture Galleries, and a Visiting Professor at Cooper Union throughout most of the 1990s. Evan Douglis received a 1999 Emerging Voice citation from the Architectural League of New York; was a participant and exhibitor in the 2004 ARCHILAB International Conference in Orléans, France; a 2006 Design Merit Award; a finalist nominee for the 2006 James Beard Foundation Restaurant Design Awards; and a recipient of the 2006 ACADIA Award for Emerging Digital Practice. His main projects include *Anamorphic Balloons* (Columbia University, New York, 2000); *Auto-Braids/ Auto Breeding*, installation for traveling Jean Prouvé exhibition (beginning in 2003); ECO Bars (Cape Verde Islands, Africa, 2003–04); *Accordion Fractals*, Lantern Restaurant, design for building proposal (New York, 2004–05); *Helioscopes*, traveling media-scape (Orléans, France, 2004–07); and the REptile–Haku Japanese Restaurant (New York, 2005, published here). Current work includes fLORA_*flex*, a new modular wall system and house prototype created for the upcoming 2007 Rotterdam Biennale.

**EVAN DOUGLIS** nahm 1980 an einem Austauschprogramm der Architectural Association in London teil, ehe er 1983 an der Cooper Union die Prüfung zum Bachelor of Arts ablegte und 1991 an der Harvard Graduate School of Design den Grad eines Master of Architecture erwarb. Von 1982 bis 1985 arbeitete er im Büro von Tod Williams und Billie Tsien in New York, von 1985 bis 1987 mit Emilio Ambasz und von 1991 bis 1992 bei Agrest and Gandelsonas. Seit seiner Gründung 1982 ist das Evan Douglis Studio ein Architektur- und interdisziplinäres Designbüro, »das sich der Erforschung und Anwendung neuer selbstgenerativer Systeme, der Membrantechnologie und modernen Fertigungstechniken verschrieben hat, wie sie bei einer Vielzahl von Projekten zur Anwendung kommen.« Douglis ist zurzeit Dekan der Undergraduate School of Architecture am Pratt Institute. Davor war er Associate Assistant Professor an der Columbia University, leitete deren Architekturgalerie und hatte fast die gesamten 1990er-Jahre hindurch eine Gastprofessur an der Cooper Union inne. 1999 erhielt er von der Architectural League of New York eine lobende Erwähnung als Emerging Voice, war 2004 als Aussteller an der ARCHILAB International Conference in Orléans, Frankreich, beteiligt, erhielt 2006 den Design Merit Award, kam 2006 in die Endauswahl der James Beard Foundation Restaurant Design Awards und wurde ebenfalls 2006 mit dem ACADIA Award for Emerging Digital Practice ausgezeichnet. Zu seinen Hauptprojekten zählen: »Anamorphic Balloons« (Columbia University, New York, 2000), »Auto-Braids/Auto Breeding«, eine Installation für die Wanderausstellung zu Jean Prouvé (Anfang 2003), ECO Bars (Kapverdische Inseln, 2003–04), »Accordion Fractals«, Lantern Restaurant, Entwurf für ein geplantes Bauwerk (New York, 2004–05), die Medienpräsentation »Helioscopes« (Orléans, 2004–05) und das hier gezeigte japanische Restaurant REptile-Haku (New York, 2005). Gegenwärtig arbeitet er an fLORA_*flex*, einem neuartigen modularen Wandsystem und Hausprototyp, geschaffen für die bevorstehende Biennale 2007 in Rotterdam.

**EVAN DOUGLIS** a participé au programme d'échanges de l'Architectural Association de Londres (1980) avant d'obtenir son B. Arch. à Cooper Union (1983) et son M. Arch. à la Harvard Graduate School of Design (1991). Il a travaillé de 1982 à 1985 chez Tod Williams et Billie Tsien à New York puis, de 1985 à 1987, avec Emilio Ambasz et enfin de 1991 à 1992 chez Agrest and Gandelsonas. Depuis sa création en 1992, l'Evan Douglis Studio se présente comme «une agence de conception interdisciplinaire d'architecture, engagée dans la recherche et l'application de nouveaux systèmes autogénérés, la technologie des membranes et les techniques contemporaines de fabrication appliquée à une vaste gamme de projets. » Douglis est actuellement président de l'Undergraduate School of Architecture du Pratt Institute. Il était Professeur assistant associé à Columbia University, directeur des galeries d'architecture de cette université et Professeur invité à Cooper Union pendant les années 1990. Il a été cité comme «Emerging Voice» en 1999 par l'Architectural League de New York, a participé et exposé à l' ARCHILAB 2004 à Orléans, France, obtenu le Design Merit Award en 2006, nominé finaliste pour les James Beard Foundation Restaurant Design Awards 2006 et a reçu le prix ACADIA 2006 pour les pratiques numériques émergentes. Parmi ses principaux projets : *Anamorphic Balloons* (Columbia University, New York, 2000) ; *Auto-Braids/Auto Breeding*, installation pour une exposition itinérante sur Jean Prouvé (2003–) ; ECO Bars dans les Îles du Cap Vert (2003–04) ; *Accordion Fractals* au Lantern Restaurant ; un projet d'immeuble, New York (2004–05) ; *Helioscopes*, média-paysage itinérant, Orléans, France (2004–05) et le restaurant japonais REptile-Haku à New York, publié ici (2005). Ses interventions récentes comprennent fLORA_*flex*, un nouveau système de mur modulaire et de prototype de maison créé pour la Biennale de Rotterdam 2007.

# REPTILE–HAKU JAPANESE RESTAURANT

*New York, New York, USA, 2005*

*Floor area: 130 m². Client: not disclosed. Cost: $325 000.*
*Project Coordinator: Eric Wong*

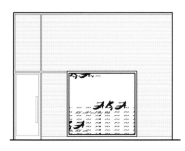

The conceptual motivation behind this sushi restaurant located on Broadway in Manhattan is derived from the architect's interest in biological mimesis, modular systems, and mass-customization. Drawing inspiration from mythology and anatomical features specific to reptiles for his Japanese restaurant, Evan Douglis went on to create a modular tile system that utilizes these effects in a new way. Through the use of 3D and animation software the tile surfaces alternate between smooth and pyramidal spike patterns producing the illusion of "architecture coming to life." Using CNC (Computer Numerical Control) milling, a set of master forms, corresponding urethane molds and liquid plastic casts were created, enabling the architect to mass-produce a unique modular and interchangeable tile system. Finished in hi-gloss red automobile paint the intricacy inscribed into the surfaces acquired a visual boldness and theatrical intensity that permeates the entire space. The 200 lights suspended above the dining tables, serve to activate the perimeter wall tiles with highlights, shadows and reflective glares. In the Haku Restaurant, Douglis creates a most unexpected and skilful blend of repetitive, modular elements, with unique characteristics generated through computer design. The fact that the entire cladding system has its origin in reptilian imagery gives another layer of meaning to the design. A custom-designed aluminum façade introduces the idea of repetition and modularity from the outside.

Die konzeptuelle Motivation für dieses Sushi-Restaurant am Broadway in Manhattan entstand aus dem Interesse des Architekten an biologischer Mimesis, Modulsystemen und individualisierte Massenfertigung. Für sein japanisches Restaurant bezog Evan Douglis Anregungen aus der Mythologie und typischen anatomischen Merkmalen von Reptilien und gestaltete ein modulares Kachelsystem, das diese Effekte neuartig verwertet. Mit Hilfe von 3D- und Animationssoftware hatten die Oberflächen der Kacheln abwechselnd glatte oder mit pyramidenförmigen Zacken besetzte Muster und erzeugen den Eindruck einer "lebendig gewordenen Architektur". Durch den Einsatz von CNC (elektronisch-numerisch gesteuerte Maschinen) entstand eine Reihe von Formvorlagen, entsprechende Polyurethanformen und Gussformen für Flüssigkunststoff, die es dem Architekten ermöglichten ein einzigartiges modulares, austauschbares Kachelsystem serienmäßig herzustellen. Überzogen mit hochglänzendem rotem Autolack, nimmt die den Oberflächen eigene Komplexität eine den ganzen Raum erfüllende visuelle Kühnheit und dramatische Intensität an. Die 200 über den Restauranttischen hängenden Beleuchtungskörper produzieren Schlaglichter, Schattierungen und Reflexe auf den Kacheln. Im Haku-Restaurant gelingt Douglis eine überraschende, geschickte Verschmelzung von sich wiederholenden, bausteinartigen Elementen mit durch computergestütztes Entwerfen möglichen außergewöhnlichen Merkmalen. Die Tatsache, dass die gesamte Innenverkleidung ihre Formgebung der Bildwelt der Reptilien verdankt, verleiht der Gestaltung eine weitere Bedeutungsebene. Eine maßgefertigte Aluminiumfassade auf der Außenseite vermittelt die Vorstellung von Wiederholung und Modularität.

La motivation conceptuelle de ce restaurant de sushi sur Broadway à Manhattan évoque l'intérêt de l'architecte pour la *mimesis* biologique, les systèmes modulaires et la customisation de masse. Tirant son inspiration de la mythologie et de caractéristiques physiques spécifiques aux reptiles pour ce restaurant japonais, Douglis a créé un système de carrelage modulaire qui utilise les effets de façon novatrice. Grâce à des logiciels de 3D et d'animation, la surface de chaque carreau peut alterner des motifs lisses ou pyramidaux pointus produisant l'illusion d'une « architecture s'animant ». Utilisant des outils à pilotage numérique, des formes matricielles, des moules en uréthane et de la fonte de plastique, il a pu produire en quantité ce système de carrelages uniques, modulaires et interchangeables. Leur finition à la peinture pour automobile rouge brillant met en valeur cette complexité d'imbrication qui fait partie de la surface même et crée une intensité théâtrale visuellement audacieuse qui se développe dans la totalité de l'espace. L'illumination produite par 200 points lumineux au-dessus des tables active des effets de soulignement, de brillances et de reflets sur les carreaux. Dans le Haku Restaurant, Douglis crée ainsi une combinaison très inattendue et habile d'éléments répétitifs modulaires dont les caractéristiques sépcifiques sont obtenues par des techniques de conception par ordinateur. Le fait que ce système de revêtement mural tire ses origines de l'imagerie reptilienne ajoute une strate de sens supplémentaire à ce projet. La façade en aluminium introduit l'idée de répétition et de modularité dès l'extérieur.

*The layout of the restaurant as seen in the plans above is quite simple. There is, however, a play on surfaces and colors that animates the space.*

*Wie an den Plänen oben zu sehen, ist die Anlage des Restaurants recht simpel. Es gibt allerdings ein den Raum belebendes Spiel mit Oberflächen und Farben.*

*Comme le montrent les plans ci-dessus, la disposition du restaurant est assez simple. On observe cependant un jeu de surfaces et de couleurs qui anime l'espace.*

*Both the lights hanging from the ceiling and the three-dimensional patterns of the wall covering give a reptilian feeling to the restaurant, justifying its name.*

*Sowohl die von der Decke hängenden Lampen als auch die dreidimensionale Wandverkleidung verschaffen dem Restaurant die den Namen rechtfertigende reptilienhafte Anmutung.*

*Les luminaires suspendus et les motifs tridimensionnels de l'habillage des murs créent une impression d'univers reptilien qui a donné son nom au restaurant.*

Even the toilet walls and light fixtures (right) conform to the style of the restaurant. The sweeping irregular patterns of the wall panels can be compared to works of art (above).

Selbst in den Waschräumen (rechts) entsprechen Wände und Beleuchtungskörper dem Stil des Restaurants. Die weitläufigen unregelmäßigen Muster der Wandpaneele können mit Kunstwerken verglichen werden (oben).

Même les murs des toilettes (à droite) et les luminaires rappellent le style du restaurant. Les motifs filants irréguliers des panneaux qui habillent les murs sont assimilables à des œuvres d'art (ci-dessus).

# MICHAEL ELMGREEN & INGAR DRAGSET

*Klosterfelde Gallery*
*Zimmerstrasse 90/91*
*10117 Berlin*
*Germany*

*Tel: +49 30 283 5305*
*Fax: +49 30 283 5306*
*E-mail: office@klosterfelde.de*
*Web: www.klosterfelde.de*

The artists **MICHAEL ELMGREEN**, born in 1961 in Copenhagen, Denmark, and **INGAR DRAGSET**, born in 1969 in Trondheim, Norway, have been working together in Berlin since 1995. Although their subject may be less architecture itself than "mechanisms of ideological control," they have frequently explored the shape of buildings in their *Powerless Structures* series. Amongst other goals, they transformed the conventions of "white cube" gallery space by creating galleries suspended from the ceiling, sunken into the ground or turned upside down. "The emphasis," as their gallery explains, "is put on the deconstruction and reconstruction of meaning in predetermined or institutionalized spaces." They have participated in the "Nuit Blanche," Musée d'Art Moderne (Paris, 1998); Manifesta III (Ljubljana, 2000); "What if…," Moderna Museet (Stockholm, 2000); Portikus (Frankfurt, 2001); and the São Paulo Bienniale (2002). More recent work includes "Utopia Station," 50th Biennale (Venice, 2003); "Blocking the View" at the Tate Modern (London, 2004); "The Welfare Show," Serpentine Gallery (London, 2006); and their Skulptur Projekte (Münster, 2007). They exhibit at the Galerie Klosterfelde (Berlin), the Galleri Nicolai Wallner (Copenhagen), as well as other galleries and institutions, and in 2005 realized *Prada Marfa* in the United States (published here).

Der 1961 in Kopenhagen geborene **MICHAEL ELMGREEN** und der 1969 in Trondheim, Norwegen, gebürtige **INGAR DRAGSET** arbeiten seit 1995 gemeinsam in Berlin. Wenngleich ihr Gegenstand wohl eher die »Mechanismen ideologischer Kontrolle« sind als die Architektur, setzen sie sich in ihrer Serie »Powerless Structures« häufig mit der Form von Gebäuden auseinander. Neben anderen Zielsetzungen transformierten sie die herkömmlichen weißen Kuben der Ausstellungsräume, indem sie von der Decke herabhängende, unter den Boden abgesenkte oder auf den Kopf gestellte Galerien schufen. Wie ihre Galerie erläutert, liegt »der Schwerpunkt auf der Dekonstruktion und Rekonstruktion von Bedeutung in prädeterminierten oder institutionalisierten Räumen«. Sie waren beteiligt an der »Nuit Blanche« im Musée d'Art Moderne (Paris, 1998), Manifesta III (Ljubljana, 2000), »What if …«, Moderna Museet (Stockholm, 2000), Portikus (Frankfurt am Main, 2001) und der Biennale in São Paulo (2002). Neuere Arbeiten sind »Utopia Station«, 50. Biennale Venedig (2003), »Blocking the View«, Tate Modern (London, 2004), »The Welfare Show«, Serpentine Gallery (London, 2006), und ihre Skulptur Projekte in Münster (2007). Sie stellen in der Galerie Klosterfelde (Berlin) aus, der Galleri Nicolai Wallner (Kopenhagen) sowie in anderen Galerien und Institutionen und realisierten 2005 in den USA das hier gezeigte Projekt »Prada Marfa«.

Les artistes **MICHAEL ELMGREEN**, né en 1961 à Copenhague, au Danemark, et **INGAR DRAGSET**, né en 1969 à Trondheim, en Norvège, travaillent ensemble à Berlin depuis 1995. Bien que leur préoccupation commune soit moins l'architecture elle-même que « les mécanismes du contrôle idéologique », ils ont fréquemment exploré les formes du bâti dans leur série *Powerless Structures*. Parmi leurs projets, ils bousculent les conventions de l'espace de galerie-cube blanc, en créant des galeries suspendues au plafond, enterrées dans le sol, ou renversées. « Ils s'intéressent, comme l'explique leur galeriste, à la déconstruction et à la reconstruction du sens dans des lieux prédéterminés ou institutionnalisés. » Ils ont participé à la manifestation « Nuit blanche » au Musée d'art moderne de la Ville de Paris (1998) ; à « Manifesta III » à Ljubljana (2000) ; « What if… » au Moderna Museet à Stockholm (2000) ; au Portikus de Francfort (2001) et à la Biennale de Sao Paulo (2002). Parmi leurs inventions plus récentes : « Utopia Station » à la 50ᵉ Biennale de Venise (2003) ; « Blocking the view » à la Tate Modern, à Londres (2004) ; « The Welfare Show » à la Serpentine Gallery, à Londres (2006), et leurs « Skulptur Projekte » à Münster (2007). Ils exposent, entre autres, à la Galerie Klosterfelde à Berlin, la Galleri Nicolai Wallner à Copenhague et, en 2005, ont réalisé aux États-Unis *Prada Marfa,* publiée ici.

# PRADA MARFA

*Valentine, Texas, USA, 2005*

*Client: Art Production Fund, New York; Ballroom Marfa, Marfa. Size: 760 x 470 x 480 cm. Cost: not disclosed.*
*Collaboration: Art Production Fund, New York; Ballroom Marfa, Marfa*

Made with "adobe bricks, plaster, paint, glass pane, aluminum frame, mdf, and carpet," *Prada Marfa* was installation art that certainly resembled architecture. The artists had already made reference to the ubiquitous Prada label in their 1998 work *Opening Soon* (Powerless Structures, Figure 242, Tanya Bonakdar Gallery, New York, 2001). With the Prada name visible from the street in this instance, they pointed out that consumerism and "culture" have become inevitably linked. Installed on a desert road near Valentine, Texas, rendered famous in the art world by the presence of Donald Judd's Chinati Foundation, the small structure erected by the artists and stocked with shoes and handbags by Prada represented a humorous and incongruous conjunction of cultural and consumer "icons." Elmgreen and Dragset described their work as a "pop architectural land art project," leaving critics to speculate on the rapport between Prada's known display minimalism and the artistic minimalism of Judd. As useless as spike heels in the desert, the shop was never intended to open to the public. Indeed, shortly after its inauguration, *Prada Marfa* was vandalized, but fortunately Ms Prada donated new items. Although it is billed as a "permanent" installation, the artists expect that *Prada Marfa* will eventually be destroyed by time and the elements.

Die Kunstinstallation »Prada Marfa«, bestehend aus »Lehmziegeln, Putz, Farbe, Glasscheiben, Aluminiumtragwerk, Hartfaserplatten und Teppich«, könnte sicherlich leicht mit Architektur verwechselt werden. Die Künstler hatten bereits 1998 in ihrem Werk »Opening Soon« (»Powerless Structures«, Figur 242, Tanya Bonakdar Gallery, New York, 2001) auf das allgegenwärtige Prada-Label angespielt. Da der Name Prada in diesem Fall von der Straße aus sichtbar ist, machen sie darauf aufmerksam, dass Konsumdenken und »Kultur« inzwischen unvermeidlich miteinander verquickt sind. Das an einer Straße durch die Wüste in der Nähe von Valentine, Texas, errichtete kleine Gebäude, das in der Kunstwelt durch die Präsenz von Donald Judds Chinati Foundation berühmt und mit von Miuccia Prada gestifteten Schuhen und Handtaschen versorgt wurde, verkörpert eine humorvolle, weil unvereinbare Verknüpfung von Kultur- und Konsumikonen. Elmgreen und Dragset bezeichnen ihr Werk als ein »pop architectural land art project« und überlassen es den Kritikern, über die Beziehung zwischen Pradas bekannt minimalistischer Werbung und dem künstlerischen Minimalismus von Judd zu spekulieren. Nutzlos wie Pfennigabsätze in der Wüste, sollte der Laden nie wirklich eröffnet werden. Tatsächlich wurde »Prada Marfa« kurz nach seiner Einweihung mutwillig zerstört, die Schuhe und Taschen gestohlen. Erfreulicherweise stiftete Frau Prada neue Ware für die Ausstellung. Obwohl »Prada Marfa« als Dauerinstallation angekündigt ist, gehen die Künstler davon aus, dass Zeit und Witterung es eines Tages zerstören werden.

« En briques d'adobe, plâtre, peinture, panneaux de verre, ossature d'aluminium, médium et moquette », *Prada Marfa* est une œuvre relevant de l'art de l'installation, non sans rapport avec l'architecture. Les artistes avaient déjà fait référence à la marque Prada, omniprésente dans leur œuvre de 1998, *Opening Soon* (Powerless Structures, Figure 242, Tanya Bonakdar Gallery, New York, 2001). À travers le nom de Prada, visible de la route, ils pointent le doigt sur le fait que le consumérisme et la « culture » sont devenus inévitablement liés. Installée au bord d'une route dans le désert près de Valentine au Texas, lieu rendu célèbre dans le monde de l'art par la présence de la Chinati Foundation de Donald Judd, la petite structure est remplie de chaussures et de sacs offerts par Miuccia Prada. Cette œuvre illustre la conjonction humoristique et incongrue d'icônes culturelle et consumériste. Elmgreen et Dragset décrivent cette œuvre comme « un projet de land art pop architectural », laissant aux critiques le loisir de spéculer sur les rapports entre le minimalisme affiché de Prada, et celui, artistique, de Judd. Aussi inutile que des talons hauts dans le désert, la boutique n'a jamais été prévue pour ouvrir au public. En fait, peu après son inauguration, elle a été vandalisée. Heureusement Madame Prada a remplacé ses cadeaux. Bien que cette installation soit « permanente », les artistes pensent qu'elle sera sans doute finalement détruite par les effets du climat et de la durée.

The contrast between the "urban myth" constituted by Prada's reputation and this desolate setting highlights both the ambiguity of the work and the clever misappropriation of the genre by the artists.

Der Kontrast zwischen dem von der Reputation Pradas konstituierten »urbanen Mythos« und diesem öden Schauplatz unterstreicht sowohl die Mehrdeutigkeit des Werkes als auch die listige Zweckentfremdung des Genres durch die Künstler.

Le contraste entre le « mythe urbain » de Prada et ce cadre désolé souligne à la fois l'ambiguïté de l'œuvre et une appropriation intelligemment détournée par les artistes.

# ANTÓN GARCÍA-ABRIL RUIZ
# & ENSAMBLE STUDIO

*Antón García-Abril Ruiz & Ensamble Studio*
*c/ Cristobal Bordiú 55, bajo*
*28003 Madrid*
*Spain*

*Tel: +34 91 541 0848*
*E-mail: anton@ensamble.info*
*Web: www.ensamble.info*

**ANTÓN GARCÍA-ABRIL RUIZ** was born in Madrid in 1969. He graduated from the ETSA in Madrid in Architecture and Urbanism in 1995 and went on to receive a doctorate from the same institution in 2000. He is currently a Professor of Architectural Projects at the ETSA. He worked in the office of Santiago Calatrava (1992) and Alberto Campo Baeza (1990–94). He created his first firm in 1995, and his present one, **ENSAMBLE STUDIO**, in 2000. García-Abril explains that the name of his firm is derived from the architectural term "assemble" and the musical designation "ensemble." "This team," he says, "develops a multidisciplinary working scheme […] to carry out the intervention of the architect in the whole process that leads to the artistic work, from the conceptual abstraction to the construction detail." Essentially this means that he has created an in-house contracting firm. His completed projects include the Musical Studies Center (Santiago de Compostela, 2002); Concert Hall and Music School (Medina del Campo, 2003); Martemar House (Málaga, 2003–05, published here); Valdés Studio (Madrid, 2004), all in Spain. Amongst his current projects: SGAE Central Office (Santiago de Compostela, 2005); La Casa del Lector Library (Madrid, 2006); Hemeroscopium House (Madrid, 2006); Berklee Tower of Music (Valencia, 2007); Liric Theater (Mexico, D. F., 2007); Fleta Theater (Saragossa, 2007); and Paraiso Theater (Shanghai, China, 2007).

**ANTÓN GARCÍA-ABRIL RUIZ** wurde 1969 in Madrid geboren. Er beendete 1995 sein Studium der Architektur und der Stadtplanung an der ETSA in Madrid und wurde 2000 von derselben Institution promoviert. Gegenwärtig ist er als Professor für Architekturprojekte an der ETSA tätig. García-Abril arbeitete in den Büros von Santiago Calatrava (1992) und Alberto Campo-Baeza (1990–94). Sein erstes Büro gründete er 1995 und das heutige **ENSAMBLE STUDIO** im Jahr 2000. García-Abril erklärt, der Name seines Büros leite sich ab von dem in der Architektur gebräuchlichen Begriff »assemble« und dem musikalischen Begriff »ensemble«. »Dieses Team«, sagt er, »entwickelt ein multidisziplinäres Arbeitsprogramm […], um die Arbeit des Architekten in dem gesamten Prozess, der zum Kunstwerk führt, zu verwirklichen – vom abstrakten Entwurf bis zum Detail der Konstruktion.« Das bedeutet im Grunde die Schaffung einer Baufirma in-house. Zu seinen realisierten Projekten zählen: das Musikalische Studienzentrum in Santiago de Compostela (2002), Konzerthalle und Musikschule in Medina del Campo (2003), Haus Martemar (Málaga, 2003–05, hier vorgestellt) und das Studio Valdés (Madrid, 2004), alle in Spanien. Aktuelle Projekte sind: die SGAE-Zentrale (Santiago de Compostela, 2005), die Bibliothek La Casa del Lector (Madrid, 2006), Haus Hemeroscopium (Madrid, 2006), Berklee Tower of Music (Valencia, 2007), Teatro Lyrico (Mexico-Stadt, 2007), Teatro Fleta (Saragossa, 2007) und das Paraiso-Theater (Shanghai, China, 2007).

**ANTÓN GARCÍA-ABRIL RUIZ** est né à Madrid, en 1969. Diplômé de l'ETSA (Madrid) en architecture et urbanisme (1995), il y poursuit ses études de doctorat (2000). Il est actuellement professeur de projets architecturaux à l'ETSA. Il a travaillé chez Santiago Calatrava (1992) et Alberto Campo Baeza (1990–94). Il crée sa première agence, en 1995, et l'actuelle, **ENSAMBLE STUDIO**, en 2000, expliquant que ce nom provient de la fusion du terme architectural « assemblage » et du terme musical « ensemble ». « Cette équipe, explique-t-il, travaille dans une orientation multidisciplinaire… pour mettre en œuvre l'intervention de l'architecte dans le processus global qui conduit à une œuvre artistique, de l'abstraction du concept aux détails de la construction… » Travaillant en quelque sorte à la façon d'une entreprise générale. Parmi ses projets réalisés, tous en Espagne : le Centre d'études musicales de Saint-Jacques de Compostelle (2002) ; une salle de concert et une école de musique, Medina del Campo (2003) ; la maison Martemar, Málaga (2003–05), publiée ici ; le Studio Valdés, Madrid (2004). Ses projets actuels comprennent : les bureaux du siège de SGAE à Saint-Jacques de Compostelle (2005) ; la bibliothèque de la Casa del Lector à Madrid (2006) ; la maison Hemeroscopium à Madrid (2006) ; la tour de musique Berklee à Valence (2007) ; le Théâtre lyrique de Mexico (2007) ; le Théâtre Fleta, Saragosse (2007), et le Théâtre Paraiso à Shanghai, Chine (2007).

# MARTEMAR HOUSE

*Benahavis, Málaga, Spain, 2003–05*

*Floor area: 1640 m². Client: Perez Arauna family. Cost: not diclosed.
Technical Architect: Javier Cuesta. Ensamble Studio: Guillermo Sevillano, Johannes Gramse,
Claudia Gans, Jorge Consuegra, Jan Goebel*

This was the first house designed by Antón García-Abril. Its elevated site gives it broad views of the sea in front and the mountains to the rear, a fact that the architect played on. As he says, "The house is like a passing viewpoint in this direction and both directions: with all the interior spaces linked to these horizons." Two porticos, one facing the sea and the other the mountains, mark the design. The sea view is framed by a sliding 25-meter-wide window. A prestressed concrete lintel weighing some 50 000 kilos was used to support five metallic trusses. This massive concrete element appears to float above the rather strictly detailed residence. As Antón García-Abril has written, he likes "the nudity of the structure, and its expression through the construction. We have incorporated solutions that are not common in residential programs and we attempt to resolve them with constructive honesty, where the systems are assembled seeking a new expression of architectural language resulting from the meeting of elements of different scales." The overall impression given by this house is one of architectural power, perhaps beyond the scale usually encountered in a house, but its essential nature is, as the architect insists, one of openness to the natural setting.

Dies ist das erste von García-Abril entworfene Haus. Sein erhöhter Standort gewährt ihm auf der Vorderseite weite Ausblicke auf das Meer, auf der Rückseite auf die Berge, ein Umstand, den der Architekt zu nutzen versteht. Er führt dazu aus: »Das Haus ist wie ein durchgehender Aussichtspunkt in diese Richtung und in beide Richtungen, bei dem sämtliche Innenräume auf diese beiden Ausblicke bezogen sind.« Zwei Vorbauten von denen einer zum Meer, der andere zu den Bergen hin gelegen ist, zeichnen den Entwurf aus. Der Blick aufs Meer wird von einem verschiebbaren, 25 m breiten Fenster gerahmt. Ein über 50 000 kg schwerer, vorgespannter Sturzträger aus Beton wurde zum Abstützen der fünf metallischen Träger verwendet. Dieses massive Betonteil scheint über dem eher streng durchgebildeten Wohnhaus zu schweben. Wie Antón García-Abril schreibt, schätzt er »die Nacktheit des Baukörpers und seines Ausdrucks durch die Konstruktion. Wir haben Lösungen einbezogen, die im Wohnhausbau nicht üblich sind, und wir versuchen, sie mit konstruktiver Ehrlichkeit anzugehen. Durch das Zusammenstellen dieser Systeme suchen wir einen neuen Ausdruck in der Architektursprache, der aus dem Aufeinandertreffen von Elementen unterschiedlicher Größenverhältnisse entsteht.« Der von diesem Haus erzeugte Gesamteindruck ist geprägt von architektonischer Kraft, vielleicht in einem für Wohnhäuser ungewöhnlichen Maß, wenngleich der Architekt beteuert, der grundlegende Charakter werde von der Offenheit zur umgebenden Landschaft bestimmt.

Première maison conçue par Antón García-Abril, elle profite de son site élevé offrant d'amples perspectives panoramiques sur la mer d'un côté et les montagnes de l'autre, situation dont l'architecte a su jouer : « Cette maison, dit-il, est comme un point de vue mobile dans une direction et dans deux directions : tous les espaces intérieurs sont liés à ces horizons. » Deux portiques, l'un face à la mer, l'autre face aux montagnes, caractérisent ce projet. La vue sur la mer est cadrée par une baie de 25 mètres de large. Le massif linteau en béton prétensionné, pesant quelque 50 tonnes, soutient cinq poutres métalliques, et semble tenir en suspension au-dessus de la maison. L'architecte aime « la nudité de la structure, et son expression par le processus constructif. Nous avons intégré des solutions qui ne sont pas courantes dans les programmes résidentiels, et avons tenté de résoudre les problèmes avec une honnêteté constructive à travers des systèmes qui s'assemblent, dans la recherche d'une nouvelle expression du langage architectural résultant de la confrontation d'éléments d'échelles différentes. » L'impression d'ensemble est celle d'une très forte présence architecturale qui va peut-être au-delà de l'échelle habituellement rencontrée dans ce type de projet, mais sa nature essentielle, sur laquelle insiste l'architecte, est « son ouverture sur son environnement naturel ».

*The house is located in a heterogeneous architectural environment and imposes its strict rectilinear form.*

*Das Haus steht in einem heterogenen architektonischen Umfeld und zwingt ihm seine Gradlinigkeit auf.*

*La maison se trouve dans un environnement architectural hétérogène et impose sa forme rectiligne.*

*To say that the Martemar House is minimalist would almost be understating the nature of its design, where a muscular Modernism expresses itself in part through materials that almost take on industrial dimensions.*

*Das Haus Martemar als minimalistisch zu bezeichnen kommt in diesem Fall, wo sich eine kraftstrotzende Moderne teilweise mittels industriell anmutender Materialien äußert, nahezu einer Untertreibung gleich.*

*Dire que la maison Martemar est minimaliste serait presque un euphémisme par rapport à sa conception : un modernisme musculeux exprimé en partie dans des matériaux qui semblent d'échelle industrielle.*

*Strong steel or concrete elements
are placed above an apparently
much more frail glass base.*

*Schwergewichtige Elemente aus Stahl
und Beton stehen auf einem scheinbar weit fragileren Unterbau.*

*Les lourds éléments de béton ou
d'acier semblent reposer sur une
base de verre fragile.*

The house appears to borrow its strength from factory-like elements that are used to create agreeable spaces.

Das Haus scheint seine Stärke aus fabrikartigen Elementen zu beziehen, die zur Schaffung angenehmer Räumlichkeiten genutzt werden.

La maison paraît tirer sa force d'éléments industriels qui permettent néanmoins de créer d'agréables volumes.

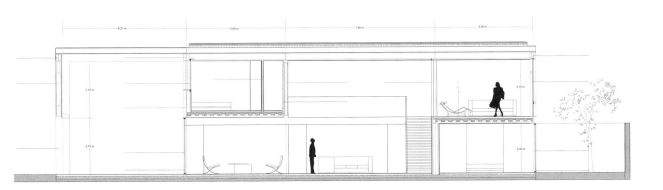

A touch of color in the form of a couch serves partially to alleviate the rigor of the structural elements. The architect has certainly ventured into uncharted territory with this house.

Die Couch als Farbtupfer dient dazu, die Strenge der konstruktiven Elemente wenigstens teilweise abzumildern. Mit diesem Haus hat der Architekt mit Gewissheit Neuland betreten.

La touche de couleur d'un canapé allège en partie la rigueur des éléments structuraux en place. L'architecte s'est aventuré ici dans un territoire jusque-là inexploré.

The dining and living area (below) exemplifies the concept of powerful steel elements hovering over a glass base with floor to ceiling glazing. Even the bathroom (above) takes up the strict, bare vocabulary of the rest of the house.

Auch im Wohn- und Essbereich (unten) wird die Konzeption der schweren Stahlträger deutlich, die über gläsernem Untergrund schweben, gepaart mit deckenhoher Verglasung. Selbst das Bad (oben) behält die strenge, karge Formensprache des übrigen Hauses bei.

Dans la zone de séjour et des repas (ci-dessous), règne le concept de puissants éléments d'acier reposant sur une base en verre prise entre sol et plafond. Même la salle de bains (ci-dessus) maintient le vocabulaire strict et épuré du reste de la maison.

# MARIO GARZANITI

Atelier d'Architecture Mario Garzaniti
Rue Wazon 95
4000 Liège
Belgium

Tel: +32 4 223 3712
Fax: +32 4 221 1162
E-mail: mariogarzaniti@skynet.be

*Social Housin*

**MARIO GARZANITI** was born in Liège in 1956. He graduated from the Institut Supérieur d'Architecture Lambert Lombard in Liège in 1981. He created the Independent Atelier in 1982 in Liège, and his present firm, Atelier d'Architecture Mario Garzaniti, in 2000. He won the 1999 competition for public housing in Schaerbeek (Brussels, 2001–03, published here) and was the winner of the 2002 competition for building a housing project on the site of the Prince Baudouin barracks in Brussels (in association with AC&T). His work includes the Dormal Houses (Villers-L'Évêque, 1990); a restoration project for medical offices (Huy, 1993); Scheuren House (Vottem, 1994); eight apartments (Grivegnée, 2004); and the Dexis Bank (Rocourt, Liège, 2004), all in Belgium. Garzaniti has also designed musical instruments—the "Oiram" flügelhorn and trumpet for Hub van Laar (Margraten, The Netherlands, 2006).

**MARIO GARZANITI** wurde 1956 in Lüttich geboren und schloss 1981 am dortigen Institut Supérieur d'Architecture Lambert Lombard sein Studium ab. 1982 gründete er in Lüttich das Independent Atelier, dem im Jahr 2000 sein heutiges Büro Atelier d'Architecture Mario Garzaniti folgte. 1999 konnte er den Wettbewerb für ein Sozialwohnungsprojekt in Schaerbeek (Brüssel, 2001–03, hier vorgestellt) für sich entscheiden und gewann ebenso den Wettbewerb für ein Wohnungsbauvorhaben auf dem Gelände der Prinz-Baudouin-Kaserne in Brüssel (in Zusammenarbeit mit AC&T). Zu seinem Werk zählen: die Dormal-Häuser (Villers-L'Evêque, 1990), ein Renovierungsprojekt für medizinische Praxen (Huy, 1993), die Scheuren-Häuser (Vottem, 1994), acht Wohnungen (Grivegnée, 2004) sowie die Dexis Bank (Rocourt, Lüttich, 2004), alle in Belgien. Darüber hinaus entwarf Mario Garzaniti auch Musikinstrumente – das Flügelhorn »Oiram« und eine Trompete für Hub van Laar (Margraten, Niederlande, 2006).

**MARIO GARZANITI**, né à Liège en 1956, est diplômé de l'Institut supérieur d'architecture Lambert Lombard à Liège (1981). Il crée son Atelier d'architecture indépendant en 1982, à Liège, et son agence actuelle, Atelier d'architecture Mario Garzaniti, en 2000. Il remporte, en 1999, un concours pour des logements sociaux à Schaerbeek, Bruxelles (2001–03) publiés ici, et un second pour des logements programmés sur le site des casernes Prince Baudouin à Bruxelles en 2002 (en association avec AC&T). Parmi ses réalisations, toutes en Belgique, les maisons Dormal à Villers-l'Évêque (1990) ; un projet de restauration de bureaux médicaux à Huy (1993) ; la maison Scheuren à Vottem (1994) ; huit appartements à Grivegnée (2004) et la banque Dexis à Rocourt, Liège (2004). Il a également dessiné des instruments de musique, un bugle et une trompette pour Hub van Laar (Margraten, Pays-Bas, 2006).

# SOCIAL HOUSING

*Schaerbeek, Brussels, Belgium, 2001–03*

*Floor area: 314 m². Client: City of Schaerbeek. Cost: €223 000.*
*Collaborators: Jean François Salée, Johanne Hubin, Alain Richard, Filip Roland*

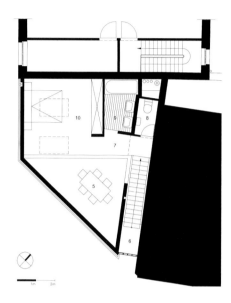
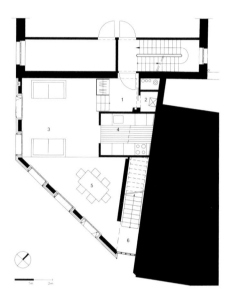

Located on a wedge-shaped site on the very visible angle of Liedts Square and Avenue de la Reine in Schaerbeek, to the northeast of the center of Brussels, this structure contains two duplex rent-controled apartments (respectively measuring 80 m² and 100 m²) and one ground-floor shop. The structure has a very small footprint—just 53 square meters. The 4-millimeter Cor-ten steel panels of the building were mounted on stainless-steel profiles on concrete walls. The windows also have perforated Cor-ten shutters which give the whole a rather abandoned aspect when they are in their closed position, lying flush with the building's surface. The reinforced-concrete roof was also clad in weathered steel. Exterior woodwork is in untreated Afzelia. Despite a notable resistance to contemporary architecture, this project was carried out with the noted support of the local mayor. Notwithstanding the rough appearance of the façade, a great deal of attention was paid to the simplicity of the detailing of the building. The monolithic appearance of the closed block may in a sense be reminiscent of large works by the American sculptor Richard Serra.

Dieses auf einem keilförmigen Grundstück an der zentralen Ecke von Liedts-Platz und Avenue de la Reine in Schaerbeek errichtete Projekt umfasst zwei 80 und 100 m² große, mietpreisgebundene Maisonettewohnungen sowie ein Ladengeschäft im Erdgeschoss. Die sehr kleine Grundfläche beschränkt sich auf nur 53 m². Die 4 mm starken Wandtafeln aus Cor-Ten-Stahl wurden mittels Edelstahlprofilen auf den Betonwänden befestigt. Auch die Fenster sind mit durchbrochenen Klappläden aus Cor-Ten-Stahl ausgestattet, die in geschlossenem Zustand bündig mit den Außenmauern, dem Ganzen eine Anmutung der Verlassenheit verleihen. Auch das Dach aus Stahlbeton wurde mit der Witterung ausgesetztem Stahl verkleidet. Für das außenliegende Holzwerk wurde unbehandeltes Afzeliaholz verwendet. Trotz eines erheblichen Widerstands gegen zeitgenössische Architektur wurde dieses Projekt mit der besonderen Unterstützung des örtlichen Bürgermeisters ausgeführt. Ungeachtet des schroffen Aussehens der Fassade wurde der schlichten architektonischen Durchbildung des Gebäudes viel Aufmerksamkeit geschenkt. Die monolithische Erscheinung des geschlossenen Blocks mag in mancher Hinsicht an großformatige Werke des amerikanischen Bildhauers Richard Serra erinnern.

Implanté sur un terrain en forme de coin, à un angle très en vue de la place Liedts et de l'avenue de la Reine à Schaerbeek, au nord-est du centre de Bruxelles, ce petit immeuble d'une emprise au sol de 53 m² seulement, comporte deux duplex à loyer modéré (80 et 100 m²) et un commerce en rez-de-chaussée. Des panneaux en acier Cor-Ten de 4 millimètres d'épaisseur ont été montés sur des profilés en acier inoxydable, contre les murs en béton. Les fenêtres sont dotées, à fleur de baie, de volets en Cor-Ten perforé qui donnent l'impression d'une forme « d'abandon » surtout lorsqu'ils sont fermés. Le toit en béton armé est également plaqué d'acier patiné. Les éléments extérieurs en bois sont en afzélia non traité. Malgré une notable résistance à son allure contemporaine, ce projet a pu être mené à bien grâce au soutien du maire local. L'aspect brut de la façade ne doit pas masquer une grande attention portée à la simplicité des détails. L'allure monolithique de ce bloc fermé pourrait presque rappeler les œuvres de grandes dimensions du sculpteur américain Richard Serra.

*The use of rusted Cor-ten steel for the façades of the building makes it look like an abandoned structure, one that fits in with a relatively difficult urban environment in an unexpected way.*

*Die Verwendung von rostigem Cor-Ten-Stahl für die Fassade des Gebäudes lässt es wie ein aufgelassenes Bauwerk wirken, das auf überraschende Weise zu seinem eher schwierigen städtischen Umfeld passt.*

*La présence d'acier Cor-Ten patiné sur les façades de l'immeuble donne l'impression d'un bâtiment abandonné, qui s'intègre de façon inattendue à son environnement urbain un peu difficile.*

Slits in the steel shutters bring a relatively agreeable light into the inner spaces of the building, belying its apparently uncompromising exterior.

Schlitze in den stählernen Klappläden lassen ein relativ angenehmes Licht in die Innenräume einfallen, das dem scheinbar abschreckenden Äußeren widerspricht.

Les fentes pratiquées dans les volets d'acier apportent un éclairage assez agréable dans les volumes intérieurs, contrairement à ce que l'aspect extérieur aurait pu faire croire.

# FRANK O. GEHRY

Gehry Partners, LLP
12541 Beatrice Street
Los Angeles, CA 90066
USA

Tel: +1 310 482 3000
Fax: +1 310 482 3006

*Hotel Marqués de Risca*

Born in Toronto, Canada, in 1929, **FRANK O. GEHRY** studied at the University of Southern California, Los Angeles (1951–54), and at Harvard (1956–57). Principal of Gehry Partners, LLP, Los Angeles, since 1962, he received the Pritzker Prize in 1989. Some of his most notable projects are the Loyola Law School (Los Angeles, 1984); Norton Residence (Venice, California, 1984); California Aerospace Museum (Los Angeles, 1984); Schnabel Residence (Brentwood, California, 1989); Festival Disney (Marne-la-Vallée, France, 1992); Guggenheim Museum (Bilbao, Spain, 1997); the unbuilt Guggenheim Museum (New York, 1998–); and Experience Music Project (Seattle, Washington, 2000). Recent completed work includes the DZ Bank Headquarters (Berlin, Germany, 2001); Fisher Center for the Performing Arts at Bard College (Annandale-on-Hudson, New York, 2003); Walt Disney Concert Hall (Los Angeles, 2003); and Massachusetts Institute of Technology Stata Complex (Cambridge, Massachusetts, 2004). Recent and current work includes the Hotel Marqués de Riscal (Elciego, Spain, 2006, published here); Ohr-O'Keefe Museums (Biloxi, Mississippi); King Alfred Leisure Centre (Brighton & Hove, UK); InterActiveCorp Headquarters (New York); Atlantic Yards (Brooklyn, New York); and New World Symphony (Miami, Florida).

Der 1929 in Toronto geborene **FRANK O. GEHRY** studierte an der University of Southern California in Los Angeles (1951–54) und in Harvard (1956–57). Er leitet seit 1962 Gehry Partners, LLP in Los Angeles und wurde 1989 mit dem Pritzker-Preis ausgezeichnet. Zu seinen denkwürdigsten Projekten zählen: die Loyola Law School (Los Angeles, 1984), die Norton Residence (Venice, Kalifornien, 1984), California Aerospace Museum (Los Angeles, 1984), Schnabel Residence (Brentwood, Kalifornien, 1989), Festival Disney (Marne-la-Vallée, Frankreich, 1992), Guggenheim Museum (Bilbao, 1997), das unrealisierte Guggenheim Museum in New York (1998–) sowie das Experience Music Project (Seattle, 2000). Zu den in den letzten Jahren fertiggestellten Arbeiten gehören: Zentrale der DZ-Bank (Berlin, 2001), Fisher Center for the Performing Arts am Bard College (Annandale-on-Hudson, New York, 2003), Walt Disney Concert Hall (Los Angeles, 2003) und Massachusetts Institute of Technology Stata Complex (Cambridge, Massachusetts, 2004). Jüngste und aktuelle Projekte sind: das Hotel Marqués de Riscal (Elciego, Spanien, 2006, hier publiziert), Ohr-O'Keefe Museum (Biloxi, Mississippi), King Alfred Leisure Centre (Brighton & Hove, Großbritannien), InterActiveCorp-Zentrale (New York), Atlantic Yards (Brooklyn, New York), und New World Symphony (Miami, Florida).

Né à Toronto, Canada, en 1929, **FRANK O. GEHRY** étudie à l'University of Southern California, Los Angeles (1951–54), puis à Harvard (1956–57). Directeur de l'agence Gehry Partners, LLP à Los Angeles, depuis 1962, il reçoit, en 1989, le Pritzker Prize. Parmi ses projets les plus remarqués : la Loyola Law School, Los Angeles (1984); la Norton Residence, Venice, Californie (1984); le California Aerospace Museum, Los Angeles (1984); la Schnabel Residence, Brentwood, Californie (1989); Festival Disney, Marne-la-Vallée, France (1992); le Guggenheim Museum, Bilbao, Espagne (1997); le Guggenheim Museum de New York qui reste à construire (1998–) et l'Experience Music Project, Seattle, Washington (2000). Parmi ses chantiers récents : le siège de la DZ Bank (Berlin, Allemagne, 2001); le Fisher Center for the Performing Arts de Bard College, Annandale-on-Hudson, New York (2003); le Walt Disney Concert Hall (Los Angeles, 2003); et le Massachusetts Institute of Technology Stata Complex, Cambridge, Massachusetts (2004). Ses projets les plus récents incluent l'Hotel Marqués de Riscal à Elciego, Espagne (2006) publié ici; le Ohr-O'Keefe Museum of Art à Biloxi, Mississippi; le Centre de loisir King Alfred, Brighton & Hove, Grande-Bretagne; le siège d'InterActiveCorp à New York; les Atlantic Yards à Brooklyn, New York, et le New World Symphony à Miami, Floride.

# HOTEL MARQUÉS DE RISCAL

*Elciego, Álava, Spain, 2003–06*

*Floor area: 3000 m². Client: Vinos de los Herederos del Marqués de Riscal.
Cost: € 16 million. Design Partner: Edwin Chan. Project Architect: Andy Liu.
Executive Architect: IDOM Architecture: César Caicoya Gómez-Morán*

Set in the Rioja area of Spain's Basque country, this winery, one of the oldest in the region, asked Frank Gehry to create a visitor's center and hotel, to be approached through the actual vineyards. The basic sandstone-clad rectilinear elements, lifted off the ground on supports including three 16.5-meter "supercolumns," are topped by sweeping pink and gold titanium panels and mirror-finish stainless steel. "It's a marvelous creature, with hair flying everywhere, which launches itself over the vineyards," says Gehry. A covered entry plaza sits below the building itself and allows for attractive views of the vineyards, the neighboring village of Elciego, and 19th-century winemaking facilities. The hotel reception is on this level and the 14 guest rooms are above. The building includes a wine-tasting room, a 172-seat Echaurren restaurant, an outdoor dining area and a private guest lounge on the upper level. Panoramic terraces are located on the roof of the structure. Numerous scale models were made and changed in the process of designing the hotel. These models were then translated into digital form and the CATIA program was used for three-dimensional modeling. These CATIA models were then used with other programs to complete the complex structural calculations. One particularly complex aspect of the project was that the third floor slab, which supports the rest of the structure, has cantilevers of up to 10 meters.

Die im baskischen Riojagebiet gelegene Weinkellerei, eine der ältesten der Region, beauftragte Gehry mit dem Entwurf eines Besucherzentrums und Hotels, die durch die Weingärten selbst zu erreichen sein sollten. Die einfachen, mit Sandstein verkleideten, rechtwinkligen Baukörper werden von Stützen, darunter drei 16,5 m dicke »Superstützen«, über den Boden angehoben und von turbulenten rosé- und goldfarbenen Platten aus Titan und verspiegeltem Edelstahl bekrönt. »Es ist ein fabelhaftes Geschöpf, dessen Haar in alle Richtungen fliegt und das sich über die Weinberge katapultiert«, sagt Gehry. Unterhalb des Gebäudes liegt eine überdachte Eingangsplaza, von der aus sich reizvolle Ausblicke auf die Weingärten, das benachbarte Dorf Elciego und aus dem 19. Jahrhundert stammende Einrichtungen zum Keltern von Wein bieten. Die Rezeption des Hotels befindet sich auf dieser Ebene, die 14 Gästezimmer sind darüber angeordnet. Zu der Anlage gehören ein Raum für Weinproben, das Restaurant Echaurren mit 172 Plätzen, eine Terrasse zum Speisen im Freien sowie eine private Gästelounge auf der oberen Ebene; auf dem Dach des Gebäudes befinden sich Panoramaterrassen. Während des Entwurfsprozesses entstanden zahlreiche maßstabsgerechte Modelle, die bei Bedarf jeweils verändert wurden. Diese Modelle wurden dann digitalisiert und mittels CATIA in dreidimensionale Form gebracht. Dann wurden sie mit anderen Programmen dazu verwendet, die komplexen konstruktiven Berechnungen auszuführen. Ein besonders diffiziler Aspekt des Projekts war die Bodenplatte der dritten Ebene, die den übrigen Bau trägt und Auskragungen von bis zu 10 m aufweist.

Située dans la province de la Rioja au nord de l'Espagne, cette exploitation viticole, une des plus anciennes de la région, avait demandé à Frank Gehry de concevoir un centre d'information pour les visiteurs et un hôtel accessibles par son vignoble. Les éléments architecturaux de base, rectilignes et habillés de grès, surélevés du sol par des piliers dont trois « super-colonnes » de 16,5 mètres, sont surmontés d'une composition de panneaux incurvés en titane rose et or et acier inoxydable poli miroir. « C'est une créature fabuleuse, dont la chevelure flotte à tous les vents, qui se projette au-dessus des vignes », commente Gehry. De l'espace entrée aménagé sous le bâtiment, le visiteur bénéficie de vues superbes sur le vignoble, sur le village voisin d'Eciego et les chais du XIXᵉ siècle. La réception de l'hôtel se trouve à ce niveau, au-dessous des 14 chambres. Le bâtiment comprend une salle de dégustation, un restaurant de 172 couverts, l'Echaurren, une aire pour les repas en plein air et un salon pour invités à l'étage supérieur. Des terrasses offrant une vue panoramique occupent le toit. De nombreuses maquettes ont été réalisées et ont permis de faire évoluer le projet. Elles ont été transférées en fichiers numériques pour le logiciel CATIA utilisé pour la modélisation en 3D qui ont ensuite servi à calculer la structure complexe de l'ensemble. Un point délicat à résoudre a été la dalle du troisième niveau qui soutient le reste de la structure et présente des porte-à-faux de 10 mètres.

*With the Hotel Marqués de Riscal, Gehry carries the idea of exuberant sculptural forms even further than in his earlier work in this style.*

*Mit dem Hotel Marqués de Riscal entwickelt Gehry die Idee üppiger plastischer Formen noch weiter als in früheren Werken dieser Art.*

*Dans cet hôtel Marqués de Riscal, Gehry pousse encore plus loin les formes exubérantes qu'il a mises au point dans de précédentes réalisations.*

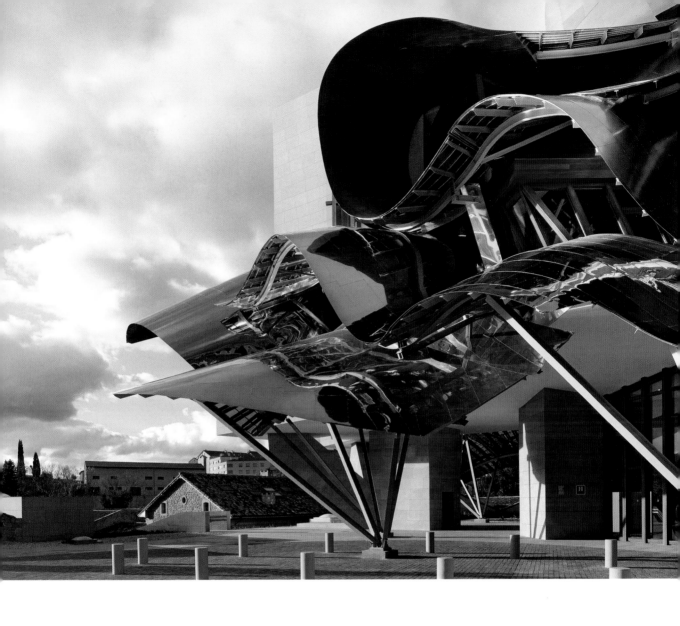

The soaring surfaces of the structure give the impression that it might be difficult to use the space inside effectively.

Die aufragenden Flächen des Gebäude lassen vermuten, dass es schwierig sein könnte, die Innenräume sinnvoll zu nutzen.

Les plans dressés du bâtiment font douter de la possibilité d'utiliser les volumes de façon efficace.

# SEAN GODSELL

Sean Godsell Architects
Level 1 49 Exhibition St
Melbourne
Victoria 3000
Australia

Tel: +61 3 9654 2677
Fax: +61 3 9654 3877
E-mail: godsell@netspace.net.au
Web: www.seangodsell.com

**SEAN GODSELL** was born in Melbourne in 1960. He graduated from the University of Melbourne in 1984 and worked from 1986 to 1988 in London with Sir Denys Lasdun. He created Godsell Associates Pty Ltd. Architects in 1994. After receiving an M.Arch degree from RMIT University in 1999, he was a finalist in the Seppelt Contemporary Art Awards held by the Museum of Contemporary Art in Sydney for his work *Future Shack*. He won the RAIA Award of Merit for new residential work for the Carter/Tucker House in 2000. He taught in the RMIT Department of Architecture from 1986 to 1997. His work has been shown in exhibitions in New York, Paris, London and Mendrisio, Switzerland, and includes the Carter/Tucker House (Breamlea, Victoria, 1999–2000); Peninsula House (Victoria, 2001–02; ar+d Prizewinner 2002; RAIA Architecture Award 2003); Woodleigh School Science Faculty (Baxter, Victoria, 2002; RAIA William Wardell Award 2003); Lewis House (Dunkeld, Victoria, 2003); Westwood House (Sydney, 2003); ACN Headquarters (Victoria, 2003); and St. Andrews Beach House (Mornington Peninsula, Victoria, 2003–05, published here), all in Australia. He has also worked on the CIPEA Housing Project (Nanjing, China, 2003); La Nada Retreat (Arizona, 2004); and in Australia, Glenburn House (Victoria, 2006); and Tanderra House (Victoria, 2006).

**SEAN GODSELL** wurde 1960 in Melbourne geboren. Er schloss 1984 sein Studium an der University of Melbourne ab und arbeitete von 1986 bis 1988 bei Sir Denys Lasdun in London. 1994 gründete er Godsell Associates Pty Ltd. Architects. Nachdem er 1999 den Grad eines M.Arch. an der RMIT University erworben hatte, kam er mit seiner Arbeit »Future Shack« in die letzte Runde des vom Museum of Contemporary Art in Sidney ausgeschriebenen Seppelt Contemporary Art Awards. Für das Carter/Tucker House erhielt er 2000 den RAIA Award of Merit für neue Wohnbebauung. Von 1986 bis 1997 lehrte er am RMIT Department of Architecture. Seine Arbeiten wurden in Ausstellungen in New York, Paris, London und dem schweizerischen Mendrisio gezeigt. Sein Œuvre umfasst: Carter/Tucker House (Breamlea, Victoria, 1999–2000), Peninsula House (Victoria, 2001–02, ar+d Prizewinner 2002, RAIA Architecture Award 2003), Woodleigh School Science Faculty (Baxter, Victoria, 2002, RAIA William Wardell Award 2003), Lewis House (Dunkeld, Victoria, 2003), Westwood House (Sydney, 2003), ACN-Zentrale (Victoria, 2003) und St. Andrews Beach House (Mornington Peninsula, Victoria, 2003–05, hier vorgestellt), alle in Australien. Außerdem arbeitete er am CIPEA Wohnungsbauprojekt (Nanjing, China, 2003), am La Nada Retreat (Arizona, 2004) und in Australien am Glenburn House und dem Tanderra House (beide in Victoria, 2006).

Né à Melbourne en 1960, **SEAN GODSELL** sort diplômé de l'Université de Melbourne en 1984, puis travaille de 1986 à 1988 à Londres chez Sir Denys Lasdun. Il crée Godsell Associates Pty Ltd. Architects en 1994. M. Arch. de RMIT University en 1999, il est finaliste des Seppelt Contemporary Art Awards organisés par le Musée d'art contemporain de Sydney pour son projet *Future Shack*. Il remporte le Prix du mérite du RAIA pour sa maison Carter/Tucker en 2000. Il enseigne au département d'architecture du RMIT de 1986 à 1997. Son œuvre a été présentée dans des expositions à New York, Paris, Londres et Mendrisio en Suisse. Parmi ses réalisations, toutes en Australie : la maison Carter/Tucker à Bremlea, Victoria (1999–2000) ; la maison Peninsula, Victoria (2001–02), Prix ar+d 2002 et Prix d'architecture du RAIA 2003 ; la faculté des sciences de Woodleigh School, Baxter, Victoria (2002), Prix RAIA 2003 ; la maison Lewis, Dunkeld, Victoria (2003) ; la maison Westwood, Sydney (2003) ; le siège d'ACN, Victoria (2003) ; et la St. Andrews Beach House, Péninsule de Mornington, Victoria (2003–05, publiée ici). Il a également travaillé sur le projet de logements CIPEA à Nankin, Chine (2003) ; sur La Nada Retreat, Arizona (2004) et, en Australie, dans l'État de Victoria, sur les maisons Glenburg et Tanderra (2006).

# ST ANDREWS BEACH HOUSE

*Mornington Peninsula, Victoria, Australia, 2003–05*

*Floor area: 280 m². Clients: Mr. and Mrs. D. McNair. Cost: not disclosed.*
*Project Team: Sean Godsell, Hayley Franklin*

Located directly opposite the ocean in one of the few areas in Australia where construction is allowed near the beach, this residence has a protective outer skin made of industrial oxidized steel floor-grating mounted as *brise-soleil* shutters. The three-bedroom family house is raised up from the ground on columns, permitting parking and storage at ground level. Kitchen, dining and living space is contained in one block and the bedrooms in the other, with a promenade deck linking the two. In a gesture that recalls Japanese residential architecture, residents are obliged to go outside to move from one area to the other. Sean Godsell explains that "this strategy was requested by the client as a way of using the weekend house to rehumanise oneself after a week of office work. It serves to de-sanitise the controlled 22°C built environment to which we have all grown accustomed and to remind the occupants of their own frailty." While the outside of the building is intended to shelter it from potentially violent storms, the unusual division of the house in two means that the owners will always be aware of the state of the natural world around them.

Dieses Wohnhaus liegt direkt am Meer in einem der wenigen Gebiete Australiens, in denen das Bauen am Strand gestattet ist. Es ist von einer schützenden Außenhaut aus oxidiertem Industriestahl umgeben, die aus Bodengittern als Sonnenblenden besteht. Das Haus mit drei Schlafräumen steht auf Stützen über dem Boden, so dass darunter Stauraum und Parkflächen entstehen. Küche, Ess- und Wohnbereich sind in dem einen Block, die Schlafräume im anderen untergebracht; das dazwischen liegende Promenadendeck verbindet die beiden Teile. Um vom einen in den anderen Bereich zu gelangen, müssen die Bewohner also ins Freie gehen, was an gewisse japanische Wohnhausarchitektur erinnert. Sean Godsell erläutert, dass »diese Strategie vom Bauherren gewünscht wurde, um das Wochenendhaus dazu zu nutzen, sich nach einer Woche Büroarbeit zu ›rehumanisieren‹. Es dient dazu, der auf 22° C klimatisierten gebauten Umwelt, an die wir uns alle gewöhnt haben, ihre Künstlichkeit zu nehmen und die Bewohner an ihre eigene Schwäche zu erinnern«. Während die Außenhaut das Haus vor möglicherweise orkanartigen Stürmen schützen soll, bedingt seine ungewöhnliche Zweiteilung, dass sich die Besitzer jederzeit des augenblicklichen Zustands ihrer Umgebung bewusst sind.

Située face à l'océan, dans l'une des rares régions australiennes où l'on peut construire sur la plage, cette résidence se caractérise par une peau de protection en caillebotis de sol industriels en acier oxydé, montés en brise-soleil. La maison repose sur des piliers qui ont permis de loger le parking et divers stockages au niveau du sol. La cuisine, le séjour et l'espace des repas sont réunis dans un bloc et les trois chambres dans un second, à l'autre extrémité, tous deux étant reliés par une terrasse-promenoir. Dans un cheminement qui rappelle l'architecture de certaines maisons japonaises, les occupants sont obligés de sortir pour aller d'une partie à l'autre. Sean Godsell explique que « cette stratégie était une attente du client qui y voyait une façon d'utiliser cette résidence de week-end pour se réhumaniser après une semaine de travail au bureau. Elle sert à rompre avec l'environnement construit à 22°C auquel nous nous sommes tous habitués, et à rappeler aux occupants leur propre fragilité. » Si l'extérieur de la maison la protège des tempêtes qui peuvent être violentes, sa division originale en deux parties signifie aussi que ses propriétaires resteront toujours conscients des forces de la nature qui les entoure.

A certain tradition of Australian contemporary architecture that hovers above on the earth informs this house, as does, undoubtedly, a reference to Asian or South Pacific designs.

Dieses Haus ist von einer bestimmten Richtung zeitgenössischer australischer Architektur beeinflusst wie zweifellos auch von asiatischen oder südpazifischen Formen.

Cette maison poursuit une tradition de l'architecture australienne récente qui cherche à la poser délicatement sur le sol, référence sans doute à des pratiques asiatiques ou du Pacifique Sud.

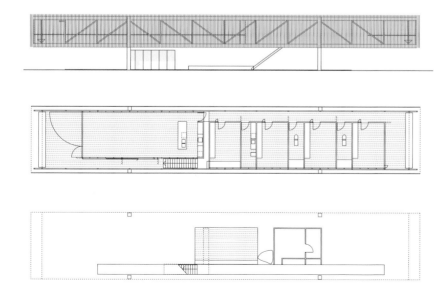

The large spaces of the house are lifted up off the ground and open onto the countryside and the water in the distance.

Die großen Räume dieses Hauses sind über den Boden angehoben und öffnen sich frei zur Landschaft und zum Meer hin.

Les grands espaces de la maison sont surelevés, offrant une vue sur le paysage, et la mer au loin.

Warm wood floors and slatted openings filter the light and make the
interior space of the house agreeable.

Lamellenöffnungen filtern das Licht
und sorgen zusammen mit den warmen Holzböden für ein angenehmes
Klima im Inneren.

Les sols en bois de couleur chaude
et les ouvertures grillagées colorent
la lumière et rendent les espaces
intérieurs agréables à vivre.

This breezy hallway runs through the house and opens out onto the surrounding countryside.

Der luftige Korridor durchzieht das Haus und öffnet sich zur Umgebung.

Ce passage aéré longe la maison d'un bout à l'autre, et ouvre sur le dehors.

The themes of lightness and simplicity that mark the exterior architecture are carried through to the interiors.

Die den Außenbau bestimmenden Motive Leichtigkeit und Schlichtheit werden auch im Inneren fortgeführt.

Les thèmes de légèreté et de simplicité remarqués à l'extérieur se retrouvent à l'intérieur.

# GRAFT

*Graft Gesellschaft von Architekten mbH*
*Heidestrasse 50 / 10557 Berlin / Germany*

*Tel: +49 30 2404 7985 / Fax: +49 30 2404 7987*
*E-mail: berlin@graftlab.com / Web: www.graftlab.com*

**GRAFT** was created in Los Angeles in 1998 "as a label for architecture, art, music, and the pursuit of happiness." Lars Krückeberg, Wolfram Putz, and Thomas Willemeit are the partners of Graft that today employs about 20 architects and artists in the United States, Europe and Asia. Graft has offices in Los Angeles, Berlin, and Beijing. Lars Krückeberg was educated at the Technical University (TU) in Braunschweig, Germany, as an engineer (1989–96), and at SCI-Arc in Los Angeles (1997–98). Wolfram Putz attended the TU in Braunschweig (1988–95), the University of Utah, Salt Lake City (1992–93), and SCI-Arc in Los Angeles (1996–98). Thomas Willemeit was also educated in Braunschweig, and at the Bauhaus Dessau (1991–92), before working in the office of Daniel Libeskind (1998–2001). Taking advantage of their German background combined with U.S. training, Graft declares: "We can see an architecture of new combinations, the grafting of different cultures and styles. The English word graft includes a variety of meanings and multiple readings. It has a particular meaning in the terminology of botany, the grafting of one shoot onto a genetically different host. The positive properties of two genetically different cultures are combined in the new biological hybrid." They have built a studio and house for the actor Brad Pitt in Los Angeles (2000–03); designed a private dental clinic (2005, published here); and Hotel Q! (2002–04) in Berlin. They have designed restaurants in the Mirage (published here) and Bellagio Casinos in Las Vegas and worked on several luxury-resort hotels in the Caribbean, including locations in the Turcs and Caicos and in the Dominican Republic. A Design Hotel in Tbilisi, Georgia, is under construction.

**GRAFT** entstand 1998 in Los Angeles »als eine Gesellschaft für Architektur, Kunst, Musik und das Streben nach Glück«. Lars Krückeberg, Wolfram Putz und Thomas Willemeit sind die Partner von Graft, die heute in den Vereinigten Staaten, Europa und Asien etwa 20 Architekten und Künstler beschäftigen und Büros in Los Angeles, Berlin und Peking unterhalten. Lars Krückeberg erhielt seine Ausbildung zum Ingenieur an der Technischen Universität Braunschweig (1989–96) und absolvierte ein Ingenieurstudium am SCI-Arc in Los Angeles (1997–98). Wolfram Putz besuchte von 1988 bis 1995 die TU Braunschweig, 1992 bis 1993 die University of Utah in Salt Lake City und schließlich SCI-Arc von 1996 bis 1998. Thomas Willemeit wurde ebenfalls in Braunschweig ausgebildet, anschließend am Bauhaus in Dessau (1991–92), ehe er im Büro von Daniel Libeskind arbeitete (1998–2001). Vor dem Hintergrund ihrer teils in Deutschland, teils in den USA absolvierten Ausbildung heißt es bei Graft: »Wir können eine Architektur neuer Kombinationen erkennen, das Kultivieren verschiedener Kulturen und Stile. Das englische Wort ›graft‹ beinhaltet verschiedene Bedeutungen und Lesarten. Im Bereich der Botanik hat es eine besondere Bedeutung, das Aufpfropfen eines Schösslings auf eine genetisch andersartige Wirtspflanze. Die positiven Eigenschaften zweier genetisch verschiedenartiger Kulturen werden in der neuen biologischen Hybride vereint.« In Los Angeles bauten sie ein Studio und ein Haus für den Schauspieler Brad Pitt (2000–03) und entwarfen die hier vorgestellte private Zahnklinik (2005) sowie das Hotel Q! (2002–04) in Berlin. Sie gestalteten Restaurants in den Kasinos Mirage (hier publiziert) sowie Bellagio in Las Vegas und arbeiteten an mehreren Luxusresorts in der Karibik, darunter an Standorten auf den Turks und Caicos-Inseln und in der Dominikanischen Republik. Ein Design-Hotel in Tiflis, Georgien, ist im Bau.

**GRAFT**, « label pour l'architecture, l'art, la musique et la poursuite du bonheur », a été créé à Los Angeles en 1998. Lars Krückeberg, Wolfram Putz et Thomas Willemeit sont les associés de cette agence qui emploie aujourd'hui environ vingt architectes et artistes aux États-Unis, en Europe et en Asie et possède des bureaux à Los Angeles, Berlin et Pékin. Lars Krückeberg a fait des études d'ingénierie à la Technische Universität de Braunschweig en Allemagne (1989–1996), et au SCI-Arc à Los Angeles (1997–98). Wolfram Putz a étudié dans la même université (1988–95), mais aussi dans celle de l'Utah à Salt Lake City (1992–93) et au SCI-Arc à Los Angeles (1996–98). Thomas Willemeit a également étudié à Braunschweig et au Bauhaus Dessau (1991–92), avant de travailler auprès de Daniel Libeskind (1998–2001). En s'appuyant sur leur formation à la fois allemande et américaine, Graft se propose « d'envisager une architecture de combinaisons nouvelles, la greffe de différents styles et cultures. Le terme anglais de *graft* offre une grande variété de sens et de lectures. Il possède un sens particulier en botanique, celui de greffage sur un hôte génétiquement différent. Les propriétés positives de deux cultures génétiquement différentes se combinent alors en un nouvel hybride biologique. » Ils ont construit un atelier et une maison pour l'acteur Brad Pitt à Los Angeles (2000–03) ; conçu une clinique dentaire privée (2005, publiée ici), et l'Hotel Q! (2002–04) à Berlin, des restaurants pour les casinos Mirage (publié ici) et Bellagio à Las Vegas et travaillé sur plusieurs projets de complexes hôteliers de luxe dans les Caraïbes, les îles Turks-et-Caicos et en République dominicaine. Un hôtel « design » est en cours de construction à Tbilissi, en Géorgie.

# DENTAL CLINIC KU64

*Kurfürstendamm 64, Berlin, Germany, 2005*

*Floor area: 940 m². Client: Dr. Stephen Ziegler. Cost: €448 000.*
*Project Architects: Tobias Hein, Karsten Sell. Architects: Sven Fuchs, Lennart Wiechell.*
*Project Team: Björn Rolle, Markus Müller*

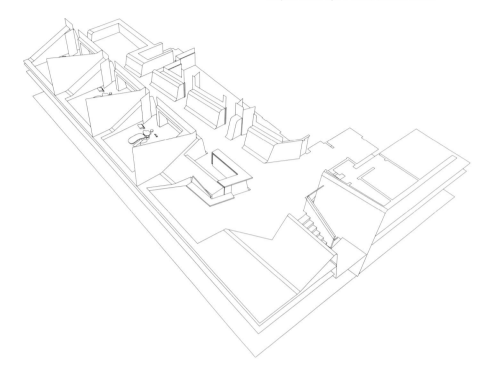

*The dental clinic as seen in this image has an atmosphere more like that of a comfortable hotel than a place to get one's teeth pulled, and that is exactly the point of the architects.*

*Die auf diesem Bild zu sehende Zahnklinik hat eher die Anmutung eines komfortablen Hotels als die eines Ortes, an dem Zähne gezogen werden, und genau das wollten die Architekten erreichen.*

*Cette clinique dentaire possède une atmosphère plus proche de celle d'un hôtel que d'un lieu où se faire retirer une dent, ce qui était exactement l'objectif des architectes.*

The architects started by affirming that few environments have as many negative connotations as the dental clinic, and attempted to move users in this instance "away from negative prejudices toward an atmosphere of art, well-being, and relaxation. The goal is to let patients forget about their fears and relax in a way they would usually expect from a spa, from cafés, restaurants or hotels." Graft configured the space into a series of metaphorical "hills" and "valleys." Anamorphic images were silk-screened onto the prevailing orange, sculptural surfaces of the clinic, treated with four layers of polyurethane. The waiting area was designed like a lounge with an adjacent exterior sundeck. Wireless Internet access, video and games for children, and the odor of burning wood and freshly ground coffee replace the normally unpleasant dental clinic atmosphere. The dental-care room "plays with the notion of purity: a water basin with its floating glass sinks is reflecting moving light onto the ceiling and the dripping waterfall fills the space with a sound of freshness, evoking a clean, futuristic image of a grotto with its own rituals." The clinic includes nine treatment spaces, as well as three offices, the reception area, lounge, dental spa, staff rooms, and storage space.

Am Anfang stand die Erkenntnis, dass kaum eine Umgebung so zahlreiche negative Konnotationen mit sich bringt wie eine Zahnklinik. Daraus ergab sich das Bestreben, die Patienten »weg von negativen Vorurteilen und hin zu einer von Kunst, Wohlbefinden und Entspannung geprägten Atmosphäre zu führen. Die Patienten sollen ihre Ängste vergessen und sich in einer Weise entspannen, die sie sonst von einem Kurort, von Cafés, Restaurants oder Hotels erwarten würden.« Graft gliederte den Raum in eine Reihe metaphorischer »Hügel« und »Täler«. Auf die vorherrschend orangefarbenen, plastischen Wandflächen, die mit einem vierfachen Polyurethananstrich versehen wurden, brachte man im Siebdruckverfahren anamorphische Bilder auf. Der Wartebereich wurde wie eine Lounge mit einer angrenzenden Sonnenterrasse gestaltet. Internet-Hotspots, Videos und Spiele für Kinder sowie die Aromen von Holzfeuer und frisch gemahlenem Kaffee treten an die Stelle der gewöhnlich unangenehmen Atmosphäre einer Zahnklinik. Der Behandlungsraum »spielt mit der Vorstellung von Reinheit: Ein Wasserbassin mit schwimmenden Glasbecken reflektiert Licht auf die Decke und der tröpfelnde Wasserfall füllt den Raum mit einem frischen Klang, der das kristallen-futuristische Bild einer Grotte mit besonderen Ritualen heraufbeschwört«. Zur Klinik gehören neben neun Behandlungszimmern drei Büroräume, Empfangsbereich, Lounge, Dental-Spa, Räume für die Mitarbeiter sowie Lagerraum.

Pour les architectes, peu d'environnements présentent autant de connotations négatives qu'une clinique dentaire. Ils se sont efforcés d'effacer « les préjugés négatifs en introduisant une atmosphère artistique de bien-être et de relaxation. L'objectif est de faire oublier aux patients leurs craintes, et de les amener à se détendre d'une façon qu'ils attendent généralement plutôt d'un spa, d'un café, d'un restaurant ou d'un hôtel ». Graft a configuré l'espace en une suite de « collines » et de « vallées » métaphoriques. Des images anamorphiques ont été sérigraphiées sur les parois sculpturales de couleur orange pour la plus grande partie, et recouvertes de quatre couches de polyuréthane. La salle d'attente est un salon à solarium extérieur. L'accès au Wi-fi, vidéos et jeux pour enfants, et odeurs de feu de bois et de café fraîchement moulu remplacent l'atmosphère désagréable des cabinets dentaires. Les salles de soins « jouent avec la notion de pureté : un bassin d'eau sur lequel flottent des lavabos de verre projette ses reflets sur le plafond et une cascade de gouttelettes emplit l'espace d'un bruit frais qui évoque une image futuriste et propre de grotte où se dérouleraient des rituels ». La clinique compte neuf postes de traitements, trois bureaux, une réception, un salon, un spa dentaire et des pièces pour le personnel.

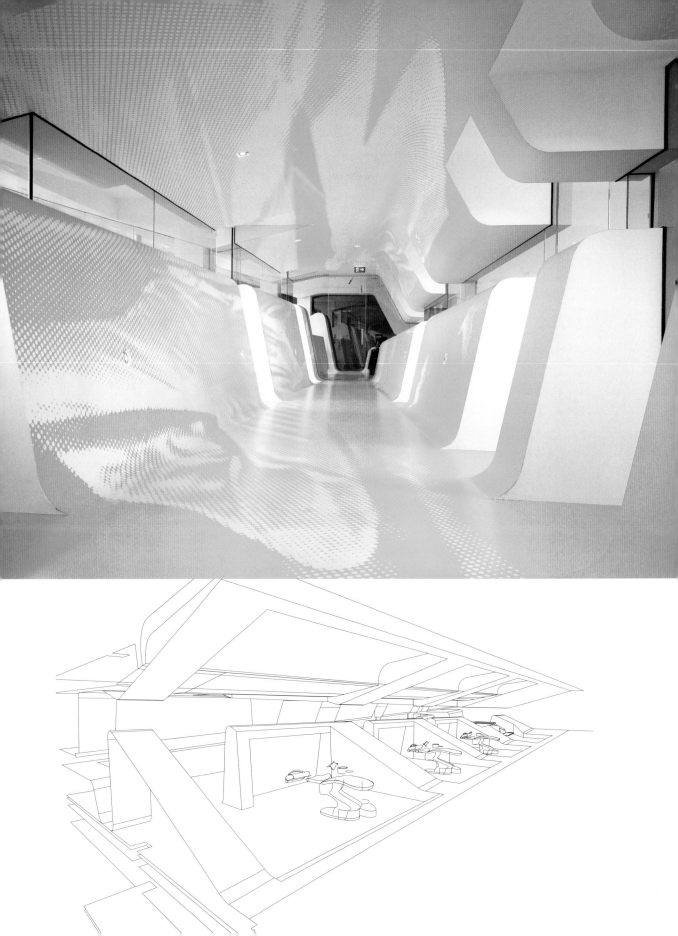

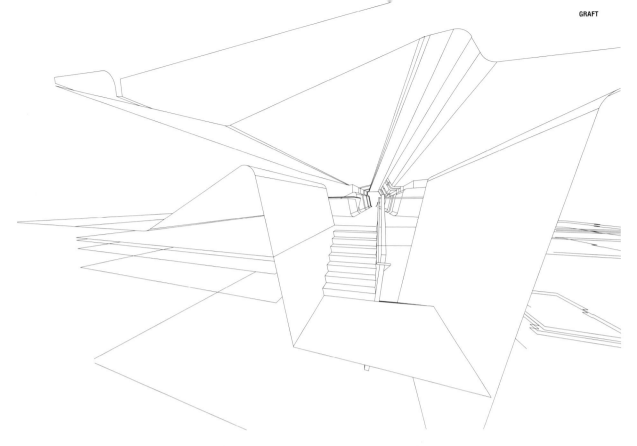

By using bright colors and a slick design, Graft pushes the dental clinic into the realm of design and dabbles in mood control as well.

Mit leuchtenden Farben und einem schicken Design versetzt Graft die Zahnklinik in den Bereich der gehobenen Innenausstattung und versucht sich außerdem im Manipulieren von Stimmungen.

Grâce à ses couleurs vives et à sa mise en forme habile, Graft fait entrer cette clinique dans le domaine du design et joue avec le contrôle des émotions.

The folded planes of the Graft design are very much in the spirit of the moment whereas their use of color may be somewhat more expected in this instance.

Die gefalteten Flächen des Designs von Graft entsprechen sehr dem aktuellen Zeitgeist, während man den Einsatz von Farbe eher erwarten kann.

Les plans pliés du projet Graft sont bien dans l'esprit du moment, mais l'utilisation de la couleur paraît un peu plus attendue.

The bright color themes are maintained throughout the clinic, with some functional variations. Even the furniture selected, like the red couch below, contributes to the cheerful aspect of the entire space.

*Das Motiv der leuchtenden Farben bleibt in der ganzen Klinik erhalten, mit einigen funktionalen Varianten. Selbst das ausgewählte Mobiliar, wie die rote Couch unten, trägt zur fröhlichen Erscheinung des gesamten Raums bei.*

*Les couleurs vives sont déclinées dans toute la clinique, y compris à travers certaines variations d'ordre fonctionnel. Même le mobilier choisi, tel le canapé rouge ci-dessous, contribue à donner un aspect joyeux à l'espace.*

# STACK RESTAURANT AND BAR, MIRAGE

*Las Vegas, Nevada, USA, 2005*

*Floor area: 539 m². Client: The Light Group, MGM Mirage Design Group. Cost: not disclosed. Project Leader: Alejandra Lillo.*
*Project Team: Sascha Krückeberg, Andrea Schütte, Narineh Mirzaeian*

As the architects describe this Las Vegas restaurant, "An enticing canyoning landscape is generated through undulating striations of seating, layered wall and bar, utilizing the generous 5.8-meter height capacity to produce a telescopic effect in depth. The horizontal layers are peeled from one another, creating variation in patterning, cantilevering, and velocity. This effect forms a visible invitation to the space, drawing the visitor in, and gradually frames multiple spatial readings, keeping the guest inside. The canyon wall is embedded with a lighting effect that reveals a random pixilated pattern once one has journeyed inside the restaurant and looks back out. The material for the layered canyon is wood paneling, giving both warmth to the space and translating the canyon feel into a contemporary formal solution." Just as they have in other projects, such as their Q! Hotel in Berlin, Graft seeks here to create an original space in which furniture, lighting, colors, and the very atmosphere become part of an architectural environment. This is certainly a case where the distinction between architecture and design becomes blurred.

Die Architekten beschreiben dieses Restaurant in Las Vegas wie folgt: »Durch die wellenförmigen Streifen der Sitzmöbel, durch die Schichtungen der Wände und Bar, die die großzügige Raumhöhe von 5,8 m nutzen, um eine teleskopische Tiefenwirkung zu erzielen, entsteht eine verlockende ›Cañonlandschaft‹. Die horizontalen Schichten lösen sich voneinander ab, wodurch wechselnde Musterungen, Überstände und Verwirbelungen entstehen. Dieser Effekt wirkt wie eine sichtbare Einladung in den Raum, sie zieht den Besucher förmlich hinein und formuliert peu à peu vielfältige räumliche Lesarten, die den Gast festhalten. Eingebettet in die ›Cañonwand‹ ist eine Beleuchtungsanlage, die eine kuriose Zufallsmusterung erkennen lässt, sobald man in das Restaurant vorgedrungen ist und zurückschaut. Der geschichtete Cañon besteht aus einer Holzverschalung, die dem Raum Wärme verleiht und das Gefühl von einer Schlucht in eine formal zeitgemäße Lösung überträgt.« Ebenso wie bei anderen Projekten, beispielsweise ihrem Hotel Q!, ist Graft auch hier bestrebt, einen Raum zu schaffen, in dem Möblierung, Beleuchtung, Farben und die Atmosphäre Teil eines architektonischen Environments werden. Hier handelt es sich gewiss um ein Projekt, bei dem die Unterscheidung zwischen Architektur und Design schwerfällt.

Ce projet de restaurant à Las Vegas représente, selon les architectes, « un fascinant paysage de canyon, reconstitué par les stries en ondulations des sièges, des murs stratifiés et du bar, ainsi que par l'utilisation de la généreuse hauteur de plafond de 5,8 mètres qui génère un effet télescopique de profondeur. Les strates horizontales sont décalées les unes des autres pour créer des variantes de motifs ou de porte-à-faux et un sentiment de vitesse. Ces effets invitent littéralement le visiteur à pénétrer dans cet espace, en lui offrant peu à peu de multiples lectures spatiales qui lui donnent envie de s'installer. Des points lumineux décrivent un motif pixellisé aléatoire. L'habillage de bois donne de la chaleur à ce volume et change l'impression de se trouver dans un canyon en une expérience formelle beaucoup plus contemporaine. » De même que dans d'autres projets comme l'Hotel Q! à Berlin, Graft a cherché ici à créer un espace original dans lequel le mobilier, l'éclairage, les couleurs contribuent à créer une atmosphère qui participe à l'environnement architectural. La distinction entre architecture et design est ici difficile à établir.

*The architects refer to "canyoning" when describing this project. Their use of layers of wood indeed brings to mind topographical maps.*

*Die Architekten sprechen bei diesem Projekt nicht zufällig von Cañons. Die Verwendung von Holzschichten erinnert in der Tat an topografische Karten.*

*Les architectes utilisent le terme de « canyon » dans ce projet. Les strates de bois évoquent en effet des cartes géologiques.*

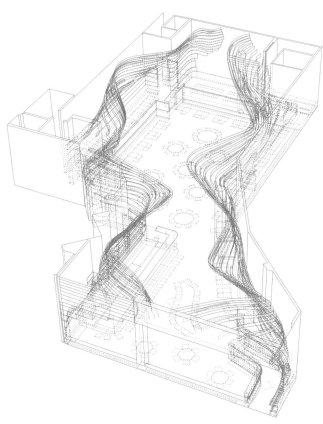

The irregular pattern and form of the interior walls is revealed in the drawing of the layout of the restaurant and bar to the left.

Die unregelmäßige Musterung und Form der Innenwände offenbart sich in der Zeichnung der Anlage von Restaurant und Bar links.

Les formes et motifs irréguliers des murs intérieurs se révèlent dans le dessin du plan du restaurant et du bar (à gauche).

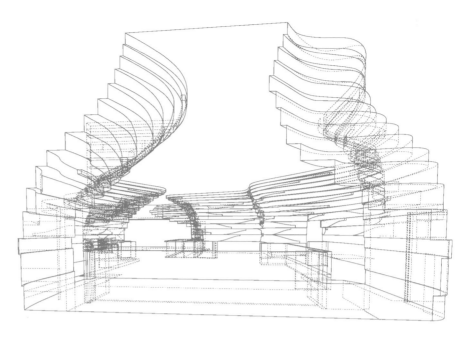

The use of continuous bands of wood gives a sense of movement to the space, while the color of the wood lends a warmth not always associated with cutting-edge contemporary architecture.

Die Verwendung durchgehender Holzstreifen lässt den Raum bewegt erscheinen, während der Farbton des Holzes eine nicht unbedingt mit neuester Architektur assoziierte Wärme hervorruft.

Les bandes de bois continues animent ce volume, tandis que la couleur même du matériau lui apporte une chaleur qui n'est pas toujours associée à l'architecture contemporaine d'avant-garde.

# ZAHA HADID

*Zaha Hadid*
*Studio 9*
*10 Bowling Green Lane*
*London EC1R OBQ*
*UK*

*Tel: +44 20 7253 5147*
*Fax: +44 20 7251 8322*
*E-mail: mail@zaha-hadid.com*
*Web: www.zaha-hadid.com*

**ZAHA HADID** studied architecture at the Architectural Association (AA) in London beginning in 1972 and was awarded the Diploma Prize in 1977. She then became a partner of Rem Koolhaas in the Office for Metropolitan Architecture (OMA) and taught at the AA. She has also taught at Harvard, the University of Chicago, in Hamburg and at Columbia University in New York. Well-known for her paintings and drawings, she has had a substantial influence, despite having built relatively few buildings. She has completed the Vitra Fire Station (Weil am Rhein, Germany, 1990–94); and exhibition designs, such as those for "The Great Utopia" (Solomon R. Guggenheim Museum, New York, 1992). Significant competition entries include her design for the Cardiff Bay Opera House (1994–96); the Habitable Bridge (London, 1996); and the Luxembourg Philharmonic Hall (1997). More recently, Hadid has entered a phase of active construction with such projects as the Bergisel Ski Jump (Innsbruck, Austria, 2001–02); Lois & Richard Rosenthal Center for Contemporary Art (Cincinnati, Ohio, 1999–2003); Phaeno Science Center (Wolfsburg, Germany, 2001–05, published here); and Central Building of the new BMW Assembly Plant (Leipzig, Germany, 2005). She is working on the Price Tower Arts Center (Bartlesville, Oklahoma); Doha Tower (Doha, Qatar); and made a proposal for the 2012 Olympic Village, New York. In 2004, Zaha Hadid became the first woman to win the coveted Pritzker Prize.

**ZAHA HADID** studierte ab 1972 an der Architectural Association (AA) in London Architektur und wurde 1977 mit dem Diploma Prize ausgezeichnet. Sie wurde dann im Office for Metropolitan Architecture (OMA) Partnerin von Rem Koolhaas und lehrte an der AA. Darüber hinaus übernahm sie Lehraufträge in Harvard, der University of Chicago, in Hamburg und an der Columbia University in New York. Hadid ist besonders durch ihre Gemälde und Zeichnungen bekannt geworden. Obwohl nur wenige ihrer Entwürfe realisiert wurden, gehört sie zu den einflussreichsten Vertreterinnen ihrer Zunft. Sie stellte u. a. die Feuerwache für Vitra (Weil am Rhein, 1990–94) fertig und Ausstellungsarchitekturen wie die für »The Great Utopia« (Solomon R. Guggenheim Museum, New York, 1992). Zu ihren wichtigen Wettbewerbsbeiträgen zählen: der Entwurf für das Cardiff Bay Opera House (1994–96), die Habitable Bridge (London, 1996) und die Philharmonie in Luxemburg (1997). In jüngerer Zeit begann für Zaha Hadid eine Phase des aktiven Bauens mit Projekten wie der Bergisel-Skischanze (Innsbruck, 2001–02), dem Lois & Richard Rosenthal Center for Contemporary Art (Cincinnati, Ohio, 1999–2003), dem hier vorgestellten Phaeno Wissenschaftszentrum (Wolfsburg, 2001–05) und dem Zentralgebäude des neuen BMW-Werks in Leipzig (2005). Gegenwärtig arbeitet sie am Price Tower Arts Center (Bartlesville, Oklahoma) sowie dem Doha Tower (Doha, Katar). Außerdem legte sie eine Planung für das Olympische Dorf 2012 in New York vor. 2004 wurde Zaha Hadid als erste Frau mit dem begehrten Pritzker-Preis ausgezeichnet.

**ZAHA HADID** a fait ses études à l'Architectural Association (AA) de Londres, de 1972 à 1977, date à laquelle elle a reçu le Diploma Prize. Elle devient ensuite partenaire dans l'agence de Rem Koolhaas, Office for Metropolitan Architecture (OMA), et enseigne à l'AA, à Harvard, à l'Université de Chicago, à Columbia University (New York) et l'Université de Hambourg. Célèbre pour ses peintures et dessins, elle exerce une réelle influence, même si elle n'a construit que peu de bâtiments. Parmi ses réalisations : un poste d'incendie pour Vitra, Weil-am-Rhein, Allemagne (1990–94), et des projets pour des expositions comme *La Grande Utopie* au Solomon R. Guggenheim Museum à New York (1992). Elle a participé à de nombreux concours dont les plus importants sont le projet pour l'Opéra de Cardiff, Pays-de-Galles (1994–96) ; un Pont habitable, Londres, (1996) et la salle de concerts philharmoniques de Luxembourg (1997). Plus récemment, elle est entrée dans une phase de grands chantiers, avec des projets comme le tremplin de ski de Bergisel à Innsbruck, Autriche (2001–02) ; le Lois & Richard Rosenthal Center for Contemporary Art, Cincinnati, Ohio (1999–2003) ; le musée scientifique Phaeno, Wolfsburg, Allemagne (2001–05) publié ici, et le bâtiment central de la nouvelle usine BMW de Leipzig (2005). Elle travaille actuellement sur le projet du Price Tower Arts Center, Bartlesville, Oklahoma ; sur la Doha Tower, Doha, Quatar, et a présenté une proposition pour le village des Jeux olympiques de New York en 2012. En 2004, elle a été la première femme à remporter le très convoité Pritzker Prize.

# PHAENO SCIENCE CENTER

*Wolfsburg, Germany, 2001–05*

*Floor area: 12 631 m². Client: City of Wolfsburg. User: Phaeno Foundation, Wolfsburg.*
*Cost: €79 million. Associated Architect: Mayer Bährle, Freie Architekten.*
*Furniture and other interior elements: Uli Guth, Dominik Wendl, G + S + W Architektur und Design, Munich*

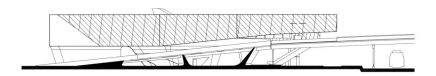

Winner of an international competition in January 2000, Zaha Hadid imagined a structure that contains no less than 27 000 cubic meters of concrete, and yet is suspended, in good part, some 7 meters above the ground. Explaining the unusual public space thus created beneath the Science Center, Zaha Hadid states, "The free ground is a Modernist idea, but it was never an animated space. That's what I try to create." Located near the town's central train station and across the tracks from the VW manufacturing plant, the new building is set up on 10 asymmetrical cones, some of which contain a shop, a bar or a bistro, as well as the museum entrance. The same cones penetrate the building and hold up the roof. The structure is nothing if not complex. Hadid states, "Phaeno is the most ambitious and complete statement of our quest for complex, dynamic, and fluid spaces. The visitor is faced with a degree of complexity and strangeness, ruled by a very specific system based on an unusual volumetric structural logic." As it is described by the users, "Phaeno provides hands-on, entertaining access to the phenomena of natural science and the principles of technology. Around 180 000 visitors are expected to play and experiment each year with its 250 exhibits in the visitor labs, in the Ideas Forum, and in the Science Theatre." Total visitor space is 9000 square meters with 5900 square meters devoted to the "exhibition landscape"; 54 square meters and 10 workplaces for the biology and chemistry lab; 118 square meters and 16 workplaces for the physics and technology lab; a 560-square-meter, 250-seat Science Theater; and the 370-square-meter Ideas Forum. Obviously sensitive to questions raised about the complexity of the building, Zaha Hadid declares, "Nobody thinks that landscape is strange because God made it, but if I make it, people think it's strange."

Als Zaha Hadid im Januar 2000 den internationalen Wettbewerb gewann, stellte sie sich ein Bauwerk vor, das nicht weniger als 27 000 m³ Beton enthalten und dennoch zu einem erheblichen Teil etwa 7 m über dem Boden hängen sollte. Zur Erläuterung des so entstandenen, ungewöhnlichen öffentlichen Raums unterhalb des Wissenschaftszentrums bemerkt Zaha Hadid: »Der freibleibende Boden ist eine Idee des Modernismus, aber er war nie ein belebter Raum. Ich versuche genau das zu gestalten.« Der neue Bau, der unweit des städtischen Hauptbahnhofs und jenseits der Gleise des VW-Werks liegt, steht auf zehn asymmetrischen Körpern, von denen einige einen Laden, eine Bar oder ein Bistro oder auch den Museumseingang enthalten. Eben diese Körper durchstoßen das hochkomplexe Gebäude und tragen das Dach. Dazu Hadid: »Bei Phaeno handelt es sich um den ehrgeizigsten und vollständigsten Ausdruck unserer Suche nach komplexen, dynamischen und fließenden Räumen. Der Besucher sieht sich einem Ausmaß von Komplexität und Fremdheit gegenüber, das von einem sehr spezifischen System bestimmt wird, das seinerseits auf einer besonderen volumetrisch-konstruktiven Logik beruht.« Die Betreiber beschreiben das Zentrum wie folgt: »Phaeno bietet interaktiven, unterhaltsamen Einblick in naturwissenschaftliche Phänomene und technische Prinzipien. Es wird erwartet, dass pro Jahr etwa 180 000 Besucher mit den 250 Versuchsanordnungen in Besucherlaboratorien, im Ideenforum und Wissenschaftstheater spielen und experimentieren werden.« Den Besuchern stehen insgesamt 9000 m² Platz zur Verfügung, die auf folgende Funktionen verteilt sind: 5900 m² »Ausstellungslandschaft«, 54 m² und 10 Arbeitsplätze im Biologie- und Chemielabor, 118 m² und 16 Arbeitsplätze im Physik- und Techniklabor, 560 m² für das Wissenschaftstheater mit 250 Sitzplätzen, 370 m² für das Ideenforum. Offensichtlich empfindlich bei Fragen zur Komplexität des Gebäudes, erklärt Zaha Hadid: »Keiner hält Landschaft für sonderbar, weil Gott sie machte, aber wenn ich etwas mache, halten die Leute es für sonderbar.«

Ce bâtiment, dont Zaha Hadid avait remporté le concours international en janvier 2000, ne représente pas moins de 27 000 m³ de béton en grande partie suspendus, jusqu'à 7 mètres au-dessus du sol. Pour expliquer la forme inhabituelle des espaces publics ouverts sous ce Centre des sciences, Zaha Hadid a déclaré : « Libérer le sol est une idée moderniste, mais cet espace n'avait jamais été vraiment animé. C'est ce que j'essaie de faire. » Situé à proximité de la gare principale de Wolfsburg, de l'autre côté des voies ferrées qui desservent l'usine Volkswagen, le musée repose sur dix cônes asymétriques dont certains contiennent une boutique, un bar, un bistro ou l'entrée du musée. Ces mêmes cônes pénètrent le bâti et soutiennent la couverture. La structure est quasiment intégrée. Selon Hadid : « Phaeno est l'affirmation la plus ambitieuse et la plus complète de nos recherches sur la complexité, la dynamique et la fluidité des espaces. Le visiteur est confronté à un certain degré de complexité et d'étrangeté soumis à un système très spécifique reposant sur une logique volumétrique structurelle peu usitée. » Selon le descriptif : « Phaeno offre un accès direct et ludique à l'explication des phénomènes des sciences naturelles et aux principes de diverses technologies. Il attend environ 180 000 visiteurs par an qui joueront et participeront à des expériences grâce à 250 attractions scientifiques, que ce soit dans les laboratoires qui leur sont réservés, le Forum des idées ou le Théâtre de la science. » L'espace ouvert au public mesure 9 000 m² dont 5 900 consacrés à une « exposition paysagée » ; 54 m² et dix postes de travail pour le laboratoire de biologie et de chimie, 118 m² et 16 postes pour la physique et la technologie, un théâtre de 250 places sur 560 m² et le Forum des idées de 370 m². Réagissant aux remarques sur la complexité de ce bâtiment, Zaha Hadid a déclaré : « Personne ne pense qu'un paysage est étrange parce que Dieu l'a fait, mais si je le fais, les gens pensent qu'il est étrange. »

With the Phaeno Science Center, Hadid confirms that she has now set out on an ambitious schedule of large-scale construction.

Mit dem Wissenschaftszentrum Phaeno bestätigt Hadid, dass sie inzwischen ein ehrgeiziges Programm großformatiger Bauten geschaffen hat.

À travers le Phaeno Science Center, Zaha Hadid confirme qu'elle s'est lancée dans un ambitieux programme de projets à grande échelle.

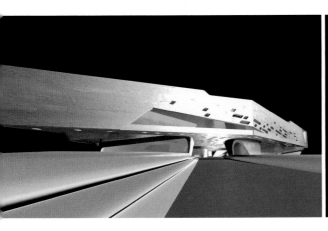

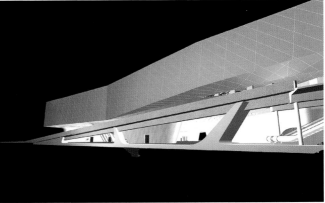

The unexpected nature of the Center's exterior is effectively carried over into the interior spaces, which are at once exciting and comprehensible for the user.

Der überraschende Außenbau des Zentrums wird auf effektive Weise in Innenräume umgesetzt, die zugleich spannend und für den Besucher nachvollziehbar sind.

L'extérieur inattendu du Centre est efficacement décliné à l'intérieur, qui est à la fois stimulant et compréhensible par l'usager.

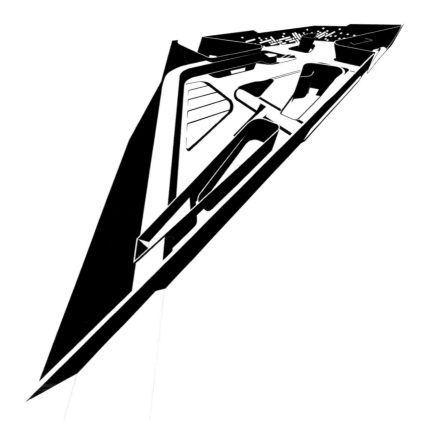

# STEVEN HARRIS

Steven Harris Architects LLP
50 Warren Street
New York, NY 10007
USA

Tel: +1 212 587 1108
E-mail: info@stevenharrisarchitects.com
Web: www.stevenharrisarchitects.com

**STEVEN HARRIS** received his B. A. degree from New College, a B. F.A. from the Rhode Island School of Design, and his M.Arch from Princeton. He taught at the Institute for Architecture and Urban Studies, Princeton, and Harvard before becoming Professor (Adjunct) at Yale. He was the co-editor with Deborah Berke of the book *Architecture of the Everyday* (Princeton Architectural Press, 1998). Steven Harris Architects was established in 1988 and has completed a large number of residential, commercial and institutional projects. Staffed in good part by the former Yale students of Harris, the office employs about 20 architects and designers, and provides interior architecture services as well. Current projects include the design of an eco-tourist resort and equestrian center on 1000 hectares southeast of Mumbai, India; a major addition to the Professional Children's School in New York City; and private houses throughout the United States, in India, and Mexico (such as the Weiss House, 2001, published here). In South Africa, the firm is currently engaged in the design of a private 8000-hectare game preserve located in the Karoo. Recent projects have included a living environment and online broadcasting studio for MTV in New York City; a beach volleyball venue for New York City's 2012 Olympics bid proposal; a pool hall, bowling alley, restaurant and bar in Queens, New York; a grocery and café in the Tribeca neighborhood of Manhattan; and a restaurant in Minneapolis highlighting foods from the "hot zones" of Latin America and China.

**STEVEN HARRIS** legte die Prüfung zum Bachelor of Arts am New College, die zum Bachelor of Fine Arts an der Rhode Island School of Design und die zum Master of Architecture in Princeton ab. Er lehrte am Institute for Architecture and Urban Studies, Princeton, und in Harvard, ehe er zum außerordentlichen Professor in Yale berufen wurde. Er war mit Deborah Berke Herausgeber des Buchs *Architecture of the Everyday* (Princeton Architectural Press, 1998). Steven Harris Architects wurde 1988 eröffnet und hat eine große Zahl von Wohn-, Geschäfts- und Institutsbauten realisiert. Das Büro beschäftigt etwa 20 Architekten und Designer, zum guten Teil ehemalige Studenten von Harris in Yale, und bietet auch innenarchitektonische Dienste an. Zu den derzeitigen Projekten gehören die Gestaltung eines Öko-Touristenhotels und Reiterzentrums auf einem 1000 ha großen Gelände südöstlich von Bombay, ein umfangreicher Anbau an die Professional Children's School in New York sowie Privathäuser in den USA, in Indien und Mexico (wie das hier publizierte Weiss House). In Südafrika ist das Büro zurzeit mit der Gestaltung eines privaten 8000 ha großen Wildreservats in der Karoo beschäftigt. Neuere Projekte umfassen eine Wohnumgebung und ein Online-Sendestudio für MTV in New York, einen Beachvolleyballplatz für die Bewerbung New Yorks für die Olympischen Spiele 2012, eine Billardhalle, Bowlingbahn, Restaurant und Bar im New Yorker Stadtteil Queens, ein Lebensmittelgeschäft und Café im Tribeca-Viertel von Manhattan und ein Restaurant in Minneapolis, das auf Gerichte aus den »heißen Zonen« Südamerikas und Chinas spezialisiert ist.

Dplomé de New College, de la Rhode Island School of Design et de Princeton, **STEVEN HARRIS** a enseigné à l'Institute for Architecture and Urban Studies de Princeton et à Harvard avant de devenir professeur-adjoint à Yale. Avec Deborah Berke, il a codirigé l'édition du livre *Architecture of the Everyday* (Princeton Architectural Press, 1998). L'agence Steven Harris Architects, créée en 1988, a signé un grand nombre de projets résidentiels, commerciaux et institutionnels. Composée en grande partie d'anciens étudiants de Harris à Yale, elle emploie environ vingt architectes et designers et intervient également en architecture intérieure. Ses projets actuels comprennent : la conception d'un centre d'écotourisme et d'équitation sur 1 000 ha au sud-est de Mumbai, en Inde ; une importante extension de la Professional Children's School à New York et des résidences privées aux États-Unis, en Inde et au Mexique, dont la maison Weiss publiée ici. Pour l'Afrique du Sud, l'agence conçoit actuellement une réserve de chasse privée de 8 000 ha dans le Karoo. Parmi ses récents projets : un studio d'émissions en ligne et un cadre d'émissions de télé-réalité pour MTV à New York ; une proposition d'installation de volley de plage pour les Jeux olympiques de New York 2012 ; une piscine couverte, des installations de bowling, un restaurant et un bar dans le Queens à New York ; une épicerie-café dans le quartier de Tribeca à Manhattan et un restaurant à Minneapolis, consacré aux spécialités des « zones chaudes » d'Amérique latine et de Chine.

# WEISS HOUSE

*Cabo San Lucas, Baja California, Mexico, 2001*

*Floor area: 836 m² under roof; 669 m² interior. Client: Weiss family. Cost: $1.5 million.*
*Architect: Steven Harris. Project Team: Tom Zook, Antonio Zaninovic.*
*Interior Design: Lucien Rees Roberts. Landscape Architect: Margie Ruddick*

As the architects describe this project, "The Weiss House is located on a rock bluff 75 meters above the Pacific Ocean in Cabo San Lucas, Mexico; it is the southernmost private residence at the foot of the Baja Peninsula, one of the few places in the world where the desert meets the sea. The natural landscape is sparsely vegetated and is characterized by desert grasses and cacti, rocky cliffs and windswept sandy soils." The proximity of the house to this rare natural setting is a key to the architecture. Approached from above, the house is entered via a ramp and an outdoor entrance pavilion with a fireplace. An irregular courtyard allows the site itself to enter the concrete house. High-strength laminated glass is used for the full-height glass walls to resist hurricane winds. Stone steps lead from the courtyard to the pool on a lower level. Still further down, on the lowest level, there is a guest suite. The configuration of this house and its integration into the natural setting has been compared to that of certain houses by Richard Neutra. The exceptional use of living areas without walls, rendered possible by the local climate, makes the symbiosis between this very modern house and its setting all the more striking and evident. Rough stone walls and natural boulders form a dramatic contrast with much more sophisticated modern surfaces and volumes.

Die Architekten beschreiben das Projekt wie folgt: »Das Weiss House steht in Cabo San Lucas, Mexico, auf einem felsigen Steilufer in 75 m Höhe über dem Pazifik. Es handelt sich dabei um das am weitesten südlich gelegene Privathaus an der Spitze der Halbinsel Baja California, einem der wenigen Orte auf der Welt, an dem Wüste und Meer zusammentreffen. Die nur spärlich mit Wüstengräsern und Kakteen bewachsene umgebende Landschaft ist gekennzeichnet von felsigen Klippen und windgepeitschten sandigen Böden.« Die unmittelbare Nähe des Hauses zu dieser ungewöhnlichen Umgebung ist der Schlüssel zu seiner Architektur. Man nähert sich dem Haus von oben und betritt es über eine Rampe und einen außenliegenden Eingangspavillon mit Kamin. Das Gelände erhält in Form eines unregelmäßig angelegten Innenhofs Zutritt zu dem Betonbau. Damit die deckenhohen Glaswände Wirbelstürmen standhalten, wurden sie aus hochfestem Verbundglas gefertigt. Vom Innenhof führt eine Steintreppe zum darunterliegenden Pool. Noch tiefer, auf der untersten Ebene, befindet sich eine Gästesuite. Die Gestaltung des Hauses und seine Integration in die Umgebung wurden mit bestimmten Häusern von Richard Neutra verglichen. Die dank des hier herrschenden Klimas mögliche außergewöhnliche Nutzung von Wohnbereichen ohne Außenwände macht die Symbiose zwischen diesem sehr modernen Haus und seiner Lage umso bemerkenswerter und augenfälliger. Unbehandelte Steinmauern und Findlinge stehen in spektakulärem Kontrast zu sehr viel subtileren, modernen Oberflächen und Räumen.

Les architectes présentent ainsi leur projet : « La maison Weiss s'élève sur une crête rocheuse qui domine de 75 mètres l'océan Pacifique à Cabo San Lucas au Mexique. C'est la résidence privée la plus méridionale construite au pied de la Baja Peninsula, l'un des rares endroits au monde où un désert rejoint la mer. Le paysage naturel est très peu végétalisé et se caractérise par des herbes et des cactées, des falaises rocheuses et un sol sableux battus par les vents. » La proximité de ce cadre inhabituel est la clé de l'architecture de cette maison. On s'en approche par le haut et y accède par une rampe et un pavillon d'entrée doté d'une cheminée. Une cour, de forme irrégulière, donne l'impression que le site même pénètre dans construction en béton. Les murs vitrés, toute hauteur, sont en verre laminé de haute-résistance en prévision des ouragans. Quelques marches de pierre conduisent de la cour à la piscine située à un niveau inférieur. Au niveau le plus bas est aménagée une suite pour invités. La configuration de la maison et son intégration au cadre naturel ont pu été comparées à celles de maisons de Richard Neutra. La présence exceptionnelle de ces espaces de séjour sans murs, rendus possibles par le climat local, rendent la symbiose entre cette résidence d'une grande modernité et son site d'autant plus frappante et presque évidente. Les murs en pierre brute et en galets contrastent avec des surfaces et des volumes d'inspiration beaucoup plus sophistiquée.

*The house is integrated into its natural setting, with rocks at close proximity to the structure and stone walls echoing the rugged site.*

*Das Haus ist in seine natürliche Umgebung mit den nahe gelegenen Felsen integriert und setzt mit seinen Steinwänden das raue Gelände fort.*

*La maison est intégrée à son cadre naturel. Les rochers à proximité immédiate et les murs de pierre rappellent la rudesse du lieu.*

Set on a cliff above the sea, the house encompasses such dramatic interior settings as this fully glazed corner looking down the shoreline.

Das auf einer Klippe hoch über dem Meer stehende Haus ermöglicht dramatische Interieureffekte wie diese vollständig verglaste Ecke mit Blick auf das Meeresufer.

Implantée sur une falaise au-dessus de la mer, la maison se prête à des effets intérieurs spectaculaires, comme cet angle de verre orienté vers la côte.

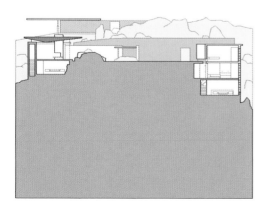

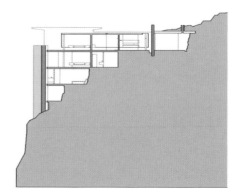

*The architecture allows for frequent surprises and encounters between built forms and natural ones, as in the stairway bottom right.*

*Die Architektur ermöglicht zahlreiche Überraschungen und Zusammentref-fen von gebauten und natürlichen Formen wie im Fall der Treppe unten rechts.*

*L'architecture réserve de nombreuses surprises et rencontres entre les formes construites et celles de la nature, comme dans l'escalier, ci-dessous à droite.*

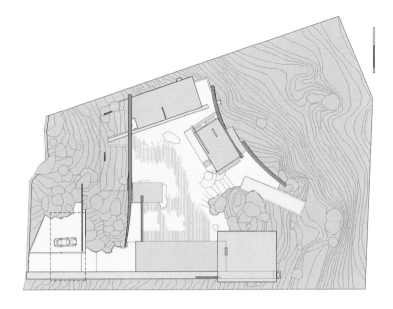

# HERTL.ARCHITEKTEN

*Hertl.Architekten ZT KEG*
*Zwischenbrücken 4*
*4400 Steyr*
*Austria*

*Tel: +43 7252 469 44*
*Fax: +43 7252 473 63*
*E-mail: steyr@hertl-architekten.com*
*Web: www.hertl-architekten.com*

*Ecker Abu Zahra Hou*

Gernot Hertl was born in Steyr, Austria, in 1971. He studied architecture at the Technical University in Graz (1992–97), before beginning to work with Joseph Steinberger (2002–03). He created Hertl.Architekten in 2003 and **HERTL.ARCHITEKTEN** ZT KEG in 2004. His major projects include: Ruby House (Christkindl, 1997–99); Indoor Bath at Farmhouse (Klein Pöchlarn, 2000–02); Storehouse Hartlauer (Amstetten, 2001); Central Plaza Passage (Steyr, 2002); Steinwendtner House (Steyr, 2002–03); Schlüsselhofgasse Town House (Steyr, 2002–03); Housing St. Magdalen (Villach, 2002–05); Boarding School Linz 8 (Linz, 2002–08); Technology House (Steyr, 2003–04, 2005–06); Enns Pumping Station (Steyr, 2004–05); Uncle Fred's Cabin (Steyr, 2004–05); Ecker Abu Zahra House (Luftenberg, 2004–06, published here); Mair Villa (Vienna, 2004–07); Krammer House (Waidhofen an der Ybbs, 2005–06); Reform Factory (Steyr, 2005–07); and Apartment and Office Building Suedpool (Steyr, 2006–08), all in Austria.

Gernot Hertl wurde 1971 in Steyr, Österrreich, geboren. Von 1992 bis 1997 studierte er an der Technischen Universität Graz Architektur und arbeitete von 2002 bis 2003 bei Joseph Steinberger. 2003 gründete er Hertl.Architekten und 2004 **HERTL.ARCHITEKTEN** ZT KEG. Zu seinen wichtigen Projekten zählen das Rubinhaus in Christkindl (1997–99), ein Swimmingpool für ein Bauernhaus (Klein-Pöchlarn, 2000–02), Verkaufsräume für Hartlauer (Amstetten, 2001), Stadtplatzpassage (Steyr, 2002), Haus Steinwendtner (Steyr, 2002–03), Stadthaus Schlüsselhofgasse (Steyr, 2002–03), Wohnungsbau St. Magdalen (Villach, 2002–05), Internat und Berufsschule Linz 8 (Linz, 2002–08), Technologiehaus (Steyr, 2003–04, 2005–06), Ennspumpstation (Steyr, 2004–05), Onkel Freds Hütte (Steyr, 2004–05), Haus Ecker Abu Zahra (Luftenberg, 2004–06, hier publiziert), Villa Mair (Wien, 2004–07), Haus Krammer (Waidhofen an der Ybbs, 2005–06), das Betriebsgebäude Reform (Steyr, 2005–07) und das Apartment- und Bürogebäude Suedpool (Steyr, 2006–08), alle in Österreich.

Gernot Hertl est né à Steyr, Autriche, en 1971. Il étudie l'architecture à l'Université Technique de Graz (1992–97) puis travaille pour Joseph Steinberger (2002–03). Il fonde Hertl Architekten en 2003 et **HERTL.ARCHITEKTEN** ZT KEG en 2004. Ses principaux projets, tous en Autriche, comprennent : la maison Ruby, Christkindl (1997–99) ; une piscine intérieure dans une ferme de Klein Pöchlarn (2000–02), l'entrepôt Hartlauer, Amstetten (2001) ; le passage de la place centrale à Steyr (2002) ; la maison Steinwendtner à Steyr (2002–03) ; la maison de ville Schlüsselhofgasse à Steyr ( 2002–03) ; des logements à St. Magdalen, Villach (2002–05) ; le pensionnat et lycée professionel Linz 8, Linz (2002–08) ; la Maison de la technologie, Steyr (2003–04, 2005–06) ; Station de pompage de Enns à Steyr (2004–05); Cabane de l'Oncle Fred à Steyr (2004–05) ; la maison Abu Zahra, Luftenberg (2004–06) publiée ici ; la villa Mair, Vienne (2004–07) ; la maison Krammer, Waidhofen an der Ybbs (2005–06) ; l'usine de Reform, Steyr (2005–07), et l'immeuble d'appartements et de bureaux Suedpool, Steyr (2006–08).

# ECKER ABU ZAHRA HOUSE

*Luftenberg, Austria, 2004–06*

*Floor area: 261 m². Client: Johann Ecker. Cost: not disclosed.*
*Collaborators: Marcel Schäfer, Lothar Bauer*

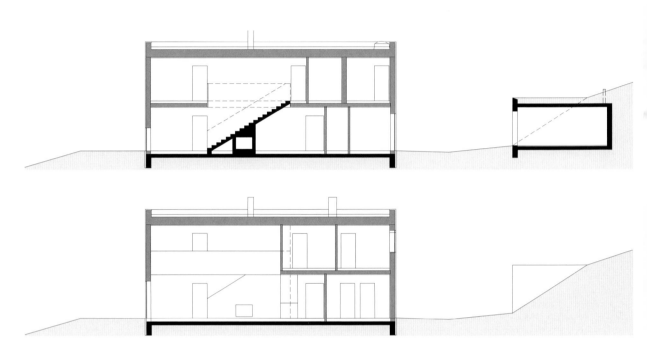

| | | |
|---|---|---|
| *Section drawings of the house reveal a far more "normal" design than the exterior of the structure would tend to indicate.* | *Schnittdarstellungen des Hauses offenbaren eine weit »normalere« Gestaltung, als sie der Außenbau vermuten lässt.* | *Les coupes de la maison révèlent un plan beaucoup plus « normal » que son apparence extérieure ne le laisse supposer.* |

Built for a teacher and a sociologist with a passion for bees, this wooden structure with a flat roof and a vertical copper-plate façade has a 15 x 15-meter ground plan. Windows and the entrance to the house are sliced into the basic cubic form, creating an impression of irregularity within the otherwise purely geometric plan. Within the house, a living space with a ceiling height of almost 6 meters cuts through the building. Floor-to-ceiling glazing opens the living area to the natural setting. On the ground floor, a library, guest room, and apiary share the space, while the bedrooms, an office, and a rooftop terrace occupy the upper level. Stockrooms for the apiary are separated from the house, as is a garage and storage area. The garden is used in large part as a flowering meadow for the bees. The 9731-square-meter site, running from east to west, is lined on both sides by forest, and the architects have made an effort to insert windows where the best views are afforded.

Dieses Holzhaus mit Flachdach und einer mit Kupferblech verkleideten Fassade entstand für einen Lehrer und eine Soziologin mit einer Vorliebe für Bienen auf einem 15 x 5 m messenden Grundriss. In die kubische Grundform des Hauses wurden Fenster und Tür eingeschnitten, so dass in dem ansonsten rein geometrischen Grundriss der Eindruck von Unregelmäßigkeit entsteht. Das Hausinnere wird von einem fast 6 m hohen Wohnraum durchbrochen. Deckenhohe Verglasung öffnet den Wohnbereich zur umgebenden Landschaft. Im Erdgeschoss teilen sich Bibliothek, Gästezimmer und Bienenhaus den Platz, während Schlafzimmer, ein Büro und eine Dachterrasse das Obergeschoss einnehmen. Ebenso wie eine Garage mit Abstellraum, sind auch zum Bienenhaus gehörige Lagerräume vom Haus getrennt. Der Garten wird zum größten Teil als Blumenwiese für die Bienen genutzt. Das von Ost nach West verlaufende, 9731 m² große Grundstück ist auf beiden Seiten von Wald umgeben und die Architekten waren bemüht, die Fenster da einzusetzen, wo sich die schönsten Ausblicke bieten.

Construite pour un enseignant et une sociologue passionnés par les abeilles, cette construction en bois à toit plat et façade verticale en cuivre couvre une empreinte au sol de 15 x 15 mètres. Les fenêtres et l'entrée de la maison sont découpées dans une forme essentiellement cubique, créant une impression d'irrégularité à l'intérieur de ce plan, par ailleurs purement géométrique. Le séjour, dont le plafond atteint près de 6 mètres de haut, est découpé dans le bâtiment. Des ouvertures toute hauteur donnent sur le cadre naturel. Une bibliothèque, une chambre d'amis et un rucher se partagent le rez-de-chaussée, tandis que les chambres, un bureau et une terrasse en toiture se répartissent à l'étage. Les pièces de stockage pour le rucher sont séparées de la maison, ainsi que le garage et l'espace de rangement. Le jardin est occupé en grande partie par une prairie fleurie laissée aux abeilles. Le terrain de 9 731 m² orienté est-ouest est bordé sur deux côtés par une forêt, et les architectes se sont efforcés de disposer les ouvertures en fonction des plus belles perspectives.

The wooden façade of the house lifts up and opens at unexpected angles, giving a certain ambiguous dynamism to the structure.

Die hölzerne Fassade des Hauses erhebt und öffnet sich in überraschenden Schrägen, was dem Bau eine gewisse vieldeutige Dynamik verleiht.

La façade en bois se relève et s'ouvre selon des angles inattendus pour créer une dynamique assez ambiguë.

The floor plans show an essentially square form, whereas the angled openings in the façades (above) give an impression that the weight of the house is suspended above nothing but a thin glass curtain wall.

Die Grundrisse zeigen eine im Wesentlichen quadratische Form, während die schrägen Öffnungen in der Fassade (oben) den Eindruck erwecken, als schwebe das Haus über nichts als einer dünnen Glasfassade.

Les plans reprennent une forme à peu près carrée, tandis que les ouvertures inclinées dans les façades (ci-dessus) donnent l'impression que le poids de la maison ne repose sur rien qu'un mince mur-rideau de verre.

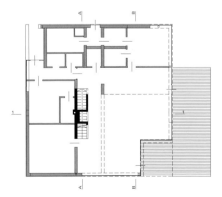
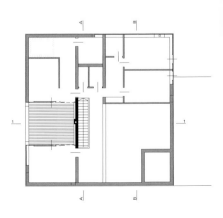

The interior spaces are much less regular in appearance than the basic plans or sections reveal, allowing ample natural light into the living spaces as well as affording views to the outside.

Die Innenräume erscheinen weit weniger regelmäßig als es Grundrisse oder Schnitte vermuten lassen und erlauben viel Tageslicht in den Wohnräumen ebenso wie Ausblicke in die Umgebung.

Les volumes intérieurs sont d'aspect beaucoup moins régulier que les plans et les coupes ne le montrent. Ils bénéficient d'un généreux éclairage naturel dans les parties de séjour et de nombreuses vues sur l'extérieur.

# HERZOG & DE MEURON

*Herzog & de Meuron*
*Rheinschanze 6*
*4056 Basel*
*Switzerland*

*Tel: +41 61 385 5757 / Fax: +41 61 385 5758*
*E-mail: info@herzogdemeuron.com*

**JACQUES HERZOG** and **PIERRE DE MEURON** were both born in Basel in 1950. They received degrees in Architecture from the ETH in Zurich in 1975, after studying with Aldo Rossi, and founded their firm Herzog & de Meuron in Basel in 1978. Harry Gugger and Christine Binswanger joined the practice as partners in 1991 and 1994 respectively, followed by Robert Hösl and Ascan Mergenthaler in 2004, and Stefan Marbach in 2006. Their built work includes the Ricola Storage Building (Laufen, Switzerland, 1987); the Goetz Collection, a gallery for a private collection of contemporary art (Munich, 1991–92); and the Ricola Europe Factory (Mulhouse, France, 1993). Most notably they were chosen early in 1995 to design the Tate Modern in London, addition to the Tate Gallery for contemporary art, situated in the Bankside Power Station, on the Thames opposite St Paul's Cathedral, which opened in May 2000 as Tate Modern. In the near future, they will be engaged in building an extension of it (published here). They were also shortlisted in the competition for the new design of the Museum of Modern Art New York (1997). More recently, they have built the Prada Aoyama Epicenter (Tokyo, 2001–03); Forum 2004 Building and Plaza (Barcelona, 2002–04); Allianz Arena (Munich, 2002–05); De Young Museum (San Francisco, California, 2002–05); and Walker Art Center, Expansion of the Museum and Cultural Center (Minneapolis, Minnesota, 2003–05). They are presently working on the CaixaForum-Madrid (Spain); the Elbe Philharmonic Hall in Hamburg (Germany); the Miami Art Museum (Miami); and the National Stadium, the Main Stadium for the 2008 Olympic Games in Beijing (China). Herzog & de Meuron have been awarded the Royal Gold Medal 2007 by the Royal Institute of British Architects (RIBA).

**JACQUES HERZOG** und **PIERRE DE MEURON** wurden beide 1950 in Basel geboren. 1975 schlossen sie ihr Architekturstudium bei Aldo Rossi an der ETH Zürich ab und gründeten 1978 in Basel ihr erstes Büro Herzog & de Meuron. 1991 und 1994 wurden Harry Gugger und Christine Binswanger Partner, 2004 folgten Robert Hösl und Ascan Mergenthaler sowie 2006 Stefan Marbach. Zu ihren realisierten Projekten gehören das Ricola-Lagergebäude (Laufen, Schweiz, 1987), die Sammlung Goetz, eine Galerie für eine Privatsammlung zeitgenössischer Kunst (München 1991–92), und das Fabrikgebäude für Ricola Europe SA in Mulhouse (Frankreich, 1993). Anfang 1995 erhielten sie den prestigeträchtigen Auftrag zum Bau der Tate Modern für zeitgenössische Kunst als Ergänzung der Tate Gallery. Der Neubau entstand in der Bankside Power Station an der Themse gegenüber von St. Paul's Cathedral und wurde im Mai 2000 eröffnet. In Kürze werden sie mit dem Bau der hier vorgestellten Museumserweiterung befasst sein. Darüber hinaus kamen sie beim Wettbewerb für die neue Gestaltung des Museum of Modern Art in New York (1997) in die engere Wahl. In den letzten Jahren bauten sie das Prada Aoyama Epicenter (Tokio 2001–03), das Gebäude und den Platz »Forum 2004« (Barcelona, 2002–04), die Allianz Arena (München, 2002–05), das De Young Museum (San Francisco, 2002–05) sowie die Erweiterung des Walker Art Center (Minneapolis, Minnesota, 2003–05). Gegenwärtig arbeiten sie am CaixaForum Madrid, der Elbphilharmonie in Hamburg, dem Miami Art Museum in Miami und dem Hauptstadion der Olympischen Spiele 2008 in Peking. 2007 erhielten Herzog & de Meuron die Goldmedaille des Royal Institute of British Architects (RIBA).

**JACQUES HERZOG** et **PIERRE DE MEURON**, tous deux nés à Bâle en 1950, sont diplômés en architecture de l'ETH de Zurich (1975) où ils étudient auprès d'Aldo Rossi. Ils fondent à Bâle, en 1978, Herzog & de Meuron. Harry Gugger et Christine Binswanger les rejoignent respectivement en 1991 et 1994, ainsi que Robert Hösl et Ascan Mergenthaler en 2004 et Stefan Marbach en 2006. Parmi leurs réalisations : entrepôt Ricola, Laufen, Suisse (1987), la collection Goetz, une galerie pour une collection privée d'art contemporain à Munich (1991–92), et l'usine Ricola Europe à Mulhouse, France (1993). Ils ont été sélectionnés, en 1995, pour l'aménagement de la Tate Modern, consacrée aux collections d'art moderne et contemporain de la Tate Gallery de Londres, dans une ancienne centrale électrique – Bankside Power Station – au bord de la Tamise, face à la cathédrale Saint-Paul, réalisation qui fut inaugurée en mai 2000. Ils se préparent à en réaliser une extension, publiée ici. Ils ont fait partie des architectes retenus pour le concours de la transformation du Museum of Modern Art de New York (1997). Plus récemment, ils ont construit le Prada Aoyama Epicenter à Tokyo (2001–03), le bâtiment et la place du Forum 2004 à Barcelone (2002–04) ; le stade Allianz Arena à Munich (2002–05) ; le De Young Museum à San Francisco, Californie (2002–05) et le Walker Art Center, extension du Museum and Cultural Center à Minneapolis, Minnesota (2003–05). Ils travaillent actuellement aux projets du CaixaForum-Madrid, de la salle philharmonique de l'Elbe à Hambourg, du Miami Art Museum à Miami, et du stade principal des Jeux olympiques qui se tiendront à Pékin en 2008. Herzog & de Meuron ont reçu la Royal Gold Medal 2007 décernée par le le Royal Institute of British Architects (RIBA).

# TRANSFORMING TATE MODERN

*Bankside, Southwark, London, UK, 2004–12*

*Floor area: 23 400 m². Client: Tate Trustees. Cost: €318 million (total project cost in 2012).*
*Partners: Jacques Herzog, Pierre de Meuron, Harry Gugger. Project Architects: Michael Casey (Associate),*
*Ben Duckworth (Associate), Jad Silvester. Landscape Design: Vogt Landscape Architects*

Tate Modern was designed by Herzog & de Meuron 15 years ago for 1.8 million visitors a year and it now receives over four million. The new plan would add 7000 square meters of exhibition space to the existing 9000 square meters of the Tate Modern (excluding the Turbine Hall). The architects propose to add a new 10-story structure near the southwest side of the present building. Ten new galleries, two new performance spaces located in former power-plant oil tanks, learning spaces, two new shops, six new cafés, bars, and restaurants are part of the plan. The Switch House, a "largely derelict" space used as an electricity substation by EDF Energy Networks, occupies one-third of the Tate Modern building, space that would be freed, allowing free entrance from the south, which has not been the case until now. Whereas the architects had intentionally used the existing brick structure of the former Bankside Power Station in the first phase of their work, they now propose "a diametrically opposed stand, satisfying the specifications of the brief by having gigantic blocks protrude out of a basically pyramidal structure." Describing the whole as giving "the impression of a rough-cast, fragmented form in progress," Herzog & de Meuron aim to use their design to allow modifications through to the end of the design process "without affecting the basic character of the building." The new structure would be visible from the north, behind Tate Modern, but not in an obtrusive way, declaring its presence without overwhelming the original building. Connected by bridges and envisaging an increased emphasis on the Turbine Hall as the "backbone of the entire complex," the new plan appears to build on the existing infrastructure while also significantly updating it, moving well beyond the successful adaptive reuse of the power plant.

Tate Modern wurde von Herzog & de Meuron vor 15 Jahren für 1,8 Millionen Besucher im Jahr konzipiert und muss jetzt über 4 Millionen verkraften. Der neue Plan sieht vor, der vorhandenen Ausstellungsfläche der Tate Modern von 9000 m² (ohne die Turbinenhalle) weitere 7000 m² hinzuzufügen. Die Architekten planen, nahe der Südwestseite des Gebäudes einen neuen zehngeschossigen Bau zu errichten. Die Planung sieht zehn neue Ausstellungsräume, zwei in den Öltanks des ehemaligen Kraftwerks untergebrachte neue Bereiche für Performances, Studienräume, zwei neue Läden sowie sechs neue Cafés, Bars und Restaurants vor. Das »Switch House«, ein weitgehend baufälliger Raum, der von EDF Energy Networks als elektrische Umspannstation genutzt wurde, nimmt ein Drittel des Gebäudes der Tate Modern ein, Raum der freigegeben werden könnte und von Süden her den bisher nicht möglichen ungehinderten Zugang erlauben würde. Während die Architekten im ersten Abschnitt ihrer Arbeit bewusst den vorhandenen Backsteinbau des aufgelassenen Kraftwerks Bankside nutzten, vertreten sie jetzt »einen diametral entgegengesetzten Standpunkt und entsprechen den Anforderungen der Ausschreibung, indem sie aus einem im Wesentlichen pyramidalen Baukörper riesige Blocks herausragen lassen«. Herzog & de Meuron, nach deren Meinung das Ganze »den Eindruck einer roh verputzten, fragmentierten, sich weiterentwickelnden Form« erweckt, wollen ihren Entwurf so verwenden, dass bis zum Abschluss des Entwurfsprozesses Modifikationen möglich sind, »ohne den grundlegenden Charakter des Gebäudes zu beeinträchtigen«. Von Norden aus wäre der Neubau hinter Tate Modern zu sehen und würde sich zu seiner Präsenz bekennen, ohne jedoch das ursprüngliche Gebäude zu überwältigen. Die durch Brücken angebundene neue Planung, die eine zunehmende Bedeutung der Turbinenhalle als »Rückgrat des Gesamtkomplexes« vorsieht, verlässt sich anscheinend auf die vorhandene Infrastruktur, die sie zugleich wesentlich modernisiert und damit über die gelungene Umnutzung des Kraftwerks hinausgeht.

La Tate Modern, conçue par Herzog & de Meuron il y a quinze ans pour recevoir 1,8 million de visiteurs par an en accueille aujourd'hui plus de 4 millions. Cette nouvelle extension accroît de 7 000 m² les 9 000 m² d'espaces d'exposition existants (hors Turbine Hall). Les architectes ont proposé d'accoler au sud-ouest du bâtiment actuel une nouvelle structure de dix niveaux. Dix galeries, deux salles pour des performances sont installées dans les anciens réservoirs de pétrole de la centrale, des espaces d'enseignement, deux boutiques, six cafés bars et un restaurant font également partie de ce plan. La Switch House, espace « en grande partie délabré » servant de sous-station pour EDF Energy Networks et qui occupait un tiers du bâtiment de la Tate Modern, sera libéré pour permettre d'aménager une entrée par le sud, impossible jusqu'à présent. Alors que les architectes avaient volontairement utilisé le bâtiment en briques de l'ancienne centrale électrique pour la première phase, ils proposent aujourd'hui « une attitude diamétralement opposée, qui satisfait aux spécifications de l'appel d'offre par des blocs gigantesques se projetant à partir d'une structure pyramidale. » Décrivant l'ensemble comme donnant « l'impression d'une forme brute de fonderie fragmentée et en devenir », Herzog & de Meuron revendiquent la liberté d'y apporter des modifications jusqu'à la fin du processus de conception « sans affecter le caractère de base du bâtiment ». La nouvelle structure sera visible du nord, derrière la Tate Modern, mais de façon non agressive, affirmant sa présence sans dominer le bâtiment d'origine auquel elle sera reliée par des passerelles. En prévoyant de mettre un nouvel accent sur le Hall de la Turbine « épine dorsale du complexe dans son ensemble », le nouveau plan s'appuie sur l'existant, tout en le rajeunissant et en allant bien au-delà de la réutilisation adaptée et réussie d'une ancienne centrale électrique.

The unusual "stacked" new extension seems to be at odds with the more staid brick architecture of the old power plant. The point of the architects is to make a statement in this instance, and to provide highly flexible museum space.

Der ungewöhnlich »gestapelte« neue Erweiterungsbau scheint im Widerspruch zur gesetzteren Backsteinarchitektur des alten Kraftwerks zu stehen. Tatsächlich wollen die Architekten hier einen Kontrapunkt setzen und gleichzeitig einen äußerst flexiblen Ausstellungsraum bereitstellen.

La curieuse apparence d'empilement de cette nouvelle extension semble se poser en contradiction avec l'architecture de brique, plus rangée, de l'ancienne centrale électrique. Les architectes ont cherché à la fois à affirmer une présence, et à offrir des espaces muséaux de grande souplesse.

# HHF

*HHF architekten GmbH*
*St. Johanns-Vorstadt 17 / 4056 Basel / Switzerland*
*Tel: +41 61 263 8080 / Fax: +41 61 263 8090*
*E-mail: info@hhf.ch / Web: www.hhf.ch*

**HHF** was founded in 2003 by Tilo Herlach, Simon Hartmann and Simon Frommenwiler. Tilo Herlach was born in 1972 in Zurich. He studied architecture from 1992 to 1998 at the ETH Zurich and at the EPFL in Lausanne. He subsequently worked with d-company in Bern (2001–03), and with Rolf Furrer Architekten (Basel, 2003). Simon Hartmann was born in 1974 in Bern, and studied architecture from 1994 to 2000 at the EPFL, at the Technical University of Berlin, and the ETH. From 1997 to 2003, he worked with Nicola di Battista in Rome, A.B.D.R., Garofalo & Miura, Steuerwald + Scheiwiller Architekten in Basel, and Rolf Furrer Architekten in Basel. Simon Frommenwiler was born in London in 1972. He attended the ETH in Zurich from 1994 to 2000, and worked subsequently with Bearth & Deplazes in Chur, ARchos Architecture in Basel, and Skidmore Owings & Merrill in New York. He was a member of the SOM-Sejima-Neutelings team for the World Trade Center competition in New York (2003). Simon Hartmann has been a teaching assistant at the ETH Studio Basel working with Jacques Herzog, Pierre de Meuron, Roger Diener, and Marcel Meili since 2002, and head of teaching there since 2005. Simon Frommenwiler has been a teaching assistant working with Harry Gugger at the EPFL in Lausanne since 2005. HFF worked on the Jinhua Architecture Park, where they completed the *Baby Dragon* in 2005, and also in China realized the Treehouse (Lijiang, Yunnan Province, 2005–07, published here). Current work under construction includes: SonVida Housing (Bottmingen, Switzerland, 2003–07); Tsai Residence (Taghkanic, New York, 2005–07); Artfarm, a showroom and storage for art (Clinton, New York, 2006–07); "Ono" Bar-Café-Lounge (Basel, Switzerland, 2006–); Cafeteria Kirschgarten High School (Basel, Switzerland, 2006–08), and a private House in Ordos (Mongolia/China, 2007–).

**HHF** wurde 2003 von Tilo Herlach, Simon Hartmann und Simon Frommenwiler gegründet. Tilo Herlach wurde 1972 in Zürich geboren und studierte von 1992 bis 1998 an der ETH Zürich und der EPFL in Lausanne Architektur. Anschließend war er von 2001 bis 2003 bei der d-company in Bern und 2003 bei Rolf Furrer Architekten in Basel tätig. Simon Hartmann wurde 1974 in Bern geboren und studierte von 1994 bis 2000 an der EPFL, der TU Berlin und der ETH Zürich Architektur. Von 1997 bis 2003 arbeitete er bei Nicola di Battista in Rom, A.B.D.R., Garofalo & Miura, Steuerwald + Scheiwiller Architekten in Basel und Rolf Furrer Architekten, ebenfalls Basel. Simon Frommenwiler wurde 1972 in London geboren, besuchte von 1994 bis 2000 die ETH Zürich, um anschließend bei Bearth & Deplazes, Chur, ARchos Architecture in Basel sowie Skidmore, Owings & Merrill in New York zu arbeiten. Beim Wettbewerb um das World Trade Center in New York 2003 gehörte er dem Team SOM-Sejima-Neutelings an. Simon Hartmann arbeitete ab 2002 als sog. Teaching Assistant am ETH Studio Basel mit Jacques Herzog, Pierre de Meuron, Roger Diener und Marcel Meili, seit 2005 als Head of Teaching. Simon Frommenwiler ist seit 2005 bei Harry Gugger als Teaching Assistant an der EPFL in Lausanne tätig. HFF arbeiteten am Architekturpark Jinhua, wo sie 2005 das »Drachenbaby« fertigstellten; ebenfalls in China realisierten sie das hier publizierte Baumhaus (Lijiang, Provinz Yunnan, 2005–07). Zurzeit im Bau befindlich sind: Wohnungsbau SonVida (Bottmingen, Schweiz, 2003–07), Tsai Residence (Taghkanic, New York, 2005–07), Artfarm, Ausstellungsraum und Lager für Kunst (Clinton, New York, 2006–07), Bar-Café-Lounge »Ono« (Basel, 2006), die Cafeteria Kirschgarten (Basel, 2006–08) sowie ein Privathaus in Ordos (Mongolei, China, 2007–).

L'agence **HHF** a été fondée en 2003 par Tilo Herlach, Simon Hartmann et Simon Frommenwiler. Tilo Herlach, né en 1972 à Zurich, a étudié l'architecture de 1992 à 1998 à l'ETH de Zurich et à l'EPFL de Lausanne. Il a ensuite travaillé pour la d-company à Berne (2001–03) et Rolf Furrer Architekten à Bâle (2003). Simon Hartmann, né en 1974 à Berne, a étudié l'architecture de 1994 à 2000 à l'EPFL, à l'Université polytechnique de Berlin et à l'ETH. De 1997 à 2003, il a travaillé pour Nicola di Battista à Rome, A.B.D.R., Garofalo & Miura, Steuerwald + Scheiwiller Architekten à Bâle et Rolf Furrer Architekten à Bâle. Simon Frommenwiler, né à Londres en 1972, a étudié à l'ETH de Zurich de 1994 à 2000 et travaillé ensuite pour Bearth & Deplazes (Chur), ARchos Architecture à Bâle et Skidmore Owings & Merrill à New York. Il a fait partie de l'équipe SOM-Sejima-Neutelings constituée pour le concours du World Trade Center à New York en 2003. Simon Hartmann a été assistant enseignant à l'ETH Studio Basel, auprès de Jacques Herzog, Pierre de Meuron, Roger Diener et Marcel Meili depuis 2002, et est responsable des enseignements depuis 2005. Simon Frommenwiler est assistant enseignant auprès de Harry Gugger à l'EPFL de Lausanne depuis 2005. Ils ont travaillé ensemble sur le projet de parc d'architecture de Jinhua, où ils ont achevé le *Baby Dragon* en 2005 et ont également réalisé en Chine la Treehouse (maison-arbre) à Lijiang, province du Yunnan (2005–07), publiée ici. Parmi leurs chantiers actuels : les logements SonVida, Bottmingen, Suisse (2003–07) ; la résidence Tsai, Taghkanic, New York (2005–07) ; l'Artfarm, showroom et stockage d'art, Clinton, New York (2006–07) ; le bar-café-lounge Ono, Bâle, Suisse (2006), la cafétéria du collège de Kirschgarten, Bâle, Suisse (2006–08), ainsi qu'une résidence privée à Ordos (Mongolia/Chine, 2007–).

# TREEHOUSE

*Lijiang, Yunnan Province, China, 2005–07*

*Floor area: 400 m². Clients: Xue Shan Shui Cheng Tourism & Real Estate Develop Co. Cost: not disclosed.*
*Architects: HHF architects in collaboration with Ai WeiWei / FAKE Design*

Intended as a guesthouse for a golf club, this two-level concrete structure is "based on a pentagonal pattern." The architects find this pattern interesting because "it is not possible to create an infinite addition of pentagons without generating leftovers. These leftovers are an essential for the house: they create interesting light situations, linking the interior to nature and integrating the existing trees on the site into the house (within the resulting courtyards). Like leaves create a space beneath a tree, lights and shadows are fundamental elements creating different qualities of space in the treehouse." Cantilevering over a small lake with a view of the mountains beyond, the structure contains an entrance courtyard, lobby, and kitchen areas, library, living room, and two bedrooms with a bathroom on the ground floor. The lower level comprises the master bedroom and bathroom. Bamboo boards were used for the cast-in-place concrete, while the floors are covered in a dark wood. The same wood is used for the windows and blinds. The roof of the structure is covered with grass in an effort to integrate it further into the natural setting.

Dieser als Gästehaus für einen Golfclub gedachte, zweistöckige Betonbau »basiert auf Fünfecken«. Die Architekten finden diese Form interessant, weil »es nicht möglich ist, Fünfecke in beliebiger Zahl aneinander zu setzen, ohne dass Restflächen entstehen. Diese Reste sind von entscheidender Bedeutung für das Haus: Sie schaffen interessante Lichtverhältnisse, indem sie den Innenraum mit der Natur verbinden und die auf dem Gelände vorhandenen Bäume in das Haus bzw. in die entstandenen Innenhöfe integrieren. So wie durch die Blätter eines Baums ein Raum entsteht, erzeugen Licht und Schatten als grundlegende Elemente unterschiedliche Raumqualitäten im Baumhaus.« Der über einen kleinen See auskragende Bau mit Blick auf die dahinter liegenden Berge umfasst auf der Eingangsebene Vorhof, Lobby, Küche, Bibliothek, Wohnraum und zwei Schlafzimmer mit Bad. Auf der unteren Ebene befinden sich die Hauptschlafzimmer und das Bad. Für den Ortbeton wurden Bambusbretter verwendet, die Böden sind mit dunklem Holz belegt. Das gleiche Holz wurde für die Fenster und Abschirmungen benutzt. Das mit Gras bewachsene Dach soll den Bau noch weiter in seine Umgebung einbinden.

Maison d'hôtes pour un club de golf, cette construction en béton sur deux niveaux est « basée sur un plan pentagonal ». Les architectes apprécient cette forme « car il est impossible de multiplier à l'infini des pentagones sans créer de vides. Ces vides sont essentiels à cette maison : ils génèrent d'intéressantes situations d'éclairage reliant l'intérieur à la nature et intégrant la maison aux arbres existants sur le terrain (dans les cours ainsi dégagées). Comme les feuilles créent un espace sous un arbre, l'ombre et la lumière sont des éléments fondamentaux qui génèrent différentes qualités d'espaces dans toute la maison ». En porte-à-faux au-dessus d'un petit lac et bénéficiant dans le lointain d'une vue sur les montagnes, le bâtiment contient une cour d'entrée, un hall d'accueil et une cuisine, une bibliothèque, un séjour et deux chambres avec salle de bains au rez-de-chaussée. Le niveau inférieur contient la chambre principale et sa salle de bains. Des planches de bambou ont été utilisées pour le coulage du béton sur place et les sols sont en bois dur. Le même matériau a servi aux fenêtres et aux écrans. Le toit recouvert d'herbes affirme une volonté d'intégration poussée au cadre naturel.

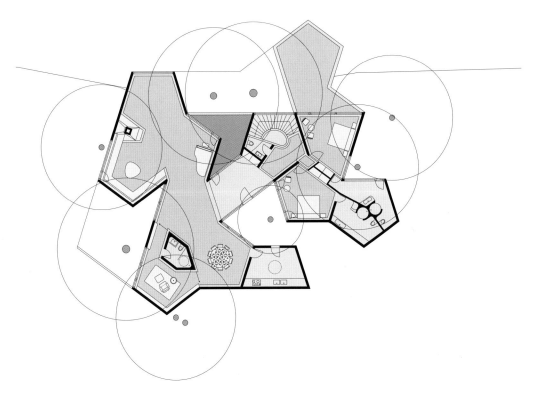

The rather complex geometric pattern of the plan for the house, seen to the left, reveals its originality even more than the computer perspectives of its situation on the water.

Die ziemlich komplexe Geometrie des Hausgrundrisses (links) offenbart dessen Originalität noch deutlicher als die Computerperspektive seiner Lage am Wasser.

Le caractère géométrique assez complexe du plan de la maison est encore plus original dans la réalité que dans les images de synthèse réalisées de son implantation sur l'eau.

# HOLODECK.AT

*HOLODECK.at*
*Friedrichstrasse 6/15 / 1010 Vienna / Austria*
*Tel: +43 1 5248 1330 / Fax: +43 1 5248 1334*
*E-mail: vienna@holodeck.at / Web: www.holodeck.at*

**HOLODECK.AT** has existed since 1998, with offices in Vienna and Berlin. Marlies Breuss studied Piano and Composition at the Landeskonservatorium Feldkirch, before obtaining her degree in Engineering from the Technical University (TU) in Vienna (1993). She went on to receive her M.Arch degree from the Southern California Institute of Architecture (SCI-Arc, 1995). She was an Associate Professor at the Institute for Housing and Design (1996–2002), and has taught a design course entitled "Building Structure and Design" at the TU in Vienna, since 2003. Michael Ogertschnig also obtained his diploma as an engineer from the TU in Vienna (1998) and did postgraduate studies at the IAAS/MACBA Barcelona (1999). He too has taught "Building Structure and Design" at the TU in Vienna (2005). The team states their approach as follows: "Architecture is a network connecting the user, location, technology, and philosophy. We collect detailed information about particularities of the site, investigate the user programs, integrate the newest technologies, and then develop the concept and process. Our architectural strategy aims to maintain the intertwined complexity and we generate buildings with new programmatic interpretations, continuity of landscape, urban context, and differentiated sequences of space." Their work includes housing projects such as "Urban Stratification" in Vienna; "22tops" in Wolfsberg; "rooftop 02" and "Urban Reflections" in Vienna; the "hall 01" Industrial Building in St. Veit; urban planning studies in Valencia, Spain; an office high-rise in Vienna; a number of single-family houses such as the Floating House in Austria, published here; and exhibition design, such as that for the show "The Modernist Book – Marzona Collection" held in Vienna.

**HOLODECK.AT** existiert seit 1998 mit Büros in Wien und Berlin. Marlies Breuss studierte am Landeskonservatorium Feldkirch Klavier und Komposition, ehe sie an der Technischen Universität Wien 1993 einen Abschluss in Ingenieurwesen erwarb. Sie setzte ihre Ausbildung am Southern California Institute of Architecture (SCI-Arc) fort, wo sie 1995 die Prüfung zum Master of Architecture ablegte. Von 1996 bis 2002 war sie als Assistentin am Institute for Housing and Design tätig und veranstaltet an der TU Wien seit 2003 einen Designkurs mit dem Titel »Baukonstruktion und Design«. Michael Ogertschnig erwarb ebenfalls ein Ingenieurdiplom an der TU Wien (1998) und setzte 1999 seine Studien am IAAS/MACBA in Barcelona fort. Auch er unterrichtete 2005 an der TU Wien zum Thema »Baukonstruktion und Design«. Die beiden legen ihre Auffassung wie folgt dar: »Architektur ist die Vernetzung von Mensch, Ort, Technologie und Philosophie. Wir sammeln detaillierte Informationen über die Eigenheiten des Ortes, analysieren die Nutzerprogramme, untersuchen die neuesten Technologien und entwickeln daraus das kontextuelle Konzept. Unser Anliegen in der Architektur liegt in der Überlagerung von Komplexitäten und wir generieren Gebäude mit programmatischen Neuinterpretationen, landschaftlicher Kontinuität, urbanem Kontext und differenzierten Raumsequenzen.« Ihr Werk umfasst Wohnungsbauprojekte wie: »Urban Stratification« in Wien, »22tops« in Wolfsberg, »rooftop 02« und »Urban Reflections« in Wien, das Industriegebäude »hall 01« in St. Veit, Stadtplanungsstudien in Valencia, ein Bürohochhaus in Wien, eine Reihe Einfamilienhäuser wie das hier vorgestellte Floating House in Österreich sowie Ausstellungsgestaltungen wie die für die in Wien gezeigte Ausstellung »Das Buch der Moderne – Architektur des 20. Jahrhunderts aus der Sammlung Marzona«.

**HOLODECK.AT**, agence présente à Vienne et Berlin existe depuis 1998. Marlies Breuss a étudié le piano et la composition musicale au Landeskonservatorium de Feldkirch, avant d'entamer des études d'ingénierie à la Technische Universität de Vienne (TU) dont elle sort diplômée en 1993. Elle reçoit son M. Arch du Southern California Institute of Architecture (SCI-Arc, 1995), puis est chargée de cours à l'Institute for Housing and Design (1996–2002) et dirige un atelier d'enseignement intitulé « Structures de construction et conception » à la TU de Vienne, depuis 2003. Michael Ogertschnig est également diplômé ingénieur de la TU de Vienne (1998) et a suivi des études supérieures au IAAS/MACBA à Barcelone (1999). Il enseigne également les « Structures de construction et conception » à la TU de Vienne (2005). Tous deux présentent leur approche de la façon suivante : « L'architecture est un réseau entre l'usager, le lieu, la technologie et la philosophie. Nous rassemblons une information détaillée sur les particularités du site, étudions les programmes des utilisateurs, intégrons les dernières technologies et mettons enfin au point le concept et le processus. Notre stratégie architecturale vise à maintenir la complexité entrelacée, et nous créons des bâtiments aux nouvelles interprétations programmatiques, incluant la continuité avec le paysage, le contexte urbain et différentes séquences spatiales. » Parmi leurs réalisations : le projet de logement « Urban Stratification » à Vienne ; « 22tops » à Wolfsberg ; « rooftop 02 » et « Urban Reflections » à Vienne ; le « hall 01 » de la construction industrielle à St. Veit ; des études d'urbanisme pour Valence, Espagne ; un immeuble de bureaux de grande hauteur à Vienne ; plusieurs résidences privées comme la Maison flottante en Autriche, publiée ici, et la conception d'expositions comme « Le Livre moderniste – la collection Marzona » organisée à Vienne.

# FLOATING HOUSE

*Siegenfeld, Austria, 2004–05*

*Floor area: 439 m². Client: H. family. Cost: €575 000.*
*Collaborators: Manuel Garcia Barbero, Sebastian Uhl, Ana Curto*

Designed as a house for a family with two children, this residence offers a surprising profile in an otherwise rather traditional area. As the architects describe it, it is a "house in the countryside serving as a refuge for urban workers. The urban context ends with the volumes of garage and office space. Then the program changes and a new concept is formed by the landscape. The movement creates a complex and multilayered continuous space, starting from the adjacent field and ending back in the landscape transformed into a reflecting projection area." Lifted off the ground and cantilevered over the garden, the gray presence of the house exudes what might be called a dynamic austerity. The rather complex and skewed plan provides for an entrance area, living room, and terrace on the ground floor and bedrooms, dining room and kitchen on the upper level. The snaking movement from one floor to the other means that these spaces are not actually located on planes, but are distributed throughout the space in a more unexpected manner. Guest and fitness rooms are located below grade.

Dieses für eine Familie mit zwei Kindern gedachte Wohnhaus zeichnet sich in einer ansonsten eher traditionellen Gegend durch eine überraschende Formgebung aus. Die Architekten bezeichnen es als »Haus auf dem Land, das als Zufluchtsort für arbeitende Stadtmenschen dient. Der urbane Kontext findet mit Garage und Büroraum ein Ende. Dann verändert sich der Plan und ein neues Konzept wird von der Landschaft geformt. Dieser Umschwung erzeugt einen komplexen und vielschichtigen zusammenhängenden Raum, der mit dem angrenzenden Feld beginnt und, umgewandelt in eine reflektierende Projektionsfläche, wieder in der Landschaft endet.« Vom Boden abgehoben und über den Garten auskragend strahlt die graue Präsenz des Hauses eine vielleicht als dynamische Nüchternheit zu bezeichnende Anmutung aus. Der recht komplexe, schräge Grundriss umfasst im Erdgeschoss einen Eingangsbereich, Wohnzimmer und Terrasse, im Obergeschoss Schlafzimmer, Esszimmer und Küche. Die gewundene, vertikale Bewegung bringt es mit sich, dass diese Räumlichkeiten sich nicht wirklich auf Ebenen befinden, sondern in unerwarteter Weise im Raum verteilt sind. Gästezimmer und Fitnessraum befinden sich im Souterrain.

Cette résidence, conçue pour une famille de cinq personnes, présente un profil surprenant pour cette région assez traditionnelle. Les architectes la présentent comme « une maison dans la campagne destinée à servir de refuge à des travailleurs urbains. Le contexte urbain se borne aux volumes du garage et du bureau. Puis le programme se transforme et un nouveau concept apparaît, issu du paysage. Le mouvement crée un espace complexe à multiples strates en continu, qui part du champ adjacent et vient s'achever dans le paysage transformé en une aire de projection réfléchissante ». Surélevée du sol et en porte-à-faux au-dessus du jardin, cette maison grise exprime ce que l'on pourrait qualifier d'une austérité dynamique. Le plan en biais assez complexe se répartit en une entrée, un séjour et une terrasse au rez-de-chaussée, des chambres, la cuisine et l'aire des repas à l'étage. Le mouvement, qui sinue d'un niveau à l'autre, signifie que ces espaces ne se trouvent pas réellement sur des plans, mais sont distribués dans le volume de façon plus inattendue. Des pièces pour invités et une salle de remise en forme occupent le sous-sol.

*Much as its name implies, the Floating House appears to hover above the earth, since the upper volume is made to look as though it is much heavier than the lighter, smaller base.*

*Seinem Namen gemäß scheint das Floating House über dem Erdboden zu schweben, eine Folge des über dem kleineren Unterbau bewusst schwer wirkenden oberen Bauteils.*

*Comme son nom l'indique, la Maison flottante semble suspendue au-dessus du sol, le volume supérieur paraissant beaucoup plus lourd que sa base, plus petite.*

# TOYO ITO

Toyo Ito & Associates, Architects
1–19–4 Shibuya, Shibuya-ku
Tokyo 150–0002
Japan

Tel: +81 3 3409 5822
Fax: +81 3 3409 5969

Born in 1941, **TOYO ITO** graduated from the University of Tokyo in 1965 and worked in the office of Kiyonori Kikutake until 1969. He created his own office, Urban Robot (URBOT), in Tokyo in 1971, assuming the name of Toyo Ito & Associates, Architects in 1979. His completed works include the Silver Hut (Tokyo, 1984); Tower of the Winds (Kanagawa, 1986); Yatsushiro Municipal Museum (Kumamoto, 1991); Old People's Home (1994); and Fire Station (1995), both located in Kyushu; Nagaoka Lyric Hall (Niigata, 1996) and Dome in Odate (Akita, 1997). One of his most successful and widely published projects, Sendai Mediatheque in Miyagi, was completed in 2001. He designed a temporary pavilion for the Serpentine Gallery in London (2002). He was given the Golden Lion for Lifetime Achievement at the 8th International Architecture Exhibition at the Venice Biennale the same year. More recently, he has completed the Tod's Omotesando Building (Tokyo, 2004); Island City Central Park Grin Grin (Fukuoka, 2005); Meiso no Mori Municipal Funeral Hall (Gifu, 2006, published here) and Mikimoto Ginza 2 in Tokyo. He is currently working on a Relaxation Park in Torrevieja; Taichung Metropolitan Opera House; and the University of California Berkeley Art Museum/Pacific Film Archive. In 2006, Ito was awarded the Royal Gold Medal by the Royal Institute of British Architects (RIBA).

Der 1941 geborene **TOYO ITO** schloss 1965 sein Studium an der Universität von Tokio ab und war danach bis 1969 im Büro von Kiyonori Kikutake tätig. Unter der Bezeichnung Urban Robot (URBOT) eröffnete er 1971 in Tokio ein eigenes Büro, das seit 1979 unter dem Namen Toyo Ito & Associates, Architects firmiert. Zu seinen realisierten Bauten zählen: Silver Hut (Tokio, 1984), der Turm der Winde (Kanagawa, 1986), das Städtische Museum Yatsushiro (Kumamoto, 1991), ein Altenheim (1994) und eine Feuerwache (1995), beide auf der Insel Kyushu, Nagaoka Lyric Hall (Niigata, 1996) und der Dome in Odate (Akita, 1997), sämtlich in Japan. Eines seiner geglück-testen, bekanntesten Projekte, die Sendai Mediathek in Miyagi, wurde 2001 fertiggestellt. Er entwarf einen temporären Pavillon für die Serpentine Gallery in London (2002) und wurde im gleichen Jahr bei der 8. Internationalen Architekturbiennale in Venedig mit dem Goldenen Löwen für sein Lebenswerk ausgezeichnet. In den letzten Jahren vollendete er das Tod's Omotesando Building (Tokio, 2004), den Island City Central Park Grin Grin (Fukuoka, 2005), Meiso no Mori Municipal Funeral Hall (Gifu, 2006, hier publiziert) sowie Mikimoto Ginza 2 in Tokio. Er arbeitet gegenwärtig an einem Erholungspark in Torrevieja; am Metropolitan Opera House in Taichung; und am Kunstmuseum/Pacific Film Archive der University of California in Berkeley. 2006 wurde Ito mit der Royal Gold Medal des Royal Institute of British Architects (RIBA) ausgezeichnet.

Né en 1941, **TOYO ITO** est diplômé de l'Université de Tokyo en 1965 et a travaillé pour l'agence de Kiyonori Kikutake jusqu'en 1969. Il a créé sa propre agence, Urban Robot (URBOT) en 1971, qui prend le nom de Toyo Ito & Associates, Architects en 1979. Parmi ses réalisations : la maison Silver Hut, Tokyo (1984) ; la Tour des vents, Kanagawa (1986) ; le Musée municipal de Yatsushiro, Kumamoto (1991) ; une maison de retraite (1994) et une caserne de pompiers (1995), les deux sur l'île de Kyushu ; la salle de concerts lyriques de Nagaoka, Niigata, Japon (1996) ; et le Dome de Odate, Akita, Japon (1997). L'un des projets les plus réussis et plus publiés est la médiathèque de Sendai à Miyagi (2001). Il a conçu un pavillon temporaire pour la Serpentine Gallery à Londres (2002) et a reçu le Lion d'or pour l'ensemble de son œuvre à la 8e Biennale internationale d'architecture de Venise la même année. Plus récemment, il a achevé l'immeuble Tod's Omotesando, Tokyo (2004) ; le parc central Grin Grin, Fukuoka (2005) ; le funérarium municipal Meiso no Mori à Gifu (2006, publié ici) ; et l'immeuble Mikimoto Ginza 2 à Tokyo. Il travaille actuellement sur un parc de relaxation à Torrevieja, l'opéra métropolitain de Taichung et l'Art Museum/Pacific Film Archive de l'Université de Californie de Berkeley. En 2006, il a reçu la Royal Gold Medal du Royal Institute of British Architects (RIBA).

# MEISO NO MORI
# MUNICIPAL FUNERAL HALL

*Kakamigahara, Gifu, Japan, 2005–06*

*Floor area: 2264 m². Client: City of Kakamigahara. Cost: not disclosed*

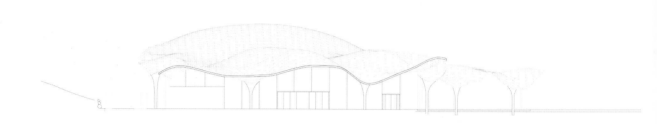

The most surprising feature of this crematorium, rebuilt in a cemetery in the city of Kakamigahara, in the central Japanese prefecture of Gifu, is undoubtedly its "spacious roof floating above the site like slowly drifting clouds creating a soft field." As the architect explains, "We investigated a freely curved reinforced-concrete shell structure to construct a roof characterized by concavities and convexities. The shape of the roof structure was determined by an algorithm intended to generate the optimum structural solution. Since this type of structural analysis resembles the growth patterns of plants that keep transforming themselves following simple natural rules, the process is called 'evolution.' Several hundred such evolutionary cycles produced the final shape. The curved line becomes landscape, in harmony with the edge silhouette of the surrounding mountains." The gently curving roof also determines the shape of the interior ceiling, and an indirect natural light suffuses the whole space during the day. Set on a 6696-square-meter site, the two-story building has a maximum height of 11.5 meters and a floor area of 2264 square meters. Working with a building type usually noted for its extreme austerity or heaviness, Toyo Ito has sought and obtained lightness and what must be a comforting space for the families and friends of the deceased.

Die überraschendste Besonderheit dieses Krematoriums, das auf einem Friedhof der Stadt Kakamigahara in der zentraljapanischen Präfektur Gifu umgebaut wurde, ist fraglos sein »weiträumiges, gleich langsam dahinziehenden Wolken über dem Baugrund schwebendes Dach«. Der Architekt erläutert: »Wir beschäftigten uns mit einem frei gekrümmten Stahlbetonschalenbau, um ein von konkaven und konvexen Wölbungen gestaltetes Dach zu konzipieren. Die Dachform wurde von einem Algorithmus berechnet, der die optimale konstruktive Lösung erbringen sollte. Da dieser Typ der konstruktiven Analyse dem Wachstum von Pflanzen ähnelt, die sich einfachen Naturgesetzen folgend beständig verändern, bezeichnet man diesen Vorgang als ›Evolution‹. Hunderte solcher evolutionären Zyklen ergaben die endgültige Form. Die gebogene Linie wird zur Landschaft, in Einklang mit der Silhouette der umgebenden Hügelketten.« Das sanft gebogene Dach bestimmt darüber hinaus die Form der inneren Decke. Tagsüber ist der gesamte Raum von indirektem Licht durchflutet. Das auf einem 6696 m² großen Baugelände stehende zweigeschossige Gebäude hat eine maximale Höhe von 11,5 m und eine Bodenfläche von 2264 m². Jenseits des in der Regel für seine extreme Nüchternheit oder Schwere bekannten Bautyps, gelang Toyo Ito die von ihm angestrebte Leichtigkeit und ein vermutlich für Familie und Freunde der Verstorbenen trostreicher Raum.

La caractéristique la plus surprenante de ce crématorium, reconstruit dans un cimetière de la ville de Kakamigahara dans la préfecture de Gifu au centre du Japon, est certainement son « vaste toit flottant au-dessus du site comme des nuages s'étirant lentement en créant un paysage adouci ». L'architecte présente ainsi son projet : « Nous avons étudié une structure en coquille de béton armé à courbes libres pour constituer ce toit caractérisé par des concavités et des convexités. Cette forme a été déterminée par un algorithme qui doit générer une solution structurelle optimale. Comme ce type d'analyse structurelle fait penser au processus de croissance des plantes qui ne cessent de se transformer en fonction de règles naturelles simples, nous l'avons appelée « évolution ». Plusieurs centaines de cycles évolutifs ont abouti à la forme finale. La ligne incurvée est un paysage en harmonie avec la silhouette effilée des montagnes environnantes. » Le toit et ses courbes douces déterminent également la forme du plafond intérieur. L'ensemble du volume est éclairé le jour par une lumière naturelle indirecte. Implantée sur un terrain de 6 696 m², cette construction sur deux niveaux présente une hauteur maximum de 11,5 mètres et une surface au sol de 2 264 m². Intervenant sur un type de construction généralement caractérisé par son extrême austérité ou sa lourdeur, Toyo Ito a cherché et obtenu un vaste espace d'une grande légèreté, dont l'atmosphère est sans doute plus réconfortante pour les familles et les amis des disparus.

*The floating canopy that covers the complex appears clearly in the drawing above. This is the defining element of the design.*

*Auf der Zeichnung oben ist das »schwebende« Schutzdach über dem Komplex deutlich zu sehen. Es ist das bestimmende Element des Entwurfs.*

*Élément qui personnalise ce projet, une sorte de canopée recouvre le complexe. Elle apparaît clairement dans le dessin ci-dessus.*

The undulation of the roof assumes a natural configuration, with images such as those of clouds brought to mind.

Die eine natürliche Gestalt annehmende, gewellte Form des Dachs erinnert an Bilder von Wolken.

L'ondulation du toit emprunte une configuration naturelle qui évoque des nuages.

*Toyo Ito is known for the lightness of his architecture, but it appears that his mature work assumes an even more ethereal quality than some of his earlier attempts to achieve a kind of architectural "weightlessness."*

*Toyo Ito ist bekannt für die Leichtigkeit seiner Bauten, aber es scheint, als sei der Charakter seiner ausgereiften Bauten noch ätherischer als seine früheren Versuche mit einer »schwerelosen« Architektur.*

*Toyo Ito est connu pour la légèreté de son architecture, mais il semble que les réalisations de sa maturité tendent à développer un aspect encore plus éthéré que ses recherches antérieures avec une sorte « d'absence de poids » architecturale.*

Conforming to the natural topography of the site, as the site plan to the right shows, the building encloses a series of relatively traditional rectangular volumes.

Wie auf dem Lageplan rechts zu sehen, umfasst der sich den natürlichen Gegebenheiten des Geländes anpassende Komplex eine Reihe relativ traditioneller rechtwinkliger Baukörper.

Prenant en compte la configuration naturelle du site, comme le montre le plan de droite, le bâtiment réunit une série de volumes rectangulaires relativement traditionnels.

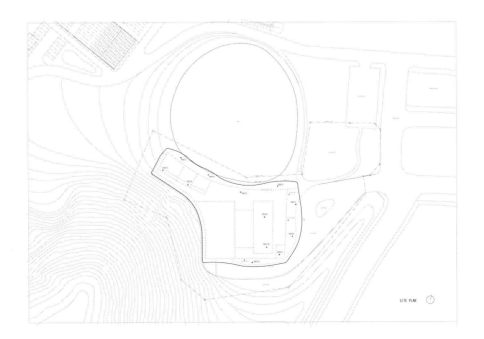

SITE PLAN

*Red House*

# JARMUND/VIGSNÆS

*Jarmund/Vigsnæs AS Architects MNAL*
*Hausmannsgate 6*
*0186 Oslo*
*Norway*

*Tel: +47 22 994 353*
*Fax: +47 22 994 353*
*E-mail: jva@jva.no*
*Web: www.jva.no*

**JARMUND/VIGSNÆS** often works on projects "related to nature and preferably in strong natural settings with a harsh climate." The principals of the office are Einar Jarmund, Håkon Vigsnæs and Alessandra Kosberg. Jarmund and Vigsnæs were born in 1962 in Oslo and graduated from the Oslo School of Architecture in 1987 and 1989. Vigsnæs spent one year at the Architectural Association (AA) in London, and Jarmund received a Master's degree from the University of Washington in Seattle. Håkon Vigsnæs worked with Sverre Fehn, while Einar Jarmund taught and worked in Seattle. Both were Visiting Professors at Washington University in St. Louis in 2004 and at University of Arizona, Tucson, in 2005. Jarmund / Vigsnæs Architects was established in 1995 after teaching and independent practice for both partners. The office today employs 15 architects. In 2004, they added a third partner, Alessandra Kosberg. She was born in 1967, graduated from the Oslo School of Architecture in 1995 and started working with JVA in 1997. Their work includes the Red House (Oslo, 2001–02, published here); Turtagrø Hotel (Jotunheimen, Norway, 2002); an apartment for the Crown Prince of Norway (2003); and Svalbard Science Center (Longyearbyen, Spitsbergen, 2005). Their current work includes the Norwegian Ministry of Defense (Akershus Fortress, Oslo, 2006); and a high-rise hotel (Fornebu, Norway, 2006). In addition, the firm has built 16 single-family houses and vacation homes and 10 more are in progress.

**JARMUND/VIGSNÆS** ist häufig mit Projekten »im Zusammenhang mit Natur und vorzugsweise in ausdrucksstarker Landschaft mit rauen klimatischen Bedingungen« befasst. Geleitet wird das Büro von Einar Jarmund, Håkon Vigsnæs und Alessandra Kosberg. Jarmund und Vigsnæs wurden 1962 in Oslo geboren und schlossen ihre Ausbildung 1987 bzw. 1989 an der Architekturschule in Oslo ab. Vigsnæs verbrachte ein Jahr an der Architectural Association in London und Jarmund erwarb einen Magisterabschluss an der University of Washington in Seattle. Håkon Vigsnæs arbeitete mit Sverre Fehn, während Einar Jarmund in Seattle lehrte und arbeitete. Beide hatten 2004 Gastprofessuren an der Washington University in St. Louis und 2005 an der University of Arizona in Tucson inne. Nach Lehraufträgen und freiberuflicher Tätigkeit wurde 1995 Jarmund/Vigsnæs eröffnet. Heute beschäftigt das Büro 15 Architekten. 2004 kam mit Alessandra Kosberg eine dritte Partnerin hinzu. Sie wurde 1967 geboren, schloss 1995 ihr Architekturstudium in Oslo ab und nahm 1997 ihre Tätigkeit bei Jarmund/Vigsnæs auf. Ihre Arbeiten umfassen das hier publizierte Rote Haus (Oslo, 2001–02), das Hotel Turtagrø (Jotunheimen, Norwegen, 2002), ein Apartment für den norwegischen Kronprinzen (2003) und das Svalbard Science Center (Longyearbyen, Spitzbergen, 2005). Neueste Projekte sind u. a. das norwegische Verteidigungsministerium (Festung Akershus, Oslo, 2006) und ein Hotelhochhaus (Fornebu, Norwegen, 2006). Darüber hinaus errichtete das Büro 16 Einfamilienhäuser und Ferienhäuser, zehn weitere sind im Bau.

**JARMUND/VIGSNÆS** travaillent souvent sur des projets « liés à la nature, de préférence dans un cadre naturel très présent et des conditions climatiques difficiles ». Les associés de l'agence sont Einar Jarmund, Håkon Vigsnæs et Alessandra Kosberg. Jarmund et Vigsnæ, nés en 1962 à Oslo, sont diplômés de l'École d'architecture de cette ville, respectivement en 1987 et 1989. Vigsnæs a étudié un an à l'Architectural Association de Londres et Jarmund a obtenu son Master d'architecture à l'Université de Washington, à Seattle. Håkon Vigsnæs a travaillé avec Sverre Fehn et Jarmund a enseigné et travaillé à Seattle. Tous deux ont été professeurs invités à Washington University, St. Louis, en 2004, et à l'Université de l'Arizona, Tucson, en 2005. L'agence Jarmund/Vigsnæs Architects, fondée en 1995, emploie quinze architectes. En 2004, Alessandra Kosberg les a rejoints en tant qu'associée. Née en 1967, diplômée de l'École d'architecture d'Oslo en 1995, elle a commencé à travailler pour JVA en 1997. Parmi leurs réalisations : Red House, Oslo (2001–02) publiée ici ; Turtagrø Hotel, Jotunheimen, Norvège (2002) ; un appartement pour le prince héritier de Norvège (2003) et le Centre scientifique Svalbard, Longyearbyen, Spitzberg (2005). Ils travaillent actuellement sur la forteresse d'Akershus, Oslo (2006) pour le ministère de la défense norvégien, et sur un projet d'une tour-hôtel à Fornebu, Norvège (2006). Ils ont également réalisé seize maisons familiales et de vacances et dix autres sont en construction.

# RED HOUSE

*Oslo, Norway, 2001–02*

*Floor area: 175 m². Client: not disclosed. Cost: not disclosed.*
*Assistant Architect: Roar Lund-Johnsen.*
*Interior: Jarmund / Vigsnæs AS Architects MNAL*

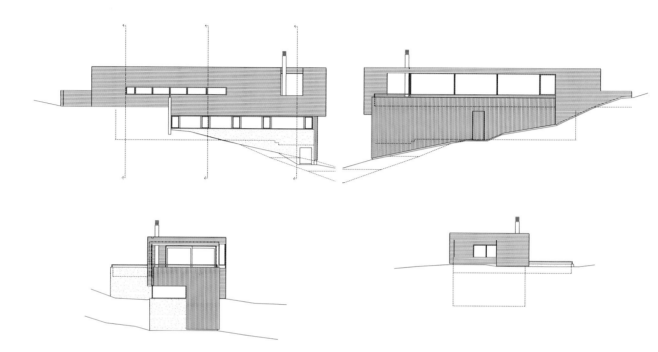

*Elevation drawings of the house show how it sits atop the slope of its site, with very straightforward lines, and two facades with large glazed openings.*

*Aufrisszeichnungen des Hauses zeigen, wie es am Hang des Grundstücks steht, mit sehr unkomplizierten Linien und zwei Fassaden mit großen Fensteröffnungen.*

*Les élévations de la maison aux lignes résolument droites montrent la façon dont elle s'appuie sur le sommet de la colline et ses deux façades aux larges ouvertures vitrées.*

Located in wooded valley to the west of Oslo, the Red House is set at right angles to a stream, in part to avoid obstructing neighbors' views. The two-story structure has living areas on the upper level oriented to the south, and a covered terrace to the west. The view toward the natural setting is assured by a 4-meter-long band window. Children's bedrooms facing the river valley to the north are on the lower floor. One aspect of the original brief is that the clients wished to have separate areas for themselves and the children. The architects explain that "the neighborhood is characterized by postwar wooden single-family houses, and this local character has inspired both the development of the spatial concept and the detailing." The color that gives its name to the house was the result of the client's request, although the area has many houses with colored wood façades. This did not keep certain neighbors from expressing surprise at the bright red tone.

Das in einem bewaldeten Tal westlich von Oslo erbaute Rote Haus wurde im rechten Winkel zu einem Fluss errichtet, u. a., um nicht die Aussicht der Nachbarn zu verstellen. In dem zweigeschossigen Bau befinden sich auf der oberen Ebene nach Süden ausgerichtete Wohnbereiche und nach Westen hin eine überdachte Terrasse. Ein 4 m langes Fensterband ermöglicht Ausblicke in die Umgebung. Auf der unteren Ebene sind Kinderzimmer mit Blick auf das im Norden liegende Flusstal untergebracht. Dem ursprünglichen Auftrag zufolge wünschten sich die Bauherren für sich und die Kinder jeweils separate Bereiche. Die Architekten führen aus, dass »die Gegend geprägt ist von nach dem Krieg erbauten Einfamilienhäusern aus Holz; dieses Lokalkolorit hat sowohl die Entwicklung des Raumkonzepts als auch die Gestaltung beeinflusst«. Die namengebende Farbe des Hauses war ein Wunsch der Bauherren, zumal es in der Gegend zahlreiche Häuser mit farbigen Holzfassaden gibt. Dies hinderte manche Nachbarn nicht daran, ihre Überraschung angesichts der leuchtend roten Farbe zu artikulieren.

Située dans une vallée boisée à l'ouest d'Oslo, cette « Maison rouge » est implantée perpendiculairement à une rivière, en partie pour éviter de gêner la vue des voisins. Le bâtiment sur deux niveaux dispose de pièces à vivre au niveau supérieur orientées au sud et d'une terrasse couverte à l'ouest. Une baie en bandeau de 4 mètres de long offre un panorama sur l'environnement naturel. Les chambres des enfants, au nord et face à la rivière, se trouvent au niveau inférieur. Un des aspects originaux du programme était le souhait exprimé par les clients d'une séparation parents / enfants. Les architectes précisent que : « Le voisinage se caractérise par des maisons individuelles en bois datant de l'après-guerre et ce caractère local a inspiré à la fois la mise au point de notre concept spatial et sa réalisation. » La couleur qui donne son nom à la maison résulte d'une demande du client, bien que de nombreuses maisons voisines soient dans des tons de bois. Certains voisins ont évidemment été surpris par ce rouge vif.

Contrary to what these images suggest, the house is not built at an angle, but sits flat on the slope. Its marking features are of course the red finish and its sculptural cut-outs.

Obgleich es auf den Abbildungen aussieht, als sei das Haus schrägstehend, steht es doch flach am Hang. Prägnante Merkmale sind der rote Anstrich und die plastischen Ausschnitte.

Contrairement à ce que ces images suggèrent, la maison est horizontale par rapport à la pente. Ses caractéristiques sont à l'évidence la couleur rouge et les découpes sculpturales.

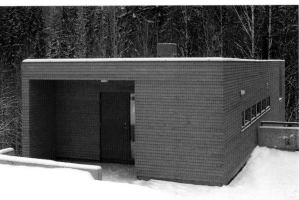

The large glazed openings of the house afford generous views to the surrounding countryside.

Die großen, verglasten Öffnungen des Hauses gestatten den Bewohnern weitreichende Ausblicke.

Les grandes ouvertures vitrées offrent à ses occupants des vues généreuses sur la campagne.

Seen from below, the wrapping red exterior of the house assumes a somewhat less traditional form, allowing for the openings that characterize the interior space.

Von unten gesehen erscheint die Form des rot gestrichenen Hauses, die die charakteristischen Öffnungen der Innenräume ermöglicht, weniger traditionell.

Vue en contre-plongée, l'enveloppe extérieure rouge prend une forme encore plus surprenante et détermine les ouvertures qui caractérisent le volume intérieur.

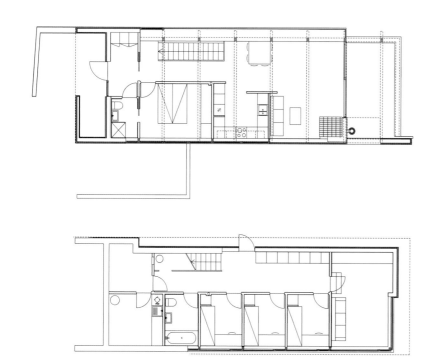

Interior design follows the geometric alignments of the overall plan, making for a variety of spaces and views beyond what the basic rectangular plan might suggest.

Die Gestaltung des Inneren folgt den geometrischen Fluchtlinien des Gesamtplans und ermöglicht so, angesichts des im Wesentlichen rechtwinkligen Grundrisses, überraschend vielfältige Räumlichkeiten und Aussichten.

L'aménagement intérieur reprend la géométrie des alignements du plan d'ensemble et détermine des espaces diversifiés et des perspectives qui vont au-delà de ce que l'on pouvait attendre de ce plan basiquement rectangulaire.

White walls and wooden floors impose a calmer color scheme inside than out, but the red of the exterior is occasionally visible, near the balconies, for example.

*Mit weißen Wänden und Holzböden ist die Farbigkeit im Inneren behutsamer als außen, aber das Rot des Außenbaus ist stellenweise – z. B. nahe den Balkonen – auch innen zu sehen.*

*Les murs blancs et les sols en bois génèrent à l'intérieur une ambiance chromatique plus calme que celle de l'extérieur, dont le rouge s'impose cependant parfois, près des balcons par exemple.*

# PATRICK JOUIN

*Agence Patrick Jouin*
*8, passage de la Bonne Graine*
*75011 Paris*
*France*

*Tel: +33 1 5528 8920*
*Fax: +33 1 5830 6070*
*E-mail: agence@patrickjouin.com*
*Web: www.patrickjouin.com*

Born in Nantes, France, in 1967, **PATRICK JOUIN** studied at the École Nationale Supérieure de Création Industrielle (ENSCI) in Paris and received his diploma in 1992. He worked in 1992 as a designer at the Compagnie des Wagons-Lits, and for the two following years at Tim Thom, Thomson Multimédia, under Philippe Starck who was then Artistic Director of the brand. From 1995 to 1999, Patrick Jouin was a designer in Philippe Starck's Paris studio. He created his own office in 1998. **SANJIT MANKU**, born in Nairobi, Kenya in 1971, and educated at Carlton University School of Architecture, became a partner in 2006, with the intention of working on architectural projects. Patrick Jouin has designed numerous objects and pieces of furniture, the firm's architectural work includes: Alain Ducasse au Plaza Athénée Restaurant (Paris, 2000); 59 Poincaré Restaurant (Paris, 2000); Plastic Products Factory (Nantes, 2001); Plaza Athénée Bar (Paris, 2001); Spoon Byblos Restaurant (Saint Tropez, 2002); Mix New York Restaurant for Alain Ducasse (2003); Chlösterli Restaurants and Club, Spoon des Neiges Restaurant (Gstaad, Switzerland, 2004); Mix Restaurant Las Vegas (2004); Terrasse Montaigne, Plaza Athénée (Paris, 2005); Gilt Restaurant and Bar (New York, 2005, published here); and house in Kuala Lumpur (Malaysia, 2004–07, published here). His Solid collection of furniture for the Belgian firm MGX uses the sophisticated technique of stereo-lithography to create remarkable, unique polymer objects.

Der 1967 in Nantes geborene **PATRICK JOUIN** studierte an der École Nationale Supérieure de Création Industrielle (ENSCI) in Paris, wo er 1992 sein Diplom erhielt. Im selben Jahr arbeitete er als Designer bei der Compagnie des Wagons-Lits und in den beiden folgenden Jahren bei Tim Thom, Thomsen Multimédia, für Philippe Starck, der damals Art Director für die Marke war. Von 1995 bis 1999 war Patrick Jouin Designer bei Philippe Starck in Paris. Er gründete 1998 sein eigenes Büro. **SANJIT MANKU**, geboren 1971 in Narobi, Kenia, studierte an der Carlton University School of Architecture. Er wurde 2006 Partner, um an Architekturprojekten zu arbeiten. Patrick Jouin entwarf zahlreiche Objekte und Möbelstücke, zu den Architekturprojekten der Agentur gehören u. a. folgende: das Restaurant Alain Ducasse im Plaza Athénée (Paris, 2000), das Restaurant 59 Poincaré (Paris, 2000), eine Fabrik für Kunststoffprodukte (Nantes, 2001), Plaza Athénée Bar (Paris, 2001), das Restaurant Spoon Byblos (Saint Tropez, 2002), das Mix Restaurant für Alain Ducasse (New York, 2003), das Chlösterli mit zwei Restaurants und Club, das Restaurant Spoon des Neiges (beide in Gstaad, Schweiz, 2004), das Mix Restaurant in Las Vegas (2004), die Terrasse Montaigne im Plaza Athénée (Paris, 2005), das hier vorgestellte Gilt Restaurant mit Bar (New York, 2005) sowie das ebenfalls vorgestellte Haus in Kuala Lumpur (Malaysia, 2004–07). Seine Möbelkollektion »Solid« für die belgische Firma MGX setzt die anspruchsvolle Technik der Stereo-Lithografie ein, um einzigartige Polymerobjekte herzustellen.

Né à Nantes en 1967, **PATRICK JOUIN** a étudié à l'École nationale supérieure de création industrielle (ENSCI) à Paris dont il est sorti diplômé en 1992. Il a ensuite travaillé pour la Compagnie des Wagons-Lits, puis les deux années suivantes pour Tim Thom, département de design de Thomson Multimédia animé par Philippe Starck, alors directeur artistique de la marque. De 1995 à 1999, il a été designer chez celui-ci. Il a crée son agence en 1998. **SANJIT MANKU**, né à Nairobi au Kenya en 1971, a fait ses études à l'École d'architecture de la Carlton University et a rejoint Patrick Jouin en 2006 pour travailler sur les projets architecturaux. Patrick Jouin a conçu de nombreux objets et meubles. Les interventions architecturales de l'agence comprennent : le restaurant Alain Ducasse du Plaza Athénée, Paris (2000) ; le restaurant 59 Poincaré, Paris (2000) ; une usine de produits en plastique, Nantes (2001) ; le bar du Plaza Athénée, Paris (2001) ; le restaurant Spoon Byblos, Saint-Tropez (2002) ; le restaurant Mix pour Alain Ducasse, New York (2003) ; les restaurants et club Chlösterli et le restaurant Spoon des Neiges à Gstaad, Suisse (2004) ; le restaurant Mix, Las Vegas (2004) ; la Terrasse Montaigne, Plaza Athénée, Paris (2005) ; le Gilt Restaurant and Bar, New York (2005) et une maison à Kuala Lumpur, Malaisie (2004–07), tous deux publiés ici. Sa collection de meubles Solid pour le fabricant belge MGX fait appel à des techniques sophistiquées de stéréolithographie pour créer de remarquables objets uniques en polymères.

# GILT RESTAURANT AND BAR

*New York, New York, USA, 2005*

*Floor area: 400 m². Client: New York Palace Hotel. Cost: not disclosed.*
*Project Manager: Marie Deroudilhe.*
*Architect of Record: Augustine Digneo*

*Patrick Jouin has transformed this restaurant and bar through the audacious addition of modern elements, such as the wood and fiberglass "Oyster," visible in the images below, near the bar.*

*Patrick Jouin verwandelte dieses Restaurant mit Bar durch die kühne Hinzufügung moderner Elemente wie die auf den Bildern unten nahe der Bar sichtbare »Auster« aus Holz und Glasfaserstoff.*

*Patrick Jouin a transformé ce bar et restaurant en insérant d'audacieux éléments contemporains, comme cette « huître » en bois et fibre de verre, visible dans les images ci-dessous, près du bar.*

Lighting effects, furniture and the unusual forms of the Oyster combine to
make an essentially "old-fashioned"
space into a dynamic new volume of
intriguing visual complexity.

Beleuchtungseffekte, Mobiliar und die
ungewöhnlichen Formen der »Auster«
verwandeln einen im Grunde traditionellen Raum in ein dynamisches
neues Ganzes von faszinierender,
visueller Komplexität.

Des effets lumineux, le mobilier et
la curieuse forme de l'huître se combinent pour faire d'un volume classiquement « démodé » un nouvel
espace d'une complexité visuelle
intrigante.

Located in the New York Palace Hotel at the corner of Madison Avenue and 50th Street, Gilt features an entrance hall in the form of a wine display. A gray-tinted glass box covers refrigerators for white wine and champagne at the top and red wines at room temperature below. Hand-veneered and sandblasted black walnut is used for the wine racks. The oval bar has a polished cameo white Corian top on a powder-coated fiberglass base. The most surprising feature of the bar is the "Oyster" shell, a faceted wood structure, fiberglass-coated, and finished with chrome paint on one side and upholstered with Kvadrat bronze sharkskin fabric on the bar side. The more formal dining room has a continuous perimeter leather banquette that rises up from the floor. The dining-room chairs were designed by Patrick Jouin specifically for Gilt (manufactured by Laval). As he has in other instances, Jouin succeeds here in creating an atmosphere that is at once luxurious and contemporary. The faceted oyster shell in the bar is very much in keeping with computer-designed forms often found in the most recent contemporary architecture.

Das im New York Palace Hotel an der Ecke von Madison Avenue und 50. Straße gelegene Gilt zeichnet sich durch eine Eingangshalle in Gestalt einer Weinaus-lage aus. Oben überdeckt ein Kasten aus grau getöntem Glas Kühlschränke für Weißwein und Champagner, während darunter Rotweine bei Raumtemperatur gelagert werden. Für die Weinregale wurde handfurniertes, sandgestrahltes Holz der schwarzen Walnuss verwendet. Die ovale Bar ist mit einer polierten Corian-Platte in »Cameo White« über einem pulverbeschichteten Fiberglassockel ausgestattet. Das überraschendste Merkmal der Bar ist die »Austernschale«, ein facettiertes Gebilde aus Holz, das mit Fiberglas beschichtet und auf einer Seite mit Chromfarbe behandelt, auf der Seite zur Bar hin mit bronzefarbenem Haifischhautgewebe von Kvadrat gepolstert ist. Entlang der Wände des konventionelleren Restaurantteils zieht sich eine aus dem Boden aufsteigende, umlaufende Polsterbank aus Leder. Die dazugehörigen Stühle wurden von Patrick Jouin eigens für Gilt entworfen und von Laval angefertigt. Wie schon bei anderen Projekten gelingt es Jouin auch hier, eine zugleich luxuriöse und zeitgemäße Atmosphäre zu schaffen. Die facettierte »Austernschale« in der Bar hat sehr viel mit den computergenerierten Formen gemein, die häufig Bestandteil von Architekturprojekten der jüngsten Zeit sind.

À l'angle de Madison Avenue et de la 50e rue, à l'intérieur du New York Palace Hotel, le restaurant Gilt est accessible par un hall d'entrée aménagé en lieu de présentation de grands crus. Une boîte en verre teinté en gris et réfrigérée contient des vins blancs et des champagnes en partie supérieure et des vins rouges à la température de la pièce en partie inférieure. Les casiers sont en noyer sablé et noirci verni au tampon. Le bar ovale est équipé d'un plan en Corian blanc laiteux poli sur socle en fibre de verre poudrée. L'élément le plus surprenant est une coque en « huître » réalisée en bois faceté, avec projection de fibre de verre et finition en pein-ture au chrome sur une partie, garni d'un tissu de chez Kvadrat « peau de requin » de couleur bronze du côté du bar. La salle à manger plus formelle est équipée d'une banquette de cuir périphérique intégrée au sol. Les sièges ont été spécialement dessinés pour ce restaurant par Jouin et fabriqués par Laval. Comme dans d'autres projets, Patrick Jouin a réussi à créer une atmosphère à la fois luxueuse et contemporaine. Sa coquille d'huître est dans l'esprit des formes conçues par ordinateur que l'on retrouve dans les réalisations architecturales les plus récentes.

From above, the bar's oval shape is seen to be placed in an asymmetrical way, adding to the visually dynamic aspect of the room.

Von oben gesehen erschließt sich die asymmetrische Platzierung der oval geformten Bar, die zur visuellen Dynamik des Raums beiträgt.

Vue de dessus, la forme ovale du bar, implanté de façon asymétrique, renforce l'aspect visuellement dynamique de la salle.

A plan shows the bar to the right of the series of rooms redesigned in their entirety by the Agence Patrick Jouin, who demonstrated a real talent for such work in Paris, at the Plaza Athénée Hotel and in other locations.

Im Grundriss sind links von der Bar mehrere Räume zu sehen, die zur Gänze von der Agence Patrick Jouin umgestaltet wurden, der beim Hotel Plaza Athénée in Paris und an anderen Orten sein Talent für dergleichen unter Beweis stellte.

Plan montrant le bar à droite d'une série de salons entièrement redessinés par l'Agence Patrick Jouin, qui avait déjà montré son talent pour ce type d'aménagements à l'hôtel Plaza Athénée à Paris, et dans d'autres lieux.

# HOUSE
*Kuala Lumpur, Malaysia, 2004–07*

*Floor area: 3000 m². Client: not disclosed. Cost: not disclosed.*
*Architect of Record: Sp. Ytl, Kuala Lumpur*

For his transition into a combination of architecture and interior design, Patrick Jouin has created this astonishing and very large residence in Malaysia with Sanjit Manku.

Dieses erstaunliche, sehr ausgedehnte Wohnhaus in Malaysia von Patrick Jouin und Sanjit Manku steht am Übergang einer Kombination von Architektur und Design.

Phase de transition personnelle entre architecture intérieure et architecture, Patrick Jouin et Sanjit Manku ont conçu cette très vaste et étonnante résidence en Malaisie.

As Sanjit Manku explains: "This private residence for a prominent family in Malaysia is one that explores complex relations between new and old cultures, sociological ideas of the image of wealth and power, the place of patron families in the development of new cities, and the redefinition of ancient building typologies, to name a few. The program given to us was one that could have been written centuries ago: to design a stately home for three current generations of an important family. The home is to be used as a residence but also as a symbol of the family's power in culture, politics, business, civil importance, and, perhaps most importantly, an icon to the family's legacy within a culture." Acting in this instance as an architect and designer, since he is also responsible for the house's interior Patrick Jouin explains that until a recent date, residences of this nature have assumed the form of "*faux* Palladian villas next to French chateaux and Spanish villas." This radically modern design thus breaks the mold and marks the emergence of the Agence Patrick Jouin as an architectural firm. The house includes nine bedrooms, two suites, two family rooms, a family kitchen and dining room, library, game room, formal dining room, reception room, ball room, and chapel, as well as two guest suites. The structure is only 5% smaller in surface area than the site, which required the architect to engage in very careful planning, dividing the house into three zones—the family house, public space in the base, and guest area in a sculptural ring-shaped form at ground level. Sanjit Manku concludes, "For this project we were searching for a spatial and formal language as dramatic as the landscape itself—to create a home that is not village house, nor a 'traditional tropical house,' yet at the same time was truly based on and almost at times mimicked the particular spatial character of the natural environment. We wished to create a project that rests with ease among the dense tropical flora."

Sanjit Manku führt aus: »Dieses Privathaus für eine prominente Familie in Malaysia ist eines, dass komplexe Beziehungen zwischen alten und neuen Kulturen, soziologische Überlegungen zum Leitbild von Wohlstand und Macht, die Bedeutung von Stifterfamilien bei der Entwicklung neuer Städte sowie die Neubestimmung uralter Bautypologien auslotet, um nur einige zu nennen. Das Bauprogramm, das man uns gab, hätte vor Jahrhunderten geschrieben sein können: ein imposantes Haus für die drei Generationen einer bedeutenden Familie zu entwerfen. Das Gebäude soll als Wohnhaus dienen, aber auch als Symbol der Macht der Familie in Kultur, Politik, Handel, bürgerschaftlichem Engagement und, vielleicht am wichtigsten, als Ikone des Vermächtnisses der Familie innerhalb einer Kultur.« Jouin, in diesem Fall Architekt und Designer, da er auch für die Innenräume verantwortlich zeichnet, erklärt, dass man bis vor Kurzem Wohnsitze dieser Art eher im Stil »palladianischer Villen, französischer Chateaux oder spanischer Villen« erbaut hätte. Der von Grund auf moderne Entwurf sprengt somit den üblichen Rahmen und markiert den Auftritt der Agence Patrick Jouin als Architekturbüro. Zum Haus gehören neun Schlafräume, zwei Suiten, zwei Mehrzweckräume, die Familienküche mit Esszimmer, Bibliothek, Freizeitraum, offizielles Speisezimmer, Empfangsraum, Ballsaal und Kapelle sowie zwei Gästesuiten. Die Gebäudefläche ist nur 5 % kleiner als das Baugrundstück, was eine sorgfältige Planung erforderte, die das Haus in drei Zonen unterteilte – Haus der Familie, öffentlicher Raum im Sockel und Gästebereich in einem skulpturalen, ringförmigen Bereich im Erdgeschoss. Abschließend äußert Sanjit Manku: »Für dieses Projekt suchten wir nach einer räumlichen und formalen Sprache, die ebenso dramatisch war wie die Landschaft selbst – um ein Heim zu gestalten, das weder ein Landhaus, noch ein ›traditionelles Tropenhaus‹ ist und sich dabei auf den besonderen räumlichen Charakter der natürlichen Umgebung bezieht und ihn manchmal fast nachahmt. Wir wollten ein Gebäude schaffen, das mühelos inmitten der dichten tropischen Flora ruht.«

Comme l'explique Sanjit Manku : « Cette résidence privée construite pour une riche famille malaise explore, entre autres, les relations complexes entre des cultures anciennes et nouvelles, à partir d'une réflexion d'ordre sociologique sur l'image de la richesse et du pouvoir, la place du mécénat familial dans le développement de villes nouvelles et la redéfinition d'une ancienne typologie de bâtiment. Le programme qui nous a été confié aurait pu être rédigé il y a des siècles : concevoir une demeure de prestige pour les trois générations d'une importante famille. La maison est une résidence, mais aussi un symbole de la puissance du rôle de cette famille dans la vie culturelle, politique et économique et peut-être, plus important encore, son rôle d'icône du patrimoine au sein de cette culture. » Intervenant ici comme architecte et designer, puisqu'il est également responsable des aménagements intérieurs, Patrick Jouin précise que, jusqu'à une certaine date, « une résidence de cette nature aurait probablement pris la forme d'une fausse villa palladienne, d'un château français ou d'une villa espagnole… » Cette conception radicalement moderne a ainsi rompu un moule et marque l'apparition de l'Agence Patrick Jouin sur la scène de l'architecture. La maison comprend neuf chambres, deux suites, deux séjours, une cuisine et salle à manger, une bibliothèque, une salle de jeux, une salle à manger de réception, un salon de réception, une salle de bal et une chapelle ainsi que deux suites pour invités. La construction occupe 95 % de la surface du terrain et l'architecte a dû se livrer à un délicat exercice de programmation pour diviser la maison en trois zones – famille, réception, invités – à l'intérieur de l'élément en forme d'anneau sculptural qui couvre le rez-de-chaussée. « Pour ce projet, nous avons recherché un langage spatial et formel aussi spectaculaire que le paysage environnant, afin de créer une demeure qui ne soit pas une maison de village ni une « maison tropicale traditionnelle » mais qui, en même temps, repose sur des données authentiques et va parfois jusqu'à imiter même le caractère particulier de cet environnement naturel. Nous avons souhaité créer un projet en harmonie avec la dense flore tropicale. »

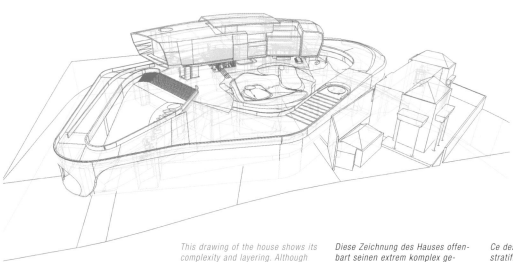

*This drawing of the house shows its complexity and layering. Although straight lines do occur in the design, they are certainly not the rule.*

*Diese Zeichnung des Hauses offenbart seinen extrem komplex geschichteten Aufbau. Die geraden Linien wirken fast wie Ausnahmen.*

*Ce dessin montre la complexité et la stratification extrêmes de la maison. Les lignes droites font presque exception.*

The house is intended for large receptions and the generous interior volumes allow for this kind of use.

Das Haus ist für große Empfänge gedacht und die großzügigen Innenräume gestatten diese Art der Nutzung.

La maison est conçue pour pouvoir donner de grandes réceptions, ce que permettent les généreux volumes intérieurs.

Jouin's drawings for the interior of the house show that its external architectural complexity is indeed reflected inside. Large openings and dramatic lighting effects reveal his intention to sculpt the space, much as he has created an unusual shell for the house.

Jouins Zeichnungen vom Inneren des Hauses zeigen, dass sich die komplexe Architektur des Äußeren tatsächlich auch im Inneren widerspiegelt. Große Öffnungen und dramatische Beleuchtungseffekte deuten an, dass er plant, den Innenraum plastisch zu gestalten ebenso wie er eine ungewöhnliche Hülle für das Haus schuf.

Les dessins de Jouin concernant l'intérieur de la maison montrent que sa complexité architecturale externe se retrouve à l'intérieur. De grandes ouvertures et de spectaculaires effets d'éclairage montrent qu'il a sculpté l'espace intérieur après avoir créé cette surprenante coquille.

# JUDD LYSENKO MARSHALL

*Judd Lysenko Marshall Architects*
*21 Gardiner Street*
*North Melbourne, Victoria 3051*
*Australia*

*Tel: +61 411 214 832*
*Fax: +61 3 9348 9923*
*E-mail: info@jlma.com.au*
*Web: www.jlma.com.au*

*Wheatsheaf Residence*

**JESSE JUDD** was born in 1975 in Melbourne. In 1995, he received a Bachelor of Planning and Design degree from the University of Melbourne, and a B.Arch in 1999 from the same institution. He became a registered architect in 2001. He worked with Edmond & Corrigan, Ivan Rijavec, Kovac Malone and Ashton Raggatt McDougall, before creating his own firm. His projects, in Australia, include M2 Fitout (Prahran, Victoria, 2000); Melbourne Docklands Masterplanning & Concept Design (2000); Trackside Apartment (Brunswick, Victoria, 2000); Marion Cultural Centre (Marion, 2001); Harbour Esplanade (Melbourne Docklands, 2001); Melbourne Zoo Masterplanning (Melbourne, 2001); Shrine of Remembrance (Melbourne, 2003); Somers House (Flinders, Victoria, 2004); and the Wheatsheaf Residence (Daylesford, Victoria, 2005, published here). Current work includes Digital Harbour (Docklands, Melbourne) and various residential projects in Melbourne and rural Victoria.

**JESSE JUDD** wurde 1975 in Melbourne geboren. An der dortigen Universität erwarb er 1995 einen Bachelor of Planning and Design und 1999 einen Bachelor of Architecture. 2001 wurde er als Architekt zugelassen. Ehe er sein eigenes Büro eröffnete, war er bei Edmond & Corrigan, Ivan Rijavec, Kovac Malone und Ashton Raggatt McDougall tätig. Zu seinen Projekten in Australien gehören: M2 Fitout (Prahran, Victoria, 2000), Melbourne Docklands, Masterplan und Entwurfskonzept (2000), Trackside Apartment (Brunswick, Victoria, 2000), Marion Kulturzentrum (Marion, 2001), Harbour Esplanade (Melbourne Docklands, 2001), Bebauungsplan für den Zoo in Melbourne (2001), Shrine of Remembrance (Melbourne, 2003), Somers House (Flinders, Victoria, 2004) und die Wheatsheaf Residence (Daylesford, Victoria, 2005, hier vorgestellt). Neuere Bauten sind Digital Harbour (Docklands, Melbourne) und verschiedene Wohnhäuser in Melbourne und dem ländlichen Victoria.

**JESSE JUDD**, né en 1975 à Melbourne, a reçu un diplôme d'urbanisme et de conception (1995) et d'architecture (1999) de l'université de cette ville. Architecte licencié en 2001, il a travaillé chez Edmond & Corrigan, Ivan Rijavec, Kovac Malone et Ashton Raggatt McDougall avant de créer sa propre agence. Ses projets en Australie comprennent : M2 Fitout, Prahran, Victoria (2000) ; Melbourne Docklands, plan directeur et concept (2000) ; Trackside Apartment, Brunswick, Victoria (2000) ; Marion Cultural Centre, Marion (2001) ; Esplanade du port, Melbourne Docklands (2001) ; plan directeur du zoo de Melbourne (2001) ; Mausolée du souvenir, Melbourne (2003) ; Somers House, Flinders, Victoria (2004), et la résidence Wheatsheaf, Daylesford, Victoria (2005), publiée ici. Parmi ses réalisations les plus récentes : Digital Harbour, Docklands, Melbourne, ainsi que de divers projets résidentiels à Melbourne et dans la campagne de l'État de Victoria.

# WHEATSHEAF RESIDENCE

*Daylesford, Victoria, Australia, 2005*

*Floor area: 170 m² interior; 135 m² deck. Client: not disclosed.
Cost: not disclosed*

As Jesse Judd explains, "The Wheatsheaf Residence investigates nomadic nature inherent in the holiday unit. Nestled in four hectares of abandoned messmate (*Eucalyptus obliqua*) forest, the extruded form sits at once comfortably within, and distinct from, its monoculture environment. The house examines the typology of the ephemeral, a stressed skin structure that seems to be spontaneously relocatable, perhaps informed by the Airstream trailer, an aircraft hull, or the folded steel bus stops inherent in Melbourne's baby-boom south-eastern suburbs." Made up of two folded planes that create a "womblike interior," the house sits above the land, allowing "native wildlife to run freely under foot." The architect compares his work to that accomplished in the California Case Study Houses in the 1950s. He maintains that the Wheatsheaf Residence reveals "an intriguing geometry, generated through a dumb plan and simple construction technologies." The corrugated steel used in the house transforms itself from wall to roof. "The result," says Judd, "is architecture as surface—three dimensionally smooth yet sufficiently complex to be legible through our increasingly logoized world of visual codes and conventional signs."

Jesse Judd bemerkt zu diesem Projekt: »Das Haus Wheatsheaf thematisiert den einem Ferienhaus inhärenten nomadischen Charakter. Eingebettet in 4 ha eines verlassenen Eukalyptusbestands liegt die extrudierte Form angenehm inmitten ihres Umfelds und zugleich davon abgetrennt. Das Haus untersucht die Typologie des Flüchtigen, eine Schalenkonstruktion, die man scheinbar spontan verlagern kann, vielleicht inspiriert vom Airstream-Wohnanhänger, von einem Flugzeugkörper oder den Bushaltestellen aus geformtem Stahl, die zu den kinderreichen Vororten im Südosten von Melbourne gehören.« Das aus zwei gefalteten Flächen bestehende Haus mit seinem »höhlenartigen Interieur« ist vom Erdboden abgehoben, sodass »die heimische Tierwelt darunter frei umherlaufen kann«. Der Architekt vergleicht seine Arbeit mit dem, was in den 1950er-Jahren mit den kalifornischen Case Study Houses erreicht wurde. Ihm zufolge offenbart die Wheatsheaf Residence »eine faszinierende Geometrie, hervorgerufen durch einen einfachen Grundriss und simple Bauverfahren«. Der für den Hausbau verwendete gewölbte Stahl verändert sich von der Wand zum Dach. »Die Folge«, sagt Jesse Judd, »ist Architektur als Fläche – dreidimensional geschmeidig und doch hinreichend komplex, um durch unsere zunehmend mit Logos versehene Welt visueller Codes und konventioneller Zeichen verständlich zu sein«.

Selon Jesse Judd : « La résidence Wheatsheaf est une recherche sur la nature nomade de la maison de vacances. Nichée au sein d'une forêt négligée de quatre hectares (Eucalyptus obliqua), sa forme extrudée s'y est confortablement intégrée tout en restant distincte de son environnement monoculturel. La maison part d'une analyse de la typologie de l'éphémère, qui est exprimée dans sa structure à peau tendue qui semble pouvoir s'installer spontanément ailleurs. Elle pourrait être inspirée de la caravane Airstream, d'un nez d'avion ou des abris de bus en tôle d'acier pliée, si fréquents dans les banlieues sud-est de Melbourne datant du baby-boom. » Composée de deux plans repliés qui génèrent un « intérieur matriciel », elle est posée au-dessus du sol, permettant « à la vie sauvage de se poursuivre librement sous ses pieds ». L'architecte compare ce travail à celui accompli dans le cadre des Case Study Houses californiennes des années 1950. Pour lui, il exprime « une géométrie intrigante, issue d'un plan banal et de technologies constructives simples ». La tôle d'acier ondulée passe du mur à la toiture. « Le résultat est une architecture qui constitue une surface tridimensionnelle lisse mais néanmoins suffisamment complexe pour être appréhendée par le prisme de notre monde de plus en plus soumis aux marques, aux codes visuels et aux signes conventionnels. »

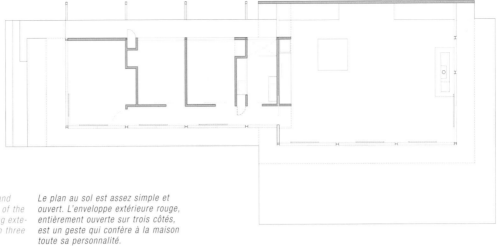

The floor plan is quite simple and open, and the defining gesture of the architecture is the red, wrapping exterior shell that opens entirely on three sides.

Le plan au sol est assez simple et ouvert. L'enveloppe extérieure rouge, entièrement ouverte sur trois côtés, est un geste qui confère à la maison toute sa personnalité.

Der Grundriss ist recht einfach und offen. Das prägende Merkmal der Architektur ist die auf drei Seiten gänzlich offene, rote äußere Umhüllung.

The red shell also defines the interior of the house, and gives it an unexpected warmth, while the glass walls allow the residents to commune with the natural setting.

Die rote Außenhaut bestimmt auch das Interieur des Hauses und verleiht ihm eine überraschende Wärme, während es den Bewohnern dank der Glaswände möglich ist, in Gemeinschaft mit der Natur zu leben.

La coque rouge définit également l'intérieur de la maison et lui apporte une chaleur inattendue, tandis que les murs de verre permettent à ses occupants de vivre pratiquement en communion avec la nature.

# ANISH KAPOOR

*Anish Kapoor Studio*
*230 Farmer's Road*
*London SE5 0TW*
*UK*

*Tel: +44 20 7735 5485*
*Fax: +44 20 7793 9234*
*E-mail: anish@kapoorstudio.f9.co.uk*

*Sky Mirror*

**ANISH KAPOOR** was born in Mumbai, India, in 1954 and has lived and worked in London since the early 1970s. Not an architect, but a sculptor, he studied at the Hornsey College of Art (1973–77) and the Chelsea School of Art (1977–78), and had his first solo exhibition in 1980. His early work centered on lightweight materials and bright colors. Subsequent to moving into a ground-floor studio space in the late 1980s, he began to experiment with stone sculpture, but in almost all cases he deals with the ambiguities of perception. As he says, "I don't want to make sculpture about form […]. I wish to make sculpture about belief, or about passion, about experience that is outside of material concern." His work has been exhibited all over the world and is held in many major international collections. He represented Britain at the 44th Biennale in Venice in 1990 and won the Turner Prize in 1991. His work *Marsyas*, exhibited in the Turbine Hall of the Tate Modern in London in 2002, was designed in collaboration with Cecil Balmond. He completed *Cloud Gate*, a large-scale stainless-steel work for Chicago's Millennium Park, in 2004, and *Sky Mirror* in New York in 2006 (published here).

**ANISH KAPOOR** kam 1954 in Mumbai zur Welt und lebt und arbeitet seit Anfang der 1970er-Jahre in London. Der nicht als Architekt, sondern als Bildhauer am Hornsey College of Art (1973–77) und der Chelsea School of Art (1977–78) ausgebildete Kapoor hatte 1980 seine erste Einzelausstellung. Seine frühen Werke beschäftigten sich mit leichten Materialien und leuchtenden Farben. Nachdem er Ende der 1980er-Jahre sein Studio in eine Erdgeschosswohnung verlegt hatte, begann er mit Steinskulpturen zu experimentieren. In fast allen Fällen beschäftigt er sich dabei mit den Mehrdeutigkeiten der Wahrnehmung. Er sagt: »Meine Skulpturen sollen sich nicht mit Form auseinandersetzen […] Ich möchte Skulpturen über Glauben machen oder über Leidenschaft, über Erfahrung, die über materielle Dinge hinausgeht.« Seine Arbeiten wurden in der ganzen Welt ausgestellt und sind Bestandteil zahlreicher bedeutender, internationaler Sammlungen. Er vertrat 1990 Großbritannien auf der 44. Biennale in Venedig und gewann 1991 den Turner-Preis. Seine 2002 in der Turbinenhalle der Tate Modern in London ausgestellte Großskulptur »Marsyas« entstand in Zusammenarbeit mit Cecil Balmond. 2002 schuf er für den Millennium Park in Chicago »Cloud Gate«, eine großformatige Skulptur aus rostfreiem Stahl, und 2006 für New York den hier vorgestellten »Sky Mirror«.

**ANISH KAPOOR**, né à Mumbai en Inde, en 1954, vit et travaille à Londres depuis le début des années 1970. Sculpteur et non pas architecte, il a étudié au Hornsey College of Art & Design (1973–77), à l'École d'art de Chelsea (1977–78), et a tenu sa première exposition personnelle en 1980. Ses premières œuvres étaient centrées sur les matériaux légers et les couleurs vives. Après s'être installé dans un vaste atelier à la fin des années 1980, il commence à s'intéresser à la sculpture sur pierre tout en poursuivant ses recherches sur les ambiguïtés de la perception : « Je ne veux pas faire de sculptures sur la forme… je souhaite faire des sculptures sur la foi, la passion, l'expérience hors de nos préoccupations matérielles. » Son œuvre a été exposée dans le monde entier et figure dans de nombreuses grandes collections internationales. Il a représenté la Grande-Bretagne à la 44e Biennale de Venise en 1990 et remporté le Turner Prize en 1991. Son œuvre, *Marsyas*, présentée au Turbine Hall de la Tate Modern à Londres en 2002, a été conçue en collaboration avec Cecil Balmond. Il a récemment réalisé *Cloud Gate*, œuvre en acier inoxydable de grandes dimensions pour le Millennium Park de Chicago en 2004, et *Sky Mirror* à New York en 2006, publié ici.

# SKY MIRROR

*New York, New York, USA, 2006*

*Diameter: 10.7-m polished stainless-steel mirror.*
*Clients: Tishman Speyer and the Public Art Fund. Cost: not disclosed*

*Sky Mirror* was a 10.7-meter-diameter polished stainless-steel mirror installed on the axis of the Rockefeller Center near Fifth Avenue in Manhattan from September 19 to October 27, 2006. The 23-ton sculpture was installed on a slightly elevated platform in full view of passersby. Its convex side faced Fifth Avenue and was angled down, while the concave side faced the tower at 30 Rockefeller Plaza. Kapoor is known for public sculptures, such as *Cloud Gate* (2004) installed in Chicago's Millennium Park. In both instances, the object of his attention is the transformative power of the mirrored surface in an architectural context. Simply put, the mirror effect of these sculptures allows passersby to view and to appreciate the neighboring architectural monuments in a different way—indeed, a way that changes substantially according to the angle at which they are approached. This particular installation was a collaboration between the artist and Tishman Speyer, the co-owner and manager of the Rockefeller Center and the Public Art Fund, New York's leading presenter of artists' projects and installations in public spaces. The Public Art Fund has previously presented works by Jonathan Borofsky, Takashi Murakami, Nam June Paik, and Jeff Koons at the Rockefeller Center. This exhibition was presented by Tumi, a luggage manufacturer.

»Sky Mirror« ist ein Spiegel aus poliertem Edelstahl mit einem Durchmesser von 10,7 m, der vom 19. September bis 27. Oktober 2006 auf der Achse des Rockefeller Center unweit der Fifth Avenue in Manhattan installiert war. Die 23 t schwere Skulptur stand auf einem leicht erhöhten Sockel direkt vor den Augen der Passanten. Die konvexe, nach unten geneigte Seite, war der Fifth Avenue zugewandt, die konkave Seite zeigte zu dem Hochhaus an der Rockefeller Plaza 30. Kapoor ist bekannt für Skulpturen im öffentlichen Raum, wie »Cloud Gate« (2004), das im Millennium Park von Chicago steht. In beiden Fällen gilt seine Aufmerksamkeit dem umgestaltenden Potenzial verspiegelter Oberflächen im Zusammenhang mit Architektur. Kurz gesagt ermöglicht die Spiegelwirkung dieser Skulpturen den Passanten, die umstehende Architektur auf andere Weise zu betrachten und zu würdigen, obendrein in einer Weise, die sich mit dem Winkel, in dem man sich den Skulpturen nähert, beträchtlich verändert. Diese Installation war das Ergebnis der Zusammenarbeit des Künstlers mit Tishman Speyer, dem Mitbesitzer und Manager des Rockefeller Center und des Public Art Fund, New Yorks führendem Veranstalter von Projekten und Installationen von Künstlern auf öffentlichen Plätzen. Zuvor wurden vom Public Art Fund Werke von Jonathan Borofsky, Takashi Murakami, Nam June Paik und Jeff Koons am Rockefeller Center präsentiert. In diesem Fall hat die Firma Tumi, Hersteller von Reisegepäck, die Ausstellung finanziert.

*Sky Mirror* est un miroir en acier poli de 10,7 mètres de diamètre, qui a été installé dans l'axe du Rockefeller Center près de la Cinquième Avenue à Manhattan, du 19 septembre au 27 octobre 2006. Cette sculpture d'un poids de 23 tonnes a été posée sur une plate-forme légèrement surélevée au milieu des passants. Sa face convexe, sur l'avenue, était légèrement inclinée, et sa face concave donnait sur la tour du 30 Rockefeller Plaza. Kapoor était déjà célèbre pour ses sculptures installées dans des espaces publics comme son *Cloud Gate* (2004) dans le Millennium Park de Chicago. Dans les deux cas, l'objet de son travail est le pouvoir de transformation d'une surface en miroir dans un contexte architectural. Plus simplement, l'effet de miroir de ces sculptures permet aux passants de voir et d'apprécier les monuments architecturaux avoisinants d'une façon différente, qui se modifie substantiellement en fonction de l'angle d'approche. Cette installation new-yorkaise est le fruit d'une collaboration entre l'artiste et Tishman Speyer, copropriétaire et directeur du Rockefeller Center et du Public Art Fund, un des principaux mécènes new-yorkais pour l'exposition de projets d'artistes et d'installations dans des lieux publics. Ce fonds avait auparavant présenté des œuvres de Jonathan Borofsky, Takashi Murakami, Nam June Paik et Jeff Koons au Rockefeller Center. Cette exposition a été financée par Tumi, un fabricant de bagages.

A temporary installation, the Sky Mirror invited thousands of New Yorkers and the numerous tourists who come to visit the Rockefeller Center to look at the architectural environment around them in a new way.

Der nur für begrenzte Zeit errichtete »Sky Mirror« lud Tausende von New Yorkern sowie die zahlreichen Touristen im Rockefeller Center dazu ein, die umgebende Architektur auf neue Weise zu sehen.

Installation temporaire, le Sky Mirror a invité des milliers de New-Yorkais et de touristes à venir au Rockefeller Center pour contempler leur environnement urbain d'un œil différent.

# BERNARD KHOURY

*DW5 / Bernard Khoury*
*3rd Floor – Street 56 – Jisr Sector 77 / PO Box 175–280*
*Beirut 20777209 / Lebanon*

*Tel: +961 1 570 670 / Fax: +961 1 570 770*
*E-mail: mailbox@bernardkhoury.com / Web: www.bernardkhoury.com*

**BERNARD KHOURY** was born in Beirut, Lebanon, in 1968. He studied architecture at the Rhode Island School of Design (B. F .A. 1990; B.Arch 1991) and received an M.Arch from Harvard University in 1993. In 2001, he received an honorable mention in the Borromini Prize, awarded by the municipality of Rome to architects under 40 years of age. He has lectured and exhibited his work in prestigious academic institutions in Europe and the United States, including a solo show of his work held by the International Forum for Contemporary Architecture at the Aedes Gallery in Berlin (2003). Khoury started an independent practice in 1993. Over the past 10 years, his office has developed an international reputation and a significant diverse portfolio of projects, both locally and abroad. He was a co-founder of Beirut Flight Architects, concerned with architecture and design and behind numerous experimental projects, including "Evolving Scars," implemented in 1993 to rebuild and progressively modify war-damaged buildings in Beirut. His best-known public commissions in Beirut include the BO18 Nightclub (1998), built on the site of the former quarantine area of the port, and the restaurant La Centrale (2001). Khoury suggests ways of implementing and developing his theoretical projects in practical projects and proposals for construction. He is in charge of the conversion of Berlin's Pfefferberg complex and the construction of various additions. He has taught architecture at Beirut's American University and lectured in various universities and prestigious academic institutions in Europe and the United States. One of his recent projects is the BlackBox Aïzone (Beirut, 2005) published here.

**BERNARD KHOURY** wurde 1968 in Beirut im Libanon geboren. Er studierte an der Rhode Island School of Design Architektur (B. F. A. 1990, B.Arch. 1991) und legte 1993 in Harvard die Prüfung zum M.Arch. ab. Beim Premio Borromini, der von der Stadt Rom an Architekten unter 40 Jahren vergeben wird, erhielt er eine lobende Erwähnung. Er machte seine Arbeit durch Vorträge und Ausstellungen in akademischen Einrichtungen in Europa und den Vereinigten Staaten bekannt, darunter eine Einzelausstellung seiner Werke, die vom International Forum for Contemporary Architecture 2003 in der Galerie aedes in Berlin veranstaltet wurde. 1993 machte er sich selbstständig. Im Lauf der letzten zehn Jahre erwarb sich sein Büro internationale Reputation und beschäftigte sich mit vielgestaltigen lokalen und internationalen Projekten. Er gehört zu den Begründern der mit Architektur und Design befassten Beirut Flight Architects, die zahlreiche experimentelle Projekte verantworten, darunter das 1993 eingerichtete »Evolving-Scars«-Programm, bei dem es um die Wiederherstellung und fortlaufende Modifikation kriegsbeschädigter Bauten in Beirut geht. Zu seinen bekanntesten öffentlichen Aufträgen in Beirut gehören der Nachtclub BO18 (1998), der auf dem Gelände der ehemaligen Quarantäne-Station des Hafens entstand, und das Restaurant La Centrale von 2001. Khoury plant Methoden, seine theoretischen Vorhaben in Form praktischer Projekte und Bauvorhaben umzusetzen und weiterzuentwickeln. Er zeichnet verantwortlich für die bauliche Veränderung des Pfefferberg-Komplexes in Berlin durch verschiedene Anbauten. Er lehrte Architektur an der American University in Beirut und hielt Vorträge in verschiedenen Universitäten und renommierten akademischen Einrichtungen in Europa und den Vereinigten Staaten. Zu seinen jüngsten Projekten zählt das hier vorgestellte Gebäude BlackBox Aïzone (Beirut, 2005).

**BERNARD KHOURY**, né à Beyrouth au Liban en 1968, a étudié l'architecture à la Rhode Island School of Design (B. F. A. 1990 ; B. Arch. 1991) et est M. Arch. d'Harvard University (1993). En 2001, il reçoit une mention honorable au Prix Borromini attribué par la Ville de Rome aux architectes de moins de 40 ans. Il a donné des conférences et présenté son travail dans de prestigieuses institutions académiques en Europe et aux États-Unis, dont une exposition personnelle lors de l'International Forum for Contemporary Architecture à la Galerie Aedes à Berlin (2003). Il travaille à son compte depuis 1993. Au cours des dix dernières années, son agence s'est fait connaître internationalement par un ensemble de projets très divers réalisés aussi bien au Liban qu'à l'étranger. Il a été co-fondateur des Beirut Flight Architects et a participé à de nombreux projets expérimentaux dont « Evolving Scars » (1993) sous forme de récupération et de modification progressive d'immeubles endommagés par la guerre à Beyrouth. Ses commandes les plus connues sont la boîte de nuit BO18 (1998) construit sur le site de l'ancienne zone de quarantaine du port de Beyrouth, et le restaurant La Centrale, dans la même ville, en 2001. Il propose des voies et des modes de mise en œuvre concrète de ses projets théoriques. Khoury est chargé de la conversion du complexe du Pfefferberg à Berlin et de la construction de diverses extensions. Il a enseigné l'architecture à l'American Academy de Beyrouth. L'un de ses plus récents projets est le BlackBox Aïzone (Beyrouth, 2005), publié ici.

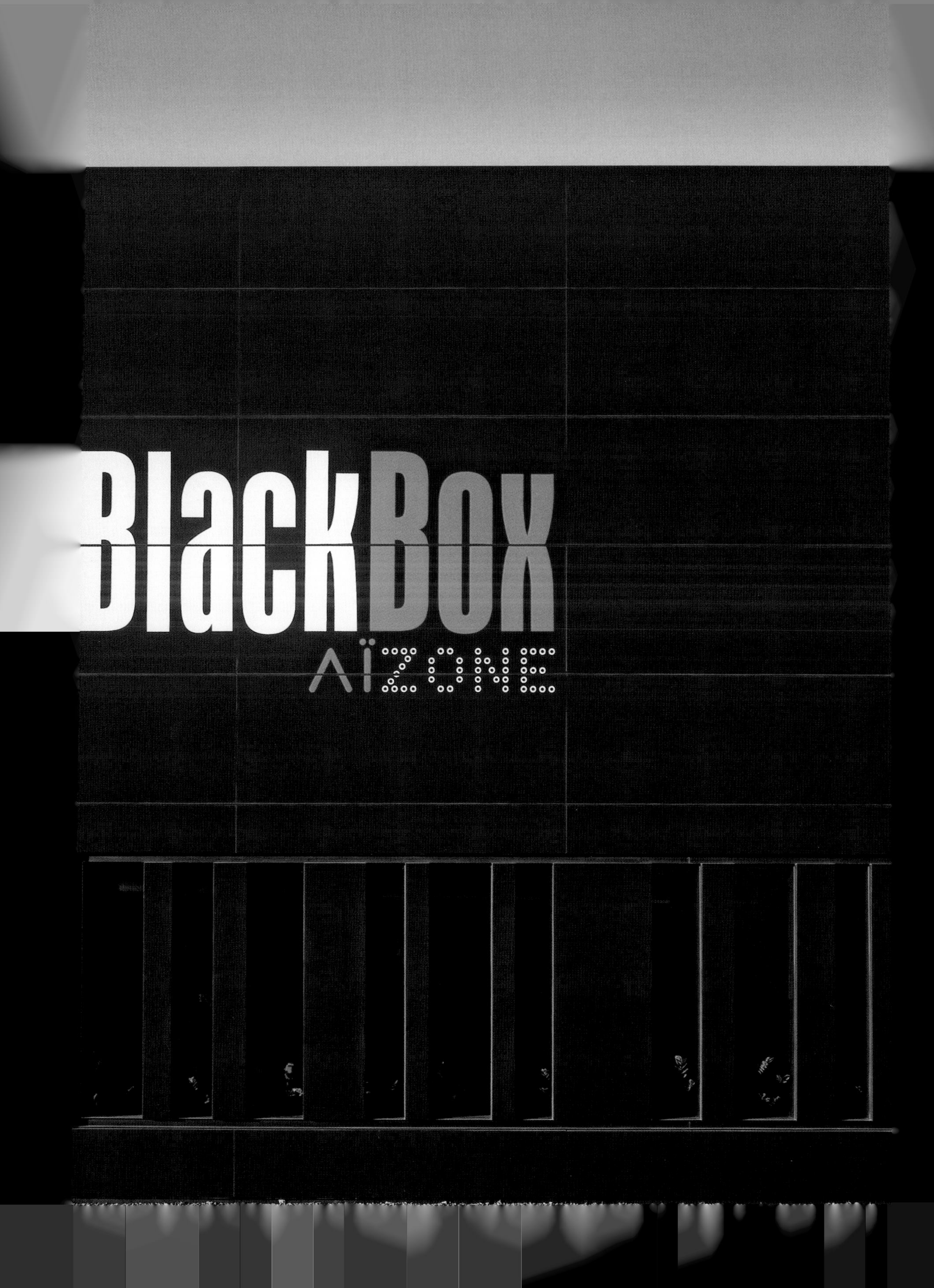
BlackBox
AÏZONE

# BLACKBOX AÏZONE

*Beirut, Lebanon, 2005*

*Floor area: 1000 m². Client: Aishti/Aïzone. Cost: not disclosed*

In its fairly rough urban setting, the BlackBox Aïzone building stands out because of its large-scale graphics and its unusual projecting sign.

Mit der riesigen Schrift auf der Fassade und der ungewöhnlichen Anzeigentafel sticht das BlackBox Aïzone aus dieser urbanen Umgebung heraus.

Grâce à son style « super-graphique » et l'installation surprenante de son écran, la BlackBox Aïzone tranche avec l'austère paysage urbain.

This structure is intended not only as a billboard aimed at motorists on the northbound section of the Greater Beirut highway but also to fulfill more practical functions. Built for the fashion retailer Aishti/Aïzone, located next door in a five-story Cor-ten steel-box building, the structure houses a diner, a kitchen, bar, and terrace, all located on the ground floor with a sea view. Large windows with a red padded recess announce the presence of the restaurant. Offices are located on the floor above with vertical slit windows. Wrapped in black aluminum composite panels, the building works as a giant sign for the store, and a steel "arm," projecting 20 meters toward the highway, containing a vitrine and a 5 x 3-meter screen for the fashion designer, accentuates this use. The tip of the arm is supported by a steel cylinder that contains a cash distributor. As the architect says, "The assemblage of the installation recognizes and amplifies contemporary society's reliance on the trendiest fashions, latest entertainment venues, and the facility of money distributors." The words "BlackBox Aïzone" painted on the façade of the building in a "super-graphic" style in white and red, contrasting with the black of the façade itself, clearly announce the presence of the building and its affiliation.

Dieser Baukörper ist ebenso sehr als Reklametafel gedacht, die sich an Autofahrer auf dem nach Norden führenden Abschnitt des Greater Beirut Highway wendet, wie für speziellere praktische Funktionen. So finden auf der unteren Ebene ein Restaurant, Küche, Bar und Terrasse mit Meerblick Platz. In rot ausgelegte Vertiefungen eingesetzte, große Fenster machen auf die Existenz des Restaurants aufmerksam. In Auftrag gegeben wurde der Container von dem Modegeschäft Aishti/Aïzone, das in dem benachbarten, fünfgeschossigen Gebäude aus Cor-Ten-Stahl seinen Sitz hat. Auf der oberen Ebene des Containers sind Büros mit vertikal eingeschnittenen Fenstern untergebracht. Der mit schwarzen Aluminiumverbundplatten verkleidete Baukörper fungiert als riesiges Ladenschild; ein 20 m zum Highway hin vorspringender stählerner »Arm«, der eine Vitrine und einen 5 x 3 m großen Bildschirm für den Modedesigner trägt, unterstreicht diese Funktion. Die Spitze des Arms wird von einem Stahlzylinder gestützt, der einen Geldautomaten enthält. Dazu der Architekt: »Die Teile der Installation kombinieren und illustrieren die Abhängigkeit der heutigen Gesellschaft von den neuesten Modetrends, den angesagtesten Treffpunkten und der Bequemlichkeit von Geldautomaten.« Die Worte »BlackBox Aïzone«, die im »Super-Graphic«-Stil in Weiß und Rot auf der Fassade erscheinen und sich von dem schwarzen Untergrund deutlich abheben, verkünden unübersehbar die Präsenz des Gebäudes und seine Zugehörigkeit.

Cette construction est autant un effet d'affichage destiné aux automobilistes roulant sur la section nord de l'axe routier du Grand Beyrouth qu'un immeuble fonctionnel. Édifiée pour le distributeur de vêtements Aishti / Aïzone installé juste à côté, dans un immeuble en forme de boîte en acier Cor-Ten, cette « boîte noire » abrite un restaurant, une cuisine, un bar et une terrasse, le tout au rez-de-chaussée avec vue sur la mer. De grandes fenêtres à embrasures rembourrées signalent la présence de ce lieu à la mode. Des bureaux occupent l'étage, derrière d'étroites fenêtres verticales. Enveloppé de panneaux en composite d'aluminium noir, le bâtiment fonctionne comme une gigantesque enseigne pour le magasin. Le « bras » en acier, se projetant de 20 mètres vers l'autoroute, soutient une vitrine, et l'écran de 5 x 3 mètres, consacré aux créateurs de mode, renforce cette impression. La pointe du bras repose sur un cylindre d'acier contenant un distributeur de billets. Pour l'architecte : « L'assemblage de cette installation prend en compte et renforce le goût de la société contemporaine pour la mode la plus avant-gardiste, les lieux de divertissement les plus récents et les facilités des distributeurs d'argent. » Les mots « Black Box Aïzone » peints sur la façade dans un style « super-graphique » en blanc et rouge contrastent avec le fond noir de la façade et annoncent clairement le lieu et son affiliation.

Bernard Khoury, one of the most interesting architects working in Lebanon, has combined industrial and high-tech elements in this unexpected building in the form of a sign. The structure contains a bar and a diner.

Bernard Khoury, einer der interessantesten im Libanon tätigen Architekten, kombinierte Industrie- und Hightechelemente zu diesem ungewöhnlichen Bauwerk in Form eines Werbeschildes. Es enthält eine Bar und ein Restaurant.

Bernard Khoury, l'un des architectes les plus intéressants à l'œuvre au Liban, a associé des éléments industriels et high-tech dans ce bâtiment inattendu en forme d'enseigne. Il contient un bar et un restaurant.

# MARCIO KOGAN

*Marcio Kogan*
*Alameida Tiete, 505*
*04616–001 São Paulo, SP*
*Brazil*

*Tel: +55 11 3081 3522*
*Fax: +55 11 3063 3424*
*E-mail: mk-mk@uol.com.br*
*Web: www.marciokogan.com.br*

*Cury Hous*

Born in 1952, **MARCIO KOGAN** graduated in 1976 from the School of Architecture at Mackenzie University in São Paulo. He received an IAB (Brazilian Architects Institute) Award for UMA Stores (1999 and 2002); Coser Studio (2002); Gama Issa House (2002) and Quinta House (2004). He also received the Record House Award for Du Plessis House (2004) and BR House (2005). In 2002, he completed a Museum of Microbiology in São Paulo and in 2003 he made a submission for the World Trade Center Site Memorial. He worked with Isay Weinfeld on the Fasano Hotel in São Paulo. He also participated with Weinfeld in the 25th São Paulo Biennale (2002) with the project for a hypothetical city named Happyland. Kogan is known for his use of boxlike forms, together with wooden shutters, trellises and exposed stone. Amongst Kogan's current residential projects are the Cury House (São Paulo, 2006, published here); the E-Home, a "super-technological" house (Santander, Spain); Warbler House (Los Angeles); a villa in Milan; an "extreme house" on an island in Paraty, Rio de Janeiro; as well as two other houses in Brasília. His office is also working on a "Green Building" in New Jersey.

Der 1952 geborene **MARCIO KOGAN** schloss 1976 an der Architekturfakultät der Universidade Mackenzie in São Paulo sein Studium ab. Er erhielt mehrfach Auszeichnungen des IAB (Instituto do Arquitetos do Brasil): für seine UMA Stores (1999 und 2002), das Coser Studio (2002), das Gama Issa House (2002) und das Quinta House (2004). Ebenfalls erhielt er den Record House Award für das Du Plessis House (2004) und das BR House (2005). 2002 stellte er das Museum für Mikrobiologie in São Paulo fertig und reichte 2003 einen Beitrag für die Gedenkstätte am ehemaligen World Trade Center ein. Mit Isay Weinfeld arbeitete er am Hotel Fasano in São Paulo. Ebenfalls mit Weinfeld beteiligte er sich mit dem Projekt für eine fiktive Stadt namens Happyland an der 25. Biennale in São Paulo (2002). Kogan ist bekannt für die Verwendung kastenförmiger Elemente zusammen mit hölzernen Jalousien und Gittern sowie Sichtstein. Unter Kogans aktuellen Wohnprojekten befinden sich das Haus Cury (São Paulo, 2006, hier publiziert), das E-Home, ein »Supertechnologiehaus« (Santander, Spanien), Warbler House (Los Angeles), ein Villa in Mailand, ein »Extremhaus« auf einer Insel in Paraty, Rio de Janeiro, sowie zwei weitere Häuser in Brasília. Außerdem arbeitet sein Büro an einem »Grünen Gebäude« in New Jersey.

Né en 1952, **MARCIO KOGAN**, diplômé en 1976 de l'École d'architecture de l'Universidade Mackenzie à São Paulo, reçoit en 1999 et 2002 un prix de l'IAB (Instituto do Arquitetos do Brazil) pour ses magasins UMA, le Studio Coser (2002), la maison Gama Issa (2002), la maison Quinta (2004), et le prix Record House pour la maison Du Plessis (2004) et la maison BR (2005). En 2002, il a achevé le Musée de microbiologie de São Paulo et, en 2003, a participé au concours pour le mémorial du World Trade Center. Il a collaboré avec Isay Weinfeld sur l'hotel Fasano ainsi qu'à la 25e Biennale de São Paulo sur un projet de ville utopique, Happyland (2002). Il est connu pour ses formes en boîtes, ses voûtes en bois, ses treillis et son utilisation de la pierre apparente. Parmi ses projets résidentiels figurent la maison Cury à São Paulo, publiée ici (2006) ; la E-Home, une maison « supertechnologique » à Santander, Espagne ; la maison Warbler à Los Angeles ; une villa à Milan ; une « maison extrême » sur une île à Paraty, Rio de Janeiro, et deux autres maisons à Brasília. Son agence travaille actuellement sur un projet d'immeuble « vert » dans le New Jersey.

# CURY HOUSE

*São Paulo, SP, Brazil, 2004–06*

*Floor area: 832 m². Clients: Luiz and Luciana Cury.*
*Cost: not disclosed*

The architect highlights the extreme attention to details that went into the construction of this three-story house. Stone, either rough or smooth, wood, water, and concrete come together in an accomplished symphony of forms and textures that fully justify the high opinion in which Marcio Kogan is held. An atrium in the entrance to the house links its various spaces—dining room, kitchen, and living room on the ground floor, with bedrooms above, and, finally, on the top of the house, "a small intimate area." From the top floor, two large wooden doors open to a deck offering a view of the city in one direction and the garden in the other. The living room has large parallel openings that allow air to flow through the residence and to give a free feeling to the entire space. Appearing to be almost entirely closed from certain angles, the Cury House in fact offers continuous openings and a communion with the garden and pools that can be fully appreciated in the often warm climate of Brazil's largest city.

Der Architekt unterstreicht die enorme Sorgfalt, die beim Bau dieses dreigeschossigen Hauses auf Details verwendet wurde. Rauer oder glatter Stein, Holz, Wasser und Beton bilden zusammen eine gelungene Sinfonie aus Formen und Strukturen, die die Hochschätzung von Marcio Kogan zur Gänze rechtfertigt. Ein Atrium im Eingang des Hauses verbindet die verschiedenen Räume – Esszimmer, Küche und Wohnraum im Erdgeschoss, darüber die Schlafräume und schließlich auf dem Dach »ein kleiner, intimer Bereich«. Vom Obergeschoss führen zwei große Holztüren auf eine Veranda, von der aus man in einer Richtung die Stadt überblickt, in der anderen den Garten. Der Wohnraum verfügt über zwei große, parallele Öffnungen, durch die Frischluft in das gesamte Haus strömen und für eine freie Atmosphäre sorgen kann. Das aus bestimmten Blickwinkeln völlig geschlossen erscheinende Haus zeichnet sich im Gegenteil durch großzügige Öffnungen und eine enge Verbindung zu Garten und Pools aus, ein Umstand, der im häufig warmen Klima von Brasiliens größter Stadt sehr schätzenswert ist.

Les architectes soulignent l'extrême attention aux détails apportée dans la construction de cette résidence de trois niveaux. La pierre, brute ou polie, le bois, l'eau et le béton se marient dans une harmonieuse symphonie de formes et de textures qui justifient pleinement la réputation dont jouit Marcio Kogan. L'atrium de l'entrée relie les divers espaces. Le séjour, la salle à manger et la cuisine sont implantés au rez-de-chaussée, les chambres au premier étage, tandis qu'au second se trouve une « petite zone d'intimité ». Là, deux grandes portes de bois ouvrent sur une terrasse dont la vue donne d'un côté sur la ville et de l'autre sur le jardin. Le séjour est encadré par deux grandes ouvertures parallèles qui permettent une agréable circulation de l'air dans toute la maison et donnent une impression de liberté. Semblant presque entièrement fermée vue sous certains angles, la maison Cury est en fait en communion permanente avec son jardin et ses bassins, si appréciables dans le climat tropical de la plus grande ville du Brésil.

*Kogan uses powerful box-like forms and alternates stone, wood, concrete and glazing to create a thoroughly unexpected house.*

*Kogan verwendet kastenartige Formen und entwirft aus Stein, Holz, Beton und Glas ein ganz und gar ausgefallenes Haus.*

*Kogan s'est servi de formes en boîte, et a alterné la pierre, le bois, le béton et le verre pour créer cette maison extrêmement intrigante.*

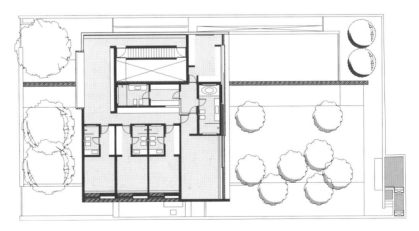

*As the external volumes would imply, the basic plan of the house is strictly rectilinear.*

*Wie schon der Außenbau andeutet, ist der Grundriss des Hauses streng geradlinig.*

*Comme ces volumes vus de l'extérieur le laissent penser, le plan de la maison est strictement orthogonal.*

Kogan uses the full openings that the Brazilian climate permits to engineer surprising transitions from interior to exterior, just as he juxtaposes materials with an evident mastery.

Dank des brasilianischen Klimas kann Kogan großflächige Öffnungen nutzen, um überraschende Übergänge von drinnen nach draußen anzulegen, so wie er mit augenscheinlicher Meisterschaft die Materialien gegeneinander setzt.

L'architecte utilise pleinement les ouvertures qu'autorise le climat brésilien pour aménager de surprenantes transitions de l'intérieur vers l'extérieur, de même qu'il juxtapose magistralement les matériaux.

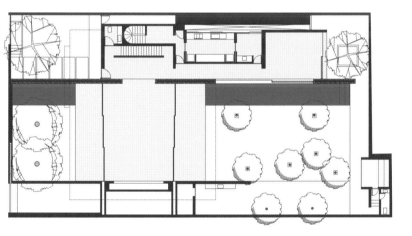

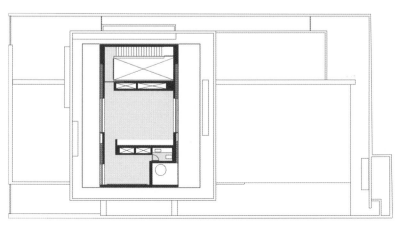

# LOCALARCHITECTURE

*Localarchitecture*
*Côtes-de-Montbenon 30*
*Case Postale*
*1002 Lausanne*
*Switzerland*

*Tel: +41 21 320 0686*
*E-mail: local@localarchitecture.ch*
*Web: www.localarchitecture.ch*

*Cow Ba*

Manuel Bieler, Antoine Robert-Grandpierre and Laurent Saurer created **LOCALARCHITECTURE** in Lausanne in 2002. Manuel Bieler was born in 1970 and received his degree in architecture from the EPFL (Federal Polytechnic Institute, Lausanne) in 1996. He received a postgraduate diploma in the economy and management of construction from the EPFL in 2002. Antoine Robert-Grandpierre was born in 1972 and also received his degree in architecture from the EPFL in 1996. Laurent Saurer, born in 1971, obtained his degree from the EPFL in 1998. They are currently working on the Fédération Internationale de Motocyclisme (Mies, 2006–); the Verdeil Foundation/Pierrefleur School (Lausanne, 2006–); housing in Lavaux (Corsy, 2006–); and the restoration of the Collégiale Neuchâtel (2005–), all in Switzerland. They have completed the Guyot House (Colombier, 2003–05); the Maison du Villaret (Colombier, 2004–05); and an ophthalmologist's office (Saint Gallen, 2004), as well as the cow barn published here. They won the Second Prize in the 2005 international competition for the new Lausanne Museum of Modern Art and a prize in the 2006 competition for the new Estonian National Museum.

2002 gründeten Manuel Bieler, Antoine Robert-Grandpierre und Laurent Saurer in Lausanne **LOCALARCHITECTURE**. Der 1970 geborene Manuel Bieler erwarb 1996 sein Architekturdiplom an der EPFL (École Polytechnique Fédérale de Lausanne). 2002 schloss er dort ein Aufbaustudium in Bauökonomie und -management mit dem Diplom ab. Auch der 1972 geborene Antoine Robert-Grandpierre erhielt 1996 seinen Abschluss in Architektur an der EPFL sowie Laurent Saurer, 1971 geboren, 1998. Gegenwärtig arbeiten sie an der Fédération Internationale de Motocyclisme (Mies, 2006–), der Fondation Verdeil/École Pierrefleur (Lausanne, seit 2006), an einem Wohnungsbau in Lavaux (Corsy, 2006–) sowie an der Restaurierung des Collégiale Neuchâtel (seit 2005), sämtlich in der Schweiz. Sie erbauten die Maison du Guyot (Colombier, 2003–05), die Maison du Villaret (Colombier, 2004–05), die Praxis eines Augenarztes (Sankt Gallen, 2004) sowie den hier publizierten Kuhstall. Im internationalen Wettbewerb für das neue Museum für Moderne Kunst in Lausanne gewannen sie 2005 den zweiten Preis sowie 2006 einen Preis im Wettbewerb für das neue Estnische Nationalmuseum.

Manuel Bieler, Antoine Robert-Grandpierre et Laurent Saurer ont créé l'agence **LOCALARCHITECTURE** à Lausanne in 2002. Manuel Bieler, né en 1970, est diplômé en 1996 en architecture de l'École Polytechnique Fédéreale de Lausanne (EPFL) et en 2002 d'études supérieures d'économie et de gestion de chantiers de l'EPFL. Antoine Robert-Grandpierre, né en 1972, est également diplômé en architecture de l'EPFL (1996), comme Laurent Saurer (né en 1971) en 1998. Ils travaillent actuellement en Suisse sur le projet du siège de la Fédération internationale de motocyclisme, Mies (2006–) ; l'école de la Fondation Verdeil-Pierrefleur, Lausanne (2006), des logements à Lavaux (Corsy, 2006–) et la restauration de la collégiale de Neuchâtel (2005). Ils avaient précédemment réalisé, toujours en Suisse, la maison Guyot, Colombier (2003–05) ; la maison du Villaret, Colombier (2004–05) ; un cabinet d'ophtalmologiste, Saint-Gall (2004) et l'étable publiée ici. Ils ont remporté en 2005 le deuxième prix au concours international pour le nouveau Musée d'Art moderne de Lausanne et en 2006, un prix au concours du Musée national d'Estonie.

# COW BARN

*Lignières, Neuchâtel, Switzerland, 2003–05*

*Floor area: 470 m². Clients: Juan Daniel and Cuche Fernand.*
*Cost: €201 000*

This barn was designed to house 30 cows and their offspring. It includes 130 square meters of stockpiling space for hay, an exterior courtyard of 150 square meters, and other related facilities. The precise program was established by the client and the Canton's Department of Agricultural Economy. As the architects explain, the client wanted a contemporary design that would nevertheless fit within the budget allocated by Swiss federal authorities for this type of building. The farmers further wished to have a facility fully adapted to organic production. Part of a large agricultural estate called the Cerisier, the site is located in an idyllic rural Swiss landscape. The barn had to be located near the existing farm, and the architects engaged in a careful analysis of local farm building types before finalizing their design. The wooden design that they came up with is both respectful of its function, the site, and the shared goal of "sustainability." The movement of earth on the site was minimized during construction and local wood was used. The architects proved that a barn can be improved by the thoughtful use of modern design.

In diesem Stall sollen 30 Kühe und ihr Nachwuchs untergebracht werden. Darüber hinaus umfasst er 130 m² Lagerraum für Heu, einen 150 m² großen Außenhof und andere zugehörige Vorrichtungen. Der genaue Bauauftrag wurde vom Bauherrn und dem kantonalen Amt für Landwirtschaft vorgegeben. Die Architekten erläutern, dass der Auftraggeber eine zeitgenössische Gestaltung wünschte, die gleichwohl im Rahmen des von der Schweizer Bundesbehörde für diese Art von Bauwerk vorgegebenen Budgets blieb. Die Betreiber wollten darüber hinaus eine völlig der ökologischen Landwirtschaft entsprechende Einrichtung. Das Gelände gehört zu einem großen landwirtschaftlichen Betrieb mit Namen Cerisier und liegt im idyllischen Schweizer Kanton Jura. Der Stall sollte in der Nähe des Bauernhauses zu stehen kommen und die Architekten beschäftigten sich eingehend mit den örtlichen Hoftypen, ehe sie ihren Entwurf abschlossen. Der von ihnen entwickelte Holzbau geht mit seiner Funktion, dem Standort und dem Ziel der »Nachhaltigkeit« gleichermaßen achtungsvoll um. Die Erdbewegungen auf dem Baugelände wurden auf das Minimum beschränkt und heimisches Holz verwendet. Die Architekten konnten beweisen, dass sich auch ein Stall durch die durchdachte Anwendung modernen Designs verbessern lässt.

Cette étable a été conçue pour un troupeau de trente vaches et leurs veaux. Elle comprend 130 m² pour le stockage du foin, une cour de 150 m² et divers locaux techniques. Un programme très précis avait été établi par le client et le département de l'économie agricole du canton. Le client souhaitait un bâtiment contemporain qui puisse entrer dans les conditions des subventions allouées par les autorités fédérales suisses pour ce type de construction ainsi que des installations adaptées à la production biologique. Appartenant à un vaste domaine agricole, Le Cerisier, le terrain est situé dans un paysage idyllique typiquement suisse. L'étable devait être implantée près de la ferme et les architectes ont étudié avec soin les divers types de bâtiments locaux avant de finaliser leur projet. La construction en bois respecte à la fois la fonction, le site et les objectifs de développement durable. Les déplacements de terre pendant le chantier ont été réduits au maximum et un bois local a été utilisé. Les architectes ont prouvé que même une étable pouvait bénéficier de principes de conception modernes et réfléchis.

*Applying the principles of contemporary architecture to a traditional building type, such as the barn, is an interesting exercise in the reconciliation of two different worlds.*

*Die Prinzipien moderner Architektur auf einen traditionellen Bautypus wie einen Stall anzuwenden, ist ein interessanter Versuch, zwei verschiedene Welten in Einklang zu bringen.*

*Appliquer les principes de l'architecture contemporaine à un type de construction traditionnel comme une étable est un intéressant exercice de réconciliation.*

The shapes of the barn are outwardly quite simple, with angles introduced to render it somewhat more dynamic than it might have been had the form of an undifferentiated shed been used.

Abgesehen von einigen Schrägen, die den Stall etwas dynamischer gestalten sollen, sind seine äußeren Formen recht einfach.

Les formes de l'étable sont assez simples vues de l'extérieur. Les pans coupés apportent un peu de dynamisme par rapport à la forme classique de ce type de construction.

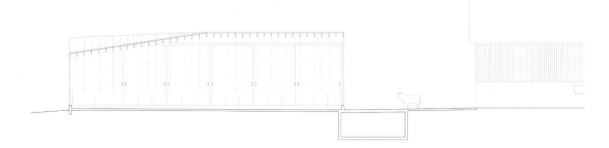

The simple wooden shapes are adapted to their intended use in farming. The Swiss maintain a high standard of workmanship in wooden architecture.

*Die schlichten hölzernen Formen sind an die landwirtschaftliche Verwendung angepasst. In der Schweiz wird im Holzbau ein hoher Standard gepflegt.*

*Les formes simples en bois sont adaptées à leur usage agricole. Les Suisses ont conservé le savoir-faire de la construction en bois.*

# GUILHERME MACHADO VAZ

*Guilherme Machado Vaz*
*Rua Dr. Ramalho Fontes 193, 5° Esq.*
*4150–630 Porto*
*Portugal*

*Tel: +351 91 785 3719*
*E-mail: gmvarq@gmail.com*

**GUILHERME MACHADO VAZ** was born in 1974 in Porto. In 1999, he graduated from the Faculdade de Arquitectura da Universidade do Porto (FAUP). The buildings of the FAUP were designed by Álvaro Siza (1987–93). Machado Vaz worked with Souto Moura Arquitectos (1997–98), before creating his own office. His main projects are: Valley House (Vieira do Minho, 1998–2004, published here); Primary School (Matosinhos, 2000–03); Grave (Porto, 2003–04); Esplanade (Matosinhos, 2004–05); and Civic Center (Matosinhos, 2002–06), all in Portugal. He is currently working on four houses as a local architect for David Chipperfield in Portugal. He won Second Prize in an international competition for the new Psychology Faculty in Coimbra, Portugal (associated with architect Nuno Graça Moura), in 2004.

**GUILHERME MACHADO VAZ** wurde 1974 in Porto geboren, wo er 1999 an der Faculdade de Arquitectura da Universidade do Porto (FAUP) sein Studium abschloss. Die Bauten der FAUP (1987–93) entstanden nach Entwürfen Álvaro Sizas. Ehe Machado Vaz sein eigenes Büro eröffnete, arbeitete er 1997 bis 1998 bei Souto Moura Arquitectos. Seine wichtigsten Projekte sind: das hier vorgestellte Valley House (Vieira do Minho, 1998–2004), Grundschule (Matosinhos, 2000–03), ein Grab (Porto, 2003–04), Esplanade (Matosinhos, 2004–05) sowie ein Verwaltungszentrum (Matosinhos, 2002–06), sämtlich in Portugal. Zurzeit arbeitet er als Architekt vor Ort für David Chipperfield an vier Häusern in Portugal. Beim internationalen Wettbewerb für die neue Psychologische Fakultät in Coimbra, Portugal, gewann er 2004 in Zusammenarbeit mit dem Architekten Nuno Graça Moura den zweiten Preis.

**GUILHERME MACHADO VAZ**, né à Porto en 1974, est diplômé en 1999 de la Faculté d'architecture de l'université de Porto (FAUP) dont les bâtiments ont été conçus par Álvaro Siza en 1987–93. Machado Vaz a travaillé pour Souto Moura Arquitectos (1997–98) avant de créer sa propre agence. Parmi ses principaux projets au Portugal : la maison de la Vallée, Vieira do Minho (1998–2004) publiée ici ; une école primaire à Matosinhos (2000–03) ; une tombe, Porto (2003–04) ; une esplanade (2004–05) et un Centre municipal à Matosinhos (2002–06). Il travaille actuellement sur quatre projets de maisons au Portugal en tant qu'architecte local pour David Chipperfield. Il a remporté le second prix d'un concours international pour la faculté de psychologie de Coimbra (en association avec Nuno Graça Moura) en 2004.

# VALLEY HOUSE

*Vieira do Minho, Portugal, 1998–2004*

*Floor area: 340 m². Client: Prof. Júlio Benfiquista.*
*Cost: € 250 000*

This house stands out as a concrete, glass, wood, and steel composition in intentional contrast to the natural surroundings. But the architect also anticipates the moment when natural aging of the construction materials will make the residence blend more fully into the site. No less than a total of 82 meters long, 8 meters wide, with a usable floor area of 340 square meters, the structure appears to echo the form of a nearby natural stone wall. The architect states that the "floor plan obeys a typical regional typology in which all the elements are gathered around a central room, the 'veranda,' that assumes the role of the 'nuclear' part of the building where family and friends congregate. The Valley House," he concludes, "is an isolated shelter that transports us to a place in time where man lived in a purely natural environment due to the lack of technical ability to transform it." Both Álvaro Siza and to an even greater extent Eduardo Souto Moura have also experimented with the close integration of modern houses into their natural settings, an undoubted influence on Guilherme Machado Vaz.

Dieses Haus steht als Komposition aus Beton, Glas, Holz und Stahl in bewusstem Kontrast zu seiner Umgebung. Der Architekt rechnet allerdings auch mit dem Zeitpunkt, wenn das Haus dank der natürlichen Alterung des Baumaterials stärker mit dem Gelände verschmilzt. Der stattliche 82 m lange, 8 m breite Bau mit einer Nutzfläche von 340 m² nimmt scheinbar die Form einer nahe gelegenen Natursteinmauer auf. Der Architekt konstatiert, dass »der Grundriss einer typischen lokalen Form folgt, bei der sich sämtliche Elemente um einen zentralen Raum, die ›Veranda‹, das Herz des Hauses, gruppieren, in dem Familie und Freunde zusammenkommen. Das Valley House«, schließt er, »gleicht einem isolierten Schutzraum, der uns an einen Ort und in eine Zeit versetzt, in der der Mensch, bedingt durch das Fehlen der technischen Fähigkeit, etwas zu verändern, in einer rein naturbelassenen Umgebung lebte.« Auch Álvaro Siza und in noch stärkerem Maß Eduardo Souto Moura haben mit der engen Einbindung moderner Häuser in ihre natürliche Umgebung experimentiert und damit zweifellos Guilherme Machado Vaz beeinflusst.

Cette maison est une composition en béton, verre, bois et acier qui se détache de son cadre naturel par contraste. L'architecte a cependant prévu le moment où le vieillissement naturel des matériaux de construction entraînera une intégration plus douce avec le site. De pas moins de 82 mètres de long, 8 mètres de large et de 340 m² de surface, cette résidence semble faire écho à l'ancien mur de pierre voisin. L'architecte précise que « le plan au sol obéit à une typologie régionale typique dans laquelle tous les éléments sont regroupés autour d'une pièce centrale, la « véranda », qui joue le rôle d'un « noyau » dans lequel famille et amis se retrouvent. Cette maison de la vallée, conclut-il, est un abri isolé qui nous transporte dans une période de l'Histoire où l'homme vivait dans un cadre purement naturel par manque de capacité technique à le transformer. » Álvaro Siza et, dans une mesure encore plus forte, Eduardo Souto Moura, qui ont également travaillé sur l'intégration étroite de maisons modernes dans un cadre naturel, ont certainement influencé Guilherme Machado Vaz.

*Despite its planar concrete walls, the house is intended to blend in with its natural setting, almost appearing to rise up out of the earth itself.*

*Ungeachtet seiner ebenen Betonwände soll das Haus mit seiner natürlichen Umgebung verschmelzen, ja sich scheinbar aus der Erde erheben.*

*Malgré ses murs plans en béton, la maison fusionne avec son cadre naturel, comme si elle sortait de la terre.*

The simple lines of the exterior architecture are echoed inside, with a living room wall opening entirely to the outdoors in the image below.

*Die einfachen Linien des Außenbaus spiegeln sich im Inneren; unten ist der auf einer Seite nach außen offene Wohnraum zu sehen.*

*Les lignes simples de l'architecture se retrouvent en écho à l'intérieur. Un mur du séjour s'ouvre entièrement vers l'extérieur (image ci-dessous).*

The landscape and swimming pool
are designed in harmony with the
house itself, planar and carefully
integrated into the natural setting.

Grünflächen und Schwimmbecken
sind in Einklang mit dem behutsam in
die natürliche Umgebung eingebette-
ten Haus gestaltet.

Le paysage et la piscine sont conçus
en harmonie avec la maison soigneusement intégrée au cadre naturel.

The plan below shows the very strict
and narrow rectangular design of the
house, corresponding to its insertion
into the existing hillside.

Der Grundriss unten zeigt die sehr
strenge, längsrechteckige Gestaltung
des Hauses, die seiner Stellung zum
vorhandenen Hang entspricht.

Le plan ci-dessous montre l'organisation de la maison sur un rectangle
long et étroit, qui correspond à son
insertion dans le flanc de la colline.

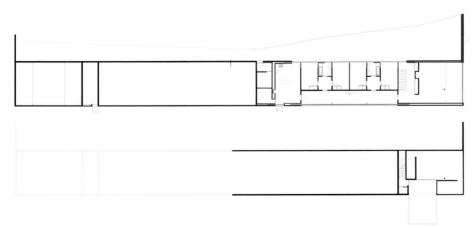

*"Ghost Lab*

# MACKAY-LYONS SWEETAPPLE

*MacKay-Lyons Sweetapple Architects Ltd.*
*2188 Gottingen Street*
*Halifax, Nova Scotia*
*Canada B3K 3B4*

*Tel: +1 902 429 1867 / Fax: +1 902 429 6276*
*E-mail: info@mlsarchitects.ca / Web: www.mlsarchitects.ca*

**BRIAN MACKAY-LYONS** was born in Arcadia, Nova Scotia. He received his B.Arch from the Technical University of Nova Scotia in 1978 and his Master of Architecture and Urban Design from UCLA. After studying in China, Japan, California, and Italy, working with Charles Moore, Barton Myers and Giancarlo De Carlo, Mac-Kay-Lyons returned to Nova Scotia in 1983. In 1985 he founded the firm Brian MacKay-Lyons Architecture Urban Design in Halifax. Twenty years later, he created a partnership with Talbot Sweetapple under the name MacKay-Lyons Sweetapple Architects Ltd., at present a 20-person firm. **TALBOT SWEETAPPLE** was born in St. John's, Newfoundland. He graduated with an M.Arch from Dalhousie University. He worked with Shin Takamatsu in Berlin, Germany, and the firm KPMB in Toronto. MacKay-Lyons is a Professor of Architecture at Dalhousie University. Significant projects, all in Canada, include: Danielson House (Cape Breton Island, Nova Scotia, 1998); House on the Nova Scotia Coast #22 (Nova Scotia, 1998); Howard House (Nova Scotia Coast, 1999); Messenger House 2 (Kingsburg, Nova Scotia, 2003); Hill House (Nova Scotia Coast, 2004); Dalhousie Faculty of Computer Science (Halifax, Nova Scotia, 1999); Academic Resource Centre, University of Toronto (Scarborough, Ontario, 2003); and Office for Mackay-Lyons Sweetapple Architects (Halifax, Nova Scotia, 2003). Current work includes: Port Campus, Nova Scotia College of Art and Design (Halifax, Nova Scotia, 2007) and the Canadian High Commission (Dhaka, Bangladesh, 2007). The "Ghost Lab," published here, is something different.

**BRIAN MACKAY-LYONS** wurde in Arcadia, Nova Scotia, geboren. Er erhielt 1978 von der Technical University of Nova Scotia den Grad eines B.Arch. An der UCLA erwarb er den Master of Architecture and Urban Design. Nach Studien in China, Japan, Kalifornien und Italien sowie nach Tätigkeiten in den Büros von Charles Moore, Barton Myers und Giancarlo De Carlo kehrte MacKay-Lyons 1983 nach Nova Scotia zurück. 1985 eröffnete er in Halifax das Büro Brian MacKay-Lyons Architecture Urban Design. 20 Jahre später ging er mit Talbot Sweetapple eine Partnerschaft unter dem Namen MacKay-Lyons Sweetapple Architects Ltd. ein, gegenwärtig ein Büro mit 20 Mitarbeitern. **TALBOT SWEETAPPLE** wurde in St. John's in Neufundland geboren. Er verließ die Dalhousie University, Halifax, mit dem Grad eines M.Arch. und arbeitete mit Shin Takamatsu in Berlin und dem Büro KPMB in Toronto. MacKay-Lyons lehrt als Architekturprofessor an der Dalhousie University. Zu den sämtlich in Kanada befindlichen, bedeutenden Projekten zählen: Danielson House (Cape Breton Island, Nova Scotia, 1998), Haus an der Küste von Nova Scotia #22 (Nova Scotia, 1998), Howard House (Nova Scotia Coast, 1999), Messenger House 2 (Kingsburg, Nova Scotia, 2003), Hill House (Nova Scotia Coast, 2004), Dalhousie University, Fakultät für Computerwissenschaft (Halifax, Nova Scotia, 1999), Academic Resource Centre, University of Toronto (Scarborough, Ontario, 2003), und das Büro für MacKay-Lyons Sweetapple Architects (Halifax, Nova Scotia, 2003). Die aktuellen Projekte sind: Port Campus, Nova Scotia College of Art and Design (Halifax, Nova Scotia, 2007), und die kanadische Gesandtschaft in Dhaka (Bangladesh, 2007). Das hier vorgestellte »Ghost Lab« verfolgt eine von diesen Projekten gänzlich unabhängige Zielsetzung.

**BRIAN MACKAY-LYONS** est né en Arcadie, Nouvelle-Écosse, Canada. Il est B. Arch. de l'Université Technique de Nouvelle-Écosse (1978) et M. Arch et urbanisme de UCLA. Après des études en Chine, au Japon, en Californie et en Italie, il a travaillé pour Charles Moore, Barton Myers et Giancarlo De Carlo. De retour en Nouvelle-Écosse en 1983, il fonde en 1985 l'agence Brian MacKay-Lyons Architecture Urban Design à Halifax. Vingt ans plus tard, il s'associe avec Talbot Sweetapple sous le nom de MacKay-Lyons Sweetapple Architects Ltd. qui emploie aujourd'hui vingt collaborateurs. **TALBOT SWEETAPPLE** est né à St. John, Newfoundland. Il est M. Arch. de Dalhousie University et a travaillé avec Shin Takamatsu à Berlin et l'agence KPMB à Toronto. MacKay-Lyons est professeur d'architecture à l'Université de Dalhousie. Parmi leurs projets les plus significatifs, tous au Canada : Danielson House, île de Cap Breton, Nouvelle-Écosse (1998) ; maison sur la côte de Nouvelle-Écosse n° 22, Nouvelle-Écosse (1998) ; Howard House, côte de Nouvelle-Écosse (1999) ; Messenger House 2, Kingsburg, Nouvelle-Écosse (2003) ; Hill House, côte de Nouvelle-Écosse (2004) ; Faculté des sciences de l'informatique Dalhousie, Halifax, Nouvelle-Écosse (1999) ; Resource Centre for Academic Technology, University of Toronto, Scarborough, Ontario (2003) ; bureaux pour Mackay-Lyons Sweetapple Architects, Halifax, Nouvelle-Écosse (2003). Parmi leurs chantiers actuels : Port Campus, Nova Scotia College of Art and Design, Halifax (2007) et la Haute Commission canadienne, Dhaka, Bangladesh (2007). Le « Ghost Lab » publié ici relève d'un autre type d'intervention.

# "GHOST LAB"

*Nova Scotia, Canada, 1994–1997, 2002–*

*The unusual wooden tower seen here was built as part of "Ghost 6" in the summer of 2004.*

*Der hier abgebildete, ungewöhnliche Holzturm wurde im Sommer 2004 als Teil von »Ghost 6« errichtet.*

*Cette curieuse tour en bois, qui fait partie du projet « Ghost 6 », a été construite pendant l'été 2004.*

Brian MacKay-Lyons describes his invention of the "Ghost Lab" as follows: "As an architectural student in my early twenties, I quickly became suspicious of the nature of the architectural education that I was receiving. While daydreaming in the classroom and looking out of the window at the life on the street outside, I felt a recurring desire to knock down the massive brick wall of the building and let the sounds and fresh air fill the academy. In 1994, as a professor in that same school, I saw an opportunity to take architectural education out of the classroom and into the landscape. The Ghost Laboratory has been conducted on the nearby 400-year-old ruins on the back of my farm on the southwest coast of Nova Scotia ever since. At first (1994–97) it began as a Dalhousie University summer studio called a 'free lab'. From 2002 to 2004 it has been an international summer internship offered by my practice in partnership with Dalhousie." The "Ghost Labs" have created their own structures where "each project is a study in light wood framing which is temporary, recycled, and biodegradable, resulting in an ephemeral quality." The emphasis of the summer programs under the direction of MacKay-Lyons is "on issues of landscape, material culture, and community." The two-week sessions consist of one week of design and one week of construction.

Brian MacKay-Lyons beschreibt seine Erfindung des »Ghost Lab« wie folgt: »Als Architekturstudent von Anfang 20 wurde mir die Art der Architekturausbildung, die ich erhielt, schnell suspekt. Während ich tagträumend im Unterricht saß und aus dem Fenster das Leben auf der Straße draußen beobachtete, empfand ich wieder und wieder das Bedürfnis, die massiven Backsteinmauern des Gebäudes einzureißen, auf dass die Akademie mit den Geräuschen und der frischen Luft von draußen erfüllt würde. Als ich dann 1994 an derselben Schule als Professor tätig war, sah ich die Gelegenheit, die Architektenausbildung aus dem Hörsaal in die Landschaft zu verlegen. Seither wird das Ghost Laboratory auf den fast 400 Jahre alten Ruinen auf dem rückwärtigen Gelände meiner Farm an der Südwestküste von Nova Scotia durchgeführt. Zu Anfang, in den Jahren 1994 bis 1997, fand es unter der Bezeichnung ›free lab‹ als Sommerkurs der Dalhousie University statt. Von 2002 bis 2004 wurde es unter Beteiligung der Universität von meinem Büro als internationales Sommerpraktikum angeboten.« Während der »Ghost Labs« entstanden jeweils eigene Bauten, von denen »ein jeder eine Studie zum Leichtholzrahmen darstellt, der temporär, recyclebar, biologisch abbaubar und damit von einer kurzlebigen Qualität geprägt ist«. In den von MacKay-Lyons geleiteten Sommerprogrammen werden schwerpunktmäßig »Fragen von Landschaft, Materialkultur und Gemeinschaft« behandelt. Die zweiwöchigen Veranstaltungen setzen sich aus einer Woche Entwerfen und einer Woche Bauen zusammen.

Brian MacKay-Lyons décrit ainsi ce « Ghost Lab » ou « labo fantôme » : « Étudiant en architecture d'une vingtaine d'années, je me suis vite posé des questions sur la nature de l'enseignement que je recevais. Tout en rêvassant pendant les cours et en regardant par la fenêtre ce qui se passait dans la rue, je ressentais le besoin récurrent de faire tomber le mur massif du bâtiment et de laisser les sons et l'air frais du dehors emplir la faculté. En 1994, professeur dans la même école, j'ai trouvé une opportunité de faire sortir l'enseignement architectural de la salle de classe et de l'attirer vers le paysage. Le Ghost Laboratory a été mis en œuvre sur des ruines datant de près de 400 ans, qui se trouvaient derrière ma ferme sur la côte sud-ouest de la Nouvelle-Écosse. » Initialement (1994–97), l'expérience débuta sous forme de stage d'été de l'université de Dalhousie appelé « free lab ». « De 2002 à 2004, il s'est transformé en stage international d'été proposé par mon agence en partenariat avec Dalhousie. » Ces « Ghost Labs » ont créé leurs propres structures dans lesquelles « chaque projet est une recherche sur les principes de l'ossature légère en bois temporaire, recyclée et biodégradable, d'où une certaine qualité d'éphémère. » L'accent mis par ces programmes d'été sous la direction de MacKay-Lyons porte « sur les enjeux du paysage, de culture matérielle et de communauté ». Les sessions d'une durée de quinze jours se répartissent entre la conception et la construction.

*"Each project," says Brian MacKay-Lyons, "acts as a landscape measuring device, reading natural and settlement patterns through a built proposition. Each project is a study in light wood framing, which is temporary, recycled, and biodegradable, resulting in an ephemeral quality."*

*»Jedes Projekt«, sagt Brian MacKay-Lyons, »fungiert als ein Messinstrument, das naturgegebene und siedlungsabhängige Muster anhand eines Bauvorhabens liest. Jedes Projekt ist ein Beispiel für das Bauen mit Leichtholzrahmen, die temporär, recyclebar, biologisch abbaubar und von ephemerer Anmutung sind.«*

*« Chaque projet, a déclaré Brian MacKay-Lyons, agit comme une mesure du paysage qui facilite la lecture de ses caractéristiques naturelles et de l'implantation à travers une proposition de construction. Chaque projet est une étude sur l'ossature légère en bois, temporaire, recyclée et biodégradable, et sa qualité éphémère. »*

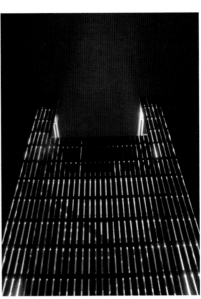

The cabins above were created for "Ghost 7" in 2005.

Die Holzhäuser oben entstanden 2005 für »Ghost 7«.

Les huttes (ci-dessus) ont été créées pour le projet « Ghost 7 », en 2005.

To the right, a view showing the "Ghost 7" cabins in the background and the structure built for "Ghost 8" in 2006, in the foreground. Below, two pictures of the cabins built during "Ghost 7".

Auf der Abbildung rechts sind im Hintergrund die Holzhäuser von »Ghost 7« und im Vordergrund der 2006 für »Ghost 8« errichtete Bau zu sehen. Unten zwei Bilder der während »Ghost 7« entstandenen Holzhäuser.

À droite, vue des huttes de « Ghost 7 », en arrière plan, et de la structure édifiée pour « Ghost 8 », en 2006, au premier plan. En bas, deux vues des huttes de « Ghost 7 ».

# MEIXNER SCHLÜTER WENDT

*Meixner Schlüter Wendt / Architekten*
*Fischerfeldstrasse 13*
*60311 Frankfurt am Main*
*Germany*

*Tel: +49 69 2102 860 / Fax: +49 69 2102 8620*
*E-mail: info@meixner-schlueter-wendt.de*
*Web: www.meixner-schlueter-wendt.de*

**CLAUDIA MEIXNER** was born in 1964 in Bad Hersfeld. She studied architecture at the Technical University in Darmstadt (1983–91), and at the Universita degli Studi in Florence (1987–88). Since 1987, she has worked on drawing and painting, holding various exhibitions. In 1991 to 1994, she was a lecturer at the Department of Construction & Design at the Technical University (TU) Darmstadt. Since 2005, she has been a member of the Advisory Council for Town and Country Planning, for Frankfurt. **FLORIAN SCHLÜTER** was born in 1959 in Karlsruhe. He studied architecture at the TU in Darmstadt (1980–88). Like Claudia Meixner, he studied at the Universita degli Studi in Florence. Since 1985, he has worked on drawing and sculpture, holding various exhibitions. In 1993–98, he was a lecturer at the Department of Sculpture at the TU Darmstadt. In 2001 he was Senior Lecturer in Architecture at the Siegen University of Applied Science. **MARTIN WENDT** was born in 1955 in Ahlen, and studied architecture at the Frankfurt University of Applied Science (1976–81). Between 1981 and 1994, he was an employee of several architecture firms. From 1994 to 1996, he worked as a self-employed Architecture Consultant for the planning and construction of several residential, industrial and public buildings. With the other two partners, he created Meixner Schlüter Wendt in 1997. Recent work, all in Germany, includes: a floating snack bar (Frankfurt, 2001–02); Schlüter Residence (Karlsruhe, 2003); Recycling Center (Frankfurt, 2003); Dornbusch Church (Frankfurt, 2004); Wohlfahrt-Laymann House (Taunus, 2004–05, published here); and Ordnungsamt Frankfurt (in progress).

**CLAUDIA MEIXNER** wurde 1964 in Bad Hersfeld geboren. Sie studierte von 1983 bis 1991 an der TU Darmstadt und von 1987 bis 1988 an der Universita degli Studi in Florenz Architektur. Seit 1987 arbeitet, zeichnet und malt sie und beschickte verschiedene Ausstellungen. In den Jahren 1991 bis 1994 war sie wissenschaftliche Mitarbeiterin am Lehrstuhl Baukonstruktion und Entwerfen der TU Darmstadt. Seit 2005 gehört sie dem Städtebaubeirat der Stadt Frankfurt an. **FLORIAN SCHLÜTER** wurde 1959 in Karlsruhe geboren und studierte von 1980 bis 1988 an der TU Darmstadt Architektur. Auch er setzte sein Studium in Florenz fort. Seit 1985 beschäftigt er sich mit Stahlplastik und Zeichnung und nahm an diversen Ausstellungen teil. Von 1993 bis 1998 war er wissenschaftlicher Mitarbeiter am Lehrstuhl Plastisches Gestalten der TU Darmstadt. 2001 hatte er eine Professur-Vertretung an der Gesamthochschule Siegen. Der Dritte im Bunde, **MARTIN WENDT**, wurde 1955 in Ahlen geboren und studierte von 1976 bis 1981 an der Fachhochschule Frankfurt. Zwischen 1981 und 1994 war er bei verschiedenen Architekturbüros angestellt. Von 1994 bis 1996 arbeitete er freischaffend als Berater an der Planung und Realisierung von Wohn- und Gewerbebauten sowie öffentlichen Gebäuden. 1997 tat er sich mit den beiden anderen zur Bürogemeinschaft Meixner Schlüter Wendt zusammen. Zu den neueren, sämtlich in Deutschland realisierten Projekten zählen: eine schwimmende Snackbar (Frankfurt, 2001–02), das Wohnhaus Schlüter (Karlsruhe, 2003), Recyclingcenter (Frankfurt, 2003), Dornbuschkirche (Frankfurt, 2004), das hier vorgestellte Wohnhaus Wohlfahrt-Laymann (Oberursel, 2004–05) sowie das im Bau befindliche Ordnungsamt Frankfurt.

**CLAUDIA MEIXNER**, née en 1964 à Bad Hersfeld, a étudié l'architecture à l'Université Technique (TU) de Darmstadt (1983–91) et à l'Universita degli Studi à Florence (1987–88). Depuis 1987, elle dessine et peint et a exposé à plusieurs reprises. En 1991–94, elle est assistante au département de construction et design à la TU de Darmstadt. Depuis 2005, elle est membre du Conseil consultatif pour la planification urbaine et rurale de Francfort. **FLORIAN SCHLÜTER**, né en 1959 à Karlsruhe, a étudié l'architecture à la TU de Darmstadt (1980–88). Comme Claudia Meixner, il a étudié à l'Universita degli Studi à Florence. Depuis 1985, il travaille le dessin et la sculpture, et donne diverses expositions. En 1993–98, il est assistant au Département de sculpture à la TU de Darmstadt, puis en 2001 est nommé assistant senior en architecture à l'Université des sciences appliquées de Siegen. **MARTIN WENDT**, né en 1955 à Ahlen, a étudié l'architecture à l'Université des sciences appliquées de Francfort (1976–81). De 1981 à 1994, il travaille pour plusieurs agences et, de 1994 à 1996, intervient comme consultant en architecture pour la programmation et la construction de plusieurs immeubles résidentiels et industriels. Avec Meixner et Schlüter, il participe, en 1997, à la fondation de l'agence Meixner Schlüter Wendt. Parmi leurs récents travaux, tous en Allemagne : un snack-bar flottant, Francfort (2001–02) ; la maison Schlüter, Karlsruhe (2003) ; un centre de recyclage à Francfort (2003) ; l'église de Dornbusch, Francfort (2004) ; la maison Wohlfahrt-Laymann, Taunus (2004–05), publiée ici, et un poste de police à Francfort (en cours).

# WOHLFAHRT-LAYMANN HOUSE

*Oberursel (Taunus), Germany, 2004–05*

*Floor area before: 180 m² / Floor area after: 290 m².*
*Client: Jürgen Wohlfahrt-Laymann. Cost: €500 000*

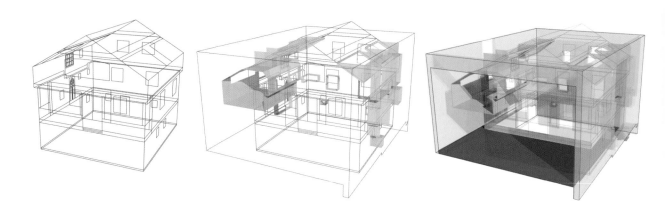

Working with a 1930s house in a wealthy but heterogeneous residential neighborhood in the Taunus hills outside Frankfurt, the architects rejected the original idea of simply tearing down the existing building and decided to use it as the basis of a more ambitious project. A shell was built around the old house, creating often curious "intermediate" spaces as well as new interior volumes. The "inner" house was broken open where light was required inside and rooftop rooms were extended upward. As the architects explain, "Paradoxes occur—from within and without—a seemingly normal reality is distorted. A simple, traditional 'cottage in the country,' which originated as a matter-of-course, is dissolved, transformed, and simultaneously fortified—in the sense of a metamorphosis." The architects, who have a background in art, refer clearly to the work of Gordon Matta-Clark in this instance, as well as to Gregor Schneider's *Ur House* (German Pavilion, Venice Biennale, 2003). Having absorbed the existing cottage into their new creation, Meixner Schlüter Wendt chose to make a closer connection than that which previously existed between the house and its natural setting. Thus, "The dark brown earth covering the garden is apparently continued in the equally dark brown flooring of the terrace and the parquet floor inside the house. The gray-green coloring of the outer shell integrates well into the colors of the surrounding woodlands."

Die Architekten, die es mit einem 1930er-Jahre-Haus in einem hochwertigen, aber heterogenen Wohnviertel im Taunus außerhalb Frankfurts zu tun hatten, verwarfen das ursprüngliche Vorhaben, das vorhandene Haus einfach abzureißen, sondern beschlossen, es als Basis für ein aufwendigeres Projekt zu verwenden. Um das alte Haus wurde eine Hülle errichtet, wodurch einige kuriose Zwischenräume wie auch neue Innenräume entstanden. Das »innere« Haus wurde da, wo Licht fehlte, aufgebrochen und Dachzimmer nach oben erweitert. Dazu die Architekten: »Es entstehen Paradoxien – von innen und außen – eine anscheinend normale Realität wird verfremdet. Ein einfaches, archetypisches ›Haus im Grünen‹, das der Tradition gemäß entstand, wird aufgelöst, umgeformt und gleichzeitig überhöht – im Sinne einer Metamorphose.« Die Architekten, die über Erfahrungen in der bildenden Kunst verfügen, beziehen sich in diesem Fall deutlich auf das Werk von Gordon Matta-Clark sowie auf »Haus Ur« von Gregor Schneider (Deutscher Pavillon, Biennale Venedig, 2003). Nachdem ihre Neuschöpfung das vorhandene Haus in sich aufgenommen hatte, beschlossen Meixner Schlüter Wendt zwischen dem Haus und seiner Umgebung eine engere Beziehung als zuvor herzustellen. So setzt sich »die dunkelbraune Erde des Gartens scheinbar im ebenfalls dunkelbraunen Bodenbelag der Terrasse und dem Parkett im Hausinneren fort. Die graugrüne Farbe der äußeren Hülle fügt sich gut in die bewaldete Umgebung ein.«

Chargés de rénover une maison des années 1930 construite dans une zone résidentielle aisée mais hétérogène des montagnes du Taunus près de Francfort, les architectes ont rejeté l'idée de départ de démolir la construction d'origine et préféré en faire la base d'un projet plus ambitieux. Une coquille a été construite autour de la vieille résidence, générant souvent de curieux espaces « intermédiaires » et de nouveaux volumes intérieurs. La maison « interne » a été ouverte lorsqu'il fallait obtenir davantage de lumière naturelle à l'intérieur et les pièces sous le toit ont gagné en hauteur. Selon les explications des architectes : « Des paradoxes se produisent – issus du dedans et du dehors – lorsqu'une réalité apparemment normale est déformée. Ce simple et traditionnel « cottage de campagne » qui semblait banal se dissout, se transforme et se fortifie simultanément en une sorte de métamorphose. » Les architectes, qui possèdent une formation artistique, se réfèrent clairement ici au travail de Gordon Matta-Clark ou de la Ur-House de Gregor Schneider (pavillon allemand de la Biennale de Venise 2003). Après avoir absorbé le cottage dans leur nouvelle création, Meixner, Schlüter et Wendt ont décidé de resserrer la connexion entre la maison et son cadre naturel. « La terre brun foncé du jardin se retrouve apparemment dans les sols tout aussi foncés de la terrasse et les parquets intérieurs. La coloration gris-vert de la coque extérieure s'intègre bien aux couleurs des bois environnants. »

*As the drawings above show, this unusual project involves the complete enclosure of an existing, very ordinary house.*

*Wie auf den Zeichnungen oben zu sehen, geht es bei diesem ungewöhnlichen Projekt darum, ein vorhandenes Haus vollständig zu umbauen.*

*Comme le montrent les dessins cidessus, cet étonnant projet consiste en l'absorption intégrale d'une maison existante très ordinaire.*

The final form of the house takes on a modern, rectilinear shape, in effect swallowing the earlier sloped roof design.

Die endgültige Form des Hauses, die das ehemalige geneigte Dach praktisch »verschluckt«, ist modern und geradlinig.

La forme finale de la maison prend un aspect moderne et rectiligne. L'ancienne toiture à double pente a été littéralement avalée.

In absorbing the earlier house, the designers have created a structure that might be compared with certain works of contemporary art that push the boundaries between architecture and art.

Indem sie das alte Haus absorbieren, schufen die Designer ein Konstrukt im Geiste mancher Werke der zeitgenössischen Kunst, die die Grenze zwischen Kunst und Architektur überschreiten.

En absorbant la maison antérieure, les architectes ont créé une structure qui n'est guère éloignée de certaines œuvres contemporaines, aux limites de l'art et de l'architecture.

*Where the contemporary volumes dominate, as in these two images, little hint is given of the underlying, traditional house.*

*Wo die modernen Bauformen beherrschend sind, wie auf diesen beiden Abbildungen, ist von dem zugrunde liegenden, traditionellen Haus kaum noch etwas zu ahnen.*

*La domination de la forme des volumes contemporains dans ces deux images ne laisse pas apparaître la moindre trace de l'ancienne maison.*

# PAULO MENDES DA ROCHA

Paulo Mendes da Rocha
Rua Bento Freitas 306 – 5º/51
CEP: 01220–000, São Paulo, SP
Brazil

Tel: +55 11 3259 3175
E-mail: pmr@sti.com.br

*Leme Gallery*

**PAULO MENDES DA ROCHA** was born in 1928 in the city of Vitória, capital of the state of Espírito Santo in Brazil. He completed his studies at the Mackenzie Architecture School in 1954. The first project outside Brazil was the Brazilian Pavilion for the International Expo in Osaka, Japan (1970). One of his best-known projects is the Brazilian Museum of Sculpture (São Paulo, 1987–92). He has also done interesting renovation work, as was the case in the State Museum of São Paulo (1993). His Patriarch Plaza and Viaduct do Chá (São Paulo, 1992), with its great, curving wing canopy, is one of the more visible architectural monuments of Brazil's largest city. Other significant works include: Paulistano Club Gymnasium (1957–61); Clubhouse of the Jockey Club of Goiás (1963); Beach Club in Guarujá (1963); House in Butantã (1964); Masetti Residence (1970); Hotel in Poxoréu (1971); Jardim Calux School (1972); Keiralla Sarhan Office Building (1984–88); and Jaraguá Apartment Building (1984–88). His more recent work includes a master plan for Vigo University in Spain, the Sesc 24 de Maio Building in the center of São Paulo, and the Leme Gallery published here. Paulo Mendes da Rocha was the 2006 winner of the Pritzker Prize.

**PAULO MENDES DA ROCHA** wurde 1928 in Vitória, der Hauptstadt des brasilianischen Bundesstaats Espírito Santo geboren. 1954 schloss er seine Ausbildung an der Architekturschule der Universidade Mackenzie ab. Sein erstes Projekt außerhalb von Brasilien war der Brasilianische Pavillon auf der Weltausstellung in Osaka (1970), einer seiner bekanntesten Bauten das Brasilianische Museum für Skulptur in São Paulo (1987–92). Ferner zeichnet er für interessante Renovierungen wie das Staatsmuseum in São Paulo (1993) verantwortlich. Die von ihm entworfene Praça do Patriarca sowie das Viadukt do Chá (São Paulo, 1992) mit seinem großartigen, geschwungenen Kragdach ist eines der prägnanteren architektonischen Monumente in der größten Stadt des Landes. Weitere bedeutende Werke sind: der Clube Atletico Paulistano (1957–61), Clubhaus des Jockeyclubs von Goiás (1963), Beachclub in Guarujá (1963), Haus in Butantã (1964), Wohnhaus Masetti (1970), Hotel in Poxoréu (1971), Jardim-Calux-Schule (1972), Bürogebäude Keiralla Sarhan (1984–88) und das Apartmenthaus Jaraguá (1984–88). Zu seinen neueren Arbeiten gehören: Gesamtplan für die Universität Vigo, Spanien, das Gebäude Sesc 24 de Maio im Zentrum von São Paulo sowie die hier vorgestellte Galerie Leme. 2006 wurde Mendes da Rocha mit dem Pritzker-Preis ausgezeichnet.

**PAULO MENDES DA ROCHA** est né en 1928 à Vitoria, capitale de l'État de l'Espírito Santo, au Brésil. Il a achevé ses études à l'École d'architecture de l'Universidade Mackenzie en 1954. Son premier projet hors du Brésil a été le Pavillon brésilien de l'International Expo d'Osaka au Japon (1970). L'une de ses œuvres les plus connues est le Musée brésilien de la sculpture, São Paulo (1987–92). Il a également réalisé d'intéressantes interventions en rénovation comme le Musée d'État de São Paulo (1993). Sa Place des Patriarches et le viaduc do Chá, São Paulo (1992), au vaste auvent en aile incurvée est l'un des monuments architecturaux les plus remarquables de la grande cité brésilienne. Parmi ses autres réalisations importantes : le Clube Atletico Paulistano (1957–61) ; le Clubhouse du Jockey Club de Goiás (1963) ; le Beach Club de Guarujá (1963) ; une maison à Butantã (1964) ; la résidence Masetti (1970) ; un hôtel à Poxoréu (1971) ; l'école du Jardim Calux (1972) ; l'immeuble de bureaux Keiralla Sarhan (1984–88) et l'immeuble résidentiel Jaraguá (1984–88). Il a récemment conçu le plan directeur de l'Université de Vigo (Espagne) ; l'immeuble Sesc 24 de Maio au centre de São Paulo et la galerie Leme, publiée ici. En 2006, il a remporté le Pritzker Prize.

# LEME GALLERY

*São Paulo, SP, Brazil, 2004*

*Floor area: 375 m². Client: Eduardo Leme. Cost: not disclosed.*
*Collaborators: Martin Corullon, Anna Ferrari, Gustavo Cedroni*

Located in the Butantã area of São Paulo, the Leme Gallery is one of the best-known contemporary art galleries in the city. Unlike most "clean" gallery spaces, the Leme Gallery was designed entirely in unpolished concrete by Paulo Mendes da Rocha. There are 150 square meters of exhibition space, and the gallery is lit in good part by a 9-meter-high skylight. Space on this scale allows Eduardo Leme to show large-scale works and to indulge his "new expansive take on leading manifestations in art that propose an aesthetics of substance." Although numerous well-known architects have tried their hands at designing galleries of contemporary art, often in carefully rebuilt industrial spaces, such as those so popular in the Chelsea area of Manhattan, it would seem that Mendes da Rocha, in collaboration with Leme, has hit upon a different way of associating cutting-edge art with contemporary architecture at the highest level.

Bei der im Butantã-Viertel von São Paulo gelegenen Galerie Leme handelt es sich um eine der bekanntesten Galerien für zeitgenössische Kunst in der Stadt. Im Gegensatz zu den meist »sauberen« Galerieräumen wurde die Galerie Leme von Paulo Mendes da Rocha zur Gänze aus unpoliertem Beton errichtet. In den vorhandenen 150 m² großen Ausstellungsraum fällt Helligkeit in erster Linie durch ein 9 m hoch liegendes Oberlicht. Räume dieser Größe ermöglichen es Eduardo Leme, großformatige Werke zu zeigen und seiner »neuen, ausgreifenden Interpretation von bedeutenden Kunstwerken, die eine Ästhetik des Wesentlichen vertreten«, zu frönen. Obgleich zahlreiche namhafte Architekten sich in der Gestaltung von Galerien für moderne Kunst versuchten, oft in umgebauten Industrieräumen, wie sie sich in der Gegend von Chelsea in Manhattan so großer Beliebtheit erfreuen, scheint es, als habe Mendes da Rocha in Zusammenarbeit mit Leme einen anderen Weg gefunden, neueste Kunst mit zeitgenössischer Architektur auf hohem Niveau in Einklang zu bringen.

Située dans le quartier de Butantã à São Paulo, la galerie Leme est l'une des galeries d'art contemporain les plus connues de la ville. À la différence de tant d'espaces d'exposition « propres » elle est entièrement en béton brut. La surface consacrée aux expositions est de 150 m² et la galerie est en grande partie éclairée par une verrière située à 9 mètres de haut. Un volume d'une telle échelle permet à Eduardo Leme de présenter des œuvres de grandes dimensions et de se prêter « à cette nouvelle tendance de manifestations artistiques qui propose une esthétique de la substance ». Bien que de nombreux architectes connus se soient essayés à la conception de galeries d'art contemporain, souvent dans d'anciens lieux industriels rénovés, comme dans le quartier de Chelsea à Manhattan, Mendes da Rocha, en collaboration avec Eduardo Leme, a opté pour une voie différente dans l'association de l'art d'avant-garde et d'une architecture contemporaine du plus haut niveau.

*The powerful concrete forms of Mendes da Rocha are certainly urban in nature, and yet even as they fit into the enormous city, they also stand out.*

*Der Charakter der machtvollen Betonformen von Mendes da Rocha kann gewiss als urban gelten. Obgleich sie sich in die riesige Stadtlandschaft einfügen, stehen sie doch für sich.*

*Les formes puissantes créées par Mendes da Rocha sont certainement de nature urbaine, mais s'en distinguent néanmoins, même quand elles s'insèrent dans une ville gigantesque.*

Clearly the client and the architect have found a way of working together and created a space adapted to the unusual approach of the Leme Gallery.

Offensichtlich fanden Auftraggeber und Architekt einen Modus der Zusammenarbeit und schufen einen dem besonderen Ansatz der Galerie Leme entsprechenden Raum.

Le client et son architecte ont su collaborer pour créer un espace adapté à l'approche artistique particulière de la galerie Leme.

With its strictly controlled natural light and rather cavernous exhibition space, this is not an indifferent "white box" style of gallery.

Mit ihrem genau dosierten Tageslicht und dem höhlenartigen Ausstellungsraum gehört die Galerie nicht zu den üblichen weiß getünchten Schachteln.

Espace d'expositions presque caverneux, éclairage naturel strictement contrôlé, il ne s'agit pas ici de l'habituelle galerie style « boîte blanche ».

# MENIS ARQUITECTOS/
# AMP ARQUITECTOS

*Fernando Menis*
*Puerta Canseco 35–2°b / 38003 Santa Cruz de Tenerife / Spain*
*Tel: +34 922 288 838 / Fax: +34 922 151 925*
*E-mail: info@menis.es / Web: www.menis.es*

*AMP Arquitectos*
*c/San José, 2 ático / 38001 Santa Cruz de Tenerife / Spain*
*Tel: +34 922 245 149 / Fax: +34 922 247 173*
*E-mail: amp@arquired.es / Web: www.amparquitectos.com*

Born in Santa Cruz de Tenerife in 1951, Fernando Menis studied architecture in Barcelona, obtaining his degree in 1975 (Escola Tècnica Superior d'Arquitectura de Barcelona, ETSAB). He went on to study Urban Planning in the same school. He worked from 1976 to 1980 on projects such as the Jardin des Halles in Paris, and housing in Marne-la-Vallée, France. He also worked with the architect Ricardo Fayos in Barcelona (1977). In 1981, he created a firm with Felipe Artengo Rufino and José María Rodriguez-Pastrana Malagón by the name of Artengo, Menis, Pastrana. In 1992 the team created a new firm called Artengo, Menis, Pastrana Arquitectos (**AMP ARQUITECTOS**). In 2004 and 2005, Menis with his new independent studio, **MENIS ARQUITECTOS**, won the First Prize in competitions for the Puerto de la Cruz Harbor, Tenerife; the Cuchillitos de Tristan Park, Tenerife; 55 social-housing units, La Laguna, Tenerife; and for the rehabilitation of the historic center of Agulo and Vallehermoso, La Gomera. His work includes: the MM/MM House (Santa Cruz de Tenerife, 1998); the Offices of the President of the Government (Santa Cruz de Tenerife, 1999); 11 Bungalows, El Guincho (Tenerife, 2002); Swimming Pool on the Spree (Berlin, Germany, 2004); Magma Arts and Congress Centre (Adeje, Tenerife, 1998–2005; published here). His Athletics Stadium (Santa Cruz de Tenerife, 2002–); and Church of the Saint Redeemer (La Laguna, 2004–) are both currently under construction.

Der 1951 in Santa Cruz de Tenerife geborene Fernando Menis studierte in Barcelona an der ETSAB (Escola Tècnica Superior d'Arquitectura de Barcelona) Architektur. Nach seinem Abschluss 1975 setzte er am gleichen Institut seine Ausbildung mit einem Studium in Stadtplanung fort. Von 1976 bis 1980 arbeitete er an Projekten wie dem Jardin des Halles in Paris und Wohnungsbauvorhaben in Marne-la-Vallée, Frankreich. Außerdem war er 1977 bei dem Architekten Ricardo Fayos in Barcelona tätig. 1981 gründete er mit Felipe Artengo Rufino und José María Rodriguez-Pastrana Malagón unter dem Namen Artengo, Menis, Pastrana ein Büro. 1992 legte sich das Team die neue Bezeichnung Artengo, Menis, Pastrana Arquitectos (**AMP ARQUITECTOS**) zu. 2004 und 2005 gewann Menis mit seinem neuen unabhängigen Studio **MENIS ARQUITECTOS** erste Preise in Wettbewerben für den Hafen Puerto de la Cruz, Teneriffa, den Park Cuchillitos de Tristan, ebenfalls Teneriffa, 55 Sozialwohnungen, La Laguna, Teneriffa, und für die Sanierung des historischen Zentrums von Agulo und Vallehermoso auf La Gomera. Des Weiteren umfasst sein Œuvre: das Haus MM/MM (Santa Cruz de Tenerife, 1998), die Büros des Regierungspräsidenten (Santa Cruz de Tenerife, 1999), elf Bungalows (El Guincho, Teneriffa, 2002), Schwimmbad an der Spree (Berlin, 2004) und das hier vorgestellte Kunst- und Kongresszentrum Magma (Adeje, Teneriffa, 1998–2005). Sein Sportstadion (Santa Cruz de Tenerife, seit 2002) und die Erlöserkirche (La Laguna, seit 2004) befinden sich derzeit im Bau.

Né à Santa Cruz de Tenerife en 1951, Fernando Menis a étudié l'architecture à l'Escola Tècnica Superior d'Arquitectura de Barcelona (ETSAB) dont il est sorti diplômé en 1975, puis l'urbanisme, dans la même école, et a travaillé de 1976 à 1980 à des projets comme le Jardin des Halles à Paris ou des logements à Marne-la-Vallée, France. Il a également collaboré avec l'architecte Ricardo Fayos à Barcelona (1977). En 1981, il crée l'agence Artengo, Menis, Pastrana en association avec Felipe Artengo Rufino et José María Rodriguez-Pastrana Malagón. En 1992, l'équipe fonde une nouvelle agence, Artengo, Menis, Pastrana Arquitectos (**AMP ARQUITECTOS**). En 2004 et 2005, Menis et sa nouvelle agence indépendante, **MENIS ARQUITECTOS**, remportent le premier prix des concours organisés à Tenerife pour le Puerto de la Cruz et le Parc Cuchillitos de Tristan, cinquante-cinq appartements sociaux à La Laguna et la réhabilitation du centre historique d' Agulo et Vallehermoso, La Gomera. Parmi ses réalisations : la maison MM/MM, Santa Cruz de Tenerife (1998) ; les bureaux du président du gouvernement, Santa Cruz de Tenerife (1999) ; onze bungalows, El Guincho, Tenerife (2002) ; une piscine sur la Spree, Berlin, Allemagne (2004) ; le Centre d'art et de congrès Magma, Adeje, Tenerife (1998–2005), publié ici. Son stade d'athlétisme pour Santa Cruz de Tenerife (2002), et son église du Saint-Rédempteur à La Laguna (2004) sont actuellement en construction.

# MAGMA ARTS AND CONGRESS CENTRE

*Adeje, Tenerife, Spain, 1998–2005*

*Floor area: 27 784 m² site; 20 434 m² built area. Client: Canarias Congress Bureau Tenerife SUR SA (CCBTS). Cost: €28 962 000.*
*Architects: Fernando Martín Menis, Felipe Artengo Rufino, José Mariá Rodríguez Pastrana.*
*Collaborators: Esther Ceballos, Andreas Weihnacht, Ana Salinas. Project Manager: Fernando Merino*

This convention center for Tenerife is located near the airport and is surrounded by hotels. The architect writes, "The semidesert landscape around it and the presence of the sea are the starting points of the concept of the building. Though it is not situated directly on the water, it does have a strong relation with the ocean, an imposing presence that frames the building with a constant view of La Gomera Island." Thirteen "geometrically shaped" blocks contain program functions, such as offices, restrooms, a cafeteria, etc. "These pieces rise up," explains Menis, "creating a fault line that produces the flow of the roof, imagined as a liquid in motion, outlining the space in every direction. The undulating surface becomes fractured, creating cracks of light and ventilation, splitting and multiplying everywhere with a sensation of lightness." Conference halls are situated between the blocks, with the main room offering 2354 square meters of space, sufficient for 2500 people. This hall can be divided into as many as nine smaller conference rooms if necessary. Menis concludes, "The flowing and undulating role of the roof inside responds to technical necessities which were determined during the construction process, with the help of collaborators, among them the director of the Symphonic Orchestra of Tenerife."

Das Kongresszentrum von Teneriffa liegt in der Nähe des Flughafens und ist von Hotels umgeben. Der Architekt schreibt: »Die wüstenartige Landschaft und die Präsenz des Meeres boten sich als Ausgangspunkte der baulichen Konzeption an. Obgleich sich das Gebäude nicht unmittelbar am Wasser befindet, hat es doch eine ausgeprägte Beziehung zum Meer, das zusammen mit dem unveränderlichen Anblick der Insel La Gomera den Bau auf imposante Weise rahmt.« 13 geometrisch geformte Baukörper enthalten Funktionen wie Büros, sanitäre Anlagen, eine Cafeteria usw. »Diese Teile erheben sich«, erläutert Menis, »und bilden eine Verwerfungslinie, die den Verlauf des Dachs ergibt, das man sich als in Bewegung befindliche Flüssigkeit vorstellen kann, die den Raum in jeder Richtung nachzeichnet. Die gewellte Oberfläche bricht und lässt Licht- und Lüftungsschlitze entstehen, die sich mit scheinbarer Leichtigkeit überall teilen und vervielfältigen.« Zwischen den Blöcken wurden Kongresssäle eingefügt, deren größter 2354 m² umfasst und Platz für 2500 Besucher bietet. Dieser Saal lässt sich bei Bedarf in neun kleinere Konferenzräume unterteilen. Abschließend bemerkt Menis: »Die fließende, gewellte Beschaffenheit des Dachs entspricht im Inneren technischen Notwendigkeiten, die im Zusammenwirken mit Spezialisten, darunter der Direktor des Sinfonieorchesters von Teneriffa, während der Bauarbeiten festgelegt wurden.«

Ce Centre de congrès pour Tenerife, entouré d'hôtels, est situé près de l'aéroport. Selon le descriptif des architectes : « Le paysage semi-désertique environnant et la présence de l'océan sont les points de départ du concept de ce bâtiment. Bien qu'il ne se trouve pas directement sur l'eau, il entretient une relation forte avec l'Atlantique, présence imposante qui donne un cadre au bâtiment et l'on voit de partout l'île de La Gomera ». Treize blocs de forme géométrique contiennent divers éléments programmatiques, bureaux, cafeteria, etc. « Ces composants s'élèvent, explique Menis, en créant une ligne de faille qui entraîne le flux de la masse de la toiture, imaginée comme liquide en mouvement qui découperait l'espace dans toutes les directions. Cette surface ondulante se fracture, s'ouvre selon des failles de lumière et de ventilation, se multiplie pour donner naissance à un sentiment de légèreté. » Les salles de conférences sont situées entre les blocs. La salle principale de 2 354 m² et 2 500 places peut se fragmenter si nécessaire en unités plus petites, jusqu'à neuf . « Le rôle du flux ondulant de la toiture à l'intérieur répond à des nécessités techniques déterminées au cours du processus de construction à l'aide de collaborations diverses, dont celle du directeur de l'Orchestre symphonique de Tenerife. »

*The tilted, sloping forms recall the volcanic landscapes of Tenerife as much as any particular style of contemporary architecture.*

*Die schrägen, geneigten Formen erinnern ebenso an die vulkanische Landschaft von Teneriffa wie an irgendeine Spielart zeitgenössischer Architektur.*

*Les formes basculées et inclinées rappellent les paysages volcaniques de Tenerife ainsi qu'un style particulier d'architecture contemporaine.*

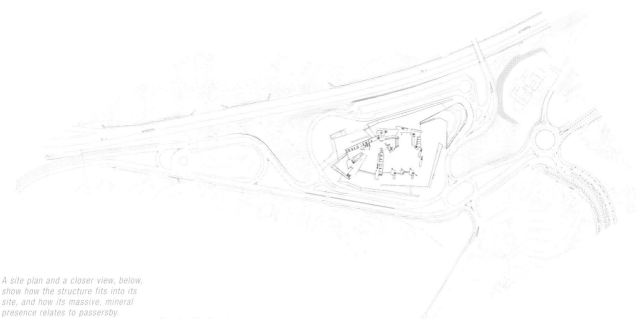

A site plan and a closer view, below, show how the structure fits into its site, and how its massive, mineral presence relates to passersby.

Ein Lageplan und die Nahsicht (unten) zeigen, wie sich der Bau in das Gelände einfügt und das Größenverhältnis seiner mächtigen, steinernen Präsenz zu den Passanten.

Un plan du site et une vue rapprochée, ci-dessous, montrent comment la structure s'intègre dans son environnement, et la relation entre les passants et cette présence massive et minérale.

*The dimensions of the walls and the ways that sun plays on them create an imposing contrast to the visitor seen on the right. On the following double-page, an interior view shows that the interior design is developed in a coherent manner.*

*Die Größe der Mauern und die Art, wie die Sonne auf ihnen spielt, stellen einen eindrucksvollen Kontrast zu der rechts sichtbaren Besucherin her. Auf der folgenden Doppelseite zeigt eine Innenansicht, dass die Innenarchitektur in kohärenter Weise gestaltet ist.*

*Les dimensions des murs et la façon dont le soleil joue sur leur surface créent un contraste impressionnant pour le visiteur (à droite). Double-page suivante : vue de l'aménagement intérieur, cohérent avec l'architecture.*

*The rough stone of the building relates it to natural rock formations but also to an almost archaic solidity.*

*Der raue Stein bringt das Bauwerk in Verbindung zu natürlichen Felsformationen, aber auch zu einer nahezu archaischen Unverwüstlichkeit.*

*La présence de la pierre brute renvoie aux formations rocheuses naturelles voisines, mais aussi à une solidité quasi archaïque.*

Interior views show rough stone surfaces and angled walls and ceilings, emphasizing the interior's cave-like or geological quality.

Auf den Innenansichten sind die rauen Steinflächen und schrägstehenden Wände und Decken zu sehen, die erneut die hier zugrunde liegende Vorstellung einer Höhle oder geologischen Formation unterstreichen.

Vues intérieures montrant les plans en pierre brute, les murs et les plafonds inclinés qui renforcent l'aspect caverneux, ou géologique, de l'approche architecturale.

The plan (right) of the building is
by no means Modernist, nor are the
strong, overhanging concrete volumes
seen in the photo below.

Der Grundriss des Gebäudes (rechts)
ist ebenso wenig modernistisch wie
die auf der Abbildung unten zu
sehenden massiven, freitragenden
Betonelemente.

Le plan (à droite) de l'immeuble n'est
en rien moderniste, pas plus que les
puissants volumes de béton en porte-
à-faux (ci-dessous).

# TOSHIKO MORI

*Toshiko Mori Architect*
*180 Varick Street, Suite 1322*
*New York, NY 10014*
*USA*

*Tel: +1 212 337 9644 / Fax: +1 212 337 9647*
*E-mail: info@tmarch.com / Web: www.tmarch.com*

**TOSHIKO MORI** attended the Cooper Union School of Art, and School of Architecture (1970–76), and received an Honorary Master of Architecture degree from the Harvard School of Design in 1996. She has worked on numerous retail stores, such as Nigel French International (New York, 1991); Comme des Garçons (New York, 1998); Kyoto Arts & Fashions (New York, 1989); as well as corporate offices, such as Sony Research Laboratories (New York, 1996). She completed the Issey Miyake Pleats Please Boutique with Gwenaël Nicolas in the SoHo area of New York in 1998. She also worked on the Issey Miyake Store on Madison Avenue, and the Comme des Garçons Shirt Store, also in Manhattan. In January 2002, Toshiko Mori was appointed to Chair of the Department of Architecture at the Harvard School of Design, where she has taught since 1995. On the occasion of her nomination, Peter Rowe, Dean of the Harvard Design School, commented, "Mori is an exceptional educator and practicing architect, and the School benefits greatly from her deep experience, knowledge, and keen exploration of topics and issues in architecture and design." Prior to joining the faculty at Harvard, Toshiko Mori taught for more than a decade at the Cooper Union. She has served as a visiting faculty member at Columbia University and Yale University, where she was the Eero Saarinen Visiting Professor in 1992. Among others, she has built: House in Connecticut I (New Canaan, Connecticut, 1994); House in Maine I (Cushing, Maine, 2001); House in Maine II (Penobscot Bay, Maine, 2004); two buildings in Casey Key (Florida), together with the house addition published here; and designed the Frank Lloyd Wright's Darwin D. Martin House Complex Visitor Center (Buffalo, New York, in progress).

**TOSHIKO MORI** studierte an der Cooper Union School of Art und School of Architecture (1970–76) und erhielt 1996 von der Harvard School of Design einen Master of Architecture ehrenhalber. Sie arbeitete an der Gestaltung zahlreicher Ladengeschäfte wie Nigel French International (New York, 1991), Comme des Garçons (New York, 1998), Kyoto Arts & Fashions (New York, 1989) sowie an Firmenbüros wie den Sony Research Laboratories (New York, 1996). 1998 vollendete sie mit Gwenaël Nicolas im SoHo-Gebiet von Manhattan die Boutique Issey Miyake Pleats Please. Darüber hinaus arbeitete sie am Issey Miyake Store an der Madison Avenue und am ebenfalls in Manhattan befindlichen Hemdengeschäft von Comme des Garçons. Im Januar 2002 wurde Toshiko Mori zur Vorsitzenden der Architekturfakultät an der Harvard School of Design berufen, wo sie seit 1995 lehrte. Anlässlich ihrer Berufung äußerte sich Peter Rowe, Dekan der Harvard School of Design: »Mori ist eine außergewöhnliche Lehrerin und praktizierende Architektin und die Schule profitiert eminent von ihrer großen Erfahrung, ihrem Wissen und ihrer scharfsinnigen Auslotung von Themen und Fragen zu Architektur und Design.« Ehe Mori den Ruf nach Harvard erhielt, hatte sie mehr als ein Jahrzehnt lang an der Cooper Union gelehrt. Sie hatte Gastprofessuren an der Columbia und der Yale University inne, wo sie 1992 Eero-Saarinen-Gastprofessorin war. Sie baute u. a.: Haus in Connecticut I (New Canaan, Connecticut, 1994), Haus in Maine I (Cushing, Maine, 2001), Haus in Maine II (Penobscot Bay, Maine, 2004), zwei Gebäude in Casey Key (Florida) zusammen mit dem hier publizierten Anbau und sie entwarf das Besucherzentrum Frank Lloyd Wright's Darwin D. Martin House (Buffalo, New York, im Bau).

**TOSHIKO MORI** a étudié à l'École d'art et à l'École d'architecture de la Cooper Union (1970–76). Elle est M. Arch honoraire de l'École de Design d'Harvard (1996). Elle a travaillé à de nombreux projets de magasins comme Nigel French International, New York (1991); Comme des Garçons, New York (1998); Kyoto Arts & Fashion, New York (1989), ainsi que des bureaux d'entreprises dont les Sony Research Laboratories, New York (1996). En 1998, elle a réalisé la boutique d'Issey Miyake, Pleats Please, en collaboration avec Gwenaël Nicolas à Soho, New York (1998), le magasin Issey Miyake de Madison Avenue et celui de Comme des Garçons Shirt, également à Manhattan. En janvier 2002, elle a été nommée à la présidence du département d'Architecture de l'École de Design d'Harvard, où elle enseignait depuis 1995. Lors de sa nomination, Peter Rowe, doyen de cette école a déclaré : «Mori est une éducatrice exceptionnelle et une architecte remarquable et très active. L'école bénéficie grandement de son expérience et de sa connaissance approfondies, ainsi que de sa volonté d'explorer avec finesse les sujets et enjeux de l'architecture et du design. » Avant de rejoindre Harvard, elle avait enseigné pendant plus de deux ans à la Cooper Union et avait été enseignante invitée à Columbia University et Yale University où elle avait été professeur invité «Eero Saarinen» en 1992. Elle a réalisé, entre autres : House in Connecticut I, New Canaan, Connecticut (1994); House in Maine I, Cushing, Maine (2001); House in Maine II, Penobscot Bay, Maine (2004); deux immeubles à Casey Key (Floride); l'extension d'une maison, publiée ici, et conçu le Frank Lloyd Wright's Darwin D. Martin House Complex Visitor Center, Buffalo, New York (projet en cours).

# ADDITION TO HOUSE
# ON THE GULF OF MEXICO I

*Casey Key, Florida, USA, 2004–05*

*Floor area: 186 m². Client: not disclosed. Cost: not disclosed*

Toshiko Mori was called on to create an addition to a house designed by the respected architect Paul Rudolph in 1957. The site, in Casey Key, Florida, to the south of Sarasota, is on a narrow sand bar. The older house is located to the south of the site, and a guest house, also designed by Toshiko Mori, is on the northern end of the plot. The new addition is set on the southeast corner of the site, and is connected to the existing house by a translucent canopy. A kitchen and dining area occupy the ground floor of the addition and open out onto a swimming pool. A master bedroom, bath, and terrace are on the upper floor. The addition, designed with glass, concrete and steel, has a fiberglass and carbon fiber exterior stairway, materials chosen "because of their resistance to the extreme climatic conditions on the site." The large glazed surface of the addition affords generous views of the garden with its large trees.

Toshiko Mori erhielt den Auftrag, einen Anbau für ein Haus zu konzipieren, das der renommierte Architekt Paul Rudolph im Jahr 1957 entworfen hatte. Der Baugrund auf Casey Key südlich von Sarasota befindet sich auf einer schmalen Sandbank. Das ältere Haus liegt im Süden des Geländes und ein ebenfalls von Toshiko Mori entworfenes Gästehaus am nördlichen Ende des Grundstücks. Der neue Anbau steht an der südwestlichen Ecke des Baugrunds und ist mit dem bestehenden Haus durch ein lichtdurchlässiges Schutzdach verbunden. Im Erdgeschoss des Anbaus sind Küche und Essbereich untergebracht, durch eine Öffnung gelangt man zum Schwimmbecken. Im Obergeschoss finden Hauptschlafraum, Bad und Terrasse Platz. Der aus Glas, Beton und Stahl errichtete Anbau verfügt über eine Außentreppe aus Fiberglas und Karbonfaser, Materialien, die »wegen ihrer Beständigkeit angesichts der hier herrschenden extremen klimatischen Bedingungen« gewählt wurden. Der großflächig verglaste Anbau erlaubt zahlreiche Ausblicke in den mit hohen Bäumen bestandenen Garten.

Toshiko Mori avait été appelée pour créer l'extension d'une maison conçue en 1957 par le très respecté Paul Rudolph. Casey Key, en Floride au sud de Sarasota, est une étroite bande de sable. La maison existante se trouve en partie sud du site et une maison d'amis, également due à Toshiko Mori, au nord. La nouvelle extension occupe l'angle sud-est du terrain et se rattache à la maison existante par un auvent translucide. La cuisine et la salle des repas se trouvent au rez-de-chaussée, ouvert sur une piscine. Une chambre principale, une salle de bains et une terrasse constituent l'étage. L'extension, en verre, béton et acier, possède un escalier extérieur en fibre de verre et de carbone, matériaux choisis « pour leur résistance aux conditions climatiques extrêmes que connaît cet endroit ». De vastes plans vitrés permettent de généreuses perspectives sur le jardin et ses grands arbres.

Toshiko Mori's elevated addition has an unobtrusive presence and is well adapted to its natural surroundings.

Toshiko Moris erhöhter Anbau scheint sich mit einer der natürlichen Umgebung angepassten, leichtgewichtigen Präsenz in die Gartenlandschaft einzufügen.

L'extension surélevée de Toshiko Mori semble s'insérer avec facilité dans le cadre du jardin. La légèreté de sa présence est adaptée à son environnement.

*Seen at night near the swimming pool, the addition is largely transparent, and is formed through a strong contrast between its vertical column elements and the horizontal floor and roof planes.*

*Nachts am Swimmingpool aufgenommen, wirkt der Anbau weitgehend transparent und ist durch den starken Kontrast zwischen seinen vertikalen Stützen und den horizontalen Geschoss- und Dachflächen geprägt.*

*Vue la nuit, près de la piscine, l'extension est en grande partie transparente, et présente de forts contrastes entre ses colonnes verticales et les plans horizontaux des sols et de la toiture.*

*Reflecting the garden and blending into it, the rectilinear forms of the addition are softened by the close presence of vegetation.*

*Die rechtwinkligen Formen des Anbaus, die den Garten reflektieren und mit ihm verschmelzen, werden durch die nahe Vegetation gemildert.*

*Réfléchissant le jardin et fusionnant avec lui, les formes orthogonales de l'extension sont adoucies par la présence de la végétation.*

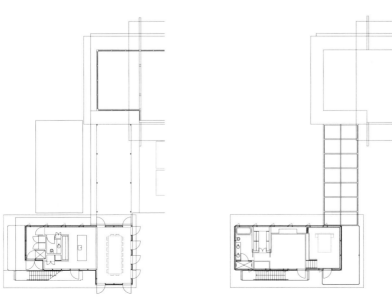

The crisp lines of the architecture are
complemented by a sober choice of
modern furniture. The floor to ceiling
glazing means that nature is
omnipresent.

*Die scharfen Linien der Architektur
werden durch klug gewähltes modernes Mobiliar ergänzt. Die deckenhohe
Verglasung führt zur ständigen Präsenz der Natur überall im Haus.*

*Les lignes tendues de l'architecture
se complètent d'un choix de mobilier
moderne et sobre. Les vitres toute
hauteur s'ouvrent sur la nature qui
entoure la maison.*

# MORPHOSIS

*Morphosis*
*2041 Colorado Avenue*
*Santa Monica, CA 90404*
*USA*

*Tel: +1 310 453 2247*
*Fax: +1 310 829 3270*
*E-mail: studio@morphosis.net*
*Web: www.morphosis.net*

**MORPHOSIS** principal Thom Mayne, born in Connecticut in 1944, received his B.Arch degree in 1968 from USC, and his M.Arch degree from Harvard in 1978. He created Morphosis in 1972 with Jim Stafford. Thom Mayne has taught at UCLA, Harvard, Yale, and SCI-Arc, of which he was a founding faculty member. Some of the main buildings by Morphosis are, in California, the Lawrence House (Hermosa Beach, 1981); Kate Mantilini Restaurant (Beverly Hills, 1986); Cedar's Sinai Comprehensive Cancer Care Center (Beverly Hills, 1987); Crawford Residence (Montecito, 1987–92); Yuzen Vintage Car Museum (project, West Hollywood, 1992); Blades Residence (Santa Barbara, 1992–97); International Elementary School (Long Beach, 1997–99); Diamond Ranch High School (Pomona, 1996–2000); as well as in Austria the Hypo Alpe-Adria Center (Klagenfurt, 1996–2002). More recent work includes the Caltrans District 7 Headquarters (Los Angeles, 2001–04); Science Center School (Los Angeles, 2004); San Francisco Federal Building; the University of Cincinnati Student Recreation Center (Cincinnati, Ohio, 1999–2005); NOAA Satellite Operation Facility in Suitland (Maryland, 2001–05); Wayne L. Morse U. S. Courthouse (Eugene, Oregon, 1999–2006); New Academic Building for the Cooper Union for the Advancement of Science and Art (New York, 2004–08); proposal for the 2012 Olympics in New York City made prior to the selection of London; and Phare Tower (Paris, 2006–12, published here). Thom Mayne was the winner of the 2005 Pritzker Prize.

Der Leiter von **MORPHOSIS**, Thom Mayne, wurde 1944 in Connecticut geboren, erwarb 1968 den Grad eines B.Arch. an der University of Southern California (USC) und 1978 den eines M.Arch. in Harvard. 1972 gründete er Morphosis mit Jim Stafford. Tom Mayne lehrte an der UCLA, in Harvard, Yale und am SCI-Arc, zu dessen Gründungsmitgliedern er gehörte. Zu den wichtigsten Bauten von Morphosis zählen in Kalifornien: Lawrence House (Hermosa Beach, 1981), Kate Mantilini Restaurant (Beverly Hills, 1986), Cedar's Sinai Krebsklinik (Beverly Hills, 1987), Wohnhaus Crawford (Montecito, 1987–92), Yuzen Vintage Automuseum (Projekt, West-Hollywood, 1992), Wohnhaus Blades (Santa Barbara, 1992–97), Internationale Grundschule (Long Beach, 1997–99), Diamond Ranch High School (Pomona, 1996–2000) und in Österreich das Hypo Alpe-Adria Center (Klagenfurt, 1996–2002). In jüngerer Zeit entstanden die Caltrans District 7 Zentrale (Los Angeles, 2001–2004), die Science Center School (Los Angeles, 2004), das San Francisco Federal Building, das Studentenzentum an der University of Cincinnati (Cincinnati, Ohio, 1999–2005), die Satellitenbetriebseinrichtung der NOAA in Suitland (Maryland, 2001–05), das Wayne L. Morse U. S. Courthouse (Eugene, Oregon, 1999–2006), das New Academic Building der Cooper Union zur Förderung von Wissenschaft und Kunst (New York, 2004–08), ein Entwurf für die Olympischen Spiele 2012 in New York City (vor der Wahl Londons als Austragungsort entstanden) sowie der Phare Tower (Paris, 2006–12, hier publiziert). Thom Mayne erhielt 2005 den Pritzker-Preis.

Le directeur de **MORPHOSIS**, Thom Mayne, né dans le Connecticut en 1944, est B. Arch de USC (1968) et M. Arch. d'Harvard (1978). Il crée Morphosis en 1972 avec Jim Stafford. Thom Mayne a enseigné à UCLA, Harvard, Yale, et SCI-Arc dont il est un des fondateurs. Parmi les principales réalisations de Morphosis, en Californie : Lawrence House, Hermosa Beach (1981) ; Kate Mantilini Restaurant, Beverly Hills (1986) ; le Cedar's Sinai Comprehensive Cancer Care Center, Beverly Hills, (1987) ; la Crawford Residence, Montecito (1987–92) ; le Yuzen Vintage Car Museum (projet, West Hollywood, 1992) ; la Blades Residence, Santa Barbara (1992–97) ; l'International Elementary School de Long Beach (1997–99) ; la Diamond Ranch High School, Pomona (1996–2000), et, en Autriche, le Hypo-Alpe Adria Center à Klagenfurt (1996–2002). Plus récemment, il a réalisé le siège de Caltrans District 7, Los Angeles (2001–04) ; le centre fédéral de San Francisco ; le centre de loisirs de l'Université de Cincinnati, Ohio (1999–2005) ; le centre opérationnel satellitaire NOAA à Suitland, Maryland (2001–05) ; le tribunal fédéral Wayne L. Morse, Eugene, Oregon (1999–2006) ; le nouvel immeuble du Cooper Union for the Advancement of Science and Art, New York (2004–08) ; une proposition pour les Jeux Olympiques 2012 à New York, avant la sélection de Londres, et le projet de la Tour Phare, Paris La Défense (2006–12) publié ici. Thom Mayne a reçu le Pritzker Prize en 2005.

# PHARE TOWER
*Paris, France, 2006–12*

Floor area: 130 000 m². Client: Unibail, EPAD. Cost: not disclosed

In November 2006, Morphosis was selected from a group of 10 international architects, including Herzog & de Meuron, Rem Koolhaas, and Jean Nouvel, to build the first, new very tall building in Paris in many years. To be located in the La Défense district, almost on the axis of the Arc of Triumph and the Champs-Elysées, the 300-meter-high, 68-story office tower has been described as a "beacon of optimism and progress." Set near the landmark CNIT building (Centre des Nouvelles Industries et Technologies, Robert Camelot, Jean de Mailly, Bernard Zehrfuss, 1956–58) and connected to it by enclosed exterior escalators, the Phare will have a 60-meter-hight lobby. In the spirit of this open public space, gardens, cafés and shops will be distributed vertically through the tower and will remain accessible to outsiders. The architects refer to the technologically innovative spirit of Gustave Eiffel, the author of the only other 300-meter-high landmark in Paris, in describing their scheme. The double-skinned structure is carefully designed to avoid undue solar gain while maximizing natural daylight. Futuristic windmills will top the building, providing "clean, alternative energy to power the fans that activate the building's natural ventilation system." Thom Mayne, the Design Director of Morphosis, concludes, "There's a fluidity, a sensuousness, a softness to the form as it reaches to the sky. Moving around the tower, it appears to shift continually, distinct from different vantage points—not a single image, but a dynamic structure that responds to its site, environment, and performance requirements."

Im November 2006 wurde Morphosis aus einer Gruppe von zehn internationalen Architekturbüros, darunter Herzog & de Meuron, Rem Koolhaas und Jean Nouvel, ausgewählt, das seit Jahren erste neue Hochhaus in Paris zu bauen. Der im Viertel La Défense fast auf der Achse des Arc de Triomphe und der Champs-Elysées geplante 300 m hohe Büroturm mit 68 Geschossen wurde als ein »Fanal des Optimismus' und Fortschritts« beschrieben. Der unweit des markanten CNIT-Gebäudes (Centre des Nouvelles Industries et Technologies, Robert Camelot, Jean de Mailly, Bernard Zehrfuss, 1956–58) entstehende und mit diesem durch geschlossene Außenaufzüge verbundene Phare Tower wird über eine 60 m hohe Lobby verfügen. Im Geiste dieses offen zugänglichen Bereichs werden im Turm vertikal Gärten, Cafés und Läden verteilt sein, die auf Dauer für die Allgemeinheit nutzbar bleiben werden. Bei der Beschreibung seiner Planung bezieht sich der Architekt auf den technisch innovativen Geist Gustave Eiffels, Schöpfer des einzigen anderen, über 300 m hohen Bauwerks in Paris. Der Phare Tower wird dank seiner doppelschaligen Beschaffenheit gegen unerwünschte Erwärmung durch Sonneneinstrahlung geschützt sein und gleichzeitig ein Maximum an Tageslicht erhalten. Futuristische Windräder werden den Turm bekrönen und »saubere alternative Energie liefern, mit der die Ventilatoren betrieben werden, die das natürliche Belüftungssystem des Gebäudes in Gang setzen«. Thom Mayne, der leitende Architekt von Morphosis, bemerkt abschließend: »Die dem Himmel zustrebende Form zeichnet sich durch ein Fließen, durch Sinnlichkeit und Weichheit aus. Beim Umrunden des Turms entsteht der Eindruck, er verschiebe sich ständig, wirke unterschiedlich aus allen Blickwinkeln – nicht ein einziges Bild, sondern ein dynamischer Bau, der auf seinen Standort, seine Umgebung und seine funktionalen Anforderungen reagiert.«

C'est en novembre 2006 que Morphosis a été sélectionnée parmi dix autres agences internationales dont Herzog & de Meuron, Rem Koolhaas et Jean Nouvel pour construire le premier immeuble de grande hauteur réalisé à Paris depuis de longues années. Située dans le quartier d'affaires de La Défense, presque dans l'axe de l'Arc de triomphe et des Champs-Elysées, cette tour de 68 niveaux et de 300 mètres de haut a été décrite comme « un phare d'optimisme et de progrès ». Implantée près du monumental CNIT (Centre des nouvelles industries et technologies, de Robert Camelot, Jean de Mailly, Bernard Zehrfuss, 1956–58) auquel elle sera reliée par ses escalators extérieurs, elle s'ouvrira sur un hall de 60 mètres de haut. Dans un esprit d'ouverture, jardins, cafés et boutiques sont organisés à la verticale de la tour et accessibles au public. Les architectes se sont inspirés de la technologie d'Eiffel, qui a construit le seul bâtiment de plus de 300 mètres de haut à Paris. La double peau de la façade a été étudiée pour limiter la chaleur du soleil, tout en optimisant la lumière du jour. Des éoliennes futuristes situées en haut du bâtiment produisent une « énergie propre, alternative, qui fournit l'électricité nécessaire au système de ventilation. » Thom Mayne, directeur artistique de Morphosis, conclut : « Il y a comme une fluidité, une sensibilité, une douceur de la forme quand elle s'approche du ciel. Suivant le point de vue où l'on se trouve, la tour change continuellement d'aspect. On n'a donc pas une image unique, mais une structure dynamique qui répond à un site, un environnement et des exigences de performances. »

Numerous attempts have been made to design large buildings for the Défense area of Paris, and it appears that the Morphosis tower, more radical in concept than most of its neighbors, will in fact be built.

Es wurden verschiedentlich Versuche unternommen, dem La-Défense-Viertel in Paris große Bauten hinzuzufügen, aber nun scheint der Turm von Morphosis, wiewohl radikaler als die meisten Nachbarbauten, tatsächlich realisiert zu werden.

De nombreuses tentatives d'immeubles de très grande hauteur ont été proposées pour le quartier de La Défense à Paris, mais il semble que cette fois la tour de Morphosis, plus radicale de concept que le plupart de ses voisines, ait toutes les chances d'être construite.

# NEUTELINGS RIEDIJK

*Neutelings Riedijk Architecten bv*
*P. O. Box 527*
*3000 AM Rotterdam*
*The Netherlands*

*Tel: +31 10 404 6677*
*Fax: +31 10 414 2712*
*E-mail: info@neutelings-riedijk.com*
*Web: www.neutelings-riedijk.com*

**WILLEM JAN NEUTELINGS** was born in 1959 in Bergen op Zoom. He studied at the Technical University in Delft (1977–81), before working for OMA with Rem Koolhaas (1981–86). He has taught at the Academy of Architecture in Rotterdam and at the Berlage Institute in Amsterdam (1990–99). **MICHIEL RIEDIJK** was born in Geldrop, The Netherlands, in 1964. He attended the Technical University in Delft (1983–89), before working with J. D. Bekkering in Amsterdam (1989–91). He has taught at the Technical Univeristy in Delft and Eindhoven, and at the Academies of Architecture in Amsterdam, Rotterdam and Maastricht. Their built, mainly in The Netherlands, work includes the Prinsenhoek Residential Complex (Sittard, 1992–95); Tilburg Housing (1993–96); Hollainhof Social Housing (Ghent, Belgium, 1993–98); Borneo Sporenburg Housing (Amsterdam, 1994–97); Lakeshore Housing, first phase (Huizen, 1994–96); and building for Veenman Printers (Ede, 1995–97). One of their most widely published projects is the Minnaert Building (Utrecht, 1994–98). They have also built fire stations in Breda (1996–98) and Maastricht (1996–99). In 2004, they won the competition for the Kolizej Centre in Ljubljana, Slovenia, which is to include a 1400-seat concert hall, 25 000 square meters of office space, 100 apartments, a shopping arcade, and a parking lot. They completed the Shipping and Transport College in Rotterdam in 2005, and the Netherlands Institute for Sound and Vision in Hilversum in 2006 (published here).

**WILLEM JAN NEUTELINGS** wurde 1959 in Bergen op Zoom geboren. Er studierte an der Technischen Universität in Delft (1977–81), ehe er von 1981 bis 1986 bei OMA mit Rem Koolhaas arbeitete. Anschließend lehrte er an der Architekturakademie in Rotterdam und am Berlage-Institut in Amsterdam (1990–99). **MICHIEL RIEDIJK** wurde 1964 in Geldorp in den Niederlanden geboren. Er besuchte die Technische Universität in Delft (1983–89), ehe er mit J. D. Bekkering in Amsterdam arbeitete (1989–91). Er lehrte an den Technischen Universitäten Delft und Eindhoven sowie an den Architekturakademien in Amsterdam, Rotterdam und Maastricht. Zu den gemeinsamen Bauten der beiden, fast alle in den Niederlanden, gehören: Wohnanlage Prinsenhoek (Sittard, 1992–95), Wohnbauten Tilburg (1993–96), Sozialwohnungen Hollainhof (Gent, Belgien, 1993–98), Wohnbauten Borneo Sporenburg (Amsterdam, 1994–97), Lakeshore Housing, erster Abschnitt (Huizen, 1994–96), und das Gebäude für Veenman Printers (Ede, 1995–97). Eines ihrer bekanntesten Projekte ist das Minnaert-Gebäude (Utrecht, 1994–98). Außerdem erbauten sie Feuerwachen in Breda (1996–98) und Maastricht (1996–99). 2004 gewannen sie den Wettbewerb für das Kolizej-Zentrum in Ljubljana, Slowenien, zu dem eine Konzerthalle mit 1400 Plätzen, 25 000 m² Bürofläche, 100 Apartments, eine Ladenpassage und ein Parkgelände gehören sollen. 2005 stellten sie die Hochschule für Schifffahrts- und Transportwesen in Rotterdam fertig und 2006 das hier vorgestellte Niederländische Institut für Bild und Ton in Hilversum.

**WILLEM JAN NEUTELINGS**, né en 1959 à Bergen Op Zoom, Pays-Bas, a étudié à l'Université Technique de Delft (1977–81) et travaillé pour l'Office for Metropolitan Architecture de Rem Koolhaas (1981–86). Il a enseigné à l'Académie d'architecture de Rotterdam et au Berlage Institute d'Amsterdam (1990–99). **MICHIEL RIEDIJK**, né à Geldrop, Pays-Bas, en 1964, a étudié à l'Université Technique de Delft (1983–89), avant de travailler avec J. D. Bekkering à Amsterdam (1989–91). Il a enseigné à l'Université Technique de Delft et d'Eindhoven et aux Académies d'architecture d'Amsterdam, Rotterdam et Maastricht. Parmi leurs réalisations, dont la plupart aux Pays-Bas : le Complexe résidentiel de Prinsenhoek, Sittard (1992–95) ; un immeuble d'appartements à Tilburg (1993–96) ; l'immeuble de logements Borneo Sporenburg, Amsterdam (1994–97) ; des logements à Lakeshore, phase 1, Huizen (1994–96) ; l'immeuble de Veenman Printers, Ede (1995–97). L'un de leurs projets les plus publiés est l'immeuble Minnaert, Utrecht (1994–98). Ils ont construit des casernes de pompiers à Breda (1996–98) et Maastricht (1996–99). En 2004, ils ont remporté le concours pour le Centre Kolizej à Ljubljana, Slovénie, comprenant une salle de concert de 1 400 places, 25 000 m² de bureaux, 100 appartements, un centre commercial et un parking. Ils ont achevé le Collège de la navigation et des transports en 2005 et l'Institut néerlandais de l'audiovisuel à Hilversum en 2006, publié ici.

# NETHERLANDS INSTITUTE FOR SOUND AND VISION

*Hilversum, The Netherlands, 2003–06*

*Floor area: 30 000 m². Client: Netherlands Institute for Sound and Vision, Hilversum. Cost: €40 million.*
*Team: Willem Jan Neutelings, Michiel Riedijk, Frank Beelen, Joost Mulders, Tania Ally, Wessel Vreugdenhil, Lennaart Sirag,*
*Bas Suijkerbuijk, Julia Söffing, Willem Bruijn, Stan Vandriessche, Wonne Ickx, Patricia Lopes Simóes.*
*Architectural Design and Façade Concept: Neutelings Riedijk Architecten in cooperation with Bureau Bouwkunde Rotterdam.*
*Graphic Design of the façade: Studio Jaap Drupsteen*

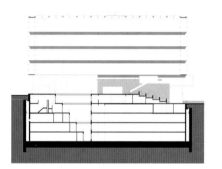 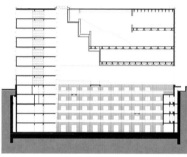 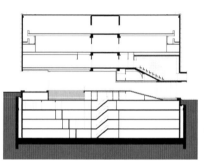

The Netherlands Institute for Sound and Vision has the task of archiving all of the audiovisual material produced in the country, from the earliest recordings to the present. The building contains five essential elements—archives, a museum, offices, client reception, and services, grouped together around a central "well" at the heart of the building. The structure was essentially divided into two horizontally because roughly half of the program was dedicated to the storage of the archives and thus required specific climatic and lighting conditions. The storage vault is located below grade, while the museum is above ground. A "canyon" in the entrance area leading down to the vault gives visitors an idea of the large scale of the facility. There are five levels underground and five above. The architects explain that "the central well culminates in an enormous void where both museum and offices show their best face. The upside-down cascade of museum levels registers as a wall sculpture that shapes and scales the internal space of the building." The unusual façade of the building depicts famous images from Dutch television, in a composition conceived by the architects with the graphic designer Jaap Drupsteen. Sophisticated new technology was used to create no less than 748 different glass panels.

Das Niederländische Institut für Bild und Ton hat die Aufgabe, alle je im Land produzierten audiovisuellen Materialien von der frühesten Aufzeichnung bis zu Gegenwart zu archivieren. Das Bauwerk umfasst fünf wesentliche Elemente – Archive, ein Museum, Büros, Kundenempfang und Serviceeinrichtungen, die um einen zentralen »Schacht« im Herzen des Gebäudes gruppiert sind. Der Bau wurde im Grunde horizontal zweigeteilt, da etwa die Hälfte des Raumprogramms der Unterbringung der Archive gewidmet ist und von daher spezifische Klima- und Lichtverhältnisse erfordert. Die Archivräume befinden sich unter, das Museum über der Erde. Ein »Schacht« im Eingangsbereich, der zu dem Gewölbe hinunterführt, vermittelt den Besuchern eine Vorstellung von der Größe der Anlage. Fünf Ebenen befinden sich unter, weitere fünf über der Erde. Die Architekten erläutern: »Der zentrale Lichtschacht mündet in einen riesigen Hohlraum, wo Museum und Büros ihre Schauseite präsentieren. Die umgekehrte Kaskade der Museumsebenen prägt sich als Wandskulptur ein, von der die Innenräume des Gebäudes Form und Maßstab erhalten.« Auf der ungewöhnlichen Fassade des Gebäudes sind in einer Komposition der Architekten und dem Grafiker Jaap Drupsteen berühmte Bilder des niederländischen Fernsehens abgebildet. Mithilfe neuester Computertechnologie wurden nicht weniger als 748 verschiedene Glasscheiben geschaffen.

L'Institut néerlandais de l'audiovisuel a pour tâche l'archivage de tous les matériaux audiovisuels produits dans le pays, des premiers enregistrements à nos jours. L'immeuble comprend cinq éléments essentiels : archives, musée, bureaux, réception des clients et services, regroupés autour d'un « puits » central. L'ensemble a été divisé à peu près horizontalement en deux parties. La moitié du programme est consacrée aux archives qui réclament des conditions d'éclairage et de climatisation particulières. Le stockage est situé en sous-sol, le musée en surface. De l'entrée, un « canyon » conduisant aux salles de conservation permet aux visiteurs de prendre conscience de la très grande échelle de ces installations. Cinq niveaux sont en sous-sol et quatre au-dessus du rez-de-chaussée. Selon les architectes : « Le puits central s'ouvre en un énorme vide où le musée et les bureaux se présentent sous leur meilleur jour. La cascade inversée des niveaux du musée se lit comme une sculpture murale donnant sa forme et son échelle au volume intérieur du bâtiment. » La curieuse façade – une composition conçue par les architectes en collaboration avec le graphiste Jaap Drupsteen – utilise des images célèbres tirées de programmes de télévision néerlandais. Une technologie nouvelle sophistiquée a servi à créer pas moins de 748 panneaux différents.

*The section drawings above show the substantial part of the structure that is located below grade, allowing the whole to appear less massive than it is in reality.*

*Auf der Schnittzeichnung oben erkennt man den erheblichen unterirdischen Anteil des Gebäudes, aufgrunddessen es weniger wuchtig wirkt.*

*Les coupes ci-dessus montrent la partie substantielle construite en sous-sol, ce qui permet de donner à l'ensemble un aspect moins massif que son volume réel.*

The multicolored façade is one of the key elements of the design. Visible both day and night, the glass design comprises television images.

Die farbenfrohe Fassade ist eines der Schlüsselelemente des Entwurfs. Das bei Tag und Nacht sichtbare Glasdekor wurde aus Fernsehbildern entwickelt.

La façade de verre multicolore est l'un des éléments-clés de ce projet. Visible de jour comme de nuit, cette composition s'inspire d'images de télévision.

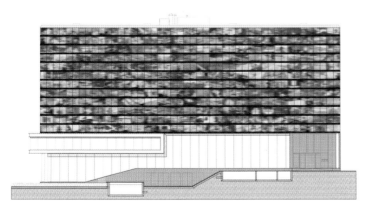

The colored glass of the façades generates a good deal more variety in the light of interior spaces than would have been the case with a more traditional cladding.

Das farbige Glas der Fassaden erzeugt eine weit größere Vielfalt der Innenbeleuchtung, als es eine herkömmliche Verkleidung gekonnt hätte.

Le verre de couleur des façades crée une grande variété d'éclairages à l'intérieur, beaucoup plus importante qu'avec un habillage plus classique.

Color, or the contrast between vivid colors and the more sober palette of interior materials, enlivens vast spaces that are intended to protect the archive's holdings from light and other sources of potential decay.

Farbe bzw. der Kontrast zwischen leuchtenden Farben und den gedämpfteren Tönen der im Inneren verwendeten Materialien belebt die riesigen Räume, die Archivmaterial vor Licht und anderen zerstörerischen Einflüssen schützen sollen.

La couleur, ou le contraste entre les couleurs vives des façades et la palette plus sobre des matériaux intérieurs, animent les vastes espaces destinés aux archives qui doivent être protégées de la lumière et autres facteurs de dégradation.

With its bridges and enigmatic red
openings, the interior space takes
on a Piranesian aspect well adapted
to its large underground storage
areas.

Mit seinen Brücken und rätselhaften
roten Öffnungen erinnert der Innenraum an Werke Piranesis, passend
zu den riesigen unterirdischen Lager-
räumen.

Avec ses passerelles et ses étranges
ouvertures rouges, l'espace intérieur
prend l'aspect d'un Piranèse bien
adapté à ces grands espaces
d'archivages souterrains.

In the image above, solid and opaque
volumes are contrasted with plunging
openings and a glazed view to the
outside. Right, the auditorium.

Im Bild oben stehen massive, opake
Elemente abgrundtiefen Öffnungen
und verglasten Ausblicken nach
draußen gegenüber; rechts das Auditorium.

Dans l'image ci-dessus, des volumes
aveugles et opaques contrastent avec
des ouvertures plongeantes et une
vue vers l'extérieur à travers une
baie vitrée. À droite, l'auditorium.

# OSCAR NIEMEYER

*Oscar Niemeyer*
*Avenida Atlântica 3940 cob. 1001*
*CEP: 22070–002, Rio de Janeiro, RJ*
*Brazil*

*Tel: +55 21 523 4890*
*Fax: +55 21 267 6388*
*E-mail: arquitetura@oscarniemeyer.com.br*

Born in Rio de Janeiro in 1907, **OSCAR NIEMEYER** studied at the Escola Nacional de Belas Artes. He graduated in 1934 and joined a team of Brazilian architects collaborating with Le Corbusier on a new Ministry of Education and Health in Rio de Janeiro. It was Lucio Costa, for whom he worked as an assistant, who introduced Niemeyer to Le Corbusier. Between 1940 and 1954, his work was based in three cities: Rio de Janeiro, São Paulo and Belo Horizonte. In 1956, Niemeyer was appointed architectural adviser to Nova Cap—an organization responsible for implementing Lucio Costa's plans for Brazil's new capital, Brasília. The following year, he became its chief architect, designing most of the city's important buildings. In 1964, he sought exile in France for political reasons. There, amongst other structures, he designed the building for the French Communist Party, in Paris. With the end of the dictatorship, he returned to Brazil, immediately resuming his professional activities. He was awarded the Gold Medal of the American Institute of Architecture in 1970 and the 1988 Pritzker Prize. Despite the fact that he will celebrate his 100th birthday at the end of 2007, Niemeyer has continued to work on numerous large projects, including an Administrative Center for the province of Minas Gerais in Belo Horizonte; an Auditorium completed in 2005 to celebrate the 50th anniversary of his Ibirapuera Park in São Paulo (published here); and Cultural Center in Goiânia completed in 2007 (also published here).

Der 1907 in Rio de Janeiro geborene **OSCAR NIEMEYER** studierte an der Escola Nacional de Belas Artes. Er machte seinen Abschluss 1934 und schloss sich einem Team brasilianischer Architekten an, die mit Le Corbusier beim Bau eines neuen Ministeriums für Erziehung und Gesundheit zusammenarbeiteten. Er war Assistent bei Lucio Costa, der ihn mit Le Corbusier bekannt machte. Zwischen 1940 und 1954 baute er in drei Städten: Rio de Janeiro, São Paulo und Belo Horizonte. 1956 wurde Niemeyer zum architektonischen Berater von Nova Cap berufen – einer Organisation, die für die Umsetzung von Lucio Costas Plänen für Brasília, die neue Hauptstadt Brasiliens, verantwortlich war. Im folgenden Jahr wurde er leitender Architekt von Nova Cap und entwarf die meisten wichtigen Bauten der Stadt. Aus politischen Gründen ging er 1964 ins Exil nach Frankreich. Dort entwarf er u. a. das Gebäude der Kommunistischen Partei Frankreichs in Paris. Nach dem Ende der Diktatur in Brasilien kehrte er dorthin zurück und nahm seine Arbeit unverzüglich wieder auf. 1970 erhielt er die Goldmedaille des American Institute of Architecture und 1988 den Pritzker-Preis. Ungeachtet der Tatsache, dass er Ende 2007 seinen 100. Geburtstag feiern wird, arbeitet Niemeyer an zahlreichen Großprojekten, darunter ein Verwaltungszentrum für die Provinz Minas Gerais in Belo Horizonte; ein zur Feier des 50. Jahrestags seines Ibirapuera Parks in São Paulo 2005 fertiggestelltes Auditorium (hier publiziert) sowie das 2007 fertig werdende Kulturzentrum von Goiânia (ebenfalls hier publiziert).

Né à Rio de Janeiro en 1907, **OSCAR NIEMEYER** étudie à la Escola Nacional de Belas Artes. Diplômé en 1934, il fait partie de l'équipe d'architectes brésiliens qui collabore avec Le Corbusier sur le projet du nouveau ministère de l'éducation et de la santé à Rio. Lucio Costa, dont il est assistant, l'introduit auprès de Le Corbusier. De 1940 à 1954, il intervient essentiellement dans trois villes : Rio de Janeiro, São Paulo et Belo Horizonte. En 1956, il est nommé conseiller pour l'architecture de Nova Cap, organisme chargé de la mise en œuvre des plans de Costa pour la nouvelle capitale, Brasília. L'année suivante, il en devient l'architecte en chef, dessinant la plupart de ses bâtiments importants. En 1964, il s'exile en France pour des raisons politiques, où il construit entre autres le siège du parti communiste à Paris. À la fin de la dictature, il retourne au Brésil, et reprend immédiatement ses responsabilités professionnelles. Il reçoit la médaille d'or de l'American Institute of Architecture en 1970 et le Pritzker Prize en 1988. Même s'il célébrera son 100e anniversaire fin 2007, Niemeyer n'en continue pas moins à travailler sur de nombreux projets, dont un Centre administratif pour l'État du Minas Gerais à Bel Horizonte ; un auditorium achevé en 2005 pour la célébration du 50e anniversaire de son parc d'Ibirapuera à São Paulo et le Centre culturel à Goiânia, achevé en 2007, tous deux publiés ici.

# IBIRAPUERA AUDITORIUM

*São Paulo, SP, Brazil, 2004–05*

*Stage area: 28 x 50 x 15 m. Floor area: 7000 m². Sponsors: TIM (Telecom Italia Mobile) and Municipality of São Paulo.*
*Cost: € 11 million. Architects: Ana Elisa Niemeyer, Jair Varela. Structure: José Carlos Sussekind, Carlos Henrique da Cruz Lima/*
*Casuarina Consultoria Ltda. Furniture: Anna Maria Niemeyer*

In 1951, Oscar Niemeyer and the landscape architect Roberto Burle Marx were commissioned to create the Ibirapuera Park planned to commemorate the 400th anniversary of the city of São Paulo. Inaugurated on August 21, 1954, Ibirapuera Park included several structures—a Palace of the Arts, Palace of Nations, Palace of Agriculture, and Palace of Industry, all linked by a curvilinear concrete canopy. The former Palace of Industry, a 250 x 50-meter rectangle, is the location for the celebrated São Paulo Biennale, the largest contemporary art event in Latin America. In 2004, 50 years after the inauguration of Ibirapuera Park, a final element—an auditorium—which had been part of Niemeyer's original plan, was built, thanks to the generosity of an Italian telephone company, TIM. Shaped like a wedge, the auditorium seats 850 persons and has a very large rear opening, allowing outdoor performances for several thousand spectators. As he often did elsewhere, the architect has created a building that resembles an object more than it does a theater in any traditional sense. Indeed, he wrote of the "necessity to add a triangular building to guarantee the white purity of the complex." Restored in part by the talented Brazilian architect Paulo Mendes da Rocha, the Ibirapuera Park complex still clearly reflects the audacious plan of Niemeyer, despite the addition of later structures. Tomie Ohtake, a noted Brazilian artist and mother of the architect Ruy Ohtake, was responsible for the gigantic red sculptural door, a work that continues inside the theater.

Im Jahr 1951 erhielten Oscar Niemeyer und der Landschaftsarchitekt Roberto Burle Marx den Auftrag zur Gestaltung des Ibirapuera Parks, mit dem des 400-jährigen Bestehens von São Paulo gedacht werden sollte. Der am 21. August 1954 eingeweihte Park umfasste mehrere Bauwerke – einen Palast der Künste, Palast der Nationen, Palast der Landwirtschaft und einen Palast der Industrie, die sämtlich durch ein gewundenes Schutzdach aus Beton verbunden waren. Der frühere Palast der Industrie, ein Rechteck von 250 x 50 m, ist der Schauplatz der berühmten Biennale von São Paulo, der größten Schau zeitgenössischer Kunst in Lateinamerika. 50 Jahre nach der Einweihung des Ibirapuera Parks wurde dank der Großzügigkeit von TIM, einer italienischen Telefongesellschaft, 2004 das bis dahin fehlende Auditorium gebaut, das Bestandteil von Niemeyers ursprünglichem Plan war. Das wie ein geschlossener Keil geformte Auditorium bietet 850 Zuschauern Platz und verfügt über eine sehr großzügig dimensionierte rückwärtige Öffnung, die Aufführungen im Freien für mehrere Tausend Besucher ermöglicht. Wie so häufig schuf der Architekt ein Gebäude, das eher einem Objekt als einem Theater im herkömmlichen Sinn gleicht. In der Tat schrieb er von der »Notwendigkeit, ein dreieckiges Gebäude hinzuzufügen, um die weiße Reinheit der Anlage zu gewährleisten«. Der z. T. vom talentierten brasilianischen Architekten Paulo Mendes da Rocha restaurierte Ibirapuera-Park-Komplex lässt trotz später hinzugekommener Bauten immer noch die kühne Planung Niemeyers erkennen. Tomie Ohtake, eine bekannte brasilianische Künstlerin und Mutter des Architekten Ruy Ohtake, zeichnet verantwortlich für das riesige rote Tor, ein skulpturales Werk, das sich im Inneren des Theaters fortsetzt.

En 1951, Oscar Niemeyer et l'architecte-paysagiste Roberto Burle Marx avaient été chargés de la conception du parc d'Ibirapuera dans le cadre des commémorations du 400ᵉ anniversaire de la fondation de São Paulo. Inauguré le 21 août 1954, ce parc compte plusieurs constructions : un palais des Arts, le palais des Nations, le palais de l'Agriculture et un palais de l'Industrie, reliés par une allée incurvée couverte par un auvent en béton. C'est dans l'ancien palais de l'Industrie, bâtiment rectangulaire de 250 x 50 mètres que se déroule la célèbre Biennale de São Paulo, plus grande manifestation d'art contemporain d'Amérique du Sud. En 2004, cinquante ans après l'inauguration, un auditorium qui faisait partie des plans d'origine de Niemeyer a été construit grâce au mécénat de la société italienne de téléphones mobiles TIM. En forme de trapèze fermé, cette salle de 850 places présente en partie arrière une très grande ouverture qui permet d'organiser des spectacles en plein air pour plusieurs milliers de spectateurs. Comme il l'a souvent fait ailleurs, l'architecte a créé ici une construction qui évoque davantage un objet qu'un théâtre traditionnel. Il a d'ailleurs parlé de « la nécessité d'ajouter à ce projet [de parc] une construction triangulaire qui confirme la pureté immaculée du complexe ». En partie restauré par le talentueux architecte brésilien Paulo Mendes da Rocha, le complexe du Parc reflète toujours l'audacieux plan de son créateur, malgré l'adjonction de quelques autres constructions. Tomie Ohtake, artiste brésilienne connue et mère de l'architecte Ruy Ohtake, a créé la gigantesque porte sculpturale rouge qui se poursuit à l'intérieur du théâtre lui-même.

*The new auditorium is essentially a large white wedge, set amongst the other buildings designed by Niemeyer in the Ibirapuera Park 50 years ago.*

*Das neue Auditorium gleicht im Grunde einem großen, weißen Keil, der inmitten der von Niemeyer vor 50 Jahren entworfenen, anderen Gebäuden im Ibirapuera Park zu stehen kommt.*

*Le nouvel auditorium se présente essentiellement sous forme d'un grand triangle, inséré parmi d'autres bâtiments conçus par Niemeyer pour le parc d'Ibirapuera cinquante ans plus tôt.*

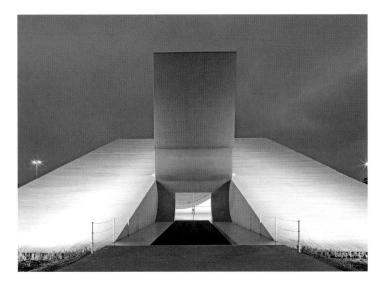

*The red, tongue-like opening of the main entrance stands out from the white, concrete building.*

*Die rote, zungengleiche Öffnung des Hauptzugangs hebt sich deutlich von dem weißen Betonbau ab.*

*L'ouverture, sorte de langue rouge dressée, contraste avec la construction blanche.*

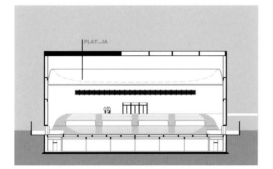

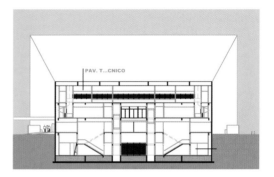

An enormous door to the rear of the stage opens out into the gardens, allowing for far larger audiences and breaking with the fundamentally closed nature of the architecture.

Ein überdimensionales Tor im hinteren Teil der Bühne öffnet sich zu den Gärten und ermöglicht damit weit höhere Besucherzahlen und durchbricht den im Grunde geschlossenen Charakter der Architektur.

À l'arrière de la scène, une énorme porte s'ouvre sur les jardins, permettant d'accueillir un beaucoup plus grand nombre de spectateurs. Elle rompt le caractère fermé de l'architecture.

The rear stage door is shown open
in the image above. To the right,
the foyer of the auditorium.

Auf der Abbildung oben steht das
hintere Bühnentor offen; rechts
das Foyer des Auditoriums.

Ci-dessus, la porte arrière de la
scène ouverte. À droite, le foyer
de l'auditorium.

The red forms imagined by the noted artist Tomie Ohtake sweep from the main exterior door into the lobby of the auditorium, where Niemeyer has installed one of his signature spiral ramps.

Die von der bekannten Künstlerin Tomie Ohtake erdachten roten Formen geleiten vom Haupteingang in die Lobby des Auditoriums, wo Niemeyer eine seiner typischen Wendeltreppen einbaute.

Les inserts rouges imaginées par l'artiste Tomie Ohtake partent de la porte principale et se développent dans le hall de l'auditorium où Niemeyer a implanté l'une de ses célèbres rampes en spirale.

Another view of the ramp and Ohtake's artwork (above) contrasts with the strict, triangular section of the building seen below.

Eine weitere Ansicht der Rampe und des Kunstwerks von Ohtake (oben) steht in Kontrast zum streng dreieckigen Schnitt des Gebäudes (unten).

Une autre vue de la rampe et de l'œuvre d'Ohtake (ci-dessus) contraste avec la coupe triangulaire du bâtiment, ci-dessous.

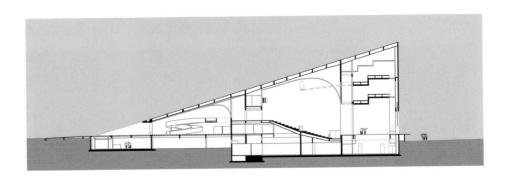

# CULTURAL CENTER

*Goiânia, Goiás, Brazil, 2003–07*

*Floor area: 16 721 m² buildings; 26 325 m² esplanade. Client: State Government of Goiás – Brazil/AGEPEL. Cost: not disclosed.*
*Collaborating Architect: João Niemeyer Arquitetura e Urbanismo (BRA)*

Goiânia is the capital of the Brazilian state of Goiás, about 200 km south-west of Brasília. Oscar Niemeyer designed the multipart center in the tradition of earlier projects like the Ibirapuera Park in São Paulo. The architect's own commentary about the complex is enlightening: "What we like the most in this project," writes Oscar Niemeyer, "is the great concrete plaque—The Cultural Esplanade. With this solution, the square and parking area became well defined. Over the plaque we built the three buildings: the large white concrete block, where the libraries are located, the Musical Center, and the Contemporary Art Museum, in the form of a white concrete cylinder. The first is a large building standing on *pilotis*. The Art Museum, served by a ramp, has a large exhibition room, a wide mezzanine floor around its perimeter, where engravings and drawings should be exposed. The Musical Center has upper and lower auditoriums and two bars with restaurant service. And complementing this complex, the final element is the Human Rights Monument, a great red concrete triangle that confers the desired importance to the whole."

Goiânia ist die Hauptstadt des brasilianischen Bundesstaats Goiás und liegt etwa 200 km südwestlich von Brasília. Oscar Niemeyer gestaltete das Mehrzweckzentrum in der Tradition früherer Projekte wie des Ibirapuera Parks in São Paulo. Der Kommentar des Architekten zu dem Komplex ist erhellend: »Was wir an diesem Projekt am meisten schätzten«, schreibt Oscar Niemeyer, »ist die große Betonplatte – die Kulturesplanade. Dank dieser Lösung wurden Platz und Parkfläche genau begrenzt. Über der Platte errichteten wir drei Bauten: einen großen, weißen Betonblock, in dem die Bibliotheken untergebracht sind, das Musikzentrum und das Museum zeitgenössischer Kunst in der Form eines weißen Betonzylinders. Bei dem erstgenannten Gebäude handelt es sich um einen großen aufgeständerten Baublock. Das über eine Rampe zugängliche Kunstmuseum verfügt über einen großen Ausstellungsraum, ein umlaufendes, breites Mezzaningeschoss, in dem Radierungen und Zeichnungen ausgestellt werden sollen. Das Musikzentrum umfasst ein oberes und unteres Auditorium sowie zwei Bars mit Restaurantservice. Vervollständigt wird dieser Komplex durch das Denkmal für die Menschenrechte, ein mächtiges, rotes Betondreieck, das dem Ganzen die gewünschte Bedeutung verleiht.«

Goiânia est la capitale de l'État de Goiás, à 200 km au sud-ouest de Brasília. Oscar Niemeyer y a conçu un centre réparti entre plusieurs bâtiments, dans l'esprit de précédentes réalisations comme le parc d'Ibirapuera à São Paulo. Il en fait un commentaire éclairant : « Ce que nous préférons dans ce projet, c'est la grande dalle de béton, l'Esplanade culturelle. Cette solution a permis une meilleure définition de la place et du parking. Sur la dalle, nous avons construit trois bâtiments, le grand bloc de béton blanc où se trouvent les bibliothèques, le Centre musical et le musée d'Art contemporain en forme de cylindre blanc. Le premier est un vaste bâtiment sur pilotis. Le musée, desservi par une rampe, possède de grandes salles d'exposition et, tout autour, un important niveau en mezzanine où l'on devrait présenter des dessins et des gravures. Le Centre musical possède deux auditoriums, haut et bas, et deux bars-restaurants. En point final vient le Monument des droits de l'homme, un grand triangle de béton rouge qui confère à l'ensemble toute l'importance souhaitée. »

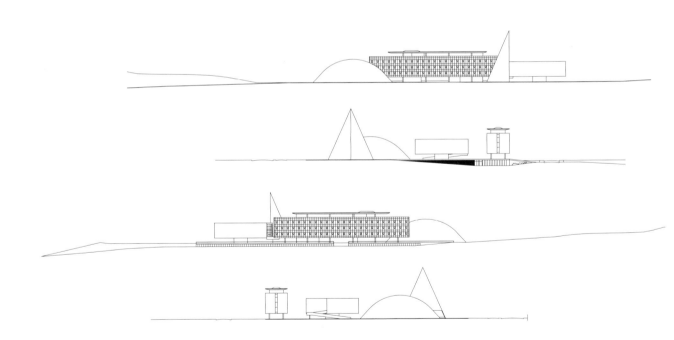

*As he has in other locations, Niemeyer here conceived a composition consisting of powerful geometric forms whose immediate utility is not always evident.*

*Wie schon andernorts, konzipierte Niemeyer hier ein Ensemble aus ausdrucksstarken, geometrischen Formen, deren Nutzen sich nicht immer sofort erschließt.*

*Comme en d'autres lieux, Niemeyer a conçu une composition à partir de formes géométriques puissantes, dont l'utilité n'est pas toujours évidente.*

The design is akin to modern sculpture on a very large scale, with the added element of a surprising contrast of color between the stark white volumes and the triangular red structure.

Die Komposition ähnelt riesigen modernen Skulpturen, mit dem zusätzlichen Element eines überraschenden farblichen Kontrasts zwischen den reinen weißen Baukörpern und dem hoch aufragenden roten Dreieck.

Le projet fait penser à une sculpture à très grande échelle, à laquelle vient s'ajouter le surprenant contraste de couleur entre les volumes blancs et la flèche triangulaire rouge.

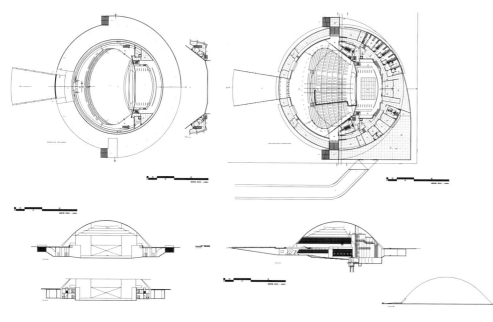

A large, round auditorium is housed in the white, hemispherical dome that recalls other, similar shapes used by Niemeyer, for example in the Ibira-puera Park.

In dem weißen, halbkugeligen Kuppel-bau, der an ähnliche, von Niemeyer beispielsweise im Ibirapuera Park gebrauchte Formen erinnert, befindet sich ein großflächiges, rundes Audi-torium.

Un vaste auditorium circulaire est logé sous la coupole hémisphérique blanche qui rappelle certaines for-mes déjà utilisées par Niemeyer, par exemple dans le parc d'Ibirapuera.

Interior views with the type of curving ramps and walls that Niemeyer is well-known for. The Goiânia Cultural Center was completed 100 years after the birth of the architect.

Innenansichten mit den für Niemeyer typischen gebogenen Rampen und Wänden; als das Kulturzentrum in Goiânia fertiggestellt wurde, war sein Erbauer 100 Jahre alt.

Vues intérieures montrant le type de rampes incurvées et de murs qui ont rendu Niemeyer célèbre. Le Centre culturel de Goiânia a été achevé cent ans après sa naissance.

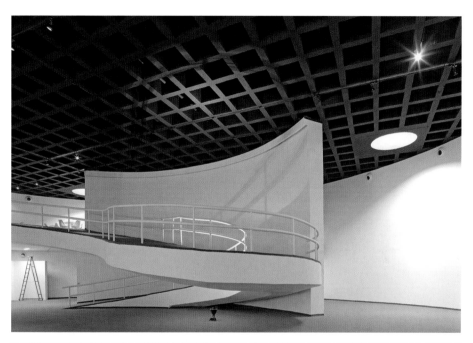

# RYUE NISHIZAWA

*Office of Ryue Nishizawa*
*2-2-35-6B, Higashi-Shinagawa*
*Shinagawa-ku*
*Tokyo 140-0002*
*Japan*

*Tel: +81 3 3450 0117*
*Fax: +81 3 3450 1757*
*E-mail: office@ryuenishizawa.com*
*Web: www.ryuenishizawa.com*

*Moriyama House*

**RYUE NISHIZAWA** was born in Tokyo in 1966, and graduated from the National University in Yokohama in 1990 with a Master's degree in Architecture. He joined Kazuyo Sejima & Associates in 1990 and established Kazuyo Sejima + Ryue Nishizawa / SANAA together with her in 1995. He also established the Office of Ryue Nishizawa in 1997 in Tokyo. He has been a Visiting Professor at the Harvard Graduate School of Design (2000), an Associate Professor at the Yokohama National University since 2001, and a Visiting Associate Professor of Architectural Design at Princeton since 2005. The Office of Ryue Nishizawa has worked on a weekend house (Gumma); the Takeo Head Office (Tokyo); Ichikawa Apartment (Chiba, 2000); a house in Kamakura (Kanagawa, 2001); a house in China (Tianjin, China, 2003–); Love Planet Museum (Okayama, 2003); Funabashi Apartment (Chiba, 2004); as well as the Moriyama House (Tokyo, 2002–05) published here. Current work includes the N Museum (Kagawa, 2005–) and the Towada Art Center (Aomori, 2005–), all in Japan unless otherwise indicated.

**RYUE NISHIZAWA** wurde 1966 in Tokio geboren und schloss 1990 sein Architekturstudium an der National University in Yokohama mit der Masterprüfung ab. Noch im selben Jahr schloss er sich Kazuyo Sejima & Associates an und begründete 1995 mit ihr das Büro Kazuyo Sejima + Ryue Nishizawa / SANAA. Darüber hinaus eröffnete er 1997 in Tokio das Büro Ryue Nishizawa. Er lehrte als Gastprofessor an der Harvard Graduate School of Design (2000), seit 2001 als Associate Professor an der Yokohama National University und seit 2005 als Visiting Associate Professor of Architectural Design in Princeton. Das Büro von Ryue Nishizawa zeichnet verantwortlich für: Wochenendhaus (Gumma), Zentrale von Takeo (Tokio), Ichikawa Apartment (Chiba, 2000), Haus in Kamakura (Kanagawa, 2001), Haus in China (Tianjin, China, 2003–), Love Planet Museum (Okayama, 2003), Funabashi Apartment (Chiba, 2004) sowie das hier vorgestellte Moriyama House (Tokio, 2002–05). Unter den aktuellen Bauten befinden sich das N Museum (Kanagawa, 2005–) und das Towada Art Center (Aomori, 2005–). Alle Projekte befinden sich in Japan, sofern nicht anders angegeben.

**RYUE NISHIZAWA**, né à Tokyo en 1966, est diplômé de l'Université nationale de Yokohama (M. Arch., 1990). Il commence à travailler avec Kazuyo Sejima & Associates la même année et ils fondent ensemble Kazuyo Sejima + Ryue Nishizawa / SANAA en 1995. Il crée également le bureau Ryue Nishizawa en 1997 à Tokyo. Il a été professeur invité à la Harvard Graduate School of Design (2000), professeur associé à l'Université nationale de Yokohama depuis 2001 et professeur associé de conception architecturale invité à Princeton depuis 2005. Le bureau Ryue Nishizawa a réalisé une maison de week-end (Gumma) ; le siège de Takeo (Tokyo) ; l'immeuble d'appartements Ichikawa, Chiba (2000) ; une maison à Kamakura, Kanagawa (2001) ; une maison à Tianjin, Chine (2003–) ; le Love Planet Museum, Okayama (2000) ; l'immeuble de logements Funabashi, Chiba (2004) et la maison Moriyama à Tokyo (2002–05), publiée ici. Il travaille actuellement aux projets du N Museum, Kagawa (2005–), et du Art Center Towada, Aomori (2005–), tous au Japon sauf exception indiquée.

# MORIYAMA HOUSE

*Tokyo, Japan, 2002–05*

*Floor area: 263 m². Client: Mr. Moriyama. Cost: not disclosed.*
*Principal Architect: Ryue Nishizawa. Associates: Ippei Takahashi, Yusuke Ohi, Kimihiko Okada*

Although it is set in a rather traditional area of Tokyo, the Moriyama House is certainly not typical. Rather than a single structure, the "house" consists of a series of 10 white boxes installed on a 290-square-meter site. Connected individual gardens occupy the spaces between the blocks. If the structures were to be identified by letters, "A, B, C, D are occupied by the client. More specifically, A is bedrooms and a study, B the kitchen and pantry, C the living room, and D the bathroom. E is the maid's quarters. F, G + H, I, J are rental units of varying size." In an interesting play on Japanese tradition, the bathroom unit can be entered only by going outside, and it has an open glass wall. Ryue Nishizawa says of the Moriyama House, "In this house, the client is given the freedom to decide which part of this cluster of rooms is to be used as a residence or as rental rooms. He may switch among the series of living and dining rooms or use several rooms at a time according to the season or other circumstances. The domain of the residence changes in accordance with his own life." Like a small city rather than an individual residence, the Moriyama House seems likely to be occupied entirely by its owner as soon as his circumstances permit. As the architects write, "All of the buildings might some day be used by Mr. Moriyama. Currently some are rented, creating a small community of little dwellings. This group of individually proportioned buildings creates a kind of new atmosphere and a landscape in and of itself."

Obwohl es in einem eher traditionellen Viertel Tokios steht, ist dieses »Haus« alles andere als typisch. Anstelle eines einzelnen Baukörpers besteht es aus zehn weißen Kästen auf einem 290 m² großen Grundstück. Die Zwischenräume werden von miteinander verbundenen einzelnen Gartenflächen eingenommen. Wenn man die Kästen zum besseren Verständnis mit Buchstaben bezeichnet, werden »A, B, C und D vom Auftraggeber genutzt. Genauer gesagt enthält A Schlafräume und ein Arbeitszimmer, B Küche und Speisekammer, C den Wohnraum und D das Bad. In E wohnt die Hausangestellte. F, G + H, I und J sind vermietete Einheiten unterschiedlicher Größe.« Das nur von außen zu betretende Bad mit einer offenen Glaswand stellt eine interessante Variante japanischer Traditionen dar. Nishizawa sagt zum Haus Moriyama: »In diesem Haus hat der Besitzer die Freiheit zu entscheiden, welcher Teil der Raumgruppen als Wohnhaus und welche als vermietete Flächen genutzt werden sollen. Er kann zwischen verschiedenen Gruppen von Wohn- und Esszimmern wechseln oder, abhängig von der Jahreszeit oder anderen Gegebenheiten, mehrere Räume gleichzeitig nutzen. Der Wohnbereich verändert sich in Einklang mit seinem eigenen Leben.« Es ist anzunehmen, dass das Haus Moriyama, das eher einer kleinen Stadt als einem Einzelhaus ähnelt, ganz von ihrem Besitzer selbst bewohnt werden wird, sobald seine Verhältnisse dies erlauben. Dazu der Architekt: »Sämtliche Gebäudeteile könnten eines Tages von Herrn Moriyama genutzt werden. Zurzeit sind einige vermietet und so entstand eine begrenzte Kommune kleiner Häuser. Diese Gruppe individuell gestalteter Bauten schafft eine neue Atmosphäre und aus sich heraus eine eigene Landschaft.«

Atypique bien que réalisé dans un quartier traditionnel de Tokyo, la « maison » ne se compose pas d'un seul élément mais d'une série de 10 boîtes blanches disposées sur un terrain de 290 m². Des jardins individuels occupent les espaces vides entre ces blocs et les relient. Si l'on devait identifier ces boîtes par une lettre, « A, B, C et D sont occupés par le client. A contient les chambres et un bureau, B la cuisine et le bureau, C le séjour et D la salle de bains. E est un bloc réservé à l'employée. F, G + H, I et J sont des espaces à louer de dimensions diverses ». Jeu intéressant avec la tradition japonaise, la salle de bains à mur de verre n'est accessible qu'en passant par l'extérieur. Selon Nishizawa : « Dans cette maison, le client a la liberté de décider quelle partie de cet ensemble de pièces il utilise pour y habiter ou pour louer. Il peut intervertir les pièces de séjour ou de repas ou utiliser plusieurs pièces à la fois, selon la saison ou les circonstances. Le domaine de sa résidence change en fonction de sa manière de vivre. » Davantage petite ville que maison individuelle, la maison Moriyama sera sans doute bientôt entièrement occupée par son propriétaire dès que les circonstances le permettront. Comme le précise l'architecte : « Tous les bâtiments pourraient un jour être utilisés par Mr. Moriyama. Actuellement, certains sont loués, ce qui crée une petite communauté répartie dans ces petits logements. Ce groupe d'immeubles individuellement proportionnés crée une atmosphère nouvelle, un paysage en soi. »

The Moriyama House is not a house in the traditional sense at all, but rather a series of related pavilions.

Das Haus Moriyama ist keineswegs ein Haus im herkömmlichen Sinn, sondern eher eine Abfolge miteinander verbundener Pavillons.

La maison Moriyama n'est pas une maison au sens traditionnel du terme, mais plutôt une série de pavillons reliés entre eux.

The architect refers to the size or basic form of nearby buildings, while remaining in a strictly modern gamut of shapes and finishes. White opacity is contrasted with large, glazed openings.

Der Architekt nimmt Bezug auf Größe und Grundform benachbarter Gebäude, bleibt jedoch bei einer strikt modernen Auswahl von Formen und Oberflächen. Weiße Opazität kontrastiert mit großflächigen, verglasten Öffnungen.

L'architecte se réfère aux dimensions ou formes des constructions voisines, tout en utilisant une gamme de formes et de finitions strictement modernes. Le blanc opaque contraste avec les grandes ouvertures vitrées.

*Levene House*

# NO.MAD ARQUITECTOS

*Eduardo Arroyo*
*NO.MAD Arquitectos*
*c/ Pez, 27–1º Izda.*
*28004 Madrid*
*Spain*

*Tel: +34 91 532 7034*
*Fax: +34 91 522 8847*
*E-mail: nomad@nomad.as*
*Web: www.nomad.as*

**EDUARDO ARROYO** was born in 1964 in Bilbao and graduated from the ETSA Madrid in 1988. He was a Professor in the same school from 1996 to 2002. He has also taught in universities in Seoul, Teheran, Paris, Lausanne, Eindhoven, Graz, Ferrara, Porto, Lisbon, Oslo, Brussels, Buenos Aires, Barcelona, Alicante, Valencia, and Seville. His recent work includes: EuskoTren Headquarters (Durango, Spain, 2003, competition entry); Visitors' Center and Elica Hotel (Fabriano, Italy, 2003); Kaleido Restaurant (Madrid, 2004); Musée des Beaux-Arts (Lausanne, Switzerland, NMBA, 2004, competition entry); Estonian National Museum (Tartu, Estonia, 2005, competition entry); urban design at El Torico Plaza (Teruel, Spain, 2005); the access and plaza for Etxebarria Park (Bilbao, 2005); Levene House (San Lorenzo de El Escorial, 2005, published here); and a Single-Family House (Calas, Spain, 2006). His current work, all in Spain, includes: Social Housing for IVVSA (Valencia, 2007); Social Housing for EMVS (Madrid, 2007); Housing Tower (Durango, 2007); and Housing and Sport Center (Valencia, 2007).

**EDUARDO ARROYO** wurde 1964 in Bilbao geboren und beendete 1988 an der ETSA in Madrid sein Studium. Von 1996 bis 2002 lehrte er dort als Professor. Außerdem unterrichtete er an den Universitäten von Seoul, Teheran, Paris, Lausanne, Eindhoven, Graz, Ferrara, Porto, Lissabon, Oslo, Brüssel, Buenos Aires, Barcelona, Alicante, Valencia und Sevilla. Zu seinen neueren Arbeiten gehören: EuskoTren-Zentrale (Durango, Spanien, 2003, Wettbewerbsbeitrag), Besucherzentrum und Elica-Hotel (Fabriano, Italien, 2003), Kaleido-Restaurant (Madrid, 2004), Musée des Beaux-Arts (Lausanne, Schweiz, NMBA, 2004, Wettbewerbsbeitrag), Estnisches Nationalmuseum (Tartu, Estland, 2005, Wettbewerbsbeitrag), Stadtplanung an der Plaza El Torico (Teruel, Spanien, 2005), Zufahrt und Plaza für den Etxebarria-Park (Bilbao, 2005), Casa Levene (San Lorenzo de El Escorial, 2005, hier publiziert) und ein Einfamilienhaus (Calas, Spanien, 2006). Zu den aktuellen, sämtlich in Spanien entstehenden Projekten zählen: Sozialwohnungen für IVVSA (Valencia, 2007), Sozialwohnungen für EMVS (Madrid, 2007), Wohnhochhaus (Durango, 2007) und ein Wohn- und Sportzentrum (Valencia, 2007).

**EDUARDO ARROYO** est né en 1964 à Bilbao et a obtenu son diplôme d'architecte de l'ETSA à Madrid en 1988. Il a enseigné dans la même école de 1996 à 2002, ainsi que dans les universités de Séoul, Téhéran, Paris, Lausanne, Eindhoven, Graz, Ferrare, Porto, Lisbonne, Oslo, Bruxelles, Buenos Aires, Barcelone, Alicante, Valence et Séville. Parmi ses récents projets : le siège d'EuskoTren, Durango, Espagne (2003, participation au concours) ; le centre des visiteurs et Elica Hotel, Fabriano, Italie (2003) ; le Restaurant Kaleido, Madrid (2004) ; le musée des Beaux-Arts, Lausanne, Suisse, NMBA (2004, participation au concours) ; Le Musée national de l'Estonie, Tartu, Estonie (2005, participation au concours) ; le plan d'urbanisme pour la Plaza del Torico, Teruel, Espagne (2005) ; l'accès et la place du parc Etxebarria, Bilbao (2005) ; la maison Levene, San Lorenzo de El Escorial, Espagne (2005) publiée ici et une maison individuelle à Calas, Espagne (2006). Ses projets actuels, tous en Espagne, comprennent des logements sociaux pour IVVSA, Valence (2007) et pour EMVS, Madrid (2007) ; une tour de logements, Durango (2007) ; des logements et un centre sportif à Valence (2007).

# LEVENE HOUSE

*San Lorenzo de El Escorial, Spain, 2002–05*

*Floor area: 400 m². Client: Richard Levene. Cost: € 1.2 million.*
*Collaborators: Francesco Monaco, Javier Tamer Elshiekh, Cristina Fidalgo*

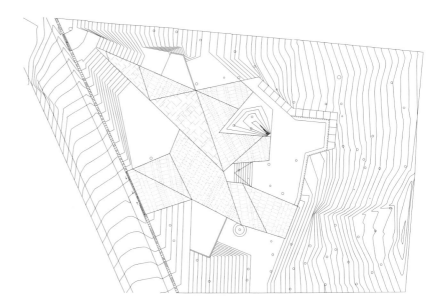

The astonishing forms of the house
are integrated into the existing
forest. A plan to the right shows the
complexity of the design.

Die ungewöhnlichen Formen des Hauses arrangieren sich mit den vorhandenen Bäumen. Ein Grundriss rechts
zeigt die Komplexität des Entwurfs.

Les formes étonnantes de la maison
s'intègrent à leur environnement
arboré. Le plan de droite expose la
complexité du projet.

In a somewhat polemical vein, Eduardo Arroyo writes, "For the concept of this home, we asked ourselves whether we were capable of building something while maintaining the utmost respect for the natural surroundings, avoiding speaking about sustainability, alternative energy or ecology as a veneer for modernity and political correctness." The volume of the house was thus integrated into the forest and the topography. Arroyo divided the general volume into what he calls "specialized fingers," or specific programmatic elements. Two of these fingers are intended for family rooms, another for an indoor pool, another for a kitchen-dining room, and so forth. The entrance from the highest level leads down to the lowest space, the master bedroom, a gym, and sauna. Openings in the façades of the house were also determined by the presence of trees. The density of the glazing, transparent, etched, or translucent, depends on the type of light in each space, thus affirming "the influence of the forest on this strange object that has invaded the tranquility of its territory." Amber resin with wooden slats is used for floors, walls, and ceilings. "A strange feature," concludes Arroyo, "slides along the upper floors, a reflection of the owner's collector behavior. Its polycarbonate structure with iridescent sheens holds a mass of tiny inhabitants whose presence filters the boring collective exterior in a personal, non-transferable interior." The tiny inhabitants referred to are the owner's collection of Action Man toy figures.

Etwas polemisch schreibt Eduardo Arroyo: »Bei der Konzeption dieses Hauses fragten wir uns, ob wir in der Lage sein würden, etwas zu bauen und dabei den größtmöglichen Respekt für die umgebende Natur zu bewahren; außerdem wollten wir die Erwähnung von Nachhaltigkeit, alternativer Energie oder Ökologie als Fassade für Modernität und ›political correctness‹ vermeiden.« Also wurde die Größe des Hauses dem Wald und der Topografie angepasst. Arroyo unterteilte den Baukörper in, wie er das nennt, »spezialisierte Finger« oder spezifische programmatische Elemente. Zwei dieser Finger sind für Wohnräume vorgesehen, ein anderer für ein Schwimmbecken, ein weiterer für eine Kombination aus Küche und Esszimmer usw. Vom Eingang auf der obersten Ebene gelangt man hinunter zu den tiefliegendsten Räumlichkeiten, dem Elternschlafzimmer, einem Fitnessraum und der Sauna. Auch die Öffnungen in der Fassade wurden von der Präsenz besonderer Bäume bestimmt. Von der Dichte des Glases, ob klar, geätzt oder halb durchscheinend, hängt die Art des Lichts in jedem Raum ab und bestätigt »den Einfluss des Waldes auf dieses fremdartige Objekt, das in die Stille seines Hoheitsgebiets eingedrungen ist«. Bernsteinfarbenes Harz und Holzbohlen wurden für Böden, Wände und Decken verwendet. »Eine Besonderheit«, berichtet Arroyo abschließend, »bewegt sich entlang der Obergeschosse und ist Ausdruck der Sammlertätigkeit des Eigentümers. Die Struktur aus Polycarbonat mit irisierendem Glanz enthält eine große Menge winziger Bewohner, deren Präsenz das langweilige Äußere insgesamt in ein individuelles, nichtübertragbares Interieur filtert.« Bei den erwähnten winzigen Bewohnern handelt es sich um des Hausherren Sammlung von Action-Man-Spielzeugfiguren.

De façon assez polémique, Eduardo Arroyo écrit : « Pour le concept de cette maison, nous nous sommes demandés si nous étions capables de construire quelque chose dans le plus grand respect pour l'environnement naturel, en évitant de parler de développement durable, d'énergies alternatives ou d'écologie, ce vernis de modernité et du politiquement correct. » Le volume de cette maison a ainsi été intégré dans la forêt et la topographie. Arroyo a divisé le volume en ce qu'il appelle des « doigts spécialisés » ou éléments programmatiques spécifiques. Deux de ces « doigts » sont destinés aux pièces familiales, un autre à une piscine intérieure, un quatrième à une cuisine-salle à manger, etc. De l'entrée, qui se fait par le haut, on descend vers le niveau inférieur, la chambre principale, une salle de gymnastique et un sauna. Les ouvertures dans les façades ont également été déterminées par la présence des arbres. La densité du verre, transparent, sablé ou translucide dépend du type de lumière nécessaire à chaque espace affirmant ainsi « l'influence de la forêt sur cet étrange objet qui a envahi la tranquillité de son territoire ». Les sols, murs et plafonds sont recouverts d'une résine ambrée et de lattes de bois. « Un élément étrange, conclut Arroyo, se glisse le long des niveaux supérieurs et illustre la passion de collectionneur du propriétaire. Cette structure en polycarbonate aux luisances iridescentes contient une foule de petits habitants dont la présence transforme cet aspect extérieur collectif et ennuyeux en un autre, intériorisé, très personnel et unique. » Ces « petits habitants » sont une collection de poupées-jouets Action-Man.

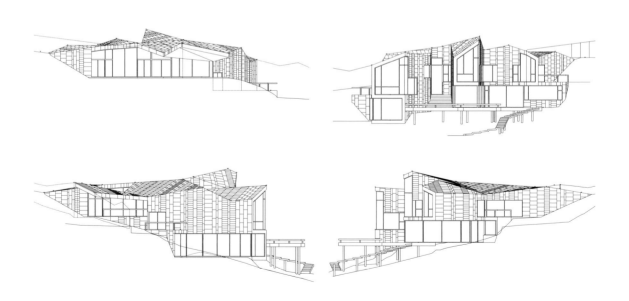

*Sections reveal the density of the design and its integration into the sloped site.*

*Schnitte zeugen von der Kompaktheit der Bebauung und von der Art, wie sie in das Gelände integriert ist.*

*Coupes montrant la densité du projet et son insertion dans la pente.*

Interior views demonstrate the continuity between the outside and the inside of the house and show the frequent openings to the forest setting.

Innenansichten vermitteln die Kontinuität zwischen dem Äußeren und Inneren des Hauses und zeigen insbesondere die zahlreichen Öffnungen zur bewaldeten Umgebung.

Ces vues de l'intérieur montrent la continuité entre l'extérieur et l'intérieur de la maison et, en particulier, les nombreuses ouvertures donnant sur le cadre boisé.

# OSA

osa – office for subversive architecture
4 Lawrence Mansions
Lordship Place
London SW3 5HU
UK

Tel: +44 79 5719 7835 / +49 177 207 3524
E-mail: mail@osa-online.net
Web: www.osa-online.net

*Kunsthülle LP*

**OSA** was founded by a group of students at the Technical University in Darmstadt in 1996. As the group describes itself, "OSA's work sits somewhere between art and architecture. The projects explore the way people use and interact with public spaces and address issues relating to urban regeneration. The work is focused on the reinterpretation of public space and generates the 'unexpected.' […] OSA subverts the common views on architecture. OSA members work individually and whenever a project comes up—self initiated or commissioned—they gather in loose formations depending on availability and interest. All projects are discussed via intranet." The members of the group are Sebastian Appl, Rotterdam (The Netherlands); Ulrich Beckefeld, Vienna (Austria); Britta Eiermann, Darmstadt (Germany); Karsten Huneck, London (UK); Oliver Langbein, Darmstadt (Germany); Anja Ohliger, Frankfurt (Germany); Anke Strittmatter, Graz (Austria); Bernd Trümpler, Munich (Germany) and London (UK). Some of their recent work includes *Urban Oasis*, a temporary installation at Broadgate Circus for Hoegaarden (London, 2005); a temporary installation for the 20th anniversary of the Schirn Kunsthalle (Frankfurt, 2006); a permanent installation at the Kunstwerk for Plan 06 (Cologne, 2006); and *Kunsthülle LPL* (Liverpool, 2006, published here).

**OSA** wurde 1996 von einer Gruppe von Studenten an der Technischen Universität Darmstadt gegründet. Die Gruppe beschreibt sich selbst wie folgt: »Die Arbeit von OSA ist irgendwo zwischen Kunst und Architektur angesiedelt. Die Projekte untersuchen die Art und Weise, in der Menschen öffentliche Räume nutzen und mit ihnen umgehen und sprechen Fragen der Stadtsanierung an. Die Arbeit konzentriert sich auf die Umdeutung öffentlichen Raums und schafft ›Unerwartetes‹ […] OSA untergräbt die üblichen Auffassungen von Architektur. Die Mitglieder arbeiten jeder für sich, und wann immer ein Projekt auftaucht – ob selbst initiiert oder als Auftrag – kommen sie, abhängig von Verfügbarkeit und Interesse, in losen Formationen zusammen. Man verständigt sich über sämtliche Projekte mittels Intranet.« Der Gruppe gehören an: Sebastian Appl (Rotterdam), Ulrich Beckefeld (Wien), Britta Eiermann (Darmstadt), Karsten Huneck (London), Oliver Langbein (Darmstadt), Anja Ohliger (Frankfurt am Main), Anke Strittmatter (Graz), Bernd Trümpler (München und London). Zu ihren neueren Arbeiten zählen: »Urban Oasis«, eine temporäre Installation am Broadgate Circus für Hoegaarden (London, 2005), eine temporäre Installation zum 20. Jahrestag der Schirn Kunsthalle (Frankfurt am Main, 2006), eine dauerhafte Installation am Kunstwerk für Plan 06 (Köln, 2006) und »Kunsthülle LPL« (Liverpool, 2006, hier publiziert).

L'agence **OSA** a été fondée par un groupe d'étudiants de l'Université Technique de Darmstadt en 1996. Selon sa présentation : « Le travail d'OSA se situe quelque part entre art et architecture. Les projets explorent la façon dont les gens utilisent l'espace public ou interagissent avec lui, et traitent des enjeux liés à la régénération de la ville. Le travail se concentre sur la réinterprétation de l'espace public et génère de « l'inattendu » […] OSA subvertit les idées courantes sur l'architecture. Ses membres travaillent individuellement et, lorsqu'un projet se présente – auto-initié ou commandité –, se réunissent en formations libres en fonction de leur disponibilité et leur intérêt. Tous les projets sont discutés en commun via intranet. » Les membres de ce groupe sont Sebastian Appl, Rotterdam ; Ulrich Beckefeld, Vienne ; Britta Eiermann, Darmstadt ; Karsten Huneck, Londres ; Oliver Langbein, Darmstadt ; Anja Ohliger, Francfort ; Anke Strittmatter, Graz ; Bernd Trümpler, Munich et Londres. Parmi leurs récentes interventions : *Urban Oasis*, une installation temporaire à Broadgate Circus pour Hoegaarden, Londres (2005) ; une autre pour le 20e anniversaire de la Schirn Kunsthalle à Francfort (2006) ; une installation permanente au Kunstwerk de Plan 06, Cologne (2006) et *Kunsthülle LPL* (Liverpool, 2006, publié ici).

# KUNSTHÜLLE LPL

*Blade Factory, Greenland Street, Liverpool, UK, 2006*

*Floor area: 252 m². Clients: A Foundation, Liverpool Biennale for Contemporary Art.
Cost: € 150 000. Project Team: Karsten Huneck and Bernd Trümpler, OSA, and Studio+44.
Structural Engineer: Darren Paine*

The internal glow of this added structure contrasts with the brick architecture of the former factory, and signals the activity within.

*Das innere Leuchten des Anbaus kontrastiert mit der Backsteinarchitektur des ehemaligen Fabrikgebäudes und kündet von der Aktivität im Inneren.*

*La radiance lumineuse de cette structure en toiture contraste avec la brique de l'ancienne usine et signale les activités qui s'y déroulent.*

*Kunsthülle LPL* was a temporary installation on the roof of the Blade Factory at Greenland Street. Greenland Street is a new venue for contemporary art created by the A Foundation in September 2006. As its organizers describe it, Greenland Street is "located within walking distance of the city center, the World Heritage Site docks area and major museums including Tate Liverpool, [and] consists of three enormous former industrial buildings located in the Baltic Triangle, Liverpool's up and coming industrial district, that have been transformed into 2500 square meters of high-quality exhibition space." *Kunsthülle LPL* was designed by OSA members Karsten Huneck and Bernd Trümpler and their London firm Studio+44 as the first of an annual series of architectural works to be installed on the roof of this converted factory and art center. Their pavilion divided the rooftop into two spaces (christened "City" and "Merseyside") using green hedges and colored PVC factory curtains. An outer white, translucent layer protected the project from the elements, whereas the inner, red layer added thermal and noise protection while giving a visual warmth to the installation as well. The resulting space was used for lectures, performances and events focusing on the relationship between art and architecture, thus taking advantage of the views from the rooftop of the Mersey and city center. Lit from within, the structure also served to signal the presence of the Blade Factory from the outside.

Bei »Kunsthülle LPL« handelt es sich um eine temporäre Installation auf dem Dach der Blade Factory in der Greenland Street. Greenland Street ist ein neues, im September 2006 von der A Foundation geschaffenes Forum für zeitgenössische Kunst. Der Beschreibung seiner Betreiber zufolge befindet sich Greenland Street »in Laufentfernung vom Stadtzentrum, dem zum Weltkulturerbe zählenden Dockgelände und bedeutenden Museen, darunter die Tate Liverpool. Es besteht aus drei gewaltigen aufgelassenen Industriebauten im Baltic Triangle, Liverpools aufstrebendem Industriebezirk, die in 2500 m² hochwertigen Ausstellungsraum umgewandelt wurden«. »Kunsthülle LPL« wurde von den OSA-Mitarbeitern Karsten Huneck und Bernd Trümpler und ihrem Londoner Büro Studio+44 als Erstes einer alljährlichen Reihe architektonischer Werke entworfen, die auf dem Dach dieser zum Kunstzentrum umgenutzten Fabrik installiert werden sollen. Ihr Pavillon unterteilte mithilfe von grünen Absperrungen und Fabrikvorhängen aus PVC das Dach in zwei, »City« und »Merseyside« genannte Räume. Eine durchscheinende, weiße Außenhülle schützte den Aufbau vor der Witterung, während eine rote innere Schicht für Wärme- und Lärmdämmung sorgte und der Installation gleichzeitig zu visueller Wärme verhalf. Der so entstandene Raum wurde für Vorträge, Aufführungen und Events genutzt, die sich um die Beziehung von Kunst und Architektur drehten und somit auch die Ausblicke vom Dach auf den Mersey und das Stadtzentrum nutzen konnten. Der von innen beleuchtete Aufbau diente darüber hinaus dazu, die Präsenz der Blade Factory nach außen zu signalisieren.

*Kunsthülle LPL* est une installation temporaire sur le toit de la Blade Factory de Greenland Street, nouveau lieu d'exposition d'art contemporain créé par la A Foundation en septembre 2006. Comme ses organisateurs l'expliquent, Greenland Street «se trouve à quelques pas du centre-ville, de la zone des docks classée au patrimoine mondial et de grands musées dont la Tate Liverpool [et] consiste en trois énormes anciens bâtiments industriels du Baltic Triangle, le quartier industriel où tout se passe à Liverpool, qui ont été transformés en 2500 m² d'espaces d'expositions de haute qualité». Le projet conçu par les membres d'OSA, Karsten Huneck et Bernd Trümpler et leur agence londonienne Studio+44, est la première matérialisation d'une série d'œuvres architecturales qui seront installées chaque année sur la toiture de ce nouveau lieu. Leur pavillon divise celle-ci en deux espaces, City et Merseyside, à l'aide de haies vertes et de rideaux industriels en plastique de couleur. Une tenture blanche translucide protège l'installation des éléments, une tenture rouge, interne, assurent la protection thermique et phonique tout en créant une atmosphère plus chaleureuse. L'espace ainsi délimité est utilisé pour des conférences, des performances et des événements sur les thèmes des relations entre art et architecture. Le lieu bénéficie de vues sur les toits de la Mersey et du centre de la ville. Éclairée de l'intérieur, la structure fait aussi office de signal pour la Blade Factory.

*PVC factory curtains partition the space and give it color, while allowing for a flexible use of the added volumes.*

*Fabrikvorhänge aus PVC, die eine flexible Nutzung der zusätzlichen Räume gestatten, gliedern den Raum und geben ihm Farbe.*

*Des rideaux industriels en PVC cloisonnent et colorent l'espace tout en en permettant une utilisation souple.*

*Red and white curtains render the presence of visitors somewhat enigmatic or fleeting, in the image to the right for example. Although other architects have used industrial materials to good effect, OSA does so here in an original spirit.*

*Rote und weiße Vorhänge machen die Anwesenheit von Besuchern wie beispielsweise auf der Abbildung rechts einigermaßen ungewiss oder flüchtig. Obgleich auch andere Architekten Industriematerialien mit guter Wirkung verwendeten, tut OSA es hier auf schöpferische Weise.*

*Les rideaux rouges et blancs rendent parfois énigmatique la présence des visiteurs comme dans l'image de droite. Si d'autres architectes ont utilisé des matériaux industriels pour en tirer certains effets, OSA le fait ici dans un esprit très original.*

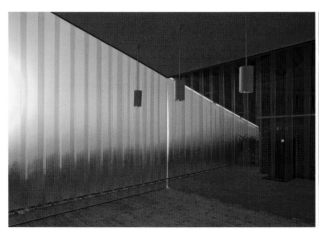

# JOHN PAWSON

*John Pawson*
*Unit B*
*70–78 York Way*
*London N1 9AG*
*UK*

*Tel: +44 20 7837 2929*
*Fax: +44 20 7837 4949*
*E-mail: email@johnpawson.co.uk*
*Web: www.johnpawson.com*

Born in Halifax in central England in 1949, **JOHN PAWSON** attended Eton and worked in his own family's textile mill before going to Japan for four years. On his return, he studied at the Architectural Association (AA) in London and set up his own firm in 1981. He has worked on numerous types of project, including the flagship store for Calvin Klein in New York, airport lounges for Cathay Pacific Airlines at the Chek Lap Kok Airport in Hong Kong, and a small apartment for the author Bruce Chatwin. Pawson may be even better known to the general public because of his 1996 book *Minimum*, which focused on such essential subjects as Light, Structure, Ritual, Landscape, and Volume. Because of this book, but also for his style, Pawson has come to be considered an essential figure in the minimalist style of recent years. Some of his current work includes: Tetsuka House (Tokyo, 2003–06, published here); Monastery of Novy Dvůr (Touzim, Czech Republic, 2004); Lansdowne Apartments (London, 2004); Baron House (Skane, Sweden, 2005); Sackler Crossing, Royal Botanic Gardens, Kew (Surrey, UK, 2006); Klein Apartment (New York, 2006); 50 Gramercy Park North (New York, 2007). He also worked on the Hotel Puerta America in Madrid.

Der 1949 in Halifax, England, geborene **JOHN PAWSON** besuchte Eton und arbeitete in der Textilfabrik seiner Familie, ehe er für vier Jahre nach Japan ging. Nach seiner Rückkehr studierte er an der AA in London und eröffnete 1981 sein eigenes Büro. Er war mit vielgestaltigen Projekten befasst, darunter der Flagship Store von Calvin Klein in New York, Flughafenlounges für Cathay Pacific am Flughafen Chek Lap Kok in Hongkong sowie ein kleines Apartment für den Schriftsteller Bruce Chatwin. Der Allgemeinheit ist Pawson besser bekannt wegen seines 1996 erschienenen Buchs *Minimum*, in dem er sich mit solch grundsätzlichen Themen wie Licht, Struktur, Ritual, Landschaft und Raum beschäftigt. Wegen dieses Buchs, aber auch wegen seines Stils gilt Pawson inzwischen als wesentlicher Vertreter des Minimalismus der letzten Jahre. Zu seinen aktuellen Projekten gehören: Haus Tetsuka (Tokio, 2003–06, hier publiziert); Kloster Novy Dvůr (Touzim, Tschechische Republik, 2004); Lansdowne Apartments (London, 2004); Haus Baron (Skane, Schweden, 2005); Sackler Crossing, Royal Botanic Gardens, Kew (Surrey, Großbritannien, 2006); Apartment Klein (New York, 2006); 50 Gramercy Park North (New York, 2007). Darüber hinaus arbeitete er am Hotel Puerta America in Madrid.

Né à Halifax en Angleterre en 1949, **JOHN PAWSON**, après des études à Eton, travaille dans l'usine textile familiale avant de séjourner quatre ans au Japon. À son retour, il étudie à l'Architectural Association de Londres et crée son agence en 1981. Il est intervenu sur de nombreux types de projets dont le principal magasin de Calvin Klein à New York, les salons de l'aéroport de Chek Lap Kok à Hongkong pour Cathay Pacific ou un petit appartement pour l'écrivain Bruce Chatwin. Il est peut-être surtout connu du grand public à travers le succès de son livre *Minimum* (1996) sur les thèmes de la lumière, de la structure, du rituel, du paysage et du volume. À la suite de ce livre, mais aussi parce que c'est son style, il a été considéré comme une figure essentielle du minimalisme contemporain. Parmi ses réalisations récentes : la maison Tetsuka, Tokyo (2003–06) publiée ici ; le monastère de Novy Dvůr, Touzim, République Tchèque (2004) ; Lansdowne Apartments, Londres (2004) ; la maison Baron, Skane, Suède (2005) ; passerelle Sackler, Royal Botanic Gardens, Kew, Surrey, Grande-Bretagne (2006) ; appartement Klein, New York (2006) ; 50 Gramercy Park North, New York (2007). Il a également participé aux aménagements de l'Hotel Puerta America à Madrid.

# TETSUKA HOUSE

*Tokyo, Japan, 2003–06*

*Floor area: 181 m². Client: Tetsuka.*
*Cost: not disclosed*

Located in the Setagaya area of Tokyo on a 195-square-meter site, the Tetsuka House is described by the architect as a "pristine box" containing a Japanese tearoom and double-height open courtyard as well as living space. Concrete with two different gray tints was used to underline the internal division between the ground and upper floors. The windows are carefully placed to offer very specific views. Cooking, dining, and relaxation spaces are "incorporated within three functionally distinct but spatially fluid zones." The tearoom, located alongside the courtyard, also serves as guest space. Pawson chose not to adhere strictly to all aspects of conventional teahouse design in this instance, but he affirms that it "stays true to its essence." The main bedroom includes an outdoor terrace. A traditional Japanese bathtub was used, creating another link between Pawson's minimal design aesthetic and Japanese culture. The architect seems quite at ease in this environment because his form of modernity has its roots in the architecture of Japan.

Das auf einem 195 m² großen Grundstück im Setayaga-Viertel von Tokio stehende Haus Tetsuka wird vom Architekten als ein »unverfälschter Kasten« beschrieben, der einen japanischen Teeraum, einen zweigeschossigen, offenen Innenhof sowie Wohnräume enthält. Zur Unterstreichung der inneren Trennung zwischen Erdgeschoss und Obergeschossen wurde Beton in zwei verschiedenen Grautönen verwendet. Die Fenster sind überlegt platziert, um ganz bestimmte Ausblicke zu bieten. Räumlichkeiten zum Kochen, Essen und Entspannen wurden »in drei funktional unterschiedliche, gleichwohl räumlich fließende Zonen integriert«. Der am Innenhof gelegene Teeraum dient darüber hinaus als Gästezimmer. In diesem Fall entschied Pawson, sich nicht streng an alle Regeln konventioneller Teehausgestaltung zu halten, versichert jedoch, dass der Raum »seinem Wesen treu bleibe«. Zum Hauptschlafzimmer gehört eine Außenterrasse. Im Haus befindet sich eine traditionelle japanische Badewanne, durch die eine weitere Verbindung zwischen Pawsons minimaler Designästhetik und japanischem Brauchtum entsteht. Augenscheinlich fühlt sich der Architekt in diesem Umfeld ganz zu Hause, wohl weil seine Ausprägung der Moderne viele Wurzeln in der Architektur Japans hat.

Située dans le quartier de Setagaya à Tokyo sur un terrain de 195 m², la maison Tetsuka est décrite par l'architecte comme une « pure boîte » contenant une maison de thé japonaise, une cour ouverte double hauteur et des espaces de vie. Le béton en deux tons de gris différents souligne la division interne entre le rez-de-chaussée et l'étage. Les fenêtres sont implantées avec soin selon des vues très calculées. La cuisine, les repas et les espaces de détente sont « intégrés dans trois zones spatialement fluides mais fonctionnellement distinctes ». La maison de thé, le long de la cour, sert également d'espace de réception. Pawson a choisi de ne pas respecter strictement toutes les règles de la conception traditionnelle d'une maison de thé, mais affirme « qu'elle est authentique dans son essence ». La chambre principale se prolonge sur une terrasse extérieure. Une baignoire japonaise traditionnelle crée un lien supplémentaire entre l'esthétique minimaliste de l'architecte et les coutumes nippones. Pawson est très à l'aise dans cet environnement car sa forme de modernité trouve de multiples racines dans l'architecture du Japon.

*John Pawson is known for his minimalist aesthetic. In the case of Japan, there is a natural continuity between this form of modernity and local building traditions.*

*Pawson ist bekannt für seine minimalistische Ästhetik. In Japan besteht eine natürliche Kontinuität zwischen dieser Ausprägung der Moderne und heimischen Traditionen.*

*John Pawson est connu pour son esthétique minimaliste. Pour ce qui est du Japon, on observe une continuité naturelle entre cette modernité et les traditions locales.*

The external appearance of the house is as minimalist as its interior, providing privacy for the residents, while admitting ample natural light.

Das äußere Erscheinungsbild des Hauses ist ebenso minimalistisch wie sein Interieur, das den Bewohnern ihre Privatsphäre bietet und doch zugleich reichlich Tageslicht einfallen lässt.

L'aspect extérieur de la maison est aussi minimaliste que ses aménagements intérieurs. Elle assure une grande intimité à ses occupants tout en laissant pénétrer généreusement la lumière naturelle.

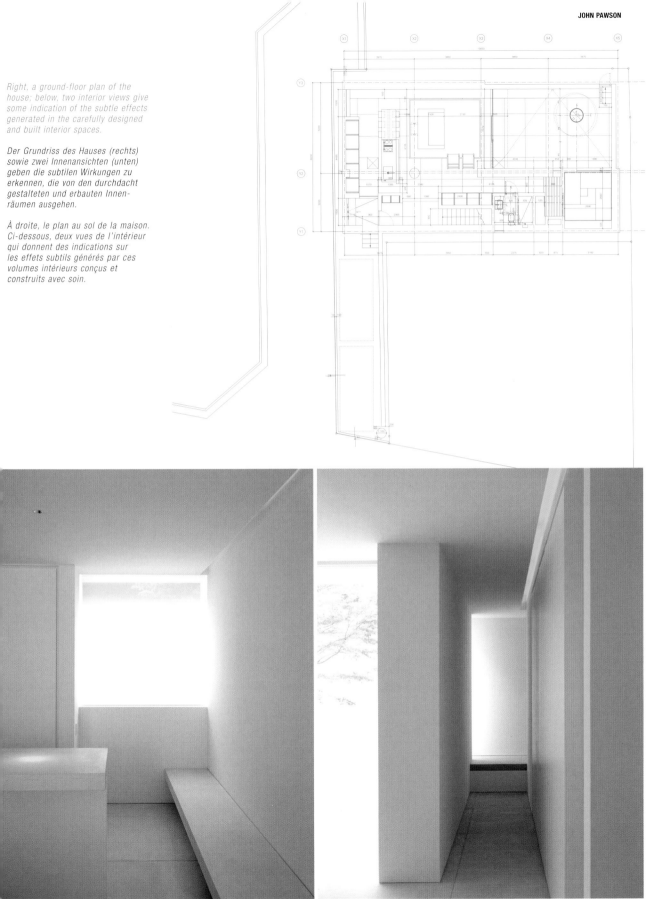

Right, a ground-floor plan of the house; below, two interior views give some indication of the subtle effects generated in the carefully designed and built interior spaces.

Der Grundriss des Hauses (rechts) sowie zwei Innenansichten (unten) geben die subtilen Wirkungen zu erkennen, die von den durchdacht gestalteten und erbauten Innen-räumen ausgehen.

À droite, le plan au sol de la maison. Ci-dessous, deux vues de l'intérieur qui donnent des indications sur les effets subtils générés par ces volumes intérieurs conçus et construits avec soin.

# PEANUTZ ARCHITEKTEN

*Peanutz Architekten*
*Brückenstrasse 1*
*10179 Berlin*
*Germany*

*Tel: +49 178 184 4098*
*E-mail: post@peanutz-architekten.de*
*Web: www.peanutz-architekten.de*

Playing on the word "nutz" (meaning "use" in German), the architects seek to act upon space in a variety of ways. Founded in 1997 by **ELKE KNÖSS** and **WOLF-GANG GRILLITSCH**, the partners have evolved a theory of "design performance" whereby they create "laboratory conditions to test the space of action." Their related idea of "tuning" consists of enhancing the use of a structure. Their first action of this kind was carried out in the Urban Issue Gallery in Berlin in 1998. For "sr-Furniture-Tuning" they used fliers to invite people to bring broken pieces of old furniture to the gallery, and then "tuned" or repaired the furniture in the gallery. Aside from their performance projects, their built work includes: Silkroom, Interior Design (Berlin, 2002); Metzer-Mix, Apartment Conversion (Berlin, 2002); Foyer Conversion, Spectrum, German Museum of Technology (Berlin, 2002); LOOPs, Design of the Campus of Donau-University (Krems, Austria, 2003–05); Trichterweiterung (Haus Eppinger Strasse, Berlin, 2005); City and Industrial Museum (Guben, Germany, 2006, published here); and Archive of Disappeared Places, Documentation Center (Forst, Horno, Germany, 2006).

Ihrer Website zufolge steht »Peanutz für räumliches Agieren mit viel NUTZ«. Das von **ELKE KNÖSS** und **WOLFGANG GRILLITSCH** 1997 gegründete Büro ist bestrebt, Raum in verschiedenster Weise zu bearbeiten und hat dazu eine Theorie des »designperformativen Arbeitens« entwickelt, mit der die Architekten »Laborbedingungen erzeugen, um den Aktionsraum zu testen.« Mit der damit verwandten Idee des »Tuning« soll der Nutzen eines Bauwerks gesteigert werden. Die erste Aktion dieser Art führten sie 1998 mit der Galerie Urban Issue in Berlin aus. Für das »sr-Furniture-Tuning« luden sie Leute mit Handzetteln dazu ein, schadhafte Möbelstücke in die Galerie zu bringen, wo sie dann »getuned« oder repariert wurden. Neben ihren Performanceprojekten haben sie sich mit folgenden architektonischen Arbeiten befasst: Silkroom, Innenraumgestaltung (Berlin, 2002), Metzer-Mix, Apartmentumnutzung (Berlin, 2002), Umnutzung eines Foyers, Spectrum, Deutsches Technikmuseum (Berlin, 2002), LOOPs, Gestaltung des Campus der Donau-Universität (Krems, Österreich, 2003–05), Trichtererweiterung (Haus Eppinger Straße, Berlin, 2005), Stadt- und Industriemuseum (Guben, Deutschland, 2006, hier vorgestellt) und Archiv der verschwunden Orte (Dokumentationszentrum Forst in der Lausitz, Neu-Horno, Deutschland, 2006).

Jouant sur le sens du mot allemand *nutz* (utilisation), les architectes veulent agir de toutes sortes de façons sur l'espace. Fondée en 1997 par **ELKE KNÖSS** et **WOLFGANG GRILLITSCH**, l'agence a développé une théorie de «la performance de conception» qui lui permet de créer «des conditions de laboratoire pour tester l'espace de l'action». Leur idée associée de *tuning* consiste à améliorer l'usage d'une structure. Leur première action de ce type a été mise en œuvre dans la galerie Urban Issue à Berlin en 1998. Lors de «sr-Furniture-Tuning», ils ont lancé des tracts pour inviter les gens à leur apporter des morceaux de vieux meubles à la galerie, puis les ont «adaptés» ou réparés sur place. En dehors de ces performances, ils ont réalisé Silkroom, un aménagement intérieur, Berlin (2002) ; Metzer-Mix, la transformation d'appartement, Berlin (2002) ; Spectrum, la transformation d'un hall d'accueil, Musée allemand de la technologie, Berlin (2002) ; LOOPs, la conception du campus l'Université du Danube, Krems, Autriche (2003–05) ; Trichterweiterung, Haus Eppinger Strasse, Berlin (2005) ; le Musée de la ville et de l'industrie, Guben, Allemagne (2006) publié ici et le Centre de documentation, archives des lieux disparus, Forst, Horno, Allemagne (2006).

# CITY AND INDUSTRIAL MUSEUM

*Guben, Germany, 2006*

*Floor area: 600 m². Client: City of Guben. Cost: €250 000.*
*Architects: Elke Knöß and Wolfgang Grillitsch with Oskar Wittich*

*The "hoods" installed in this former hat factory by the architects create pleasant and flexible exhibition spaces without undue cost.*

*Die in diesem ehemaligen Fabrikgebäude von den Architekten errichteten »Hauben« schaffen ohne übermäßige Kosten angenehme, flexible Ausstellungsräume.*

*Les « capuchons » imaginés par les architectes dans cette ancienne fabrique de chapeaux créent des cellules d'exposition agréables et souples, sans investissement excessif.*

Guben is a city on the Lusatian Neisse River in the state of Brandenburg. It is a divided city on the border between Germany and Poland, having been separated into Guben and Gubin in 1945. The architects installed a series of 14 large hoods ranging from 1 x 1.5 meters up to 7 x 4 meters in a former hat factory. Each of these hoods contains material dealing with a specific topic, including the history of the city, its industry, and the "cultural history of hats." Part of a new city-center project including a town hall, library, and music school, the museum offers a lively installation for topics that might otherwise have seemed somewhat difficult for some visitors. The variety of the shapes and colors of the hoods animates the space and creates a certain intimacy without creating a network of solid walls.

Die Stadt Guben liegt an der Lausitzer Neiße im Land Brandenburg. Die an der Grenze zwischen Deutschland und Polen liegende Stadt wurde 1945 in Guben und Gubin geteilt. In einer ehemaligen Hutfabrik installierten die Architekten eine Reihe von 14 großen »Hauben«, die zwischen 1 x 1,5 m und 7 x 4 m messen. Jede dieser Hauben enthält Material, das sich mit einer bestimmten Thematik befasst, darunter die Stadtgeschichte, ihre Industrie und »die Kulturgeschichte von Hüten«. Das Museum gehört zu einem Projekt zur Umgestaltung des Stadtzentrums, das auch Rathaus, Bibliothek und Musikschule umfasst und bietet seinen Besuchern einen leichten Zugang zu sonst eher »trockenen« Themenkreisen. Die Vielfalt von Formen und Farben der Hauben belebt den Raum und erzeugt ohne feste Wände eine gewisse Intimität.

Guben est une ville de l'État du Brandenburg, au bord de la Neisse. Elle a été divisée par la frontière entre l'Allemagne et la Pologne en Guben et Gubin, en 1945. Les architectes ont installé une succession de quatorze grands «capuchons» de 1 x 1,5 mètres à 7 x 4 mètres dans une ancienne fabrique de chapeaux. Chacun contient des informations sur un sujet particulier comme l'histoire de la ville, son industrie et «l'histoire culturelle du chapeau». Élément du projet d'un nouveau centre urbain comprenant l'hôtel de ville, une bibliothèque et une école de musique, ce musée offre une présentation très vivante de sujets qui auraient pu sembler d'accès difficile à certains visiteurs. La variété des formes et des couleurs des «capuchons» anime l'espace et crée une certaine intimité sans recourir à des murs fixes.

Typography or images can easily be introduced on either the exterior or the interior of the exhibition hoods.

Schrift oder Bilder lassen sich außen oder innen an den Ausstellungshauben leicht anbringen.

Des typographies ou des images peuvent être facilement introduites à l'intérieur ou à l'extérieur des « capuchons » d'exposition.

The different color patters and angles of the hoods chosen by the architects enliven the space and, as the image above shows, can provide for very different moods in each area.

Die von den Architekten gewählten unterschiedlichen Farbmuster und Neigungswinkel der Hauben beleben den Raum und können, wie die Abbildung oben zeigt, in jedem Bereich eine andere Atmosphäre erzeugen.

Les couleurs et les inclinaisons variées de ces capuchons animent l'espace et, comme le montre l'image ci-dessus, créent des atmosphères très diverses.

# ARSENIO PÉREZ AMARAL

*Corona y P. Amaral Arquitectos*
*Avda. Los Pescaditos*
*Edif. Litoral Oficina 1 Maria Jiménez*
*38180 Santa Cruz de Tenerife*
*Spain*

*Tel: +34 922 598 002*
*Fax: +34 922 596 829*
*E-mail: estudio@coronaypamaral.com*
*Web: www.coronaypamaral.com*

**ARSENIO PÉREZ AMARAL** was born in Santa Cruz de Tenerife in 1958. He received his degree as an architect from the ETSA in Madrid in 1982. He did postgraduate work at Cornell (1983), before becoming a partner in the firm N Tres Arquitectos (1984–2002). He was a founding partner of Corona y P. Amaral Arquitectos. He was a Guest Professor at the Escuela de Arquitectura de Las Palmas de Gran Canaria (2006–07). His recent work includes the Jet Foil Maritime Station (Santa Cruz de Tenerife, 1989); Tenerife North Airport (La Laguna, Tenerife, 2002); Central Workshop and Offices of Ground Transportation System (Santa Cruz de Tenerife, 2002); 270 Dwelling Building (Santa Cruz de Tenerife, 2003); 99 Los Molinos Building (Santa Cruz de Tenerife, 2003); and Jardín Del Sol House (Tacoronte, Tenerife, 2005, published here).

**ARSENIO PÉREZ AMARAL** wurde 1958 in Santa Cruz de Tenerife geboren. Er schloss sein Architekturstudium 1982 an der ETSA in Madrid ab. An der Cornell University setzte er seine Studien 1983 fort und wurde dann Partner im Büro N Tres Arquitectos (1984–2002). Er war Gründungspartner von Corona y P. Amaral Arquitectos. Von 2006 bis 2007 hatte er eine Gastprofessur an der Escuela de Arquitectura de Las Palmas de Gran Canaria inne. Zu seinen Bauten gehören: Jet Foil Maritime Station (Santa Cruz de Tenerife, 1989), Nordflughafen auf Teneriffa (La Laguna, Teneriffa, 2002), Zentralwerkstatt und Büros des Bodentransportsystems (Santa Cruz de Tenerife, 2002), Wohnanlage 270 (Santa Cruz de Tenerife, 2003), Wohnanlage Los Molinos 99 (Santa Cruz de Tenerife, 2003) sowie die Casa Jardín del Sol (Tacoronte, Teneriffa, 2005, hier vorgestellt).

**ARSENIO PÉREZ AMARAL**, né à Santa Cruz de Tenerife in 1958, est architecte diplômé de l'ETSA à Madrid (1982). Il fait des études supérieures à Cornell (1983) avant d'entrer comme partenaire dans l'agence N Tres Arquitectos (1984–2002). Il est associé fondateur de Corona y P. Amaral Arquitectos. Il a été professeur invité à la Escuela de Arquitectura de Las Palmas de Gran Canaria (2006–07). Parmi ses réalisations : la gare maritime d'hydroglisseurs de Santa Cruz de Tenerife (1989) ; l'aéroport nord de Tenerife, La Laguna, Tenerife (2002) ; les ateliers et bureaux du réseau de transports en commun de Santa Cruz de Tenerife (2002) ; un immeuble de 270 logements, Santa Cruz de Tenerife (2003) ; l'immeuble du 99 Los Molinos, Santa Cruz de Tenerife (2003) et la maison Jardín del Sol, Tacoronte, Tenerife (2005), publiée ici.

# JARDÍN DEL SOL HOUSE

*Tacoronte, Tenerife, Canary Islands, Spain, 2003–05*

*Floor area: 317 m². Client: Arsenio Pérez Amaral.*
*Cost: €450 000*

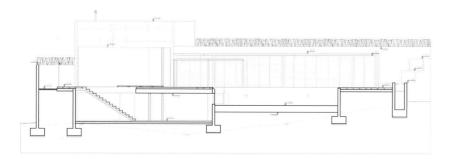

*The extreme simplicity and planar character of the architecture allows it to blend almost seamlessly with the horizon.*

*Die äußerste Schlichtheit und Flächigkeit der Architektur lassen sie fast nahtlos mit dem Horizont verschmelzen.*

*L'extrême simplicité et la construction par plans de cette architecture lui permettent de se fondre presque invisiblement avec l'horizon.*

There is almost no distinction in these images between the deck, swimming pool and the sea beyond. The simplicity of the architectural design contributes to this effect.

Auf diesen Bildern ist nahezu kein Unterschied zwischen dem Schwimmbecken und dem dahinter liegenden Meer erkennbar. Die Schlichtheit der Architektur trägt zu dieser Wirkung bei.

On ne fait pratiquement pas la distinction dans ces images entre la terrasse de la piscine et la mer. La simplicité de la conception architecturale contribue à cet effet.

The architect set out to create "a monolithic concrete and glass volume over a timber platform, located at the edge of a 300-meter cliff in order to enjoy the amazing view of the cliff, a kilometer-long black-sand beach, Mount Teide, and the north coast of Tenerife Island." The bedroom and services areas are located in a one-story rectangular volume that intersects a double-height volume containing the living room, studio, and kitchen. The two volumes create the L-shaped plan around the black pond located at the edge of the platform "so that the surface of the water blends with that of the sea." "All the areas of the house thus enjoy views underlined by wood and water," says the architect. A gym with direct access from the terrace is located in the basement. A view into the pond is offered through a glass wall. Timber shutters protect the bedroom area and outside canvas shades are used in the living room. A freestanding canopy made of steel and wood shelters the central section of the terrace. The house, located on a 626-square-meter site, appears to be perfectly integrated into the cliff.

Der Architekt plante, »einen am Rand einer 300 m hohen Klippe gelegenen, monolithischen Baukörper aus Beton und Glas auf einer hölzernen Terrassenfläche [zu entwerfen], um die fantastischen Aussichten auf Klippe, einen Kilometer schwarzen Sandstrands, Pico de Teide und die Nordküste von Teneriffa zu genießen«. Schlafzimmer und Funktionsräume befinden sich in einem eingeschossigen, rechtwinkligen Baukörper, der an einen anderen Bauteil mit doppelter Geschosshöhe stößt, in dem Wohnraum, Studio und Küche untergebracht sind. Die beiden Elemente ergeben den L-förmigen Grundriss um das schwarze Wasserbecken herum, das am Rand der Plattform liegt, »so dass die Wasseroberfläche in die des Meeres übergeht«. Dem Architekten zufolge »profitieren somit sämtliche Bereiche des Hauses von durch Wald und Wasser akzentuierten Ausblicken«. Ein direkt von der Terrasse aus zugänglicher Fitnessraum befindet sich im Souterrain. Eine verglaste Wand ermöglicht Ausblicke auf das Wasserbecken. Hölzerne Läden schützen den Schlafzimmerbereich, beim Wohnzimmer kommen außen angebrachte Segeltuchschirme zum Einsatz. Ein freistehendes Dach aus Stahl und Holz schützt den zentralen Abschnitt der Terrasse. Das auf einem 626 m² großen Grundstück stehende Haus wirkt, als sei es direkt in die Feldwand eingefügt.

L'architecte a réussi à créer ici un « volume monolithique en verre et béton sur une plate-forme de bois, en bordure d'une falaise de 300 mètres de haut pour profiter de la vue stupéfiante de kilomètres de plages de sable noir, le mont Teide et la côte septentrionale de l'île de Tenerife ». La chambre et les pièces de service se trouvent dans le volume rectangulaire sur un seul niveau qui vient interrompre un second volume de deux niveaux contenant le séjour, un studio et la cuisine. Ces deux éléments s'articulent en « L » autour d'une piscine noire en bordure de la plate-forme visible à travers un mur de verre « de telle façon que la surface de l'eau se fond avec celle de la mer. ». « Toutes les parties de la maison bénéficient de vues mises en valeur par le bois et l'eau », précise l'architecte. Une salle de gymnastique avec accès direct à la terrasse se trouve en sous-sol. Des volets en bois protègent la zone des chambres, et des stores extérieurs en toile, le séjour. Un auvent en bois et acier abrite la partie centrale de la terrasse. La maison, implantée sur un terrain de 626 m², semble être insérée dans la falaise.

*Another image shows that the house is not quite as splendidly isolated as the previous double page might lead one to believe, yet the openness of the residence remains remarkable.*

*Dieses Bild zeigt, dass das Haus nicht ganz so herrlich abgeschieden ist, wie die vorstehende Doppelseite glauben lässt, und doch bleibt die Offenheit des Hauses bemerkenswert.*

*Autre image montrant que la maison ne se trouve pas dans le splendide isolement que la double-page précédente laisse croire. Mais son ouverture reste remarquable.*

The plan to the right is slightly
angled to take advantage of the site.
Above, the kitchen and dining area
are very close to each other.

Der Grundriss ist leicht verdreht oder
verschoben, um das Gelände auszu-
nutzen. Oben liegen Küche und Essbereich nahe beeinander.

Le plan est légèrement en biseau pour
mieux tirer parti du site. Ci-dessus,
la cuisine et la zone des repas, très
proches l'une de l'autre.

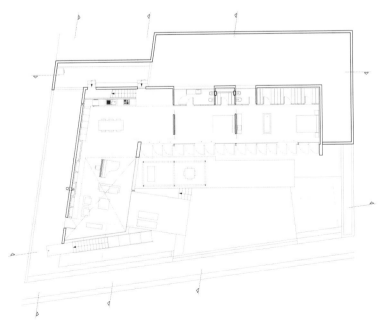

# PEZO VON ELLRICHSHAUSEN ARQUITECTOS

*Pezo von Ellrichshausen Arquitectos*
*Lo Pequén 502*
*Concepción*
*Chile*

*Tel: +56 41 221 0281*
*E-mail: info@pezo.cl*
*Web: www.pezo.cl*

**PEZO VON ELLRICHSHAUSEN ARQUITECTOS** was founded in Buenos Aires, Argentina, in 2001 by Mauricio Pezo and Sofía von Ellrichshausen. They were awarded the Commended Prize at the AR Awards for Emerging Architecture (London, 2005) and the Best Work by Young Architects Prize at the Fifth Ibero-American Architecture Bienniale (Montevideo, 2006). Projects such as Rivo House (Valdivia, 2003), 120 Doors (Concepción, 2003), Poli House (Coliumo Peninsula, Chile, 2005, published here), and numerous public art projects have been widely published in magazines (*The Architectural Review, Domus, A+U, Detail, Architectural Record*, etc). Mauricio Pezo was born in Chile in 1973 and completed his Masters in Architecture at the Catholic University of Chile (Santiago, 1998). He graduated from the University of Bío-Bío with a degree in Architecture (Concepción, 1999). He is a visual artist and director of the Movimiento Artista del Sur (MAS). He teaches at the School of Architecture of the Bío-Bío University, at the University of Las Américas and at the University of Talca. Pezo was awarded the Young Chilean Architect Prize 2006. Sofía von Ellrichshausen was born in Argentina in 1976. She holds a degree in Architecture from the University of Buenos Aires (2002). She teaches at the School of Architecture of the University of Las Américas and at the University of Talca.

**PEZO VON ELLRICHSHAUSEN ARQUITECTOS** wurde 2001 von Mauricio Pezo und Sofía von Ellrichshausen in Argentinien gegründet. Bei den AR Awards for Emerging Architecture erhielten sie 2005 in London den Commended Prize und 2006 in Montevideo anlässlich der 5. Ibero-Amerikanischen Architekturbiennale den Preis Best Work by Young Architects. Projekte wie die Casa Rivo (Valdivia, 2003), 120 Türen (Concepción, 2003), Casa Poli (Península de Coliumo, 2005, hier publiziert) sowie zahlreiche Projekte von Kunst im öffentlichen Raum wurden in Zeitschriften wie *The Architectural Review, Domus, A+U, Detail, Architectural Record* usw. vielfach dokumentiert. Mauricio Pezo wurde 1973 in Chile geboren und schloss 1998 sein Architekturstudium an der Universidad Católica de Chile in Santiago ab. Die Universidad del Bío-Bío in Concepción verließ er 1999 mit einem Diplom in Architektur. Er ist bildender Künstler und Direktor des Movimiento Artista del Sur (MAS). Darüber hinaus lehrt er an der Architekturfakultät der Universidad del Bío-Bío, an der Universidad de Las Américas und der Universidad de Talca. Pezo wurde 2006 mit dem Preis für junge chilenische Architekten ausgezeichnet. Sofía von Ellrichshausen wurde 1978 in Argentinien geboren. 2002 schloss sie an der Universidad de Buenos Aires ihr Architekturstudium ab. Sie unterrichtet an der Architekturfakultät der Universidad de Las Américas und der Universidad de Talca.

L'agence **PEZO VON ELLRICHSHAUSEN ARQUITECTOS** a été fondée à Buenos Aires, Argentine, en 2001 par Mauricio Pezo et Sofía von Ellrichshausen. Ils ont reçu le Commended Prize de l'AR Awards for Emerging Architecture à Londres en 2005 et le prix de la meilleure œuvre de jeunes architectes à la 5e Biennale ibéro-américaine d'architecture de Montevideo en 2006. Leurs réalisations comme la maison Rivo, Valdivia (2003), 120 Doors, Concepción (2003), la maison Poli, Péninsule de Coliumo (2005), publiée ici, et de nombreux projets artistiques pour lieux publics ont été largement repris par des magazines comme *The Architectural Review, Domus, A+U, Detail, Architectural Record*, etc. Mauricio Pezo, né au Chili en 1973, a reçu son master d'architecture à l'Université catholique du Chili, Santiago (1998) et est aussi diplômé d'architecture de l'Universidad del Bío-Bío, Concepción (1999). Il est artiste plasticien et directeur du Movimiento Artista del Sur (MAS). Il enseigne à l'École d'architecture de l'Universidad del Bío-Bío, à l'Universidad de Las Américas et à l'Université de Talca. Il a reçu le Prix des jeunes architectes chiliens en 2006. Sofía von Ellrichshausen, née en Argentine en 1976, est diplômée en architecture de l'Université de Buenos Aires (2002). Elle enseigne à l'École d'architecture de l'Universidad de Las Américas ainsi qu'à celle de Talca.

# POLI HOUSE

*Coliumo Peninsula, Chile, 2003–05*

*Floor area: 180 m². Client: Eduardo Meissner, Rosmarie Prim (Casapoli Cultural Center).
Cost: $66 600*

Located 550 kilometers south of Santiago, this house was conceived as a "multipurpose space; both as cultural center and temporary residence." Local technology, non-specialized workers, and hand-made concrete were used, as well as the wood frames employed for the concrete that were then recycled for interior insulation. The architects placed the structure as close as possible to the cliff edge on the 10 000-square-meter site. This location was selected "in order to capture two things: both the sensation of a natural podium surrounded by vastness and the morbid and unavoidable sight of the foot of the cliffs, where the sea explodes against the rocks." The interior floor is divided into three platforms that "adapt to the slope in a zigzagging way." A triple-height space is set on the lower platform, oriented to the northwest. The use of the structure as both a summer house and as a cultural center required the architects to reconcile domestic and "monumental" scales. The service functions (kitchen, bathrooms, closets, vertical circulation) are located at the perimeter, inside a thick wall that acts as a buffer and can be used for furniture storage. Sliding wood panels can be used to close the house entirely.

Dieses 550 km südlich von Santiago gelegene Haus war als »Mehrzweckraum [konzipiert] und sollte sowohl als Kulturzentrum wie als zeitweiliges Wohnhaus dienen«. Es wurde mit heimischer Technologie, ohne Facharbeiter und mit von Hand hergestelltem Beton errichtet, außerdem wurden die für den Beton verwendeten Holzrahmen anschließend für die Dämmung des Innenraums weiterverwendet. Die Architekten platzierten den Bau so nah wie möglich an die meerseitige Abbruchkante des 10 000 m² großen Grundstücks. Man wählte den Ort, »um zwei Phänomene einzufangen: Das Empfinden eines von unermesslicher Weite umgebenen natürlichen Podiums und den morbiden und unvermeidlichen Anblick des am Fuß der Klippe gegen die Felsen donnernden Meeres«. Der Innenraum verteilt sich auf drei Ebenen, die »sich zickzackförmig an den Abhang anpassen«. Auf der untersten Ebene befindet sich ein nach Nordwesten ausgerichteter Raum mit dreifacher Deckenhöhe. Aufgrund der zweifachen Nutzung des Gebäudes als Sommerhaus wie auch als Kulturzentrum waren die Architekten gezwungen, häusliche und »monumentale« Größenordnungen miteinander in Einklang zu bringen. Die Funktionsräume (Küche, Bäder, Schränke, vertikale Erschließung) befinden sich am Außenrand im Inneren einer massiven Wand, die als Puffer dient und auch zum Lagern von Möbelstücken verwendet werden kann. Mittels verschiebbarer Holzplatten lässt sich das Haus komplett verschließen.

Située à 550 km au sud de Santiago du Chili, cette maison construite sur un terrain de 10 000 m² a été conçue comme un espace « polyvalent, à la fois centre culturel et résidence temporaire ». Sa construction a fait appel aux technologies maîtrisables localement, à des ouvriers non spécialisés et du béton préparé in situ dont le bois de coffrage a été recyclé pour l'isolation intérieure. Les architectes ont rapproché autant que possible la construction du bord de la falaise. Le lieu a été choisi « pour capter deux choses : la sensation d'un podium naturel entouré de l'immensité et la vue fascinante du pied des falaises où la mer explose contre les rochers ». Le volume intérieur est divisé en trois plates-formes qui « s'adaptent à la pente en zigzag ». Un espace triple-hauteur occupe la plate-forme inférieure, orientée vers le nord-ouest. La double fonction de centre culturel et de résidence d'été entraînait la conciliation des échelles domestique et « monumentale ». Les services (cuisine, salles de bains, placards, circulation verticale) ont été reportés en périmétrie dans la masse d'un mur qui joue le rôle de tampon et peut également servir au stockage de mobilier. Des panneaux de bois coulissants permettent de clore entièrement la maison.

The house sits above the Pacific, and offers a grandiose view of the setting sun.

*Das Haus liegt über dem Pazifik und bietet eine grandiose Aussicht auf die untergehende Sonne.*

*La maison qui domine le Pacifique offre des couchers de soleil grandioses.*

The basic floor plan is a perfect square, but the architects have introduced an unusual double-shell system that means that the walls are in effect inhabited.

Der Grundriss ist im Grunde quadratisch, aber die Architekten verwenden eine ungewöhnliche doppelschalige Bauweise, das heißt, die Wandzwischenräume sind Teil der Wohnfläche.

Le plan au sol est un carré parfait, mais les architectes ont introduit un système de double-coque qui fait que les murs sont utilisés dans leur épaisseur même.

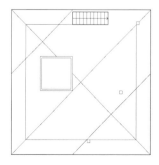

The rough finishing of the house makes it well adapted to its spectacular, but rocky, natural setting.

Die rohe Oberfläche des Hauses passt gut zu seinem grandiosen, wenngleich felsigen Standort.

La finition brute de la maison semble bien adaptée à son cadre naturel spectaculaire et rocheux.

Windows of various sizes and set at unexpected levels animate the interior space and allow views of the ocean, while also admitting ample natural light.

Die unterschiedlich großen und in unregelmäßigen Abständen eingeschnittenen Fenster sorgen für reichlich Tageslicht, variieren den Innenraum und gestatten Ausblicke auf den Ozean.

Des fenêtres de dimensions variées, percées à des niveaux inattendus, animent l'espace intérieur et favorisent les perspectives sur l'océan, tout en laissant pénétrer une généreuse lumière naturelle.

*The house encourages communion with the remarkable natural setting, while providing the necessary level of comfort.*

*Das Haus scheint gut geeignet für eine Verbindung mit seinem bemerkenswerten Standort, während es gleichzeitig den nötigen Komfort bietet.*

*La maison est en communion réelle avec son remarquable cadre naturel, en offrant cependant le niveau de confort nécessaire.*

# RENZO PIANO

*Renzo Piano Building Workshop*
*34, rue des Archives*
*75004 Paris*
*France*

*Tel: +33 1 4461 4900 / Fax: +33 1 4278 0198*
*E-mail: info@rpbw.com / Web: www.rpbw.com*

**RENZO PIANO** was born in 1937 in Genoa, Italy. He studied at the University of Florence, and at the Polytechnic Institute, Milan (1964). He formed his own practice (Studio Piano) in 1965, then associated with Richard Rogers (Piano & Rogers, 1971–78). Piano completed the Pompidou Center in Paris in 1977. From 1978 to 1980, he worked with Peter Rice (Piano & Rice Associates). He created the Renzo Piano Building Workshop in 1981 in Genoa and Paris. Piano received the RIBA Gold Medal, 1989. His built work includes: Menil Collection Museum (Houston, Texas, 1981–86); conversion of the Lingotto Factory Complex (Turin, Italy, 1983–2003); Cité Internationale de Lyon (Lyon, France, 1985–96); San Nicola Stadium (Bari, Italy, 1987–90); the 1988–90 extension of the IRCAM (Paris); Kansai International Airport Terminal (Osaka, Japan, 1988–94); Beyeler Foundation Museum (Riehen, Basel, Switzerland, 1991–97); Jean-Marie Tjibaou Cultural Center (New Caledonia, 1991–98); Padre Pio Pilgrimage Church (San Giovanni Rotondo, Foggia, Italy, 1991–2004); Potsdamer Platz reconstruction (Berlin, Germany, 1992–2000); Mercedes-Benz Center (Stuttgart, Germany, 1993–98); Rome Auditorium (Italy, 1994–2002); Parma Auditorium (Italy, 1997–2001); Maison Hermès (Tokyo, Japan, 1998–2001); and renovation and expansion of the Morgan Library (New York, New York, 2000–06, published here). Current projects include: New York Times Tower (New York, New York, 2004–07); Whitney Museum of American Art (New York); Woodruff Arts Center Expansion (Atlanta, Georgia); London Bridge Tower (London); California Academy of Sciences (San Francisco); and The Chicago Art Institute Expansion (Chicago).

**RENZO PIANO** wurde 1937 in Genua geboren. Er studierte an der Universität von Florenz und am Polytechnischen Institut in Mailand (1964). 1965 eröffnete er unter dem Namen Studio Piano ein eigenes Büro und schloss sich dann mit Richard Rogers zu Piano & Rogers zusammen (1971–78). 1977 errichteten sie das Centre Pompidou in Paris. Von 1978 bis 1980 arbeitete er mit Peter Rice (Piano & Rice Associates). 1981 eröffnete er in Genua und Paris den Renzo Piano Building Workshop. 1989 erhielt Piano die Goldmedaille der RIBA. Zu seinen realisierten Bauten gehören: Menil Collection Museum (Houston, Texas, 1981–86), Umbau des Fiat-Werks Lingotto (Turin, 1983–2003), Cité Internationale de Lyon (Lyon, 1985–96), Stadion San Nicola (Bari, 1987–90), die Erweiterung des IRCAM (Paris, 1988–90), Kansai International Airport Terminal (Osaka, 1988–94), Museum der Fondation Beyeler (Riehen bei Basel, 1991–97), Kulturzentrum Jean-Marie Tjibaou (Neukaledonien, 1991–98), Pilgerkirche Padre Pio (San Giovanni Rotondo, Foggia, Italien, 1991–2004), Wiederaufbau des Potsdamer Platzes (Berlin, 1992–2000), Mercedes-Benz-Center (Stuttgart, 1993–98), Auditorium in Rom (1994–2002), Auditorium in Parma (1997–2001), Maison Hermès (Tokio, 1998–2001) und Renovierung und Ausbau der Morgan Library (New York, 2000–06 hier publiziert). Aktuelle Projekte sind: New York Times Tower (New York, 2004–07), Whitney Museum of American Art (New York), Erweiterung des Woodruff Arts Center (Atlanta, Georgia), London Bridge Tower (London), California Academy of Sciences (San Francisco) und die Erweiterung des Chicago Art Institute (Chicago).

**RENZO PIANO** né en 1937 à Gênes, Italie étudie à l'Université de Florence et à l'Institut Polytechnique de Milan (1964). Il crée son agence, Studio Piano, en 1965, puis s'associe à Richard Rogers (Piano & Rogers, 1971–78). Ils achèvent le Centre Pompidou à Paris en 1977. De 1978 à 1980, il collabore avec Peter Rice (Piano & Rice Associates). Il fonde le Renzo Piano Building Workshop en 1981 à Gênes et Paris. Il a reçu la médaille d'or du RIBA en 1989. Parmi ses réalisations : le Menil Collection Museum, Houston, Texas (1981–86) ; la conversion de l'usine du Lingotto, Turin, Italie (1983–2003) ; la Cité Internationale de Lyon, France (1985–96) ; le stade San Nicola, Bari, Italie (1987–90) ; l'extension de l'IRCAM, Paris (1988–90) ; le terminal de l'aéroport international du Kansai Airport, Osaka, Japon (1988–94) ; le musée de la Fondation Beyeler, Riehen, Bâle, Suisse (1991–97) ; le Centre culturel Jean-Marie Tjibaou, Nouvelle-Calédonie (1991–98) ; l'église de pèlerinage Padre Pio (San Giovanni Rotondo, Foggia, Italie (1991–2004) ; la reconstruction de la Potsdamer Platz, Berlin (1992–2000) ; le Centre Mercedes-Benz, Stuttgart, Allemagne (1993–98) ; l'auditorium de Rome (1994–2002) ; l'auditorium de Parme (1997–2001), la Maison Hermès, Tokyo (1998–2001), et la rénovation et l'agrandissement de la Morgan Library (New York, 2000–06) publiés ici. Ses projets les plus récents comprennent : la New York Times Tower (New York, 2004–07) ; le Whitney Museum of American Art (New York) ; l'agrandissement du Woodruff Arts Center (Atlanta, Georgie) ; la London Bridge Tower (Londres) ; la California Academy of Sciences (San Francisco) et l'agrandissement du Chicago Art Institute (Chicago).

# RENOVATION AND EXPANSION
# OF THE MORGAN LIBRARY

*New York, New York, USA, 2000–06*

*Floor area: 8341 m² (gross space in new building). Client: The Morgan Library. Cost: not disclosed.*
*Collaboration with Beyer Blinder Belle LLP (New York).*
*Design Team: G. Bianchi (partner in charge), T. Sahlmann, K. Doerr, A. Knapp, Y. Pages, M. Reale and P. Bruzzone,*
*M. Cook, S. Abe, M. Aloisini, L. Bouwman, J. Hart, H. Kybicova, M. Leon. Models: Y. Kyrkos, C. Colson, O. Aubert*

Serving as both a museum and a library, the Morgan Library is home to one of the world's largest and finest collections of rare medieval and Renaissance literary and musical manuscripts, books, prints, and drawings. Created by the financier J. P. Morgan (1837–1913), the library was housed in a building designed by New York architects McKim, Mead & White in 1903. The Morgan Library later extended to the Morgan Library Annex Building, built in 1928, and subsequently to a series of other extensions, including the former mansion of the Morgan family (1853), forming a complex assemblage of spaces. With the goal of rendering this situation more rational and also of increasing visitor and storage space, the library called on the Renzo Piano Building Workshop. The architects succeeded in expanding the Morgan by roughly one-third without exceeding the height of the historic structures. This was accomplished in good part by digging into the bedrock beneath the library. A 229-seat auditorium, a three-level storage vault, and mechanical spaces were thus housed below grade in new space. Above ground a new glazed "piazza" creates a sense of unity and coherence between the old and new areas. A new public entrance on Madison Avenue was created, and the existing buildings significantly renovated. A 6-meter cube was added at ground level for the display of the Morgan's masterpieces and as an element that unites the earlier McKim and Annex buildings. A new four-story building directly connected to the Morgan Mansion was added on the north side for offices that face the piazza and 37th Street. The Annex Building was made into the main gallery space, and a new bookshop, café, and small restaurant were also added.

Die sowohl als Museum wie auch als Bibliothek dienende Morgan Library verfügt über die weltweit größte und wertvollste Sammlung seltener literarischer und musikalischer Manuskripte, Bücher, Drucke und Zeichnungen aus Mittelalter und Renaissance. Das von dem Finanzier John Pierpont Morgan (1837–1913) ins Leben gerufene Institut hatte seinen Sitz in einem 1903 von den New Yorker Architekten McKim, Mead & White entworfenen Gebäude. Es wurde 1928 durch das Morgan Library Annex Building erweitert und in der Folge durch eine Reihe anderer Erweiterungsbauten, darunter das 1853 erbaute Herrenhaus der Familie Morgan vergrößert, die zusammen eine komplexe Ansammlung von Räumlichkeiten ergaben. Mit dem Ziel, diese Situation rationeller zu gestalten und darüber hinaus den Raum für Besucher und das Depot zu vergrößern, wandte sich die Bibliothek an Renzo Pianos Building Workshop. Den Architekten gelang es, die Bibliothek um etwa ein Drittel ihres Raums zu erweitern, ohne die Höhe der historischen Bauten zu überschreiten. Das war zum größten Teil dadurch möglich, dass sie die Felssohle unter der Bibliothek aus-schachteten. So entstanden in dem neuen unterirdischen Raum ein Auditorium mit 229 Plätzen, ein dreistöckiges Lager sowie Räume für die Haustechnik. Oberirdisch lässt eine neue verglaste »Piazza« zwischen den alten und neuen Gebäudeteilen ein Gefühl der Einheitlichkeit und Stimmigkeit entstehen. Die bestehenden Baulichkeiten wurden umfassend renoviert, an der Madison Avenue entstand ein neuer öffentlicher Zugang. Zur Ausstellung von Morgans Kostbarkeiten und auch als ein Element, die früheren Bauten McKims und die Anbauten zusammenschließt, kam ebenerdig ein Kubus von 6 m Seitenlänge hinzu. An der Nordseite entstand ein direkt mit dem Wohnhaus der Morgans verbundenes, viergeschossiges Gebäude, in dem Büros mit Blick auf die Piazza und die 37. Straße untergebracht sind. Das Annexgebäude wurde zum Hauptausstellungsraum. Darüber hinaus wurde der Komplex um einen neuen Buchladen, ein Café und ein kleines Restaurant ergänzt.

Musée et bibliothèque, la Morgan Library abrite l'une des plus vastes et plus belles collections au monde de manuscrits littéraires et musicaux rares, de livres, d'estampes et de dessins du Moyen Âge et de la Renaissance. Fondée par le financier J. P. Morgan (1837–1913), la bibliothèque était logée dans un bâtiment de 1903 conçu par les architectes new-yorkais McKim, Mead & White. Elle s'étendit par la suite dans une annexe édifiée en 1928, puis dans d'autres extensions, dont l'ancienne résidence de la famille Morgan (1853), pour finir par constituer un assemblage complexe de volumes. Pour le rationaliser et multiplier le nombre de visiteurs et la capa-cité des réserves, la Bibliothèque fit appel à Renzo Piano qui réussit à accroître l'ensemble d'environ un tiers sans dépasser la hauteur des bâtiments anciens. Ceci a pu se faire en grande partie grâce au creusement en souterrain. Un auditorium de 229 places, un magasin de stockage de trois niveaux et des espaces techniques ont ainsi été créés en sous-sol. Au-dessus, une nouvelle *piazza* vitrée suscite un sentiment d'unité et de cohérence entre les parties anciennes et nouvelles. Une nouvelle entrée du public a été ouverte sur Madison Avenue et les bâtiments existants rénovés en profondeur. Un cube de 6 mètres de côté a été installé au rez-de-chaussée pour pré-senter des chefs-d'œuvre des collections, et établir un lien entre les bâtiments McKim et l'annexe. Un nouvel immeuble de bureaux sur quatre niveaux, directement relié à la résidence Morgan, a été ajouté au nord face à la *piazza* et sur la 37e rue. L'annexe est devenue la galerie principale et une nouvelle librairie, un café et un petit restaurant sont venus compléter ce dispositif.

Models and a photograph of the completed entrance on Madison Avenue show how Piano has integrated his expansion into a block of existing houses, themselves integrated over time into the Morgan Library complex.

Modelle und eine Fotografie des fertiggestellten Eingangs an der Madison Avenue zeigen, wie Piano seine Erweiterung in einen vorhandenen Häuserblock, der seinerseits über die Jahre mit dem Komplex der Morgan Library verschmolzen war, integrierte.

Les maquettes et une photographie de l'entrée sur Madison Avenue montrent comment Piano a inséré son extension dans un bloc d'immeubles existants, eux-mêmes intégrés avec le temps dans le complexe de la Morgan Library.

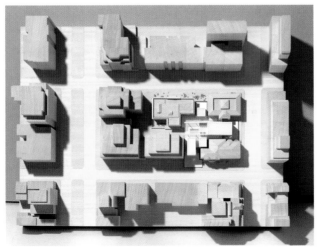

The interior "piazza" of the Morgan Library is the element that unites its formerly disparate parts. Below, sections show the large spaces carved out of the bedrock of Manhattan for the storage and auditorium areas.

Die innere »Piazza« der Morgan Library ist das verbindende Element ihrer vormals disparaten Bestandteile. Die unten abgebildeten Schnitte zeigen, wie die großen Räume für Lager und Auditorium aus dem Untergrund Manhattans ausgeschnitten wurden.

La « piazza » intérieure de la Morgan Library réunit des éléments auparavant disparates. Ci-dessous, des coupes montrent les vastes volumes creusés dans le socle rocheux de Manhattan pour les réserves et les auditoriums.

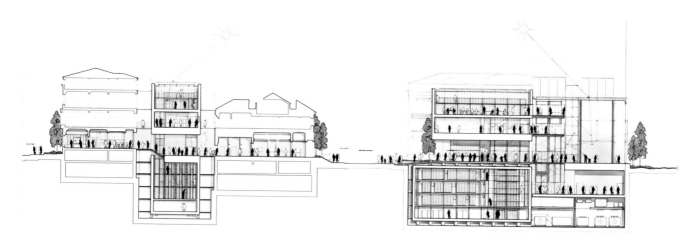

Piano's addition appears at various points around the block, integrating the library's different parts, made up of a heterogeneous set of stone and brick houses.

Pianos Anbau kommt an verschiedenen Stellen rund um den Straßenblock herum zum Vorschein und integriert die verschiedenen Teile der Bibliothek, die aus einer heterogenen Ansammlung von Stein- und Backsteinhäusern besteht.

L'extension apparaît à divers endroits, intégrant les différentes parties du complexe composé de constructions diverses en pierre ou en brique.

*Above, the auditorium and reading room for precious manuscripts.*

*Oben Auditorium und Leseraum der Handschriftensammlung.*

*En haut, l'auditorium et la salle de lecture des manuscrits précieux.*

*Below and left, the interior piazza of the library created by Piano. The image below was taken looking straight up.*

*Unten und links die von Piano geschaffene, innere »Piazza« der Bibliothek. Das untenstehende Bild zeigt den Blick direkt nach oben.*

*En bas et à gauche, la place intérieure créée par Renzo Piano. L'image ci-dessous a été prise en regardant vers le haut.*

# PIVNICE LTD.

*Pivnice Ltd. Architecture*
*Level 4, AA Building 210 Hereford St.*
*P. O. Box 13825*
*Christchurch 8011*
*New Zealand*

*Tel: +64 3 377 9293*
*Fax: +64 3 377 9294*
*E-mail: pivnice@ihug.co.nz*
*Web: www.pivnice.co.nz*

Jason Mill was born in Gore, Southland, New Zealand, in 1969. He attended Christchurch Polytech (1990), and received his B.Arch degree from the University of Auckland in 1994. He worked with Goodwin Stevens Architecture (Christchurch, 1987–92), Jackson Architects (British Columbia, Canada, 1994), Barclay Hodgeskin Architects (Christchurch, 1995) and Sheppard & Rout Architects (Christchurch, 1995–96), before forming Pivnice Group Architecture in 1996 with Duane Kolkrabs in Christchurch, New Zealand. He has been the Director of **PIVNICE LTD.** since its creation in 2001. The practice has a current staff of five persons. A subsidiary called ZNO, making 3D models for Google Earth, has grown at a rapid rate. Current work, in New Zealand, includes: Mahana House (Mahana, 2005–06, published here); Drummond Studio (Woollston, Christchurch, 2007); Greening House (Scarborough, Christchurch, 2007); Edwards Apartment (Lyttleton, 2007); WaiTapu (Sacred Water) House (Bay of Islands, 2007); AA Apartments (Christchurch, 2007); 5 Star Winery Lodge (Nelson, 2008); NG/Logan House II (Christchurch, 2008). International projects include: Pacific Modernism Development with 2500 dwellings (Pacific Islands, 2008); Pacific Stadium: 3 waterfront stadiums and A1 track development (Pacific Islands, 2010); and a 5000-bed hotel chain development (Pacific Islands/Macau/Las Vegas, 2010).

Jason Mill wurde 1969 in Gore, Southland, Neuseeland geboren. Er besuchte das Polytechnikum in Christchurch (1990) und erwarb 1994 den Grad des B. Arch. an der University of Auckland. Er war bei Goodwin Stevens Architecture (Christchurch, 1987–92), Jackson Architects (British Columbia, Kanada, 1994), Barclay Hodgeskin Architects (Christchurch, 1995) und et Sheppard & Rout Architects (Christchurch, 1995–96) tätig, ehe er 1996 mit Duane Kolkrabs in Christchurch Pivnice Group Architecture gründete. Seit der Gründung von **PIVNICE LTD.** in 2001 hat er die Position des Direktors inne und leitet derzeit einen Mitarbeiterstab von fünf Personen. Eine unter der Bezeichnung ZNO arbeitende Zweigstelle fertigt 3D-Modelle für Google Earth und verzeichnet ein schnelles Wachstum. Neuere Projekte in Neuseeland umfassen: Mahana House (Mahana, 2005–06, hier publiziert), Drummond Studio (Woollston, Christchurch, 2007), Greening House (Scarborough, Christchurch, 2007), Edwards Apartment (Lyttleton, 2007), WaiTapu (Sacred Water) House (Bay of Islands, 2007), AA Apartments (Christchurch, 2007), 5 Star Winery Lodge (Nelson, 2008), NG/Logan House II (Christchurch, 2008). Zu den internationalen Projekten zählen: Pacific Modernism Development mit 2500 Wohnungen (Pacific Islands, 2008), Pacific Stadium – drei Stadien am Ufer und Planung der Formel-1-Rennstrecke (Pacific Islands, 2010) sowie die Entwicklung einer Hotelkette mit 5000-Betten-Häusern (Pacific Islands/Macau/Las Vegas, 2010).

Jason Mill né à Gore, Southland, Nouvelle-Zélande, en 1969 a étudié à Christchurch Polytech (1990). Il est B. Arch. de l'Université d'Auckland (1994). Il a travaillé chez Goodwin Stevens Architecture (Christchurch, 1987–92), Jackson Architects (British Columbia, Canada, 1994), Barclay Hodgeskin Architects, Christchurch (1995) et Sheppard & Rout Architects (Christchurch, 1995–96), avant de fonder l'agence Pivnice Group Architecture en 1996 avec Duane Kolkrabs à Christchurch. Il dirige l'agence **PIVNICE LTD.** depuis sa création en 2001 et emploie cinq personnes. Une filiale, ZNO, réalise des modèles 3D pour Google Earth, et se developpe rapidement. Parmi ses réalisations actuelles en Nouvelle-Zélande : maison Mahana, Mahana (2006), publiée ici ; Drummond Studio, Woollston, Christchurch (2007) ; maison Greening, Scarborough, Christchurch (2007) ; Edwards Apartment, Lyttleton (2007) ; maison WaiTapu (Eau sacrée), Bay of Islands (2007) ; AA Apartments, Christchurch (2008) ; la 5 Star Winery Lodge, Nelson (2008) ; NG/Logan House II, Christchurch (2007–08). Parmi les projets internationaux : Pacific Modernism Development, un complexe de 2500 appartements, Pacific Islands (2008); Pacific Stadium, trois stades en front de mer et piste de Formule I, Pacific Islands (2010), et des hôtels de chaîne de 5000 lits à Pacific Islands, Macau et Las Vegas (2010).

# MAHANA HOUSE

*Mahana, New Zealand, 2005–06*

*Floor area: 572 m² addition; 1052 m² total. Client: not disclosed.*
*Cost: not disclosed*

The Mahana House is located on the Woollaston Estate Winery in the Upper Moutere Valley. An existing structure was to be developed into a residence for a director and his extended family. The owner developed a sculpture program in conjunction with the winery, and the architects were contacted early in 2005 by the New Zealand sculptor Andrew Drummond, artistic adviser for the winery. The client wished to give a new visual cohesiveness to the architecture "informed by a modern aesthetic." Letting themselves be inspired by the art collection of the client, including works by Donald Judd, the "reduction and simplicity of line and form" became the theme for their intervention. An upper level containing a large gallery, office, library, master bedroom, and guest suite, together with extensive decks, were added to the top of the existing house. The existing house employed cedar weatherboards and corrugated zincalume (zinc/aluminum alloy-coated steel). The new addition uses cedar screen, steel framing, zincalume and corked teak decking. The two levels are intentionally distinctively different in exterior footprint and interior finish. The need to employ lightweight construction allowed the architects "to make a strong reference to traditional NZ building forms and their timber-based lightweight construction."

Das Mahana House liegt auf dem Gelände des Weinguts Woollaston im Upper Moutere Valley. Ein vorhandenes Gebäude sollte zu einem Wohnhaus für einen Direktor und seine erweiterte Familie umgestaltet werden. Der Eigentümer entwickelte in Verbindung mit dem Weingut ein Skulpturenprogramm und Anfang 2005 nahm der neuseeländische Bildhauer Andrew Drummond, künstlerischer Berater des Weinguts, Kontakt mit den Architekten auf. Der Auftraggeber wünschte sich für die Architektur einen »von einer modernen Ästhetik durchdrungenen« neuen visuellen Zusammenhalt. Inspiriert von der Kunstsammlung des Bauherrn, machten sich die Architekten »Reduktion und Einfachheit von Linie und Form« zum Leitmotiv. Auf dem Dach des vorhandenen Hauses entstand ein Obergeschoss mit einer geräumigen Galerie, Büro, Bibliothek, Hauptschlafraum und Gästesuite sowie ausgedehnten Freiflächen. Das alte Haus war mit Zedernholz und gewelltem Zincalume (mit Zink-Aluminiumlegierung beschichteter Stahl) verkleidet. Bei dem neuen Anbau wurden Zedernholzgitter, Stahlskelett, Zincalume und Teakholzbelag verwendet. Die Notwendigkeit, Leichtbaustoffe zu verwenden, ermöglichte es den Architekten »sich deutlich auf traditionelle neuseeländische Bauformen und ihre auf Holz basierende Leichtbauweise zu beziehen«.

La maison Mahana se trouve dans le domaine viticole de Woollaston dans la Upper Moutere Valley. Le projet consistait en la transformation d'une construction existante en résidence pour le directeur et sa grande famille, qui souhaitait également développer un programme de sculpture en liaison avec l'exploitation viticole. Les architectes furent d'ailleurs contactés en 2005 par le sculpteur néo-zélandais Andrew Drummond, conseiller artistique de la Woolaston Estate Winery. Le client recherchait également une cohésion visuelle architecturale nouvelle, « nourrie d'une esthétique moderne ». Inspirées de la collection d'art de leur client, la « réduction et la simplicité de ligne et de forme » devinrent ainsi le thème de cette intervention. Un niveau supérieur contenant une grande galerie d'expositions, des bureaux, une bibliothèque, la chambre principale et une suite pour invités ainsi que de grandes terrasses a été ajouté au-dessus de la maison existante. Celle-ci utilisait le cèdre patiné et le Zincalume ondulé (acier enrobé d'un alliage de zinc et d'aluminium). L'addition a fait appel à une ossature en acier, des écrans en cèdre, du Zincalume et des terrasses en teck bouchonné. Les deux niveaux se présentent volontairement de façon très différente dasn leur spect et leur finition intérieure. La nécessité d'une construction légère a encouragé les architectes à « faire référence aux formes traditionnelles du bâti néo-zélandais et ses constructions légères à base de bois ».

*Above, the house with the newly added section to the left. The architects have both respected the original structure and added an element with a considerable amount of originality.*

*Oben: das Haus mit dem neuen Anbau zur Linken. Die Architekten haben sowohl den ursprünglichen Bau respektiert als auch ein Element von beträchtlicher Eigenständigkeit hinzugefügt.*

*En haut, la maison et sa partie ajoutée, à gauche. Les architectes ont à la fois respecté la construction d'origine et ajouté un élément d'une très grande originalité.*

The addition seen here appears almost to be an independent house, with its main volume lifted in part off the site on thin pilotis, emphasizing its lightness. As the elevations below show, the house takes into account a change in levels of the site.

Hier wirkt der Anbau fast wie ein freistehendes Haus, dessen Hauptbaukörper auf dünnen Stützen über das Baugelände angehoben ist, was seine Leichtbauweise unterstreicht. Wie die Aufrisse unten zeigen, passt sich das Haus dem Höhenunterschied des Geländes an.

L'extension semble constituer une maison pratiquement indépendante. Son volume principal est en partie surélevé sur des pilotis, ce qui met en valeur sa légèreté. Comme l'élévation ci-dessous le montre, elle prend en compte les différences de niveau du terrain.

Thin columns and horizontal cedar slats engender a feeling of lightness that corresponds to the intentions of the architects and allows for considerable light and air to enter the structure.

*Dünne Stützen und horizontal angebrachte Lamellen aus Zedernholz sorgen für das vom Architekten intendierte Gefühl der Leichtigkeit und für eine gute Helligkeit und Durchlüftung des Gebäudes.*

*Les fines colonnes et les lattes de cèdres donnent un sentiment de légèreté qui répond aux intentions de l'architecte, et permettent à l'air et à la lumière de s'écouler à travers la maison.*

Light, bright spaces looking out to the natural setting and making space for the owners' collection of modern art are clearly the goals of this scheme, as these images show.

Wie diese Abbildungen zeigen, waren lichte, helle Räume mit Blick auf die umgebende Landschaft und mit Raum für die vom Besitzer gesammelte moderne Kunst eindeutig Ziel dieses Entwurfs.

Les espaces clairs et lumineux donnant sur l'environnement naturel sont adaptés à la collection d'œuvres d'art moderne des propriétaires. Ces qualités faisaient partie des objectifs du projet comme le montrent ces images.

# PORNCHAI BOONSOM

*Pornchai Boonsom Architect*
*288 Srivara Road*
*Soi Lad Phrao 94*
*Wangthonglang, Bangkok 10310*
*Thailand*

*Tel: +66 08 1310 6696*
*Fax: +66 02 530 3795*
*E-mail: nopparat_sur@yahoo.com*
*Web: www.thelastdesing.com*

*MnG House*

**PORNCHAI BOONSOM** was born in 1964 in Songkhla, in southern Thailand near the Malaysian border. He received his B.Arch degree from the Southern California Institute of Architecture (SCI-Arc) in 1985, his M.Arch degree from the University of Michigan at Ann Arbor (1987), and had a Fellowship at the same institution in Interior Design (1990). He then worked successively in the offices of Craig Hodgetts, Neil Denari, Peter Eisenman, and Morphosis. Aside from the MnG House published here, he has worked on the A House (Chiang Rai, 1998–99); and on the interior space of the Science Museum (Bangkok, 1999, in collaboration with Pealong Associates). Recent work includes the Bn House (Bangkok, 2003–04); Coffee Pavillion, Art/4d (Bangkok, 2004); a Media Showroom (Bangkok, 2007); and Is House (Bangkok, 2007), all in Thailand.

**PORNCHAI BOONSOM** wurde 1964 in Songkhla in Südthailand nahe der malaysischen Grenze geboren. 1985 erhielt er seinen Bachelor in Architektur vom Southern California Institute of Architecture, 1987 gefolgt von einem M.Arch. an der University of Michigan in Ann Arbor, wo er 1990 ein Stipendium in Innenarchitektur erhielt. Anschließend arbeitete er nacheinander in den Büros von Craig Hodgetts, Neil Denari, Peter Eisenman und Morphosis. Neben dem hier publizierten MnG House arbeitete er am A House (Chiang Rai, 1998–99) sowie an den Innenräumen des Wissenschaftsmuseums in Bangkok (1999 in Zusammenarbeit mit Pealong Associates). Zu seinen neueren Arbeiten zählen Bn House (Bangkok, 2003–04), der Kaffeepavillon Art/4d (Bangkok, 2004), ein Medien-Ausstellungsraum (Bangkok, 2007) und das Is House (Bangkok, 2007), alle in Thailand.

**PORNCHAI BOONSOM** est né en 1964 à Songkhla, dans le sud de la Thaïlande près de la frontière malaise. Il est B. Arch. du Southern California Institute of Architecture (SCI-Arc, 1985), M. Arch. de l'Université du Michigan à Ann Arbor (1987), et enseigne l'architecture intérieure dans la même institution (1990). Il a ensuite travaillé successivement dans les agences de Craig Hodgetts, Neil Denari, Peter Eisenman, et Morphosis. En dehors de la maison MnG publiée ici, il est l'auteur du projet de la maison A, Chiang Rai (1998–99) et de l'aménagement intérieur du Musée des sciences de Bangkok, en collaboration avec Pealong Associates (1999). Parmi ses interventions récentes, toutes en Thaïlande : la maison Bn, Bangkok (2003–04) ; un Pavillon de café, Art/4d, Bangkok (2004) ; un showroom pour médias, Bangkok (2007) et la maison Is, Bangkok (2007).

# MNG HOUSE

*Bangkok, Thailand, 2001–02*

Floor area: 600 m². Client: Suphanee Sethapotra. Cost: $600 000

The complex shapes and angular forms of the MnG House make it stand out from its environment and indeed from many works of contemporary architecture.

Die komplexen, eckigen Formen des MnG House heben es von seiner Umgebung und ebenso von vielen zeitgenössischen Bauten ab.

Les formes complexes et anguleuses de la maison MnG la détachent de son environnement et la distinguent également de nombreuses réalisations architecturales contemporaines.

"The MnG House," says the architect, "is based on the exploration in time and dynamic movement of interactive forces. It is a specific reflection on the philosophical concept and an architectural experiment in time as different from the space-time relationship in modern architecture." The geometry of the house is composed of an assemblage of cubic volumes. The continuity of floor, wall, and ceiling on the first floor is seen by Pornchai Boonsom as being part of his reflection on time and space. Located on a 480-square-meter site, the house is three-and-a-half floors high and has a total floor space of 600 square meters. The architect's intention was to maximize the usable area and the complex design comprises a series of seven steps or levels. It contains office space, a reception room, dining room, multipurpose room, family and maids' rooms, a prayer room, four bedrooms, and a parking area. The office area occupies two floors and has its own private stairway. The MnG House is a beam-column structure built with massive reinforced concrete. No less than 500 cubic meters of concrete were used for the construction. Other construction materials are structural steel, brick, glass, aluminum and timber. The house is 14 meters wide, 23 meters long, and 13.7 meters high.

»Das MnG House«, sagt der Architekt, »basiert auf der Auslotung interaktiver Kräfte in Zeit und dynamischer Bewegung. Es handelt sich um eine spezifische Überlegung zum philosophischen Konzept und um ein architektonisches Experiment in der Zeit so verschieden von der Raum-Zeit-Beziehung in der modernen Architektur.« Das Haus besteht aus einer Ansammlung kubischer Baukörper. Die im ersten Geschoss herrschende Kontinuität von Boden, Wand und Decke wird von Pornchai Boonsom als Teil seiner Überlegungen zu Zeit und Raum betrachtet. Das auf einem 480 m² großen Grundstück stehende Haus hat dreieinhalb Geschosse und eine Gesamtfläche von 600 m². Absicht des Architekten war es, die Nutzfläche zu maximieren, und die komplexe Gestaltung entstand in einer Folge von sieben Stufen oder Ebenen. Das Haus verfügt über Büroräume, einen Empfang, Speisezimmer, Mehrzweckraum, Zimmer für Familie und Hausangestellte, Andachtsraum, vier Schlafräume und eine Parkfläche. Der Bürobereich umfasst zwei Stockwerke und verfügt über eine eigene Treppe. Bei dem MnG House handelt es sich um einen Träger-Stützen-Bau aus massivem Stahlbeton, für den insgesamt 500 m³ Beton verwendet wurden. Außerdem wurden Baustahl, Backstein, Glas, Aluminium und Holz benutzt. Das Haus ist 14 m breit, 23 m lang und 13,7 m hoch.

«La maison MnG, explique l'architecte, est issue d'une exploration du temps et du mouvement dynamique de forces interactives. C'est une réflexion spécifique sur un concept philosophique et une expérimentation architecturale dans le temps aussi différente que celle de la relation espace-temps par l'architecture moderne. » La maison se présente sous la forme d'un assemblage de volumes cubiques. La continuité des sols, murs et plafonds du rez-de-chaussée intègre cette réflexion sur le temps et l'espace. Située sur un terrain de 480 m², la résidence compte trois niveaux et demi pour une surface totale de 600 m². L'intention de l'architecte était d'obtenir la plus grande surface utile possible et son plan complexe se développe en une succession de sept marches ou niveaux. Elle contient un bureau, une salle à manger, une salle multifonctions, des pièces pour la famille et les domestiques, une pièce de prière, quatre chambres et une aire de parking. Le bureau occupe deux niveaux et possède son propre escalier d'accès. La maison possède une structure en massives colonnes de béton armé. Pas moins de 500 m³ de béton ont d'ailleurs été utilisés sur ce chantier. Les autres matériaux de base sont l'acier structurel, la brique, le verre, l'aluminium et le bois. Elle mesure 14 mètres de large, 23 mètres de long et 13,7 mètres de haut.

The external shapes of the house, here seen in a broader context than opposite, confirm the initial impression of angular complexity—a certain "prickliness" that intrigues but may also lead some to reject this structure.

Die hier in größerem Zusammenhang zu sehenden äußeren Formen des Hauses bestätigen den anfänglichen Eindruck verwinkelter Komplexität – eine gewisse, faszinierende »Stacheligkeit«, die allerdings manchen dieses Gebäude ablehnen lässt.

La forme extérieure de la maison, vue ici dans un contexte plus large que ci-contre, confirme l'impression initiale de complexité anguleuse, d'une sorte de « hérissement » qui intrigue, mais peut également provoquer un rejet.

*The external complexity of the house
is clearly echoed in its interior as
seen in these views.*

*Wie man auf diesen Bildern sieht,
spiegelt sich die äußere Komplexität
deutlich im Inneren.*

*La complexité externe de la maison
se retrouve à l'intérieur, comme le
montrent ces photographies.*

*Curves are nowhere in site in these
interior photographs, but open, inter-
penetrating spaces define and inform
the architecture.*

*Auf diesen Innenaufnahmen erkennt
man sich gegenseitig durchdringende
Räume, die die Architektur definieren
und formen, nirgendwo jedoch gebogene Linien.*

*Pas de courbes, mais des espaces
ouverts qui s'interpénètrent et définissent l'organisation interne.*

# MUTI RANDOLPH

Muti Randolph
Praia de Botafogo, 68/601
22250–040
Rio de Janeiro
Brazil

Tel: +55 21 2551 2692
Fax: +55 21 9179 6290
E-mail: m@muti.cx
Web: www.muti.cx

**MUTI RANDOLPH** is an illustrator, graphic art designer, set maker, and creator of a number of noted interiors. His clubs, like D-Edge or U-Turn, are inspired by "computers and electronic equipment" as well as the "unique freedom and playfulness" of the 1960s. "The main concept of my party and club projects is giving shape and color to the music," he says. Born in 1967 in Rio de Janeiro, Muti Randolph studied Visual Communications and Industrial Design at the Pontificia Universidade Católica do Rio de Janeiro. He started his career as a graphic designer and illustrator in the late 1980s. One of the pioneers in computer art, 3D illustration and animation in Brazil, he began shifting from virtual 3D to real 3D spaces. His interest in music and technology is very apparent in his projects, where he explores the relationship between music and space. He has been developing a software to synch live music and video used in some current permanent and temporary projects. Some of his noted projects are: U-Turn Nightclub (São Paulo, 1997); Tozen Nightclub (Campo Grande, 2001); D-Edge Nightclub (São Paulo, 2003, published here); Galeria Melissa (São Paulo, 2005); São Paulo Fashion Week (2005); and I Capuleti e i Montecchi Opera at the Teatro Municipal do Rio de Janeiro (2006). He is presently working on an extension of D-Edge, including a second dance floor and bar, a private lounge and an open terrace.

**MUTI RANDOLPH** ist ein Illustrator, Grafiker, Bühnenbildner und Gestalter einer Reihe bekannter Interieurs. Seine Clubs, wie D-Edge oder U-Turn. sind angeregt von »Computern und elektronischem Gerät«, wie auch von der »einzigartigen Freiheit und Verspieltheit« der 1960er-Jahre. »Die Hauptidee meiner Party- und Clubprojekte besteht darin, der Musik Form und Farbe zu geben«, sagt er. Der 1967 in Rio de Janeiro geborene Randolph studierte an der Pontificia Universidade Católica do Rio de Janeiro Visuelle Kommunikation und Industriedesign. Ende der 1980er-Jahre begann er seine Laufbahn als Grafiker und Illustrator. Als einer der Pioniere in Computerkunst, 3D-Abbildung und Animation in Brasilien fing er an, seine Tätigkeit von virtuellen auf reale 3D-Räume zu verlegen. Sein Interesse an Musik und Technik kommt in seinen Projekten, mit denen er die Beziehung zwischen Musik und Raum erforscht, sehr deutlich zum Ausdruck. Er entwickelte eine Software zur Synchronisierung von Live-Musik und Video, die zurzeit bei einigen permanenten und temporären Projekten verwendet wird. Zu seinen bekannten Projekten zählen: der Nachtclub U-Turn (São Paulo, 1997), Nachtclub Tozen (Campo Grande, 2001), Nachtclub D-Edge (São Paulo, 2003, hier publiziert), Galeria Melissa (São Paulo, 2005), São Paulo Modewoche (2005) und die Oper »I Capuleti e i Montecchi« am Teatro Municipal do Rio de Janeiro (2006). Zurzeit arbeitet er an der Erweiterung des D-Edge, mit einer zweiten Tanzfläche und Bar, einer Private Lounge und Außenterrasse.

**MUTI RANDOLPH** est illustrateur, graphiste, typographe et créateur de plusieurs aménagements intérieurs remarqués. Les clubs qu'il a réalisés, dont le D-Edge ou le U-Turn sont inspirés par « des équipements informatiques et électroniques » et, dit-il, « la liberté et le goût du jeu unique » des années 1960. « Le principal concept de mes projets de soirées et de clubs est de donner forme et couleur à la musique. » Né en 1967 à Rio de Janeiro, il a étudié la communication visuelle et le design industriel à la Pontificia Universidade Católica de Rio de Janeiro. Il a débuté sa carrière comme graphiste et illustrateur à la fin des années 1980. Un des pionniers de l'art numérique, de l'illustration en 3D et de l'animation au Brésil, il commence à passer de la 3D virtuelle aux vrais espaces tridimensionnels. Son intérêt pour la musique et la technologie est très présent dans ses projets où il explore les relations entre la musique et l'espace. Il a développé un logiciel pour synchroniser en direct musique et vidéo qu'il utilise dans certains projets permanents ou temporaires. Parmi ses réalisations remarquées : Nightclub U-Turn, São Paulo (1997) ; Nightclub Tozen, Campo Grande (2001) ; Nightclub D-Edge, São Paulo (2003) publié ici ; la Galeria Melissa, São Paulo (2005) ; la semaine de la mode de São Paulo (2005) ; les décors de l'opéra de Bellini I Capuleti e i Montecchi au Teatro Municipal de Rio de Janeiro (2006). Il travaille actuellement à une extension du D-Edge comprenant une seconde piste de danse, un bar, un salon privé et une terrasse ouverte.

# D-EDGE

*São Paulo, SP, Brazil, 2003*

Floor area: 300 m². Client: Renato Ratier. Cost: not disclosed

The interior of D-Edge is formed in good part by the architect's innovative use of light and sound.

Die Gestaltung des Innenraums von D-Edge ergibt sich überwiegend durch die innovative Verwendung von Licht und Klang.

L'intérieur du club D-Edge vient en grande partie de l'utilisation novatrice du son et de la lumière.

D-Edge is a fashionable São Paulo nightclub that can accommodate up to 400 people at a time. The materials here are concrete, resin, wood, metalon, Plexiglas, and fluorescent and LED lighting. The concrete floor treated with black resin is the least obvious of Muti Randolph's interventions. As he has said, "The computer is to me what the mirror was to Alice." By bringing his Alice in Wonderland vision of the computer together with light and sound, Muti Randolph forms D-Edge more specifically than any more substantial architectural gesture might. The architect writes that "the space is determined by the light, and the light is determined by the music. The main idea is to show the relation between music and space through lighting, using software that analyzes the sound and makes the light change accordingly." At a time when architects all over the world are seeking to find ways to make their buildings dissolve or change according to lighting conditions for example, Randolph has taken the process a step further, forming space with computer software, light, and sound. Any architecture in the more traditional sense of the word is just a backdrop or a container for his intriguing manipulations of the perception of space.

D-Edge ist ein sehr angesagter Nachtclub in São Paulo, in dem bis zu 400 Besucher gleichzeitig Platz finden. Die hier verwendeten Materialien sind Beton, Kunstharz, Holz, Metalon, Plexiglas sowie fluoreszierende und LED-Beleuchtungskörper. Der am wenigsten augenfällige Beitrag Randolphs ist der mit schwarzem Kunstharz behandelte Betonboden. In Randolphs Worten »ist für mich der Computer, was der Spiegel für Alice war«. Indem er seine Alice-im-Wunderland-Vision des Computers mit Licht und Klang zusammenbringt, prägt Muti Randolph D-Edge deutlicher als jeder substanziellere architektonische Eingriff. Der Architekt schreibt, dass »der Raum vom Licht und das Licht von der Musik bestimmt wird. Die wichtigste Idee besteht darin, die Beziehung von Musik und Raum durch Beleuchtung zu zeigen und dabei Software einzusetzen, die den Sound analysiert und die Beleuchtung entsprechend verändert«. Zu einem Zeitpunkt, an dem Architekten weltweit bestrebt sind, Methoden zu finden, durch die ihre Bauten sich auflösen oder sich z. B. den Beleuchtungsverhältnissen gemäß verändern, hat Randolph das ganze Verfahren einen Schritt weiter geführt, indem er Raum mit Computersoftware, Licht und Klang formt. Jegliche Architektur im traditionelleren Sinn ist nur ein Hintergrund oder Behälter für seine faszinierenden Manipulationen der Wahrnehmung von Raum.

D-Edge est un nightclub à la mode de São Paulo qui peut recevoir jusqu'à 400 personnes. Les matériaux utilisés sont le béton, la résine, le bois, le Métalon, le Plexiglas et un éclairage à base de LED et de tubes fluorescents. Le sol en béton et résine noire est la moins spectaculaire des interventions de Randolph : «Pour moi, l'ordinateur est ce que le miroir était pour Alice. » En rapprochant cette vision de l'informatique de la lumière et du son, il a donné à D-Edge une forme plus spécifique que n'aurait pu le faire un geste classiquement architectural. Il précise que « l'espace est déterminé par la lumière et la lumière déterminée par la musique. L'idée principale est de montrer la relation entre la musique et l'espace via l'éclairage, à partir d'un logiciel qui analyse les sons et modifie la musique en fonction de la lumière. » Dans un contexte où les architectes du monde entier cherchent le moyen d'amener leurs projets à se dissoudre visuellement ou à se transformer en fonction des conditions d'éclairage, Randolph fait avancer ce processus. Toute architecture au sens plus traditionnel du terme ne peut être qu'un fond ou un contenant pour ses étranges manipulations de l'espace.

The lighting patterns of the space vary according to the music being played, creating an ambiance that changes while the basic architectural shell is relatively innocuous.

*Die gerade laufende Musik beeinflusst die Beleuchtungsmuster und erzeugt so ein sich veränderndes Ambiente, wogegen die architektonische Hülle eher konventionell wirkt.*

*Les éclairages varient selon la musique diffusée pour créer une ambiance en modification permanente, à l'intérieur d'une coquille relativement neutre.*

# RICHARD ROGERS

*Rogers Stirk Harbour + Partners*
*Thames Wharf*
*Rainville Road*
*London W6 9HA*
*UK*

*Tel: +44 20 7385 1235*
*Fax: +44 20 7385 8409*
*E-mail: enquiries@rsh-p.com*
*Web: www.rsh-p.com*

**RICHARD ROGERS** was born in Florence in 1933. He studied at the Architectural Association (AA) in London, and received his M.Arch degree from Yale (1954–59). He was the recipient of the 1985 RIBA Gold Medal and the 2000 Praemium Imperiale. He is an Honorary Trustee of the Museum of Modern Art in New York. He founded his present firm Rogers Stirk Harbour + Partners in 1977, just after the completion of the Pompidou Center. "We were young and we wanted to shock them," says Renzo Piano, describing the design of the Georges Pompidou Center (Paris, 1971–77) that he worked on with Rogers. This goal was attained. Piano and Rogers both joined the ranks of the best-known architects in the world, known for a "high-tech" style that Rogers affirmed with very visible structures like the Lloyd's of London Headquarters (1978–86). Rogers subsequently refined his visually complex assemblages in buildings like the Channel 4 Television Headquarters (London, 1990–94), and his Law Courts in Bordeaux (France, 1992–98). Rogers has also participated in large-scale urban schemes like the Lu Jia Zui Masterplan (Shanghai, China, 1992–). Recent and current work includes the Madrid Barajas Airport (Spain, 1997–2005); Hesperia Hotel and Conference Center (Barcelona, 1999–2006); Maggie's Centre (London, 2001–06); and Terminal 5, Heathrow Airport (London, 1989–2008). Another high-profile project is the National Assembly for Wales building in Cardiff (1998–2005, published here).

**RICHARD ROGERS** wurde 1933 in Florenz geboren. Er studierte Architektur an der Architectural Association in London und legte die Prüfung zum M.Arch. in Yale (1954–59) ab. 1985 wurde er mit der Goldmedaille der RIBA und im Jahr 2000 mit dem Praemium Imperiale ausgezeichnet. Er ist Treuhänder ehrenhalber des Museum of Modern Art in New York. Sein jetziges Büro Rogers Stirk Harbour + Partners gründete er 1977, unmittelbar nach Fertigstellung des Centre Pompidou. »Wir waren jung und wollten schockieren«, sagt Renzo Piano, als er den Entwurf des Centre Georges Pompidou (Paris, 1971–77) beschreibt, das er zusammen mit Richard Rogers baute. Dieses Ziel erreichten sie. Piano und Rogers gehören zu den weltweit bekanntesten Architekten, berühmt für ihren Hightechstil, den Rogers mit sehr prägnanten Bauten wie der Zentrale von Lloyd's of London (1978–86) bestätigte. Rogers verfeinerte in der Folge seine visuell komplexen Projekte bei Bauten wie der Zentrale des Fernsehsenders Channel 4 (London, 1990–94) und seinem Gerichtsgebäude in Bordeaux (1992–98). Darüber hinaus beteiligte sich Richard Rogers an großflächigen Stadtprojekten wie dem Gesamtplan Lu Jia Zui (Shanghai, China, seit 1992). Zu neueren bzw. im Bau befindlichen Projekten zählen der Flughafen Barajas, Madrid (1997–2005), Hesperia-Hotel mit Konferenzzentrum (Barcelona, 1999–2006), Maggie's Centre (London, 2001–06) und Terminal 5, Flughafen Heathrow (London, 1989–2008). Ein weiteres vielbeachtetes Projekt ist das hier publizierte Gebäude der National Assembly for Wales in Cardiff (1998–2005).

Né à Florence, Italie, en 1933, **RICHARD ROGERS** étudie à l'Architectural Association de Londres et passe son M. Arch. à la Yale University School of Architecture (1954–59). Il reçoit la médaille d'or du RIBA en 1985 et le Praemium Imperiale en 2000. Il est administrateur honoraire du Museum of Modern Art de New York. Il fonde son agence actuelle, Rogers Stirk Harbour + Partners, en 1977, juste après l'achèvement du Centre Pompidou. «Nous étions jeunes et nous voulions les choquer », dit Renzo Piano pour décrire ce projet parisien (1971–77) dont il est le co-auteur. Le but fut atteint. Piano et Rogers rejoignirent alors les rangs des architectes les plus célèbres du monde, connus pour ce nouveau style *high-tech* que Rogers poursuit dans des réalisations très vues comme le siège des Lloyd's, Londres (1978–86) ; le siège de Channel 4, Londres (1990–94) et le Palais de justice de Bordeaux (1992–98). Richard Rogers a également participé à des projets d'urbanisme à grande échelle comme le plan directeur du district de Lu Jia Zui, Shanghai, Chine (1992–). Parmi ses réalisations récentes : l'aéroport de Barajas à Madrid (1997–2005) ; l'Hesperia Hotel and Conference Center, Barcelone (1999–2006) ; le Maggie's Centre, Londres (2001–06), et le Terminal 5 de l'aéroport d'Heathrow, Londres (1989–2008). Son projet pour l'Assemblée nationale du Pays de Galles à Cardiff (1998–2005), publié ici, a été très remarqué.

# NATIONAL ASSEMBLY FOR WALES

*Cardiff, Wales, UK, 1998–2005*

*Floor area: 4000 m². Client: National Assembly for Wales.*
*Cost: € 60 586 000*

The brief for the April 1998 international design competition for this project, won by Richard Rogers, set out the desire of the client to create "an open democratic building, appropriate for the 21st century." It was further stipulated that the building should have a minimum life-span of 100 years, and that Welsh materials should be used wherever possible. Set in the Cardiff Bay area, the building was inaugurated by the Queen on March 1, 2006. The brief required a 610-square-meter debating chamber, three committee rooms, offices, a media briefing room, members' lounge, public galleries, and a main reception hall. Prefabrication techniques with off-site assembly were used to the greatest extent possible for reasons of cost control. Natural materials such as timber, slate and stone were chosen for their durability. Natural ventilation also features in the design. Other environment-friendly elements include the collection of rain water and the use of a Ground Source Heat Pump system. The three-level building, also known as the Senedd, rises from a slate plinth and succeeds in mixing a great deal of transparency with acknowledged energy efficiency and more than a passing reference to Greek temples, albeit in a thoroughly modern mode.

In der Ausschreibung für den im April 1998 veranstalteten, internationalen Wettbewerb für dieses Projekt, den Richard Rogers für sich entscheiden konnte, war von dem Wunsch des Auftraggebers die Rede, »ein dem 21. Jahrhundert angemessenes, offenes, demokratisches Gebäude« zu schaffen. Darüber hinaus hieß es, der Bau müsse mindestens 100 Jahre überdauern und es sollten wo immer möglich aus Wales kommende Materialien Verwendung finden. Das in der Bucht von Cardiff errichtete Bauwerk wurde am 1. März 2006 von der Queen eingeweiht. Die Ausschreibung forderte einen 610 m² großen Sitzungssaal, drei Räume für Ausschüsse, Büros, einen Presseraum, eine Lounge für die Abgeordneten, Zuhörertribünen sowie eine Hauptempfangshalle. Aus Gründen der Kostenbegrenzung wurde soweit möglich auf fertig montierte, vorgefertigte Teile zurückgegriffen. Wegen ihrer Dauerhaftigkeit wählte man Naturmaterialien wie Holz, Schiefer und Stein. Auch wurde in dem Entwurf vorzugsweise natürliche Belüftung eingeplant. Zu weiteren umweltfreundlichen Elementen zählen die Aufbereitung von Regenwasser und die Nutzung von Erdwärme durch Wärmepumpen. Das auch als Senedd bekannte dreigeschossige Gebäude erhebt sich über einem Schiefersockel und präsentiert eine gelungene Mischung aus viel Transparenz, hoher Energieeffizienz und einer mehr als flüchtigen Anspielung auf griechische Tempel, wenn auch in gänzlich moderner Auffassung.

L'appel d'offres d'avril 1998 pour le concours international organisé pour ce projet, remporté par Richard Rogers, spécifiait la volonté de construire « un immeuble démocratique ouvert, adapté au XXIᵉ siècle ». Par ailleurs, il devait posséder une espérance de vie minimale de cent ans et utiliser dans la mesure du possible des matériaux d'origine galloise. En bordure de la baie de Cardiff, ce parlement, inauguré par la reine le 1ᵉʳ mars 2006, comprend une salle des débats de 610 m², trois salles de commissions, des bureaux, une salle pour les médias, un salon pour les députés, des galeries pour le public et un grand hall de réception. Des techniques de préfabrication à assemblage hors site ont été utilisées pour des raisons de coût. Les matériaux naturels comme le bois, l'ardoise et la pierre ont été préférés pour leur durabilité et la ventilation naturelle privilégiée dans l'ensemble du projet. Les préoccupations écologiques sont également présentes dans la récupération des eaux de pluie et l'utilisation d'une pompe à chaleur géothermique. Le bâtiment de trois niveaux, appelé le Senedd, s'élève au-dessus d'une plinthe en ardoise et réussit à associer une forte transparence au contrôle de la consommation d'énergie. Il fait plus que référence aux temples grecs, mais dans un esprit résolument moderne.

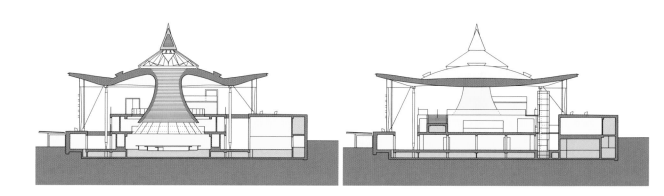

*With the National Assembly for Wales, Richard Rogers seems quite far removed from the Pompidou Center in Paris, which he designed with Renzo Piano (1977).*

*Mit der National Assembly for Wales hat sich Richard Rogers offensichtlich weit vom Centre Pompidou in Paris entfernt, das er 1977 gemeinsam mit Renzo Piano entwarf.*

*À travers l'Assemblée nationale du Pays de Galles, Richard Rogers semble s'être vraiment éloigné du Centre Pompidou à Paris qu'il avait conçu avec Renzo Piano en 1977.*

The sweeping roof of the building covers an essentially rectangular floor plan as seen in the image above and the site plan to the right.

*Das ausladende Dach des Gebäudes bedeckt einen im Wesentlichen recht-eckigen Grundriss, wie man auf der Abbildung oben und dem Lageplan rechts sieht.*

*Le toit incurvé recouvre un plan au sol pratiquement rectangulaire, comme le montre l'image ci-dessus et le plan à droite.*

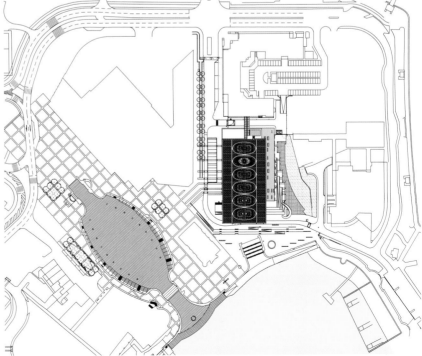

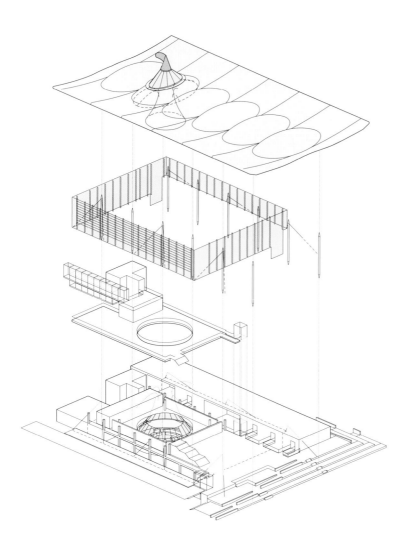

An exploded axonometric drawing
(left) shows how the building is
centered on its round debating
chamber.

*Auf einer auseinandergezogenen
Axonometrie (links) erkennt man,
wie das Gebäude um den kreisförmigen Sitzungssaal zentriert ist.*

*Un éclaté axonométrique (à gauche)
montre comment le bâtiment est cen-
tré sur la salle des débats circulaire.*

Sections of the building show its unusual roof and the relationship of the
structure to neighboring architecture
near Cardiff Bay.

*Schnitte des Gebäudes zeigen das
auffallende Dach und die Beziehung
des Gebäudes zur benachbarten
Bebauung unweit der Cardiff Bay.*

*Des coupes montrent la curieuse toi-
ture et la relation entre le bâtiment
et les bâtiments voisins en bordure
de la baie de Cardiff.*

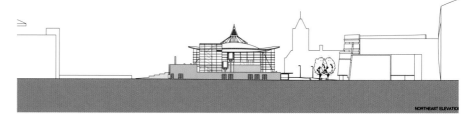

NORTHEAST ELEVATION

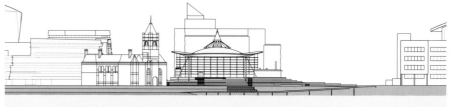

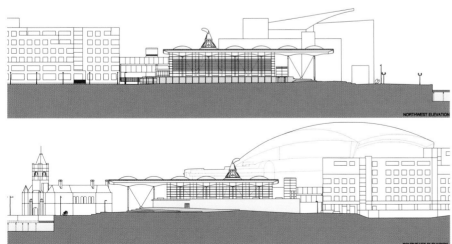

The undulating wood-slat roof seen above cascades onto the floor of the building, emphasizing the relationship between the different planes of the building. Glazed openings offer a close visual connection to the city and the bay.

Das oben zu sehende, gewellte Holzlamellendach reicht in Kaskaden bis auf den Boden des Gebäudes hinunter und stellt damit eine Verbindung zwischen den verschiedenen Ebenen her. Verglaste Öffnungen bieten direkten visuellen Kontakt zu Stadt und Bay.

Le toit en lattis de bois plonge jusqu'au niveau du sol, créant une relation entre les différents niveaux du Parlement. De vastes baies vitrées font connexion avec la ville et la baie.

# STANLEY SAITOWITZ

*Stanley Saitowitz / Natoma Architects Inc.*
*1022 Natoma Street, Unit 3*
*San Francisco, CA 94103*
*USA*

*Tel: +1 415 626 8977*
*Fax: +1 415 626 8978*
*E-mail: info@saitowitz.com*
*Web: www.saitowitz.com*

**STANLEY SAITOWITZ** is Professor of Architecture at the University of California, Berkeley, and Principal of Stanley Saitowitz / Natoma Architects Inc. He was born in Johannesburg, South Africa, and received his B.Arch degree from the University of Witwatersrand, Johannesburg, in 1975, and his M.Arch from the University of California, Berkeley, in 1977. He began his practice in South Africa in 1975. Completed projects, all in California unless stated otherwise, include the California Museum of Photography in Riverside (1990); residences at Stinson Beach, Los Gatos (1991), and other locations; New England Holocaust Memorial in Boston (1991); San Francisco Embarcadero Promenade (1991); Oxbow Art School in Napa (2001); and houses in San Francisco, Berkeley, Napa, and Marin, such as the Shaw Residence (2001–03) published here. Recent projects include the Visual Arts Library and Wurster Hall Fourth Floor Link at the University of California (Berkeley, 2002); University of Waterloo School of Architecture (Ontario, Canada, 2002); City Hall Plaza in Henderson (Nevada, 2003); Building 23B at the UCSF Mission Bay (2006); Beth El Synagogue in La Jolla (2006); and Beth Sholom Synagogue in San Francisco (2007). Aside from his work at the University of California, Berkley, he has taught at a number of schools, including the Harvard Graduate School of Design (Eliot Noyes Professor 1991–92), University of Oklahoma (Bruce Goff Professor, 1993), SCI-Arc, UCLA, the University of Texas and the University of the Witwatersrand.

**STANLEY SAITOWITZ** lehrt als Professor für Architektur an der University of California in Berkeley und ist Chef von Stanley Saitowitz / Natoma Architects Inc. Er wurde in Johannesburg in Südafrika geboren und erhielt 1975 den Grad des B.Arch. von der University of Witwatersrand, Johannesburg, und 1977 seinen M.Arch. von der University of California in Berkeley. 1975 eröffnete er ein Büro in Südafrika. Zu seinen fertiggestellten Projekten, die sich, wenn nicht anders vermerkt, alle in Kalifornien befinden, gehören: das California Museum of Photography in Riverside (1990), Wohnhäuser in Stinson Beach, Los Gatos (1991), und weiteren Orten, das New England Holocaust Memorial in Boston (1991), die San Francisco Embarcadero Promenade (1991), die Oxbow Art School in Napa (2001) sowie Häuser in San Francisco, Berkeley, Napa und Marin, wie die hier publizierte Shaw Residence (2001–03). Neuere Projekte sind: Visual Arts Library und Wurster Hall Fourth Floor Link an der University of California (Berkeley, 2002), die Architekturschule der University of Waterloo (Ontario, Kanada, 2002), die City Hall Plaza in Henderson (Nevada, 2003), Gebäude 23B an der UCSF Mission Bay (2006), die Beth-El-Synagoge in La Jolla (2006) und die Beth-Sholom-Synagoge in San Francisco (2007). Neben seiner Lehrtätigkeit an der University of California in Berkeley unterrichtete er an einer Reihe von Instituten, darunter die Harvard Graduate School of Design (Eliot-Noyes-Professor, 1991–92), University of Oklahoma (Bruce-Goff-Professor, 1993), SCI-Arc, UCLA, University of Texas und University of Witwatersrand.

**STANLEY SAITOWITZ** est professeur d'architecture à l'Université de Californie, Berkeley, et dirige Stanley Saitowitz / Natoma Architects Inc. Né à Johannesburg, Afrique du Sud, il est B. Arch. de l'Université de Witwatersrand, Johannesburg (1975) et M. Arch. de l'Université de Californie, Berkeley (1977). Il a commencé à travailler en Afrique du Sud en 1975. Ses projets réalisés, tous en Californie, sauf exception signalée, comprennent : le California Museum of Photography, Riverside (1990) ; des résidences à Stinson Beach, Los Gatos (1991), et autres lieux ; le New England Holocaust Memorial, Boston (1991) ; la San Francisco Embarcadero Promenade (1991) ; l'Oxbow Art School, Napa (2001) ; des maisons à San Francisco, Berkeley, Napa, et Marin, dont la Shaw Residence (2001–03) publiée ici. Parmi ses projets récents : la Visual Arts Library et le Wurster Hall Fourth Floor Link à l'Université de Californie, Berkeley (2002) ; l'Université de Waterloo School of Architecture, Ontario, Canada (2002) ; le City Hall Plaza à Henderson, Nevada (2003) ; l'immeuble 23B de la UCSF Mission Bay (2006) ; la synagogue Beth El, La Jolla (2006) ; et la synagogue Beth Sholom, San Francisco (2007). En dehors de Berkeley, il a enseigné dans plusieurs écoles, dont la Harvard Graduate School of Design (Professeur Eliot Noyes 1991–92), l'Université de l'Oklahoma (Professeur Bruce Goff, 1993), la SCI-Arc, UCLA, l'Université du Texas, et l'University de Witwatersrand.

# SHAW RESIDENCE

*San Francisco, California, USA, 2001–03*

*Floor area: 444 m². Client: John Shaw. Cost: not disclosed*

*As can be seen on the preceding page, this house offers a very modern environment in the midst of a more traditional architectural context.*

*Die vorstehende Seite zeigt, wie dieses Haus inmitten eines traditionellen architektonischen Kontextes ein höchst modernes Umfeld ermöglicht.*

*Comme le montre la page précédente, la maison impose sa modernité au milieu d'un contexte architectural plus traditionnel.*

This four-level house is located on the top of Russian Hill in San Francisco on a 288-square-meter site. The architect stripped and rebuilt an existing 1960s house, retaining its original zoning envelope, but modifying the materials and opening. The interior of the house was completely renovated, creating "a quiet world of stone and glass." A garage is located on the first level, with a garden room and space for a caretaker and pets above. The next level up contains a bedroom, dressing area, and bathroom, as well as a media and music room. A kitchen and formal dining room are topped by a living room and windows "framing a panorama of the bay." The overall color scheme is muted, contributing to an overall impression of modernity and calm. A rooftop terrace is walled in etched glass and also offers spectacular views of the city and bay. The architect concludes that the renovated house is "serene, reflective, and empty, providing a tranquil refuge in the city."

Dieses Haus mit vier Ebenen steht auf einem 288 m² großen Grundstück auf der Kuppe des Russian Hill in San Francisco. Der Architekt baute ein vorhandenes Haus aus den 1960er-Jahren um, behielt die ursprüngliche Aufteilung bei, modifizierte jedoch Materialien und Öffnungen. Das Hausinnere wurde komplett renoviert, wobei »eine ruhige Welt aus Stein und Glas« entstand. Auf der ersten Ebene befindet sich eine Garage, darüber ein Gartenraum sowie Platz für den Hausmeister und Haustiere. Auf der darüberliegenden Ebene finden Schlafzimmer, Ankleidezimmer und Bad sowie ein Medien- und Musikzimmer Platz. Über Küche und offiziellem Speisezimmer liegt ein Wohnzimmer mit Fenstern, »die einen Panoramablick auf die Bucht rahmen«. Die Farbigkeit ist insgesamt gedeckt und trägt damit zur modernen, ruhigen Anmutung des Hauses bei. Die Dachterrasse ist von einer Brüstung aus geätztem Glas umgeben und ermöglicht ebenfalls eindrucksvolle Ausblicke auf Bucht und Stadt. Abschließend findet der Architekt, das renovierte Haus sei »heiter, besinnlich und leer und biete eine ruhige Zuflucht in der Stadt«.

Cette maison sur quatre niveaux se dresse sur une parcelle de 288 m² au sommet de Russian Hill, à San Francisco. L'architecte a démonté et reconstruit une maison existante des années 1960, n'en conservant que l'enveloppe d'origine mais en modifiant les matériaux et le caractère d'ouverture. L'intérieur a été entièrement rénové pour créer «un univers serein de pierre et de verre». Le garage se trouve au rez-de-chaussée ainsi qu'une pièce donnant sur le jardin et une autre pour le concierge et les animaux de compagnie au-dessus. Le premier étage contient une chambre, un dressing et une salle de bains ainsi qu'une pièce pour la musique et les médias. La cuisine et la salle à manger de réception se trouvent sous le séjour dont les fenêtres «cadrent un panorama de la baie». Une gamme de couleurs assourdies contribue à un sentiment général de modernité et de calme. La terrasse sur le toit est encerclée de verre givré, et offre, elle aussi, des vues spectaculaires sur la ville et la baie. L'architecte conclut que cette maison rénovée est «calme, réfléchie et vide, un refuge de tranquillité au cœur de la ville».

The plans of the house are rectangular, with an interior décor that echoes the modern façade. Muted colors and simple forms confirm the contemporary feel of the residence.

*Die Grundrisse des Hauses sind rechtwinklig. Die Innenraumgestaltung setzt die moderne Fassade fort. Gedämpfte Farben und schlichte Formen passen zur zeitgenössischen Anmutung des Hauses.*

Les plans de la maison sont rectangulaires, le décor intérieur fait écho à la façade moderne. Les couleurs assourdies et les formes simples confirment le sentiment de grande modernité.

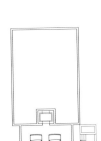

# KAZUYO SEJIMA + RYUE NISHIZAWA / SANAA

*Kazuyo Sejima + Ryue Nishizawa / S A N A A*
*7-A Shinagawa-Soko / 2–2-35 Higashi-Shinagawa / Shinagawa-ku / Tokyo 140 / Japan*

*Tel: +81 3 3450 1754 / Fax: +81 3 3450 757*
*E-mail: sanaa@sanaa.co.jp / Web: www.sanaa.co.jp*

Born in Ibaraki Prefecture in 1956, Kazuyo Sejima received her M.Arch from the Japan Women's University in 1981 and went to work in the office of Toyo Ito the same year. She established Kazuyo Sejima and Associates in Tokyo in 1987. She has been a Visiting Lecturer at Japan Women's University and at Waseda University since 1994. Ryue Nishizawa was born in Tokyo in 1966, and graduated from the National University in Yokohama in 1990. He began working with Sejima the same year, and the pair created the new firm **KAZUYO SEJIMA + RYUE NISHIZAWA / S A N A A** in 1995. He has been a Visiting Professor at the Harvard School of Design and at the National University in Yokohama. The built work of Kazuyo Sejima includes the Saishunkan Seiyaku Women's Dormitory (Kumamoto, 1990–91); Pachinko Parlor I (Hitachi, Ibaraki, 1992–93); Pachinko Parlor II (Nakamachi, Ibaraki, 1993); Villa in the Forest (Tateshina, Nagano, 1993–94); Chofu Station Police Box (Tokyo, 1993–94); Pachinko Parlor III (Hitachi, Ibaraki, 1995), all in Japan. The work of S A N A A includes the 21st Century Museum of Contemporary Art (Kanazawa, Ishikawa, 2002–04); Moriyama House (Tokyo, 2002–05); Glass Pavilion, Toledo Museum of Art (Ohio, 2003–06, published here); theater and cultural center in Almere, extension of the Valencia Institute of Modern Art (IVAM); and building for the New Museum of Contemporary Art in New York. Kazuyo Sejima and Ryue Nishizawa won the competitions to design the Learning Center of the EPFL in Lausanne, Switzerland, and the new building of the Louvre in Lens, France.

Die 1956 in der Präfektur Ibaraki geborene Kazuyo Sejima erhielt 1981 den M. Arch. von der japanischen Frauenuniversität und arbeitete noch im gleichen Jahr im Büro von Toyo Ito. 1987 eröffnete sie in Tokio Kazuyo Sejima and Associates. Seit 1994 ist sie als Gastprofessorin an der Frauenuniversität und an der Universität Waseda tätig. Ryue Nishizawa wurde 1966 in Tokio geboren und legte 1990 seine Abschlussprüfung an der Nationaluniversität in Yokohama ab. Noch im gleichen Jahr nahm er seine Arbeit bei Sejima auf. Zusammen gründeten sie 1995 das neue Büro **KAZUYO SEJIMA + RYUE NISHIZAWA / S A N A A**. Er hatte eine Gastprofessur an der Harvard School of Design und der Nationaluniversität in Yokohama. Zu den realisierten Bauten von Kazuyo Sejima zählen: das Frauenwohnheim Saishunkan Seiyaku (Kumamoto, 1990–91), Pachinko Parlor I (Hitachi, Ibaraki, 1992–93), Pachinko Parlor II (Nakamachi, Ibaraki, 1993), die Villa im Wald (Tateshina, Nagano, 1993–94), Polizeistaton Bahnhof Chofu (Tokio, 1993–94), Pachinko Parlor III (Hitachi, Ibaraki, 1995), alle in Japan. Zum Werk von S A N A A zählen: Museum für die Kunst des 21. Jahrhunderts (Kanazawa, Ishikawa, 2002–04), Haus Moriyama (Tokio, 2002–05), Glaspavillon am Toledo Museum of Art (Ohio, 2003–06, hier publiziert), Theater und Kulturzentrum in Almere, Erweiterung des Instituts für moderne Kunst (IVAM) in Valencia sowie Gebäude für das New Museum of Contemporary Art in New York. Kazuyo Sejima und Ryue Nishizawa gewannen die Wettbewerbe zum Bau des Lernzentrums der EPFL in Lausanne, Schweiz, und für das neue Gebäude des Louvre in Lens, Frankreich.

Née dans la préfecture d'Ibaraki en 1956, Kazuyo Sejima obtient son M. Arch. de l'Université féminine du Japon en 1981 et est engagée par l'agence de Toyo Ito la même année. Elle crée Kazuyo Sejima and Associates à Tokyo en 1987. Elle a été chargée de cours invitée à l'Université féminine et à l'Université Waseda depuis 1994. Ryue Nishizawa, née à Tokyo en 1966, est diplômée de l'Université nationale de Yokohama (1990). Il a commencé à travailler pour Sejima la même année et ils ont fondé ensemble **KAZUYO SEJIMA + RYUE NISHIZAWA / S A N A A** en 1995. Il a été professeur invité à la Harvard School of Design et à l'Université nationale de Yokohama. Les réalisations de Kazuyo Sejima comprennent le dortoir Saishunkan Seiyaku, Kumamoto (1990–91); Pachinko Parlor I, Hitachi, Ibaraki (1992–93); Pachinko Parlor II, Nakamachi, Ibaraki (1993); la Villa en forêt, Tateshina, Nagano (1993–94); le poste de police de Chofu, Tokyo (1993–94); Pachinko Parlor III, Hitachi, Ibaraki (1995), tous au Japon. Parmi les références de S A N A A : le Musée d'art contemporain du XXIe siècle, Kanazawa, Ishikawa (2002–04); la maison Moriyama, Tokyo, (2002–05); le pavillon de verre du Toledo Museum of Art, Toledo, Ohio (2003–06), publié ici; un théâtre et centre culturel à Almere; une extension de l'Institut d'art moderne de Valence (IVAM) et un immeuble pour le New Museum of Contemporary Art à New York. Kazuyo Sejima et Ryue Nishizawa ont remporté les concours pour le Centre d'enseignement de l'EPFL à Lausanne, Suisse, et des nouvelles installations du Louvre à Lens, France.

# GLASS PAVILION,
# TOLEDO MUSEUM OF ART

*Toledo, Ohio, USA, 2003–06*

*Floor area: 7060 m². Client: Toledo Museum of Art. Cost: $30 million.*
*Project Architects: Toshihiro Oki, Florian Idenburg, Takayuki Hasegawa. Executive Architect: Kendall Heaton Associates*

The first building designed in the United States by S A N A A, the Glass Pavilion was intended as an annex located across the street from the Toledo Museum of Art on a 20 317-square-meter site with 150-year-old trees for the institution's extensive collections of glass, as temporary exhibition space, and as a glass-making facility. As the architects describe their scheme, "Conceived as a single one-story volume penetrated by courtyards with sightlines through layers of transparent walls, the visitor's experience will always involve the surrounding greenery. Individually, each space is enclosed in clear glass, resulting in cavity walls that act as buffer zones between different climates: museum exhibition spaces, the glass-making hot-shop, and the outdoors. The plan is derived from a grid of various rectilinear shapes, with room-to-room connections achieved using curving glass surfaces. Glass wraps the spaces forming continuous elevations, uninterrupted by corners. The visitor flows with the form through a series of interconnected bubbles." A total of 2972 square meters of glass surfaces were used, originating from Germany, but curved and laminated in China. Thin solid steel columns support the structure, and solid 1.9-centimeter-thick plate-steel walls were used for lateral bracing. Both these devices, together with the large glazed surface of the building, serve to give it a remarkably light, transparent appearance.

Das erste von S A N A A entworfene Gebäude in den Vereinigten Staaten ist der dem Toledo Museum of Art gegenüberliegende Glaspavillon. Er steht auf einem 20 317 m² großen Gelände mit 150 Jahre alten Bäumen und enthält die umfangreiche Glassammlung des Museums sowie eine kleine Schauwerkstatt zur Glasherstellung. Die Architekten beschreiben ihr Projekt folgendermaßen: »Da der von Innenhöfen durchsetzte, eingeschossige Baukörper seitlich deckenhoch verglast ist, werden Besucher immer auch die umgebende Botanik wahrnehmen. Jeder einzelne Raum ist rundum verglast, wodurch zweischalige Wände entstehen, die als Puffer zwischen klimatisch unterschiedlichen Bereichen, den Ausstellungsräumen, Glaswerkstatt und Außenraum, dienen. Der Grundriss besteht aus einem Raster verschiedener rechtwinkliger Räume; Verbindungen zwischen den Räumen gewährleisten gebogene Glaswände. Diese die Räume umgebenden Glaswände bilden nicht von Ecken unterbrochene, durchgehende Ansichten. Der Besucher gleitet mit der Form durch eine Abfolge miteinander verbundener Blasen.« Insgesamt wurden 2972 m² in Deutschland hergestelltes und in China gebogenes und beschichtetes Glas verwendet. Schlanke, massive Stahlstützen tragen den Bau; den Wandverband übernehmen massive, 1,9 cm starke Wände aus Stahlblech. Zusammen mit den großen Glasflächen sorgt dies für das bemerkenswert leichte, transparente Erscheinungsbild dieses Gebäudes.

Première réalisation de S A N A A aux États-Unis, ce pavillon de verre est une annexe du Musée d'art de Toledo située face à celui-ci, sur un terrain de 20 317 m² entouré d'arbres séculaires. Il contient les vastes collections d'art du verre du musée, des espaces pour expositions temporaires et un atelier de verrerie. Les architectes en décrivent ainsi le projet : « Volume d'un seul niveau pénétré par des cours et des perspectives filant à travers des strates de murs transparents, ce bâtiment intègre en permanence la présence de la verdure extérieure. Chaque espace pris individuellement est clos de verre clair, constituant des murs qui font tampon entre les différents climats y régnant : celui des zones d'exposition, de l'atelier de verrerie et de l'extérieur. Le plan utilise une trame de diverses formes orthogonales. Les connexions d'une salle à l'autre sont assurées par des plans de verre incurvés. Le verre enveloppe ainsi les espaces par des élévations continues, non interrompues par des angles. Le visiteur se déplace dans une série de bulles interconnectées. » Une surface de 2 972 m² de murs est en verre produit en Allemagne, mais feuilleté et courbé en Chine. Des colonnes d'acier filiformes soutiennent la structure et des murs en tôle d'acier de 1,9 cm d'épaisseur servent de contreventements latéraux. Ces deux techniques ainsi que les vastes surfaces vitrées confèrent à ce petit bâtiment une légèreté et une transparence remarquables.

*Using curved glass walls like those seen in the Kanazawa Museum of 21st Century Art, S A N A A uses a basically square plan and inserts the museum spaces in freer forms inscribed within those limits.*

*Wie beim Museum für die Kunst des 21. Jahrhunderts in Kanazawa verwendet S A N A A gebogene Glaswände bei einem prinzipiell quadratischen Grundriss und fügt die freier gestalteten Museumsräume in diese Begrenzung ein.*

*À partir d'un plan presque carré et de murs de verre incurvés comme dans le Musée du XXIe siècle de Kanazawa, S A N A A peut inscrire des formes presque libres dans ces limites strictes.*

The transparency and use of glass in the building are particularly appropriate given that the structure is intended for the display of works in glass.

Die Transparenz und die Verwendung von Glas liegen bei diesem Bauwerk besonders nahe, da es zur Ausstellung von Werken aus Glas gedacht ist.

La transparence et le verre sont particulièrement appropriés pour un musée consacré à la présentation d'œuvres de verriers.

There is an undeniable flexibility and lightness associated with this architecture, confirmed not only by the use of glass, but also by the extremely thin column seen above, for example.

Mit dieser Architektur bringt man Flexibilität und Leichtigkeit in Verbindung, zum einen wegen der Verwendung von Glas, zum anderen aufgrund der oben abgebildeten, extrem schlanken Stützen.

Cette architecture affirme sa souplesse et sa légèreté, grâce à l'utilisation du verre mais aussi à celle de colonnes extrêmement fines, comme ci-dessus.

The similarity of this building to the Kanazawa Museum also by S A N A A is apparent, both in the free forms inscribed within the basic geometric plan, but also in the ambiguity imposed by the layering of glass walls, with their reflections and varying degrees of translucency depending on lighting conditions.

Die Ähnlichkeit dieses Gebäudes mit dem ebenfalls von S A N A A konzipierten Museum in Kanazawa ist augenfällig, sowohl was die in den geometrischen Grundriss eingeschriebenen freien Formen betrifft als auch in der Mehrdeutigkeit, bedingt durch die Glaswandschichten mit ihren Reflexionen und der von den Lichtverhältnissen abhängigen, wechselnden Transluzenz.

La similarité de ce bâtiment avec le Musée de Kanazawa, également de S A N A A, apparaît à la fois dans les formes libres inscrites dans un plan géométrique et dans l'ambiguïté créée par la stratification de parois de verre, leurs reflets et leurs divers degrés de translucidité selon les conditions d'éclairage.

A building made largely of glass makes an ideal showcase for "The Art of Glass" announced in the entrance (above). An inner courtyard brings light into the center of the structure.

Ein vorwiegend aus Glas bestehendes Gebäude ergibt einen idealen Ausstellungsraum für die am Eingang (oben) angekündigte »Kunst aus Glas«. Ein Innenhof bringt Licht ins Zentrum des Gebäudes.

Ce bâtiment en grande partie en verre est une vitrine idéale pour l'exposition « l'Art du verre » annoncé dans l'entrée (ci-dessus). Une cour intérieure fait pénétrer la lumière au centre du bâtiment.

# SANAKSENAHO ARCHITECTS

*Sanaksenaho Arkkitehdit Oy*
*Tehtaankatu 27–29 D*
*00150 Helsinki*
*Finland*

*Tel: +358 9 177 341*
*Fax: +358 9 630 636*
*E-mail: ark@sanaksenaho.com*
*Web: www.kolumbus.fi/sanaksenaho*

Matti Sanaksenaho was born in Helsinki in 1966. He obtained his M.Arch degree from the Helsinki University of Technology (HUT, 1993), and was a partner in the architectural office Monark (1990–92) when he founded **SANAKSENAHO ARCHITECTS** in 1991. He has been a Guest Professor at the Architecture School in Århus, Denmark (1996), and a guest teacher at the Royal Danish Academy of Fine Arts, Copenhagen, Denmark (1996, 1997, 1999); the Royal Academy of Fine Arts, Stockholm, Sweden (1997); the Nancy School of Architecture, France (1999); the Norwegian University of Science and Technology, Trondheim, Norway (2001); and the Architecture School of Versailles, France (2004). Pirjo Sanaksenaho was born in 1966 in Turku, Finland. She studied at the HUT and obtained her architect's degree in 1993. She became a partner in Sanaksenaho Architects in 1997. She has been teaching Housing Design at HUT Department of Architecture since 2000. Matti Sanaksenaho built the Finnish Pavilion in Seville (Spain, 1992, with Monark); while Sanaksenaho Architects completed the Hackman Design Shop (Helsinki, 1999); Tammimaki House (Espoo, 2001); Mahlberg House (Lake Lohja, 2002); Villa Aho (Lapland, 2003); St. Henry's Ecumenical Art Chapel (Turku, 2005, published here); and a Home for the Elderly and Daycare Center (Espoo, 2006), all in Finland. They have also designed a villa in Nanjing (China International Practical Exhibition for Architecture, CIPEA, 2005).

Matti Sanaksenaho wurde 1966 in Helsinki geboren. Er erhielt 1993 den Grad des M.Arch. von der Technischen Universität Helsinki (HUT) und war von 1990 bis 1992 Partner des Architekturbüros Monark, als er 1991 **SANAKSENAHO ARCHITECTS** gründete. 1996 nahm er eine Gastprofessur an der Architekturfakultät in Århus, Dänemark wahr, außerdem war er 1996, 1997 und 1999 Gastdozent an der Königlichen dänischen Akademie der bildenden Künste in Kopenhagen, 1997 an der Königlichen Akademie der bildenden Künste in Stockholm, 1999 an der Architekturfakultät in Nancy, 2001 an der Norwegischen Universität für Wissenschaft und Technik in Trondheim und schließlich 2004 an der École d'Architecture de Versailles in Frankreich. Pirjo Sanaksenaho wurde 1966 in Turku, Finnland, geboren. Sie studierte an der HUT und legte 1993 ihre Architekturprüfung ab. 1997 wurde sie Partnerin im Büro Sanaksenaho. Seit 2000 lehrt sie Wohnbaudesign an der Architekturfakultät der HUT. Matti Sanaksenaho errichtete den Finnischen Pavillon in Sevilla (1992 mit Monark); Sanaksenaho Architects bauten den Hackman Design Shop (Helsinki, 1999), Haus Tammimaki (Espoo, 2001), Haus Mahlberg (Lohja-See, 2002), Villa Aho (Lappland, 2003), die ökumenische Kapelle St. Heinrich (Turku, 2005, hier vorgestellt) sowie ein Altenheim mit Zentrum für Tagespflege (Espoo, 2006), alle in Finnland. Ebenfalls entwarfen sie eine Villa in Nanjing (China International Practical Exhibition for Architecture, CIPEA, 2005).

Matti Sanaksenaho, né à Helsinki en 1966, est M. Arch. de l'Université de technologie de cette ville (HUT, 1993), puis devient associé de l'agence Monark (1990–92), et fonde **SANAKSENAHO ARCHITECTS**, en 1991. Il a été professeur invité à l'École d'architecture d'Århus, Danemark (1996), à l'Académie royale danoise des Beaux-Arts, Copenhague (1996, 1997, 1999) ; à l'Académie royale des Beaux-Arts de Stockholm (1997) ; à l'École d'architecture de Nancy, France (1999) ; à l'Université norvégienne des sciences et technologies, Trondheim (2001) et à l'École d'architecture de Versailles, France (2004). Pirjo Sanaksenaho, née en 1966 à Turku, Finlande, a étudié à l'HUT et obtenu son diplôme d'architecte in 1993. Elle s'associe à Sanaksenaho Architects en 1997. Elle enseigne la conception de logements dans le département d'architecture de l'HUT depuis 2000. Matti Sanaksenaho a construit le pavillon finlandais à Séville, Espagne (1992, avec Monark) ; et Sanaksenaho Architects : le magasin de design Hackman, Helsinki (1999) ; la maison Tammimaki, Espoo (2001) ; la maison Mahlberg, Lake Lohja (2002) ; la villa Aho, Laponie (2003) ; la chapelle d'art œcuménique de St. Henry, Turku (2005, publiée ici), et une maison et dispensaire pour personnes âgées à Espoo (2006), toutes réalisations en Finlande. Ils ont également réalisé une villa à Nankin (China International Practical Exhibition for Architecture, CIPEA, 2005).

# ST HENRY'S ECUMENICAL ART CHAPEL

*Turku, Finland, 2004–05*

*Floor area: 300 m². Client: St. Henry's Chapel Association. Cost: €1.6 million.*
*Project Team: Sari Lehtonen, Enrico Garbin, Teemu Kurkela, Juha Jääskeläinen, Maria Isotupa, Jaana Hellinen,*
*Jari Mänttäri, Kain Tapper. Glass Artist: Hanu Konola*

This chapel is set on an east-west alignment on top of a wooded hill on the island of Hirvensalo. It is in the midst of a group of buildings that form a cancer clinic. Copper cladding was chosen to make the chapel blend in with the trees more as its surface oxidizes. The architects write: "The form of the chapel speaks quietly. The intention was to create a large landscape sculpture and a small building." A small foyer leads to a large hall that the architects call "the stomach of the fish" in reference to the early Christian symbol. Indeed, the entire plan of the chapel resembles the form of a fish. The main interior material is pine, with successive ribs forming the actual nave. Indirect natural light comes in from both sides of the chapel, with an altar window created by the artist Hanu Konola. Indeed, art is an integral part of this chapel. The architects explain, "The exhibition of art and religious ceremonies coexist within the same space. The symbiosis of art and ceremony is well known from Renaissance churches, which are still used in this way. Visitors view the art at the rear of the space, while religious ceremonies occur in the front of the chapel."

Diese Kapelle steht in ost-westlicher Ausrichtung auf der Spitze eines bewaldeten Hügels auf der Insel Hirvensalo, mitten zwischen den Gebäuden einer Krebsklinik. Die Wahl fiel auf eine Kupferverkleidung, damit sich die Kapelle mit zunehmender Oxidierung der Oberfläche den umstehenden Bäumen anpasst. Die Architekten schreiben: »Die Form der Kapelle spricht leise. Wir wollten eine weithin wirkende Landschaftsskulptur und ein kleines Gebäude schaffen.« Durch ein kleines Foyer gelangt man in eine große Halle, die von den Architekten in Bezug auf das frühchristliche Symbol als »der Bauch des Fisches« bezeichnet wird. Tatsächlich ähnelt der ganze Grundriss der Kapelle der Form eines Fisches. Der Innenraum ist überwiegend mit Kiefernholz verkleidet, wobei das eigentliche Kirchenschiff von fortlaufenden Rippen gebildet wird. Von beiden Seiten dringt indirektes Tageslicht in die Kapelle ein, das Altarfenster wurde von dem Künstler Hanu Konola gestaltet. Kunst ist in der Tat ein integraler Bestandteil dieser Kapelle. Die Architekten erläutern: »Die Ausstellung von Kunst und die Gottesdienste koexistieren im selben Raum. Die Symbiose von Kunst und Zeremonie ist aus Kirchen der Renaissance, die noch heute so genutzt werden, wohlbekannt. Besucher betrachten die Kunst im hinteren Teil der Kirche, während vorne in der Kapelle religiöse Zeremonien stattfinden.«

Cette chapelle implantée sur la crête orientée est-ouest d'une colline boisée de l'île d'Hirvensalo s'élève dans un ensemble de bâtiments qui constituent une clinique pour le traitement du cancer. L'habillage de cuivre a été choisi pour qu'elle se fonde dans les arbres au fur et à mesure de son oxydation. Pour les architectes : « La forme de la chapelle s'exprime avec calme. L'intention était de créer une sculpture dans le paysage et un bâtiment de faibles dimensions. » Une petite entrée mène à la grande salle que les architectes dénomment « l'estomac du poisson », en référence au symbole des premiers chrétiens. Le plan de la chapelle tout entière, dont la nef est soutenue par une succession de « nervures », fait d'ailleurs penser à la forme d'un poisson. Le principal matériau utilisé pour l'intérieur est le pin. La lumière naturelle arrive indirectement des deux côtés, et par un vitrail d'autel dessiné par l'artiste Hanu Konola. L'art fait partie intégrante du lieu. Pour les architectes : « L'exposition d'art et les cérémonies religieuses coexistent dans un même espace. La symbiose de l'art et du rituel est connue depuis les églises de la Renaissance qui restent utilisées dans cet esprit. Les visiteurs peuvent regarder les pièces artistiques disposées au fond de la chapelle pendant que les cérémonies se déroulent dans la partie avant. »

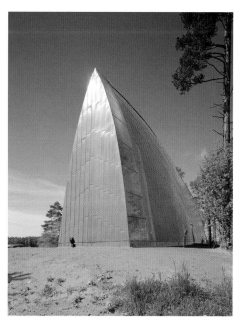

*The basic shape of the chapel is not specifically related to Christian tradition as such, and yet the idea of a boat hull is, of course, present in much religious architecture.*

*Zwischen der Form der Kapelle und christlicher Tradition besteht keine spezifische Verbindung, und doch ist die Idee eines Bootskörpers in vielen kirchlichen Bauwerken präsent.*

*La forme basique de la chapelle n'est pas spécifiquement liée à la tradition chrétienne, mais déjà l'idée de coque de bâteau rappelle l'architecture religieuse.*

In this instance, the inverted hull, or even fish shape, discernable in the floor plan does connect to Christian imagery of the fisherman. Without being explicitly religious in its external forms, the building is nonetheless readily identifiable as a chapel.

In diesem Fall ist die im Grundriss erkennbare Boots- oder Fischform mit der christlichen Symbolik des Fischers verbunden. Auch ohne explizit religiöse äußere Formen ist der Bau doch sofort als Kapelle erkennbar.

Ici, la coque inversée, ou même la forme de poisson du plan au sol, fait lien avec l'iconographie chrétienne du pêcheur. Sans être explicitement religieux dans sa forme extérieure, ce petit bâtiment n'en est pas moins identifiable en tant que chapelle.

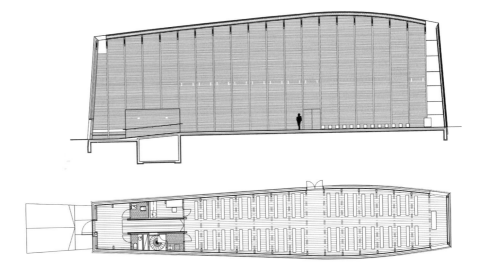

Interior spaces may evoke the imagery of the forest, or even, of hands folded in prayer. The successive arches of the nave are almost unadorned, leaving light as a quintessential expression of spirituality.

Die Innenräume könnten an einen Wald oder gefaltete Hände erinnern. Die aufeinander folgenden Bögen im Kirchenschiff sind nahezu schmucklos und betonen damit das Licht als reinsten Ausdruck von Spiritualität.

Les espaces intérieurs peuvent évoquer l'image d'une forêt ou de mains en position de prière. La succession d'arcs de la nef ne présente aucun décor. La lumière est ici l'expression de la spiritualité.

# ÁLVARO LEITE SIZA VIEIRA

*Álvaro Leite Siza Vieira*
*Rua do Aleixo 53 – Cave A*
*4150 – 043 Porto*
*Portugal*

*Tel: +351 22 610 8575*
*Fax: +351 22 610 8574*
*E-mail: alvarinhosiza@sapo.pt*

*Tóló House*

**ÁLVARO LEITE SIZA VIEIRA** was born in Porto, in 1962. He worked with his father, Álvaro Siza Vieira, on the first projects for the Chiado area of Lisbon (1987), and with the office of Eduardo Souto de Moura on the Vanzeller House in Afife (1992), before graduating from the Faculty of Architecture of the University of Porto (FAUP) in 1994. His own work includes the Estado Novo Discotheque (Matosinhos, 1996); Garrett House (Foz do Douro, Porto, 1998); Francisco Ramos Pinto House (Francelos, 2000); and Leite Faria House (Porto, 2001), all in Portugal. His current work includes the Rua de Fez Houses (Porto); Tóló House (Freguesia de Cerva, 2005, published here); and an urban project for Fontaínhas Lane and Park (Porto, 2006).

**ÁLVARO LEITE SIZA VIEIRA** wurde 1962 in Porto geboren. Er arbeitete mit seinem Vater Álvaro Siza Viera an den ersten Projekten für das Chiado-Viertel in Lissabon (1987) und mit dem Büro Eduardo Souto de Moura am Haus Vanzeller in Afife (1992), ehe er an der Architekturfakultät der Universität Porto (FAUP) 1994 sein Studium abschloss. Zu seinen eigenen Bauten gehören: Diskothek Estado Novo (Matosinhos, 1996), Haus Garrett (Foz do Douro, Porto, 1998), Haus Francisco Ramos Pinto (Francelos, 2000) und Haus Leite Faria (Porto, 2001), alle in Portugal. Neuere Werke sind die Häuser Rua de Fez (Porto), Haus Tóló (Freguesia de Cerva, 2005, hier vorgestellt) sowie ein urbanes Projekt für Fontaínhas-Straße und -Park (Porto, 2006).

**ÁLVARO LEITE SIZA VIEIRA**, né à Porto in 1962, a travaillé avec son père, Álvaro Siza Vieira, sur les premiers projets pour le quartier du Chiado à Lisbonne (1987) et dans l'agence d'Eduardo Souto de Moura sur le projet de la maison Vanzeller à Afife (1992), avant même d'être diplômé de la Faculté d'architecture de l'Université de Porto (FAUP) en 1994. Ses propres réalisations comprennent la discothèque Estado Novo, Matosinhos (1996) ; la maison Garrett, Foz do Douro, Porto (1998) ; la maison Francisco Ramos Pinto, Francelo (2000) et la maison Leite Faria, Porto (2001), toutes au Portugal. Actuellement, il réalise les maisons Rua de Fez, Porto ; la maison Tóló, Freguesia de Cerva (2005) publiée ici et le projet d'urbanisme de l'avenue et du parc Fontaínhas à Porto (2006).

# TÓLÓ HOUSE

*Lugar das Carvalhinhas – Alvite, Freguesia de Cerva, Portugal, 2000–05*

*Floor area: 180 m². Client: Luís Marinho Leite Barbosa da Silva.*
*Cost: not disclosed*

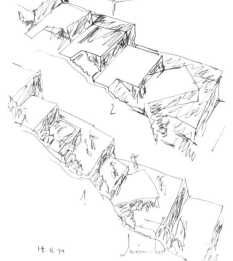

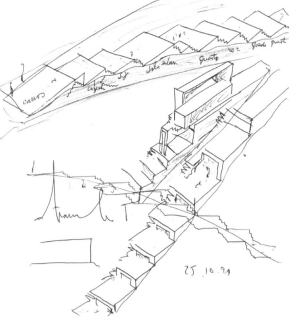

Set on a steeply inclined, 1000-square-meter site, this is a three-bedroom holiday house, including a living room, dining room, kitchen, and a small outdoor pool. Given the topography of the site, the architect decided to create a long, narrow plan facing south for optimum solar exposure. The entrance is at the northern, or higher, end of the lot, and the house is fragmented into a series of small interconnected volumes. The roof serves as a support for gardens, and an attempt was made to preserve all existing trees on the site. An outdoor path links the top and bottom of the house, but as the architect says, "The house itself is a path." A relatively low budget suggested that part of the house should be buried, for reasons of thermal conservation and security. "The choice of exposed concrete," explains the architect, "creates an idea like that of massive stones appearing naturally on the site. In this way, expressiveness is extracted from a continuous structure of reinforced concrete, the most efficient on the lot with these characteristics, and making optimum use of the modest economic resources available." PVC canvas was used to seal the foundations because of a high water-table on the site. Non-load-bearing walls were built with cement blocks filled with sand, plastered, and painted white inside. Interior floors and doors are made of wood; exterior doors and windows of metal with double-glazing, for reasons of thermal and acoustic insulation.

Dieses Ferienhaus mit drei Schlafzimmern, Wohn- und Essraum, Küche und kleinem Außenpool liegt auf einem steil abfallenden, 1000 m² großen Gelände. Angesichts der Topografie entschied sich der Architekt für einen langen, schmalen Grundriss, der wegen der Sonne nach Süden ausgerichtet ist. Der Eingang befindet sich am nördlichen, höheren Ende des Grundstücks und das Haus ist in eine Abfolge kleinerer, miteinander verbundener Baukörper gegliedert, deren Dachflächen für Gartenanlagen genutzt werden. Beim Bau des Hauses wurde größtmögliche Rücksicht auf vorhandene Bäume genommen. Ein im Freien verlaufender Weg verbindet die beiden Enden des Hauses, aber wie der Architekt sagt, »ist das Haus selbst ein Weg«. Aufgrund eines eher begrenzten Budgets wurden Teile des Hauses unter die Erde verlegt, um Wärmedämmung und Sicherheit zu gewährleisten. Nach Meinung des Architekten »entsteht durch das Material Sichtbeton der Eindruck natürlich auf dem Gelände vorhandener Steinblöcke. Aus dem fortlaufenden Baukörper aus Stahlbeton entsteht Expressivität und die bescheidenen ökonomischen Mittel werden optimal genutzt«. Wegen des hohen Grundwasserspiegels auf dem Gelände wurden die Fundamente sorgfältig mit PVC-beschichteten Planen abgedichtet. Nichttragende Wände wurden aus sandgefüllten Betonblöcken errichtet, verputzt und innen weiß gestrichen. Fußböden und Türen im Inneren wurden aus Holz gefertigt, Außentüren und Fenster aus Metall mit Doppelverglasung zur besseren Wärme- und Geräuschdämmung.

Implantée sur un terrain très incliné de 1 000 m², cette maison de vacances contient quatre chambres, un séjour, une salle à manger, une cuisine et une petite piscine extérieure. Etant donné la topographie, l'architecte a opté pour un plan allongé et étroit face au sud afin d'obtenir une exposition solaire maximale. L'entrée se fait par le nord, à l'extrémité haute de la parcelle, et la maison se fragmente en une succession de petits volumes interconnectés. Le toit sert de soutien aux jardins, et la plupart des arbres existants ont été conservés. Un passage extérieur relie le haut et le bas de la maison, mais, comme l'architecte le dit lui-même « cette maison est en soi un cheminement ». Pour des raisons de protection thermique, de sécurité et de budget, une partie a été enterrée. « Le choix du béton apparent, précise l'architecte, évoque d'une certaine façon les blocs de pierre massifs présents sur le site. Ainsi l'expressivité vient-elle de cette structure continue en béton armé, forme la plus efficace pour un terrain présentant ces caractéristiques et pour tirer un parti maximum du modeste budget alloué. » Une toile en PVC a permis d'étanchéifier les fondations, une nécessité du fait de la proximité de la nappe phréatique. Les murs non porteurs ont été construits en parpaings de ciment remplis de sable, plâtrés et peints sur leur face intérieure. Les sols et les portes intérieurs sont en bois, les portes et les fenêtres extérieures en métal à double vitrage, pour une meilleure isolation thermique et acoustique.

Álvaro Leite Siza's house is inscribed into the hillside, in a gesture that may recall the natural integration of houses, such as those by Eduardo Souto de Moura, for example, while remaining original nonetheless.

Álvaro Leite Sizas Haus schmiegt sich auf eine Art an den Hang, die an in die Landschaft integrierte Häuser wie die von Eduardo Souto de Moura erinnert, und bleibt doch gänzlich originell.

La maison d'Álvaro Leite Siza s'inscrit dans le flanc d'une colline, en un geste qui peut évoquer des réalisations comme celles d'Eduardo Souto de Moura par exemple, tout en restant néanmoins originale.

Simple wooden furniture echoes the use of wood planks for the steps here.

Schlichte Holzmöbel greifen die hölzernen Treppenstufen auf.

Un simple mobilier de bois vient en écho aux planches utilisées pour les escaliers.

The numerous windows looking out onto the leafy surroundings and the constant presence of openings and stairways imposed by the sloped terrain allow light into the space.

Die zahlreichen Fenster mit Blick auf die grüne Umgebung und die vom abschüssigen Terrain bedingten allgegenwärtigen Öffnungen und Treppen lassen Licht in die Räume.

Les nombreuses fenêtres qui donnent sur la verdure environnante, et la présence constante d'ouvertures et d'escaliers imposés par la pente du terrain facilitent la pénétration de la lumière.

The very site creates a variety of the forms in the architecture, while careful attention is paid to the visual communication of the light and passageways.

*Das Baugelände selbst bedingt die vielfältigen Formen der Architektur; große Aufmerksamkeit wird der von Licht oder Durchgängen ermöglichten visuellen Kommunikation gewidmet.*

*Le terrain lui-même génère les différentes formes architecturales. L'attention a été portée à la communication visuelle née de l'éclairage et de la lumière naturelle.*

Narrow stairs pass through brightly lit spaces in the house whose basic form is that of a cascade of pavilions connected by steps.

In dem Haus, das aus einer Folge von durch Treppen verbundenen Pavillons besteht, erschließen schmale Treppen hell erleuchtete Räume.

D'étroits escaliers traversent les volumes lumineux de la maison, qui est constituée d'une cascade de pavillons connectés par des marches.

# SPILLMANN ECHSLE ARCHITEKTEN

*spillmann echsle architekten*
*Jupiterstrasse 26*
*8032 Zurich*
*Switzerland*

*Tel: +41 44 272 2727*
*Fax: +41 44 272 2737*
*E-mail: mail@spillmannechsle.ch*
*Web: www.spillmannechsle.ch*

*Freitag Flagship Store*

**ANNETTE SPILLMANN** studied Sociology and Film at the University of Zurich (1990–94), and architecture at the ETH in Zurich (1994–2000). She worked for Bétrix & Consolascio architects, Erlenbach (1997–99), and Pfister Schiess Tropeano architects (Zurich, 2000–01). She has been Head of Architecture at art-tv since 2004, and an Assistant Professor in Design and Construction at the Basel University of Applied Sciences since 2005. In 2002, she co-founded spillmann echsle architekten in Zurich with **HARALD ECHSLE**. Harald Echsle studied architecture at the Frank Lloyd Wright School of Architecture (Taliesin, Wisconsin, 1991) and at the ETH in Zurich (1991–97). He won the Swiss Steel Construction Prize for the SEW Pavilion (Zurich, 1996). From 1993 to 1995, he worked for Franz Staffelbach architects, Zurich. From 1997 to 2001, he was a project manager at Bétrix & Consolascio architects, Erlenbach. Current work includes planned single-family residences, such as Lebensraum House (Stallikon, 2006) and Höhenweg House (Wollerau, 2006), both in Switzerland; and the Freitag Flagship Store (Zurich, 2006, published here).

**ANNETTE SPILLMANN** studierte an der Universität Zürich von 1990 bis 1994 Soziologie und Filmwissenschaft und anschließend von 1994 bis 2000 an der ETH Zürich Architektur. Von 1997 bis 1999 arbeitete sie bei Bétrix & Consolascio Architekten, Erlenbach, und von 2000 bis 2001 bei Pfister Schiess Tropeano Architekten in Zürich. Sie ist seit 2004 bei art-tv für die Architekturbeiträge verantwortlich und seit 2005 als Lehrbeauftragte im Bereich Design und Bauen an der Fachhochschule in Basel tätig. 2002 gründete sie mit **HARALD ECHSLE** in Zürich spillmann echsle architekten. Harald Echsle studierte 1991 an der Frank Lloyd Wright School of Architecture in Taliesin, Wisconsin, und anschließend von 1991 bis 1997 an der ETH Zürich Architektur. 1996 gewann er für den SEW Pavillon in Zürich den Schweizer Stahlbaupreis. Von 1993 bis 1995 arbeitete er bei Franz Staffelbach Architekten, Zürich. Von 1997 bis 2001 fungierte er als Projektleiter bei Bétrix & Consolascio Architekten, Erlenbach. Aktuelle Projekte sind: Einfamilienhäuser wie das Lebensraum-Haus (Stallikon, 2006) und das Höhenweg-Haus (Wollerau, 2006), beide in der Schweiz, sowie der hier vorgestellte Freitag Flagship Store (Zürich, 2006).

**ANNETTE SPILLMANN** a étudié la sociologie et le cinéma à l'Université de Zurich (1990–94) et l'architecture à l'ETH Zurich (1994–2000). Elle a travaillé pour Bétrix & Consolascio, Erlenbach (1997–99), et Pfister Schiess Tropeano, Zurich (2000–01). Elle est responsable de l'architecture à art-tv depuis 2004, et professeur assistant de conception et de construction à l'Université des sciences appliquées de Bâle depuis 2005. En 2002, elle a cofondé spillmann echsle architekten à Zurich avec **HARALD ECHSLE**. Harald Echsle a étudié l'architecture à la Frank Lloyd Wright School of Architecture, Taliesin, Wisconsin (1991) et à l'ETH Zurich (1991–97). Il a remporté le Prix suisse de la construction en acier pour le pavillon SEW, Zurich (1996). De 1993 à 1995, il a travaillé pour Franz Staffelbach, Zurich. Puis, de 1997 à 2001, il a été directeur de projet chez Bétrix & Consolascio, Erlenbach. L'agence a réalisé récemment des maisons individuelles, comme la maison Lebensraum, Stallikon (2006) et la maison Höhenweg, Wollerau (2006), toutes deux en Suisse, ainsi que le Freitag Flagship Store, Zurich (2006) publié ici.

# FREITAG FLAGSHIP STORE

*Zurich, Zurich, Switzerland, 2006*

*Floor area: 100 m². Client: FREITAG lab. ag. Cost: not disclosed.*
*Realization: Raumbau AG, Zurich*

*The Freitag Flagship Store is made up of a stack of shipping containers. Although containers have been used by architects such as Shigeru Ban, they have rarely, if ever, been made into a towering store.*

*Der Freitag Flagship Store besteht aus aufeinander gestapelten Schiffscontainern. Obgleich Architekten wie Shigeru Ban bereits Container verwendet haben, wurde aus ihnen bisher doch selten oder nie ein Ladenturm errichtet.*

*Le Freitag Flagship Store se compose d'une accumulation de conteneurs de transport maritime. Si ce type de conteneur a déjà été utilisé par des architectes comme Shigeru Ban, ils n'avaient encore jamais servi à élever une tour.*

Inaugurated on May 18, 2006, the Freitag Flagship Store is a 26-meter-high tower made with 17 shipping containers. The containers are stacked and held in place using material only from the shipping industry. The shop, which is intended to be permanent, includes four floors and steps to a rooftop platform. The idea for this shop came from the owners and graphic designers Daniel and Markus Freitag, and the structure was created with "rusty, recycled freight containers […] gutted, reinforced, piled up, and secured." Low enough not to violate the city's restriction on high-rise buildings; high enough to send shivers down anyone's spine: located on Geroldstrasse between two of the city's main thoroughfares—the Hardbrücke flyover and Geroldrampe approach road to one side, and the railway viaduct and central train station approach tracks to the other—the store has a site befitting of its image. Indeed, the fit with Freitag's products is quite natural since they produce and market "bags and accessories made from used materials and found on the road: old truck tarpaulins tanned by exhaust fumes, cycle inner tubes, and used seat belts, as well as the new resource of used airbags."

Bei dem am 18. Mai 2006 eingeweihten Freitag Flagship Store handelt es sich um einen 26 m hohen Turm aus 17 Schiffscontainern. Die gestapelten Container sind nur mit Materialien aus dem Schiffsbau befestigt. Der als dauerhafte Einrichtung gedachte Laden umfasst vier Ebenen und Treppen auf eine Dachterrasse. Die Idee für diesen Laden stammt von den Eigentümern und Grafikern Daniel und Markus Freitag und er entstand aus »rostigen, gebrauchten Frachtcontainern […], die verstärkt, gestapelt und befestigt wurden«. Die Höhe der Konstruktion überschreitet nicht die städtischen Richtlinien zu Hochhäusern, ist aber ausreichend, um jeden zu beeindrucken. Zwischen zwei der Hauptverbindungslinien der Stadt – Überführung Hardbrücke und Geroldrampe auf der einen, Eisenbahnviadukt und Einfahrtsgleise zum Hauptbahnhof auf der anderen Seite – an der Geroldstraße gelegen, hat der Laden eine zum Image passende Lage. Zudem ergibt sich ganz natürlich der Bezug zu den Freitag-Produkten, da sie »Taschen und Accessoires aus gebrauchten und auf der Straße gefundenen Materialien [produzieren und vermarkten]: alte, von Abgasen verfärbte Lastwagenplanen, Radschläuche und gebrauchte Sicherheitsgurte sowie als neue Ressource gebrauchte Airbags«.

Inauguré le 18 mai 2006, le Freitag Flagship Store est une tour de 26 mètres de haut faite de 17 conteneurs maritimes. Ils sont empilés et solidarisés par des matériaux de récupération exclusivement issus de la construction navale. Le magasin, qui devrait être permanent, compte quatre niveaux et un escalier conduisant à une plate-forme aménagée à son sommet. Son idée, qui vient à l'origine des propriétaires et graphistes Daniel et Markus Freitag, est de créer une structure faite « de conteneurs de fret rouillés recyclés… nettoyés, renforcés, empilés et maintenus ensemble ». Suffisamment bas pour ne pas enfreindre la réglementation locale sur les immeubles de grande hauteur, cette structure est assez haute pour faire trembler les visiteurs. Situé Geroldstrasse entre deux des principaux axes de communication de la ville – l'enjambement du Hardbrücke et la rampe Gerold d'un côté, le viaduc de chemin de fer et les voies d'arrivées vers la gare principale de l'autre – le magasin a certainement trouvé le site qui convenait à son image. La concordance avec les produits Freitag est assez naturelle puisqu'il s'agit « de sacs et d'accessoires réalisés en matériaux utilisés et trouvés : vieilles bâches de camions tannées par des gaz d'échappement, chambres à air de vélos, ceintures de sécurité récupérées, sans oublier les ressources nouvelles offertes par les vieux « airbags ».

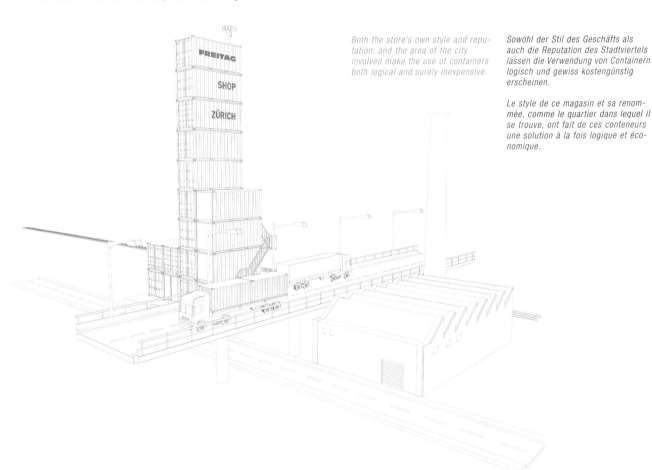

*Both the store's own style and reputation, and the area of the city involved make the use of containers both logical and surely inexpensive.*

*Sowohl der Stil des Geschäfts als auch die Reputation des Stadtviertels lassen die Verwendung von Containern logisch und gewiss kostengünstig erscheinen.*

*Le style de ce magasin et sa renommée, comme le quartier dans lequel il se trouve, ont fait de ces conteneurs une solution à la fois logique et économique.*

The interior space is far more practical than the exterior might imply and the industrial vocabulary of the products finds a natural echo in the substance of the architecture.

Der Innenraum ist weit praktischer als es der äußere Anschein impliziert und vor allem passen das industrielle Vokabular der Produkte und die Materialität der Architektur bestens zusammen.

Le volume intérieur est beaucoup plus pratique que ce que l'aspect extérieur laisse deviner. Le vocabulaire industriel des produits présentés trouve son écho dans cette architecture.

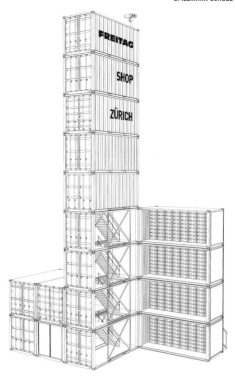

# PHILIPPE STARCK

*Ubik*
*18/20, rue du Faubourg du Temple*
*75011 Paris*
*France*


*Tel: +33 1 4807 5454*
*Fax: +33 1 4807 5464*
*E-mail: info@philippe-starck.com*
*Web: www.philippe-starck.com*

**PHILIPPE STARCK** was born in 1949 and attended the École Nissim de Camondo in Paris. Though he is of course best known as a furniture and object designer, his projects as an architect include the Café Costes (Paris, 1984); Laguiole Knife Factory (Laguiole, France, 1987); Royalton Hotel (New York, 1988); Nani Nani Building (Tokyo, 1989); Asahi Beer Building (Tokyo, 1989); Teatriz Restaurant (Madrid, 1990); Paramount Hotel (New York, 1990); and the Baron Vert Building (Osaka, 1990). He has also designed a number of private houses and apartment blocks, for example Lemoult in Paris (1987); Angle in Antwerp (1991); apartment buildings in Los Angeles (1991); and a private house in Madrid (1991). He was responsible for the interior design of the Saint Martin's Lane and Sanderson Hotels in London, the Delano in Miami, the Mondrian in Los Angeles, the Hudson in New York and the Clift in San Francisco. In 2006, the Japanese restaurant Katsuya opened in Los Angeles. He has also worked on the design of condominium apartments in Toronto (75 Portland Street), and the 24-story JIA boutique hotel in Hong Kong. The 40 000-square-meter Alhondiga in Bilbao, a "place of discovery, exchange and living," is due to open in 2008. Starck's other ventures include his role as Creative Director of Yoo, a property development company in which he is associated with the developer John Hitchcox and Jade Jagger.

**PHILIPPE STARCK** wurde 1949 geboren und besuchte die École Nissim de Camondo in Paris. Obgleich er natürlich mit seinen Möbel- und Objektentwürfen am bekanntesten wurde, umfassen seine architektonischen Projekte das Café Costes (Paris, 1984), Messerfabrik Forge de Laguiole (Laguiole, Frankreich, 1987), Royalton Hotel (New York, 1988), Nani Nani Building (Tokio, 1989), Asahi Beer Building (Tokio, 1989), Teatriz Restaurant (Madrid, 1990), Paramound Hotel (New York, 1990) und das Baron Vert Building (Osaka, 1990). Darüber hinaus entwarf er eine Reihe von Privathäusern und Wohnungsbauten, zum Beispiel Lemoult in Paris (1987), Angle in Antwerpen (1991), Apartmenthäuser in Los Angeles (1991) sowie ein Privathaus in Madrid (1991). Er war verantwortlich für den Innenausbau der Saint Martin's Lane und Sanderson Hotels in London, des Delano in Miami, des Mondrian in Los Angeles, des Hudson in New York und des Clift in San Francisco. 2006 wurde in Los Angeles das japanische Restaurant Katsuya eröffnet. Außerdem war er am Ausbau von Eigentumswohnung in Toronto (75 Portland Street) und des 24-geschossigen JIA Boutique Hotels in Hong Kong beteiligt. Die Eröffnung des 40 000 m$^2$ umfassenden Alhondiga in Bilbao, einem »Ort für Entdeckung, Austausch und Leben«, ist für 2008 geplant. Zu Starcks sonstigen Unternehmungen zählt seine Rolle als Creative Director von Yoo, einer Wohnungsbaufirma, bei der er Partner des Bauunternehmers John Hitchcox und Jade Jagger ist.

**PHILIPPE STARCK** est né en 1949 et a étudié à l'École Nissim de Camondo à Paris. Bien qu'il soit surtout connu comme designer d'objets et de meubles, il a réalisé un certain nombre de projets d'architecture comme le Café Costes, Paris (1984) ; la manufacture Forge de Laguiole, Laguiole, France (1987) ; le Royalton Hotel, New York (1988) ; l'immeuble Nani Nani, Tokyo (1989) ; l'immeuble Asahi Beer, Tokyo (1989) ; le restaurant Teatriz, Madrid (1990) ; le Paramount Hotel, New York (1990) ; et l'immeuble Baron Vert, Osaka (1990). Il a également conçu un certain nombre de résidences privées et d'immeubles d'appartements, par exemple la maison Lemoult à Paris (1987) ; l'Angle à Anvers (1991) ; un immeuble d'appartements à Los Angeles (1991) et une maison privée à Madrid (1991). Il a été responsable des aménagements intérieurs des hôtels Saint Martin's Lane et Sanderson à Londres, le Delano à Miami, le Mondrian à Los Angeles, l'Hudson à New York et le Clift à San Francisco. En 2006, son restaurant japonais Katsuya a ouvert ses portes à Los Angeles. Il a également travaillé à la conception d'un immeuble d'appartements en copropriété à Toronto (75 Portland Street) et le boutique hôtel de 24 niveaux JIA à Hong Kong. L'Alhondiga de 40 000 m$^2$, un « lieu de découverte, d'échange et de vie » devrait ouvrir à Bilbao en 2008. Parmi ses autres engagements figure son rôle de Directeur de la création de Yoo, une société de promotion immobilière dans laquelle il s'est associé avec le promoteur John Hitchcox et Jade Jagger.

# TASCHEN STORE

*Greene Street, New York, New York, USA, 2006–07*

*Floor area: 252 m².*
*Artwork: Beatriz Milhazes.*

This store, located at 107 Greene Street in Manhattan's busy SoHo area, is the third design by Philippe Starck for the publisher, after Paris (2001) and Beverly Hills (2003). Set in a building completed just two years ago, the overall steel and rivet façade (not the work of the designer) gives the impression that it fits in perfectly with the former warehouse area. The long, relatively narrow space of the store itself has a high ceiling and a concrete floor. The custom-made pear wood display shelves are mounted on steel bases that "grow" out of the floor. Each of the main shelves along the wall has two video screens. The wall paintings, on the sides and to the rear of the space, are works of Beatriz Milhazes, a Brazilian artist born in 1960 in Rio de Janeiro, who is noted for a wall mural in the Tate Modern restaurant in London, entitled *Guanabara*. A lower level exhibition space with free-standing concrete walls and an overhead skylight marks the rear of the shop. Office and storage space on the basement level complete the installation.

Bei diesem Ladengeschäft an der Greene Street 107 in Manhattans quirligem Bezirk SoHo handelt es sich nach Paris (2001) und Beverly Hills (2003) um die dritte Arbeit Starcks für den Verleger. Die in ein erst vor zwei Jahren fertiggestelltes Gebäude eingesetzte, gänzlich aus Stahl und Nieten bestehende Fassade (nicht von Starck) passt perfekt zu der vormals von Lagerhäusern geprägten Gegend. Der langgezogene, eher schmale Ladenraum selbst zeichnet sich durch hohe Decken und einen Betonboden aus. Die eigens angefertigten Schauregale aus Birnbaum sind auf stählerne Unterbauten montiert, die aus dem Boden zu »wachsen« scheinen. Die Wandgemälde an den Seiten und der Rückwand des Raumes sind Werke der 1960 in Rio de Janeiro geborenen brasilianischen Künstlerin Beatriz Milhazes, von der man auch im Restaurant der Tate Modern in London ein Wandgemälde (»Guanabara«) findet. Eine niedriger liegende Ausstellungsebene mit freistehenden Betonwänden und einem Oberlicht markiert den hinteren Ladenteil. Büro- und Lagerraum im Untergeschoss vervollständigen die Einrichtung.

Ce magasin, situé 107 Greene Street dans le très animé quartier de SoHo à Manhattan est le troisième conçu par Philippe Starck pour l'éditeur après celui de Paris (2001) et Beverly Hills (2003). Implanté dans un immeuble achevé deux ans plus tôt, sa façade en acier riveté (qui n'est pas l'œuvre du designer) donne l'impression d'être parfaitement adaptée à son voisinage d'entrepôts. L'espace de vente long et relativement étroit possède une grande hauteur de plafond et un sol un béton. Les étagères et meubles de présentation en poirier spécialement dessinés pour le lieu sont montés sur des socles d'acier qui « poussent » du sol. Chacune des étagères principales le long des murs est dotée de deux écrans vidéo. Les peintures murales sur les côtés et dans le fond sont l'œuvre de Beatriz Milhazes, artiste brésilienne née en 1960 à Rio de Janeiro qui peut également être contemplée au restaurant de la Tate Modern à Londres, ou se trouve sa fresque *Guanabara*. Un espace d'exposition en contrebas, à murs autoporteurs et verrière zénithale, occupe le fond du magasin. Des bureaux et des réserves complètent les installations en sous-sol.

*Above, the Greene Street façade of the store and the bright, high, interior space, with the wall murals by Beatriz Milhazes visible. The pear-wood shelves and tables are set on steel bases that appear to surge up from the concrete floors.*

*Oben die Fassade des Ladens an der Greene Street und der helle, hohe Innenraum mit den Wandgemälden Beatriz Milhazes'. Die Regale und Tische aus Birnbaum sind auf Stahlsockeln montiert, die sich scheinbar aus dem Betonboden erheben.*

*Ci-dessus, la façade sur Greene Street et le vaste volume lumineux dans lequel sont visibles les fresques de Beatriz Milhazes. Les étagères et tables en poirier reposent sur des bases en acier qui semblent jaillir des sols en béton.*

Above, the main space of the store, with a mural by Beatriz Milhazes at the rear. Below left, the lower level exhibition space, with sofa and armchairs by Joaquim Tenreiro, and right, an Arne Jacobsen Egg chair.

Oben der Hauptraum des Ladens mit einem Wandgemälde von Beatriz Milhazes im rückwärtigen Teil. Unten links der Ausstellungsraum mit Sitzmöbeln von Joaquim Tenreiro; rechts ein Egg-Chair von Arne Jacobsen.

Ci-dessus, le magasin avec une fresque de Beatriz Milhazes. Ci-dessous, à gauche, l'espace d'exposition avec un canapé et des fauteuils de Joaquim Tenreiro et, à droite, un fauteuil « Egg » d'Arne Jacobsen.

# ROSS STEVENS

Ross Stevens
Lot 5
Pounui Ridge
RD3 Western Lake Rd
Featherston, 5773
New Zealand

Tel: +64 6 307 7678
E-mail: ross.e.stevens@gmail.com

Container House

**ROSS STEVENS** was born in 1966 in Wairo, New Zealand. He received an Industrial Design diploma from Wellington Polytechnic in 1986. He holds a Master's degree in Industrial Design from Victoria University, Wellington. He was an industrial designer at Fisher and Paykel in Wellington (1987–91). He has been an Industrial Design Consultant for B&W Loudspeakers (UK, 1992–95); Thomson Consumer Electronics and Philippe Starck (1992–95); and an exhibition designer for Te Papa MONZ (New Zealand, 1994–96). He is Design Director for Plinius Audible Technology (New Zealand). The Container House published here is his only built work.

**ROSS STEVENS** wurde 1966 in Wairo, Neuseeland, geboren. 1986 erwarb er am Wellington Polytechnikum ein Diplom in Industriedesign. An der Victoria University in Wellington hat er seinem Abschluss als Master in Industriedesign gemacht. Von 1987 bis 1991 war er bei Fisher und Paykel in Wellington als Industriedesigner angestellt. Von 1992 bis 1995 war er bei der Firma B & W Loudspeakers in England, bei Thomson Consumer Electronics und Philippe Starck als beratender Industriedesigner tätig, sowie von 1994 bis 1996 als Ausstellungsdesigner für Te Papa MONZ (Neuseeland). Bei Plinius Audible Technology (Neuseeland) ist er als leitender Designer beschäftigt. Das hier publizierte Containerhaus ist sein einziges gebautes Werk.

**ROSS STEVENS**, né en 1966 à Wairo, Nouvelle-Zélande, est diplômé en design industriel de l'École polytechnique de Wellington (1986), et est titulaire d'un mastère dans la même discipline à la Victoria University, Wellington. Il a travaillé comme designer pour Fisher and Paykel à Wellington (1987–91), designer consultant pour B&W Loudspeakers (Grande-Bretagne, 1992–95) ; puis pour Thomson Consumer Electronics et Philippe Starck (1992–95), et a conçu des expositions pour Te Papa MONZ, Nouvelle-Zélande (1994–96). Il est directeur du design pour Plinius Audible Technology, Nouvelle-Zélande. La maison Container, publiée ici, est son unique réalisation architecturale.

# CONTAINER HOUSE

*Owhiro Bay, Wellington, New Zealand, 2000–07*

*Floor area: 90 m² interior; 45 m² covered deck; 60 m² garage. Client: Ross Stevens.*
*Cost: $170 000 (not including personal labor)*

This house is made up of 3 x 30-square-meter insulated refrigeration containers. It has a large covered deck made of 3 x 15-square-meter shipping platforms. These units were placed on three industrial tower crane sections. As Ross Stevens explains, "I am an industrial designer, so the idea of making architecture out of standard industrial components allowed me to work in a way more similar to industrial design while on the scale of architecture." The site of the Container House is an irregular hole in a rock, which required the 50-millimeter-thick steel deck (industrial waste) to be cut with a gap of no more than 100 millimeters from the rock. In this way, Stevens avoided the legal requirement to erect a fence around the house. He explains, "Personally I have no one belief of good design so I enjoy clashing different styles: for example modular with site specific, high-tech with decorative, or new and immaculate with old and decaying."

Dieses Haus besteht aus drei jeweils 30 m² großen, isolierten Kühlbehältern. Es verfügt über eine große, überdachte Fläche aus drei je 15 m² großen Schiffsrampen. Diese Einheiten wurden auf drei Teile von serienmäßigen Industrieturmkränen platziert. Dazu Ross Stevens: »Ich bin Industriedesigner, so dass mir die Idee, mit genormten Industriekomponenten Architektur herzustellen, ermöglichte, in einer dem Industriedesign ähnlichen Weise und doch in der Größenordnung von Architektur zu arbeiten.« Der Standplatz des Containerhauses befindet sich in einem unregelmäßigen Einschnitt in eine Felswand, die es erforderlich machte, die 50 mm starke Bodenplatte aus Stahl (Industrieabfall) mit höchstens 100 mm Abstand zur Felswand zu schneiden. Auf diese Weise umging Stevens den gesetzlich vorgeschriebenen Zaun um das Haus. »Ich persönlich habe keine feste Vorstellung von gutem Design, also macht es mir Spaß, unterschiedliche Stile aufeinanderprallen zu lassen: z. B. standardisiert mit ortsspezifisch, hightech mit dekorativ, oder neu und makellos mit alt und zerfallend.«

Cette maison est constituée de trois conteneurs réfrigérants de 30 m². Elle possède une vaste terrasse couverte comprenant trois plates-formes d'expédition de 15 m². Ces éléments ont été fixés sur trois sections de grues industrielles. Selon Stevens : « Je suis designer industriel, et l'idée de faire de l'architecture à partir de composants industriels standard m'a permis de travailler de façon assez similaire à celle du design industriel, mais à l'échelle architecturale. » Le site de cette maison Conteneur est un trou de forme irrégulière pratiqué dans la roche qui a demandé de découper la plate-forme en acier de 50 mm d'épaisseur de telle sorte que l'interstice laissé entre elle et le rocher ne dépasse pas 100 mm. De cette façon, Stevens a pu contourner l'obligation de dresser une barrière autour de sa maison. « Personnellement, je ne crois pas à un « bon » design, et j'aime les heurts entre différents styles, par exemple, le modulaire et le spécifique, le high-tech avec le décoratif, ou le nouveau et l'immaculé avec le vieux et le délabré. »

*The Container House is much more sophisticated than the Freitag Store reproduced on page 502, and yet the basic idea is quite similar—an industrial volume used for purposes other than those it was originally intended for.*

*Das Containerhaus ist weit anspruchsvoller als der auf Seite 502 abgebildete Freitag Store und doch ist der Grundgedanke ganz ähnlich – ein Industriebehältnis wird für andere als die ursprünglich vorgesehenen Zwecke genutzt.*

*La maison Conteneur est beaucoup plus sophistiquée que le magasin Freitag reproduit page 502, même si l'idée de base est à peu près similaire : utiliser des matériaux industriels pour d'autres fonctions que celles pour lesquelles ils ont été conçus.*

The insertion of the house into the rocky site required a great deal of precision, particularly in the cut-out form of the rear terrace.

Das Einfügen des Hauses in die Fels-wand erforderte ein Höchstmaß an Präzision, insbesondere die Ausschnit-te auf der rückseitigen Terrasse.

L'insertion de la maison dans ce site rocheux exigeait une grande préci-sion, en particulier dans la découpe de la terrasse arrière.

There is something of the practical spirit of Charles and Ray Eames in the Container House, and the engineering background of Ross Stevens, who is an industrial designer rather than an architect.

Im Containerhaus ist etwas vom praktischen Geist von Charles und Ray Eames spürbar und von Ross Stevens' Hintergrund als Industriedesigner und nicht Architekt.

On retrouve quelque chose de l'esprit pratique de Charles et Ray Eames dans cette maison comme dans la formation de designer industriel et non d'architecte de Stevens.

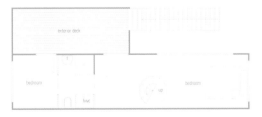

The idea of a technical or, more precisely, machine-like metal environment is understandably appealing to an industrial designer. His house and office space thus become a reflection of his profession.

Die Vorstellung einer technisch oder präziser maschinell gefertigten Umgebung aus Metall sagt einem Industriedesigner verständlicherweise zu. Derart werden sein Haus und Büro zum Spiegelbild seiner Profession.

L'idée d'un environnement technique, ou plus précisément métallique, est sans doute séduisant pour un designer industriel. Sa maison et son bureau reflètent ainsi sa profession.

# PHILIPPE STUEBI

*Philippe Stuebi Architekten GmbH*
*Hardstrasse 219*
*8005 Zurich*
*Switzerland*

*Tel: +41 44 440 7777*
*Fax: +41 44 440 7779*
*E-mail: ps@philippestuebi.ch*
*Web: www.philippestuebi.ch*

**PHILIPPE STUEBI** was born in Lausanne in 1963, and received his degree in Architecture from the Swiss Federal Institute of Technology (ETH) in Zurich in 1993, where he studied under Hans Kollhoff. He set up his own office, Philippe Stuebi Architekten GmbH, in Zurich in 1996, with the goal of creating "networked architecture," linking issues like art, lifestyle, ecology and economics, designing every project down to the smallest interior details. His built work includes: Restaurant/Bar Josef und Maria (Zurich, 1998); Maison Draeger (Corsica, 2000); Villa Polana (Uitikon, 2000); Beaufort 12, Expo '02 Pavilion (Neuchâtel, 2002); Würzgraben Housing Estate for the building authority of Zurich (2003); and the L House (Zollikon, 2005, published here), all in Switzerland. Philippe Stuebi was a co-founder and associate of the Kunstclub HeiQell in Zurich (1988–93), a gallery for contemporary art. He is currently working on the T Collection in Zurich, a chapel in Unterbäch, a villa near Lake Lucerne, a house at the waterfront of Lake Zurich, all in Switzerland, as well as on a house in Croatia.

**PHILIPPE STUEBI** wurde 1963 in Lausanne geboren und schloss sein Architekturstudium 1993 an der ETH in Zürich ab, wo er bei Hans Kollhoff studiert hatte. Er eröffnete 1996 in Zürich sein eigenes Büro, Philippe Stuebi Architekten GmbH, mit dem Ziel »vernetzte Architektur« zu schaffen, bei der sich Themen wie Kunst, Lifestyle, Ökologie und Ökonomie verbinden sollten und er bei jedem Projekt auch für das kleinste Detail der Innenausstattung zuständig sein sollte. Zu seinen realisierten Bauten zählen: Restaurant/Bar Josef und Maria (Zürich, 1998), Maison Draeger (Korsika, 2000), Villa Polana (Uitikon, 2000), Beaufort 12, Pavillon für die Expo '02 (Neuchâtel, 2002), Würzgraben-Wohnanlage für die Baubehörde von Zürich (2003) und das Haus L (Zollikon, 2005, hier publiziert), alle in der Schweiz. Philippe Stuebi gehört zu den Gründern und Gesellschaftern des Kunstclubs HeiQell in Zürich (1988–93), einer Galerie für zeitgenössische Kunst. Zurzeit arbeitet er an der T Collection in Zürich, an einer Kapelle in Unterbäch, einer Villa nahe dem Vierwaldstättersee und einem Haus am Ufer des Zürichsees, alle in der Schweiz, sowie an einem Haus in Kroatien.

**PHILIPPE STUEBI**, né à Lausanne en 1963, est diplômé d'architecture de l'ETH à Zurich (1993) où il étudie sous la direction de Hans Kollhoff. Il crée son agence, Philippe Stuebi Architekten GmbH à Zurich, en 1996, pour pratiquer une « architecture en réseau », combinant des enjeux d'art, style de vie, d'écologie et d'économie et concevant chaque projet jusque dans les plus petits détails de son aménagement intérieur. Parmi ses réalisations, toutes en Suisse : le Restaurant-bar Josef und Maria, Zurich (1998) ; la maison Draeger, Corse (2000) ; la villa Polana, Uitikon (2000) ; Beaufort 12, pavillon d'Expo '02, Neuchâtel (2002) ; logements de Würzgraben, Zurich (2003) et la maison L, Zollikon (2005), publiée ici. Philippe Stuebi a été cofondateur et associé du Kunstclub HeiQell à Zurich (1988–93), galerie d'art contemporain. Il travaille actuellement, toujours en Suisse, au projet de la T Collection à Zurich, d'une chapelle à Unterbäch, d'une villa proche du lac des Quatre Cantons, d'une maison sur le lac de Zurich ainsi qu'au projet d'une maison en Croatie.

# L HOUSE

*Zollikon, Zurich, Switzerland, 2003–05*

*Floor area: 380 m². Client: private. Cost: not disclosed*

This design called for a maximum amount of usable space to be built on a limited site. The architect explains, "The space allocation plan was incorporated into a sculptural body by the method of hollowing out. The concept was to string together the requested spaces in one movement going through the house: stretching, extending, narrowing, grinding out from its mass, until a coherent sequence of spaces emerged according to the principle of the enfilade." Each room has a specific character, most notably the double-height polygonal library with its three sides glazed with partially reflective glass. Depending on external or internal lighting conditions, this library becomes visible or reflects the garden. The ground-floor exterior walls are made with a mixture of white Carrara marble and white cement with frequent floor-to-ceiling glazing. A bright fuschia color is used in the upper-level window wells. Interior floors are covered in polished Carrara marble.

Hier sollte auf einer begrenzten Fläche ein Maximum an nutzbarem Raum entstehen. Der Architekt führt hierzu aus: »Dem skulpturalen Baukörper wurde mit der Methode des Aushöhlens das Raumprogramm einverleibt. Die Grundrissentwicklung war eine Arbeit der Aneinanderreihung der geforderten Räume zu einer durchs Haus durchgehenden Bewegung; Dehnen, Weiten, Verengen, Ausschleiffen von Masse zu einer zusammenhängenden Raumfolge nach dem Prinzip der Enfilade.« Jeder Raum hat einen speziellen Charakter, besonders die polygonale Bibliothek mit doppelter Raumhöhe, deren drei Seiten mit teilweise beschichtetem Glas geschlossen sind. Abhängig von den externen oder internen Beleuchtungsverhältnissen ist diese Bibliothek sichtbar oder reflektiert den Garten. Die Außenwände des Erdgeschosses bestehen aus einer Mischung aus weißem Carrara-Marmor und weißem Zement mit häufig deckenhoch verglasten Zonen. Die Fensternischen des Obergeschosses sind in einem leuchtenden Fuchsiaton gehalten, die Fußböden im Inneren mit poliertem Carrara-Marmor belegt.

L'enjeu de ce projet était de tirer le maximum d'espace utile d'un terrain de dimensions réduites. L'architecte explique ainsi sa démarche : « Le plan d'allocation d'espace a été intégré dans un corps structurel par la méthode du creusement-dégagement. Le concept était de lier les espaces voulus dans un seul mouvement traversant la maison : étirement, extension, étroitisation, meulage de la masse, jusqu'à ce qu'émerge une séquence cohérente d'espaces, selon le principe de l'enfilade. » Chaque pièce présente un caractère spécifique, en particulier la bibliothèque polygonale double-hauteur aux trois côtés en verre en partie réfléchissant. Selon les conditions d'éclairage interne ou externe, elle devient visible ou reflète le jardin. Les murs extérieurs du rez-de-chaussée sont réalisés dans un mélange de marbre de Carrare blanc et de ciment blanc, avec de fréquentes interruptions par des panneaux de verre toute hauteur. Un fuschia vif est utilisé pour la peinture des retraits des baies de l'étage. Les sols intérieurs sont recouverts de marbre de Carrare poli.

*The visible external surfaces of the house as seen from the street (above) give an impression of strict rectilinear Modernism.*

*Die von der Straße aus sichtbaren Außenflächen des Hauses (oben) vermitteln einen Eindruck von streng geradlinigem Modernismus.*

*Les extérieurs de la maison vus de la rue (ci-dessus) donnent une impression de strict modernisme orthogonal.*

Garden-side views somewhat compli-
cate the original impression, with a
bright lavender balcony disturbing the
whiteness of the house and a tapering
glass-walled projection containing the
client's library.

Ansichten von der Gartenseite verfäl-
schen den ursprünglichen Eindruck
mit einem lavendelfarbenen Balkon,
der von dem reinweißen Haus ablenkt,
und einem polygonal vorspringenden,
verglasten Bauteil, in dem der Besitzer
seine Bibliothek untergebracht hat.

La façade côté jardin complexifie
l'impression générale, avec un balcon
couleur lavande qui dérange la blancheur de la maison et un mur de
verre qui laisse apparaître la bibliothèque de ce client.

Inside like outside the house, whiteness is contrasted with this fuschia,
angled doorway, which breaks the
pattern of simple rectilinearity that
might be expected on the basis of the
street façade.

Im Inneren steht der weißen Fläche
dieser schräg eingesetzte, fuchsia-
farben gestrichene Eingang gegenüber und unterbricht die schlichte
Geradlinigkeit, die unten an der
Straßenfassade zu erwarten wäre.

À l'intérieur, la blancheur d'ensemble
contraste avec une porte fuschia
inclinée, qui rompt le caractère rectiligne auquel on s'attendait après la
façade sur rue.

The garden-side façade with its view into the library gives a glimpse of both the Modernist aspects of the house and its slightly unexpected plan (seen to the right).

Die Gartenseite mit dem Blick in die Bibliothek gewährt einen flüchtigen Eindruck von den modernistischen Aspekten des Hauses und dem etwas überraschenden Grundriss (rechts).

La façade côté jardin et sa vue sur la bibliothèque donnent une vision des aspects modernistes de cette maison et de son plan un peu inattendu (à droite).

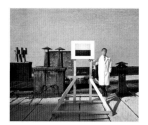

# HIROSHI SUGIMOTO

*Gallery Koyanagi*
*1–7–5 Ginza, 8th Floor*
*Chuo-ku*
*1040061 Tokyo*
*Japan*

*Tel: +81 3 3561 1896*
*Fax: +81 3 3563 3236*
*E-mail: mail@gallerykoyanagi.com*
*Web: www.gallerykoyanagi.com*

**HIROSHI SUGIMOTO**, born in Tokyo in 1948, attended Saint Paul's University in Tokyo (1966–70), then studied Photography at the Art Center College of Design in Los Angeles, receiving a B. F. A. in 1974. He moved to New York, where he currently resides, in 1974. Six main photographic series characterize his work thus far: the *Dioramas* and *Theaters* (both 1975); the *Seascapes* (1980); the *Wax Museums* (1994); *Sanjusangendo, Hall of 33 Bays* (sculptures of the Buddhist temple Sanjusangendo, 1995); and *Architecture* (1997). His large, usually black-and-white images have been presented in numerous art galleries, such as the White Cube in London and the Sonnabend Gallery in New York. Sugimoto has had exhibitions at the Metropolitan Museum of Art, New York; The Museum of Modern Art, New York; Museum of Contemporary Art, Los Angeles; Contemporary Arts Museum, Houston, Texas; MCA, Chicago; and Hara Museum of Contemporary Art, Tokyo, among others. The Hirshhorn Museum and Sculpture Garden, Washington, D. C., and the Mori Art Museum, Tokyo, were joint organizers of a 2005 Sugimoto retrospective. Hiroshi Sugimoto has shown a consistent interest in architecture, first in his photography, but also in actual works of architecture, such as his Go'o Shrine (Naoshima, Japan), or the Shirogane Apartment (published here), where he participated actively in the design.

Der 1948 in Tokio geborene **HIROSHI SUGIMOTO** besuchte von 1966 bis 1970 die St. Paul's University in Tokio und studierte im Anschluss am Arts Center College in Los Angeles Fotografie, wo er 1974 den Grad eines B. F. A. erwarb. 1974 zog er an seinen heutigen Wohnort New York. Bislang wird sein Schaffen von sechs Fotografieserien bestimmt: »Dioramas« und »Theaters« (beide 1975), »Seascapes« (1980), »Wax Museums« (1994), »Sanjusangendo, Halle der 33 Buchten« (Skulpturen des buddhistischen Tempels Sanjusangendo, 1995) und »Architecture« (1997). Seine großformatigen, in der Regel schwarz-weißen Fotografien wurden in zahlreichen Kunstgalerien wie White Cube in London und der Sonnabend Gallery in New York ausgestellt. Sugimoto hatte Ausstellungen u. a. am Metropolitan Museum of Art in New York, am Museum of Modern Art, ebenfalls in New York, am Museum of Contemporary Art in Los Angeles, am Contemporary Arts Museum in Houston, Texas, am MCA in Chicago sowie am Hara-Museum für zeitgenössische Kunst in Tokio. Das Hirshhorn Museum and Sculpture Garden in Washington, D. C., und das Mori-Kunstmuseum in Tokio veranstalteten 2005 gemeinsam eine Retrospektive mit Werken Sugimotos. Der Künstler hat ein beständiges Interesse an Architektur, zunächst bei seinen Fotografien, aber auch bei architektonischen Werken selbst, wie seinem Go'o Schrein (Naoshima, Japan) oder dem hier vorgestellten Shirogane-Apartment, an dessen Gestaltung er aktiv beteiligt war.

**HIROSHI SUGIMOTO**, né à Tokyo in 1948, a suivi les cours de Saint Paul's University à Tokyo (1966–70), puis étudié la photographie à l'Art Center College of Design à Los Angeles, dont il a reçu un B. F. A. en 1974. En 1974, il s'installe à New York, où il réside actuellement. Six grandes séries de photographies marquent son œuvre jusqu'à aujourd'hui : *Dioramas* et *Theaters* (depuis 1975) ; *Seascapes* (1980) ; *Wax Museums* (1994) ; *Sanjusangendo, Hall of 33 Bays* (sculptures du temple bouddhiste Sanjusangendo, 1995) ainsi qu'*Architecture* (1997). Ses images de grandes dimensions, généralement en noir et blanc, ont été exposées dans de nombreuses galeries d'art tels que le White Cube à Londres et la Sonnabend Gallery à New York. Il a bénéficié d'expositions entre autres au Metropolitan Museum of Art, New York, Museum of Modern Art, New York, au Museum of Contemporary Art, Los Angeles, au Contemporary Arts Museum, Houston, au MCA, Chicago, et au Musée Hara d'art contemporain, Tokyo. Le Hirshhorn Museum et Sculpture Garden, Washington D. C., et le Musée d'art Mori, Tokyo, ont conjointement organisé une rétrospective de son œuvre en 2005. Hiroshi Sugimoto s'est toujours intéressé à l'architecture, d'abord dans sa photographie, mais aussi dans des interventions architecturales concrètes comme le mausolée Go'o à Naoshima ou l'appartement Shirogane, publié ici, à la conception desquels il a activement participé.

# COLORS OF SHADOW

*Shirogane Apartment, Tokyo, Japan, 2004–06*

*Floor area: 228 m². Client: Hiroshi Sugimoto.*
*Cost: not disclosed*

In a Tokyo apartment he owns and has designed, the photographer Hiroshi Sugimoto has taken a series of photos that he calls *Colors of Shadow*. These are very subtle variants of the light and shade produced on walls of the apartment at different times and angles. As he explains, "When surfaces receive light, the light effects vary according to the angle of exposure. Selecting three distinct angles—90º, 55º, and 35º—I had the walls surfaced using traditional Japanese *shikkui* (plaster finishing), which absorbs and reflects light most evenly. In the morning light, the shadows play freely over the surfaces, now appearing, now vanishing. On rainy days, they take on a deeper, more evocative cast. I've only just begun my observations, but already I've discovered a sublime variety in shadow hues." As for the apartment itself, which has also been photographed here without direct reference to the actual *Colors of Shadow* series, Sugimoto makes clear that "this is not my work environment, not a photo studio, but a space designed for watching shadows […]. I'm also using this space for architectural experiments. I designed all the hanging rails, which are not for commercial production. For the floor, I bought more than 40 tree trunks of *kusunoki* (camphor wood), had them sliced 1.5 inches thick, then piled the planks to dry out for a year and a half before installing them. The floor does not touch the stucco wall. I wanted to leave a narrow space between them so that the shadow cast on the wall by the edge of the floor would be a sharp line. One policy is that everything has to be solid; nothing is just surface. This table I made, with a 4-inch top, is heavy wood. I work with a team of very good craftsmen who have skills that are no longer popular since they are so time consuming. Building a house used to take two to three years, but now people want it in six months. It took me four years to get to this point, and I keep paying the craftsmen by the hour. They like working with me because they can prove themselves in an authentic way."

In einem von ihm gestalteten und bewohnten Apartment in Tokio hat der Fotograf Hiroshi Sugimoto eine Reihe von Aufnahmen gemacht, die er »Colors of Shadow« nennt. Dabei handelt es sich um äußerst subtile Variationen der von den Wänden des Apartments zu verschiedenen Zeiten und unter verschiedenen Blickwinkeln produzierten Licht- und Schattenwirkungen. Er erläutert dazu: »Wenn Licht auf Oberflächen fällt, verändern sich die Lichteffekte gemäß dem Einfallswinkel. Nachdem ich drei verschiedene Winkel – 90, 55 und 35 Grad – gewählt hatte, ließ ich die Wände mit traditionellem japanischem shikkui (Verputz) anlegen, der Licht am gleichmäßigsten absorbiert und reflektiert. Im Morgenlicht bewegen sich die Schatten am ungehindertsten über die Flächen, kurz auftauchend und gleich wieder verschwindend. An regnerischen Tagen nehmen sie einen tieferen, plastischeren Farbton an. Ich habe mit meinen Beobachtungen gerade erst begonnen, habe aber bereits eine sublime Vielfalt von Schattierungen entdeckt.« Was die Wohnung selbst betrifft, die hier ohne direkten Bezug zu der Serie »Colors of Shadow« fotografiert wurde, stellt Sugimoto klar, dass »dies nicht mein Arbeitsumfeld und kein Fotostudio ist, sondern ein Raum zum Beobachten von Schatten […] Darüber hinaus nutze ich den Raum für architektonische Experimente. Ich habe sämtliche, nicht für gewerbliche Produktion gedachte Hängeschienen entworfen. Für den Boden erwarb ich über 40 Baumstämme aus kusunoki (Kampferholz), ließ sie in knapp 4 cm dicke Scheiben sägen, die ich dann anderthalb Jahre trocknen ließ, ehe ich sie verarbeitete. Der Boden berührt nicht die verputzten Wände. Ich wollte dazwischen einen schmalen Abstand lassen, so dass der vom Rand des Bodenbelags auf die Wand geworfene Schatten eine deutliche Linie sein würde. Ein Grundsatz ist, dass alles massiv sein muss, nichts ist nur Oberfläche. Dieser von mir gemachte Tisch mit seiner 10 cm dicken Platte, besteht aus massivem Holz. Ich arbeite mit einem Team sehr guter Handwerker, die über nur noch wenig verbreitete, weil zu zeitaufwendige Fähigkeiten verfügen. Früher dauerte es drei bis vier Jahre, ein Haus zu bauen, heute wollen es die Leute in sechs Monaten. Ich brauchte vier Jahre, um an diesen Punkt zu kommen und ich bezahle die Handwerker immer noch stundenweise. Sie arbeiten gerne mit mir, weil sie sich auf glaubwürdige Art beweisen können.«

Dans un appartement tokyoïte dont il est propriétaire et qu'il a conçu, Sugimoto a pris une série de photographies intitulées *Colors of Shadow* (Couleurs de l'ombre). Ce sont des variantes très subtiles sur l'ombre et la lumière produites sur les murs à différents moments de la journée et sous différents angles. Il explique ainsi son travail : « Lorsqu'une surface reçoit de la lumière, l'effet lumineux varie selon l'angle de prise de vue. Après avoir appliqué aux murs la technique japonaise ancienne du *shikkui* (finition au plâtre) qui absorbe et reflète la lumière de façon extrêmement égale, j'ai sélectionné des angles différents, 90°, 55° et 35°. Dans la lumière du matin, l'ombre joue en liberté sur les surfaces, qui tantôt apparaissent, tantôt disparaissent. Par temps pluvieux, elles prennent un aspect plus profond, plus évocateur. J'ai à peine commencé mes observations, mais j'ai déjà découvert une sublime variété de nuances d'ombres ». Sur l'appartement, photographié ici sans référence au travail sur les ombres, Sugimoto précise que « ce n'est pas mon environnement de travail, pas un studio photo, mais un espace conçu pour regarder l'ombre… je m'en sers également pour des expérimentations architecturales. J'ai conçu tous les rails d'accrochage, qui ne sont pas destinés à être produits commercialement. Pour les sols, j'ai acheté plus de quarante troncs de *kusunoki* (camphrier), les ai fait découper en planches de presque 4 cm d'épaisseur, puis j'ai mis ces dernières à sécher pendant un an et demi avant de les poser. Le sol ne touche pas le mur en stuc. Je voulais laisser un étroit espace entre eux de telle façon que l'ombre projetée sur le mur par l'angle du plancher décrive une ligne nette. Tout doit être massif, rien n'est qu'une simple surface. J'ai fabriqué cette table à plateau de 10 cm d'épaisseur en bois lourd. Je travaille avec une équipe d'excellents artisans qui possèdent des capacités de moins en moins répandues car elles prennent beaucoup de temps. Construire une maison prenait jadis de deux à trois ans, aujourd'hui, les gens la veulent en six mois. Il m'a fallu quatre ans pour arriver à ce résultat, et je paye les artisans à l'heure. Ils aiment travailler avec moi parce qu'ils peuvent se réaliser de façon plus authentique. »

*Colors of Shadow is the title of the photo series taken by Hiroshi Sugimoto in his Tokyo apartment, but this series is not meant to illustrate what the apartment looks like. Instead he sees the images as a study of light and shadow.*

*»Colors of Shadow« ist der Titel einer von Hiroshi Sugimoto in seinem Apartment in Tokio aufgenommenen Fotoserie, die jedoch nicht das Aussehen des Apartments wiedergeben soll. Sugimoto versteht sie als eine Studie von Licht und Schatten.*

*« Les couleurs de l'ombre » est le titre d'une séquence de photos prises par Hiroshi Sugimoto dans son appartement, sans en être en rien l'illustration. Il voit dans ces images une étude sur le thème de l'ombre et de la lumière.*

Sugimoto sees his apartment itself as a separate architectural space and experience. The pictures above show what the actual space looks like. Sugimoto does not consider these images as part of his artwork, whereas the Colors of Shadow picture to the right is a work of art.

Sugimoto sieht sein Apartment als separaten architektonischen Raum und Erfahrung. Die Fotos oben, die zeigen, wie die Wohnung aussieht, sind nicht Teil des künstlerischen Werks Sugimotos, im Gegensatz zu dem Foto rechts aus der Serie »Colors of Shadow«.

Sugimoto considère son appartement comme un volume architectural et une expérience que tentent de faire partager ses photos. Les photos ci-dessus ne sont pas des œuvres d'art, contrairement à la photographie de la série « Colors of Shadow », à droite.

# SYSTEMARCHITECTS

*SYSTEMarchitects*
*9 Desbrosses Street No. 512A*
*New York, NY 10013*
*USA*

*Tel: +1 212 239 8001*
*Fax: +1 800 796 4152*
*E-mail: system@systemarchitects.net*
*Web: www.systemarchitects.net*

**SYSTEMARCHITECTS** was created by Jeremy Edmiston and Douglas Gauthier in New York in 1998. Jeremy Edmiston received his B.Arch from the University of Technology, Sydney (1989), and his M.Arch from Columbia University (1992). A 1992 research project on environmental architecture earned him a Harkness Fellowship and Fulbright Scholarship. He has served as Visiting Professor in the Schools of Architecture at Columbia University, Syracuse, Roger Williams University, and City College. Douglas Gauthier holds degrees from Columbia University and the University of Notre Dame. He was a 1994 Fulbright Architectural Scholar to the Czech and Slovak Republics for research entitled "Parallel Modernism: Building Practices in the Former East Bloc." He has taught and lectured at Columbia, Parsons, Syracuse, Barnard, Yale, and Princeton. Their work includes participation in the P. S. 1 / MoMA 2003 Warm-Up Young Architect Series (Queens, New York, 2003); the New Housing New York competition (Third Prize, 2004); as well as completion of the kit home BURST*003 (North Haven, Australia, 2005, published here).

**SYSTEMARCHITECTS** wurde 1998 von Jeremy Edmiston und Douglas Gauthier in New York ins Leben gerufen. Jeremy Edmiston erwarb seinen B.Arch. 1989 an der University of Technology in Sydney und 1992 seinen M.Arch. an der Columbia University in New York. Ein Forschungsprojekt zu umweltgerechter Architektur brachte ihm 1992 eine Harkness Fellowship und ein Fulbright-Stipendium ein. Er war als Gastprofessor an den Architekturfakultäten der Columbia University, Syracuse, der Roger Williams University und am City College tätig. Douglas Gauthier besitzt Abschlüsse der Columbia University und der University of Notre Dame. Für Forschungen zum Thema »Parallele Moderne: Architekturpraxis im früheren Ostblock« hielt er sich 1994 als Fulbrightprofessor in Tschechien und Slowakien auf. Er hielt Vorlesungen und Vorträge in Columbia, Parsons, Syracuse, Barnard, Yale und Princeton. Gemeinsam beteiligten sich Edmiston und Gauthier 2003 an der P. S. 1/MoMA 2003 Warm-Up Young Architect Series (Queens, New York, 2003), am Wettbewerb für neuen Wohnungsbau in New York (3. Preis, 2004) und stellten das hier publizierte Bausatzhaus BURST*003 fertig (North Haven, Australien, 2005).

**SYSTEMARCHITECTS** a été créé par Jeremy Edmiston et Douglas Gauthier à New York en 1998. Jeremy Edmiston est B. Arch. de l'Université de technologie de Sydney (1989), et M. Arch. de Columbia University (1992). Son projet de recherche de 1992 sur l'architecture environnementale lui a valu une bourse Harkness et une bourse Fulbright. Il a été professeur invité des écoles d'architecture de Columbia University, Syracuse, Roger Williams University, et City College. Douglas Gauthier est diplômé de Columbia University et de l'Université Notre-Dame. En 1994, il a été « Fulbright Architectural Scholar » en République tchèque et slovaque pour sa recherche intitulée « Modernisme parallèle : Pratiques constructives dans l'ancien bloc de l'Est ». Il a enseigné et donné des conférences à Columbia, Parsons, Syracuse, Barnard, Yale et Princeton. Parmi leurs travaux : participation à la P. S. 1/MoMA 2003 Warm-Up Young Architect Series, Queens, New York ; au concours New Housing New York (troisième prix, 2004) ; et à la maison en kit BURST*003, North Haven, Australie (2005), publiée ici.

# BURST*003

*North Haven, New South Wales, Australia, 2005*

*Floor area: 93 m² of interior space with 46 m² of exterior deck and bleachers. Clients: Andrew Katay and Catriona Grant.*
*Cost: $250 000. Project Team: Sarkis Arakelyan, Amber Lynn Bard, Ayat Fadaifard, Sara Goldsmith,*
*Henry Grosman, Kobi Jakov, Joseph Jelinek, Ginny Hyo-jin Kang, Gen Kato, Yarek Karawczyk, Ioanna Karagiannakou, Tony Su.*
*Site Architects: Robin Edmiston & Associates. Site/Project Architect: Chris Knapp*

Built for a young family with three children on a 725-square-meter lot three hours from Sydney, BURST*003 is a prototype kit home. The plywood rib structure of the three-bedroom house was cut from 25-millimeter plywood by a computer-controlled laser. The architects explain that "each piece is pre-cut and numbered, delivered to the site, and assembled. Using digital processes, the geometry is complex and the form responsive to the relationship between natural forces on the site and the program. This relationship produces a low energy house that uses construction material and labor in a highly efficient manner." Local building regulations required that the residence be lifted 1.8 meters off the ground because it is located close to the shore. The architects conclude, "In the BURST* project, architecture successfully spatializes the outdoors. Through a series of deliberate overlaps, gaps, and slits within the building's skin, one's eye obliquely captures the surrounding landscape to interiorize the exterior. The human figure moves within, over, and under the folded skin, ambiguously occupying inside and outside. BURST*003 was built in 2005 and is being developed into a responsive parametric housing system that is earthquake, hurricane, and flood resistant." The house received the 2006 RAIA Wilkinson Award.

Das auf einem 725 m² großen Grundstück drei Stunden von Sydney entfernt stehende BURST*003 ist der Prototyp eines Bausatzhauses für eine junge Familie mit drei Kindern. Die Rippenkonstruktion des Hauses mit drei Schlafräumen wurde von einem computergesteuerten Laser aus 25 mm starkem Sperrholz geschnitten. Die Architekten erläutern: »Jedes Teil wird vorgeschnitten und nummeriert an den Bauplatz geliefert und dort montiert. Dank der Nutzung digitaler Prozesse ist die Geometrie komplex und die Form reagiert auf die Beziehung zwischen natürlichen Kräften vor Ort und dem Programm. Diese Beziehung ergibt ein Niedrigenergiehaus, das Baumaterial und Arbeitskraft höchst effizient nutzt.« Lokalen Bauvorschriften entsprechend muss das Wohnhaus 1,8 m über den Boden angehoben werden, weil es nahe am Ufer liegt. »Mit dem BURST*-Projekt gelingt es der Architektur, den Außenraum zu ›verräumlichen‹. Durch eine Reihe von absichtlichen Überschneidungen, Lücken und Schlitzen in der Außenhaut nimmt das Auge die umgebende Landschaft indirekt wahr und verinnerlicht die Außenwelt. Die menschliche Figur bewegt sich in, über und unter der gefalteten Haut und nimmt dabei das Innen und Außen vieldeutig in Anspruch. BURST*003 wurde 2005 gebaut und wird zurzeit zu einem elastischen parametrischen Wohnsystem entwickelt, das Erdbeben, Hurrikans und Überflutungen standhalten kann.« Das Haus erhielt 2006 den RAIA Wilkinson Award.

La maison BURST*003, construite pour une famille de trois enfants sur une parcelle de 725 m², située à trois heures de Sydney, est un prototype à construire soi-même. Sa structure, en nervures de contreplaqué, a été découpée au laser à commande numérique dans du contreplaqué de 25 mm d'épaisseur : « Chaque pièce est prédécoupée et numérotée, livrée sur site et assemblée. La géométrie complexe fait appel à des processus numériques et la forme répond à une relation entre les forces naturelles présentes sur le terrain et le programme. Cette relation donne naissance à une maison à faible consommation énergétique, qui utilise les matériaux de construction et la main d'œuvre nécessaires de façon extrêmement efficace. » La réglementation locale de la construction voulait que la maison soit surélevée de 1,8 mètres par rapport au sol, à cause de la côte très proche. Pour les architectes : « L'architecture « spatialise » avec succès l'extérieur. Grâce à une série de superpositions, de manques et de fentes aménagés dans la peau du bâti, le regard est capté obliquement par le paysage environnant pour intérioriser l'extérieur. L'habitant se déplace dans, sur et sous cette peau pliée, en occupant, non sans ambiguïté, l'intérieur et l'extérieur. BURST*003 a été construite en 2005 et sert de base à un système de logements paramétrés, résistant aux tremblements de terre, aux ouragans et aux marées. » La maison a reçu le RAIA Wilkinson Award 2006.

Lifted up off the ground because of the potential danger of flooding, the house is made in good part of computer-cut plywood. Despite its unusual appearance, BURST*003 is a kit house that can be assembled quickly.

Wegen möglicher Überflutung angehoben, besteht BURST*003 zum Großteil aus vom Computer zugeschnittenem Sperrholz. Trotz des ungewöhnlichen Aussehens handelt es sich um ein Baukastenhaus, das sich schnell montieren lässt.

Suspendue au-dessus du sol pour limiter les dangers d'inondation, la maison est en grande partie composée de contreplaqué découpé par ordinateur. Malgré son aspect inhabituel, c'est une maison en kit qui peut s'assembler rapidement.

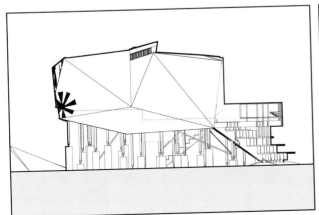

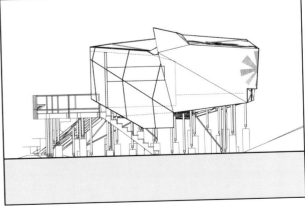

Kit houses generally lack originality or unusual spaces. In this instance, computer technology has been used to render both the design and the production of the residence simpler, allowing for greater spatial experimentation.

Baukastenhäusern fehlt es in der Regel an Originalität oder besonderen Räumen. In diesem Fall wurde die Computertechnik genutzt, um Design und Produktion des Wohnhauses einfacher zu gestalten und so räumliches Experimentieren zu ermöglichen.

Les maisons à monter manquent généralement d'originalité. Ici, la technologie numérique a servi à simplifier la conception et la production de ce projet et à profiter d'une plus grande liberté d'expérimentation spatiale.

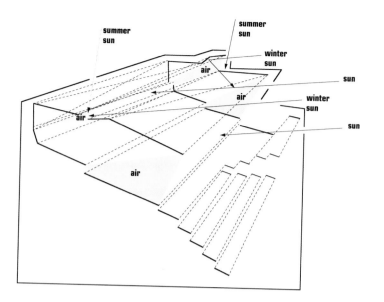

*The assembly pattern of the plywood panels is related to the original computer-driven design and production process, making unusual forms much easier to deal with than in the past.*

*Die Montageweise der Sperrholzplatten steht in Verbindung zum ursprünglichen, computergesteuerten Entwurf, wodurch die Herstellung ungewöhnlicher Formen sehr viel einfacher ist als früher.*

*Le processus d'assemblage des panneaux de contreplaqué vient de la conception et de la production assistées par ordinateur, qui rendent les formes inhabituelles beaucoup plus faciles à gérer que par le passé.*

*BURST\*003 has something of the atmosphere of a beach house, and is both cheerful and dynamic in ways that were previously unattainable for kit houses.*

*Wenngleich es etwas von der Atmosphäre eines Strandhauses hat, wirkt BURST\*003 auf eine Weise fröhlich und dynamisch, die man von früheren Baukastenhäusern nicht kennt.*

*Bien qu'elle soit une sorte de maison de plage, BURST\*003 est chaleureuse et dynamique d'une manière jusque-là inconnue pour une maison en kit.*

# UNSTUDIO

UNStudio
Stadhouderskade 113
1073 AX Amsterdam
The Netherlands

Tel: +31 20 570 2040
Fax: +31 20 570 2041
E-mail: info@unstudio.com
Web: www.unstudio.com

Ben van Berkel was born in Utrecht in 1957 and studied at the Rietveld Academy in Amsterdam and at the Architectural Association (AA) in London, receiving the AA Diploma with honors in 1987. After working briefly in the office of Santiago Calatrava in 1988, he set up his own practice in Amsterdam with Caroline Bos. He has been a Visiting Professor at Columbia and a visiting lecturer at Princeton (1994). He was a Diploma Unit Master at the AA (1994–95) and at Berlage Institute in Rotterdam. As well as the Erasmus Bridge in Rotterdam (inaugurated in 1996), **UNSTUDIO** has built the Karbouw and ACOM office buildings (1989–93), and the REMU Electricity Station (1989–93), all in Amersfoort; and housing projects and the Aedes East Gallery for Kristin Feireiss in Berlin. More recent projects include an extension of the Rijksmuseum Twente (Enschede, 1992–96); Möbius House (Naarden, 1993–98); and Het Valkhof Museum (Nijmegen, 1998), all in The Netherlands; a Switching Station (Innsbruck, Austria, 1998–2001); a music theater (Graz, Austria, 1998–2007); NMR Laboratory (Utrecht, The Netherlands, 2000); Arnhem Station (The Netherlands, 1986–2007); VilLA NM (Upstate New York, 2000–06); and Mercedes-Benz Museum (Stuttgart, 2003–06), both published here. UNStudio was also a participant in the competition for the new World Trade Center in New York, in collaboration with Foreign Office Architects, Greg Lynn FORM, Imaginary Forces, Kevin Kennon and Reiser + Umemoto RUR Architecture, under the name of United Architects, and realized *Holiday Home* in 2006, published here.

Ben van Berkel wurde 1957 in Utrecht geboren, studierte an der Rietveld-Akademie in Amsterdam und an der Architectural Association (AA) in London, wo er 1987 das Diplom mit Auszeichnung erhielt. Nach einem kurzen Arbeitseinsatz 1988 im Büro von Santiago Calatrava gründete er mit Caroline Bos sein Büro in Amsterdam. Er war Gastprofessor in Columbia und Gastdozent in Princeton (1994). 1994 bis 1995 war er Diploma Unit Master an der AA und am Berlage Institute in Rotterdam. Neben der 1996 eingeweihten Erasmusbrücke in Rotterdam errichtete **UNSTUDIO** in Amersfoort die Bürobauten für Karbouw und ACOM (1989–93) und das Kraftwerk REMU (1989–93) sowie in Berlin Wohnungsbauprojekte und die Galerie Aedes East für Kristin Feireiss. Unter den neueren Projekten finden sich die Erweiterung für das Rijksmuseum Twente (Enschede, 1992–96), Haus Möbius (Naarden, 1993–98) sowie das Museum Het Valkhof (Nimwegen, 1998), alle in den Niederlanden, eine Umschaltstation (Innsbruck, 1998–2001), ein Musiktheater (Graz, 1998–2007), NMR-Labor (Utrecht, 2000), Bahnhof Arnheim (1986–2007), VilLA NM (bei New York, 2000–06) sowie das Mercedes-Benz-Museum (Stuttgart, 2003–06), die beiden letzten Projekte sind in diesem Band besprochen. UNStudio beteiligte sich darüber hinaus am Wettbewerb für das neue World Trade Center in New York in Zusammenarbeit mit Foreign Office Architects, Greg Lynn FORM, Imaginary Forces, Kevin Kennon und Reiser + Umemoto RUR Architecture, unter dem Namen United Architects, und sie errichteten 2006 das hier vorgestellte »Holiday Home«. Ben van Berkel

Ben van Berkel, né à Utrecht en 1957, étudie à la Rietveld Academie d'Amsterdam, ainsi qu'à l'Architectural Association (AA) de Londres, dont il sort diplômé avec mention en 1987. Après avoir brièvement travaillé pour Santiago Calatrava en 1988, il ouvre son agence à Amsterdam, en association avec Caroline Bos. Il a été Professeur invité à la Columbia University, New York, et à Princeton en 1994, et Diploma Unit Master pour l'AA en 1994–95 et pour le Berlage Institute à Rotterdam. En dehors du pont Érasme à Rotterdam (inauguré en 1996), **UNSTUDIO** a construit les immeubles de bureaux Karbouw et ACOM (1989–93), le poste d'électricité REMU (1989–93), le tout à Amersfoort, ainsi que des logements et la galerie Aedes East de Kristin Feireiss à Berlin. Parmi leurs projets plus récents : l'extension du Rijksmuseum Twente, Enschede (1992–96), la maison Möbius, Naarden (1993–98), le musée Het Valkhof, Nimègue (1998), tous au Pays-Bas ; une sous-station à Innsbruck (Autriche, 1998–2001) ; une salle de musique à Graz, Autriche (1998–2007) ; le laboratoire NMR, Utrecht (2000) ; la gare d'Arnhem (Pays-Bas, 1986–2007) ; la vilLA NM, État de New York (2000–06) et le Mercedes-Benz Museum, Stuttgart (2003–06), tous deux publiés ici. UNStudio a participé au récent concours pour le World Trade Center à New York, en collaboration avec les Foreign Office Architects, Greg Lynn FORM, Imaginary Forces, Kevin Kennon et Reiser + Umemoto RUR Architecture, sous le nom de United Architects, et a réalisé l'installation *Holiday Home* en 2006, publiée ici.

# MERCEDES-BENZ MUSEUM

*Stuttgart, Germany, 2003–06*

*Floor area: 35 000 m². Client: DaimlerChrysler Immobilien (DCI) GmbH. Cost: €150 million.*
*Design: UNStudio: Ben van Berkel, Caroline Bos with Tobias Wallisser. Realization: UNStudio with Wenzel + Wenzel, Stuttgart.*
*Exhibition Concept and Design: H. G. Merz, Stuttgart. Interior Architecture: UNStudio with*
*Concrete Architectural Associates. Special Elements: Inside Outside – Petra Blaisse, Amsterdam*

"Architecture is no longer about the image," declares Ben van Berkel, "it is about the after image, about objects that appear uncomplicated, but nonetheless generate rich spatial and visual experiences like hopeful shadows." The Mercedes-Benz Museum is set at the entrance to the city, next to the B14 motorway and in the grounds of the historic Untertürkheim manufacturing plant. At a cost of approximately 150 million euros, it redefines the way museums work, and does so using the most sophisticated technology available. Created in 1923, the former Mercedes-Benz Museum attracted 480 000 visitors a year. A January 2002 architectural competition for a new building brought together some of the most prestigious names in international architecture. The second prize went to the Tokyo architects Sejima + Nishizawa / S A N A A. Van Berkel's astonishing design consists of a nine-level heart-like structure with interior double-helix spiraling ramps that allow visitors to walk through a chronological presentation of the company's production. After walking into the vaulted 47-meter atrium, visitors are carried to the top of the building in specially designed elevators that Van Berkel says remind him of Fritz Lang's iconic 1927 film *Metropolis*. Ben van Berkel admits that the parametric modeling of the Mercedes Museum reaches a degree of complexity that only computer specialists can fully grasp, but the upshot of this system is that unique parts can be fitted into the whole design without engaging in the kind of cost overruns that were typical in the past of such innovative buildings. No less than 38 000 working drawings were required for the construction and entirely new software was conceived during construction to deal with the intricacy of the task. Working with the celebrated Stuttgart engineer Werner Sobek, the exhibition designer H. G. Merz, the Amsterdam designer Petra Blaisse (Inside Outside), and Concrete Architectural Associates, Amsterdam, UNStudio maintained a high degree of control over the entire project, including the associated outside spaces.

»Architektur hat nichts mehr mit dem Bild zu tun«, verkündet Ben van Berkel, »es geht um das Nach-Bild, um Objekte, die unkompliziert scheinen, aber gleichwohl wie hoffnungsvolle Schatten vielfältige räumliche und visuelle Erfahrungen generieren.« Das Mercedes-Benz-Museum steht am Eingang zur Stadt, an der B 14 auf dem Gelände des historischen Werks in Untertürkheim. Für den Preis von etwa 150 Millionen Euro legt es die Art, wie Museen funktionieren, neu fest und bedient sich dazu hoch entwickelter Technik. Das 1923 entstandene frühere Mercedes-Benz-Museum zog jährlich 480 000 Besucher an. Der im Januar 2002 ausgeschriebene Wettbewerb für einen Neubau vereinte einige der renommiertesten Namen der internationalen Architekturszene. Der zweite Preis ging an das in Tokio ansässige Büro Sejima + Nishizawa / S A N A A. Der verblüffende Entwurf van Berkels besteht aus einem neungeschossigen Baukörper auf herzförmigem Grundriss, durch dessen Inneres sich spiralförmige Rampen wie eine Doppelhelix schrauben, die es Besuchern ermöglichen, eine chronologische Präsentation der Firmenerzeugnisse zu durchlaufen. Nachdem sie das 47 m hohe Atrium betreten haben, werden die Besucher in eigens gestalteten Fahrstühlen, von denen van Berkel sagt, sie erinnerten ihn an Fritz Langs 1927 entstandene Filmikone »Metropolis«, auf die oberste Ebene befördert. Ben van Berkel räumt ein, dass mit der parametrischen Formgebung des Mercedes-Museums ein Grad von Komplexität erreicht ist, der sich nur Computerspezialisten vollständig erschließt; im Ergebnis bedeutet dieses System jedoch, dass einzelne Teile in den Gesamtentwurf eingepasst werden können, ohne die in der Vergangenheit bei innovativen Bauten dieser Art üblichen überzogenen Kosten. Nicht weniger als 38 000 Arbeitszeichnungen waren für den Bau erforderlich und während der Arbeiten wurde völlig neue Software entwickelt, um die diffizilen Probleme der Aufgabe zu bewältigen. Bei der Zusammenarbeit mit dem renommierten Stuttgarter Ingenieur Werner Sobek, dem Ausstellungsarchitekten H. G. Merz, der Amsterdamer Designerin Petra Blaisse (Inside Outside) sowie der Concrete Architectural Association, Amsterdam, behielt UNStudio die Leitung des Gesamtprojekts, inklusive der zugehörigen Außenräume, weitestgehend in der Hand.

«L'architecture n'est plus un problème d'image, déclare Ben van Berkel, mais de ce qui se produit après l'image dans des objets qui ne semblent pas compliqués, mais qui génèrent néanmoins des expériences visuelles et spatiales riches, comme des ombres pleines d'espérance.» Le musée Mercedes-Benz, qui a coûté environ 150 millions d'euros, s'élève à l'entrée de la ville, près de l'autoroute B14, et sur les terrains de l'usine historique d'Untertürkheim. Il redéfinit la manière dont fonctionne un musée, et le fait en utilisant les technologies les plus sophistiquées du moment. Créé en 1923, l'ancien musée attirait 480 000 visiteurs par an. Un concours, organisé en janvier 2002 pour un nouveau bâtiment, a réuni certains des représentants les plus prestigieux de l'architecture internationale. Le second prix fut remporté par les architectes japonais Sejima + Nishizawa / S A N A A. L'étonnant projet de van Berkel consiste en une structure en forme de cœur de neuf niveaux à rampes internes en spirale, qui permettent aux visiteurs de suivre une présentation chronologique de la production du constructeur. Après avoir traversé l'atrium voûté de 47 mètres de haut, ils sont transportés au sommet du bâtiment par des ascenseurs de conception spécifique, qui rappellent à van Berkel le film culte de Fritz Lang, *Metropolis* (1927). L'architecte admet que la modélisation paramétrique de ce musée a atteint un tel degré de complexité que seuls des informaticiens spécialisés peuvent l'appréhender, mais la conséquence heureuse de ce système réside dans le fait que des pièces uniques peuvent être introduites dans le projet, sans entraîner les dépassements de coût typiques dans le passé de ce genre de bâtiment innovant. Pas moins de 38 000 dessins d'exécution ont été réalisés, et un logiciel entièrement nouveau a été conçu pour répondre à la complexité de la tâche. UNStudio, en collaborant avec le célèbre ingénieur de Stuttgart Werner Sobek, le concepteur d'expositions H. G. Merz, la designer amstellodamoise Petra Blaisse (Inside Outside) et Concrete Architectural Associates, Amsterdam, a conservé un contrôle très élevé sur la totalité du projet, y compris les espaces extérieurs qui lui sont liés.

*The wrapping, very contemporary forms of the Museum are intended to be seen from the neighboring highway, itself a symbol of automobile traffic. Right, a section shows the ways in which ramps lead from one level to the next.*

*Die geschlossenen, ultramodernen Formen des Museums sollen von der benachbarten Autobahn aus, selbst Symbol des Autoverkehrs, sichtbar sein. Der Schnitt (rechts) zeigt, wie die Rampen von einer Ebene zur nächsten führen.*

*Les formes enveloppantes très contemporaines du musée sont faites pour être vues de l'autoroute voisine, elle-même symbole de la circulation automobile. À droite, une coupe montre le parcours des rampes d'un niveau à l'autre.*

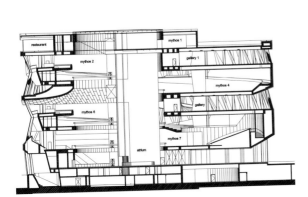

The building is the product of fully computer-driven design processes and the complexity of its various elements could not have been attained in a short construction period until very recently.

Das Bauwerk ist Ergebnis eines vollständig computergesteuerten Entwurfsprozesses und die Komplexität seiner verschiedenen Elemente hätte sich noch bis vor Kurzem nicht in so knapper Bauzeit umsetzen lassen.

Le bâtiment est issu d'un processus de conception assistée par ordinateur. Jusqu'à très récemment, la complexité de ses divers éléments n'aurait pu être obtenue dans un laps de temps aussi court.

The exhibition space is on two continuous loops that tell the story of Mercedes Benz beginning at the top of the museum.

Die Ausstellungsflächen befinden sich auf zwei fortlaufenden Schleifen und erzählen, auf der oberen Ebene beginnend, die Geschichte von Mercedes-Benz.

Les espaces d'expositions se répartissent le long des deux boucles continues qui racontent l'histoire de Mercedes Benz en commençant par le haut du musée.

Above, the spectacular central space of the museum is the first view that visitors have before being carried up to the top of the building, where the exhibition circuit begins.

Der oben zu sehende phänomenale, zentrale Raum des Museums ist der erste Eindruck der Besucher, ehe sie nach oben befördert werden, wo der Ausstellungsrundweg beginnt.

En haut, le spectaculaire espace central du musée est la première vision des visiteurs avant d'accéder au sommet de l'immeuble où débute le circuit d'exposition.

The exhibition loops, visible in the heart-shaped plans to the right, carry visitors down through the building, following the history of the brand since its inception.

Die Ausstellungsschleifen, auf den herzförmigen Grundrissen rechts, führen die Besucher durch das Gebäude und folgen dabei der Geschichte der Marke seit ihrer Gründung.

Les boucles d'expositions, visibles sur les plans en forme de cœur à droite, guident les visiteurs à travers le musée et suivent l'histoire de la marque depuis sa création.

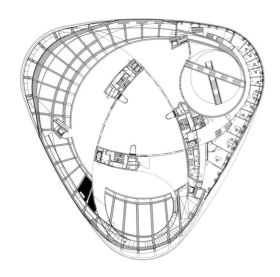

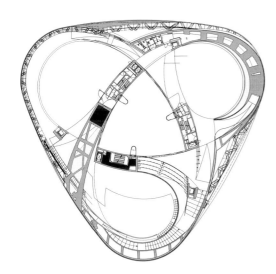

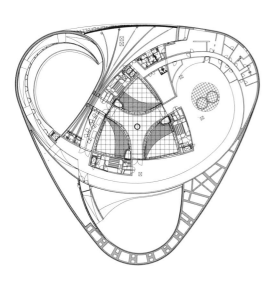

# HOLIDAY HOME

*Institute of Contemporary Art, University of Pennsylvania, Philadelphia,*
*Pennsylvania, USA, January 21–March 26, 2006*

*Floor area: 100 m². Client: Institute of Contemporary Art. Cost: $60 000.*
*Visual Media: Imaginary Forces (New York/Los Angeles)*

This was a site-specific installation created for the Philadelphia Institute of Contemporary Art (ICA), and an unexpected response to the question of what a holiday home might look like. As the ICA describes the work, "The *Holiday Home* is an experiential installation exploring and quantifying areas in which the holiday home departs from modern design conventions. The orthogonal surfaces of the archetypal house are extruded and skewed creating the sculptural armature within which the dichotomies of home and holiday home are played out. The new architectural shape emulates escapism, the expectation of a holiday as removed from the everyday experiential routine. The interplay of what is real and what is virtual transpires on a number of levels touching on ideas of collective memory and phenomenological perceptions." UNStudio has made frequent use of light, color and spatial effects in their work and this exploration of "nothing," which is to say light and color, even above form, is an extension of this interest.

Bei diesem Projekt handelt es sich um eine für das Philadelphia Institute of Contemporary Art (ICA) entworfene, standortspezifische Installation und eine überraschende Antwort auf die Frage, was ein Ferienhaus darstellen könnte. Das ICA beschreibt das Werk wie folgt: »Das ›Holiday Home‹ ist eine empirische Installation, die Bereiche erforscht und quantifiziert, in denen das Ferienhaus von den Konventionen des modernen Designs abweicht. Die orthogonalen Flächen des typischen Hauses werden extrudiert und abgeschrägt und so das plastische Gerüst geschaffen, in dem die Unterschiede zwischen Wohnhaus und Ferienhaus ausgespielt werden. Die neue architektonische Form bildet den Eskapismus nach, die Erwartung eines Urlaubs jenseits der empirischen Alltagsroutine. Das Wechselspiel zwischen Realem und Virtuellem findet auf mehreren Ebenen statt und rührt an Vorstellungen des kollektiven Gedächtnisses und an phänomenologische Wahrnehmungen.« UNStudio hat in seiner Arbeit häufig Gebrauch von Licht, Farbe und räumlichen Effekten gemacht und diese Erkundung des »Nichts«, will heißen von Farbe und Licht noch vor der Form, stellt eine Erweiterung dieses Interesses dar.

Cette installation spécifique a été créée pour l'ICA de Philadelphie. Elle apporte une réponse inattendue à ce qu'une maison de vacances pourrait représenter. Selon le descriptif de l'ICA : « La *Holiday Home* est une installation expérimentale explorant et quantifiant des zones au sein desquelles ce type de résidence se sépare des conventions de la conception moderne. Les surfaces orthogonales de la maison archétypique sont extrudées et mises en oblique pour créer une armature structurelle à l'intérieur de laquelle les dichotomies entre maison et maison de vacances son évacuées. Cette nouvelle forme architecturale stimule la fuite, l'attente de vacances éloignées de la routine de l'expérience quotidienne. L'interaction de ce qui est réel et de ce qui est virtuel apparaît à un certain nombre de niveaux et touche à des idées de mémoire collective et de perceptions phénoménologiques. » UNStudio a souvent utilisé la lumière, la couleur et les effets spéciaux dans ses recherches et son exploration du « rien ». La lumière et la couleur, au-delà même de la forme, sont des extensions de ces travaux.

*Intended for a temporary exhibition, the UNStudio* Holiday Home *is more a spatial concept than a real house. Color and angled forms set aside most of the rectilinear traditions of the house as we know it.*

*Das für eine temporäre Ausstellung gedachte »Holiday Home« von UNStudio ist eher als Raumkonzept denn als wirkliches Wohnhaus gedacht. Farbe und schräge Formen heben die geradlinigen Formen uns vertrauter Häuser auf.*

*Prévue pour une exposition temporaire, la* Holiday Home *d'UNStudio est davantage un concept spatial qu'une vraie maison. Sa couleur et ses formes penchées la placent à part des traditions de la maison telles que nous les connaissons.*

The saturated color of the interior, but also its unexpected angles and openings, suggest a certain amount of "escapism" in the holiday home, as the architects state themselves.

*Die satten Farben des Interieurs wie auch die überraschenden Schrägen und Öffnungen schließen in dem Ferienhaus einen Großteil Eskapismus ein, wie die Architekten selbst äußern.*

*La saturation de la couleur intérieure, mais aussi des basculements et des ouvertures inattendus, évoquent peut-être une forme d'évasion que symbolise la maison de vacances, comme le font remarquer les architectes.*

With computer-based design, manufacturing and construction methods,
architecture, even that of the modest
individual house, need no longer
follow the cookie-cutter patterns
imposed by old methods.

Mithilfe computergesteuerter
Entwurfs-, Herstellungs- und Bauverfahren muss selbst die Architektur
bescheidener Wohnhäuser nicht mehr
den von veralteten Methoden aufge-
zwungenen Schablonen entsprechen.

Grâce à des méthodes de conception,
de fabrication et de construction
numérisées, l'architecture, même
celle d'une modeste maison
individuelle, n'a plus à suivre les
méthodes artisanales anciennes.

# VILLA NM

*Upstate New York, New York, USA, 2000–06*

*Floor area: 230 m². Client: not disclosed. Cost: not disclosed.*
*Design Team: Ben van Berkel with Olaf Gipser and Andrew Benn, Colette Parras, Jacco van Wengerden,*
*Jan Debelius, Olga Vazquez-Ruano, Martin Kuitert. Local Consultant: Roemer Pierik*

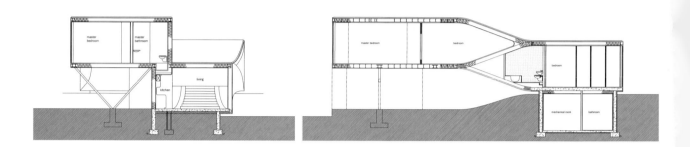

Located about two hours' drive from New York City, near Sullivan County, the area where this house was built has become popular for younger city-dwellers looking for a place to build. The sloping 7000-square-meter site has a 360° view of forest and meadowlands. The architects used a combination of concrete and glass with a light metal construction. One volume of the house follows the northern slope, another is "lifted above the hill" and contains a covered parking area. Bathrooms, kitchen, and fireplace are located in the vertical axis. Some rooms are partially closed off from the outside for privacy; others have large glazed surfaces. As the architects describe the house, "The volumetric transition is generated by a set of five parallel walls that rotate along a horizontal axis from vertical to horizontal. The walls become floor and vice versa. The ruled surface maintaining this transition is repeated five times in the building. Standardizing and pre-fabricating this structural element lowered the building costs without reducing the spatial quality of the interior. The interior space also takes advantage of the split-level organization. The kitchen and dining area on the ground floor are connected by a ramp to the living space above, the 1.5-meter height change allowing for a tremendous view over the valley. A similar ramp connects the living area to the master and the children's bedrooms on the second floor."

Die Gegend, in der dieses Haus errichtet wurde, etwa eine zweistündige Autofahrt von New York City entfernt unweit von Sullivan County gelegen, ist in letzter Zeit bei jüngeren Stadtbewohnern beliebt, die nach einem Bauplatz suchen. Das abschüssige, 7000 m² große Grundstück bietet eine Rundumsicht auf Wald und Wiesen. Die Architekten kombinierten Beton und Glas mit Leichtmetallbauweise. Ein Teil des Hauses folgt dem Abhang nach Norden, ein weiterer ist »über den Hügel angehoben« und enthält eine überdachte Parkfläche. Bäder, Küche und Kamin befinden sich auf der vertikalen Achse. Um Privatheit zu schaffen, sind einige Räume teilweise nach außen geschlossen, andere zeichnen sich durch große Glasflächen aus. Die Architekten beschreiben das Haus wie folgt: »Der volumetrische Übergang wird durch eine Gruppe von fünf parallelen Wänden geschaffen, die entlang einer horizontalen Achse von der Vertikale in die Horizontale verschwenkt werden. Die Wände werden zu Fußböden und umgekehrt. Dieser Übergang wiederholt sich im Gebäude fünfmal. Standardisierung und Vorfertigung dieses konstruktiven Elements senkten die Baukosten, ohne die räumliche Qualität des Innenraums zu mindern. Dieser macht sich die Anordnung auf versetzten Ebenen zunutze. Küche und Essbereich im Erdgeschoss sind durch eine Rampe mit dem darüberliegenden Wohnbereich verbunden, wobei der Höhenunterschied von 1,5 m einen fulminanten Blick über das Tal ermöglicht. Eine ähnliche Rampe verbindet den Wohnbereich mit dem Elternschlafzimmer und den Kinderzimmern im zweiten Stock.«

Située à deux heures de voiture de New York, près du comté de Sullivan, la région dans laquelle cette maison a été édifiée est très recherchée par les jeunes citadins qui cherchent un terrain pour construire. La parcelle de 700 m² en pente bénéficie d'une vue à 360° sur la forêt et les pâturages. Les architectes ont combiné le béton, le verre et une structure légère en métal. Un des volumes de la maison suit la pente nord, l'autre «se soulève au-dessus de la colline» et dégage la place nécessaire au garage couvert. Les salles de bains, la cuisine et la cheminée sont regroupées dans l'axe vertical. Certaines pièces présentent d'importantes parois vitrées. Selon l'architecte : « La transition volumétrique se fait grâce à un ensemble de cinq murs parallèles qui pivotent le long d'un axe horizontal de la verticale à l'horizontale. Les murs deviennent ainsi des sols et vice versa. Cette surface de transition se répète à cinq reprises. La standardisation et la préfabrication de cet élément structurel a permis d'abaisser ses coûts de construction, sans porter atteinte à la qualité spatiale intérieure. Le volume interne bénéficie également de cette organisation décalée de l'espace. La cuisine et l'aire des repas au rez-de-chaussée sont connectées par une rampe au séjour situé, la différence de hauteur de 1,5 mètres ménageant une vue splendide sur la vallée. Une rampe similaire relie le séjour à la chambre principale et à celle des enfants à l'étage. »

*Taking up in many ways where the architects' Möbius House left off, the VilLA NM represents a study of the intersection of different volumes, rendering both plan and section dynamic and surprising.*

*Die VilLA NM, die in vieler Hinsicht da einsetzt, wo das Haus Möbius der Architekten endete, stellt eine Studie sich durchschneidender, unterschiedlicher Baukörper dar, was einen dynamischen, überraschenden Grundriss und Schnitt zur Folge hat.*

*Partant à plusieurs égards de là où les architectes avaient laissé leur maison Möbius, la VilLA NM représente une étude sur l'intersection de divers volumes qui dynamise à la fois les plans et les coupes.*

With its large, mirrored glass openings, the house both connects with and reflects its environment. Its unusual cantilevered forms give an impression not of disequilibrium but of potential movement.

Mit seinen großen, verspiegelten Fensteröffnungen reflektiert das Haus seine Umgebung und nimmt so Verbindung zu ihr auf. Die ungewöhnlich vorkragenden Formen wirken keineswegs unausgewogen, sondern erzeugen den Eindruck potenzieller Bewegung.

Dotée de grandes ouvertures en verre réfléchissant, la maison se connecte à l'environnement qu'elle reflète. Ses formes étranges en porte-à-faux donnent l'impression non pas d'un déséquilibre mais d'une potentialité de mouvement.

Above, the almost cyclopean cantilevered volume of the living room,
visible to the right on the plan
reproduced here.

Der oben zu sehende, riesig wirkende auskragende Wohnraum ist auf
dem rechts reproduzierten Grundriss
erkennbar.

Ci-dessus, les volumes quasi cyclo-
péens du séjour en porte-à-faux,
visible à droite sur le plan.

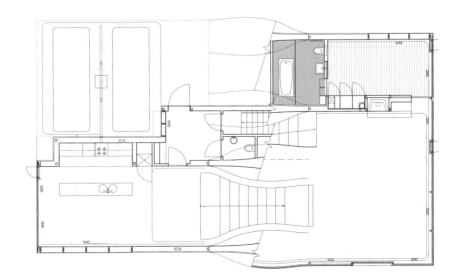

Interior spaces flow into each other, and create unusual, almost cavern-like volumes that open, as is the case above, onto a bright, fully glazed area, in this case the living room.

Innenräume gehen ineinander über und schaffen ungewöhnliche, fast höhlenartige Räumlichkeiten, die sich wie oben zum hellen, voll verglasten Wohnbereich hin öffnen.

Les espaces intérieurs s'interpénètrent et créent des volumes inhabituels, presque caverneux qui donnent, comme ci-dessus, sur la zone lumineuse largement ouverte du séjour.

The openings and passageways in the house are irregular, almost as if they had been designed by hand rather than carefully crafted with the most sophisticated computer programs available.

Die Öffnungen und Durchgänge im Haus sind uneinheitlich, fast als seien sie von Hand und nicht mit den kompliziertesten, verfügbaren Computerprogrammen entworfen.

Les ouvertures et les passages sont irréguliers, comme s'ils avaient été plutôt dessinés à la main que mis au point par certains des logiciels informatiques les plus sophistiqués du moment.

The architects have given the house its basic furnishings, leaving spaces that are fully defined in architectural terms. Wires replace a handrail on the stairway.

Die Architekten haben das Haus mit seiner Grundmöblierung ausgestattet und dabei in architektonischer Hinsicht komplett festgelegte Räume hinterlassen. An der Treppe ersetzen Drähte den Handlauf.

Les architectes ont meublé simplement la maison, laissant des espaces parfaitement définis en termes d'architecture. Des câbles remplacent une main courant le long de l'escalier.

# WANDEL HOEFER LORCH + HIRSCH

*Wandel Hoefer Lorch + Hirsch*
*Dolomitenweg 19*
*66119 Saarbrücken*
*Germany*

*Tel: +49 681 926 550*
*Fax: +49 681 926 5595*
*E-mail: info@wandel-hoefer-lorch.de*
*Web: www.wandel-hoefer-lorch.de*

*Hinzert Documentation Center ▶*

**WOLFGANG LORCH** was born in 1960 in Nürtingen am Neckar. He studied Architecture in Darmstadt and at the ETSA, Barcelona. He has taught at the Stuttgart University of Applied Sciences and at the Technical University (TU) of Darmstadt. **NIKOLAUS HIRSCH** was born in 1964 and studied at the TU in Darmstadt. He is a Unit Master at the Architectural Association in London and a Visiting Professor at the University of Pennsylvania (2005). **ANDREA WANDEL** was born in 1963 in Saarbrücken and studied Architecture at the Technical University in Kaiserslautern and the TU in Darmstadt. **RENA WANDEL-HOEFER** was born in 1959 in Saarbrücken and also studied at the TU in Darmstadt. **ANDREAS HOEFER** was born in 1955 in Hamburg and studied in Berlin and at the TU in Darmstadt. Their work includes a memorial at the Börneplatz (Frankfurt, 1995); a monument at the deportation train station at Berlin-Grunewald (1998); a synagogue in Dresden (2001); the Hinzert Documentation Center (Hinzert, 2003–05, published here); and the Jakobsplatz Museum-Synagogue (Munich, 2006), all in Germany. Current work includes the Tschavtschavadze Avenue (Tibilisi, Georgia).

**WOLFGANG LORCH** wurde 1960 in Nürtingen am Neckar geboren. Er studierte an der TU in Darmstadt und der ETSA in Barcelona Architektur. Er lehrte an der Hochschule für Technik in Stuttgart und an der TU in Darmstadt. **NIKOLAUS HIRSCH** wurde 1964 geboren und studierte an der TU Darmstadt. Er ist Unit Master an der Architectural Association in London und Gastprofessor an der University of Pennsylvania (2005). **ANDREA WANDEL** wurde 1963 in Saarbrücken geboren und studierte an der TU Kaiserslautern und der TU Darmstadt Architektur. **RENA WANDEL-HOEFER** wurde 1959 in Saarbrücken geboren und studierte ebenfalls an der TU Darmstadt. **ANDREAS HOEFER** wurde 1955 in Hamburg geboren und studierte in Berlin und an der TU Darmstadt. Zu ihrem Werk gehören eine Gedenkstätte am Börneplatz (Frankfurt am Main, 1995), das Mahnmal für die Deportierten am Bahnhof Berlin-Grunewald (1998), die Neue Synagoge in Dresden (2001), das hier gezeigte Dokumentationszentrum in Hinzert (2003–05) sowie das Jüdische Zentrum am St.-Jakobs-Platz in München (2006 eingeweiht). Zu den aktuellen Projekten zählt die Tschavtschavadze-Allee in Tiflis, Georgien.

**WOLFGANG LORCH**, né en 1960 à Nürtingen am Neckar, a étudié l'architecture à Darmstadt et à l'ETSA de Barcelone. Il a enseigné à l'Université des sciences appliquées de Stuttgart et à l'Université Technique (TU) de Darmstadt. **NIKOLAUS HIRSCH**, né en 1964, a étudié à la TU de Darmstadt. Il est responsable d'unité à l'Architectural Association de Londres et professeur invité à l'Université de Pennsylvanie (2005). **ANDREA WANDEL**, né en 1963 à Saarbruck, a étudié l'architecture à l'Université Technique de Kaiserslautern et à la TU de Darmstadt. **RENA WANDEL-HOEFER**, née en 1959 à Saarbruck, a également étudié à la TU de Darmstadt. **ANDREAS HOEFER**, né en 1955 à Hambourg, a fait ses études à Berlin et à la TU de Darmstadt. Parmi leurs réalisations, toutes en Allemagne : un mémorial Börneplatz, Francfort (1995) ; un monument dédié à la déportation dans la gare de Berlin-Grunewald (1998) ; une synagogue à Dresde (2001) ; le Centre de documentation d'Hinzert (2003–05), publié ici ; et le Musée-synagogue de la Jakobsplatz à Munich (2006). Ils travaillent actuellement au projet de l'avenue Tschavtschavadze à Tbilissi, en Géorgie.

# HINZERT DOCUMENTATION CENTER

*Hinzert, Germany, 2003–05*

*Floor area: 370 m². Client: Landeszentrale für Politische Bildung Rheinland-Pfalz. Cost: €2.5 million.*
*Project Team: Wolfgang Lorch, Nikolaus Hirsch, Andrea Wandel, Christine Biesel, Alexander Keuper*

This project is a documentation center on the former SS Sonderlager/KZ Hinzert or Hinzert Special SS Concentration Camp that was located near the German city of Trier. Made of Cor-ten steel, the new structure commemorates the fate of approximately 13 000 people who were held in the camp between its creation in 1939 and the arrival of the Allied forces in 1945. The building appears to be more sculptural than structured in a traditional way, and it is located in a rural setting that belies its function and nature. Made of 3000 different 12-millimeter sheets of steel, cut with computer-guided tools, the structure was treated with hot paraffin to give the surface of the steel more "depth." Plans for a documentation center on the site had been made as early as 1994, but the architects won a competition in 2003 and succeeded in erecting the structure in less than two years. The windows of the center that look out onto the landscape are screen-printed with images of the former prisoner's huts.

Dieses Projekt ist ein Dokumentationszentrum im früheren SS-Sonderlager Hinzert in der Nähe von Trier. Der aus Cor-Ten-Stahl bestehende neue Bau gedenkt des Schicksals von etwa 13 000 Menschen, die in dem Lager zwischen seiner Einrichtung 1939 und der Ankunft der Alliierten 1945 interniert waren. Der Bau erscheint eher skulptural als in herkömmlicher Weise gebaut und steht in einer ländlichen Umgebung, die mit seiner Funktion und seinem Charakter kontrastiert. Das aus 3000 verschiedenen, 12 mm starken, mit computergesteuerten Werkzeugen zugeschnittenen Stahlblechen bestehende Zentrum wurde mit heißem Paraffin behandelt, um der Oberfläche des Stahls mehr »Tiefe« zu verleihen. Bereits 1994 gab es Pläne für ein Dokumentationszentrum an diesem Ort, aber erst 2003 gewannen die Architekten einen Wettbewerb und konnten die Einrichtung in weniger als zwei Jahren fertigstellen. Die auf die umliegende Landschaft schauenden Fenster des Zentrums sind mit Siebdruckbildern der ehemaligen Gefangenenbaracken bedruckt.

Ce Centre de documentation a été construit sur l'ancien SS Sonderlager/KZ Hinzert camp de concentration spécial SS d'Hinzert, près de la ville allemande de Trèves. Réalisé en acier Cor-Ten, ce bâtiment commémore le destin tragique d'environ 13 000 personnes qui y ont été détenues entre son ouverture en 1939 et l'arrivée des Alliés en 1945. Situé dans un cadre rural qui pourrait faire oublier sa fonction et sa nature, il semble plus sculptural que structurel au sens traditionnel du terme. Montée à partir de 3 000 tôles d'acier différentes de 12 mm d'épaisseur, découpée par outils à commande numérique, la structure a été traitée à la paraffine chaude pour donner plus de « profondeur » à la surface de l'acier. Des plans de construction d'un centre de documentation sur ce site existaient depuis 1994, et les architectes qui en ont remporté le concours en 2003 ont réussi à réaliser leur projet en moins de deux ans. Les fenêtres centrales, qui donnent sur le paysage, sont sérigraphiées avec des images d'anciennes huttes de prisonniers.

*The snake-like Cor-ten steel exterior is punctuated by a certain number of triangular or square windows, but retains an ambiguity in harmony with the building's function.*

*Die schlangengleiche Außenhaut aus Cor-Ten-Stahl weist dreieckige oder quadratische Fenster auf, bewahrt jedoch in Einklang mit seiner Funktion eine gewisse Ambiguität.*

*L'extérieur du musée en acier Cor-Ten est ponctué d'un certain nombre de fenêtres triangulaires ou carrées, mais conserve une ambiguïté en harmonie avec la fonction du bâtiment.*

*Seen in the countryside, the building almost appears to be a rock formation, or perhaps an old fortification wall.*

*Im Gelände gesehen gleicht das Gebäude fast einer Felsformation oder vielleicht einer alten Befestigungsmauer.*

*En pleine campagne, le bâtiment ressemble presque à une formation rocheuse ou à un vestige de fortification.*

The structural web seen below allows for a sufficient number of triangular openings to let light into the building. Angular walls or ceilings create a dynamic, or perhaps slightly oppressive, interior.

Die unten abgebildete tragende Außenhaut erlaubt eine hinreichende Anzahl von dreieckigen Öffnungen für den Lichteinfall. Schräge Wände oder Decken erzeugen ein dynamisches, vielleicht etwas beunruhigendes Interieur.

Le réseau structurel vu ci-dessous permet à un nombre suffisant d'ouvertures triangulaires d'éclairer le bâtiment. Les murs et les plafonds anguleux créent un intérieur dynamique, peut-être légèrement inquiétant.

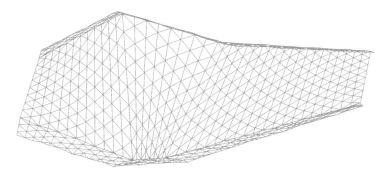

Morde in Hinzert
Executions in Hinzert / Exécutions à Hinzert

„Ihr seid hierher gekommen, um zu verrecken,
und ich gebe Euch mein Wort darauf,
dass ihr verrecken werdet!" Paul Sporrenberg

Video screens, images or texts printed directly on the walls tell the harrowing story of this place. The architects rightly stop short of allowing their design to dominate the exhibition.

Videomonitore, Bilder und direkt auf die Wände gedruckte Schrift erzählen die traurige Geschichte dieses Ortes. Die Architekten sehen richtigerweise davon ab, das Ausgestellte mit ihrem Bau zu übertrumpfen.

Des écrans vidéo, des images ou des typographies imprimées directement sur les murs racontent l'histoire du lieu. Les architectes ont su s'arrêter à temps pour que leur intervention ne domine pas l'exposition.

# WHITE

*White arkitekter AB*
*P. O. Box 2502*
*40317 Göteborg*
*Sweden*

*Tel: +46 31 608 600*
*Fax: +46 31 608 610*
*E-mail: info@white.se*
*Web: www.white.se*

*Kastrup Sea Bath* ▶

**WHITE** is one of Scandinavia's large architectural companies, with 460 employees working at 11 offices in Göteborg, Stockholm, Malmö, Linköping, Halmstadt, Örebro, Uppsala, Umeå, Copenhagen, Ringsted and Naestved. As they say, "We see ourselves as a large, employee-owned ideas factory. Our owner-system acts as an engine, a dynamo, a stabilizer, and a direction indicator, all at the same time. Shared ownership means a shared commitment. Our range of expertise embraces architecture, urban planning, landscaping, interior design, the environmental settings, and project management." Fredrik Pettersson, in charge of the Kastrup Sea Bath project of 2005 (published here), was born in 1972 in Lund, Sweden. He obtained his architectural degrees from Lund University and in Århus. He started at White in Göteborg in 1999, but got a transfer in 2002 to the Copenhagen office. The company's recent work in Sweden includes the Drottningtornet Tower (Linköping, 2006); and the future 16-story Klara Hotel (Stockholm, 2006–10).

**WHITE** ist mit 460 Angestellten, die in elf Büros in Göteborg, Stockholm, Malmö, Linköping, Halmstadt, Örebro, Uppsala, Umeå, Kopenhagen, Ringsted und Naestved arbeiten, eine der größten Architekturfirmen Skandinaviens. Aus den eigenen Reihen heißt es: »Wir verstehen uns als große Ideenfabrik im Besitz ihrer Angestellten. Unser Eignersystem fungiert gleichzeitig als Motor, Dynamo, Stabilisator und Richtungsweiser. Geteilter Besitz bedeutet geteilte Verantwortung. Die Bandbreite unserer Fachkenntnisse umfasst Architektur, Stadtplanung, Landschaftsgestaltung, Innenarchitektur, umweltgerechte Anlagen sowie Projektleitung.« Fredrik Petterson, Leiter des hier vorgestellten Projekts Seebad Kastrup von 2005, wurde 1972 in Lund, Schweden, geboren. Er studierte Architektur an der Universität von Lund und in Århus. 1999 eröffnete er das Büro White in Göteborg, wechselte jedoch 2002 in das Kopenhagener Büro. Zu ihren neuesten Bauten in Schweden zählen: Hochhaus Drottningtornet (Linköping, 2006) sowie das 16-geschossige Hotel Klara (Stockholm, 2006–10).

**WHITE** est l'une des plus importantes agences d'architecture scandinaves, qui emploie 460 collaborateurs travaillant dans ses onze bureaux de Göteborg, Stockholm, Malmö, Linköping, Halmstadt, Örebro, Uppsala, Umeå, Copenhague, Ringsted et Naestved. « Nous nous considérons comme une vaste usine à idées coopératives. Notre système de propriété est tout à la fois un moteur, une dynamo, un stabilisateur et un indicateur de direction. Ce partage de propriété permet l'engagement de tous. Notre champ d'expertise embrasse l'architecture, l'urbanisme, le paysagisme, l'architecture intérieure, le cadre environnemental et la gestion de projets. » Fredrik Pettersson, responsable du projet de la jetée de bains de mer de Kastrup (2005), publié ici, est né en 1972, à Lund, Suède. Il est diplômé en architecture des universités de Lund et Århus. Il a fait ses débuts chez White, à Göteborg, en 1999, puis a été transféré en 2002 au bureau de Copenhague. Parmi leurs récentes réalisations érigées en Suède figurent la tour de Drottningtornet, Linköping (2006) et le futur Klara Hotel de quinze étages à Stockholm (2006–10).

# KASTRUP SEA BATH

*Kastrup, Denmark, 2005*

*Floor area: 870 m² wooden deck; 70 m² changing area; 90 m² service building on land. Client: City of Kastrup.*
*Cost: €1.2 million. Landscape Design: White arkitekter AB: Fredrik Pettersson (head of project),*
*Rasmus Skaarup, Pernille Vermund, Göran Wihl, Henrik Haremst, Johnny Gere*

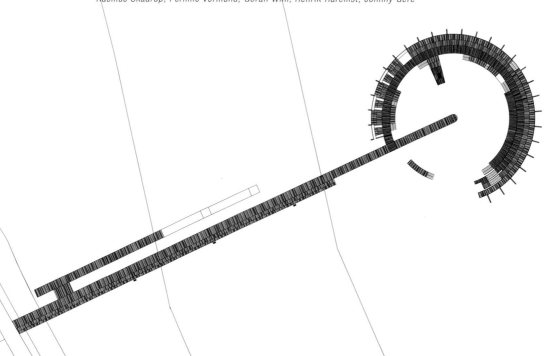

Made from Azobé wood chosen for its durability in salt water, the Kastrup Sea Bath consists of a main building located on the water, a beach, and an adjoining services building with lavatories and a changing room for the handicapped. Visitors move in a circular pattern, gradually rising from the sea's surface and ending up at a 5-meter diving platform. Of this feature, the architect Fredrik Pettersson says, "All art is self-expression, and here I've designed a path that inevitably leads to a drop of 5 meters. I've not dared to jump yet. But the construction is mine, which is a good start." The firm writes, "The Bath is conceived as a sculptural dynamic form, which can be seen from the beach, the sea, and the air. Its silhouette gradually changes as the beholder moves around it. The circular shape creates a concentrated interior, shelter from the winds, and concentrates the sun. The shape opens up toward the landside to connect to the beach and to invite visitors inside. A continuous bench runs along the pier, thus creating an additional rest and leisure area." Careful attention was paid to the night lighting of the facility, making it stand out from its surroundings. Uplights on the interior of the semicircular wall and lines of LED spots running along the pier are the essential elements of the night lighting.

Das wegen seiner Haltbarkeit in Salzwasser aus Azobéholz gefertigte Seebad Kastrup besteht aus einem am Meer stehenden Hauptgebäude, einem Strandabschnitt und einem Servicegebäude mit Toiletten und einem behindertengerechten Umkleideraum. Die Anlage wird durch kreisförmig verlaufende Wege erschlossen, über die Besucher sich vom Wasser bis zu einem 5 m hohen Sprungbrett bewegen. Architekt Fredrik Pettersson meint dazu: »Alle Kunst ist Ausdruck der eigenen Persönlichkeit und ich habe hier einen Weg gestaltet, der zwangsläufig zu einem Fall aus 5 m Höhe führt. Ich habe mich bislang nicht zu springen getraut. Aber die Konstruktion stammt von mir und das ist ein guter Anfang.« Das Büro schreibt: »Das Bad ist als plastische, dynamische Form konzipiert, die man vom Strand, vom Meer und aus der Luft sehen kann. Während der Betrachter es umrundet, verändert sich seine Silhouette allmählich. Die Kreisform erzeugt einen konzentrierten Innenraum, schirmt den Wind ab und sammelt die Sonne. Die Form öffnet sich zum Land hin, um den Strand anzubinden und Besucher einzuladen. Der Pier ist von einer durchgehenden Bank gesäumt, die einen weiteren Bereich zum Ausruhen und Entspannen schafft.« Der nächtlichen Beleuchtung widmete man große Sorgfalt, um die Anlage von ihrer Umgebung abzuheben. Auf die Innenseite der halbkreisförmigen Wand gerichtete Strahler sowie entlang des Piers verlaufende LED-Spots sind die wesentlichen Elemente der Nachtbeleuchtung.

Construite en azobé, bois choisi pour sa résistance à l'eau de mer, cette jetée pour bains de mer consiste en un bâtiment principal sur l'eau, une plage, un bâtiment de services adjacent comprenant des toilettes et un vestiaire pour handicapés. Les visiteurs se déplacent le long d'un parcours circulaire, s'élevant peu à peu du niveau de la mer jusqu'à un plongeoir de 5 mètres de haut. L'architecte Fredrik Pettersson commente ainsi son projet : « Tout art est une expression de soi et, ici, j'ai conçu un cheminement qui conduit inévitablement à une chute de 5 mètres. Je n'ai pas encore osé sauter, mais la construction est bien de moi, ce qui est un bon point de départ. » Pour l'agence : « Ce «Bain» est une forme sculpturale dynamique qui peut se voir de la mer, de la plage, et du ciel. Sa silhouette se modifie petit à petit, lorsque le spectateur se déplace autour d'elle. La forme circulaire génère une concentration vers l'intérieur, un abri par rapport au vent et une concentration solaire. Elle s'ouvre vers la terre pour se connecter à la plage et invite le visiteur à la fouler. Un banc continu s'étend le long de la jetée, créant un lieu de détente et de repos supplémentaire. » Un soin particulier a été porté à l'éclairage nocturne, qui met en valeur les installations par rapport à leur environnement. Des projecteurs dirigés vers le haut illuminent la face intérieure semi-circulaire du mur et les lignes de LED, posées le long de la jetée, jouent un rôle essentiel.

With its extremely simple plan and its wooden design, lifted up off the water, the Sea Bath allies modernity with a bow to local traditions.

Mit seiner ausgesprochen schlichten Anlage und dem über das Wasser angehobenen Holzbau verbinden sich im Seebad die Moderne mit lokalen Traditionen.

Sur un plan extrêmement simple et construits en bois sur pilotis au-dessus de l'eau, ces Bains de mer allient modernité et tradit-ions locales.

Although White is a large architec-tural firm, this structure was largely the work of a talented individual architect, Fredrik Pettersson. It is somewhat quirky and unexpected in ways that a more "corporate" approach would not have allowed.

Obgleich White ein großes Architek-turbüro ist, scheint dieser Bau eher das Werk des begabten Individualis-ten Fredrik Pettersson zu sein. Es ist in einer Weise schrullig und spontan, die eine »unternehmerische« Einstellung nicht zugelassen hätte.

Bien que White soit une grande agen-ce, cette construction semble davan-tage l'œuvre d'une personnalité de talent, Fredrik Pettersson. Elle est plus bizarre et inattendue que pour-rait l'être le produit d'une approche « institutionnelle ».

Gangplanks and stairs leading to the water in the warmer months accompany the sweeping round movement of the main structure.

*Laufstege und Treppen, die für das sommerliche Baden zum Wasser hinunterführen, begleiten die ausgreifende Rundung des Hauptbaukörpers.*

*Des appontements et des escaliers pour descendre vers l'eau à la belle saison accompagnent le mouvement en courbe de la structure principale.*

The presence of water is a constant factor of the architecture. The architect's unusual idea to lead visitors to a five-meter diving platform appears to have frightened him as much as many users.

*Die Präsenz von Wasser ist bei dieser Architektur eine Konstante. Die ungewöhnliche Idee des Architekten, Besucher zu einem 5 m hohen Sprungturm zu leiten, scheint ihn ebenso erschreckt zu haben wie viele Benutzer.*

*La présence d'eau est un facteur constant dans cette architecture. L'idée de l'architecte de faire monter les amateurs à un plongeoir à cinq mètres de haut semble leur faire aussi peur qu'à lui-même.*

# MAKOTO YOKOMIZO

AAT + Makoto Yokomizo, Architects Inc.
4–1 Kikuicho, Shinjuku-ku
Tokyo 162–0044
Japan

Tel: +81 3 3205 9580
Fax: +81 3 3205 9589
E-mail: mya@aatplus.com
Web: www.aatplus.com

**MAKOTO YOKOMIZO** was born in 1962 in Kanagawa, Japan. He graduated in 1984 from the Tokyo National University of Fine Arts, Department of Architecture, and completed his M.A. degree at the same institution two years later. In 1988, he went to work at Toyo Ito & Associates, remaining there until 2000 and working in particular on the Old People's Home in Yatsushiro (Kumamoto, 1994) and the Sendai Mediatheque (2000). In 2001, he created AAT + Makoto Yokomizo, Architects Inc. His projects since then have included stage designs for Kota Yamazaki dance performances; *Hyper Ballad*, New National Theatre Tokyo; and *Cholon*, Theatre Cocoon Tokyo, all in 2001. In 2002, he worked on Brussels Kamiya-cho, Tokyo; HEM, Tokyo; and Les Hydropathes, Tokyo. His work in 2003 included FUN, Chiba; and HAB, Chiba; while in 2004, he worked on three projects: MEM, Chiba; TEM, Tokyo; and MSH, Tokyo. In 2005, he completed the Tomihiro Art Museum, Gunma, and in 2006, GSH, published here. He has been a part-time Lecturer at the Tokyo National University of Fine Arts, the University of Tokyo, Tokai University, Hosei University, and Tokyo University of Science.

**MAKOTO YOKOMIZO** wurde 1962 in Kanagawa, Japan, geboren. 1984 machte er seinen Abschluss an der Architekturfakultät der Nationaluniversität für bildende Kunst in Tokio, zwei Jahre später folgte ein Masterabschluss am gleichen Institut. 1988 nahm er eine Tätigkeit bei Toyo Ito & Associates auf, wo er bis 2000 arbeitete, vornehmlich am Altenheim in Yatsushiro (Kumamoto, 1994) und der Mediathek von Sendai (2000). 2001 gründete er AAT + Makoto Yokomizo, Architects Inc. Seither zeichnet er verantwortlich für Bühnenbilder für Tanzaufführungen von Kota Yamazaki: »Hyper Ballad«, Neues Nationaltheater Tokio, und »Cholon«, Cocoon-Theatre Tokio, beide 2001. 2002 arbeitete er in Tokio an Brussels Kamiya-cho, HEM und Les Hydropathes. 2003 entstanden FUN, Chiba, und HAB, Chiba, während er 2004 mit drei Projekten befasst war: MEM, Chiba, TEM, Tokio, und MSH, Tokio. 2005 stellte er das Kunstmuseum Tomihiro in Gunma fertig und 2006 das hier vorgestellte GSH-Gebäude. Neben seiner Arbeit als Architekt hält er Vorlesungen an der Nationaluniversität für bildende Kunst in Tokio, den Universitäten Tokai, Hosei sowie der Universität der Wissenschaften in Tokio.

**MAKOTO YOKOMIZO** est né en 1962 à Kanagawa, Japon. Diplômé en 1984 de l'Université national des Beaux-arts de Tokyo, département d'architecture, il a obtenu son M.A. de la même institution deux ans plus tard. De 1988 à 2000, il a travaillé pour l'agence Toyo Ito & Associates, intervenant en particulier sur le foyer pour personnes âgées de Yatsushiro, Kumamoto (1994) et la médiathèque de Sendai (2000). En 2001, il a fondé AAT + Makoto Yokomizo, Architects Inc. Parmi ses projets depuis lors : en 2001, des décors de scène pour les performances de danse de Kota Yamazaki ; *Hyper Ballad*, Nouveau théâtre national, Tokyo ; *Cholon*, Théâtre Cocoon, Tokyo. En 2002, il a travaillé sur le projet de Brussels Kamiya-cho, Tokyo ; HEM, Tokyo ; et *Les Hydropathes*, Tokyo. En 2003, FUN, Chiba ; HAB, Chiba ; en 2004, MEM, Chiba ; TEM, Tokyo et MSH, Tokyo. Il a achevé le Musée d'art Tomihiro, Gunma, en 2005, et, en 2006, la maison GSH, publiée ici. Il a été enseignant à temps partiel aux Université nationale des Beaux-arts de Tokyo, Université de Tokyo, Université Tokay, Université Hosei et Université des sciences de Tokyo.

# GSH

*Minato-ku, Tokyo, Japan, 2005–06*

*Floor area: 289 m². Client: not disclosed.*
*Cost: $800 000*

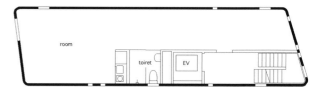

As is often the case with Tokyo buildings, GSH was built on a very small site, measuring only 72 square meters and just 4 meters wide. The five-story, 15-meter-high steel structure has a footprint of only 58 square meters. As the architect explains, the building is to be considered a "prototype of architecture for small narrow urban sites." The first and second floors are occupied by a shop, the third and fourth by offices, and the top level is the client's residence. The exterior walls of the building are made of 13 manufactured 4.5-millimeter-steel plates reinforced by steel ribs placed at irregular intervals. The building was entirely assembled at a factory, then transported in pieces and "welded together to form a semi-monocoque structure." The unusual nature of the building is further heightened by the random placement of its small and large circular windows.

Wie so häufig in Tokio wurde auch GSH auf einem sehr kleinen Grundstück von 72 m² und 4 m Breite errichtet. Das fünfstöckige, stählerne Bauwerk hat eine Grundfläche von nur 58 m². Dem Architekten zufolge soll das Gebäude als »Prototyp einer Architektur für kleine, schmale Stadtgrundstücke« gelten. Erdgeschoss und erster Stock werden als Läden genutzt, zweiter und dritter Stock als Büros und die oberste Ebene bewohnt der Bauherr. Die Außenwände des Gebäudes bestehen aus 13 eigens gefertigten, 4,5 mm starken Stahlblechen, die durch Stahlrippen in unregelmäßigen Abständen verstärkt wurden. Das Gebäude wurde in einer Fabrik komplett montiert, dann in Teile zerlegt transportiert und »zu einem Halbschalenbau zusammengeschweißt«. Der ungewöhnliche Charakter des Gebäudes wird durch die willkürliche Platzierung der unterschiedlich großen kreisförmigen Fensteröffnungen noch unterstrichen.

Comme c'est souvent le cas à Tokyo, la maison GSH a été édifiée sur une très petite parcelle de 72 m² et 4 mètres de large seulement. Cette construction sur cinq niveaux et 15 mètres de haut, à ossature en acier, n'occupe que 58 m² au sol. Ainsi que l'explique l'architecte, elle doit être considérée comme « un prototype d'architecture pour de petites parcelles urbaines étroites ». Les premier et second niveaux sont occupés par une boutique, les troisième et quatrième par des bureaux et le cinquième par la résidence du client. Les murs extérieurs sont constitués de treize plaques de tôle d'acier de 4,5 mm d'épaisseur, renforcées par des nervures d'acier disposées à intervalles irréguliers. L'ensemble a été entièrement assemblé en usine, puis transporté par morceaux et « soudé ensemble pour former une structure semi-monocoque ». La nature inhabituelle de ce micro-immeuble est soulignée par la disposition aléatoire des fenêtres circulaires, grandes et petites.

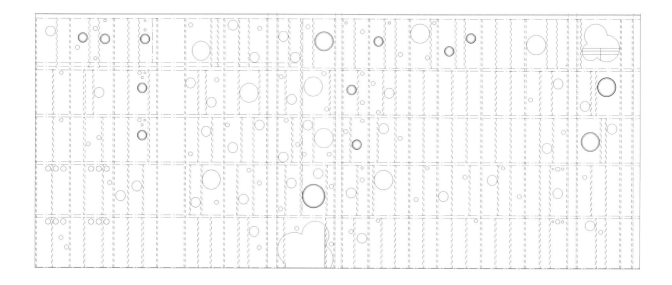

Working with very little land, the architect has introduced a surprising variety in both the façade and the interior of this building, creating a series of irregular round openings.

Auf diesem sehr kleinen Grundstück gelang es dem Architekten, Fassade und Innenräume überraschend abwechslungsreich zu gestalten, indem er eine Reihe unregelmäßiger, runder Öffnungen einsetzte.

Sur cette parcelle minuscule, l'architecte a introduit une étonnante dynamique dans la façade comme dans les aménagements intérieurs par la multiplication d'ouvertures circulaires de dimensions diverses.

# INDEX OF ARCHITECTS / BUILDINGS / PLACES

# CREDITS